The Story of
PHILOSOPHY

*The Lives and Opinions of
the Great Philosophers
of the Western World*

by
WILL DURANT

SIMON & SCHUSTER PAPERBACKS
New York   London   Toronto   Sydney

TO MY WIFE

Grow strong, my comrade . . . that you may stand
Unshaken when I fall; that I may know
The shattered fragments of my song will come
At last to finer melody in you;
That I may tell my heart that you begin
Where passing I leave off, and fathom more.

SIMON & SCHUSTER PAPERBACKS
ROCKEFELLER CENTER
1230 AVENUE OF THE AMERICAS
NEW YORK, NY 10020

FIRST SIMON & SCHUSTER PAPERBACK EDITION 2005

SIMON & SCHUSTER PAPERBACKS AND COLOPHON
ARE REGISTERED TRADEMARKS OF SIMON & SCHUSTER, INC.

FOR INFORMATION REGARDING SPECIAL DISCOUNTS FOR BULK PURCHASES,
PLEASE CONTACT SIMON & SCHUSTER SPECIAL SALES AT
1-800-456-6798 OR BUSINESS@SIMONANDSCHUSTER.COM.

ISBN 978-0-671-69500-2
ISBN 978-0-671-20159-3 (PBK)
MANUFACTURED IN THE UNITED STATES OF AMERICA

49 50 48

PREFACE TO THE SECOND EDITION

Apologia Pro Libro Suo

I

My publishers have asked me to use the occasion given by a new edition of The Story of Philosophy *to discuss the general question of "outlines," and to consider some of the shortcomings of the volume. I am glad of this opportunity to acknowledge these, and to express with all the weakness of mere words the gratitude that I must always feel for the generosity with which, despite so many defects, the American public has received this book.*

The "outlines" came because a million voices called for them. Human knowledge had become unmanageably vast; every science had begotten a dozen more, each subtler than the rest; the telescope revealed stars and systems beyond the mind of man to number or to name; geology spoke in terms of millions of years, where men before had thought in terms of thousands; physics found a universe in the atom, and biology found a microcosm in the cell; physiology discovered inexhaustible mystery in every organ, and psychology in every dream; anthropology reconstructed the unsuspected antiquity of man, archeology unearthed buried cities and forgotten states, history proved all history false, and painted a canvas which only a Spengler or an Eduard Meyer could vision as a whole; theology crumbled, and political theory cracked; invention complicated life and war, and economic creeds overturned governments and inflamed the world; philosophy itself, which had once summoned all sciences to its aid in making a coherent image of the world and an alluring picture of the good, found its task of coördination too stupendous for its courage, ran away from all these battlefronts of truth, and hid itself in recondite and narrow lanes, timidly secure from the issues and responsibilities of life. Human knowledge had become too great for the human mind.

All that remained was the scientific specialist, who knew "more and more about less and less," and the philosophical speculator, who knew less and less about more and more. The specialist put on blinders in order to shut out from his vision all the world but one little spot, to which he glued his nose. Perspective was lost. "Facts" replaced understanding; and knowledge, split into a thousand isolated fragments, no longer generated wisdom. Every science, and every branch of philosophy, developed a technical terminology intelligible only to its exclusive devotees; as men learned more about the world, they found themselves ever less capable of expressing to their educated fellow-men what it was that they had learned. The gap between life and knowledge grew wider and wider; those who governed could not understand those who thought, and those who wanted to know could not understand those who knew. In the midst of unprecedented learning popular ignorance flourished, and chose its exemplars to rule the great cities of the world; in the midst of sciences endowed and enthroned as never before, new religions were born every day, and old superstitions recaptured the ground they had lost. The common man found himself forced to choose between a scientific priesthood mumbling unintelligible pessimism, and a theological priesthood mumbling incredible hopes.

In this situation the function of the professional teacher was clear. It should have been to mediate between the specialist and the nation; to learn the specialist's language, as the specialist had learned nature's, in order to break down the barriers between knowledge and need, and find for new truths old terms that all literate people might understand. For if knowledge became too great for communication, it would degenerate into scholasticism, and the weak acceptance of authority; mankind would slip into a new age of faith, worshiping at a respectful distance its new priests; and civilization, which had hoped to raise itself upon education disseminated far and wide, would be left precariously based upon a technical erudition that had become the monopoly of an esoteric class monastically isolated from the world by the high birth rate of terminology. No wonder that all the world applauded when James Harvey Robinson sounded the call for the removal of these barriers and the humanization of modern knowledge.

II

The first "outlines," the first efforts at the humanization of knowledge, were Plato's Dialogues. The pundits possibly know that the Master wrote two sets of works—one in technical language for his students at the Academy; the other a group of popular dialogues designed to lure the average literate Athenian into philosophy's "dear delight." It did not seem to Plato any insult to philosophy that it should be transformed into literature, realized as drama, and beautified with style; nor any derogation to its dignity that it should apply itself, even intelligibly, to living problems of morality and the state. By the humor of history, his technical works were lost, and his popular works remain. By the irony of history it is these popular dialogues that have given Plato his reputation in the schools. For us, however, the career of the outline begins with H. G. Wells. The historians did not quite know what to do with The Outline of History; *Professor Schapiro described it as full of errors, and a liberal education. It was full of errors, as any book of large scope is bound to be; but it was an astonishing and stimulating performance for one mind. The journalistic genius of Mr. Wells had tied the volumes up with the movement towards international peace, and had entered them as an important team in the "race between education and catastrophe." No one wanted catastrophe, and every one bought the book. History became popular, and historians became alarmed. Now it would be necessary for them to write as interestingly as H. G. Wells.*

*Strange to say, two of them did. Professor Breasted, of Chicago and Egypt, revised and improved an old text-book, and Professor Robinson did the same; an enterprising publishing firm gathered their work into two handsome volumes, gave them a captivating title—*The Human Adventure*—and issued the best outline of all, a masterpiece of exposition as authoritative as a German and as clear as a Gaul. Nothing in their field has equaled those volumes to date.*

Meanwhile Hendrik Willem van Loon had romped over the same ground with a pen in one hand, a pencil in the other, and a twinkle in his eyes. He cared nothing for dignity, and loved a joke surpassing well; he went laughing down the centuries, and pointed his moral with drawings and smiles. Adults bought The Story of Mankind *for their children, and surreptitiously read it themselves. The world was becoming scandalously informed about history.*

The appetite of the layman grew by what it fed on. There were in America millions of men and women who had been unable to go to college, and who thirsted for the findings of history and science; even those who had gone through college showed a moderate hunger for knowledge. When John Macy published The Story of the World's Literature *thousands welcomed it as a genial and illuminating survey of a fascinating field. And when* The Story of Philosophy *appeared it had the good fortune to catch this wave of curiosity on the rise, and to be lifted to an undreamed-of popularity. Readers were astonished to find that philosophy was interesting because it was, literally, a matter of life and death. They passed along the word to their friends, and soon it became the fashion to praise, to buy, even, occasionally, to read, this book that had been written for a few. All in all it was such a success as no author who has known it once can ever hope to know again.*

Then came the flood. Outline followed outline, "story" followed "story"; science and art, religion and law, had their storiographers, and Bekker's slight essay was avidly transformed into The Story of Religion. *One author produced in one volume an outline of all knowledge, thereby making Wells, van Loon, Macy, Slosson, Breasted and the rest superfluous. The public appetite was quickly satiated; critics and professors com-*

*plained of superficiality and haste, and an undertow of resentment set in,
which reached every outline from the last to the first. As quickly as it had
come, the fashion changed; no one dared any longer say a word for the
humanization of knowledge; the denunciation of outlines was now the
easy road to critical repute; it became the style to speak with a delicate
superiority of any non-fiction book that could be understood. The snob
movement in literature began.*

III

*Many of the criticisms were disagreeably just. The Story of Philosophy
was, and is, shot through with defects. First of all, it was incomplete. The
total omission of scholastic philosophy was an outrage, forgivable only in
one who had suffered much from it in college and seminary, and resented
it thereafter as rather a disguised theology than an honest philosophy. It
is true that in some cases (Schopenhauer, Nietzsche, Spencer, Voltaire)
the exposition of doctrine was more complete than in most histories of
philosophy, regardless of their length. And it is true that the very first
page frankly announced:*

> *This book is not a complete history of philosophy. It is an attempt to
> humanize knowledge by centering the story of speculative thought around
> certain dominant personalities. Certain lesser figures have been omitted in
> order that those selected might have the space required to make them live.
> (Preface.)*

*Nevertheless the incompleteness remained. The worst sin of all—though
the critics do not seem to have noticed it—was the omission of Chinese
and Hindu philosophy. Even a "story" of philosophy that begins with
Socrates, and has nothing to say about Lao-tze and Confucius, Mencius
and Chwang-tze, Buddha and Shankara, is provincially incomplete.[1] As
for the word* Story, *which has since been so abused with use, it was chosen
partly to indicate that the record would concern itself chiefly with the
more vital philosophers, partly to convey the sense that the development
of thought was a romance as stirring as any in history.*

*No apology is offered for the neglect of epistemology. That dismal
science received its due in the chapter on Kant, where for forty pages the
reader was invited to consider the puzzles of perception. This chapter
should have pleased the young pundit, for it came very near to obscurity.
(However, one professor of philosophy, in a Midwest university, sent in
the information that he had been teaching Kant for fifteen years, and had
never understood Kant's meaning until he read this elementary chapter.)
For the rest, the book suggested unamiably that the nature of the knowl-*

---

[1] *The first volume of* The Story of Civilization *attempts to atone for this omission.*

edge process was but one of the many problems of philosophy; that this single problem was unfit to absorb the attention which the savants and the Germans had lavished upon it; and that its weary exploitation was largely responsible for the decadence of philosophy. The French have never yielded to this craze for epistemology to the exclusion of moral and political, historical and religious philosophy; and today even the Germans are recovering from it. Hear Keyserling: "Philosophy is essentially the completion of science in the synthesis of wisdom. . . . Epistemology, phenomenology, logic, etc., certainly are important branches of science." (Precisely; they are branches of science, like chemistry or anatomy.) "But it was an unmitigated evil that as the result of this, the sense for the living synthesis should have disappeared." (Creative Understanding, New York, 1929, p. 125.) This from a German—a Daniel come to judgment. And Spengler describes the earlier Chinese philosophers, down to Confucius, as "statesmen, regents, lawgivers, like Pythagoras and Parmenides, like Hobbes and Leibniz. . . . They were sturdy philosophers for whom epistemology was the knowledge of the important relations of actual life." (Decline of the West, vol. i, p. 42.) Doubtless now that epistemology is dying in Germany, it will be exported to America, as a fit return for the gift of democracy.

The Chinese philosophers were not only averse to epistemology, they had an almost Gallic disdain for prolonged metaphysics. No young metaphysician could admit that Confucius is a philosopher, for he says nothing about metaphysics, and less about epistemology; he is as positivistic as Spencer or Comte; his concern is always for morals and the state. Worse than that, he is disreputably intelligible; and nothing could be so damaging to a philosopher. But we "moderns" have become so accustomed to windy verbiage in philosophy that when philosophy is presented without the verbiage we can with difficulty recognize it. One must pay a penalty for having a prejudice against obscurity.

The Story tried to salt itself with a seasoning of humor, not only because wisdom is not wise if it scares away merriment, but because a sense of humor, being born of perspective, bears a near kinship to philosophy; each is the soul of the other. But this appears to have displeased the pundits; nothing so hurt the book with them as its smiles. A reputation for humor is disastrous to statesmen and philosophers: Germany could not forgive Schopenhauer his story of Unzelmann, and only France has recognized the depth behind the wit and brilliance of Voltaire.

I trust that the book never misled its readers into supposing that by reading it they would become philosophers overnight, or that they would be saved the trouble, or pleasure, of reading the philosophers themselves. God knows there is no short-cut to knowledge; after forty years of seeking her one finds "Truth" still veiled, and what she shows of herself most disconcerting. Instead of aiming to be a substitute for philosophers, the

Story *explicitly offered itself as an introduction and an invitation; it quoted the philosophers lavishly, so that the taste for them might linger when the book was closed; time and again it prodded the reader to the original texts (e. g., on pp. 22, 67, 121, 289, 331, 425, 438); and warning was given that one reading of them would hardly be enough. Cf. p. 186:*

> *Spinoza is not to be read, he is to be studied; you must approach him as you would approach Euclid, recognizing that in these brief two hundred pages a man has written down his lifetime's thought with stoic sculptory of everything superfluous. Do not think to find its core by running over it rapidly. . . . Read the book not all at once, but in small portions at many sittings. And having finished it, consider that you have but begun to understand it. Read then some commentary, like Pollock's Spinoza, or Martineau's Study of Spinoza, or, better, both. Finally, read the Ethics again; it will be a new book to you. When you have finished it a second time you will remain forever a lover of philosophy.*

It is comforting to learn that the sales of the philosophical classics increased some two hundred per cent. after the publication of the Story. Many publishers have issued new editions, particularly of Plato, Spinoza, Voltaire, Schopenhauer and Nietzsche. A high official of the New York Public Library, who asks to be unnamed, reports that

> *ever since the publication of the Story of Philosophy we have had a wide and increasing demand from the public for the philosophical classics, and our stock of them in the branch libraries has been gradually increased. . . . Formerly, current books about philosophy were purchased in small quantities for the system; but in the last two or three years a readable new book about philosophy is purchased very generally at the outset, in anticipation of a demand which eventually does develop, and quickly at that.*

Let us not, then, be ashamed of teaching the people. Those jealous ones who would guard their knowledge from the world have only themselves to blame if their exclusiveness and their barbarous terminology have led the world to seek in books, in lectures, and in adult education, the instruction which they themselves have failed to give. Let them be grateful that their halting efforts are aided by amateurs who love life enough to let it humanize their teaching. Perhaps each kind of teacher can be of aid to the other: the cautious scholar to check our enthusiasm with accuracy, and the enthusiast to pour warmth and blood into the fruits of scholarship. Between us we might build up in America an audience fit to listen to geniuses, and therefore ready to produce them. We are all imperfect teachers, but we may be forgiven if we have advanced the matter a little, and have done our best. We announce the prologue, and retire; after us better players will come.

THE STORY OF PHILOSOPHY has been translated into German, French, Swedish, Danish, Yugoslavian, Chinese, Japanese, Hungarian and Hindi.

Contents

CHAPTER I

PLATO

CHAPTER II

ARISTOTLE AND GREEK SCIENCE

CHAPTER III
FRANCIS BACON

CHAPTER IV
SPINOZA

CHAPTER VIII

HERBERT SPENCER

CHAPTER IX

FRIEDRICH NIETZSCHE

CHAPTER X

CONTEMPORARY EUROPEAN PHILOSOPHERS

CHAPTER XI

CONTEMPORARY AMERICAN PHILOSOPHERS

TO THE READER

This book is not a complete history of philosophy. It is an attempt to humanize knowledge by centering the story of speculative thought around certain dominant personalities. Certain lesser figures have been omitted in order that those selected might have the space required to make them live. Hence the inadequate treatment of the half-legendary pre-Socratics, the Stoics and Epicureans, the Scholastics, and the epistemologists. The author believes that epistemology has kidnapped modern philosophy, and well nigh ruined it; he hopes for the time when the study of the knowledge-process will be recognized as the business of the science of psychology, and when philosophy will again be understood as the synthetic interpretation of all experience rather than the analytic description of the mode and process of experience itself. Analysis belongs to science, and gives us knowledge; philosophy must provide a synthesis for wisdom.

The author would like to record here a debt which he can never repay, to Alden Freeman, who gave him education, travel, and the inspiration of a noble and enlightened life. May this best of friends find in these pages—incidental and imperfect though they are—something not quite unworthy of his generosity and his faith.

WILL DURANT

New York, 1926.

INTRODUCTION

On the Uses of Philosophy

THERE IS A PLEASURE in philosophy, and a lure even in the mirages of metaphysics, which every student feels until the coarse necessities of physical existence drag him from the heights of thought into the mart of economic strife and gain. Most of us have known some golden days in the June of life when philosophy was in fact what Plato calls it, "that dear delight"; when the love of a modestly elusive Truth seemed more glorious, incomparably, than the lust for the ways of the flesh and the dross of the world. And there is always some wistful remnant in us of that early wooing of wisdom. "Life has meaning," we feel with Browning—"to find its meaning is my meat and drink." So much of our lives is meaningless, a self-cancelling vacillation and futility; we strive with the chaos about us and within; but we would believe all the while that there is something vital and significant in us, could we but decipher our own souls. We want to understand; "life means for us constantly to transform into light and flame all that we are or meet with";[1] we are like Mitya in *The Brothers Karamazov*—"one of those who don't want millions, but an answer to their questions"; we want to seize the value and perspective of passing things, and so to pull ourselves up out of the maelstrom of daily circumstance. We want to know that the little things are little, and the big things big, before it is too late; we want to see things now as they will seem forever—"in the light of eternity." We want to learn to laugh in the face of the inevitable, to smile even at the looming of death. We want to be whole, to coördinate our energies by criticizing and harmonizing our desires; for coördinated energy is the last word in ethics and politics, and perhaps in logic and metaphysics too. "To be a philosopher," said Thoreau, "is not merely to have subtle thoughts, nor even to found a school, but so to love wisdom as to live, according to its dictates, a life of simplicity, independence, magnanimity, and trust." We may be sure that if we can but find wisdom, all things else will be added unto us. "Seek ye first the good things of the mind," Bacon admonishes us, "and the rest will either be supplied or its loss will not be felt."[2] Truth will not make us rich, but it will make us free.

[1] Nietzsche, *The Joyful Wisdom*, pref.   [2] *De Augmentis Scientiarum*, VIII, 2.

Some ungentle reader will check us here by informing us that philosophy is as useless as chess, as obscure as ignorance, and as stagnant as content. "There is nothing so absurd," said Cicero, "but that it may be found in the books of the philosophers." Doubtless some philosophers have had all sorts of wisdom except common sense; and many a philosophic flight has been due to the elevating power of thin air. Let us resolve, on this voyage of ours, to put in only at the ports of light, to keep out of the muddy streams of metaphysics and the "many-sounding seas" of theological dispute. But is philosophy stagnant? Science seems always to advance, while philosophy seems always to lose ground. Yet this is only because philosophy accepts the hard and hazardous task of dealing with problems not yet open to the methods of science—problems like good and evil, beauty and ugliness, order and freedom, life and death; so soon as a field of inquiry yields knowledge susceptible of exact formulation it is called science. Every science begins as philosophy and ends as art; it arises in hypothesis and flows into achievement. Philosophy is a hypothetical interpretation of the unknown (as in metaphysics), or of the inexactly known (as in ethics or political philosophy) ; it is the front trench in the siege of truth. Science is the captured territory; and behind it are those secure regions in which knowledge and art build our imperfect and marvelous world. Philosophy seems to stand still, perplexed; but only because she leaves the fruits of victory to her daughters the sciences, and herself passes on, divinely discontent, to the uncertain and unexplored.

Shall we be more technical? Science is analytical description, philosophy is synthetic interpretation. Science wishes to resolve the whole into parts, the organism into organs, the obscure into the known. It does not inquire into the values and ideal possibilities of things, nor into their total and final significance; it is content to show their present actuality and operation, it narrows its gaze resolutely to the nature and process of things as they are. The scientist is as impartial as Nature in Turgenev's poem: he is as interested in the leg of a flea as in the creative throes of a genius. But the philosopher is not content to describe the fact; he wishes to ascertain its relation to experience in general, and thereby to get at its meaning and its worth; he combines things in interpretive synthesis; he tries to put together, better than before, that great universe-watch which the inquisitive scientist has analytically taken apart. Science tells us how to heal and how to kill; it reduces the death rate in retail and then kills us wholesale in war; but only wisdom—desire coördinated in the light of all experience—can tell us when to heal and when to kill. To observe processes and to construct means is science; to criticize and coördinate ends is philosophy: and because in these days our means and instruments have multiplied beyond our interpretation and synthesis of ideals and ends, our life is full of sound and fury, signifying nothing. For a fact is nothing except in relation to desire; it is not complete except in relation to a purpose and a whole. Science without philosophy, facts without perspective and valuation, cannot save us from havoc and despair. Science gives us knowledge, but only philosophy can give us wisdom.

Specifically, philosophy means and includes five fields of study and discourse: logic, esthetics, ethics, politics, and metaphysics. *Logic* is the study of ideal method in thought and research: observation and introspection, deduction and induction, hypothesis and experiment, analysis and synthesis—such are the forms of human activity which logic tries to understand and guide; it is a dull study for most of us, and yet the great events in the history of thought are the improvements men have made in their methods of thinking and research. *Esthetics* is the study of ideal form, or beauty; it is the philosophy of art. *Ethics* is the study of ideal conduct; the highest knowledge, said Socrates, is the knowledge of good and evil, the knowledge of the wisdom of life. *Politics* is the study of ideal social organization (it is not, as one might suppose, the art and science of capturing and keeping office); monarchy, aristocracy, democracy, socialism, anarchism, feminism—these are the *dramatis personae* of political philosophy. And lastly, *metaphysics* (which gets into so much trouble because it is not, like the other forms of philosophy, an attempt to coördinate the real in the light of the ideal) is the study of the "ultimate reality" of all things: of the real and final nature of "matter" (ontology), of "mind" (philosophical psychology), and of the interrelation of "mind" and "matter" in the processes of perception and knowledge (epistemology).

These are the parts of philosophy; but so dismembered it loses its beauty and its joy. We shall seek it not in its shrivelled abstractness and formality, but clothed in the living form of genius; we shall study not merely philosophies, but philosophers; we shall spend our time with the saints and martyrs of thought, letting their radiant spirit play about us until perhaps we too, in some measure, shall partake of what Leonardo called "the noblest pleasure, the joy of understanding." Each of these philosophers has some lesson for us, if we approach him properly. "Do you know," asks Emerson, "the secret of the true scholar? In every man there is something wherein I may learn of him; and in that I am his pupil." Well, surely we may take this attitude to the master minds of history without hurt to our pride! And we may flatter ourselves with that other thought of Emerson's, that when genius speaks to us we feel a ghostly reminiscence of having ourselves, in our distant youth, had vaguely this self-same thought which genius now speaks, but which we had not art or courage to clothe with form and utterance. And indeed, great men speak to us only so far as we have ears and souls to hear them; only so far as we have in us the roots, at least, of that which flowers out in them. We too have had the experiences they had, but we did not suck those experiences dry of their secret and subtle meanings: we were not sensitive to the overtones of the reality that hummed about us. Genius hears the overtones, and the music of the spheres; genius knows what Pythagoras meant when he said that philosophy is the highest music.

So let us listen to these men, ready to forgive them their passing errors, and eager to learn the lessons which they are so eager to teach. "Do you then be reasonable," said old Socrates to Crito, "and do not mind whether the teachers of philosophy are good or bad, but think only of Philosophy herself. Try to examine her well and truly; and if she be evil, seek to turn away all men from her; but if she be what I believe she is, then follow her and serve her, and be of good cheer."

CHAPTER I

Plato

I. THE CONTEXT OF PLATO

IF YOU look at a map of Europe you will observe that Greece is a skeleton-like hand stretching its crooked fingers out into the Mediterranean Sea. South of it lies the great island of Crete, from which those grasping fingers captured, in the second millennium before Christ, the beginnings of civilization and culture. To the east, across the Ægean Sea, lies Asia Minor, quiet and apathetic now, but throbbing, in pre-Platonic days, with industry, commerce and speculation. To the west, across the Ionian, Italy stands, like a leaning tower in the sea, and Sicily and Spain, each in those days with thriving Greek colonies; and at the end, the "Pillars of Hercules" (which we call Gibraltar), that sombre portal through which not many an ancient mariner dared to pass. And on the north those still untamed and half-barbaric regions, then named Thessaly and Epirus and Macedonia, from which or through which the vigorous bands had come which fathered the geniuses of Homeric and Periclean Greece.

Look again at the map, and you see countless indentations of coast and elevations of land; everywhere gulfs and bays and the intrusive sea; and all the earth tumbled and tossed into mountains and hills. Greece was broken into isolated fragments by these natural barriers of sea and soil; travel and communication were far more difficult and dangerous then than now; every valley therefore developed its own self-sufficient economic life, its own sovereign government, its own institutions and dialect and religion and culture. In each case one or two cities, and around them, stretching up the mountainslopes, an agricultural hinterland: such were the "city-states" of Eubœa, and Locris, and Ætolia, and Phocis, and Bœotia, and Achæa, and Argolis, and Elis, and Arcadia, and Messenia, and Laconia—with its Sparta, and Attica—with its Athens.

Look at the map a last time, and observe the position of Athens: it is the farthest east of the larger cities of Greece. It was favorably placed to be the door through which the Greeks passed out to the busy cities of Asia Minor, and through which those elder cities sent their luxuries and their culture to adolescent Greece. It had an admirable port, Piræus, where countless vessels might find a haven from the rough waters of the sea. And it had a great maritime fleet.

5

In 490–470 B. C. Sparta and Athens, forgetting their jealousies and joining their forces, fought off the effort of the Persians under Darius and Xerxes to turn Greece into a colony of an Asiatic empire. In this struggle of youthful Europe against the senile East, Sparta provided the army and Athens the navy. The war over, Sparta demobilized her troops, and suffered the economic disturbances natural to that process; while Athens turned her navy into a merchant fleet, and became one of the greatest trading cities of the ancient world. Sparta relapsed into agricultural seclusion and stagnation, while Athens became a busy mart and port, the meeting place of many races of men and of diverse cults and customs, whose contact and rivalry begot comparison, analysis and thought.

Traditions and dogmas rub one another down to a minimum in such centers of varied intercourse; where there are a thousand faiths we are apt to become sceptical of them all. Probably the traders were the first sceptics; they had seen too much to believe too much; and the general disposition of merchants to classify all men as either fools or knaves inclined them to question every creed. Gradually, too, they were developing science; mathematics grew with the increasing complexity of exchange, astronomy with the increasing audacity of navigation. The growth of wealth brought the leisure and security which are the prerequisite of research and speculation; men now asked the stars not only for guidance on the seas but as well for an answer to the riddles of the universe; the first Greek philosophers were astronomers. "Proud of their achievements," says Aristotle,[1] "men pushed farther afield after the Persian wars; they took all knowledge for their province, and sought ever wider studies." Men grew bold enough to attempt natural explanations of processes and events before attributed to supernatural agencies and powers; magic and ritual slowly gave way to science and control; and philosophy began.

At first this philosophy was physical; it looked out upon the material world and asked what was the final and irreducible constituent of things. The natural termination of this line of thought was the materialism of Democritus (460–360 B. C.)—"in reality there is nothing but atoms and space." This was one of the main streams of Greek speculation; it passed underground for a time in Plato's day, but emerged in Epicurus (342–270), and became a torrent of eloquence in Lucretius (98–55 B. C.). But the most characteristic and fertile developments of Greek philosophy took form with the Sophists, travelling teachers of wisdom, who looked within upon their own thought and nature, rather than out upon the world of things. They were all clever men (Gorgias and Hippias, for example), and many of them were profound (Protagoras, Prodicus); there is hardly a problem or a solution in our current philosophy of mind and conduct which they did not realize and discuss. They asked questions about anything; they stood unafraid in the presence of religious or political taboos;

[1] *Politics*, 1341.

and boldly subpoenaed every creed and institution to appear before the judgment-seat of reason. In politics they divided into two schools. One, like Rousseau, argued that nature is good, and civilization bad; that by nature all men are equal, becoming unequal only by class-made institutions: and that law is an invention of the strong to chain and rule the weak. Another school, like Nietzsche, claimed that nature is beyond good and evil; that by nature all men are unequal; that morality is an invention of the weak to limit and deter the strong; that power is the supreme virtue and the supreme desire of man; and that of all forms of government the wisest and most natural is aristocracy.

No doubt this attack on democracy reflected the rise of a wealthy minority at Athens which called itself the Oligarchical Party, and denounced democracy as an incompetent sham. In a sense there was not much democracy to denounce; for of the 400,000 inhabitants of Athens 250,000 were slaves, without political rights of any kind; and of the 150,000 freemen or citizens only a small number presented themselves at the Ecclesia, or general assembly, where the policies of the state were discussed and determined. Yet what democracy they had was as thorough as never since; the general assembly was the supreme power; and the highest official body, the Dikasteria, or supreme court, consisted of over a thousand members (to make bribery expensive), selected by alphabetical rote from the roll of all the citizens. No institution could have been more democratic, nor, said its opponents, more absurd.

During the great generation-long Peloponnesian war (430–400 B. C.), in which the military power of Sparta fought and at last defeated the naval power of Athens, the Athenian oligarchic party, led by Critias, advocated the abandonment of democracy on the score of its inefficiency in war, and secretly lauded the aristocratic government of Sparta. Many of the oligarchic leaders were exiled; but when at last Athens surrendered, one of the peace conditions imposed by Sparta was the recall of these exiled aristocrats. They had hardly returned when, with Critias at their head, they declared a rich man's revolution against the "democratic" party that had ruled during the disastrous war. The revolution failed, and Critias was killed on the field of battle.

Now Critias was a pupil of Socrates, and an uncle of Plato.

II. SOCRATES

If we may judge from the bust that has come down to us as part of the ruins of ancient sculpture, Socrates was as far from being handsome as even a philosopher can be. A bald head, a great round face, deepset staring eyes, a broad and flowery nose that gave vivid testimony to many a Symposium—it was rather the head of a porter than that of the most famous of philosophers. But if we look again we see, through

the crudity of the stone, something of that human kindliness and un-
assuming simplicity which made this homely thinker a teacher beloved
of the finest youths in Athens. We know so little about him, and yet we
know him so much more intimately than the aristocratic Plato or the
reserved and scholarly Aristotle. Across two thousand three hundred
years we can yet see his ungainly figure, clad always in the same rumpled
tunic, walking leisurely through the agora, undisturbed by the bedlam of
politics, buttonholing his prey, gathering the young and the learned about
him, luring them into some shady nook of the temple porticos, and asking
them to define their terms.

They were a motley crowd, these youths who flocked about him and
helped him to create European philosophy. There were rich young men
like Plato and Alcibiades, who relished his satirical analysis of Athenian
democracy; there were socialists like Antisthenes, who liked the master's
careless poverty, and made a religion of it; there was even an anarchist
or two among them, like Aristippus, who aspired to a world in which
there would be neither masters nor slaves, and all would be as worri-
lessly free as Socrates. All the problems that agitate human society
to-day, and provide the material of youth's endless debate, agitated as
well that little band of thinkers and talkers, who felt, with their teacher,
that life without discourse would be unworthy of a man. Every school
of social thought had there its representative, and perhaps its origin.

How the master lived hardly anybody knew. He never worked, and he
took no thought of the morrow. He ate when his disciples asked him to
honor their tables; they must have liked his company, for he gave every
indication of physiological prosperity. He was not so welcome at home,
for he neglected his wife and children; and from Xanthippe's point of
view he was a good-for-nothing idler who brought to his family more
notoriety than bread. Xanthippe liked to talk almost as much as Socrates
did; and they seem to have had some dialogues which Plato failed to
record. Yet she, too, loved him, and could not contentedly see him die
even after three-score years and ten.

Why did his pupils reverence him so? Perhaps because he was a man
as well as a philosopher: he had at great risk saved the life of Alcibiades
in battle; and he could drink like a gentleman—without fear and without
excess. But no doubt they liked best in him the modesty of his wisdom: he
did not claim to have wisdom, but only to seek it lovingly; he was
wisdom's *amateur*, not its professional. It was said that the oracle at
Delphi, with unusual good sense, had pronounced him the wisest of the
Greeks; and he had interpreted this as an approval of the agnosticism
which was the starting-point of his philosophy—"One thing only I know,
and that is that I know nothing." Philosophy begins when one learns
to doubt—particularly to doubt one's cherished beliefs, one's dogmas
and one's axioms. Who knows how these cherished beliefs became cer-

tainties with us, and whether some secret wish did not furtively beget them, clothing desire in the dress of thought? There is no real philosophy until the mind turns round and examines itself. *Gnothi seauton,* said Socrates: Know thyself.

There had been philosophers before him, of course: strong men like Thales and Heraclitus, subtle men like Parmenides and Zeno of Elea, seers like Pythagoras and Empedocles; but for the most part they had been physical philosophers; they had sought for the *physis* or nature of external things, the laws and constituents of the material and measurable world. That is very good, said Socrates; but there is an infinitely worthier subject for philosophers than all these trees and stones, and even all those stars; there is the mind of man. What is man, and what can he become?

So he went about prying into the human soul, uncovering assumptions and questioning certainties. If men discoursed too readily of justice, he asked them, quietly, *tò tí?*—what is it? What do you mean by these abstract words with which you so easily settle the problems of life and death? What do you mean by honor, virtue, morality, patriotism? What do you mean by your*self?* It was with such moral and psychological questions that Socrates loved to deal. Some who suffered from this "Socratic method," this demand for accurate definitions, and clear thinking, and exact analysis, objected that he asked more than he answered, and left men's minds more confused than before. Nevertheless he bequeathed to philosophy two very definite answers to two of our most difficult problems —What is the meaning of virtue? and What is the best state?

No topics could have been more vital than these to the young Athenians of that generation. The Sophists had destroyed the faith these youths had once had in the gods and goddesses of Olympus, and in the moral code that had taken its sanction so largely from the fear men had for these ubiquitous and innumerable deities; apparently there was no reason now why a man should not do as he pleased, so long as he remained within the law. A disintegrating individualism had weakened the Athenian character, and left the city a prey at last to the sternly-nurtured Spartans. And as for the state, what could have been more ridiculous than this mob-led, passion-ridden democracy, this government by a debating-society, this precipitate selection and dismissal and execution of generals, this un-choice choice of simple farmers and tradesmen, in alphabetical rotation, as members of the supreme court of the land? How could a new and natural morality be developed in Athens, and how could the state be saved?

It was his reply to these questions that gave Socrates death and immortality. The older citizens would have honored him had he tried to restore the ancient polytheistic faith; if he had led his band of emancipated souls to the temples and the sacred groves, and bade them sacrifice again to the gods of their fathers. But he felt that that was a hopeless and suicidal policy, a progress backward, into and not "over the tombs." He had his own religious faith: he believed in one God, and hoped in his modest way that death would not quite destroy him;[2] but he knew that a lasting moral code could not be based upon so uncertain a theology. If one could build a system of morality absolutely independent of religious doctrine, as valid for the atheist as for the pietist, then theologies might come and go without loosening the moral cement that makes of wilful individuals the peaceful citizens of a community.

If, for example, *good* meant *intelligent,* and *virtue* meant *wisdom;* if men could be taught to see clearly their real interests, to see afar the distant results of their deeds, to criticize and coördinate their desires out of a self-cancelling chaos into a purposive and creative harmony—this, perhaps, would provide for the educated and sophisticated man the morality which in the unlettered relies on reiterated precepts and external control. Perhaps all sin is error, partial vision, foolishness? The intelligent man may have the same violent and unsocial impulses as the ignorant man, but surely he will control them better, and slip less often into imitation of the beast. And in an intelligently administered society—one that returned to the individual, in widened powers, more than it took from him in restricted liberty—the advantage of every man would lie in social and loyal conduct, and only clear sight would be needed to ensure peace and order and good will.

But if the government itself is a chaos and an absurdity, if it rules without helping, and commands without leading,—how can we persuade the individual, in such a state, to obey the laws and confine his self-seeking within the circle of the total good? No wonder an Alcibiades turns against a state that distrusts ability, and reverences number more than knowledge. No wonder there is chaos where there is no thought, and the crowd decides in haste and ignorance, to repent at leisure and in desolation. Is it not a base superstition that mere numbers will give wisdom? On the contrary is it not universally seen that men in crowds are more foolish and more violent and more cruel than men separate and alone? Is it not shameful that men should be ruled by orators, who "go ringing on in long harangues, like brazen pots which, when struck, continue to sound till a hand is put upon them"?[3] Surely the management of a state is a matter for which men cannot be too intelligent, a matter that needs the unhindered thought of the finest minds. How can a society be saved, or be strong, except it be led by its wisest men?

Imagine the reaction of the popular party at Athens to this aristocratic gospel at a time when war seemed to require the silencing of all criticism,

---

[2] Cf. Voltaire's story of the two Athenians conversing about Socrates: "That is the atheist who says there is only one God." *Philosophical Dictionary,* art. "Socrates."
[3] Plato's *Protagoras,* sect. 329.

and when the wealthy and lettered minority were plotting a revolution. Consider the feelings of Anytus, the democratic leader whose son had become a pupil of Socrates, and had then turned against the gods of his father, and laughed in his father's face. Had not Aristophanes predicted precisely such a result from this specious replacement of the old virtues by unsocial intelligence?[4]

Then the revolution came, and men fought for it and against, bitterly and to the death. When the democracy won, the fate of Socrates was decided: he was the intellectual leader of the revolting party, however pacific he might himself have been; he was the source of the hated aristocratic philosophy; he was the corrupter of youths drunk with debate. It would be better, said Anytus and Meletus, that Socrates should die.

The rest of the story all the world knows, for Plato wrote it down in prose more beautiful than poetry. We are privileged to read for ourselves that simple and courageous (if not legendary) "apology," or defence, in which the first martyr of philosophy proclaimed the rights and necessity of free thought, upheld his value to the state, and refused to beg for mercy from the crowd whom he had always contemned. They had the power to pardon him; he disdained to make the appeal. It was a singular confirmation of his theories, that the judges should wish to let him go, while the angry crowd voted for his death. Had he not denied the gods? Woe to him who teaches men faster than they can learn.

So they decreed that he should drink the hemlock. His friends came to his prison and offered him an easy escape; they had bribed all the officials who stood between him and liberty. He refused. He was seventy years old now (399 B. C.); perhaps he thought it was time for him to die, and that he could never again die so usefully. "Be of good cheer," he told his sorrowing friends, "and say that you are burying my body only." "When he had spoken these words," says Plato, in one of the great passages of the world's literature,[5]

he arose and went into the bath-chamber with Crito, who bade us wait; and we waited, talking and thinking of . . . the greatness of our sorrow; he was like a father of whom we were being bereaved, and we were about to pass the rest of our lives as orphans. . . . Now the hour of sunset was near, for a good deal of time had passed while he was within. When he came out, he sat down with us again, . . . but not much was said. Soon the jailer . . .

[4] In *The Clouds* (423 B. C.) Aristophanes had made great fun of Socrates and his "Thinking-shop," where one learned the art of proving one's self right, however wrong. Phidippides beats his father on the ground that his father used to beat him, and every debt should be repaid. The satire seems to have been good-natured enough: we find Aristophanes frequently in the company of Socrates; they agreed in their scorn of democracy; and Plato recommended *The Clouds* to Dionysius. As the play was brought out twenty-four years before the trial of Socrates, it could have had no great share in bringing the tragic dénouement of the philosopher's life.

[5] *Phaedo,* sections 116–118, tr. Jowett.

entered and stood by him, saying: "To you, Socrates, whom I know to be the noblest and gentlest and best of all who ever came to this place, I will not impute the angry feelings of other men, who rage and swear at me when, in obedience to the authorities, I bid them drink the poison—indeed I am sure that you will not be angry with me; for others, as you are aware, and not I, are the guilty cause. And so fare you well, and try to bear lightly what must needs be; you know my errand." Then bursting into tears he turned away and went out.

Socrates looked at him and said: "I return your good wishes, and will do as you bid." Then turning to us, he said, "How charming the man is; since I have been in prison he has always been coming to see me, and now see how generously he sorrows for me. But we must do as he says, Crito; let the cup be brought, if the poison is prepared; if not, let the attendant prepare some."

"Yet," said Crito, "the sun is still upon the hill-tops, and many a one has taken the draught late; and after the announcement has been made to him he has eaten and drunk, and indulged in sensual delights; do not hasten then, there is still time."

Socrates said: "Yes, Crito, and they of whom you speak are right in doing thus, for they think that they will gain by the delay; but I am right in not doing thus, for I do not think that I should gain anything by drinking the poison a little later; I should be sparing and saving a life which is already gone; I could only laugh at myself for this. Please then to do as I say, and not to refuse me."

Crito, when he heard this, made a sign to the servant; and the servant went in, and remained for some time, and then returned with the jailer carrying the cup of poison. Socrates said: "You, my good friend, who are experienced in these matters, shall give me directions how I am to proceed." The man answered: "You have only to walk about until your legs are heavy, and then to lie down, and the poison will act." At the same time he handed the cup to Socrates, who in the easiest and gentlest manner, without the least fear or change of color or feature, looking at the man with all his eyes, as his manner was, took the cup and said: "What do you say about making a libation out of this cup to any god? May I, or not?" The man answered: "We only prepare, Socrates, just so much as we deem enough." "I understand," he said; "yet I may and must pray to the gods to prosper my journey from this to that other world—may this then, which is my prayer, be granted to me." Then, holding the cup to his lips, quite readily and cheerfully he drank the poison.

And hitherto most of us had been able to control our sorrow; but now when we saw him drinking, and saw too that he had finished the draught, we could no longer forbear, and in spite of myself my own tears were flowing fast; so that I covered my face and wept over myself; for certainly I was not weeping over him, but at the thought of my own calamity in having lost such a companion. Nor was I the first, for Crito, when he found himself unable to restrain his tears, had got up and moved away, and I followed; and at that moment Apollodorus, who had been weeping all the time, broke out into a loud cry which made cowards of us all. Socrates alone retained his calmness: "What is this strange outcry?" he said. "I sent away the women mainly in order that they might not offend in this way, for I have heard that a man should die in peace. Be quiet, then, and have patience." When we heard that, we were ashamed, and restrained our tears; and he walked about until, as he said, his legs began to fail, and then he lay on his back, according to the directions, and the man who gave him the poison now and then looked at his feet and legs; and after a while he pressed his foot hard and asked him if he could feel; and he said, "No"; and then his leg, and so upwards and upwards, and showed us that he was cold and stiff. And then Socrates felt them himself, and said, "When the poison reaches the heart, that will be the end." He was beginning to grow cold about the groin, when he uncovered his face (for he had covered himself up) and said,— they were his last words,—"Crito, I owe a cock to Asclepius; will you remember to pay the debt?" "The debt shall be paid," said Crito; "is there anything else?" There was no answer to this question; but in a minute or two a movement was heard, and the attendant uncovered him; his eyes were set, and Crito closed his eyes and mouth.

Such was the end of our friend, whom I may truly call the wisest, the justest, and best of all the men whom I have ever known.

III. THE PREPARATION OF PLATO

Plato's meeting with Socrates had been a turning point in his life. He had been brought up in comfort, and perhaps in wealth; he was a handsome and vigorous youth—called Plato, it is said, because of the breadth of his shoulders; he had excelled as a soldier, and had twice won prizes at the Isthmian games. Philosophers are not apt to develop out of such an adolescence. But Plato's subtle soul had found a new joy in the "dialectic" game of Socrates; it was a delight to behold the master deflating dogmas and puncturing presumptions with the sharp point of his questions; Plato entered into this sport as he had in a coarser kind of wrestling; and under the guidance of the old "gad-fly" (as Socrates called himself) he passed from mere debate to careful analysis and fruitful discussion. He became a very passionate lover of wisdom, and of his teacher. "I thank God," he used to say, "that I was born Greek and not barbarian, freeman and not slave, man and not woman; but above all, that I was born in the age of Socrates."

He was twenty-eight when the master died; and this tragic end of a quiet life left its mark on every phase of the pupil's thought. It filled him with such a scorn of democracy, such a hatred of the mob, as even his aristocratic lineage and breeding had hardly engendered in him; it led him to a Catonic resolve that democracy must be destroyed, to be replaced by the rule of the wisest and the best. It became the absorbing problem of his life to find a method whereby the wisest and the best might be discovered, and then enabled and persuaded to rule.

Meanwhile his efforts to save Socrates had marked him out for suspicion by the democratic leaders; his friends urged that Athens was unsafe for him, that it was an admirably propitious moment for him to see the world. And so, in that year 399 B. C., he set out. Where he went we cannot for certain say; there is a merry war of the authorities for every turn of his route. He seems to have gone first to Egypt; and was somewhat shocked to hear from the priestly class which ruled that land, that Greece was an infant-state, without stabilizing traditions or profound culture, not yet therefore to be taken seriously by these sphinxly pundits of the Nile. But nothing so educates us as a shock; the memory of this learned caste, theocratically ruling a static agricultural people, remained alive in Plato's thought, and played its part in writing his Utopia. And then off he sailed to Sicily, and to Italy; there he joined for a time the school or sect which the great Pythagoras had founded; and once again his susceptible mind was marked with the memory of a small group of men set aside for scholarship and rule, living a plain life despite the possession of power. Twelve years he wandered, imbibing wisdom from every source, sitting at every shrine, tasting every creed. Some would have it that he went to Judea and was moulded for a while by the tradition of the almost socialistic prophets; and even that he found his way to the banks of the Ganges, and learned the mystic meditations of the Hindus. We do not know.

He returned to Athens in 387 B. C., a man of forty now, ripened to maturity by the variety of many peoples and the wisdom of many lands. He had lost a little of the hot enthusiasms of youth, but he had gained a perspective of thought in which every extreme was seen as a half-truth, and the many aspects of every problem blended into a distributive justice to every facet of the truth. He had knowledge, and he had art; for once the philosopher and the poet lived in one soul; and he created for himself a medium of expression in which both beauty and truth might find room and play—the dialogue. Never before, we may believe, had philosophy assumed so brilliant a garb; and surely never since. Even in translation this style shines and sparkles and leaps and bubbles over. "Plato," says one of his lovers, Shelley, "exhibits the rare union of close and subtle logic with the Pythian enthusiasm of poetry, melted by the splendor and harmony of his periods into one irresistible stream of musical impressions, which hurry the persuasions onward as in a breathless career."[6] It was not for nothing that the young philosopher had begun as a dramatist.

The difficulty in understanding Plato lies precisely in this intoxicating mixture of philosophy and poetry, of science and art; we cannot always tell in which character of the dialogue the author speaks, nor in which form; whether he is literal or speaks in metaphor, whether he jests or is in earnest. His love of jest and irony and myth leaves us at times baffled;

6Quoted by Barker, *Greek Political Theory*, London, 1918, p. 5.

almost we could say of him that he did not teach except in parables. "Shall I, as an older person, speak to you, as younger men, in apologue or myth?" asks his Protagoras.[7] These dialogues, we are told, were written by Plato for the general reading public of his day: by their conversational method, their lively war of *pros* and *cons,* and their gradual development and frequent repetition of every important argument, they were explicitly adapted (obscure though they may seem to us now) to the understanding of the man who must taste philosophy as an occasional luxury, and who is compelled by the brevity of life to read as he who runs may read. Therefore we must be prepared to find in these dialogues much that is playful and metaphorical; much that is unintelligible except to scholars learned in the social and literary minutiae of Plato's time; much that today will seem irrelevant and fanciful, but might well have served as the very sauce and flavor by which a heavy dish of thought was made digestible for minds unused to philosophic fare.

Let us confess, too, that Plato has in sufficient abundance the qualities which he condemns. He inveighs against poets and their myths, and proceeds to add one to the number of poets and hundreds to the number of myths. He complains of the priests (who go about preaching hell and offering redemption from it for a consideration—cf. *The Republic,* 364), but he himself is a priest, a theologian, a preacher, a supermoralist, a Savonarola denouncing art and inviting vanities to the fire. He acknowledges, Shakespeare-like, that "comparisons are slippery" (*Sophist,* 231), but he slips out of one into another and another and another; he condemns the Sophists as phrase-mongering disputants, but he himself is not above chopping logic like a sophomore. Faguet parodies him: "The whole is greater than the part?—Surely.—And the part is less than the whole?—Yes.—. . . Therefore, clearly, philosophers should rule the state?—What is that?—It is evident; let us go over it again."[8]

But this is the worst that we can say of him; and after it is said, the *Dialogues* remain one of the priceless treasures of the world.[9] The best of them, *The Republic,* is a complete treatise in itself, Plato reduced to a book; here we shall find his metaphysics, his theology, his ethics, his psychology, his pedagogy, his politics, his theory of art. Here we shall find problems reeking with modernity and contemporary savor: communism and socialism, feminism and birth-control and eugenics, Nietzschean problems of morality and aristocracy, Rousseauian problems of return to

[7]*Protagoras,* 320.

[8]*Pour qu'on lise Platon,* Paris, 1905, p. 4.

[9]The most important of the dialogues are: *The Apology of Socrates, Crito, Phædo, The Symposium, Phædrus, Gorgias, Parmenides,* and *The Statesman.* The most important parts of *The Republic* (references are to marginally-numbered sections, not to pages) are 327–32, 336–77, 384–5, 392–426, 433–5, 441–76, 481–3, 512–20, 572–94. The best edition is Jowett's; the most convenient is in the Everyman series. References are to *The Republic* unless otherwise stated.

nature and libertarian education, Bergsonian *élan vital* and Freudian psychoanalysis—everything is here. It is a feast for the *élite*, served by an unstinting host. "Plato is philosophy, and philosophy Plato," says Emerson; and awards to *The Republic* the words of Omar about the *Koran*: "Burn the libraries, for their value is in this book."[10]

Let us study *The Republic*.

IV. THE ETHICAL PROBLEM

The discussion takes place in the house of Cephalus, a wealthy aristocrat. In the group are Glaucon and Adeimantus, brothers of Plato; and Thrasymachus, a gruff and excitable Sophist. Socrates, who serves as the mouthpiece of Plato in the dialogue, asks Cephalus:

"What do you consider to be the greatest blessing which you have reaped from wealth?"

Cephalus answers that wealth is a blessing to him chiefly because it enables him to be generous and honest and just. Socrates, after his sly fashion, asks him just what he means by justice; and therewith lets loose the dogs of philosophic war. For nothing is so difficult as definition, nor anything so severe a test and exercise of mental clarity and skill. Socrates finds it a simple matter to destroy one after another the definitions offered him; until at last Thrasymachus, less patient than the rest, breaks out "with a roar":

"What folly has possessed you, Socrates? And why do you others all drop down at one another's feet in this silly way? I say that if you want to know what justice is, you should answer and not ask, and shouldn't pride yourself on refuting others. . . . For there are many who can ask but cannot answer" (336).

Socrates is not frightened; he continues to ask rather than answer; and after a minute of parry and thrust he provokes the unwary Thrasymachus to commit himself to a definition:

"Listen, then," says the angry Sophist, "I proclaim that might is right, and justice is the interest of the stronger. . . . The different forms of government make laws, democratic, aristocratic, or autocratic, with a view to their respective interests; and these laws, so made by them to serve their interests, they deliver to their subjects as 'justice,' and punish as 'unjust' anyone who transgresses them. . . . I am speaking of injustice on a large scale; and my meaning will be most clearly seen in autocracy, which by fraud and force takes away the property of others, not retail but wholesale. Now when a man has taken away the money of the citizens and made slaves of them, then, instead of swindler and thief he is called happy and blessed by all. For injustice is censured because those who censure it are afraid of suffering, and not from any scruple they might have of doing injustice themselves" (338-44).

[10]*Representative Men*, p. 41.

This, of course, is the doctrine which our own day more or less correctly associates with the name of Nietzsche. "Verily I laughed many a time over the weaklings who thought themselves good because they had lame paws."[11] Stirner expressed the idea briefly when he said that "a handful of might is better than a bagful of right." Perhaps nowhere in the history of philosophy is the doctrine better formulated than by Plato himself in another dialogue, *Gorgias*, (483 f), where the Sophist Callicles denounces morality as an invention of the weak to neutralize the strength of the strong.

> They distribute praise and censure with a view to their own interests; they say that dishonesty is shameful and unjust—meaning by dishonesty the desire to have more than their neighbors; for knowing their own inferiority, they would be only too glad to have equality. . . . But if there were a man who had sufficient force (enter the Superman), he would shake off and break through and escape from all this; he would trample under foot all our formulas and spells and charms, and all our laws, that sin against nature. . . . He who would truly live ought to allow his desires to wax to the uttermost; but when they have grown to their greatest he should have courage and intelligence to minister to them, and to satisfy all his longings. And this I affirm to be natural justice and nobility. But the many cannot do this; and therefore they blame such persons, because they are ashamed of their own inability, which they desire to conceal; and hence they call intemperance base. . . . They enslave the nobler natures, and they praise justice only because they are cowards.

This justice is a morality not for men but for foot-men (*oude gar andros all' andrapodou tinos*); it is a slave-morality, not a hero-morality; the real virtues of a man are courage (*andreia*) and intelligence (*phronesis*).[12]

Perhaps this hard "immoralism" reflects the development of imperialism in the foreign policy of Athens, and its ruthless treatment of weaker states.[13] "Your empire," said Pericles in the oration which Thucydides invents for him, "is based on your own strength rather than the good will of your subjects." And the same historian reports the Athenian envoys coercing Melos into joining Athens in the war against Sparta: "You know as well as we do that right, as the world goes, is only in question for equals in power; the strong do what they can, and the weak suffer what they must."[14] We have here the fundamental problem of ethics, the crux of the theory of moral conduct. What is justice?—shall we seek righteousness, or shall we seek power?—is it better to be good, or to be strong?

How does Socrates—i. e., Plato—meet the challenge of this theory? At

---

[11]*Thus Spake Zarathustra*, New York, 1906, p. 166.
[12]*Gorgias* 491; cf. Machiavelli's definition of *virtù* as intellect plus force.
[13]Barker, p. 73.
[14]*History of the Peloponnesian War*, v. 105.

first he does not meet it at all. He points out that justice is a relation among individuals, depending on social organization; and that in consequence it can be studied better as part of the structure of a community than as a quality of personal conduct. If, he suggests, we can picture a just state, we shall be in a better position to describe a just individual. Plato excuses himself for this digression on the score that in testing a man's vision we make him read first large type, then smaller; so, he argues, it is easier to analyze justice on a large scale than on the small scale of individual behavior. But we need not be deceived: in truth the Master is patching two books together, and uses the argument as a seam. He wishes not only to discuss the problems of personal morality, but the problems of social and political reconstruction as well. He has a Utopia up his sleeve, and is resolved to produce it. It is easy to forgive him, for the digression forms the core and value of his book.

V. THE POLITICAL PROBLEM

Justice would be a simple matter, says Plato, if men were simple; an anarchist communism would suffice. For a moment he gives his imagination reign:

First, then, let us consider what will be their way of life. . . . Will they not produce corn, and wine, and clothes, and shoes, and build houses for themselves? And when they are housed they will work in summer commonly stripped and barefoot, but in winter substantially clothed and shod. They will feed on barley and wheat, baking the wheat and kneading the flour, making noble puddings and loaves; these they will serve up on a mat of reed or clean leaves, themselves reclining the while upon beds of yew or myrtle boughs. And they and their children will feast, drinking of the wine which they have made, wearing garlands on their heads, and having the praises of the gods on their lips, living in sweet society, and having a care that their families do not exceed their means; for they will have an eye to poverty or war. . . . Of course they will have a relish—salt, and olives, and cheese, and onions, and cabbages or other country herbs which are fit for boiling; and we shall give them a dessert of figs, and pulse, and beans, and myrtle-berries, and beechnuts, which they will roast at the fire, drinking in moderation. And with such a diet they may be expected to live in peace to a good old age, and bequeath a similar life to their children after them (372).

Observe here the passing reference to the control of population (by infanticide, presumably), to vegetarianism, and to a "return to nature," to the primitive simplicity which Hebrew legend pictures in the Garden of Eden. The whole has the sound of Diogenes the "Cynic," who, as the epithet implied, thought we should "turn and live with the animals, they are so placid and self-contained"; and for a moment we are likely to classify Plato with St. Simon and Fourier and William Morris and Tolstoi.

But he is a little more sceptical than these men of kindly faith; he passes quietly on to the question, Why is it that such a simple paradise as he has described never comes?—why is it that these Utopias never arrive upon the map?

He answers, because of greed and luxury. Men are not content with a simple life: they are acquisitive, ambitious, competitive, and jealous; they soon tire of what they have, and pine for what they have not; and they seldom desire anything unless it belongs to others. The result is the encroachment of one group upon the territory of another, the rivalry of groups for the resources of the soil, and then war. Trade and finance develop, and bring new class-divisions. "Any ordinary city is in fact two cities, one the city of the poor, the other of the rich, each at war with the other; and in either division there are smaller ones—you would make a great mistake if you treated them as single states" (423). A mercantile bourgeoisie arises, whose members seek social position through wealth and conspicuous consumption: "they will spend large sums of money on their wives" (548). These changes in the distribution of wealth produce political changes: as the wealth of the merchant over-reaches that of the land-owner, aristocracy gives way to a plutocratic oligarchy—wealthy traders and bankers rule the state. Then statesmanship, which is the co-ordination of social forces and the adjustment of policy to growth, is replaced by politics, which is the strategy of party and the lust for the spoils of office.

Every form of government tends to perish by excess of its basic principle. Aristocracy ruins itself by limiting too narrowly the circle within which power is confined; oligarchy ruins itself by the incautious scramble for immediate wealth. In either case the end is revolution. When revolution comes it may seem to arise from little causes and petty whims; but though it may spring from slight occasions it is the precipitate result of grave and accumulated wrongs; when a body is weakened by neglected ills, the merest exposure may bring serious disease (556). "Then democracy comes: the poor overcome their opponents, slaughtering some and banishing the rest; and give to the people an equal share of freedom and power" (557).

But even democracy ruins itself by excess—of democracy. Its basic principle is the equal right of all to hold office and determine public policy. This is at first glance a delightful arrangement; it becomes disastrous because the people are not properly equipped by education to select the best rulers and the wisest courses (588). "As to the people they have no understanding, and only repeat what their rulers are pleased to tell them" (*Protagoras*, 317); to get a doctrine accepted or rejected it is only necessary to have it praised or ridiculed in a popular play (a hit, no doubt, at Aristophanes, whose comedies attacked almost every new idea). Mob-rule is a rough sea for the ship of state to ride; every wind of oratory stirs up the waters and deflects the course. The upshot of such a democracy is tyranny or autocracy; the crowd so loves flattery, it is so "hungry for honey," that at last the wiliest and most unscrupulous flatterer, calling himself the "protector of the people" rises to supreme power (565). (Consider the history of Rome.)

The more Plato thinks of it, the more astounded he is at the folly of leaving to mob caprice and gullibility the selection of political officials—not to speak of leaving it to those shady and wealth-serving strategists who pull the oligarchic wires behind the democratic stage. Plato complains that whereas in simpler matters—like shoe-making—we think only a specially-trained person will serve our purpose, in politics we presume that every one who knows how to get votes knows how to administer a city or a state. When we are ill we call for a trained physician, whose degree is a guarantee of specific preparation and technical competence—we do not ask for the handsomest physician, or the most eloquent one; well then, when the whole state is ill should we not look for the service and guidance of the wisest and the best? To devise a method of barring incompetence and knavery from public office, and of selecting and preparing the best to rule for the common good—that is the problem of political philosophy.

VI. THE PSYCHOLOGICAL PROBLEM

But behind these political problems lies the nature of man; to understand politics, we must, unfortunately, understand psychology. "Like man, like state" (575); "governments vary as the characters of men vary; . . . states are made out of the human natures which are in them" (544); the state is what it is because its citizens are what they are. Therefore we need not expect to have better states until we have better men; till then all changes will leave every essential thing unchanged. "How charming people are!—always doctoring, increasing and complicating their disorders, fancying they will be cured by some nostrum which somebody advises them to try, never getting better, but always growing worse. . . . Are they not as good as a play, trying their hand at legislation, and imagining that by reforms they will make an end to the dishonesties and rascalities of mankind—not knowing that in reality they are cutting away at the heads of a hydra?" (425).

Let us examine for a moment the human material with which political philosophy must deal.

Human behavior, says Plato, flows from three main sources: desire, emotion, and knowledge. Desire, appetite, impulse, instinct—these are one; emotion, spirit, ambition, courage—these are one; knowledge, thought, intellect, reason—these are one. Desire has its seat in the loins; it is a bursting reservoir of energy, fundamentally sexual. Emotion has its seat in the heart, in the flow and force of the blood; it is the organic resonance of experience and desire. Knowledge has its seat in the head; it is the eye of desire, and can become the pilot of the soul.

These powers and qualities are all in all men, but in divers degrees. Some men are but the embodiment of desire; restless and acquisitive souls, who are absorbed in material quests and quarrels, who burn with lust of luxuries and show, and who rate their gains always as naught compared with their ever-receding goals: these are the men who dominate and manipulate industry. But there are others who are temples of feeling and courage, who care not so much what they fight for, as for victory "in and for itself"; they are pugnacious rather than acquisitive; their pride is in power rather than in possession, their joy is on the battle-field rather than in the mart: these are the men who make the armies and navies of the world. And last are the few whose delight is in meditation and understanding; who yearn not for goods, nor for victory, but for knowledge; who leave both market and battle-field to lose themselves in the quiet clarity of secluded thought; whose will is a light rather than a fire, whose haven is not power but truth: these are the men of wisdom, who stand aside unused by the world.

Now just as effective individual action implies that desire, though warmed with emotion, is guided by knowledge; so in the perfect state the industrial forces would produce but they would not rule; the military forces would protect but they would not rule; the forces of knowledge and science and philosophy would be nourished and protected, and they would rule. Unguided by knowledge, the people are a multitude without order, like desires in disarray; the people need the guidance of philosophers as desires need the enlightenment of knowledge. "Ruin comes when the trader, whose heart is lifted up by wealth, becomes ruler" (434); or when the general uses his army to establish a military dictatorship. The producer is at his best in the economic field, the warrior is at his best in battle; they are both at their worst in public office; and in their crude hands politics submerges statesmanship. For statesmanship is a science and an art; one must have lived for it and been long prepared. Only a philosopher-king is fit to guide a nation. "Until philosophers are kings, or the kings and princes of this world have the spirit and power of philosophy, and wisdom and political leadership meet in the same man, . . . cities will never cease from ill, nor the human race" (473). This is the key-stone of the arch of Plato's thought.

VII. THE PSYCHOLOGICAL SOLUTION

Well, then, what is to be done?

We must begin by "sending out into the country all the inhabitants of the city who are more than ten years old, and by taking possession of the

children, who will thus be protected from the habits of their parents"
(540). We cannot build Utopia with young people corrupted at every
turn by the example of their elders. We must start, so far as we can, with
a clean slate. It is quite possible that some enlightened ruler will empower
us to make such a beginning with some part or colony of his realm. (One
ruler did, as we shall see.) In any case we must give to every child, and
from the outset, full equality of educational opportunity; there is no
telling where the light of talent or genius will break out; we must seek
it impartially everywhere, in every rank and race. The first turn on our
road is universal education.

For the first ten years of life, education shall be predominantly physical;
every school is to have a gymnasium and a playground; play and sport are
to be the entire curriculum; and in this first decade such health will be
stored up as will make all medicine unnecessary. "To require the help of
medicine because by lives of indolence and luxury men have filled themselves like pools with waters and winds, . . . flatulence and catarrh—is
not this a disgrace? . . . Our present system of medicine may be said to
educate diseases," to draw them out into a long existence, rather than to
cure them. But this is an absurdity of the idle rich. "When a carpenter
is ill he asks the physician for a rough and ready remedy—an emetic, or a
purge, or cautery, or the knife. And if anyone tells him that he must go
through a course of dietetics, and swathe and swaddle his head, and all
that sort of thing, he replies at once that he has no time to be ill, and that
he sees no good in a life that is spent in nursing his disease to the neglect
of his ordinary calling; and therefore, saying good-bye to this sort of
physicians, he resumes his customary diet, and either gets well and lives
and does his business, or, if his constitution fails, he dies and has done
with it" (405–6). We cannot afford to have a nation of malingerers and
invalids; Utopia must begin in the body of man.

But mere athletics and gymnastics would make a man too one-sided.
"How shall we find a gentle nature which has also great courage?—for
they seem to be inconsistent with each other" (375). We do not want a
nation of prize-fighters and weight-lifters. Perhaps music will solve our
problem: through music the soul learns harmony and rhythm, and even
a disposition to justice; for "can he who is harmoniously constituted ever
be unjust? Is not this, Glaucon, why musical training is so powerful,
because rhythm and harmony find their way into the secret places of the
soul, bearing grace in their movements and making the soul graceful?"
(401; *Protagoras*, 326). Music moulds character, and therefore shares in
determining social and political issues. "Damon tells me—and I can quite
believe it—that when modes of music change, the fundamental laws of
the state change with them."[15]

[15]Cf. Daniel O'Connell: "Let me write the songs of a nation, and I care not who
makes its laws."

Music is valuable not only because it brings refinement of feeling and character, but also because it preserves and restores health. There are some diseases which can be treated only through the mind (*Charmides*, 157): so the Corybantic priest treated hysterical women with wild pipe music, which excited them to dance and dance till they fell to the ground exhausted, and went to sleep; when they awoke they were cured. The unconscious sources of human thought are touched and soothed by such methods; and it is in these substrata of behavior and feeling that genius sinks its roots. "No man when conscious attains to true or inspired intuition, but rather when the power of intellect is fettered in sleep or by disease or dementia"; the prophet (*mantike*) or genius is akin to the madman (*manike*) (*Phædrus*, 244).

Plato passes on to a remarkable anticipation of "psychoanalysis." Our political psychology is perplexed, he argues, because we have not adequately studied the various appetites or instincts of man. Dreams may give us a clue to some of the subtle and more elusive of these dispositions.

> Certain of the unnecessary pleasures and instincts are deemed to be unlawful; every man appears to have them, but in some persons they are subjected to the control of law and reason ["sublimated"], and the better desires prevailing over them, they are either wholly suppressed, or reduced in strength and number; while in other persons these desires are stronger and more abundant. I mean particularly those desires which are awake when the reasoning and taming and ruling power ["censor"] of the personality is asleep; the wild beast in our nature, gorged with meat and drink, starts up and walks about naked, and surfeits at his will; and there is no conceivable folly or crime, however shameless or unnatural—not excepting incest or parricide ["Œdipus complex"]—of which such a nature may not be guilty. . . . But when a man's pulse is healthy and temperate, and he goes to sleep cool and rational, . . . having indulged his appetites neither too much nor too little, but just enough to lay them to sleep, . . . he is then least likely to be the sport of fanciful and lawless visions. . . . In all of us, even in good men, there is such a latent wild beast nature, which peers out in sleep (571–2).

Music and measure lend grace and health to the soul and to the body; but again, too much music is as dangerous as too much athletics. To be merely an athlete is to be nearly a savage; and to be merely a musician is to be "melted and softened beyond what is good" (410). The two must be combined; and after sixteen the individual practice of music must be abandoned, though choral singing, like communal games, will go on throughout life. Nor is music to be merely music; it must be used to provide attractive forms for the sometimes unappetizing contents of mathematics, history and science; there is no reason why for the young these difficult studies should not be smoothed into verse and beautified with song. Even then these studies are not to be forced upon an unwilling mind; within limits a libertarian spirit must prevail.

> The elements of instruction . . . should be presented to the mind in childhood, but not with any compulsion; for a freeman should be a freeman too in the acquisition of knowledge. . . . . Knowledge which is acquired under compulsion has no hold on the mind. Therefore do not use compulsion, but let early education be rather a sort of amusement; this will better enable you to find out the natural bent of the child (536).

With minds so freely growing, and bodies made strong by sport and outdoor life of every kind, our ideal state would have a firm psychological and physiological base broad enough for every possibility and every development. But a moral basis must be provided as well; the members of the community must make a unity; they must learn that they are members of one another; that they owe to one another certain amenities and obligations. Now since men are by nature acquisitive, jealous, combative, and erotic, how shall we persuade them to behave themselves? By the policeman's omnipresent club? It is a brutal method, costly and irritating. There is a better way, and that is by lending to the moral requirements of the community the sanction of supernatural authority. We must have a religion.

Plato believes that a nation cannot be strong unless it believes in God. A mere cosmic force, or first cause, or *élan vital,* that was not a person, could hardly inspire hope, or devotion, or sacrifice; it could not offer comfort to the hearts of the distressed, nor courage to embattled souls. But a living God can do all this, and can stir or frighten the self-seeking individualist into some moderation of his greed, some control of his passion. All the more so if to belief in God is added belief in personal immortality: the hope of another life gives us courage to meet our own death, and to bear with the death of our loved ones; we are twice armed if we fight with faith. Granted that none of the beliefs can be demonstrated; that God may be after all only the personified ideal of our love and our hope, and that the soul is like the music of the lyre, and dies with the instrument that gave it form: yet surely (so runs the argument, Pascal-like, of the *Phaedo*) it will do us no harm to believe, and it may do us and our children immeasurable good.

For we are likely to have trouble with these children of ours if we undertake to explain and justify everything to their simple minds. We shall have an especially hard time when they arrive at the age of twenty, and face the first scrutiny and test of what they have learned in all their years of equal education. Then will come a ruthless weeding out; the Great Elimination, we might call it. That test will be no mere academic examination; it will be practical as well as theoretical: "there shall also be toils and pains and conflicts prescribed for them" (413). Every kind of ability will have a chance to show itself, and every sort of stupidity will be hunted out into the light. Those who fail will be assigned to the economic work of the nation; they will be business men, and clerks, and factory workers, and farmers. The test will be impartial and impersonal; whether one is to be a farmer or a philosopher will be determined not by monopolized opportunity or nepotic favoritism; the selection will be more democratic than democracy.

Those who pass this first test will receive ten more years of education and training, in body and mind and character. And then they will face a second test, far severer than the first. Those who fail will become the auxiliaries, or executive aides and military officers of the state. Now it is just in these great eliminations that we shall need every resource of persuasion to get the eliminated to accept their fate with urbanity and peace. For what is to prevent that great unselected majority, in the first test, and that lesser but more vigorous and capable second group of Eliminees, from shouldering arms and smashing this Utopia of ours into a mouldering reminiscence? What is to prevent them from establishing there and then a world in which again mere number or mere force will rule, and the sickly comedy of a sham democracy will reënact itself *da capo ad nauseam?* Then religion and faith will be our only salvation: we shall tell these young people that the divisions into which they have fallen are God-decreed and irrevocable—not all their tears shall wipe out one word of it. We shall tell them the myth of the metals:

"Citizens, you are brothers, yet God has framed you differently. Some of you have the power of command; and these he has made of gold, wherefore they have the greatest honor; others of silver, to be auxiliaries; others again, who are to be husbandmen and craftsmen, he has made of brass and iron; and the species will generally be preserved in the children. But as you are of the same original family, a golden parent will sometimes have a silver son, or a silver parent a golden son. And God proclaims . . . that if the son of a golden or a silver parent has an admixture of brass or iron, then nature requires a transposition of ranks; and the eye of the ruler must not be pitiful towards his child because he has to descend in the scale to become a husbandman or an artisan, just as there may be others sprung from the artisan class who are raised to honor, and become guardians and auxiliaries. For an oracle says that when a man of brass or iron guards the state, it will be destroyed" (415).

Perhaps with this "royal fable" we shall secure a fairly general consent to the furtherance of our plan.

But now what of the lucky remnant that ride these successive waves of selection?

They are taught philosophy. They have now reached the age of thirty; it would not have been wise to let them "taste the dear delight too early; . . . for young men, when they first get the taste of philosophy in their mouths, argue for amusement, and are always contradicting and refuting, . . . like puppy-dogs who delight to tear and pull at all who come near them" (539). This dear delight, philosophy, means two things chiefly: to think clearly, which is metaphysics; and to rule wisely, which is politics. First then, our young Elite must learn to think clearly. For that purpose they shall study the doctrine of Ideas.

But this famous doctrine of Ideas, embellished and obscured by the fancy and poetry of Plato, is a discouraging maze to the modern student, and must have offered another severe test to the survivors of many siftings. The Idea of a thing might be the "general idea" of the class to which it belongs (the Idea of John, or Dick, or Harry, is Man); or it might be the law or laws according to which the thing operates (the Idea of John would be the reduction of all his behavior to "natural laws"); or it might be the perfect purpose and ideal towards which the thing and its class may develop (the Idea of John is the John of Utopia). Very probably the Idea is all of these—idea, law and ideal. Behind the surface phenomena and particulars which greet our senses, are generalizations, regularities, and directions of development, unperceived by sensation but conceived by reason and thought. These ideas, laws and ideals are more permanent—and therefore more "real"—than the sense-perceived particular things through which we conceive and deduce them: Man is more permanent than Tom, or Dick, or Harry; this circle is born with the movement of my pencil and dies under the attrition of my eraser, but the conception Circle goes on forever. This tree stands, and that tree falls; but the laws which determine what bodies shall fall, and when, and how, were without beginning, are now, and ever shall be, without end. There is, as the gentle Spinoza would say, a world of things perceived by sense, and a world of laws inferred by thought; we do not see the law of inverse squares but it is there, and everywhere; it was before anything began, and will survive when all the world of things is a finished tale. Here is a bridge: the sense perceives concrete and iron to a hundred million tons; but the mathematician sees, with the mind's eye, the daring and delicate adjustment of all this mass of material to the laws of mechanics and mathematics and engineering, those laws according to which all good bridges that are made must be made; if the mathematician be also a poet, he will see these laws upholding the bridge; if the laws were violated the bridge would collapse into the stream beneath; the laws are the God that holds up the bridge in the hollow of his hand. Aristotle hints something of this when he says that by Ideas Plato meant what Pythagoras meant by "number" when he taught that this is a world of numbers (meaning presumably that the world is ruled by mathematical constancies and regularities). Plutarch tells us that according to Plato "God always geometrizes"; or, as Spinoza puts the same thought, God and the universal laws of structure and operation are one and the same reality. To Plato, as to Bertrand Russell, mathematics is therefore the indispensable prelude to philosophy, and its highest form; over the doors of his Academy Plato placed, Dantesquely, these words, "Let no man ignorant of geometry enter here."[16]

Without these Ideas—these generalizations, regularities and ideals—the world would be to us as it must seem to the first-opened eyes of the child, a mass of unclassified and unmeaning particulars of sensation; for meaning can be given to things only by classifying and generalizing them, by finding the laws of their beings, and the purposes and goals of their activity. Or the world without Ideas would be a heap of book-titles fallen haphazard out of the catalogue, as compared to the same titles arranged in order according to their classes, their sequences and their purposes; it would be the shadows in a cave as compared with the sunlit realities without, which cast those fantastic and deceptive shadows within (514). Therefore the essence of a higher education is the search for Ideas: for generalizations, laws of sequence, and ideals of development; behind things we must discover their relation and meaning, their mode and law of operation, the function and ideal they serve or adumbrate; we must classify and coördinate our sense experience in terms of law and purpose; only for lack of this does the mind of the imbecile differ from the mind of Caesar.

Well, after five years of training in this recondite doctrine of Ideas, this art of perceiving significant forms and causal sequences and ideal potentialities amid the welter and hazard of sensation; after five years of training in the application of this principle to the behavior of men and the conduct of states; after this long preparation from childhood through youth and into the maturity of thirty-five; surely now these perfect products are ready to assume the royal purple and the highest functions of public life?—surely they are at last the philosopher-kings who are to rule and to free the human race?

Alas! not yet. Their education is still unfinished. For after all it has been, in the main, a theoretical education: something else is needed. Let these Ph.D.'s pass down now from the heights of philosophy into the "cave" of the world of men and things; generalizations and abstractions are worthless except they be tested by this concrete world; let our students enter that world with no favor shown them; they shall compete with men of business, with hard-headed grasping individualists, with men of brawn and men of cunning; in this mart of strife they shall learn from the book of life itself; they shall hurt their fingers and scratch their philosophic

[16]The details of the argument for the interpretation here given of the doctrine of Ideas may be followed in D. G. Ritchie's *Plato*, Edinburgh, 1902, especially pp. 49 and 85.

shins on the crude realities of the world; they shall earn their bread and
butter by the sweat of their high brows. And this last and sharpest test
shall go on ruthlessly for fifteen long years. Some of our perfect products
will break under the pressure, and be submerged by this last great wave of
elimination. Those that survive, scarred and fifty, sobered and self-reliant,
shorn of scholastic vanity by the merciless friction of life, and armed now
with all the wisdom that tradition and experience, culture and conflict,
can coöperate to give—these men at last shall automatically become the
rulers of the state.

VIII. THE POLITICAL SOLUTION

Automatically—without any hypocrisy of voting. Democracy means
perfect equality of opportunity, especially in education; not the rotation
of every Tom, Dick and Harry in public office. Every man shall have an
equal chance to make himself fit for the complex tasks of administration;
but only those who have proved their mettle (or, in our myth, their
metal), and have emerged from all tests with the insignia of skill, shall
be eligible to rule. Public officials shall be chosen not by votes, nor by
secret cliques pulling the unseen wires of democratic pretense, but by
their own ability as demonstrated in the fundamental democracy of an
equal race. Nor shall any man hold office without specific training, nor
hold high office till he has first filled a lower office well (*Gorgias,* 514–5).

Is this aristocracy? Well, we need not be afraid of the word, if the
reality is good which it betokens: words are wise men's counters, without
value of their own; they are the money only of fools and politicians. We
want to be ruled by the best, which is what aristocracy means; have we
not, Carlyle-like, yearned and prayed to be ruled by the best? But we have
come to think of aristocracies as hereditary: let it be carefully noted that
this Platonic aristocracy is not of that kind; one would rather call it a
democratic aristocracy. For the people, instead of blindly electing the
lesser of two evils presented to them as candidates by nominating cliques,
will here be themselves, every one of them, the candidates; and will
receive an equal chance of *educational election* to public office. There is
no caste here; no inheritance of position or privilege; no stoppage of
talent impecuniously born; the son of a ruler begins on the same level,
and receives the same treatment and opportunity, as the son of a boot-
black; if the ruler's son is a dolt he falls at the first shearing; if the boot-
black's son is a man of ability the way is clear for him to become a
guardian of the state (423). Career will be open to talent wherever it is
born. This is a democracy of the schools—a hundredfold more honest
and more effective than a democracy of the polls.

And so, "setting aside every other business, the guardians will dedicate
themselves wholly to the maintenance of freedom in the state, making

this their craft and engaging in no work which does not bear upon this end" (395). They shall be legislature and executive and court in one; even the laws shall not bind them to a dogma in the face of altered circumstance; the rule of the guardians shall be a flexible intelligence unbound by precedent.

But how can men of fifty have a flexible intelligence? Will they not be mentally plaster-casted by routine? Adeimantus (echoing, no doubt, some hot brotherly debate in Plato's home) objects that philosophers are dolts or rogues, who would rule either foolishly, or selfishly, or both. "The votaries of philosophy who carry on the study not only in youth with a view to education, but as the pursuit of their maturer years—these men for the most part grow into very strange beings, not to say utter scoundrels; and the result with those who may be considered the best of them is, that they are made useless to the world by the very study which you extol" (487). This is a fair enough description of some bespectacled modern philosophers; but Plato answers that he has guarded against this difficulty by giving his philosophers the training of life as well as the erudition of the schools; that they will in consequence be men of action rather than merely men of thought—men seasoned to high purposes and noble temper by long experience and trial. By philosophy Plato means an active culture, wisdom that mixes with the concrete busyness of life; he does not mean a closeted and impractical metaphysician; Plato "is the man who least resembles Kant, which is (with all respect) a considerable merit."[17]

So much for incompetence; as for rascality we may provide against that by establishing among the guardians a system of communism:

In the first place none of them should have any property beyond what is absolutely necessary; neither should they have a private house, with bars and bolts, closed against any one who has a mind to enter; their provisions should be only such as are required by trained warriors, who are men of temperance and courage; their agreement is to receive from the citizens a fixed rate of pay, enough to meet the expenses of the year, and no more; and they will have common meals and live together, like soldiers in a camp. Gold and silver we will tell them that they have from God; the diviner metal is within them, and they have therefore no need of that earthly dross which passes under the name of gold, and ought not to pollute the divine by earthly admixture, for that commoner metal has been the source of many unholy deeds; but their own is undefiled. And they alone of all the citizens may not touch or handle silver or gold, or be under the same roof with them, or wear them, or drink from them. And this will be their salvation, and the salvation of the State. But should they ever acquire homes or lands or moneys of their own, they will become housekeepers and husbandmen instead of guardians; enemies and tyrants instead of allies of the other citizens; hating and being hated, plotting and being plotted against, they will pass through

[17]Faguet, p. 10.

life in much greater terror of internal than of external enemies; and the
hour of ruin, both to themselves and to the rest of the State, will be at
hand (416-17).

This arrangement will make it unprofitable, as well as dangerous, for
the guardians to rule as a clique seeking the good of their class rather
than that of the community as a whole. For they will be protected from
want; the necessities and modest luxuries of a noble life will be theirs
in regular provision, without the searing and wrinkling care of economic
worry. But by the same token they will be precluded from cupidity and
sordid ambitions; they will always have just so much of the world's goods,
and no more; they will be like physicians establishing, and themselves
accepting, a dietary for a nation. They will eat together, like consecrated
men; they will sleep together in single barracks, like soldiers sworn to
simplicity. "Friends should have all things in common," as Pythagoras
used to say (*Laws* 807). So the authority of the guardians will be steril-
ized, and their power made poisonless; their sole reward will be honor
and the sense of service to the group. And they will be such men as from
the beginning have deliberately consented to so materially limited a
career; and such men as at the end of their stern training will have
learned to value the high repute of the statesman above the crass emolu-
ments of the office-seeking politicians or the "economic man." At their
coming the battles of party politics will be no more.

But what will their wives say to all this? Will they be content to forego
the luxuries of life and the conspicuous consumption of goods? The
guardians will have no wives. Their communism is to be of women as
well as of goods. They are to be freed not only from the egoism of self,
but from the egoism of family; they are not to be narrowed to the anxious
acquisitiveness of the prodded husband; they are to be devoted not to a
woman but to the community. Even their children shall not be specifically
or distinguishably theirs; all children of guardians shall be taken from
their mothers at birth and brought up in common; their particular
parentage will be lost in the scuffle (460). All the guardian-mothers
will care for all the guardian-children; the brotherhood of man, within
these limits, will graduate from phrase to fact; every boy will be a brother
to every other boy, every girl a sister, every man a father, and every
woman a mother.

But whence will these women come? Some, no doubt, the guardians
will woo out of the industrial or military classes; others will have become,
by their own right, members of the guardian class. For there is to be no
sex barrier of any kind in this community; least of all in education—the
girl shall have the same intellectual opportunities as the boy, the same
chance to rise to the highest positions in the state. When Glaucon objects
(453 f) that this admission of woman to any office, provided she has

passed the tests, violates the principle of the division of labor, he receives
the sharp reply that division of labor must be by aptitude and ability,
not by sex; if a woman shows herself capable of political administration,
let her rule; if a man shows himself to be capable only of washing dishes,
let him fulfil the function to which Providence has assigned him.

Community of wives does not mean indiscriminate mating; rather
there is to be strict eugenic supervision of all reproductive relations. The
argument from the breeding of animals here starts its wandering career:
if we get such good results in breeding cattle selectively for qualities
desired, and from breeding only from the best in each generation, why
should we not apply similar principles to the matings of mankind? (459).
For it is not enough to educate the child properly; he must be properly
born, of select and healthy ancestry; "education should begin before
birth" (*Laws*, 789). Therefore no man or woman shall procreate unless
in perfect health; a health certificate is to be required of every bride and
groom (*Laws*, 772). Men may reproduce only when they are above thirty
and under forty-five; women only when they are above twenty and
under forty. Men unmarried by thirty-five are to be taxed into felicity
(*Laws*, 771). Offspring born of unlicensed matings, or deformed, are to
be exposed and left to die. Before and after the ages specified for procreation, mating is to be free, on condition that the foetus be aborted.
"We grant this permission with strict orders to the parties to do all in
their power to prevent any embryo from seeing the light; and if any
should force its way to birth, they must understand that the offspring
of such a union cannot be maintained, and they must make their arrangements accordingly" (461). The marriage of relatives is prohibited,
as inducing degeneration (310). "The best of either sex should be united
with the best as often as possible, and the inferior with the inferior; and
they are to rear the offspring of the one sort but not that of the other;
for this is the only way of keeping the flock in prime condition. . . . Our
braver and better youth, beside their other honors and rewards, are to
be permitted a greater variety of mates; for such fathers ought to have as
many sons as possible" (459-60).

But our eugenic society must be protected not only from disease and
deterioration within, but from enemies without. It must be ready, if need
be, to wage successful war. Our model community would of course be
pacific, for it would restrict population within the means of subsistence;
but neighboring states not so managed might well look upon the orderly
prosperity of our Utopia as an invitation to raid and rapine. Hence, while
deploring the necessity, we shall have, in our intermediate class, a
sufficient number of well-trained soldiers, living a hard and simple life
like the guardians, on a stated modicum of goods supplied by their "main-
tainers and fore-fathers," the people. At the same time every precaution
must be taken to avoid the occasions of war. The primary occasion is

overpopulation (373); the second is foreign trade, with the inevitable disputes that interrupt it. Indeed, competitive trade is really a form of war; "peace is only a name" (*Laws,* 622). It will be well then to situate our ideal state considerably inland, so that it shall be shut out from any high development of foreign commerce. "The sea fills a country with merchandise and money-making and bargaining; it breeds in men's minds habits of financial greed and faithlessness, alike in its internal and in its foreign relations" (*Laws,* 704-7). Foreign trade requires a large navy to protect it; and navalism is as bad as militarism. "In every case the guilt of war is confined to a few persons, and the many are friends" (471). The most frequent wars are precisely the vilest—civil wars, wars of Greek against Greek; let the Greeks form a pan-Hellenic league of nations, uniting lest "the whole Greek race some day fall under the yoke of barbarian peoples" (469).

So our political structure will be topped with a small class of guardians; it will be protected by a large class of soldiers and "auxiliaries"; and it will rest on the broad base of a commercial, industrial, and agricultural population. This last or economic class will retain private property, private mates, and private families. But trade and industry will be regulated by the guardians to prevent excessive individual wealth or poverty; any one acquiring more than four times the average possession of the citizens must relinquish the excess to the state (*Laws,* 714 f). Perhaps interest will be forbidden, and profits limited (*Laws,* 920). The communism of the guardians is impracticable for the economic class; the distinguishing characteristics of this class are powerful instincts of acquisition and competition; some noble souls among them will be free from this fever of combative possession, but the majority of men are consumed with it; they hunger and thirst not after righteousness, nor after honor, but after possessions endlessly multiplied. Now men engrossed in the pursuit of money are unfit to rule a state; and our entire plan rests on the hope that if the guardians rule well and live simply, the economic man will be willing to let them monopolize administration if they permit him to monopolize luxury. In short, the perfect society would be that in which each class and each unit would be doing the work to which its nature and aptitude best adapted it; in which no class or individual would interfere with others, but all would coöperate in difference to produce an efficient and harmonious whole (433-4). That would be a just state.

IX. THE ETHICAL SOLUTION

And now our political digression is ended, and we are ready at last to answer the question with which we began—What is justice? There are only three things worth while in this world—justice, beauty and truth;

and perhaps none of them can be defined. Four hundred years after Plato a Roman procurator of Judea asked, helplessly, "What is truth?"—and philosophers have not yet answered, nor told us what is beauty. But for justice Plato ventures a definition. "Justice," he says, "is the having and doing what is one's own" (433).

This has a disappointing sound; after so much delay we expected an infallible revelation. What does the definition mean? Simply that each man shall receive the equivalent of what he produces, and shall perform the function for which he is best fit. A just man is a man in just the right place, doing his best, and giving the full equivalent of what he receives. A society of just men would be therefore a highly harmonious and efficient group; for every element would be in its place, fulfilling its appropriate function like the pieces in a perfect orchestra. Justice in a society would be like that harmony of relationships whereby the planets are held together in their orderly (or, as Pythagoras would have said, their musical) movement. So organized, a society is fit for survival; and justice receives a kind of Darwinian sanction. Where men are out of their natural places, where the business man subordinates the statesman, or the soldier usurps the position of the king—there the coördination of parts is destroyed, the joints decay, the society disintegrates and dissolves. Justice is effective coördination.

And in the individual too, justice is effective coördination, the harmonious functioning of the elements in a man, each in its fit place and each making its coöperative contribution to behavior. Every individual is a cosmos or a chaos of desires, emotions and ideas; let these fall into harmony, and the individual survives and succeeds; let them lose their proper place and function, let emotion try to become the light of action as well as its heat (as in the fanatic), or let thought try to become the heat of action as well as its light (as in the intellectual)—and disintegration of personality begins, failure advances like the inevitable night. Justice is a *taxis kai kosmos*—an order and beauty—of the parts of the soul; it is to the soul as health is to the body. All evil is disharmony: between man and nature, or man and men, or man and himself.

So Plato replies to Thrasymachus and Callicles, and to all Nietzscheans forever: Justice is not mere strength, but harmonious strength—desires and men falling into that order which constitutes intelligence and organization; justice is not the right of the stronger, but the effective harmony of the whole. It is true that the individual who gets out of the place to which his nature and talents adapt him may for a time seize some profit and advantage; but an inescapable Nemesis pursues him—as Anaxagoras spoke of the Furies pursuing any planet that should wander out of its orbit; the terrible *baton* of the Nature of Things drives the refractory instrument back to its place and its pitch and its natural note. The Corsican lieutenant may try to rule Europe with a ceremonious despotism fitted better to an ancient monarchy than to a dynasty born overnight; but he ends on a prison-rock in the sea, ruefully recognizing that he is "the slave of the Nature of Things." Injustice will out.

There is nothing bizarrely new in this conception; and indeed we shall do well to suspect, in philosophy, any doctrine which plumes itself on novelty. Truth changes her garments frequently (like every seemly lady), but under the new habit she remains always the same. In morals we need not expect startling innovations: despite the interesting adventures of Sophists and Nietzscheans, all moral conceptions revolve about the good of the whole. Morality begins with association and interdependence and organization; life in society requires the concession of some part of the individual's sovereignty to the common order; and ultimately the norm of conduct becomes the welfare of the group. Nature will have it so, and her judgment is always final; a group survives, in competition or conflict with another group, according to its unity and power, according to the ability of its members to coöperate for common ends. And what better coöperation could there be than that each should be doing that which he can do best? This is the goal of organization which every society must seek, if it would have life. Morality, said Jesus, is kindness to the weak; morality, said Nietzsche, is the bravery of the strong; morality, says Plato, is the effective harmony of the whole. Probably all three doctrines must be combined to find a perfect ethic; but can we doubt which of the elements is fundamental?

X. CRITICISM

And now what shall we say of this whole Utopia? Is it feasible? And if not, has it any practicable features which we could turn to contemporary use? Has it ever in any place or measure been realized?

At least the last question must be answered in Plato's favor. For a thousand years Europe was ruled by an order of guardians considerably like that which was visioned by our philosopher. During the Middle Ages it was customary to classify the population of Christendom into *laboratores* (workers), *bellatores* (soldiers), and *oratores* (clergy). The last group, though small in number, monopolized the instruments and opportunities of culture, and ruled with almost unlimited sway half of the most powerful continent on the globe. The clergy, like Plato's guardians, were placed in authority not by the suffrages of the people, but by their talent as shown in ecclesiastical studies and administration, by their disposition to a life of meditation and simplicity, and (perhaps it should be added) by the influence of their relatives with the powers of state and church. In the latter half of the period in which they ruled, the clergy were as free from family cares as even Plato could desire; and in some cases, it would seem, they enjoyed no little of the reproductive freedom accorded to the guardians. Celibacy was part of the psycho-logical structure of the power of the clergy; for on the one hand they were unimpeded by the narrowing egoism of the family, and on the other their apparent superiority to the call of the flesh added to the awe in which lay sinners held them, and to the readiness of these sinners to bare their lives in the confessional.

Much of the politics of Catholicism was derived from Plato's "royal lies," or influenced by them: the ideas of heaven, purgatory, and hell, in their medieval form, are traceable to the last book of the *Republic;* the cosmology of scholasticism comes largely from the *Timæus;* the doctrine of realism (the objective reality of general ideas) was an interpretation of the doctrine of Ideas; even the educational "quadrivium" (arithmetic, geometry, astronomy and music) was modeled on the curriculum outlined in Plato. With this body of doctrine the people of Europe were ruled with hardly any resort to force; and they accepted this rule so readily that for a thousand years they contributed plentiful material support to their rulers, and asked no voice in the government. Nor was this acquiescence confined to the general population; merchants and soldiers, feudal chieftains and civil powers all bent the knee to Rome. It was an aristocracy of no mean political sagacity; it built probably the most marvelous and powerful organization which the world has ever known.

The Jesuits who for a time ruled Paraguay were semi-Platonic guard-ians, a clerical oligarchy empowered by the possession of knowledge and skill in the midst of a barbarian population. And for a time the Com-munist Party which ruled Russia after the revolution of November, 1917, took a form strangely reminiscent of the *Republic.* They were a small minority, held together almost by religious conviction, wielding the weapons of orthodoxy and excommunication, as sternly devoted to their cause as any saint to his, and living a frugal existence while ruling half the soil of Europe.

Such examples indicate that within limits and with modifications, Plato's plan is practicable; and indeed he himself had derived it largely from actual practice as seen on his travels. He had been impressed by the Egyptian theocracy: here was a great and ancient civilization ruled by a small priestly class; and compared with the bickering and tyranny and incompetence of the Athenian *Ecclesia* Plato felt that the Egyptian government represented a much higher form of state (*Laws,* 819). In Italy he had stayed for a time with a Pythagorean community, vegetarian and communist, which had for generations controlled the Greek colony in which it lived. In Sparta he had seen a small ruling class living a hard and simple life in common in the midst of a subject population; eating together, restricting mating for eugenic ends, and giving to the brave the privilege of many wives. He had no doubt heard Euripides advocate a community of wives, the liberation of slaves, and the pacification of the Greek world by an Hellenic league (*Medea,* 230; *Fragm.,* 655); no doubt, too, he knew some of the Cynics who had developed a strong communist movement among what one would now call the Socratic Left. In short, Plato must have felt that in propounding his plan he was not making an impossible advance on realities which his eyes had seen.

Yet critics from Aristotle's day to ours have found in the *Republic* many an opening for objection and doubt. "These things and many others," says the Stagyrite, with cynical brevity, "have been invented several times over in the course of ages." It is very pretty to plan a society in which all men will be brothers; but to extend such a term to all our male contemporaries is to water out of it all warmth and significance. So with common property: it would mean a dilution of responsibility; when everything belongs to everybody nobody will take care of anything. And finally, argues the great conservative, communism would fling people into an intolerable continuity of contact; it would leave no room for privacy or individuality; and it would presume such virtues of patience and coöperation as only a saintly minority possess. "We must neither assume a standard of virtue which is above ordinary persons, nor an education which is exceptionally favored by nature and circumstance; but we must have regard to the life which the majority can share, and to the forms of government to which states in general can attain."

So far Plato's greatest (and most jealous) pupil; and most of the criticisms of later date strike the same chord. Plato underrated, we are told, the force of custom accumulated in the institution of monogamy, and in the moral code attached to that institution; he underestimated the possessive jealousy of males in supposing that a man would be content to have merely an aliquot portion of a wife; he minimized the maternal instinct in supposing that mothers would agree to have their children taken from them and brought up in a heartless anonymity. And above all he forgot that in abolishing the family he was destroying the great nurse of morals and the chief source of those coöperative and communistic habits which would have to be the psychological basis of his state; with unrivaled eloquence he sawed off the branch on which he sat.

To all these criticisms one can reply very simply, that they destroy a straw man. Plato explicitly exempts the majority from his communistic plan; he recognizes clearly enough that only a few are capable of the material self-denial which he proposes for his ruling class; only the guardians will call every guardian brother or sister; only the guardians will be without gold or goods. The vast majority will retain all respectable institutions—property, money, luxury, competition, and whatever privacy they may desire. They will have marriage as monogamic as they can bear, and all the morals derived from it and from the family; the fathers shall keep their wives and the mothers shall keep their children *ad libitum* and *nauseam.* As to the guardians, their need is not so much communistic disposition as a sense of honor, and love of it; pride and not kindness is to hold them up. And as for the maternal instinct, it is not strong before the birth, or even the growth, of the child; the average mother accepts the newborn babe rather with resignation than with joy; love for it is a development, not a sudden miracle, and grows as the child grows, as it takes form under the painstaking care of the mother; not until it has become the embodiment of maternal artistry does it irrevocably catch the heart.

Other objections are economic rather than psychological. Plato's republic, it is argued, denounces the division of every city into two cities, and then offers us a city divided into three. The answer is that the division in the first case is by economic conflict; in Plato's state the guardian and auxiliary classes are specifically excluded from participation in this competition for gold and goods. But then the guardians would have power without responsibility; and would not this lead to tyranny? Not at all; they have political power and direction, but no economic power or wealth; the economic class, if dissatisfied with the guardians' mode of rule, could hold up the food supply, as Parliaments control executives by holding up the budget. Well, then, if the guardians have political but not economic power, how can they maintain their rule? Have not Harrington and Marx and many others shown that political power is a reflex of economic power, and becomes precarious as soon as economic power passes to a politically subject group—as to the middle classes in the eighteenth century?

This is a very fundamental objection, and perhaps a fatal one. The answer might be made that the power of the Roman Catholic Church, which brought even kings to kneel at Canossa, was based, in its earlier centuries of rule, rather on the inculcation of dogmas than on the strategy of wealth. But it may be that the long dominion of the Church was due to the agricultural condition of Europe: an agricultural population is inclined to supernatural belief by its helpless dependence on the caprice of the elements, and by that inability to control nature which always leads to fear and thence to worship; when industry and commerce developed, a new type of mind and man arose, more realistic and terrestrial, and the power of the Church began to crumble as soon as it came into conflict with this new economic fact. Political power must repeatedly readjust itself to the changing balance of economic forces. The economic dependence of Plato's guardians on the economic class would very soon reduce them to the controlled political executives of that class; even the manipulation of military power would not long forestall this inevitable issue—any more than the military forces of revolutionary Russia could prevent the development of a proprietary individualism among the peasants who controlled the growth of food, and therefore the fate of the nation. Only this would remain to Plato: that even though political policies must be determined by the economically dominant group, it is better that those policies should be administered by officials specifically prepared for the purpose, than by men who stumble out of commerce or manufacturing into political office without any training in the arts of statesmanship.

What Plato lacks above all, perhaps, is the Heracleitean sense of flux and change; he is too anxious to have the moving picture of this world become a fixed and still tableau. He loves order exclusively, like any timid philosopher; he has been frightened by the democratic turbulence of Athens into an extreme neglect of individual values; he arranges men in classes like an entomologist classifying flies; and he is not averse to using priestly humbug to secure his ends. His state is static; it might easily become an old-fogey society, ruled by inflexible octogenarians hostile to invention and jealous of change. It is mere science without art; it exalts order, so dear to the scientific mind, and quite neglects that liberty which is the soul of art; it worships the name of beauty, but exiles the artists who alone can make beauty or point it out. It is a Sparta or a Prussia, not an ideal state.

And now that these unpleasant necessities are candidly written down, it remains to do willing homage to the power and profundity of Plato's conception. Essentially he is right—is he not?—what this world needs is to be ruled by its wisest men. It is our business to adapt his thought to our own times and limitations. Today we must take democracy for granted: we cannot limit the suffrage as Plato proposed; but we can put restrictions on the holding of office, and in this way secure that mixture of democracy and aristocracy which Plato seems to have in mind. We may accept without quarrel his contention that statesmen should be as specifically and thoroughly trained as physicians; we might establish departments of political science and administration in our universities; and when these departments have begun to function adequately we might make men ineligible for nomination to political office unless they were graduates of such political schools. We might even make every man eligible for an office who had been trained for it, and thereby eliminate entirely that complex system of nominations in which the corruption of our democracy has its seat; let the electorate choose any man who, properly trained and qualified, announces himself as a candidate. In this way democratic choice would be immeasurably wider than now, when Tweedledum and Tweedledee stage their quadrennial show and sham. Only one amendment would be required to make quite democratic this plan for the restriction of office to graduates in administrative technique; and that would be such equality of educational opportunity as would open to all men and women, irrespective of the means of their parents, the road to university training and political advancement. It would be very simple to have municipalities and counties and states offer scholarships to all graduates of grammar school, high school and college who had shown a certain standard of ability, and whose parents were financially unable to see them through the next stage of the educational process. That would be a democracy worthy of the name.

Finally, it is only fair to add that Plato understands that his Utopia does not quite fall within the practicable realm. He admits that he has described an ideal difficult of attainment; he answers that there is nevertheless a value in painting these pictures of our desire; man's significance is that he can image a better world, and will some part of it at least into reality; man is an animal that makes Utopias. "We look before and after and pine for what is not." Nor is it all without result: many a dream has grown limbs and walked, or grown wings and flown, like the dream of Icarus that men might fly. After all, even if we have but drawn a picture, it may serve as goal and model of our movement and behavior; when sufficient of us see the picture and follow its gleam, Utopia will find its way upon the map. Meanwhile "in heaven there is laid up a pattern of such a city, and he who desires may behold it, and beholding, govern himself accordingly. But whether there really is or ever will be such a city on earth, . . . he will act according to the laws of that city, and no other" (592). The good man will apply even in the imperfect state, the perfect law.

Nevertheless, with all these concessions to doubt, the Master was bold enough to risk himself when a chance offered to realize his plan. In the years 387 B. C. Plato received an invitation from Dionysius, ruler of the then flourishing and powerful Syracuse, capital of Sicily, to come and turn his kingdom into Utopia; and the philosopher, thinking like Turgot that it was easier to educate one man—even though a king—than a whole people, consented. But when Dionysius found that the plan required either that he should become a philosopher or cease to be a king, he balked; and the upshot was a bitter quarrel. Story has it that Plato was sold into slavery, to be rescued by his friend and pupil Anniceris; who, when Plato's Athenian followers wished to reimburse him for the ransom he had paid, refused, saying that they should not be the only ones privileged to help philosophy. This (and, if we may believe Diogenes Laertius, another similar) experience may account for the disillusioned conservatism of Plato's last work, the *Laws*.

And yet the closing years of his long life must have been fairly happy. His pupils had gone out in every direction, and their success had made him honored everywhere. He was at peace in his Academe, walking from group to group of his students and giving them problems and tasks on which they were to make research and, when he came to them again, give report and answer. La Rochefoucauld said that "few know how to grow old." Plato knew: to learn like Solon and to teach like Socrates; to guide the eager young, and find the intellectual love of comrades. For his students loved him as he loved them; he was their friend as well as their philosopher and guide.

One of his pupils, facing that great abyss called marriage, invited the Master to his wedding feast. Plato came, rich with his eighty years, and joined the merry-makers gladly. But as the hours laughed themselves away, the old philosopher retired into a quiet corner of the house, and sat down on a chair to win a little sleep. In the morning, when the feast was over, the tired revellers came to wake him. They found that during the night, quietly and without ado, he had passed from a little sleep to an endless one. All Athens followed him to the grave.

CHAPTER II

Aristotle and Greek Science

I. THE HISTORICAL BACKGROUND

ARISTOTLE was born at Stagira, a Macedonian city some two hundred miles to the north of Athens, in the year 384 B. C. His father was friend and physician to Amyntas, King of Macedon and grandfather of Alexander. Aristotle himself seems to have become a member of the great medical fraternity of Asclepiads. He was brought up in the odor of medicine as many later philosophers were brought up in the odor of sanctity; he had every opportunity and encouragement to develop a scientific bent of mind; he was prepared from the beginning to become the founder of science.

We have a choice of stories for his youth. One narrative represents him as squandering his patrimony in riotous living, joining the army to avoid starvation, returning to Stagira to practice medicine, and going to Athens at the age of thirty to study philosophy under Plato. A more dignified story takes him to Athens at the age of eighteen, and puts him at once under the tutelage of the great Master; but even in this likelier account there is sufficient echo of a reckless and irregular youth, living rapidly.[1] The scandalized reader may console himself by observing that in either story our philosopher anchors at last in the quiet groves of the Academy.

Under Plato he studied eight—or twenty—years; and indeed the pervasive Platonism of Aristotle's speculations—even of those most anti-Platonic—suggests the longer period. One would like to imagine these as very happy years; a brilliant pupil guided by an incomparable teacher, walking like Greek lovers in the gardens of philosophy. But they were both geniuses; and it is notorious that geniuses accord with one another as harmoniously as dynamite with fire. Almost half a century separated them; it was difficult for understanding to bridge the gap of years and cancel the incompatibility of souls. Plato recognized the greatness of this strange new pupil from the supposedly barbarian north, and spoke of him once as the *Nous* of the Academy,—as if to say, Intelligence personified. Aristotle had spent money lavishly in the collection of books (that is, in those printless days, manuscripts); he was the first, after Euripides, to

---

[1] Grote, *Aristotle*, London, 1872, p. 4; Zeller, *Aristotle and the Earlier Peripatetics*, London, 1897, vol. i, pp. 6 f.

gather together a library; and the foundation of the principles of library classification was among his many contributions to scholarship. Therefore Plato spoke of Aristotle's home as "the house of the reader," and seems to have meant the sincerest compliment; but some ancient gossip will have it that the Master intended a sly but vigorous dig at a certain book-wormishness in Aristotle. A more authentic quarrel seems to have arisen towards the end of Plato's life. Our ambitious youth apparently developed an "Œdipus complex" against his spiritual father for the favors and affections of philosophy, and began to hint that wisdom would not die with Plato; while the old sage spoke of his pupil as a foal that kicks his mother after draining her dry.[2] The learned Zeller,[3] in whose pages Aristotle almost achieves the Nirvana of respectability, would have us reject these stories; but we may presume that where there is still so much smoke there was once a flame.

The other incidents of this Athenian period are still more problematical. Some biographers tell us that Aristotle founded a school of oratory to rival Isocrates; and that he had among his pupils in this school the wealthy Hermias, who was soon to become autocrat of the city-state of Atarneus. After reaching this elevation Hermias invited Aristotle to his court; and in the year 344 B. C. he rewarded his teacher for past favors by bestowing upon him a sister (or a niece) in marriage. One might suspect this as a Greek gift; but the historians hasten to assure us that Aristotle, despite his genius, lived happily enough with his wife, and spoke of her most affectionately in his will. It was just a year later that Philip, King of Macedon, called Aristotle to the court at Pella to undertake the education of Alexander. It bespeaks the rising repute of our philosopher that the greatest monarch of the time, looking about for the greatest teacher, should single out Aristotle to be the tutor of the future master of the world.

Philip was determined that his son should have every educational advantage, for he had made for him illimitable designs. His conquest of Thrace in 356 B. C. had given him command of gold mines which at once began to yield him precious metal to ten times the amount then coming to Athens from the failing silver of Laurium; his people were vigorous peasants and warriors, as yet unspoiled by city luxury and vice: here was the combination that would make possible the subjugation of a hundred petty city-states and the political unification of Greece. Philip had no sympathy with the individualism that had fostered the art and intellect of Greece but had at the same time disintegrated her social order; in all these little capitals he saw not the exhilarating culture and the unsurpassable art, but the commercial corruption and the political chaos; he saw insatiable merchants and bankers absorbing the vital re-

[2] Benn, *The Greek Philosophers*, London, 1882, vol. i, p. 283.
[3] Vol. i. p. 11.

sources of the nation, incompetent politicians and clever orators misleading a busy populace into disastrous plots and wars, factions cleaving classes
and classes congealing into castes: this, said Philip, was not a nation but
only a welter of individuals—geniuses and slaves; he would bring the hand
of order down upon this turmoil, and make all Greece stand up united and
strong as the political center and basis of the world. In his youth in
Thebes he had learned the arts of military strategy and civil organization
under the noble Epaminondas; and now, with courage as boundless as
his ambition, he bettered the instruction. In 338 B. C. he defeated the
Athenians at Chæronea, and saw at last a Greece united, though with
chains. And then, as he stood upon this victory, and planned how he
and his son should master and unify the world, he fell under an assassin's
hand.

Alexander, when Aristotle came, was a wild youth of thirteen; passionate, epileptic, almost alcoholic; it was his pastime to tame horses untama-
ble by men. The efforts of the philosopher to cool the fires of this budding
volcano were not of much avail; Alexander had better success with
Bucephalus than Aristotle with Alexander. "For a while," says Plutarch,
"Alexander loved and cherished Aristotle no less than as if he had been
his own father; saying that though he had received life from the one,
the other had taught him the art of living." ("Life," says a fine Greek
adage, "is the gift of nature; but beautiful living is the gift of wisdom.")
"For my part," said Alexander in a letter to Aristotle, "I had rather excel
in the knowledge of what is good than in the extent of my power and
dominion." But this was probably no more than a royal-youthful compliment; beneath the enthusiastic tyro of philosophy was the fiery son of a
barbarian princess and an untamed king; the restraints of reason were
too delicate to hold these ancestral passions in leash; and Alexander left
philosophy after two years to mount the throne and ride the world.
History leaves us free to believe (though we should suspect these pleasant
thoughts) that Alexander's unifying passion derived some of its force and
grandeur from his teacher, the most synthetic thinker in the history of
thought; and that the conquest of order in the political realm by the
pupil, and in the philosophic realm by the master, were but diverse sides
of one noble and epic project—two magnificent Macedonians unifying
two chaotic worlds.

Setting out to conquer Asia, Alexander left behind him, in the cities
of Greece, governments favorable to him but populations resolutely
hostile. The long tradition of a free and once imperial Athens made subjection—even to a brilliant world-conquering despot—intolerable; and
the bitter eloquence of Demosthenes kept the Assembly always on the
edge of revolt against the "Macedonian party" that held the reins of city
power. Now when Aristotle, after another period of travel, returned to
Athens in the year 334 B. C., he very naturally associated with this

Macedonian group, and took no pains to conceal his approval of Alexander's unifying rule. As we study the remarkable succession of works, in speculation and research, which Aristotle proceeded to unfold in the last twelve years of his life; and as we watch him in his multifold tasks of organizing his school, and of coördinating such a wealth of knowledge as probably never before had passed through the mind of one man; let us occasionally remember that this was no quiet and secure pursuit of truth; that at any minute the political sky might change, and precipitate a storm in this peaceful philosophic life. Only with this situation in mind shall we understand Aristotle's political philosophy, and his tragic end.

II. THE WORK OF ARISTOTLE

It was not hard for the instructor of the king of kings to find pupils even in so hostile a city as Athens. When, in the fifty-third year of his age, Aristotle established his school, the Lyceum, so many students flocked to him that it became necessary to make complicated regulations for the maintenance of order. The students themselves determined the rules, and elected, every ten days, one of their numbr to supervise the School. But we must not think of it as a place of rigid discipline; rather the picture which comes down to us is of scholars eating their meals in common with the master, and learning from him as he and they strolled up and down the Walk along the athletic field from which the Lyceum took its name.[4]

The new School was no mere replica of that which Plato had left behind him. The Academy was devoted above all to mathematics and to speculative and political philosophy; the Lyceum had rather a tendency to biology and the natural sciences. If we may believe Pliny,[5] Alexander instructed his hunters, gamekeepers, gardeners and fishermen to furnish Aristotle with all the zoological and botanical material he might desire; other ancient writers tell us that at one time he had at his disposal a thousand men scattered throughout Greece and Asia, collecting for him specimens of the fauna and flora of every land. With this wealth of material he was enabled to establish the first great zoological garden that the world had seen. We can hardly exaggerate the influence of this collection upon his science and his philosophy.

Where did Aristotle derive the funds to finance these undertakings? He was himself, by this time, a man of spacious income; and he had married into the fortune of one of the most powerful public men in Greece. Athenæus (no doubt with some exaggeration) relates that Alexander

---

[4]The Walk was called *Peripatos;* hence the later name, Peripatetic School. The athletic field was part of the grounds of the temple of Apollo Lyceus—the protector of the flock against the wolf (*lycos*).

[5]*Hist. Nat.*, viii, 16; in Lewes, *Aristotle, a Chapter from the History of Science*, London, 1864, p. 15.

gave Aristotle, for physical and biological equipment and research, the sum of 800 talents (in modern purchasing power, some $4,000,000).ᵛ It was at Aristotle's suggestion, some think, that Alexander sent a costly expedition to explore the sources of the Nile and discover the causes of its periodical overflow.[7] Such works as the digest of 158 political constitutions, drawn up for Aristotle, indicate a considerable corps of aides and secretaries. In short we have here the first example in European history of the large-scale financing of science by public wealth. What knowledge would we not win if modern states were to support research on a proportionately lavish scale!

Yet we should do Aristotle injustice if we were to ignore the almost fatal limitations of equipment which accompanied these unprecedented resources and facilities. He was compelled "to fix time without a watch, to compare degrees of heat without a thermometer, to observe the heavens without a telescope, and the weather without a barometer. . . . Of all our mathematical, optical and physical instruments he possessed only the rule and compass, together with the most imperfect substitutes for some few others. Chemical analysis, correct measurements and weights, and a thorough application of mathematics to physics, were unknown. The attractive force of matter, the law of gravitation, electrical phenomena, the conditions of chemical combination, pressure of air and its effects, the nature of light, heat, combustion, etc., in short, all the facts on which the physical theories of modern science are based were wholly, or almost wholly, undiscovered."[8]

See, here, how inventions make history: for lack of a telescope Aristotle's astronomy is a tissue of childish romance; for lack of a microscope his biology wanders endlessly astray. Indeed, it was in industrial and technical invention that Greece fell farthest below the general standard of its unparalleled achievements. The Greek disdain of manual work kept everybody but the listless slave from direct acquaintance with the processes of production, from that stimulating contact with machinery which reveals defects and prefigures possibilities; technical invention was possible only to those who had no interest in it, and could not derive from it any material reward. Perhaps the very cheapness of the slaves made invention lag; muscle was still less costly than machines. And so, while Greek commerce conquered the Mediterranean Sea, and Greek philosophy conquered the Mediterranean mind, Greek science straggled, and Greek industry remained almost where Ægean industry had been when the invading Greeks had come down upon it, at Cnossus, at Tiryns and Mycene, a thousand years before. No doubt we have here the reason why

[6]Grant, *Aristotle,* Edinburgh, 1877, p. 18.
[7]The expedition reported that the inundations were due to the melting of the snow on the mountains of Abyssinia.
[8]Zeller, i, 264, 443.

Aristotle so seldom appeals to experiment; the mechanisms of experiment had not yet been made; and the best he could do was to achieve an almost universal and continuous observation. Nevertheless the vast body of data gathered by him and his assistants became the groundwork of the progress of science, the text-book of knowledge for two thousand years; one of the wonders of the work of man.

Aristotle's writings ran into the hundreds. Some ancient authors credit him with four hundred volumes, others with a thousand. What remains is but a part, and yet it is a library in itself—conceive the scope and grandeur of the whole. There are, first, the *Logical* works: "Categories," "Topics," "Prior" and "Posterior Analytics," "Propositions," and "Sophistical Refutation"; these works were collected and edited by the later Peripatetics under the general title of Aristotle's "Organon,"—that is, the organ or instrument of correct thinking. Secondly, there are the *Scientific* works: "Physics," "On the Heavens," "Growth and Decay," "Meteorology," "Natural History," "On the Soul," "The Parts of Animals," "The Movements of Animals," and "The Generation of Animals." There are, thirdly, the *Esthetic* works: "Rhetoric" and "Poetics." And fourthly come the more strictly *Philosophical* works: "Ethics," "Politics," and "Metaphysics."[9]

Here, evidently, is the Encyclopedia Britannica of Greece: every problem under the sun and about it finds a place; no wonder there are more errors and absurdities in Aristotle than in any other philosopher who ever wrote. Here is such a synthesis of knowledge and theory as no man would ever achieve again till Spencer's day, and even then not half so magnificently; here, better than Alexander's fitful and brutal victory, was a conquest of the world. If philosophy is the quest of unity Aristotle deserves the high name that twenty centuries gave him—*Ille Philosophus:* The Philosopher.

Naturally, in a mind of such scientific turn, poesy was lacking. We must not expect of Aristotle such literary brilliance as floods the pages of the dramatist-philosopher Plato. Instead of giving us great literature, in which philosophy is embodied (and obscured) in myth and imagery, Aristotle gives us science, technical, abstract, concentrated; if we go to him for entertainment we shall sue for the return of our money. Instead of giving terms to literature, as Plato did, he built the terminology of science and philosophy; we can hardly speak of any science today without employing terms which he invented; they lie like fossils in the strata of our speech: *faculty, mean, maxim,* (meaning, in Aristotle, the major premise of a syllogism), *category, energy, actuality, motive, end, principle, form*—these indispensable coins of philosophic thought were minted in his mind. And perhaps this passage from delightful dialogue to precise

---

[9]This is the chronological order, so far as known (Zeller, i, 156 f). Our discussion will follow this order except in the case of the "Metaphysics."

scientific treatise was a necessary step in the development of philosophy; and science, which is the basis and backbone of philosophy, could not grow until it had evolved its own strict methods of precedure and expression. Aristotle, too, wrote literary dialogues, as highly reputed in their day as Plato's; but they are lost, just as the scientific treatises of Plato have perished. Probably time has preserved of each man the better part.

Finally, it is possible that the writings attributed to Aristotle were not his, but were largely the compilations of students and followers who had embalmed the unadorned substance of his lectures in their notes. It does not appear that Aristotle published in his life-time any technical writings except those on logic and rhetoric; and the present form of the logical treatises is due to later editing. In the case of the *Metaphysics* and the *Politics* the notes left by Aristotle seem to have been put together by his executors without revision or alteration. Even the unity of style which marks Aristotle's writings, and offers an argument to those who defend his direct authorship, may be, after all, merely a unity given them through common editing by the Peripatetic School. About this matter there rages a sort of Homeric question, of almost epic scope, into which the busy reader will not care to go, and on which a modest student will not undertake to judge.[10] We may at all events be sure that Aristotle is the spiritual author of all these books that bear his name: that the hand may be in some cases another's hand, but that the head and the heart are his.[11]

III. THE FOUNDATION OF LOGIC

The first great distinction of Aristotle is that almost without predecessors, almost entirely by his own hard thinking, he created a new science— Logic. Renan[12] speaks of "the ill training of every mind that has not, directly or indirectly, come under Greek discipline"; but in truth the Greek intellect itself was undisciplined and chaotic till the ruthless formulas of Aristotle provided a ready method for the test and correction of thought. Even Plato (if a lover may so far presume) was an unruly and irregular soul, caught up too frequently in a cloud of myth, and letting beauty too richly veil the face of truth. Aristotle himself, as we shall see, violated his own canons plentifully; but then he was the product of his past, and not of that future which his thought would build. The

[10]Cf. Zeller, ii, 204, note; and Shule: *History of the Aristotelian Writings.*

[11]The reader who wishes to go to the philosopher himself will find the *Meteorology* an interesting example of Aristotle's scientific work; he will derive much practical instruction from the *Rhetoric;* and he will find Aristotle at his best in books i–ii of the *Ethics,* and books i–iv of the *Politics.* The best translation of the *Ethics* is Welldon's; of the *Politics,* Jowett's. Sir Alexander Grant's *Aristotle* is a simple book; Zeller's *Aristotle* (vols. iii–iv in his *Greek Philosophy*), is scholarly but dry; Gomprez's *Greek Thinkers* (vol. iv) is masterly but difficult.

[12]*History of the People of Israel,* vol. v, p. 338.

political and economic decay of Greece brought a weakening of the Hellenic mind and character after Aristotle; but when a new race, after a millennium of barbaric darkness, found again the leisure and ability for speculation, it was Aristotle's "Organon" of logic, translated by Boethius (470–525 A. D.), that became the very mould of medieval thought, the strict mother of that scholastic philosophy which, though rendered sterile by encircling dogmas, nevertheless trained the intellect of adolescent Europe to reasoning and subtlety, constructed the terminology of modern science, and laid the bases of that same maturity of mind which was to outgrow and overthrow the very system and methods which had given it birth and sustenance.

Logic means, simply, the art and method of correct thinking. It is the *logy* or method of every science, of every discipline and every art; and even music harbors it. It is a science because to a considerable extent the processes of correct thinking can be reduced to rules like physics and geometry, and taught to any normal mind; it is an art because by practice it gives to thought, at last, that unconscious and immediate accuracy which guides the fingers of the pianist over his instrument to effortless harmonies. Nothing is so dull as logic, and nothing is so important.

There was a hint of this new science in Socrates' maddening insistence on definitions, and in Plato's constant refining of every concept. Aristotle's little treatise on *Definitions* shows how his logic found nourishment at this source. "If you wish to converse with me," said Voltaire, "define your terms." How many a debate would have been deflated into a paragraph if the disputants had dared to define their terms! This is the alpha and omega of logic, the heart and soul of it, that every important term in serious discourse shall be subjected to strictest scrutiny and definition. It is difficult, and ruthlessly tests the mind; but once done it is half of any task.

How shall we proceed to define an object or a term? Aristotle answers that every good definition has two parts, stands on two solid feet: first, it assigns the object in question to a class or group whose general characteristics are also its own—so man is, first of all, an animal; and secondly, it indicates wherein the object differs from all the other members in its class—so man, in the Aristotelian system, is a *rational* animal, his "specific difference" is that unlike all other animals he is rational (here is the origin of a pretty legend). Aristotle drops an object into the ocean of its class, then takes it out all dripping with generic meaning, with the marks of its kind and group; while its individuality and difference shine out all the more clearly for this juxtaposition with other objects that resemble it so much and are so different.

Passing out from this rear line of logic we come into the great battle-field on which Aristotle fought out with Plato the dread question of "universals"; it was the first conflict in a war which was to last till our own day, and make all medieval Europe ring with the clash of "realists" and "nominalists."[18] A universal, to Aristotle, is any common noun, any name capable of universal application to the members of a class: so *animal, man, book, tree,* are universals. But these universals are subjective notions, not tangibly objective realities; they are *nomina* (names), not *res* (things); all that exists outside us is a world of individual and specific objects, not of generic and universal things; men exist, and trees, and animals; but man-in-general, or the universal man, does not exist, except in thought; he is a handy mental abstraction, not an external presence or *re*-ality.

Now Aristotle understands Plato to have held that universals have objective existence; and indeed Plato had said that the universal is incomparably more lasting and important and substantial than the individual,—the latter being but a little wavelet in a ceaseless surf; *men* come and go, but *man* goes on forever. Aristotle's is a matter-of-fact mind; as William James would say, a tough, not a tender, mind; he sees the root of endless mysticism and scholarly nonsense in this Platonic "realism"; and he attacks it with all the vigor of a first polemic. As Brutus loved not Cæsar less but Rome more, so Aristotle says, *Amicus Plato, sed magis amica veritas*—"Dear is Plato, but dearer still is truth."

A hostile commentator might remark that Aristotle (like Nietzsche) criticizes Plato so keenly because he is conscious of having borrowed from him generously; no man is a hero to his debtors. But Aristotle has a healthy attitude, nevertheless; he is a realist almost in the modern sense; he is resolved to concern himself with the objective present, while Plato is absorbed in a subjective future. There was, in the Socratic-Platonic demand for definitions, a tendency away from things and facts to theories and ideas, from particulars to generalities, from science to scholasticism; at last Plato became so devoted to generalities that they began to determine his particulars, so devoted to ideas that they began to define or select his facts. Aristotle preaches a return to things, to the "unwithered face of nature" and reality; he had a lusty preference for the concrete particular, for the flesh and blood individual. But Plato so loved the general and universal that in the *Republic* he destroyed the individual to make a perfect state.

Yet, as is the usual humor of history, the young warrior takes over many of the qualities of the old master whom he assails. We have always goodly stock in us of that which we condemn: as only similars can be profitably contrasted, so only similar people quarrel, and the bitterest wars are over the slightest variations of purpose or belief. The knightly Crusaders found in Saladin a gentleman with whom they could quarrel amicably; but when the Christians of Europe broke into hostile camps

[18]It was in reference to this debate that Friedrich Schlegel said, "Every man is born either a Platonist or an Aristotelian" (in Benn, i, 291).

there was no quarter for even the courtliest foe. Aristotle is so ruthless with Plato because there is so much of Plato in him; he too remains a lover of abstractions and generalities, repeatedly betraying the simple fact for some speciously bedizened theory, and compelled to a continuous struggle to conquer his philosophic passion for exploring the empyrean.

There is a heavy trace of this in the most characteristic and original of Aristotle's contributions to philosophy—the doctrine of the syllogism. A syllogism is a trio of propositions of which the third (the conclusion) follows from the conceded truth of the other two (the "major" and "minor" premisses). E. g., man is a rational animal; but Socrates is a man; therefore Socrates is a rational animal. The mathematical reader will see at once that the structure of the syllogism resembles the proposition that two things equal to the same thing are equal to each other; if A is B, and C is A, then C is B. As in the mathematical case the conclusion is reached by canceling from both premisses their common term, A; so in our syllogism the conclusion is reached by canceling from both premisses their common term "man," and combining what remains. The difficulty, as logicians have pointed out from the days of Pyrrho to those of Stuart Mill, lies in this, that the major premiss of the syllogism takes for granted precisely the point to be proved; for if Socrates is not rational (and no one questions that he is a man) it is not universally true that man is a rational animal. Aristotle would reply, no doubt, that where an individual is found to have a large number of qualities characteristic of a class ("Socrates is a man"), a strong presumption is established that the individual has the other qualities characteristic of the class ("rationality"). But apparently the syllogism is not a mechanism for the discovery of truth so much as for the clarification of exposition and thought.

All this, like the many other items of the Organon, has its value: "Aristotle has discovered and formulated every canon of theoretical consistency, and every artifice of dialectical debate, with an industry and acuteness which cannot be too highly extolled; and his labors in this direction have perhaps contributed more than any other single writer to the intellectual stimulation of after ages."[14] But no man ever lived who could lift logic to a lofty strain: a guide to correct reasoning is as elevating as a manual of etiquette; we may use it, but it hardly spurs us to nobility. Not even the bravest philosopher would sing to a book of logic underneath the bough. One always feels towards logic as Virgil bade Dante feel towards those who had been damned because of their colorless neutrality: *Non ragionam di lor, ma guarda e passa*[15]—"Let us think no more about them, but look once and pass on."

[14]*Benn, i, 307.*   [15]*Inferno, iii, 60.*

IV. THE ORGANIZATION OF SCIENCE

1. GREEK SCIENCE BEFORE ARISTOTLE

"Socrates," says Renan,[16] "gave philosophy to mankind, and Aristotle gave it science. There was philosophy before Socrates, and science before Aristotle; and since Socrates and since Aristotle, philosophy and science have made immense advances. But all has been built upon the foundation which they laid." Before Aristotle, science was in embryo; with him it was born.

Earlier civilizations than the Greek had made attempts at science; but so far as we can catch their thought through their still obscure cuneiform and hieroglyphic script, their science was indistinguishable from theology. That is to say, these pre-Hellenic peoples explained every obscure operation in nature by some supernatural agency; everywhere there were gods. Apparently it was the Ionian Greeks who first dared to give natural explanations of cosmic complexities and mysterious events: they sought in physics the natural causes of particular incidents, and in philosophy a natural theory of the whole. Thales (640–550 B. C.), the "Father of Philosophy," was primarily an astronomer, who astonished the natives of Miletus by informing them that the sun and stars (which they were wont to worship as gods) were merely balls of fire. His pupil Anaximander (610–540 B. C.), the first Greek to make astronomical and geographical charts, believed that the universe had begun as an undifferentiated mass, from which all things had arisen by the separation of opposites; that astronomic history periodically repeated itself in the evolution and dissolution of an infinite number of worlds; that the earth was at rest in space by a balance of internal impulsions (like Buridan's ass); that all our planets had once been fluid, but had been evaporated by the sun; that life had first been formed in the sea, but had been driven upon the land by the subsidence of the water; that of these stranded animals some had developed the capacity to breathe air, and had so become the progenitors of all later land life; that man could not from the beginning have been what he now was, for if man, on his first appearance, had been so helpless at birth, and had required so long an adolescence, as in these later days, he could not possibly have survived. Anaximenes, another Milesian (fl. 450 B. C.), described the primeval condition of things as a very rarefied mass, gradually condensing into wind, cloud, water, earth, and stone; the three forms of matter—gas, liquid and solid—were progressive stages of condensation; heat and cold were merely rarefaction and condensation; earthquakes were due to the solidification of an originally fluid earth; life and soul were one, an animating and expansive force present in everything everywhere. Anaxagoras (500–428 B. C.),

[16]*Life of Jesus,* ch. 28.

teacher of Pericles, seems to have given a correct explanation of solar
and lunar eclipses; he discovered the processes of respiration in plants
and fishes; and he explained man's intelligence by the power of manipulation that came when the fore-limbs were freed from the tasks of locomotion. Slowly, in these men, knowledge grew into science.

Heraclitus (530–470 B. C.), who left wealth and its cares to live a
life of poverty and study in the shade of the temple porticoes at Ephesus,
turned science from astronomy to earthlier concerns. All things forever
flow and change, he said; even in the stillest matter there is unseen flux
and movement. Cosmic history runs in repetitious cycles, each beginning
and ending in fire (here is one source of the Stoic and Christian doctrine
of last judgment and hell). "Through strife," says Heraclitus, "all things
arise and pass away. . . . War is the father and king of all: some he has
made gods, and some men; some slaves, and some free." Where there is
no strife there is decay: "the mixture which is not shaken decomposes."
In this flux of change and struggle and selection, only one thing is constant, and that is law. "This order, the same for all things, no one of gods
or men has made; but it always was, and is, and shall be." Empedocles
(fl. 445 B. C., in Sicily) developed to a further stage the idea of evolution.[17] Organs arise not by design but by selection. Nature makes many
trials and experiments with organisms, combining organs variously;
where the combination meets environmental needs the organism survives
and perpetuates its like; where the combination fails, the organism is
weeded out; as time goes on, organisms are more and more intricately
and successfully adapted to their surroundings. Finally, in Leucippus (fl.
445 B. C.) and Democritus (460–360 B. C.), master and pupil in Thracian
Abdera, we get the last stage of pre-Aristotelian science—materialistic,
deterministic atomism. "Everything," said Leucippus, "is driven by necessity." "In reality," said Democritus, "there are only atoms and the void."
Perception is due to the expulsion of atoms from the object upon the sense
organ. There is or have been or will be an infinite number of worlds; at
every moment planets are colliding and dying, and new worlds are rising
out of chaos by the selective aggregation of atoms of similar size and
shape. There is no design; the universe is a machine.

This, in dizzy and superficial summary, is the story of Greek science
before Aristotle. Its cruder items can be well forgiven when we consider the narrow circle of experimental and observational equipment
within which these pioneers were compelled to work. The stagnation of
Greek industry under the incubus of slavery prevented the full development of these magnificent beginnings; and the rapid complication of
political life in Athens turned the Sophists and Socrates and Plato away
from physical and biological research into the paths of ethical and
political theory. It is one of the many glories of Aristotle that he was

[17]Cf. Osborn, *From the Greeks to Darwin;* and M. Arnold, *Empedocles on Etna.*

broad and brave enough to compass and combine these two lines of Greek thought, the physical and the moral; that going back beyond his teacher, he caught again the thread of scientific development in the pre-Socratic Greeks, carried on their work with more resolute detail and more varied observation, and brought together all the accumulated results in a magnificent body of organized science.

2. ARISTOTLE AS A NATURALIST

If we begin here chronologically, with his *Physics,* we shall be disappointed; for we find that this treatise is really a *metaphysics,* an abstruse analysis of matter, motion, space, time, infinity, cause, and other such "ultimate concepts." One of the more lively passages is an attack on Democritus' "void": there can be no void or vacuum in nature, says Aristotle, for in a vacuum all bodies would fall with equal velocity; this being impossible, "the supposed void turns out to have nothing in it"— an instance at once of Aristotle's very occasional humor, his addiction to unproved assumptions, and his tendency to disparage his predecessors in philosophy. It was the habit of our philosopher to preface his works with historical sketches of previous contributions to the subject in hand, and to add to every contribution an annihilating refutation. "Aristotle, after the Ottoman manner," says Bacon, "thought he could not reign secure without putting all his brethren to death."[18] But to this fratricidal mania we owe much of our knowledge of pre-Socratic thought.

For reasons already given, Aristotle's astronomy represents very little advance upon his predecessors. He rejects the view of Pythagoras that the sun is the center of our system; he prefers to give that honor to the earth. But the little treatise on meteorology is full of brilliant observations, and even its speculations strike illuminating fire. This is a cyclic world, says our philosopher: the sun forever evaporates the sea, dries up rivers and springs, and transforms at last the boundless ocean into the barest rock; while conversely the uplifted moisture, gathered into clouds, falls and renews the rivers and the seas. Everywhere change goes on, imperceptibly but effectively. Egypt is "the work of the Nile," the product of its deposits through a thousand centuries. Here the sea encroaches upon the land, there the land reaches out timidly into the sea; new continents and new oceans rise, old oceans and old continents disappear, and all the face of the world is changed and rechanged in a great systole and diastole of growth and dissolution. Sometimes these vast effects occur suddenly, and destroy the geological and material bases of civilization and even of life; great catastrophes have periodically denuded the earth and reduced man again to his first beginnings; like Sisyphus, civilization has repeatedly neared its zenith only to fall back into barbarism and begin *da capo* its

[18]*Advancement of Learning,* bk. iii, ch.

upward travail. Hence the almost "eternal recurrence," in civilization after civilization, of the same inventions and discoveries, the same "dark ages" of slow economic and cultural accumulation, the same rebirths of learning and science and art. No doubt some popular myths are vague traditions surviving from earlier cultures. So the story of man runs in a dreary circle, because he is not yet master of the earth that holds him.

3. THE FOUNDATION OF BIOLOGY

As Aristotle walked wondering through his great zoological garden, he became convinced that the infinite variety of life could be arranged in a continuous series in which each link would be almost indistinguishable from the next. In all respects, whether in structure, or mode of life, or reproduction and rearing, or sensation and feeling, there are minute gradations and progressions from the lowest organisms to the highest.[19] At the bottom of the scale we can scarcely divide the living from the "dead"; "nature makes so gradual a transition from the inanimate to the animate kingdom that the boundary lines which separate them are indistinct and doubtful"; and perhaps a degree of life exists even in the inorganic. Again, many species cannot with certainty be called plants or animals. And as in these lower organisms it is almost impossible at times to assign them to their proper genus and species, so similar are they; so in every order of life the continuity of gradations and differences is as remarkable as the diversity of functions and forms. But in the midst of this bewildering richness of structures certain things stand out convincingly: that life has grown steadily in complexity and in power;[20] that intelligence has progressed in correlation with complexity of structure and mobility of form;[21] that there has been an increasing specialization of function, and a continuous centralization of physiological control.[22] Slowly life created for itself a nervous system and a brain; and mind moved resolutely on towards the mastery of its environment.

The remarkable fact here is that with all these gradations and similarities leaping to Aristotle's eyes, he does not come to the theory of evolution. He rejects Empedocles' doctrine that all organs and organisms are a survival of the fittest,[23] and Anaxagoras' idea that man became intelligent by using his hands for manipulation rather than for movement; Aristotle thinks, on the contrary, that man so used his hands because he had become intelligent.[24] Indeed, Aristotle makes as many mistakes as possible for a man who is founding the science of biology. He thinks, for example, that the male element in reproduction merely stimulates and quickens; it does not occur to him (what we now know from experiments in

[19]*Hist. Animalium*, viii.
[21]*De Partibus Animalium*, i, 7; ii, 10.
[20]*De Anima*, ii, 4.
[20]*De Anima*, ii, 2.
[22]*Ibid*, iv, 5–6.
[24]*De Part, An.*, iv, 10.

parthenogenesis) that the essential function of the sperm is not so much to fertilize the ovum as to provide the embryo with the heritable qualities of the male parent, and so permit the offspring to be a vigorous variant, a new admixture of two ancestral lines. As human dissection was not practised in his time, he is particularly fertile in physiological errors: he knows nothing of muscles, not even of their existence; he does not distinguish arteries from veins; he thinks the brain is an organ for cooling the blood; he believes, forgivably, that man has more sutures in the skull than woman; he believes, less forgivably, that man has only eight ribs on each side; he believes, incredibly, and unforgivably, that woman has fewer teeth than man.[25] Apparently his relations with women were of the most amicable kind.

Yet he makes a greater total advance in biology than any Greek before or after him. He perceives that birds and reptiles are near allied in structure; that the monkey is in form intermediate between quadrupeds and man; and once he boldly declares that man belongs in one group of animals with the viviparous quadrupeds (our "mammals").[26] He remarks that the soul in infancy is scarcely distinguishable from the soul of animals.[27] He makes the illuminating observation that diet often determines the mode of life; "for of beasts some are gregarious, and others solitary—they live in the way which is best adapted to . . . obtain the food of their choice."[28] He anticipates Von Baer's famous law that characters common to the genus (like eyes and ears) appear in the developing organism before characters peculiar to its species (like the "formula" of the teeth), or to its individual self (like the final color of the eyes);[29] and he reaches out across two thousand years to anticipate Spencer's generalization that individuation varies inversely as genesis—that is, that the more highly developed and specialized a species or an individual happens to be, the smaller will be the number of its offspring.[30] He notices and explains reversion to type—the tendency of a prominent variation (like genius) to be diluted in mating and lost in successive generations. He makes many zoological observations which, temporarily rejected by later biologists, have been confirmed by modern research—of fishes that make nests, for example, and sharks that boast of a placenta.

And finally he establishes the science of embryology. "He who sees things grow from their beginning," he writes, "will have the finest view of them." Hippocrates (b. 460 B. C.), greatest of Greek physicians, had given a fine example of the experimental method, by breaking a hen's eggs at various stages of incubation; and had applied the results of these studies in his treatise "On the Origin of the Child." Aristotle followed this lead and performed experiments that enabled him to give a description

[25]Gomperz, iv, 57; Zeller, i, 262, note; Lewes, 158, 165, etc.
[26]*Hist. An.* i, 6; ii, 8.   [27]*Ibid.*, viii, 1.   [28]*Politics*, 1, 8.
[29]*Hist. An.* i, 6; ii, 8.   [30]*De Generatione Animalium*, ii, 12.

of the development of the chick which even today arouses the admiration of embryologists.[31] He must have performed some novel experiments in genetics, for he disproves the theory that the sex of the child depends on what testis supplies the reproductive fluid, by quoting a case where the right testis of the father had been tied and yet the children had been of different sexes.[32] He raises some very modern problems of heredity. A woman of Elis had married a negro; her children were all whites, but in the next generation negroes reappeared; where, asks Aristotle, was the blackness hidden in the middle generation?[33] There was but a step from such a vital and intelligent query to the epochal experiments of Gregor Mendel (1822–1882). *Prudens quæstio dimidium scientiæ*—to know what to ask is already to know half. Surely, despite the errors that mar these biological works, they form the greatest monument ever raised to the science by any one man. When we consider that before Aristotle there had been, so far as we know, no biology beyond scattered observations, we perceive that this achievement alone might have sufficed for one lifetime, and would have given immortality. But Aristotle had only begun.

V. METAPHYSICS AND THE NATURE OF GOD

His metaphysics grew out of his biology. Everything in the world is moved by an inner urge to become something greater than it is. Everything is both the *form* or reality which has grown out of something which was its *matter* or raw material; and it may in its turn be the matter out of which still higher forms will grow. So the man is the form of which the child was the matter; the child is the form and its embryo the matter; the embryo the form, the ovum the matter; and so back till we reach in a vague way the conception of matter without form at all. But such a formless matter would be no-thing, for every thing has a form. Matter, in its widest sense, is the possibility of form; form is the actuality, the finished reality, of matter. Matter obstructs, form constructs. Form is not merely the shape but the shaping force, an inner necessity and impulse which moulds mere material to a specific figure and purpose; it is the realization of a potential capacity of matter; it is the sum of the powers residing in anything to do, to be, or to become. Nature is the conquest of matter by form, the constant progression and victory of life.[34]

Everything in the world moves naturally to a specific fulfilment. Of the varied causes which determine an event, the final cause, which determines the purpose, is the most decisive and important. The mistakes and futili-

[31]*De Part*, An., iii, 4.   [32]Lewes, 112.   [33]Gomprez, iv, 169.

[34]Half of our readers will be pleased, and the other half amused, to learn that among Aristotle's favorite examples of matter and form are woman and man; the male is the active, formative principle; the female is passive clay, waiting to be formed. Female offspring are the result of the failure of form to dominate matter (*De Gen. An.*, i, 2).

ties of nature are due to the inertia of matter resisting the forming force of purpose—hence the abortions and monsters that mar the panorama of life. Development is not haphazard or accidental (else how could we explain the almost universal appearance and transmission of useful organs?); everything is guided in a certain direction from within, by its nature and structure and entelechy;[35] the egg of the hen is internally designed or destined to become not a duck but a chick; the acorn becomes not a willow but an oak. This does not mean for Aristotle that there is an external providence designing earthly structures and events; rather the design is internal, and arises from the type and function of the thing. "Divine Providence coincides completely for Aristotle with the operation of natural causes."[36]

Yet there is a God, though not perhaps the simple and human god conceived by the forgivable anthropomorphism of the adolescent mind. Aristotle approaches the problem from the old puzzle about motion— how, he asks, does motion begin? He will not accept the possibility that motion is as beginningless as he conceives matter to be: matter may be eternal, because it is merely the everlasting possibility of future forms; but when and how did that vast process of motion and formation begin which at last filled the wide universe with an infinity of shapes? Surely motion has a source, says Aristotle; and if we are not to plunge drearily into an infinite regress, putting back our problem step by step endlessly, we must posit a prime mover unmoved (*primum mobile immotum*), a being incorporeal, indivisible, spaceless, sexless, passionless, changeless, perfect and eternal. God does not create, but he moves, the world; and he moves it not as a mechanical force but as the total motive of all operations in the world; "God moves the world as the beloved object moves the lover."[37] He is the final cause of nature, the drive and purpose of things, the form of the world; the principle of its life, the sum of its vital processes and powers, the inherent goal of its growth, the energizing entelechy of the whole. He is pure energy;[38] the Scholastic *Actus Purus*— activity *per se;* perhaps the mystic "Force" of modern physics and philosophy. He is not so much a person as a magnetic power.[39]

Yet, with his usual inconsistency, Aristotle represents God as self-conscious spirit. A rather mysterious spirit; for Aristotle's God never does anything; he has no desires, no will, no purpose; he is activity so pure that he never acts. He is absolutely perfect; therefore he cannot desire anything; therefore he does nothing. His only occupation is to contemplate the essence of things; and since he himself is the essence of all things, the form of all forms, his sole employment is the contemplation of him-

---

[35]*Entelecheia*—having (*echo*) its purpose (*telos*) within (*entos*); one of those magnificent Aristotelian terms which gather up into themselves a whole philosophy.
[36]*Ethics*, i, 10; Zeller, ii, 329.   [37]*Metaphysics*, ix, 7.
[38]*Ibid.*, xii, 8.   [39]Grant, 173.

self.[40] Poor Aristotelian God!—he is a *roi fainéant*, a do-nothing king; "the king reigns, but he does not rule." No wonder the British like Aristotle; his God is obviously copied from their king.

Or from Aristotle himself. Our philosopher so loved contemplation that he sacrificed to it his conception of divinity. His God is of the quiet Aristotelian type, nothing romantic, withdrawn to his ivory tower from the strife and stain of things; all the world away from the philosopher-kings of Plato, or from the stern flesh-and-blood reality of Yahveh, or the gentle and solicitous fatherhood of the Christian God.

VI. PSYCHOLOGY AND THE NATURE OF ART

Aristotle's psychology is marred with similar obscurity and vacillation. There are many interesting passages: the power of habit is emphasized, and is for the first time called "second nature"; and the laws of association, though not developed, find here a definite formulation. But both the crucial problems of philosophical psychology—the freedom of the will and the immortality of the soul—are left in haze and doubt. Aristotle talks at times like a determinist—"We cannot directly will to be different from what we are"; but he goes on to argue, against determinism, that we can choose what we shall be, by choosing now the environment that shall mould us; so we are free in the sense that we mould our own characters by our choice of friends, books, occupations, and amusements.[41] He does not anticipate the determinist's ready reply that these formative choices are themselves determined by our antecedent character, and this at last by unchosen heredity and early environment. He presses the point that our persistent use of praise and blame presupposes moral responsibility and free will; it does not occur to him that the determinist might reach from the same premisses a precisely opposite conclusion—that praise and blame are given that they may be part of the factors determining subsequent action.

Aristotle's theory of the soul begins with an interesting definition. The soul is the entire vital principle of any organism, the sum of its powers and processes. In plants the soul is merely a nutritive and reproductive power; in animals it is also a sensitive and locomotor power; in man it is as well the power of reason and thought.[42] The soul, as the sum of the powers of the body, cannot exist without it; the two are as form and wax, separable only in thought, but in reality one organic whole; the soul is not put into the body like the quick-silver inserted by Daedalus into the images of Venus to make "stand-ups" of them. A personal and particular soul can exist only in its own body. Nevertheless the soul is not material, as Democritus would have it; nor does it all die. Part of the rational power of the human soul is passive: it is bound up with memory, and dies

[40] *Meta,* xii, 8; *Ethics,* x, 8.   [41] *Ethics,* iii, 7.   [42] *De Anima,* ii.

with the body that bore the memory; but the "active reason," the pure power of thought, is independent of memory and is untouched with decay. The active reason is the universal as distinguished from the individual element in man; what survives is not the personality, with its transitory affections and desires, but mind in its most abstract and impersonal form.[43] In short, Aristotle destroys the soul in order to give it immortality; the immortal soul is "pure thought," undefiled with reality, just as Aristotle's God is pure activity, undefiled with action. Let him who can, be comforted with this theology. One wonders sometimes whether this metaphysical eating of one's cake and keeping it is not Aristotle's subtle way of saving himself from anti-Macedonian hemlock?

In a safer field of psychology he writes more originally and to the point, and almost creates the study of esthetics, the theory of beauty and art. Artistic creation, says Aristotle, springs from the formative impulse and the craving for emotional expression. Essentially the form of art is an imitation of reality; it holds the mirror up to nature.[44] There is in man a pleasure in imitation, apparently missing in lower animals. Yet the aim of art is to represent not the outward appearance of things, but their inward significance; for this, and not the external mannerism and detail, is their reality. There may be more human verity in the sternly classic moderation of the *Œdipus Rex* than in all the realistic tears of the *Trojan. Women.*

The noblest art appeals to the intellect as well as to the feelings (as a symphony appeals to us not only by its harmonies and sequences but by its structure and development) ; and this intellectual pleasure is the highest form of joy to which a man can rise. Hence a work of art should aim at form, and above all at unity, which is the backbone of structure and the focus of form. A drama, e. g., should have unity of action: there should be no confusing sub-plots, nor any digressive episodes.[45] But above all, the function of art is catharsis, purification: emotions accumulated in us under the pressure of social restraints, and liable to sudden issue in unsocial and destructive action, are touched off and sluiced away in the harmless form of theatrical excitement; so tragedy, "through pity and fear, effects the proper purgation of these emotions."[46] Aristotle misses certain features of tragedy (e. g., the conflict of principles and personalities) ; but in this theory of catharsis he has made a suggestion endlessly fertile in the understanding of the almost mystic power of art. It is an illuminating instance of his ability to enter every field of speculation, and to adorn whatever he touches.

---

[43]*De Anima,* ii, 4; i, 4; iii, 5.   [44]*Poetics,* i, 1447.
[45]Aristotle gives only one sentence to unity of time; and does not mention unity of place; so that the "three unities" commonly foisted upon him are later inventions (Norwood, *Greek Tragedy,* p. 42, note).
[46]*Poetics,* vi, 1449.

VII. ETHICS AND THE NATURE OF HAPPINESS

And yet, as Aristotle developed, and young men crowded about him to be taught and formed, more and more his mind turned from the details of science to the larger and vaguer problems of conduct and character. It came to him more clearly that above all questions of the physical world there loomed the question of questions—what is the best life?—what is life's supreme good?—what is virtue?—how shall we find happiness and fulfilment?

He is realistically simple in his ethics. His scientific training keeps him from the preachment of superhuman ideals and empty counsels of perfection. "In Aristotle," says Santayana, "the conception of human nature is perfectly sound; every ideal has a natural basis, and everything natural has an ideal development." Aristotle begins by frankly recognizing that the aim of life is not goodness for its own sake, but happiness. "For we choose happiness for itself, and never with a view to anything further; whereas we choose honor, pleasure, intellect . . . because we believe that through them we shall be made happy."[47] But he realizes that to call happiness the supreme good is a mere truism; what is wanted is some clearer account of the nature of happiness, and the way to it. He hopes to find this way by asking wherein man differs from other beings; and by presuming that man's happiness will lie in the full functioning of this specifically human quality. Now the peculiar excellence of man is his power of thought; it is by this that he surpasses and rules all other forms of life; and as the growth of this faculty has given him his supremacy, so, we may presume, its development will give him fulfilment and happiness.

The chief condition of happiness, then, barring certain physical prerequisites, is the life of reason—the specific glory and power of man. Virtue, or rather excellence,[48] will depend on clear judgment, self-control, symmetry of desire, artistry of means; it is not the possession of the simple man, nor the gift of innocent intent, but the achievement of experience in the fully developed man. Yet there is a road to it, a guide to excellence, which may save many detours and delays: it is the middle way, the golden mean. The qualities of character can be arranged in triads, in each of which the first and last qualities will be extremes and vices, and the middle quality a virtue or an excellence. So between cowardice and rashness is courage; between stinginess and extravagance is liberality; between sloth and greed is ambition; between humility and pride is modesty; be-

---

[47]*Ethics*, i, 7.

[48]The word *excellence* is probably the fittest translation of the Greek *arete*, usually mistranslated *virtue*. The reader will avoid misunderstanding Plato and Aristotle if, where translators write *virtue*, he will substitute *excellence*, *ability*, or *capacity*. The Greek *arete* is the Roman *virtus*; both imply a masculine sort of excellence (*Ares*, god of war; *vir*, a male). Classical antiquity conceived virtue in terms of man, just as medieval Christianity conceived it in terms of woman.

tween secrecy and loquacity, honesty; between moroseness and buffoonery, good humor; between quarrelsomeness and flattery, friendship; between Hamlet's indecisiveness and Quixote's impulsiveness is self-control.[49] "Right," then, in ethics or conduct, is not different from "right" in mathematics or engineering; it means correct, fit, what works best to the best result.

The golden mean, however, is not, like the mathematical mean, an exact average of two precisely calculable extremes; it fluctuates with the collateral circumstances of each situation, and discovers itself only to mature and flexible reason. Excellence is an art won by training and habituation: we do not act rightly because we have virtue or excellence, but we rather have these because we have acted rightly; "these virtues are formed in man by his doing the actions";[50] we are what we repeatedly do. Excellence, then, is not an act but a habit: "the good of man is a working of the soul in the way of excellence in a complete life; . . . for as it is not one swallow or one fine day that makes a spring, so it is not one day or a short time that makes a man blessed and happy."[51]

Youth is the age of extremes: "if the young commit a fault it is always on the side of excess and exaggeration." The great difficulty of youth (and of many of youth's elders) is to get out of one extreme without falling into its opposite. For one extreme easily passes into the other, whether through "over-correction" or elsewise: insincerity doth protest too much, and humility hovers on the precipice of conceit.[52] Those who are consciously at one extreme will give the name of virtue not to the mean but to the opposite extreme. Sometimes this is well; for if we are conscious of erring in one extreme "we should aim at the other, and so we may reach the middle position, . . . as men do in straightening bent timber."[53] But unconscious extremists look upon the golden mean as the greatest vice; they "expel towards each other the man in the middle position; the brave man is called rash by the coward, and cowardly by the rash man, and in other cases accordingly";[54] so in modern politics the "liberal" is called "conservative" and "radical" by the radical and the conservative.

It is obvious that this doctrine of the mean is the formulation of a characteristic attitude which appears in almost every system of Greek philosophy. Plato had had it in mind when he called virtue harmonious action; Socrates when he identified virtue with knowledge. The Seven Wise Men had established the tradition by engraving, on the temple of Apollo at Delphi, the motto *meden agan*,—nothing in excess. Perhaps, as Nietzsche claims,[55] all these were attempts of the Greeks to check their

[49]*Ethics*, i, 7.   [50]*Ethics*, ii, 4.   [51]*Ibid.*, i, 7.
[52] "The vanity of Antisthenes" the Cynic, said Plato, "peeps out through the holes in his cloak."
[53]*Ethics*, ii, 9.   [54]*Ibid.*, ii, 8.   [55]*The Birth of Tragedy.*

own violence and impulsiveness of character; more truly, they reflected the Greek feeling that passions are not of themselves vices, but the raw material of both vice and virtue, according as they function in excess and disproportion, or in measure and harmony.[56]

But the golden mean, says our matter-of-fact philosopher, is not all of the secret of happiness. We must have, too, a fair degree of worldly goods: poverty makes one stingy and grasping; while possessions give one that freedom from care and greed which is the source of aristocratic ease and charm. The noblest of these external aids to happiness is friendship. Indeed, friendship is more necessary to the happy than to the unhappy; for happiness is multiplied by being shared. It is more important than justice: for "when men are friends, justice is unnecessary; but when men are just, friendship is still a boon." "A friend is one soul in two bodies." Yet friendship implies few friends rather than many; "he who has many friends has no friend"; and "to be a friend to many people in the way of perfect friendship is impossible." Fine friendship requires duration rather than fitful intensity; and this implies stability of character; it is to altered character that we must attribute the dissolving kaleidoscope of friendship. And friendship requires equality; for gratitude gives it at best a slippery basis. "Benefactors are commonly held to have more friendship for the objects of their kindness than these for them. The account of the matter which satisfies most persons is that the one are debtors and the others creditors, . . . and that the debtors wish their creditors out of the way, while the creditors are anxious that their debtors should be preserved." Aristotle rejects this interpretation; he prefers to believe that the greater tenderness of the benefactor is to be explained on the analogy of the artist's affection for his work, or the mother's for her child. We love that which we have made.[57]

And yet, though external goods and relationships are necessary to happiness, its essence remains within us, in rounded knowledge and clarity of soul. Surely sense pleasure is not the way: that road is a circle: as Socrates phrased the coarser Epicurean idea, we scratch that we may itch, and itch that we may scratch. Nor can a political career be the way; for therein we walk subject to the whims of the people; and nothing is so fickle as the crowd. No, happiness must be a pleasure of the mind; and we may trust it only when it comes from the pursuit or the capture of truth. "The operation of the intellect . . . aims at no end beyond itself, and finds in itself the pleasure which stimulates it to further operation;

[56]Cf. a sociological formulation of the same idea: "Values are never absolute, but only relative. . . . A certain quality in human nature is deemed to be less abundant than it ought to be; therefore we place a value upon it, and . . . encourage and cultivate it. As a result of this valuation we call it a virtue; but if the same quality should become superabundant we should call it a vice and try to repress it."—Carver, *Essays in Social Justice*.

[57]*Ethics*, viii and ix.

and since the attributes of self-sufficiency, unweariedness, and capacity for rest, . . . plainly belong to this occupation, in it must lie perfect happiness."[58]

Aristotle's ideal man, however, is no mere metaphysician.

He does not expose himself needlessly to danger, since there are few things for which he cares sufficiently; but he is willing, in great crises, to give even his life,—knowing that under certain conditions it is not worth while to live. He is of a disposition to do men service, though he is ashamed to have a service done to him. To confer a kindness is a mark of superiority; to receive one is a mark of subordination . . . He does not take part in public displays . . . He is open in his dislikes and preferences; he talks and acts frankly, because of his contempt for men and things . . . He is never fired with admiration, since there is nothing great in his eyes. He cannot live in complaisance with others, except it be a friend; complaisance is the characteristic of a slave. . . . He never feels malice, and always forgets and passes over injuries. . . . He is not fond of talking. . . . It is no concern of his that he should be praised, or that others should be blamed. He does not speak evil of others, even of his enemies, unless it be to themselves. His carriage is sedate, his voice deep, his speech measured; he is not given to hurry, for he is concerned about only a few things; he is not prone to vehemence, for he thinks nothing very important. A shrill voice and hasty steps come to a man through care. . . . He bears the accidents of life with dignity and grace, making the best of his circumstances, like a skilful general who marshals his limited forces with all the strategy of war. . . . He is his own best friend, and takes delight in privacy whereas the man of no virtue or ability is his own worst enemy, and is afraid of solitude.[59]

Such is the Superman of Aristotle.

VIII. POLITICS

1. COMMUNISM AND CONSERVATISM

From so aristocratic an ethic there naturally follows (or was the sequence the other way?) a severely aristocratic political philosophy. It was not to be expected that the tutor of an emperor and the husband of a princess would have any exaggerated attachment to the common people, or even to the mercantile bourgeoisie; our philosophy is where our treasure lies. But further, Aristotle was honestly conservative because of the turmoil and disaster that had come out of Athenian democracy; like a typical scholar he longed for order, security, and peace; this, he felt, was no time for political extravaganzas. Radicalism is a luxury of stability; we may dare to change things only when things lie steady under our hands. And in general, says Aristotle, "the habit of lightly changing the laws is an evil; and when the advantage of change is small, some defects whether in the law or in the ruler had better be met with philosophic toleration.

[58] *Ibid.*, x, 7.   [59] *Ethics*, iv, 3.

The citizen will gain less by the change than he will lose by acquiring the habit of disobedience."[60] The power of the law to secure observance, and therefore to maintain political stability, rests very largely on custom; and "to pass lightly from old laws to new ones is a certain means of weakening the inmost essence of all law whatever."[61] "Let us not disregard the experience of ages: surely, in the multitude of years, these things, if they were good, would not have remained unknown."[62]

"These things," of course, means chiefly Plato's communistic republic. Aristotle fights the realism of Plato about universals, and idealism of Plato about government. He finds many dark spots in the picture painted by the Master. He does not relish the barrack-like continuity of contact to which Plato apparently condemned his guardian philosophers; conservative though he is, Aristotle values individual quality, privacy, and liberty above social efficiency and power. He would not care to call every contemporary brother or sister, nor every elder person father or mother; if all are your brothers, none is; and "how much better it is to be the real cousin of somebody than to be a son after Plato's fashion!"[63] In a state having women and children in common, "love will be watery. . . . Of the two qualities which chiefly inspire regard and affection—that a thing is your own, and that it awakens real love in you—neither can exist in such a state" as Plato's.[64]

Perhaps there was, in the dim past, a communistic society, when the family was the only state, and pasturage or simple tillage the only form of life. But "in a more divided state of society," where the division of labor into unequally important functions elicits and enlarges the natural inequality of men, communism breaks down because it provides no adequate incentive for the exertion of superior abilities. The stimulus of gain is necessary to arduous work; and the stimulus of ownership is necessary to proper industry, husbandry and care. When everybody owns everything nobody will take care of anything. "That which is common to the greatest number has the least attention bestowed upon it. Everyone thinks chiefly of his own, hardly ever of the public, interest."[65] And "there is always a difficulty in living together, or having things in common, but especially in having common property. The partnerships of fellow-travellers" (to say nothing of the arduous communism of marriage), "are an example to the point; for they generally fall out by the way, and quarrel about any trifle that turns up."[66]

"Men readily listen" to Utopias, "and are easily induced to believe that in some wonderful manner everybody will become everybody's friend, especially when some one is heard denouncing the evils now existing, . . . which are said to arise out of the possession of private property. These evils, however, arise from quite another source—the

[60]*Politics*, ii, 8.   [61]*Ibid.*, v. 8.   [62]*Ibid.*, ii, 5.   [63]*Ibid.*, ii, 3.
[64]*Ibid.*, ii, 4.   [65]*Politics*, ii, 3.   [66]*Ibid.*, ii, 5.

wickedness of human nature."[67] Political science does not make men, but must take them as they come from nature.[68]

And human nature, the human average, is nearer to the beast than to the god. The great majority of men are natural dunces and sluggards; in any system whatever these men will sink to the bottom; and to help them with state subsidies is "like pouring water into a leaking cask." Such people must be ruled in politics and directed in industry; with their consent if possible, without it if necessary. "From the hour of their birth some are marked out for subjection, and others for command."[69] "For he who can foresee with his mind is by nature intended to be lord and master; and he who can work only with his body is by nature a slave."[70] The slave is to the master what the body is to the mind; and as the body should be subject to the mind, so "it is better for all inferiors that they should be under the rule of a master."[71] "The slave is a tool with life in it, the tool is a lifeless slave." And then our hard-hearted philosopher, with a glimmer of possibilities which the Industrial Revolution has opened to our hands, writes for a moment with wistful hope: "If every instrument would accomplish its own work, obeying or anticipating the will of others, . . . if the shuttle would weave, or the plectrum touch the lyre, without a hand to guide them, then chief workmen would not need assistants, nor masters slaves."[72]

This philosophy typifies the Greek disdain for manual labor. Such work in Athens had not become so complicated as it is today, when the intelligence demanded in many manual trades is at times much greater than that required for the operations of the lower middle class, and even a college professor may look upon an automobile mechanic (in certain exigencies) as a very god; manual work was then merely manual, and Aristotle looked down upon it, from the heights of philosophy, as belonging to men without minds, as only fit for slaves, and only fitting men for slavery. Manual labor, he believes, dulls and deteriorates the mind, and leaves neither time nor energy for political intelligence; it seems to Aristotle a reasonable corollary that only persons of some leisure should have a voice in government.[73] "The best form of state will not admit mechanics to citizenship. . . . At Thebes there was a law that no man could hold office who had not retired from business ten years before."[74]

---

[67]*Ibid.* Note that conservatives are pessimists, and radicals are optimists, about human nature, which is probably neither so good nor so bad as they would like to believe, and may be not so much nature as early training and environment.

[68]*Ibid.*, i, 10.   [69]*Ibid.*, i, 5.

[70]*Ibid.*, i, 2. Perhaps *slave* is too harsh a rendering of *doulos;* the word was merely a frank recognition of a brutal fact which in our day is perfumed with talk about the dignity of labor and the brotherhood of man. We easily excel the ancients in making phrases.

[71]*Ibid.*, i, 5.   [72]*Ibid.*, i, 4.
[73]*Politics.* iii, 3; vii, 8.   [74]*Ibid.*, iii, 5.

Even merchants and financiers are classed by Aristotle among slaves. "Retail trade is unnatural, . . . and a mode by which men gain from one another. The most hated sort of such exchange is . . . usury, which makes a gain out of money itself, and not from its natural use. For money was intended as an instrument of exchange, and not as the mother of interest. This usury (*tokos*), which means the birth of money from money, . . . is of all modes of gain the most unnatural."[75] Money should not breed. Hence "the discussion of the theory of finance is not unworthy of philosophy; but to be engaged in finance, or in money-making, is unworthy of a free man."[76]

2. MARRIAGE AND EDUCATION

Woman is to man as the slave to the master, the manual to the mental worker, the barbarian to the Greek. Woman is an unfinished man, left standing on a lower step in the scale of development.[77] The male is by nature superior, and the female inferior; the one rules and the other is ruled; and this principle extends, of necessity, to all mankind. Woman is weak of will, and therefore incapable of independence of character or position; her best condition is a quiet home life in which, while ruled by the man in her external relations, she may be in domestic affairs supreme. Women should not be made more like men, as in Plato's republic; rather the dissimilarity should be increased; nothing is so attractive as the different. "The courage of a man and that of a woman are not, as Socrates supposed, the same: the courage of a man is shown in commanding; that of a woman in obeying. . . . As the poet says, 'Silence is a woman's glory.' "[78]

Aristotle seems to suspect that this ideal enslavement of woman is a rare achievement for man, and that as often as not the sceptre is with the tongue rather than with the arm. As if to give the male an indispensable advantage, he advises him to defer marriage till the vicinity of thirty-seven, and then to marry a lass of some twenty years. A girl who is rounding the twenties is usually the equal of a man of thirty, but may perhaps be managed by a seasoned warrior of thirty-seven. What attracts

[75] *Ibid.*, i, 10. This view influenced the medieval prohibition of interest.

[76] *Ibid.*, i, 11. Aristotle adds that philosophers could succeed in such fields if they cared to descend into them; and he proudly points to Thales, who, foreseeing a good harvest, bought up all the reapers in his city, and then, at harvest time, sold them at his own sweet price; whereupon Aristotle observes that the universal secret of great riches is the creation of a monopoly.

[77] *De Gen. Animalium*, ii, 3; *Hist. Animalium*, viii, 1; *Pol.*, i, 5. Cf. Weininger; and Meredith's "Woman will be the last thing civilized by man" (*Ordeal of Richard Feverel*, p. 1). It appears, however, that man was (or will be) the last thing civilized by woman; for the great civilizing agencies are the family and a settled economic life; and both of these are the creations of woman.

[78] *Politics*, i, 13.

Aristotle to this matrimonial mathematics is the consideration that two such disparate persons will lose their reproductive power and passions at approximately the same time. "If the man is still able to beget children while the woman is unable to bear them, or *vice versa*, quarrels and differences will arise. . . . Since the time of generation is commonly limited within the age of seventy years in the man, and fifty in the woman, the commencement of their union should conform to these periods. The union of male and female when too young is bad for the creation of children; in all animals the off-spring of the young are small and ill-developed, and generally female." Health is more important than love. Further, "it conduces to temperance not to marry too soon; for women who marry early are apt to be wanton; and in men too the bodily frame is stunted if they marry while they are growing."[79] These matters should not be left to youthful caprice, they should be under state supervision and control: the state should determine the minimum and maximum ages of marriage for each sex, the best seasons for conception, and the rate of increase in population. If the natural rate of increase is too high, the cruel practice of infanticide may be replaced by abortion; and "let abortion be procured before sense and life have begun."[80] There is an ideal number of population for every state, varying with its position and resources. "A state when composed of too few is not, as a state should be, self-sufficing; while if it has too many . . . it becomes a nation and not a state, and is almost incapable of constitutional government," or of ethnic or political unity.[81] Anything in excess of a population of 10,000 is undesirable.

Education, too, should be in the hands of the state. "That which most contributes to the permanence of constitutions is the adaptation of education to the form of government. . . . The citizen should be moulded to the form of government under which he lives."[82] By state control of schools we might divert men from industry and trade to agriculture; and we might train men, while keeping property private, to open their possessions to discriminately common use. "Among good men, with respect to the use of property, the proverb will hold, that 'friends should have all things in common.' "[83] But above all, the growing citizen must be taught obedience to law, else a state is impossible. "It has been well said that 'he who has never learned to obey cannot be a good commander.' . . . The good citizen should be capable of both." And only a state system of schools can achieve social unity amid ethnic heterogeneity; the state is a plurality which must be made into a unity and a community by education.[84] Let youth be taught, too, the great boon it has in the state, the

---

[79]*Ibid.*, vii, 16. It is apparent that Aristotle has in mind only the temperance of women; the moral effect of deferred marriage upon men does not seem to agitate him.

[80]*Politics*, vii, 16.   [81]*Ibid.*, vii, 4.   [82]*Ibid.*, v, 9; viii, 1.
[83]*Ibid.*, vi, 4; ii, 5.   [84]*Ibid.*, iii, 4; ii, 5.

unappreciated security which comes of social organization, the freedom that comes of law. "Man, when perfected, is the best of animals; but when isolated he is the worst of all; for injustice is more dangerous when armed, and man is equipped at birth with the weapon of intelligence, and with qualities of character which he may use for the vilest ends. Wherefore if he have not virtue he is the most unholy and savage of animals, full of gluttony and lust." And only social control can give him virtue. Through speech man evolved society; through society, intelligence; through intelligence, order; and through order, civilization. In such an ordered state the individual has a thousand opportunities and avenues of development open to him which a solitary life would never give. "To live alone," then, "one must be either an animal or a god."[85]

Hence revolution is almost always unwise; it may achieve some good, but at the cost of many evils, the chief of which is the disturbance, and perhaps the dissolution, of that social order and structure on which every political good depends. The direct consequences of revolutionary innovations may be calculable and salutary; but the indirect are generally incalculable, and not seldom disastrous. "They who take only a few points into account find it easy to pronounce judgment"; and a man can make up his mind quickly if he has only a little to make up. "Young men are easily deceived, for they are quick to hope." The suppression of longestablished habits brings the overthrow of innovating governments because the old habits persist among the people; characters are not so easily changed as laws. If a constitution is to be permanent, all the parts of a society must desire it to be maintained. Therefore a ruler who would avoid revolution should prevent extremes of poverty and wealth,—"a condition which is most often the result of war"; he should (like the English) encourage colonization as an outlet for a dangerously congested population; and he should foster and practice religion. An autocratic ruler particularly "should appear to be earnest in the worship of the gods; for if men think that a ruler is religious and reveres the gods, they are less afraid of suffering injustice at his hands, and are less disposed to conspire against him, since they believe that the gods themselves are fighting on his side."[86]

3. DEMOCRACY AND ARISTOCRACY

With such safeguards in religion, in education, and in the ordering of family life, almost any of the traditional forms of government will serve. All forms have good and bad commingled in them, and are severally adapted to various conditions. Theoretically, the ideal form of government would be the centralization of all political power in the one best

---

[85]*Politics*, i, 2. "Or," adds Nietzsche, who takes nearly all of his political philosophy from Aristotle, "one must be both—that is, a philosopher."

[86]*Politics*, iv, 5; ii, 9; v, 7; ii, 11.

man. Homer is right: "Bad is the lordship of many; let one be your ruler and master." For such a man law would be rather an instrument than a limit: "for men of eminent ability there is no law—they are themselves a law." Anyone would be ridiculous who should attempt to make laws for them; they would probably retort what, in the fable of Antisthenes, the lions said to the hares when, in the council of beasts, the latter began haranguing and claiming equality for all—"Where are your claws?"[87]

But in practice, monarchy is usually the worst form of government, for great strength and great virtue are not near allied. Hence the best practicable polity is aristocracy, the rule of the informed and capable few. Government is too complex a thing to have its issues decided by number, when lesser issues are reserved for knowledge and ability. "As the physician ought to be judged by the physician, so ought men in general to be judged by their peers. . . . Now does not this same principle apply to elections? For a right election can only be made by those who have knowledge: a geometrician, e. g., will choose rightly in matters of geometry; or a pilot in matters of navigation. . . .[88] So that neither the election of magistrates nor the calling of them to account should be entrusted to the many."

The difficulty with hereditary aristocracy is that it has no permanent economic base; the eternal recurrence of the *nouveaux riches* puts political office sooner or later at the disposal of the highest bidder. "It is surely a bad thing that the greatest offices . . . should be bought. The law which permits this abuse makes wealth of more account than ability, and the whole state becomes avaricious. For whenever the chiefs of the state deem anything honorable, the other citizens are sure to follow their example" (the "prestige imitation" of modern social psychology); "and where ability has not the first place there is no real aristocracy."[89]

Democracy is usually the result of a revolution against plutocracy. "Love of gain in the ruling classes tends constantly to diminish their number" (Marx's "elimination of the middle class"), "and so to strengthen the masses, who in the end set upon their masters and establish democracies." This "rule by the poor" has some advantages. "The people, though individually they may be worse judges than those who have special knowledge, are collectively as good. Moreover, there are some artists whose works are best judged not by themselves alone, but by those who do not possess the art; e. g., the user or master of a house will be a better judge of it than the builder; . . . and the guest will be a better judge of a feast than the cook."[90] And "the many are more incorruptible

[87]*Ibid.*, iii, 13. Aristotle probably had Alexander or Philip in mind while writing this passage, just as Nietzsche seems to have been influenced towards similar conclusions by the alluring careers of Bismarck and Napoleon.
[88]*Politics*, iii, 11. Cf. the modern argument for "occupational representation."
[89]*Ibid.*, ii, 11.   [90]*Ibid.*, iii, 15, 8, 11.

than the few; they are like the greater quantity of water which is less easily spoiled than a little. The individual is liable to be overcome by anger, or by some other passion, and then his judgment is necessarily perverted; but it is hardly to be supposed that a great number of persons would all get into a passion and go wrong at the same moment."[91]

Yet democracy is on the whole inferior to aristocracy.[92] For it is based on a false assumption of equality; it "arises out of the notion that those who are equal in one respect (e. g., in respect of the law) are equal in all respects; because men are equally free they claim to be absolutely equal." The upshot is that ability is sacrified to number, while numbers are manipulated by trickery. Because the people are so easily misled, and so fickle in their views, the ballot should be limited to the intelligent. What we need is a combination of aristocracy and democracy.

Constitutional government offers this happy union. It is not the best conceivable government—that would be an aristocracy of education—but it is the best possible state. "We must ask what is the best constitution for most states, and the best life for most men; neither assuming a standard of excellence which will be above ordinary persons, nor an education exceptionally favored by nature or circumstance, nor yet an ideal state which will be only an aspiration; but having in mind such a life as the majority will be able to share, and a form of government to which states in general can attain." "It is necessary to begin by assuming a principle of general application, namely, that that part of the state which desires the continuance of the government must be stronger than that which does not";[93] and strength consists neither in number alone, nor in property alone, nor in military or political ability alone, but in a combination of these, so that regard has to be taken of "freedom, wealth, culture and noble birth, as well as of mere numerical superiority." Now where shall we find such an *economic* majority to support our constitutional government? Perhaps best in the middle class: here again we have the golden mean, just as constitutional government itself would be a mean between democracy and aristocracy. Our state will be sufficiently democratic if the road to every office is open to all; and sufficiently aristocratic if the offices themselves are closed except to those who have traveled the road and arrived fully prepared. From whatever angle we approach our eternal political problem we monotonously reach the same conclusion: that the community should determine the ends to be pursued, but that only experts should select and apply the means; that choice should be democratically spread, but that office should be rigidly reserved for the equipped and winnowed best.

---

[91] *Politics,* iii, 15. Tarde, Le Bon and other social psychologists assert precisely the contrary; and though they exaggerate the vices of the crowd, they might find better support than Aristotle in the behavior of the Athenian Assembly 430–330 B. C.

[92] *Ibid.,* ii, 9.   [93] *Ibid.,* iv, 11, 10.

IX. CRITICISM

What shall we say of this philosophy? Perhaps nothing rapturous. It is difficult to be enthusiastic about Aristotle, because it was difficult for him to be enthusiastic about anything; and *si vis me flere, primum tibi flendum.*[94] His motto is *nil admirari*—to admire or marvel at nothing; and we hesitate to violate his motto in his case. We miss in him the reforming zeal of Plato, the angry love of humanity which made the great idealist denounce his fellow-men. We miss the daring originality of his teacher, the lofty imagination, the capacity for generous delusion. And yet, after reading Plato, nothing could be so salutary for us as Aristotle's sceptic calm.

Let us summarize our disagreement. We are bothered, at the outset, with his insistence on logic. He thinks the syllogism a description of man's way of reasoning, whereas it merely describes man's way of dressing up his reasoning for the persuasion of another mind; he supposes that thought begins with premises and seeks their conclusions, when actually thought begins with hypothetical conclusions and seeks their justifying premises,—and seeks them best by the observation of particular events under the controlled and isolated conditions of experiment. Yet how foolish we should be to forget that two thousand years have changed merely the incidentals of Aristotle's logic, that Occam and Bacon and Whewell and Mill and a hundred others have but found spots in his sun, and that Aristotle's creation of this new discipline of thought, and his firm establishment of its essential lines, remain among the lasting achievements of the human mind.

It is again the absence of experiment and fruitful hypothesis that leaves Aristotle's natural science a mass of undigested observations. His specialty is the collection and classification of data; in every field he wields his categories and produces catalogues. But side by side with this bent and talent for observation goes a Platonic addiction to metaphysics; this trips him up in every science, and inveigles him into the wildest presuppositions. Here indeed was the great defect of the Greek mind: it was not disciplined; it lacked limiting and steadying traditions; it moved freely in an uncharted field, and ran too readily to theories and conclusions. So Greek philosophy leaped on to heights unreached again, while Greek science limped behind. Our modern danger is precisely opposite; inductive data fall upon us from all sides like the lava of Vesuvius; we suffocate with uncoördinated facts; our minds are overwhelmed with sciences breeding and multiplying into specialistic chaos for want of synthetic thought and a unifying philosophy. We are all mere fragments of what a man might be.

[94] "If you wish me to weep you must weep first"—Horace (*Ars Poetica*) to actors and writers.

Aristotle's ethics is a branch of his logic: the ideal life is like a proper syllogism. He gives us a handbook of propriety rather than a stimulus to improvement. An ancient critic spoke of him as "moderate to excess." An extremist might call the *Ethics* the champion collection of platitudes in all literature; and an Anglophobe would be consoled with the thought that Englishmen in their youth had done advance penance for the imperialistic sins of their adult years, since both at Cambridge and at Oxford they had been compelled to read every word of the Nicomachean Ethics. We long to mingle fresh green *Leaves of Grass* with these drier pages, to add Whitman's exhilarating justification of sense joy to Aristotle's exaltation of a purely intellectual happiness. We wonder if this Aristotelian ideal of immoderate moderation has had anything to do with the colorless virtue, the starched perfection, the expressionless good form, of the British aristocracy. Matthew Arnold tells us that in his time Oxford tutors looked upon the *Ethics* as infallible. For three hundred years this book and the *Politics* have formed the ruling British mind, perhaps to great and noble achievements, but certainly to a hard and cold efficiency. What would the result have been if the masters of the greatest of empires had been nurtured, instead, on the holy fervor and the constructive passion of the *Republic*?

After all, Aristotle was not quite Greek; he had been settled and formed before coming to Athens; there was nothing Athenian about him, nothing of the hasty and inspiriting experimentalism which made Athens throb with political *élan* and at last helped to subject her to a unifying despot. He realized too completely the Delphic command to avoid excess: he is so anxious to pare away extremes that at last nothing is left. He is so fearful of disorder that he forgets to be fearful of slavery; he is so timid of uncertain change that he prefers a certain changelessness that near resembles death. He lacks that Heraclitean sense of flux which justifies the conservative in believing that all permanent change is gradual, and justifies the radical in believing that no changelessness is permanent. He forgets that Plato's communism was meant only for the élite, the unselfish and ungreedy few; and he comes deviously to a Platonic result when he says that though property should be private, its use should be as far as possible common. He does not see (and perhaps he could not be expected in his early day to see) that individual control of the means of production was stimulating and salutary only when these means were so simple as to be purchasable by any man; and that their increasing complexity and cost lead to a dangerous centralization of ownership and power, and to an artificial and finally disruptive inequality.

But after all, these are quite inessential criticisms of what remains the most marvelous and influential system of thought ever put together by any single mind. It may be doubted if any other thinker has contributed so much to the enlightenment of the world. Every later age has drawn upon Aristotle, and stood upon his shoulders to see the truth. The varied and magnificent culture of Alexandria found its scientific inspiration in him. His *Organon* played a central rôle in shaping the minds of the medieval barbarians into disciplined and consistent thought. The other works, translated by Nestorian Christians into Syriac in the fifth century A. D., and thence into Arabic and Hebrew in the tenth century, and thence into Latin towards 1225, turned scholasticism from its eloquent beginnings in Abélard to encyclopedic completion in Thomas Aquinas. The Crusaders brought back more accurate Greek copies of the philosopher's texts; and the Greek scholars of Constantinople brought further Aristotelian treasures with them when, after 1453, they fled from the besieging Turks. The works of Aristotle came to be for European philosophy what the Bible was for theology—an almost infallible text, with solutions for every problem. In 1215 the Papal legate at Paris forbade teachers to lecture on his works; in 1231 Gregory IX appointed a commission to expurgate him; by 1260 he was *de rigueur* in every Christian school, and ecclesiastical assemblies penalized deviations from his views. Chaucer describes his student as happy by having

> *At his beddes hed*
> *Twenty bookes clothed in blake or red,*
> *Of Aristotle and his philosophie;*

and in the first circles of Hell, says Dante,

> *I saw the Master there of those who know,*
> *Amid the philosophic family,*
> *By all admired, and by all reverenced;*
> *There Plato too I saw, and Socrates,*
> *Who stood beside him closer than the rest.*

Such lines give us some inkling of the honor which a thousand years offered to the Stagirite. Not till new instruments, accumulated observations, and patient experiments remade science and gave irresistible weapons to Occam and Ramus, to Roger and Francis Bacon, was the reign of Aristotle ended. No other mind had for so long a time ruled the intellect of mankind.

X. LATER LIFE AND DEATH

Meanwhile life had become unmanageably complicated for our philosopher. He found himself on the one hand embroiled with Alexander for protesting against the execution of Calisthenes (a nephew of Aristotle), who had refused to worship Alexander as a god; and Alexander had answered the protest by hinting that it was quite within his omnipotence to put even philosophers to death. At the same time Aristotle was busy

defending Alexander among the Athenians. He preferred Greek solidarity
to city patriotism, and thought culture and science would flourish better
when petty sovereignties and disputes were ended; and he saw in Alexander what Goethe was to see in Napoleon—the philosophic unity of a
chaotic and intolerably manifold world. The Athenians, hungering for
liberty, growled at Aristotle, and became bitter when Alexander had a
statue of the philosopher put up in the heart of the hostile city. In this
turmoil we get an impression of Aristotle quite contrary to that left upon
us by his *Ethics:* here is a man not cold and inhumanly calm, but a
fighter, pursuing his Titanic work in a circle of enemies on every side.
The successors of Plato at the Academy, the oratorical school of Isocrates,
and the angry crowds that hung on Demosthenes' acid eloquence, in-
trigued and clamored for his exile or his death.

And then, suddenly (323 B. C.), Alexander died. Athens went wild
with patriotic joy; the Macedonian party was overthrown, and Athenian
independence was proclaimed. Antipater, successor of Alexander and intimate friend of Aristotle, marched upon the rebellious city. Most of the
Macedonian party fled. Eurymedon, a chief priest, brought in an indictment against Aristotle, charging him with having taught that prayer and
sacrifice were of no avail. Aristotle saw himself fated to be tried by juries
and crowds incomparably more hostile than those that had murdered
Socrates. Very wisely, he left the city, saying that he would not give
Athens a chance to sin a second time against philosophy. There was no
cowardice in this; an accused person at Athens had always the option
of preferring exile.[95] Arrived at Chalcis, Aristotle fell ill; Diogenes Laertius tells us that the old philosopher, in utter disappointment with the
turn of all things against him, committed suicide by drinking hemlock.[96]
However induced, his illness proved fatal; and a few months after leaving Athens (322 B. C.) the lonely Aristotle died.

In the same year, and at the same age, sixty-two, Demosthenes, greatest of Alexander's enemies, drank poison. Within twelve months Greece
had lost her greatest ruler, her greatest orator, and her greatest philosopher. The glory that had been Greece faded now in the dawn of the
Roman sun; and the grandeur that was Rome was the pomp of power
rather than the light of thought. Then that grandeur too decayed, that
little light went almost out. For a thousand years darkness brooded over
the face of Europe. All the world awaited the resurrection of philosophy.

[95]Grote, 20.   [96]Grote, 22; Zeller, 1, 37 note.

CHAPTER III

Francis Bacon

I. FROM ARISTOTLE TO THE RENAISSANCE

WHEN Sparta blockaded and defeated Athens towards the close of the fifth century B. C., political supremacy passed from the mother of Greek philosophy and art, and the vigor and independence of the Athenian mind decayed. When, in 399 B. C., Socrates was put to death, the soul of Athens died with him, lingering only in his proud pupil, Plato. And when Philip of Macedon defeated the Athenians at Chæronea in 338 B. C., and Alexander burned the great city of Thebes to the ground three years later, even the ostentatious sparing of Pindar's home could not cover up the fact that Athenian independence, in government and in thought, was irrevocably destroyed. The domination of Greek philosophy by the Macedonian Aristotle mirrored the political subjection of Greece by the virile and younger peoples of the north.

The death of Alexander (323 B. C.) quickened this process of decay. The boy-emperor, barbarian though he remained after all of Aristotle's tutoring, had yet learned to revere the rich culture of Greece, and had dreamed of spreading that culture through the Orient in the wake of his victorious armies. The development of Greek commerce, and the multiplication of Greek trading posts throughout Asia Minor, had provided an economic basis for the unification of this region as part of an Hellenic empire; and Alexander hoped that from these busy stations Greek thought, as well as Greek goods, would radiate and conquer. But he had underrated the inertia and resistance of the Oriental mind, and the mass and depth of Oriental culture. It was only a youthful fancy, after all, to suppose that so immature and unstable a civilization as that of Greece could be imposed upon a civilization immeasurably more widespread, and rooted in the most venerable traditions. The quantity of Asia proved too much for the quality of Greece. Alexander himself, in the hour of his triumph, was conquered by the soul of the East; he married (among several ladies) the daughter of Darius; he adopted the Persian diadem and robe of state; he introduced into Europe the Oriental notior of the divine right of kings; and at last he astonished a sceptic Greece by announcing, in magnificent Eastern style, that he was a god. Greece laughed; and Alexander drank himself to death.

This subtle infusion of an Asiatic soul into the wearied body of tha master Greek was followed rapidly by the pouring of Oriental cults and faiths into Greece along those very lines of communication which the young conqueror had opened up; the broken dykes let in the ocean of Eastern thought upon the lowlands of the still adolescent European mind. The mystic and superstitious faiths which had taken root among the poorer people of Hellas were reinforced and spread about; and the Oriental spirit of apathy and resignation found a ready soil in decadent and despondent Greece. The introduction of the Stoic philosophy into Athens by the Phoenician merchant Zeno (about 310 B. C.) was but one of a multitude of Oriental infiltrations. Both Stoicism and Epicureanism —the apathetic acceptance of defeat, and the effort to forget defeat in the arms of pleasure—were theories as to how one might yet be happy though subjugated or enslaved; precisely as the pessimistic Oriental stoicism of Schopenhauer and the despondent epicureanism of Renan were in the nineteenth century the symbols of a shattered Revolution and a broken France.

Not that these natural antitheses of ethical theory were quite new to Greece. One finds them in the gloomy Heraclitus and the "laughing philosopher" Democritus; and one sees the pupils of Socrates dividing into Cynics and Cyrenaics under the lead of Antisthenes and Aristippus, and extolling, the one school apathy, the other happiness. Yet these were even then almost exotic modes of thought: imperial Athens did not take to them. But when Greece had seen Chæronea in blood and Thebes in ashes, it listened to Diogenes; and when the glory had departed from Athens she was ripe for Zeno and Epicurus.[1]

Zeno built his philosophy of *apatheia* on a determinism which a later Stoic, Chrysippus, found it hard to distinguish from Oriental fatalism. When Zeno, who did not believe in slavery, was beating his slave for some offense, the slave pleaded, in mitigation, that by his master's philosophy he had been destined from all eternity to commit this fault; to which Zeno replied, with the calm of a sage, that on the same philosophy he, Zeno, had been destined to beat him for it. As Schopenhauer deemed it useless for the individual will to fight the universal will, so the Stoic argued that philosophic indifference was the only reasonable attitude to a life in which the struggle for existence is so unfairly doomed to inevitable defeat. If victory is quite impossible it should be scorned. The secret of peace is not to make our achievements equal to our desires, but to lower our desires to the level of our achievements. "If what you have seems insufficient to you," said the Roman Stoic Seneca (d. 65 A. D.), "then, though you possess the world, you will yet be miserable."

Such a principle cried out to heaven for its opposite, and Epicurus, though himself as Stoic in life as Zeno, supplied it. Epicurus, says Fen-

[1] The table on pages 80–81 indicates approximately the main lines of philosophical development in Europe and America.

elon,[2] "bought a fair garden, which he tilled himself. There it was he set up his school, and there he lived a gentle and agreeable life with his disciples, whom he taught as he walked and worked. . . . He was gentle and affable to all men . . . He held there was nothing nobler than to apply one's self to philosophy." His starting point is a conviction that apathy is impossible, and that pleasure—though not necessarily sensual pleasure—is the only conceivable, and quite legitimate, end of life and action. "Nature leads every organism to prefer its own good to every other good";—even the Stoic finds a subtle pleasure in renunciation. "We must not avoid pleasures, but we must select them." Epicurus, then, is no epicurean; he exalts the joys of intellect rather than those of sense; he warns against pleasures that excite and disturb the soul which they should rather quiet and appease. In the end he proposes to seek not pleasure in its usual sense, but *ataraxia*—tranquillity, equanimity, repose of mind; all of which trembles on the verge of Zeno's "apathy."

The Romans, coming to despoil Hellas in 146 B. C., found these rival schools dividing the philosophic field; and having neither leisure nor subtlety for speculation themselves, brought back these philosophies with their other spoils to Rome. Great organizers, as much as inevitable slaves, tend to stoic moods: it is difficult to be either master or servant if one is sensitive. So such philosophy as Rome had was mostly of Zeno's school, whether in Marcus Aurelius the emperor or in Epictetus the slave; and even Lucretius talked epicureanism stoically (like Heine's Englishman taking his pleasures sadly), and concluded his stern gospel of pleasure by committing suicide. His noble epic "On the Nature of Things,"[3] follows Epicurus in damning pleasure with faint praise. Almost contemporary with Cæsar and Pompey, he lived in the midst of turmoil and alarms; his nervous pen is forever inditing prayers to tranquillity and peace. One pictures him as a timid soul whose youth had been darkened with religious fears; for he never tires of telling his readers that there is no hell, except here, and that there are no gods except gentlemanly ones who live in a garden of Epicurus in the clouds, and never intrude in the affairs of men. To the rising cult of heaven and hell among the people of Rome he opposes a ruthless materialism. Soul and mind are evolved with the body, grow with its growth, ail with its ailments, and die with its death. Nothing exists but atoms, space, and law; and the law of laws is that of evolution and dissolution everywhere.

> No single thing abides, but all things flow.
> Fragment to fragment clings; the things thus grow
>   Until we know and name them. By degrees
>   They melt, and are no more the things we know.

[2] Quoted as motto on the title-page of Anatole France's *Garden of Epicures.*
[3] Professor Shotwell (*Introduction to the History of History*) calls it "the most marvelous performance in all antique literature."

> *Globed from the atoms, falling slow or swift*
> *I see the suns, I see the systems lift*
>   *Their forms; and even the systems and their suns*
> *Shall go back slowly to the eternal drift.*
>
> *Thou too, O Earth—thine empires, lands and seas—*
> *Least, with thy stars, of all the galaxies,*
>   *Globed from the drift like these, like these thou too*
> *Shalt go. Thou art going, hour by hour, like these.*
>
> *Nothing abides. Thy seas in delicate haze*
> *Go off; those moonèd sands forsake their place;*
>   *And where they are shall other seas in turn*
> *Mow with their scythes of whiteness other bays.*[4]

To astronomical evolution and dissolution add the origin and elimina-tion of species.

Many monsters too the earth of old tried to produce, things of strange face and limbs; . . . some without feet, some without hands, some with-out mouth, some without eyes. . . . Every other monster . . . of this kind earth would produce, but in vain; for nature set a ban on their increase, they could not reach the coveted flower of age, nor find food, nor be united in marriage; . . . and many races of living things must then have died out and been unable to beget and continue their breed. For in the case of all things which you see breathing the breath of life, either craft or courage or speed has from the beginning of its existence protected and preserved each particular race. . . . Those to whom nature has granted none of these qualities would lie exposed as a prey and booty to others, until nature brought their kind to extinction.[5]

Nations, too, like individuals, slowly grow and surely die: "some nations wax, others wane, and in a brief space the races of living things are changed, and like runners hand over the lamp of life." In the face of warfare and inevitable death, there is no wisdom but in *ataraxia,*—"to look on all things with a mind at peace." Here, clearly, the old pagan joy of life is gone, and an almost exotic spirit touches a broken lyre. History, which is nothing if not humorous, was never so facetious as when she gave to this abstemious and epic pessimist the name of Epicurean.

And if this is the spirit of the follower of Epicurus, imagine the ex-hilarating optimism of explicit Stoics like Aurelius or Epictetus. Nothing in all literature is so depressing as the "Dissertations" of the slave, unless it be the "Meditations" of the emperor. "Seek not to have things happen as you choose them, but rather choose that they should happen as they do; and you shall live prosperously."[6] No doubt one can in this manner dic-tate the future, and play royal highness to the universe. Story has it that Epictetus' master, who treated him with consistent cruelty, one day took

[4]Paraphrase by Mallock: *Lucretius on Life and Death,* pp. 15-16.
[5]V., 830 f., translation by Munro.
[6]*Enchiridion and Dissertations of Epictetus;* ed. Rolleston; p. 81.

to twisting Epictetus' leg to pass the time away. "If you go on," said
Epictetus calmly, "you will break my leg." The master went on, and the
leg was broken. "Did I not tell you," Epictetus observed mildly, "that you
would break my leg?"[7] Yet there is a certain mystic nobility in this
philosophy, as in the quiet courage of some Dostoievskian pacifist. "Never
in any case say, I have lost such a thing; but, I have returned it. Is thy
child dead?—it is returned. Is thy wife dead?—she is returned. Art
thou deprived of thy estate?—is not this also returned?"[8] In such passages
we feel the proximity of Christianity and its dauntless martyrs; indeed
were not the Christian ethic of self-denial, the Christian political ideal of
an almost communistic brotherhood of man, and the Christian eschatol-
ogy of the final conflagration of all the world, fragments of Stoic doctrine
floating on the stream of thought? In Epictetus the Greco-Roman soul
has lost its paganism, and is ready for a new faith. His book had the distinction of being adopted as a religious manual by the early Christian
Church. From these "Dissertations" and Aurelius' "Meditations" there is
but a step to "The Imitation of Christ."

Meanwhile the historical background was melting into newer scenes.
There is a remarkable passage in Lucretius[9] which describes the decay
of agriculture in the Roman state, and attributes it to the exhaustion of
the soil. Whatever the cause, the wealth of Rome passed into poverty,
the organization into disintegration, the power and pride into decadence
and apathy. Cities faded back into the undistinguished hinterland; the
roads fell into disrepair and no longer hummed with trade; the small
families of the educated Romans were outbred by the vigorous and un-
tutored German stocks that crept, year after year, across the frontier;
pagan culture yielded to Oriental cults; and almost imperceptibly the
Empire passed into the Papacy.

The Church, supported in its earlier centuries by the emperors whose
powers it gradually absorbed, grew rapidly in numbers, wealth, and range
of influence. By the thirteenth century it owned one-third of the soil of
Europe,[10] and its coffers bulged with donations of rich and poor. For a
thousand years it united, with the magic of an unvarying creed, most of
the peoples of a continent; never before or since was organization so
widespread or so pacific. But this unity demanded, as the Church thought,
a common faith exalted by supernatural sanctions beyond the changes
and corrosions of time; therefore dogma, definite and defined, was cast
like a shell over the adolescent mind of medieval Europe. It was within
this shell that Scholastic philosophy moved narrowly from faith to reason
and back again, in a baffling circuit of uncriticized assumptions and pre-

---

[7]*Ibid.*, xxxvi.   [8]*Ibid.*, 86.

[9]II, 1170. This oldest is also the latest theory of the decline of Rome; cf. Simkho-
vitch: *Toward the Understanding of Jesus;* New York, 1921.

[10]Robinson and Beard: *Outlines of European History;* Boston, 1914, i, 443.

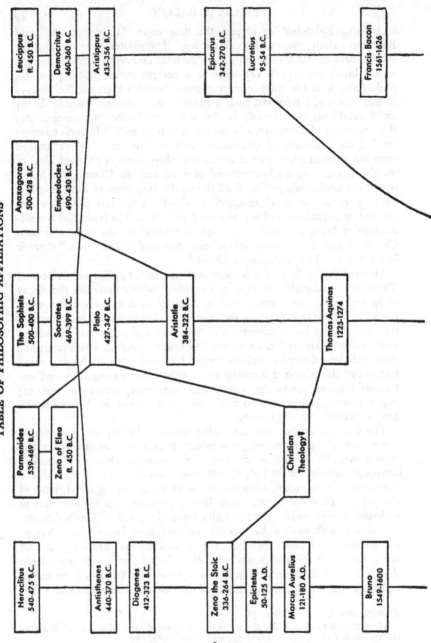

TABLE OF PHILOSOPHIC AFFILIATIONS

Leucippus fl. 450 B.C.	Democritus 460-360 B.C.	Aristippus 435-356 B.C.	Epicurus 342-270 B.C.	Lucretius 95-54 B.C.	Francis Bacon 1561-1626

| Anaxagoras 500-428 B.C. | Empedocles 490-430 B.C. |

| The Sophists 500-400 B.C. | Socrates 469-399 B.C. | Plato 427-347 B.C. | Aristotle 384-322 B.C. | Thomas Aquinas 1225-1274 |

| Parmenides 539-469 B.C. | Zeno of Elea fl. 450 B.C. | Christian Theology? |

| Heraclitus 540-475 B.C. | Antisthenes 440-370 B.C. | Diogenes 412-323 B.C. | Zeno the Stoic 336-264 B.C. | Epictetus 50-125 A.D. | Marcus Aurelius 121-180 A.D. | Bruno 1549-1600 |

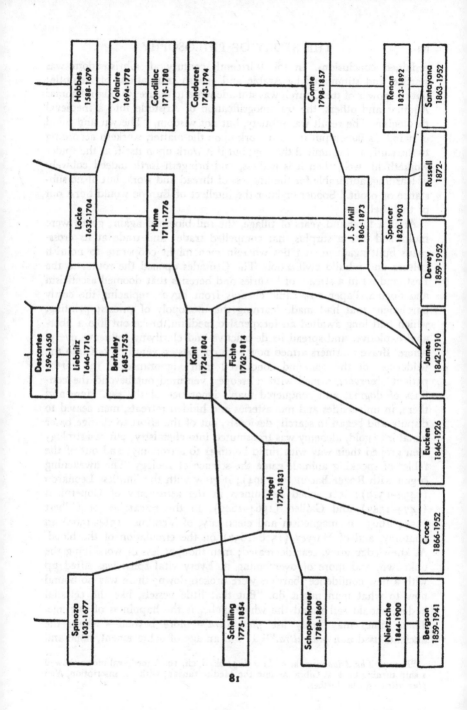

ordained conclusions. In the thirteenth century all Christendom was startled and stimulated by Arabic and Jewish translations of Aristotle; but the power of the Church was still adequate to secure, through Thomas Aquinas and others, the transmogrification of Aristotle into a medieval theologian. The result was subtlety, but not wisdom. "The wit and mind of man," as Bacon put it, "if it work upon the matter, worketh according to the stuff, and is limited thereby; but if it work upon itself, as the spider worketh his web, then it is endless, and bringeth forth indeed cobwebs of learning, admirable for the fineness of thread and work, but of no substance or profit." Sooner or later the intellect of Europe would burst out of this shell.

After a thousand years of tillage, the soil bloomed again; goods were multiplied into a surplus that compelled trade; and trade at its crossroads built again great cities wherein men might coöperate to nourish culture and rebuild civilization. The Crusades opened the routes to the East, and let in a stream of luxuries and heresies that doomed asceticism and dogma. Paper now came cheaply from Egypt, replacing the costly parchment that had made learning the monopoly of priests; printing, which had long awaited an inexpensive medium, broke out like a liberated explosive, and spread its destructive and clarifying influence everywhere. Brave mariners armed now with compasses, ventured out into the wilderness of the sea, and conquered man's ignorance of the earth; patient observers, armed with telescopes, ventured out beyond the confines of dogma, and conquered man's ignorance of the sky. Here and there, in universities and monasteries and hidden retreats, men ceased to dispute and began to search; deviously, out of the effort to change baser metal into gold, alchemy was transmuted into chemistry; out of astrology men groped their way with timid boldness to astronomy; and out of the fables of speaking animals came the science of zoology. The awakening began with Roger Bacon (d. 1294); it grew with the limitless Leonardo (1452-1519); it reached its fulness in the astronomy of Copernicus (1473-1543) and Galileo (1564-1642), in the researches of Gilbert (1544-1603) in magnetism and electricity, of Vesalius (1514-1564) in anatomy, and of Harvey (1578-1657) on the circulation of the blood. As knowledge grew, fear decreased; men thought less of worshiping the unknown, and more of overcoming it. Every vital spirit was lifted up with a new confidence; barriers were broken down; there was no bound now to what man might do. "But that little vessels, like the celestial bodies, should sail round the whole globe, is the happiness of our age. These times may justly use *plus ultra*"—more beyond—"where the ancients used *non plus ultra*."[11] It was an age of achievement, hope and

---

[11] Bacon: *The Advancement of Learning;* bk. ii, ch, 10. A medieval motto showed a ship turning back at Gibraltar into the Mediterranean, with the inscription, *Non plus ultra*—go no farther.

vigor; of new beginnings and enterprises in every field; an age that waited for a voice, some synthetic soul to sum up its spirit and resolve. It was Francis Bacon, "the most powerful mind of modern times,"[12] who "rang the bell that called the wits together," and announced that Europe had come of age.

II. THE POLITICAL CAREER OF FRANCIS BACON

Bacon was born on January 22, 1561, at York House, London, the residence of his father, Sir Nicholas Bacon, who for the first twenty years of Elizabeth's reign had been Keeper of the Great Seal. "The fame of the father," says Macaulay, "has been thrown into the shade by that of the son. But Sir Nicholas was no ordinary man."[13] It is as one might have suspected; for genius is an apex, to which a family builds itself through talent, and through talent in the genius's offspring subsides again towards the mediocrity of man. Bacon's mother was Lady Anne Cooke, sister-in-law of Sir William Cecil, Lord Burghley, who was Elizabeth's Lord Treasurer, and one of the most powerful men in England. Her father had been chief tutor of King Edward VI; she herself was a linguist and a theologian, and thought nothing of corresponding in Greek with bishops. She made herself instructress of her son, and spared no pains in his education.

But the real nurse of Bacon's greatness was Elizabethan England, the greatest age of the most powerful of modern nations. The discovery of America had diverted trade from the Mediterranean to the Atlantic, had raised the Atlantic nations—Spain and France and Holland and England—to that commercial and financial supremacy which had been Italy's when half of Europe had made her its port of entry and exit in the Eastern trade; and with this change the Renaissance had passed from Florence and Rome and Milan and Venice to Madrid and Paris and Amsterdam and London. After the destruction of the Spanish naval power in 1588, the commerce of England spread over every sea, her towns throve with domestic industry, her sailors circumnavigated the globe and her captains won America. Her literature blossomed into Spenser's poetry and Sidney's prose; her stage throbbed with the dramas of Shakespeare and Marlowe and Ben Jonson and a hundred vigorous pens. No man could fail to flourish in such a time and country, if there was seed in him at all.

At the age of twelve Bacon was sent to Trinity College, Cambridge. He stayed there three years, and left it with a strong dislike of its texts and methods, a confirmed hostility to the cult of Aristotle, and a resolve to set philosophy into a more fertile path, to turn it from scholastic dispu-

---

[12]E. J. Payne in *The Cambridge Modern History*, i, 65.
[13]*Essays:* New York, 1860: iii, 342.

tation to the illumination and increase of human good. Though still a
lad of sixteen, he was offered an appointment to the staff of the English
ambassador in France; and after careful casting up of *pros* and *cons,* he
accepted. In the Proem to *The Interpretation of Nature,* he discusses this
fateful decision that turned him from philosophy to politics. It is an indispensable passage:

> Whereas, I believed myself born for the service of mankind, and reckoned
> the care of the common weal to be among those duties that are of public
> right, open to all alike, even as the waters and the air, I therefore asked
> myself what could most advantage mankind, and for the performance of
> what tasks I seemed to be shaped by nature. But when I searched, I found
> no work so meritorious as the discovery and development of the arts and
> inventions that tend to civilize the life of man. . . . Above all, if any man
> could succeed—not merely in bringing to light some one particular inven-
> tion, however useful—but in kindling in nature a luminary which would,
> at its first rising, shed some light on the present limits and borders of human
> discoveries, and which afterwards, as it rose still higher, would reveal and
> bring into clear view every nook and cranny of darkness, it seemed to me
> that such a discoverer would deserve to be called the true Extender of the
> Kingdom of Man over the universe, the Champion of human liberty, and
> the Exterminator of the necessities that now keep men in bondage. More-
> over, I found in my own nature a special adaptation for the contemplation
> of truth. For I had a mind at once versatile enough for that most important
> object—I mean the recognition of similitudes—and at the same time suffi-
> ciently steady and concentrated for the observation of subtle shades of dif-
> ference. I possessed a passion for research, a power of suspending judgment
> with patience, of meditating with pleasure, of assenting with caution, of
> correcting false impressions with readiness, and of arranging my thoughts
> with scrupulous pains. I had no hankering after novelty, no blind admira-
> tion for antiquity. Imposture in every shape I utterly detested. For all these
> reasons I considered that my nature and disposition had, as it were, a kind
> of kinship and connection with truth.
>
> But my birth, my rearing and education, had all pointed, not toward
> philosophy, but towards politics: I had been, as it were, imbued in politics
> from childhood. And as is not unfrequently the case with young men, I
> was sometimes shaken in my mind by opinions. I also thought that my duty
> towards my country had special claims upon me, such as could not be urged
> by other duties of life. Lastly, I conceived the hope that, if I held some
> honorable office in the state, I might have secure helps and supports to aid
> my labors, with a view to the accomplishment of my destined task. With
> these motives I applied myself to politics.[14]

Sir Nicholas Bacon died suddenly in 1579. He had intended to provide
Francis with an estate; but death overreached his plans, and the young
diplomat, called hurriedly to London, saw himself, at the age of eighteen,
fatherless and penniless. He had become accustomed to most of the lux-

[14] Translation by Abbott: *Francis Bacon;* London, 1885; p. 37.

uries of the age, and he found it hard to reconcile himself now to a forced simplicity of life. He took up the practice of law, while he importuned his influential relatives to advance him to some political office which would liberate him from economic worry. His almost begging letters had small result, considering the grace and vigor of their style, and the proved ability of their author. Perhaps it was because Bacon did not underrate this ability, and looked upon position as his due, that Burghley failed to make the desired response; and perhaps, also, these letters protested too much the past, present and future loyalty of the writer to the honorable Lord: in politics, as in love, it does not do to give one's self wholly; one should at all times give, but at no time all. Gratitude is nourished with expectation.

Eventually, Bacon climbed without being lifted from above; but every step cost him many years. In 1583 he was elected to Parliament for Taunton; and his constituents liked him so well that they returned him to his seat in election after election. He had a terse and vivid eloquence in debate, and was an orator without oratory. "No man," said Ben Jonson, "ever spoke more neatly, more (com)pressedly, more weightily, or suffered less emptiness, less idleness in what he uttered. No member of his speech but consisted of its own graces. His hearers could not cough or look aside from him without loss. He commanded where he spoke. . . . No man had their affections more in his power. The fear of every man that heard him was lest that he should make an end."[15] Enviable orator!

One powerful friend was generous to him—that handsome Earl of Essex whom Elizabeth loved unsuccessfully, and so learned to hate. In 1595 Essex, to atone for his failure in securing a political post for Bacon, presented him with a pretty estate at Twickenham. It was a magnificent gift, which one might presume would bind Bacon to Essex for life; but it did not. A few years later Essex organized a conspiracy to imprison Elizabeth and select her successor to the throne. Bacon wrote letter after letter to his benefactor, protesting against this treason; and when Essex persisted, Bacon warned him that he would put loyalty to his Queen above even gratitude to his friend. Essex made his effort, failed, and was arrested. Bacon pled with the Queen in his behalf so incessantly that at last she bade him "speak of any other subject." When Essex, temporarily freed, gathered armed forces about him, marched into London, and tried to rouse its populace to revolution, Bacon turned against him angrily. Meanwhile he had been given a place in the prosecuting office of the realm; and when Essex, again arrested, was tried for treason, Bacon took active part in the prosecution of the man who had been his unstinting friend.[16]

[15]Nichol: *Francis Bacon;* Edinburgh, 1907; i, 27.

[16]Hundreds of volumes have been written on this aspect of Bacon's career. The case against Bacon, as "the wisest and meanest mankind" (so Pope called him),

Essex was found guilty, and was put to death. Bacon's part in the trial made him for a while unpopular; and from this time on he lived in the midst of enemies watching for a chance to destroy him. His insatiable ambition left him no rest; he was ever discontent, and always a year or so ahead of his income. He was lavish in his expenditures; display was to him a part of policy. When, at the age of forty-five, he married, the pompous and costly ceremony made a great gap in the dowry which had constituted one of the lady's attractions. In 1598 he was arrested for debt. Nevertheless, he continued to advance. His varied ability and almost endless knowledge made him a valuable member of every important committee; gradually higher offices were opened to him: in 1606 he was made Solicitor-General; in 1613 he became Attorney-General; in 1618, at the age of fifty-seven, he was at last Lord Chancellor.

III. THE ESSAYS[17]

His elevation seemed to realize Plato's dreams of a philosopher-king. For, step by step with his climb to political power, Bacon had been mounting the summits of philosophy. It is almost incredible that the vast learning and literary achievements of this man were but the incidents and diversions of a turbulent political career. It was his motto that one lived best by the hidden life—*bene vixit qui bene latuit*. He could not quite make up his mind whether he liked more the contemplative or the active life. His hope was to be philosopher and statesman, too, like Seneca; though he suspected that this double direction of his life would shorten his reach and lessen his attainment. "It is hard to say," he writes,[18] "whether mixture of contemplations with an active life, or retiring wholly to contemplations, do disable or hinder the mind more." He felt that studies could not be either end or wisdom in themselves, and that knowledge unapplied in action was a pale academic vanity. "To spend too much time in studies is sloth; to use them too much for ornament is affectation; to make judgment wholly by their rules is the humor of a scholar. . . . Crafty men condemn studies, simple men admire them, and wise men use them; for they teach not their own use; but that is a wisdom without them, and above them, won by observation."[19] Here is

will be found in Macaulay's essay, and more circumstantially in Abbott's *Francis Bacon;* these would apply to him his own words: "Wisdom for a man's self is the wisdom of rats, that will be sure to leave a house somewhat before it falls" (Essay "Of Wisdom for a Man's Self"). The case for Bacon is given in Spedding's *Life and Times of Francis Bacon,* and in his *Evenings with a Reviewer* (a detailed reply to Macaulay). *In medio veritas.*

[17]The author has thought it better in this section to make no attempt to concentrate further the already compact thought of Bacon, and has preferred to put the philosopher's wisdom in his own incomparable English rather than to take probably greater space to say the same things with less clarity, beauty, and force.

[18]*Valerius Terminus, ad fin.*   [19]"Of Studies."

a new note, which marks the end of scholasticism—i. e., the divorce of knowledge from use and observation—and places that emphasis on experience and results which distinguishes English philosophy, and culminates in pragmatism. Not that Bacon for a moment ceased to love books and meditation; in words reminiscent of Socrates he writes, "without philosophy I care not to live";[20] and he describes himself as after all "a man naturally fitted rather for literature than for anything else, and borne by some destiny, against the inclination of his genius" (i. e., character), "into active life."[21] Almost his first publication was called "The Praise of Knowledge" (1592); its enthusiasm for philosophy compels quotation:

> My praise shall be dedicate to the mind itself. The mind is the man, and knowledge mind; a man is but what he knoweth. . . . Are not the pleasures of the affections greater than the pleasures of the senses, and are not the pleasures of the intellect greater than the pleasures of the affections? Is not that only a true and natural pleasure whereof there is no satiety? Is not that knowledge alone that doth clear the mind of all perturbations? How many things be there which we imagine are not? How many things do we esteem and value more than they are? These vain imaginations, these ill-proportioned estimations, these be the clouds of error that turn into the storms of perturbations. Is there then any such happiness as for a man's mind to be raised above the confusion of things, where he may have a respect of the order of nature and the error of men? Is there but a view only of delight and not of discovery? Of contentment and not of benefit? Shall we not discern as well the riches of nature's warehouse as the beauty of her shop? Is truth barren? Shall we not thereby be able to produce worthy effects, and to endow the life of man with infinite commodities?

His finest literary product, the *Essays* (1597-1623), show him still torn between these two loves, for politics and for philosophy. In the "Essay of Honor and Reputation" he gives all the degrees of honor to political and military achievements, none to the literary or the philosophical. But in the essay "Of Truth" he writes: "The inquiry of truth, which is the love-making or wooing of it; the knowledge of truth, which is the praise of it; and the belief of truth, which is the enjoying of it, is the sovereign good of human natures." In books "we converse with the wise, as in action with fools." That is, if we know how to select our books. "Some books are to be tasted," reads a famous passage, "others to be swallowed, and some few to be chewed and digested"; all these groups forming, no doubt, an infinitesimal portion of the oceans and cataracts of ink in which the world is daily bathed and poisoned and drowned.

Surely the *Essays* must be numbered among the few books that deserve to be chewed and digested. Rarely shall you find so much meat, so admirably dressed and flavored, in so small a dish. Bacon abhors padding,

---

[20]Dedication of *Wisdom of the Ancients.*   [21]*De Augmentis,* viii, 3.

and disdains to waste a word; he offers us infinite riches in a little phrase; each of these essays gives in a page or two the distilled subtlety of a master mind on a major issue of life. It is difficult to say whether the matter or the manner more excels; for here is language as supreme in prose as Shakespeare's is in verse. It is a style like sturdy Tacitus', compact yet polished; and indeed some of its conciseness is due to the skillful adaptation of Latin idiom and phrase. But its wealth of metaphor is characteristically Elizabethan, and reflects the exuberance of the Renais. sance; no man in English literature is so fertile in pregnant and pithy comparisons. Their lavish array is the one defect of Bacon's style: the endless metaphors and allegories and allusions fall like whips upon our nerves and tire us out at last. The *Essays* are like rich and heavy food, which cannot be digested in large quantities at once; but taken four or five at a time they are the finest intellectual nourishment in English.[22]

What shall we extract from this extracted wisdom? Perhaps the best starting point, and the most arresting deviation from the fashions of medieval philosophy, is Bacon's frank acceptance of the Epicurean ethic. "That philosophical progression, 'Use not that you may not wish, wish not that you may not fear,' seems an indication of a weak, diffident and timorous mind. And indeed most doctrines of the philosophers appear to be too distrustful, and to take more care of mankind than the nature of the thing requires. Thus they increase the fears of death by the remedies they bring against it; for whilst they make the life of man little more than a preparation and discipline for death, it is impossible but the enemy must appear terrible when there is no end of the defense to be made against him."[23] Nothing could be so injurious to health as the Stoic repression of desire; what is the use of prolonging a life which apathy has turned into premature death? And besides, it is an impossible philosophy; for instinct will out. "Nature is often hidden; sometimes overcome; seldom extinguished. Force maketh nature more violent in the return; doctrine and discourse maketh nature less importune; but custom only doth alter or subdue nature. . . . But let not a man trust his victory over his nature too far; for nature will lay buried a great time, and yet revive upon the occasion or temptation. Like as it was with Æsop's damsel, turned from a cat to a woman, who sat very demurely at the board's end, till a mouse ran before her. Therefore let a man either avoid the occasion altogether, or put himself often to it, that he may be little moved with it."[24] Indeed Bacon thinks the body should be inured to excesses as well as to restraint; else even a moment of unrestraint may ruin it. (So one

---

[22] The author's preference is for Essays 2, 7, 8, 11, 12, 16, 18, 20, 27, 29, 38, 39, 42, 46, 48, 50, 52, 54.

[23] *Adv. of L.*, vii, 2. Certain passages from this book are brought in here, to avoid a repetition of topics under each work.

[24] "Of Nature in Men."

accustomed to the purest and most digestible foods is easily upset when forgetfulness or necessity diverts him from perfection.) Yet "variety of delights rather than surfeit of them"; for "strength of nature in youth passeth over many excesses which are owing a man till his age";[25] a man's maturity pays the price of his youth. One royal road to health is a garden; Bacon agrees with the author of *Genesis* that "God Almighty first planted a garden"; and with Voltaire that we must cultivate our back yards.

The moral philosophy of the *Essays* smacks rather of Machiavelli than of the Christianity to which Bacon made so many astute obeisances. "We are beholden to *Machiavel,* and writers of that kind, who openly and unmasked declare what men do in fact, and not what they ought to do; for it is impossible to join the wisdom of the serpent and the innocence of the dove, without a previous knowledge of the nature of evil; as, without this, virtue lies exposed and unguarded."[26] "The Italians have an ungracious proverb, *Tanto buon che val niente,*"—so good that he is good for nothing.[27] Bacon accords his preaching with his practice, and advises a judicious mixture of dissimulation with honesty, like an alloy that will make the purer but softer metal capable of longer life. He wants a full and varied career, giving acquaintance with everything that can broaden, deepen, strengthen or sharpen the mind. He does not admire the merely contemplative life; like Goethe he scorns knowledge that does not lead to action: "men ought to know that in the theatre of human life it is only for Gods and angels to be spectators."[28]

His religion is patriotically like the King's. Though he was more than once accused of atheism, and the whole trend of his philosophy is secular and rationalistic, he makes an eloquent and apparently sincere disclaimer of unbelief. "I had rather believe all the fables in the Legend, and the Talmud and the Alcoran, than that this universal frame is without a mind. . . . A little philosophy inclineth a man's mind to atheism; but depth in philosophy bringeth men's minds about to religion. For while the mind of man looketh upon second causes scattered, it may sometimes rest in them and go no further; but when it beholdeth the chain of them, confederate and linked together, it must needs fly to Providence and Deity."[29] Religious indifference is due to a multiplicity of factions. "The causes of atheism are, divisions in religion, if they be many; for any one division addeth zeal to both sides; but many divisions introduce atheism. . . . And lastly, learned times, especially with peace and prosperity; for troubles and adversities do more bow men's minds to religion."[30]

But Bacon's value lies less in theology and ethics than in psychology. He is an undeceivable analyst of human nature, and sends his shaft into every heart. On the stalest subject in the world he is refreshingly original.

[25]"Of Regiment of Health."   [26]*Adv. of L.,* xii, 2.   [27]"Of Goodness."
[28]*Adv. of L.,* vii, 1.   [29]"Of Atheism."   [30]*Ibid.*

"A married man is seven years older in his thoughts the first day."[31] "It is often seen that bad husbands have good wives." (Bacon was an exception.) "A single life doth well with churchmen, for charity will hardly water the ground where it must first fill a pool. . . . He that hath wife and children hath given hostages to fortune; for they are impediments to great enterprises, either of virtue or mischief."[32] Bacon seems to have worked too hard to have had time for love, and perhaps he never quite felt it to its depth. "It is a strange thing to note the excess of this passion. . . . There was never proud man thought so absurdly well of himself as the lover doth of the person beloved. . . . You may observe that amongst all the great and worthy persons (whereof the memory remaineth either ancient or recent), there is not one that hath been transported to the mad degree of love; which shows that great spirits and great business do keep out this weak passion."[33]

He values friendship more than love, though of friendship too he can be sceptical. "There is little friendship in the world, and least of all between equals, which was wont to be magnified. That that is, is between superior and inferior, whose fortunes may comprehend the one the other. . . . A principal fruit of friendship is the ease and discharge of the fullness and swellings of the heart, which passions of all kinds do cause and induce." A friend is an ear. "Those that want friends to open themselves unto are cannibals of their own hearts. . . . Whoever hath his mind fraught with many thoughts, his wits and understanding do clarify and break up in the communicating and discoursing with another; he tosseth his thoughts more easily; he marshaleth them more orderly; he seeth how they look when they are turned into words; finally he waxeth wiser than himself; and that more by one hour's discourse than by a day's meditation."[34]

In the essay "Of Youth and Age" he puts a book into a paragraph. "Young men are fitter to invent than to judge, fitter for execution than for counsel, and fitter for new projects than for settled business; for the experience of age in things that fall within the compass of it, directeth them; but in new things abuseth them. . . . Young men, in the conduct and management of actions, embrace more than they can hold, stir more than they can quiet; fly to the end without consideration of the means and degrees; pursue absurdly some few principles which they have chanced upon; care not to" (i. e., how they) "innovate, which draws unknown inconveniences. . . . Men of age object too much, consult too long, adventure too little, repent too soon, and seldom drive business home to the full period, but content themselves with a mediocrity of suc-

---

[31] Letter to Lord Burghley, 1606.

[32] "Of Marriage and Single Life." Contrast the more pleasing phrase of Shakespeare, that "Love gives to every power a double power."

[33] "Of Love."   [34] "Of Followers and Friends"; "Of Friendship."

cess. Certainly it is good to compel employments of both, . . . because the virtues of either may correct the defects of both." He thinks, nevertheless, that youth and childhood may get too great liberty, and so grow disordered and lax. "Let parents choose betimes the vocations and courses they mean their children should take, for then they are most flexible; and let them not too much apply themselves to the disposition of their children, as thinking they will take best to that which they have most mind to. It is true that, if the affections or aptness of the children be extraordinary, then it is good not to cross it; but generally the precept" of the Pythagoreans "is good, *Optimum lege, suave et facile illud faciet consuetudo*,"—choose the best; custom will make it pleasant and easy.[85] For "custom is the principal magistrate of man's life."[86]

The politics of the *Essays* preach a conservatism natural in one who aspired to rule. Bacon wants a strong central power. Monarchy is the best form of government; and usually the efficiency of a state varies with the concentration of power. "There be three points of business" in government: "the preparation; the debate or examination; and the perfection" (or execution). "Whereof, if you look for dispatch, let the middle only be the work of many, and the first and last the work of a few."[87] He is an outspoken militarist; he deplores the growth of industry as unfitting men for war, and bewails long peace as lulling the warrior in man. Nevertheless, he recognizes the importance of raw materials: "Solon said well to Crœsus (when in ostentation Crœsus showed him his gold), 'Sir, if any other come that hath better iron than you, he will be master of all this gold.' "[88]

Like Aristotle, he has some advice on avoiding revolutions. "The surest way to prevent seditions . . . is to take away the matter of them; for if there be fuel prepared, it is hard to tell whence the spark shall come that shall set it on fire. . . . Neither doth it follow that the suppressing of fames" (i. e., discussion) "with too much severity should be a remedy of troubles; for the despising of them many times checks them best, and the going about to stop them but makes a wonder long-lived. . . . The matter of sedition is of two kinds: much poverty and much discontentment. . . . The causes and motives of seditions are, innovation in religion; taxes; alteration of laws and customs; breaking of privileges; general oppression; advancement of unworthy persons, strangers; dearths; disbanded soldiers; factions grown desperate; and whatsoever in offending a people joineth them in a common cause." The cue of every leader, of course, is to divide his enemies and to unite his friends. "Generally, the dividing and breaking of all factions . . . that are adverse to the state, and setting them at a distance, or at least distrust, among themselves, is not one of the worst remedies; for it is a desperate case, if those that hold

---

[85] "Of Parents and Children."   [86] "Of Custom."
[87] "Of Dispatch."   [88] "Of the True Greatness of Kingdoms."

with the proceeding of the state be full of discord and faction, and those
that are against it be entire and united."[39] A better recipe for the avoid-
ance of revolutions is an equitable distribution of wealth: "Money is like
muck, not good unless it be spread."[40] But this does not mean socialism,
or even democracy; Bacon distrusts the people, who were in his day quite
without access to education; "the lowest of all flatteries is the flattery of
the common people";[41] and "Phocion took it right, who, being applauded
by the multitude, asked, What had he done amiss?"[42] What Bacon wants
is first a yeomanry of owning farmers; then an aristocracy for administration; and above all a philosopher-king. "It is almost without instance that
any government was unprosperous under learned governors."[43] He men-
tions Seneca, Antoninus Pius and Aurelius; it was his hope that to their
names posterity would add his own.

IV. THE GREAT RECONSTRUCTION

Unconsciously, in the midst of his triumphs, his heart was with philosophy. It had been his nurse in youth, it was his companion in office, it
was to be his consolation in prison and disgrace. He lamented the ill-
repute into which, he thought, philosophy had fallen, and blamed an arid
scholasticism. "People are very apt to contemn truth, on account of the
controversies raised about it, and to think those all in a wrong way who
never meet."[44] "The sciences . . . stand almost at a stay, without receiving any augmentations worthy of the human race; . . . and all the
tradition and succession of schools is still a succession of masters and
scholars, not of inventors. . . . In what is now done in the matter of
science there is only a whirling about, and perpetual agitation, ending
where it began."[45] All through the years of his rise and exaltation he
brooded over the restoration or reconstruction of philosophy; "*Meditor
Instaurationem philosophiae.*"[46]

He planned to centre all his studies around this task. First of all, he
tells us in his "Plan of the Work," he would write some *Introductory
Treatises,* explaining the stagnation of philosophy through the posthu-
mous persistence of old methods, and outlining his proposals for a new
beginning. Secondly he would attempt a new *Classification of the
Sciences,* allocating their material to them, and listing the unsolved
problems in each field. Thirdly, he would describe his new method for the
Interpretation of Nature. Fourthly, he would try his busy hand at actual
natural science, and investigate the *Phenomena of Nature.* Fifthly, he
would show the *Ladder of the Intellect,* by which the writers of the

[39]"Of Seditions and Troubles."   [40]*Ibid.*
[41]In Nichol, ii, 149.   [43]*Adv. of L.,* vi, 3.
[42]*Ibid.,* i.   [44]*Ibid.*
[45]Preface to *Magna Instauratio.*   [46]*Redargutio Philosophiarum.*

past had mounted towards the truths that were now taking form out of the background of medieval verbiage. Sixthly, he would attempt certain *Anticipations* of the scientific results which he was confident would come from the use of his method. And lastly, as *Second* (or *Applied*) *Philosophy*, he would picture the utopia which would flower out of all this budding science of which he hoped to be the prophet. The whole would constitute the *Magna Instauratio*, the Great Reconstruction of Philosophy.[47]

It was a magnificent enterprise, and—except for Aristotle—without precedent in the history of thought. It would differ from every other philosophy in aiming at practice rather than at theory, at specific concrete goods rather than at speculative symmetry. Knowledge is power, not mere argument or ornament; "it is not an opinion to be held . . . but a work to be done; and I . . . am laboring to lay the foundation not of any sect or doctrine, but of utility and power."[48] Here, for the first time, are the voice and tone of modern science.

1. The Advancement of Learning

To produce works, one must have knowledge. "Nature cannot be commanded except by being obeyed."[49] Let us learn the laws of nature, and we shall be her masters, as we are now, in ignorance, her thralls; science is the road to utopia. But in what condition this road is—tortuous, unlit, turning back upon itself, lost in useless by-paths, and leading not to light but to chaos. Let us then begin by making a survey of the state of the sciences, and marking out for them their proper and distinctive fields; let us "seat the sciences each in its proper place";[50] examine their defects, their needs, and their possibilities; indicate the new problems that await

[47] Bacon's actual works under the foregoing heads are chiefly these:

I. *De Interpretatione Naturae Proemium* (Introduction to the Interpretation of Nature, 1603); *Redargutio Philosophiarum* (A Criticism of Philosophies, 1609).

II. *The Advancement of Learning* (1603–5); translated as *De Augmentis Scientiarum*, 1622).

III. *Cogitata et Visa* (Things Thought and Seen, 1607); *Filum Labyrinthi* (Thread of the Labyrinth, 1606); *Novum Organum* (The New Organon, 1608–20).

IV. *Historia Naturalis* (Natural History, 1622); *Descriptio Globi Intellectualis* (Description of the Intellectual Globe, 1612).

V. *Sylva Sylvarum* (Forest of Forests, 1624).

VI. *De Principiis* (On Origins, 1621).

VII. *The New Atlantis* (1624).

Note.—All of the above but *The New Atlantis* and *The Advancement of Learning* were written in Latin; and the latter was translated into Latin by Bacon and his aides, to win for it a European audience. Since historians and critics always use the Latin titles in their references, these are here given for the convenience of the student.

[48] Preface to *Magna Instauratio*. [49] "Plan of the Work." [50] *Adv. of L.,* iv, 2.

their light; and in general "open and stir the earth a little about the roots" of them.[51]

This is the task which Bacon set himself in *The Advancement of Learning.* "It is my intention," he writes, like a king entering his realm, "to make the circuit of knowledge, noticing what parts lie waste and uncultivated, and abandoned by the industry of man; with a view to engage, by a faithful mapping out of the deserted tracts, the energies of public and private persons in their improvement."[52] He would be the royal surveyor of the weed-grown soil, making straight the road, and dividing the fields among the laborers. It was a plan audacious to the edge of immodesty; but Bacon was still young enough (forty-two is young in a philosopher) to plan great voyages. "I have taken all knowledge to be my province," he had written to Burghley in 1592; not meaning that he would make himself a premature edition of the *Encyclopedia Britannica,* but implying merely that his work would bring him into every field, as the critic and coördinator of every science in the task of social reconstruction. The very magnitude of his purpose gives a stately magnificence to his style, and brings him at times to the height of English prose.

So he ranges over the vast battle-ground in which human research struggles with natural hindrance and human ignorance; and in every field he sheds illumination. He attaches great importance to physiology and medicine; he exalts the latter as regulating "a musical instrument of much and exquisite workmanship easily put out of tune."[53] But he objects to the lax empiricism of contemporary doctors, and their facile tendency to treat all ailments with the same prescription—usually physic. "Our physicians are like bishops, that have the keys of binding and loosing, but no more."[54] They rely too much on mere haphazard, uncoördinated individual experience; let them experiment more widely, let them illuminate human with comparative anatomy, let them dissect and if necessary vivisect; and above all, let them construct an easily accessible and intelligible record of experiments and results. Bacon believes that the medical profession should be permitted to ease and quicken death (euthanasy) where the end would be otherwise only delayed for a few days and at the cost of great pain; but he urges the physicians to give more study to the art of prolonging life. "This is a new part" of medicine, "and deficient, though the most noble of all; for if it may be supplied, medicine will not then be wholly versed in sordid cures, nor physicians be honored only for necessity, but as dispensers of the greatest earthly happiness that could well be conferred on mortals."[55] One can hear some sour Schopenhauerian protesting, at this point, against the assumption that longer life would be a boon, and urging, on the contrary, that the speed with which some physicians put an *end* to our illnesses is a con-

[51]*Ibid.,* vi, 3.   [53]*Ibid.,* ii, 1.   [55]*De Aug.,* iv.
[54]*Adv. of L.,* iv, 2.   [52]*Ibid.*

summation devoutly to be praised. But Bacon, worried and married and harassed though he was, never doubted that life was a very fine thing after all.

In psychology he is almost a "behaviorist": he demands a strict study of cause and effect in human action, and wishes to eliminate the word *chance* from the vocabulary of science. "*Chance* is the name of a thing that does not exist."[56] And "what chance is in the universe, so will is in man."[57] Here is a world of meaning, and a challenge of war, all in a little line: the Scholastic doctrine of free will is pushed aside as beneath discussion; and the universal assumption of a "will" distinct from the "intellect" is discarded. These are leads which Bacon does not follow up;[58] it is not the only case in which he puts a book into a phrase and then passes blithely on.

Again in a few words, Bacon invents a new science—social psychology. "Philosophers should diligently inquire into the powers and energy of custom, exercise, habit, education, example, imitation, emulation, company, friendship, praise, reproof, exhortation, reputation, laws, books, studies etc.; for these are the things that reign in men's morals; by these agents the mind is formed and subdued."[59] So closely has this outline been followed by the new science that it reads almost like a table of contents for the works of Tarde, Le Bon, Ross, Wallas, and Durkheim.

Nothing is beneath science, nor above it. Sorceries, dreams, predictions, telepathic communications, "psychical phenomena" in general must be subjected to scientific examination; "for it is not known in what cases, and how far, effects attributed to superstition participate of natural causes."[60] Despite his strong naturalistic bent he feels the fascination of these problems; nothing human is alien to him. Who knows what unsuspected truth, what new science, indeed, may grow out of these investigations, as chemistry budded out from alchemy? "Alchemy may be compared to the man who told his sons he had left them gold buried somewhere in his vineyard; where they, by digging, found no gold, but by turning up the mould about the roots of the vines, procured a plentiful vintage. So the search and endeavors to make gold have brought many useful inventions and instructive experiments to light."[61]

Still another science grows to form in Book VIII: the science of success in life. Not yet having fallen from power, Bacon offers some preliminary hints on how to rise in the world. The first requisite is knowledge: of ourselves and of others. *Gnothe seauton* is but half; know thyself is valuable chiefly as a means of knowing others. We must diligently

inform ourselves of the particular persons we have to deal with—their tempers, desires, views, customs, habits; the assistances, helps and assur-

[56]*Novum Organum,* i, 60.   [57]*De Interpretatione Naturae,* in Nichol, ii, 118.
[58]They are developed in Spinoza's *Ethics,* Appendix to Book I.
[59]*Adv. of L.,* vii, 3.   [60]*De Aug.,* ix, in Nichol, ii, 129.   [61]*Adv. of L.,* i.

ances whereon they principally rely, and whence they received their power; their defects and weaknesses, whereat they chiefly lie open and are accessible; their friends, factions, patrons, dependants, enemies, enviers, rivals; their times and manners of access. . . . But the surest key for unlocking the minds of others turns upon searching and sifting either their tempers and natures, or their ends and designs; and the more weak and simple are best judged by their temper, but the more prudent and close by their designs. . . . But the shortest way to this whole inquiry rests upon three particulars; viz.— 1. In procuring numerous friendships. . . . 2. In observing a prudent mean and moderation between freedom of discourse and silence. . . . But above all, nothing conduces more to the well-representing of a man's self, and securing his own right, than not to disarm one's self by too much sweetness and good-nature, which exposes a man to injuries and reproaches; but rather . . . at times to dart out some sparks of a free and generous mind, that have no less of the sting than the honey.[62]

Friends are for Bacon chiefly a means to power; he shares with Machiavelli a point of view which one is at first inclined to attribute to the Renaissance, till one thinks of the fine and uncalculating friendships of Michaelangelo and Cavalieri, Montaigne and La Boetie, Sir Philip Sidney and Hubert Languet.[63] Perhaps this very practical assessment of friendship helps to explain Bacon's fall from power, as similar views help to explain Napoleon's; for a man's friends will seldom practice a higher philosophy in their relations with him than that which he professes in his treatment of them. Bacon goes on to quote Bias, one of the Seven Wise Men of ancient Greece: "Love your friend as if he were to become your enemy, and your enemy as if he were to become your friend."[64] Do not betray even to your friend too much of your real purposes and thoughts; in conversation, ask questions oftener than you express opinions; and when you speak, offer data and information rather than beliefs and judgments.[65] Manifest pride is a help to advancement; and "ostentation is a fault in ethics rather than in politics."[66] Here again one is reminded of Napoleon; Bacon, like the little Corsican, was a simple man enough within his walls, but outside them he affected a ceremony and display which he thought indispensable to public repute.

So Bacon runs from field to field, pouring the seed of his thought into every science. At the end of his survey he comes to the conclusion that science by itself is not enough: there must be a force and discipline outside the sciences to coördinate them and point them to a goal. "There is another great and powerful cause why the sciences have made but little progress, which is this. It is not possible to run a course aright when the goal itself has not been rightly placed."[67] What science needs is philos-

[62]*Ibid.*, viii, 2.
[63]Cf. Edward Carpenter's delightful *Iolaüs: an Anthology of Friendship.*
[64]*Adv. of L.*, viii, 2.   [66]*Essays* "Of Dissimulation" and "Of Discourse."
[65]*Adv. of L.*, viii, 2.   [67]*Adv. of L.*, i, 81.

ophy—the analysis of scientific method, and the coördination of scientific purposes and results; without this, any science must be superficial. "For as no perfect view of a country can be taken from a flat; so it is impossible to discover the remote and deep parts of any science by standing upon the level of the same science, or without ascending to a higher."[68] He condemns the habit of looking at isolated facts out of their context, without considering the unity of nature; as if, he says, one should carry a small candle about the corners of a room radiant with a central light.

Philosophy, rather than science, is in the long run Bacon's love; it is only philosophy which can give even to a life of turmoil and grief the stately peace that comes of understanding. "Learning conquers or mitigates the fear of death and adverse fortune." He quotes Virgil's great lines:

> *Felix qui potuit rerum cognoscere causas,*
> *Quique metus omnes, et inexorabile fatum,*
> *Subjecit pedibus, strepitumque Acherontis avari—*

"happy the man who has learned the causes of things, and has put under his feet all fears, and inexorable fate, and the noisy strife of the hell of greed." It is perhaps the best fruit of philosophy that through it we unlearn the lesson of endless acquisition which an industrial environment so insistently repeats. "Philosophy directs us first to seek the goods of the mind, and the rest will either be supplied, or not much wanted."[69] A bit of wisdom is a joy forever.

Government suffers, precisely like science, for lack of philosophy. Philosophy bears to science the same relationship which statesmanship bears to politics: movement guided by total knowledge and perspective, as against aimless and individual seeking. Just as the pursuit of knowledge becomes scholasticism when divorced from the actual needs of men and life, so the pursuit of politics becomes a destructive bedlam when divorced from science and philosophy. "It is wrong to trust the natural body to empirics, who commonly have a few receipts whereon they rely, but who know neither the cause of the disease, nor the constitution of patients, nor the danger of accidents, nor the true methods of cure. And so it must needs be dangerous to have the civil body of states managed by empirical statesmen, unless well mixed with others who are grounded in learning. . . . Though he might be thought partial to his profession who said, 'States would then be happy, when either kings were philosophers or philosophers kings,' yet so much is verified by experience, that the best times have happened under wise and learned princes."[70] And he reminds us of the great emperors who ruled Rome after Domitian and before Commodus.

So Bacon, like Plato and us all, exalted his hobby, and offered it as the

[68]*Ibid.* i.   [69]*Ibid.,* viii, 2.   [70]*Ibid.,* i.

salvation of man. But he recognized, much more clearly than Plato (and the distinction announces the modern age), the necessity of specialist science, and of soldiers and armies of specialist research. No one mind, not even Bacon's, could cover the whole field, though he should look from Olympus' top itself. He knew he needed help, and keenly felt his loneliness in the mountain-air of his unaided enterprise. "What comrades have you in your work?" he asks a friend. "As for me, I am in the completest solitude."[71] He dreams of scientists coördinated in specialization by constant communion and coöperation, and by some great organization holding them together to a goal. "Consider what may be expected from men abounding in leisure, and from association of labors, and from successions of ages; the rather because it is not a way over which only one man can pass at a time (as is the case with that of reasoning), but within which the labors and industries of men (especially as regards the collecting of experience) may with the best effort be collected and distributed, and then combined. For then only will men begin to know their strength when, instead of great numbers doing all the same things, one shall take charge of one thing, and another of another."[72] Science, which is the organization of knowledge, must itself be organized.

And this organization must be international; let it pass freely over the frontiers, and it may make Europe intellectually one. "The next want I discover is the little sympathy and correspondence which exists between colleges and universities, as well throughout Europe as in the same state and kingdom."[73] Let all these universities allot subjects and problems among themselves, and coöperate both in research and in publication. So organized and correlated, the universities might be deemed worthy of such royal support as would make them what they shall be in Utopia— centers of impartial learning ruling the world. Bacon notes "the mean salaries apportioned to public lectureships, whether in the sciences or the arts";[74] and he feels that this will continue till governments take over the great tasks of education. "The wisdom of the ancientest and best times always complained that states were too busy with laws, and too remiss in point of education."[75] His great dream is the socialization of science for the conquest of nature and the enlargement of the power of man.

And so he appeals to James I, showering upon him the flattery which he knew his Royal Highness loved to sip. James was a scholar as well as a monarch, prouder of his pen than of his sceptre or his sword; something might be expected of so literary and erudite a king. Bacon tells James that the plans he has sketched are "indeed *opera basilica*,"—kingly tasks —"towards which the endeavors of one man can be but as an image on a cross-road, which points out the way but cannot tread it." Certainly these

[71]In Nichol, ii, 4.   [72]*Nov. Org.*, i, 113.   [73]*Ibid.*
[74]*Adv. of L.*. ii, 1.   [75]*Ibid.*, i.

royal undertakings will involve expense; but "as the secretaries and spies
of princes and states bring in bills for intelligence, so you must allow the
spies and intelligencers of nature to bring in their bills if you would not
be ignorant of many things worthy to be known. And if Alexander placed
so large a treasure at Aristotle's command for the support of hunters,
fowlers, fishers, and the like, in much more need do they stand of this
beneficence who unfold the labyrinths of nature."[76] With such royal aid
the Great Reconstruction can be completed in a few years; without it the
task will require generations.

What is refreshingly new in Bacon is the magnificent assurance with
which he predicts the conquest of nature by man: "I stake all on the
victory of art over nature in the race." That which men have done is "but
an earnest of the things they shall do." But why this great hope? Had not
men been seeking truth, and exploring the paths of science, these two
thousand years? Why should one hope now for such great success where
so long a time had given so modest a result?—Yes, Bacon answers; but
what if the methods men have used have been wrong and useless? What if
the road has been lost, and research has gone into by-paths ending in
the air? We need a ruthless revolution in our methods of research and
thought, in our system of science and logic; we need a new Organon,
better than Aristotle's, fit for this larger world.

And so Bacon offers us his supreme book.

2. THE NEW ORGANON

"Bacon's greatest performance," says his bitterest critic, "is the first
book of the *Novum Organum*."[77] Never did a man put more life into
logic, making induction an epic adventure and a conquest. If one must
study logic, let him begin with this book. "This part of human philosophy
which regards logic is disagreeable to the taste of many, as appearing to
them no other than a net, and a snare of thorny subtlety. . . . But if
we would rate things according to their real worth, the rational sciences
are the keys to all the rest."[78]

Philosophy has been barren so long, says Bacon, because she needed a
new method to make her fertile. The great mistake of the Greek philosophers was that they spent so much time in theory, so little in observation.
But thought should be the aide of observation, not its substitute. "Man,"
says the first aphorism of the *Novum Organum*, as if flinging a challenge
to all metaphysics,—"Man, as the minister and interpreter of nature,
does and understands as much as his observations on the order of nature
. . . permit him; and neither knows nor is capable of more." The predecessors of Socrates were in this matter sounder than his followers; Democritus, in particular, had a nose for facts, rather than an eye for the

[76]*Ibid.*, ii, 1.   [77]Macaulay, *op. cit.*, p. 92.   [78]*Adv. of L., v,* 1.

clouds. No wonder that philosophy has advanced so little since Aristotle's day; it has been using Aristotle's methods. "To go beyond Aristotle by the light of Aristotle is to think that a borrowed light can increase the original light from which it is taken."[79] Now, after two thousand years of logic-chopping with the machinery invented by Aristotle, philosophy has fallen so low that none will do her reverence. All these medieval theories, theorems and disputations must be cast out and forgotten; to renew herself philosophy must begin again with a clean slate and a cleansed mind.

The first step, therefore, is the Expurgation of the Intellect. We must become as little children, innocent of isms and abstractions, washed clear of prejudices and preconceptions. We must destroy the Idols of the mind.

An idol, as Bacon uses the word (reflecting perhaps the Protestant rejection of image-worship), is a picture taken for a reality, a thought mistaken for a thing. Errors come under this head; and the first problem of logic is to trace and dam the sources of these errors. Bacon proceeds now to a justly famous analysis of fallacies; "no man," said Condillac, "has better known than Bacon the causes of human error."

These errors are, first, *Idols of the Tribe,*—fallacies natural to humanity in general. "For man's sense is falsely asserted" (by Protagoras' "Man is the measure of all things") "to be the standard of things: on the contrary, all the perceptions, both of the senses and the mind, bear reference to man and not to the universe; and the human mind resembles those uneven mirrors which impart their own properties to different objects . . . and distort and disfigure them."[80] Our thoughts are pictures rather of ourselves than of their objects. For example, "the human understanding, from its peculiar nature, easily supposes a greater degree of order and regularity in things than it really finds. . . . Hence the fiction that all celestial bodies move in perfect circles."[81] Again,

> the human understanding, when any proposition has been once laid down (either from general admission and belief, or from the pleasure it affords), forces everything else to add fresh support and confirmation: and although most cogent and abundant instances may exist to the contrary, yet either does not observe, or despises them, or it gets rid of and rejects them by some distinction, with violent and injurious prejudice, rather than sacrifice the authority of its first conclusions. It was well answered by him who was shown in a temple the votive tablets suspended by such as had escaped the peril of shipwreck, and was pressed as to whether he would then recognize the power of the gods. . . . "But where are the portraits of those that have perished in spite of their vows?" All superstition is much the same, whether it be that of astrology, dreams, omens, retributive judgment, or the like, in all of which the deluded believers observe events which are fulfilled, but neglect and pass over their failure, though it be much more common.[82]

[79] *Valerius Terminus.*   [80] *Nov. Org.,* i, 41.
[81] *Ibid.,* i, 45.   [82] *Ibid* , i, 46.

"Having first determined the question according to his will, man *then* resorts to experience; and bending her into conformity with his placets, leads her about like a captive in a procession."[83] In short, "the human understanding is no dry light, but receives an infusion from the will and affections, whence proceed sciences which may be called 'sciences as one would.' . . . For what a man had rather were true, he more readily believes."[84] Is it not so?

Bacon gives at this point a word of golden counsel. "In general let every student of nature take this as a rule—that whatever his mind seizes and dwells upon with peculiar satisfaction, is to be held in suspicion; and that so much the more care is to be taken, in dealing with such questions, to keep the understanding even and clear."[85] "The understanding must not be allowed to jump and fly from particulars to remote axioms and of almost the highest generality; . . . it must not be supplied with wings, but rather hung with weights to keep it from leaping and flying."[86] The imagination may be the greatest enemy of the intellect, whereas it should be only its tentative and experiment.

A second class of errors Bacon calls *Idols of the Cave*—errors peculiar to the individual man. "For every one . . . has a cave or den of his own, which refracts and discolors the light of nature"; this is his character as formed by nature and nurture, and by his mood or condition of body and mind. Some minds, e. g., are constitutionally analytic, and see differences everywhere; others are constitutionally synthetic, and see resemblances; so we have the scientist and the painter on the one hand, and on the other hand the poet and the philosopher. Again, "some dispositions evince an unbounded admiration for antiquity, others eagerly embrace novelty; only a few can preserve the just medium, and neither tear up what the ancients have correctly established, nor despise the just innovations of the moderns."[87] Truth knows no parties.

Thirdly, *Idols of the Market-place,* arising "from the commerce and association of men with one another. For men converse by means of language; but words are imposed according to the understanding of the crowd; and there arises from a bad and inapt formation of words, a wonderful obstruction to the mind."[88] Philosophers deal out infinites with the careless assurance of grammarians handling infinitives; and yet does any man know what this "infinite" is, or whether it has even taken the precaution of existing? Philosophers talk about "first cause uncaused," or "first mover unmoved"; but are not these again fig-leaf phrases used to cover naked ignorance, and perhaps indicative of a guilty conscience in the user? Every clear and honest head knows that no cause can be causeless, nor any mover unmoved. Perhaps the greatest reconstruction in philosophy would be simply this—that we should stop lying.

[83]*Ibid.,* i, 63.   [84]*Ibid.,* i, 49.   [85]*Ibid.,* i, 58.
[86]*Ibid.,* i, 104.   [87]*Ibid.,* i, 56.   [88]*Ibid.,* i, 49.

"Lastly, there are idols which have migrated into men's minds from the various dogmas of philosophers, and also from wrong laws of demonstration. These I call *Idols of the Theatre,* because in my judgment all the received systems of philosophy are but so many stage-plays, representing worlds of their own creation after an unreal and scenic fashion. . . . And in the plays of this philosophic theater you may observe the same thing which is found in the theater of the poets,—that stories invented for the stage are more compact and elegant, and more as we would wish them to be, than true stories out of history."[89] The world as Plato describes it is merely a world constructed by Plato, and pictures Plato rather than the world.

We shall never get far along towards the truth if these idols are still to trip us up, even the best of us, at every turn. We need new modes of reasoning, new tools for the understanding. "And as the immense regions of the West Indies had never been discovered, if the use of the compass had not first been known, it is no wonder that the discovery and advancement of arts hath made no greater progress, when the art of inventing and discovering of the sciences remains hitherto unknown."[90] "And surely it would be disgraceful, if, while the regions of the material globe . . . have been in our times laid widely open and revealed, the intellectual globe should remain shut up within the narrow limits of old discoveries."[91]

Ultimately, our troubles are due to dogma and deduction; we find no new truth because we take some venerable but questionable proposition as an indubitable starting-point, and never think of putting this assumption itself to the test of observation or experiment. Now "if a man will begin with certainties, he shall end in doubts; but if he will be content to begin in doubts he shall end in certainties" (alas, it is not quite inevitable). Here is a note common in the youth of modern philosophy, part of its declaration of independence; Descartes too would presently talk of the necessity of "methodic doubt" as the cobweb-clearing pre-requisite of honest thought.

Bacon proceeds to give an admirable description of the scientific method of inquiry. "There remains *simple experience;* which, if taken as it comes, is called accident" ("empirical"), "if sought for, experiment. . . . The true method of experience first lights the candle" (hypothesis), "and then by means of the candle shows the way" (arranges and delimits the experiment); "commencing as it does with experience duly ordered and digested, not bungling nor erratic, and from it educing axioms, and from established axioms again new experiments."[92] (We have here—as again in a later passage[93] which speaks of the results of initial experiments as a "first vintage" to guide further research—an explicit, though

[89] *Ibid.,* i, 44.   [90] *Adv. of L.,* v, 2.   [91] *Nov. Org.,* i, 84.
[92] *Ibid.,* i, 82.   [93] *Ibid.,* ii, 20.

perhaps inadequate, recognition of that need for hypothesis, experiment and deduction which some of Bacon's critics suppose him to have entirely overlooked.) We must go to nature instead of to books, traditions and authorities; we must "put nature on the rack and compel her to bear witness" even against herself, so that we may control her to our ends. We must gather together from every quarter a "natural history" of the world, built by the united research of Europe's scientists. We must have induction.

But induction does not mean "simple enumeration" of all the data; conceivably, this might be endless, and useless; no mass of material can by itself make science. This would be like "chasing a quarry over an open country"; we must narrow and enclose our field in order to capture our prey. The method of induction must include a technique for the classification of data and the elimination of hypotheses; so that by the progressive canceling of possible explanations one only shall at last remain. Perhaps the most useful item in this technique is the "table of more or less," which lists instances in which two qualities or conditions increase or decrease together, and so reveals, presumably, a causal relation between the simultaneously varying phenomena. So Bacon, asking, What is heat? —seeks for some factor that increases with the increase of heat, and decreases with its decrease; he finds, after long analysis, an exact correlation between heat and motion; and his conclusion that heat is a form of motion constitutes one of his few specific contributions to natural science.

By this insistent accumulation and analysis of data we come, in Bacon's phrase, to the *form* of the phenomenon which we study,—to its secret nature and its inner essence. The theory of forms in Bacon is very much like the theory of ideas in Plato: a metaphysics of science. "When we speak of forms we mean nothing else than those laws and regulations of simple action which arrange and constitute any simple nature. . . . The form of heat or the form of light, therefore, means no more than the law of heat or the law of light."[94] (In a similar strain Spinoza was to say that the law of the circle is its *substance*.) "For although nothing exists in nature except individual bodies exhibiting clear individual effects according to particular laws; yet, in each branch of learning, those very laws—their investigation, discovery and development—are the foundation both of theory and of practice."[95] Of theory and of practice; one without the other is useless and perilous; knowledge that does not generate achievement is a pale and bloodless thing, unworthy of mankind. We strive to learn the forms of things not for the sake of the forms but because by knowing the forms, the laws, we may remake things in the image of our desire. So we study mathematics in order to reckon quantities and build bridges; we study psychology in order to find our way in the jungle of society. When science has sufficiently ferreted out the forms of

Ibid., ii, 13, 17.   *Ibid.*, ii, 2.

things, the world will be merely the raw material of whatever utopia man may decide to make.

3. THE UTOPIA OF SCIENCE

To perfect science so, and then to perfect social order by putting science in control, would itself be utopia enough. Such is the world described for us in Bacon's brief fragment and last work, *The New Atlantis,* published two years before his death. Wells thinks it Bacon's "greatest service to science"[96] to have drawn for us, even so sketchily, the picture of a society in which at last science has its proper place as the master of things; it was a royal act of imagination by which for three centuries one goal has been held in view by the great army of warriors in the battle of knowledge and invention against ignorance and poverty. Here in these few pages we have the essence and the "form" of Francis Bacon, the law of his being and his life, the secret and continuous aspiration of his soul.

Plato in the *Timaeus*[97] had told of the old legend of Atlantis, the sunken continent in the Western seas. Bacon and others identified the new America of Columbus and Cabot with this old Atlantis; the great continent had not sunk after all, but only men's courage to navigate the sea. Since this old Atlantis was now known, and seemed inhabited by a race vigorous enough, but not quite like the brilliant Utopians of Bacon's fancy, he conceived of a new Atlantis, an isle in that distant Pacific which only Drake and Magellan had traversed, an isle distant enough from Europe and from knowledge to give generous scope to the Utopian imagination.

The story begins in the most artfully artless way, like the great tales of Defoe and Swift. "We sailed from Peru (where we had continued for the space of one whole year), for China and Japan by the South Sea." Came a great calm, in which the ships for weeks lay quietly on the boundless ocean like specks upon a mirror, while the provisions of the adventurers ebbed away. And then resistless winds drove the vessels pitilessly north and north and north, out of the island-dotted south into an endless wilderness of sea. The rations were reduced, and reduced again, and again reduced; and disease took hold of the crew. At last, when they had resigned themselves to death, they saw, almost unbelieving, a fair island looming up under the sky. On the shore, as their vessel neared it, they saw not savages, but men simply and yet beautifully clothed, clean, and manifestly of developed intelligence. They were permitted to land, but were told that the island government allowed no strangers to remain. Nevertheless, since some of the crew were sick, they might all stay till these were well again.

During the weeks of convalescence the wanderers unraveled, day by

[96]*Outline of History,* ch. xxxv, sect. 6.   [97]Sect. 25.

day, the mystery of the New Atlantis. "There reigned in this island about nineteen hundred years ago," one of the inhabitants tells them, "a King whose memory above all others we most adore. . . . His name was Solamona, and we esteem him as the Law-giver of our nation. This King had a large heart . . . and was wholly bent to make his kingdom and people happy."[98] "Among the excellent acts of that King one above all hath the preëminence. It was the creation and institution of the Order, or Society, which is called Solomon's House; the noblest foundation, as we think, that was ever upon the earth; and the lantherne of this kingdom."[99]

There follows a description of Solomon's House, too complicated for a quoted abstract, but eloquent enough to draw from the hostile Macaulay the judgment that "there is not to be found in any human composition a passage more eminently distinguished by profound and serene wisdom."[100] Solomon's House takes the place, in the New Atlantis, of the Houses of Parliament in London; it is the home of the island government. But there are no politicians there, no insolent "elected persons," no "national palaver," as Carlyle would say; no parties, caucuses, primaries, conventions, campaigns, buttons, lithographs, editorials, speeches, lies, and elections; the idea of filling public office by such dramatic methods seems never to have entered the heads of these Atlantans. But the road to the heights of scientific repute is open to all, and only those who have traveled the road sit in the councils of the state. It is a government of the people and for the people by the selected best of the people; a government by technicians, architects, astronomers, geologists, biologists, physicians chemists, economists, sociologists, psychologists and philosophers. Complicated enough; but think of a government without politicians!

Indeed there is little government at all in the New Atlantis; these governors are engaged rather in controlling nature than in ruling man. "The End of Our Foundation is the Knowledge of Causes and secret motions of things; and the enlarging of the bounds of human empire, to the effecting of all things possible."[101] This is the key-sentence of the book, and of Francis Bacon. We find the governors engaged in such undignified tasks as studying the stars, arranging to utilize for industry the power of falling water, developing gases for the cure of various ailments,[102] experimenting on animals for surgical knowledge, growing new varieties of plants and animals by cross-breeding, etc. "We imitate the flights of birds; we have some degree of flying in the air. We have ships and boats for going under water." There is foreign trade, but of an unusual sort; the island produces what it consumes, and consumes what

[98]The New Atlantis, Cambridge University Press, 1900; p. 20.
[99]Ibid., p. 22.   [100]Ibid., p. xxv.   [101]Ibid., p. 34.
[102]Cf. The New York Times of May 2, 1923, for a report of War Department chemists on the use of war gases to cure diseases.

it produces; it does not go to war for foreign markets. "We maintain a trade, not of gold, silver, or jewels, nor for silks, nor for spices, nor for any other commodity or matter; but only for God's first creature, which was light; to have light of the growth of all parts of the world."[103] These "Merchants of Light" are members of Solomon's House who are sent abroad every twelve years to live among foreign peoples of every quarter of the civilized globe; to learn their language and study their sciences and industries and literatures; and to return, at the end of the twelve years, to report their findings to the leaders of Solomon's House; while their places abroad are taken by a new group of scientific explorers. In this way the best of all the world comes soon to the New Atlantis.

Brief as the picture is, we see in it again the outline of every philosopher's utopia—a people guided in peace and modest plenty by their wisest men. The dream of every thinker is to replace the politician by the scientist; why does it remain only a dream after so many incarnations? Is it because the thinker is too dreamily intellectual to go out into the arena of affairs and build his concept into reality? Is it because the hard ambition of the narrowly acquisitive soul is forever destined to overcome the gentle and scrupulous aspirations of philosophers and saints? Or is it that science is not yet grown to maturity and conscious power?—that only in our day do physicists and chemists and technicians begin to see that the rising rôle of science in industry and war gives them a pivotal position in social strategy, and points to the time when their organized strength will persuade the world to call them to leadership? Perhaps science has not yet merited the mastery of the world; and perhaps in a little while it will.

V. CRITICISM

And now how shall we appraise this philosophy of Francis Bacon's?

Is there anything new in it? Macaulay thinks that induction as described by Bacon is a very old-fashioned affair, over which there is no need of raising any commotion, much less a monument. "Induction has been practiced from morning till night by every human being since the world began. The man who infers that mince pies disagreed with him because he was ill when he ate them, well when he ate them not, most ill when he ate most and least ill when he ate least, has employed, unconsciously but sufficiently, all the tables of the *Novum Organum*."[104] But John Smith hardly handles his "table of more or less" so accurately, and more probably will continue his mince-pies despite the seismic disturbances of his lower strata. And even were John Smith so wise, it would not shear Bacon of his merit; for what does logic do but formulate the experience and methods of the wise?—what does any discipline do but try by rules to turn the art of a few into a science teachable to all?

[103]*New Atlantis.* p. 24.   [104]*Op. cit.*, p. 471.

But is the formulation Bacon's own? Is not the Socratic method inductive? Is not Aristotle's biology inductive? Did not Roger Bacon practise as well as preach the inductive method which Francis Bacon merely preached? Did not Galileo formulate better the procedure that science has actually used? True of Roger Bacon, less true of Galileo, less true yet of Aristotle, least true of Socrates. Galileo outlined the aim rather than the method of science, holding up before its followers the goal of mathematical and quantitative formulation of all experience and relationships; Aristotle practised induction when there was nothing else for him to do, and where the material did not lend itself to his penchant for the deduction of specific conclusions from magnificently general assumptions; and Socrates did not so much practise induction—the gathering of data—as analysis—the definition and discrimination of words and ideas.

Bacon makes no claim to parthenogenetic originality; like Shakespeare he takes with a lordly hand, and with the same excuse, that he adorns whatever he touches. Every man has his sources, as every organism has its food; what is his is the way in which he digests them and turns them into flesh and blood. As Rawley puts it, Bacon "contemned no man's observations, but would light his torch at every man's candle."[105] But Bacon acknowledges these debts: he refers to "that useful method of Hippocrates,"[106]—so sending us at once to the real source of inductive logic among the Greeks; and "Plato," he writes (where less accurately we write "Socrates"), "giveth good example of inquiry by induction and view of particulars; though in such a wandering manner as is of no force or fruit."[107] He would have disdained to dispute his obligations to these predecessors; and we should disdain to exaggerate them.

But then again, is the Baconian method correct? Is it the method most fruitfully used in modern science? No: generally, science has used, with best result, not the accumulation of data ("natural history") and their manipulation by the complicated tables of the *Novum Organum,* but the simpler method of hypothesis, deduction and experiment. So Darwin, reading Malthus' *Essay on Population,* conceived the idea of applying to all organisms the Malthusian hypothesis that population tends to increase faster than the means of subsistence; deduced from this hypothesis the probable conclusion that the pressure of population on the food-supply results in a struggle for existence in which the fittest survive, and by which in each generation every species is changed into closer adaptation to its environment; and finally (having by hypothesis and deduction limited his problem and his field of observation) turned to "the unwithered face of nature" and made for twenty years a patient inductive examination of the facts. Again, Einstein conceived, or took from New-

---

[105]Quoted by J. M. Robertson, Introduction to *The Philosophical Works of Francis Bacon;* p. 7.

[106]*Adv. of L.,* iv, 2.   [107]*Fil. Lab., ad fin.*

ton, the hypothesis that light travels in curved, not straight lines; deduced from it the conclusion that a star appearing to be (on the straight-line theory) in a certain position in the heavens is really a little to one side of that position; and he invited experiment and observation to test the conclusion. Obviously the function of hypothesis and imagination is greater than Bacon supposed; and the proceduce of science is more direct and circumscribed than in the Baconian scheme. Bacon himself anticipated the superannuation of his method; the actual practice of science would discover better modes of investigation than could be worked out in the interludes of statesmanship. "These things require some ages for the ripening of them."

Even a lover of the Baconian spirit must concede, too, that the great Chancellor, while laying down the law for science, failed to keep abreast of the science of his time. He rejected Copernicus and ignored Kepler and Tycho Brahe; he depreciated Gilbert and seemed unaware of Harvey. In truth, he loved discourse better than research; or perhaps he had no time for toilsome investigations. Such work as he did in philosophy and science was left in fragments and chaos at his death; full of repetitions, contradictions, aspirations, and introductions. *Ars longa, vita brevis*—art is long and time is fleeting: this is the tragedy of every great soul.

To assign to so overworked a man, whose reconstruction of philosophy had to be crowded into the crevices of a harassed and a burdened political career, the vast and complicated creations of Shakespeare, is to waste the time of students with the parlor controversies of idle theorists. Shakespeare lacks just that which distinguishes the lordly Chancellor—erudition and philosophy. Shakespeare has an impressive smattering of many sciences, and a mastery of none; in all of them he speaks with the eloquence of an amateur. He accepts astrology: "This huge state . . . whereon the stars in secret influence comment."[108] He is forever making mistakes which the learned Bacon could not possibly have made: his Hector quotes Aristotle and his Coriolanus alludes to Cato; he supposes the Lupercalia to be a hill; and he understands Cæsar about as profoundly as Cæsar is understood by H. G. Wells. He makes countless references to his early life and his matrimonial tribulations. He perpetrates vulgarities, obscenities and puns natural enough in the gentle roisterer who could not quite outlive the Stratford rioter and the butcher's son, but hardly to be expected in the cold and calm philosopher. Carlyle calls Shakespeare the greatest of intellects; but he was rather the greatest of imaginations, and the keenest eye. He is an inescapable psychologist, but he is not a philosopher: he has no structure of thought unified by a purpose for his own life and for mankind. He is immersed in love and its problems, and thinks of philosophy, through Montaigne's phrases, only when his heart is broken. Otherwise

[108]Sonnet xv.

he accepts the world blithely enough; he is not consumed with the re-constructive vision that ennobled Plato, or Nietzsche, or Bacon.

Now the greatness and the weakness of Bacon lay precisely in his pas-sion for unity, his desire to spread the wings of his coördinating genius over a hundred sciences. He aspired to be like Plato, "a man of sublime genius, who took a view of everything as from a lofty rock." He broke down under the weight of the tasks he had laid upon himself; he failed forgivably because he undertook so much. He could not enter the promised land of science, but as Cowley's epitaph expressed it, he could at least stand upon its border and point out its fair features in the distance.

His achievement was not the less great because it was indirect. His philosophical works, though little read now, "moved the intellects which moved the world."[109] He made himself the eloquent voice of the optimism and resolution of the Renaissance. Never was any man so great a stimulus to other thinkers. King James, it is true, refused to accept his suggestion for the support of science, and said of the *Novum Organum* that "it was like the peace of God, which passeth all understanding." But better men, in 1662, founding that Royal Society which was to become the greatest association of scientists in the world, named Bacon as their model and inspiration; they hoped that this organization of English research would lead the way toward that Europe-wide association which the *Advance-ment of Learning* had taught them to desire. And when the great minds of the French Enlightenment undertook that masterpiece of intellectual enterprise, the *Encyclopédie,* they dedicated it to Francis Bacon. "If," said Diderot in the Prospectus, "we have come of it successfully, we shall owe most to the Chancellor Bacon, who threw out the plan of an universal dictionary of sciences and arts, at a time when, so to say, neither arts nor sciences existed. That extraordinary genius, when it was impossible to write a history of what was known, wrote one of what it was necessary to learn." D'Alembert called Bacon "the greatest, the most universal, and the most eloquent of philosophers." The Convention published the works of Bacon at the expense of the state.[110] The whole tenor and career of British thought have followed the philosophy of Bacon. His tendency to conceive the world in Democritean mechanical terms gave to his secretary, Hobbes, the starting-point for a thorough-going materialism; his induc-tive method gave to Locke the idea of an empirical psychology, bound by observation and freed from theology and metaphysics; and his emphasis on "commodities" and "fruits" found formulation in Bentham's identifi-cation of the useful and the good.

Wherever the spirit of control has overcome the spirit of resignation, Bacon's influence has been felt. He is the voice of all those Europeans who have changed a continent from a forest into a treasure-land of art and

[109]Macaulay, p. 491.   [110]Nichol, ii. 225.

science, and have made their little peninsula the center of the world. "Men are not animals erect," said Bacon, "but immortal gods." "The Creator has given us souls equal to all the world, and yet satiable not even with a world." Everything is possible to man. Time is young; give us some little centuries, and we shall control and remake all things. We shall perhaps at last learn the noblest lesson of all, that man must not fight man, but must make war only on the obstacles that nature offers to the triumph of man. "It will not be amiss," writes Bacon, in one of his finest passages, "to distinguish the three kinds, and as it were grades, of ambition in mankind. The first is of those who desire to extend their power in their native country; which kind is vulgar and degenerate. The second is of those who labor to extend the power of their country and its dominion among men; this certainly has more dignity, but not less covetousness. But if a man endeavor to establish and extend the power and dominion of the human race itself over the universe, his ambition is without doubt both a more wholesome thing and a nobler than the other two."[111] It was Bacon's fate to be torn to pieces by these hostile ambitions struggling for his soul.

VI. EPILOGUE

"Men in great place are thrice servants; servants to the sovereign or state, servants of fame, and servants of business, so as they have no freedom, neither in their persons nor in their action, nor in their time. . . . The rising unto place is laborious, and by pains men come to greater pains; and it is sometimes base, and by indignities men come to dignities. The standing is slippery, and the regress is either a downfall or at least an eclipse."[112] What a wistful summary of Bacon's epilogue!

"A man's shortcomings," said Goethe, "are taken from his epoch; his virtues and greatness belong to himself." This seems a little unfair to the *Zeitgeist*, but it is exceptionally just in the case of Bacon. Abbott,[113] after a painstaking study of the morals prevalent at Elizabeth's court, concludes that all the leading figures, male and female, were disciples of Machiavelli. Roger Ascham described in doggerel the four cardinal virtues in demand at the court of the Queen:

> Cog, lie, flatter and face,
> Four ways in Court to win men grace.
> If thou be thrall to none of these,
> Away, good Piers! Home, John Cheese!

It was one of the customs of those lively days for judges to take "presents" from persons trying cases in their courts. Bacon was not above the age in this matter; and his tendency to keep his expenditure several

[111]*Nov. Org.*, i, 129.   [112]Essay "Of Great Place."   [113]*Francis Bacon*, ch. i.

years in advance of his income forbade him the luxury of scruples. It might have passed unnoticed, except that he had made enemies in Essex' case, and by his readiness to sabre foes with his speech. A friend had warned him that "it is too common in every man's mouth in Court that . . . as your tongue hath been a razor to some, so shall theirs be to you."[114] But he left the warnings unnoticed. He seemed to be in good favor with the King; he had been made Baron Verulam of Verulam in 1618, and Viscount St. Albans in 1621; and for three years he had been Chancellor.

Then suddenly the blow came. In 1621 a disappointed suitor charged him with taking money for the despatch of a suit; it was no unusual matter, but Bacon knew at once that if his enemies wished to press it they could force his fall. He retired to his home, and waited developments. When he learned that all his foes were clamoring for his dismissal, he sent in his "confession and humble submission" to the King. James, yielding to pressure from the now victorious Parliament against which Bacon had too persistently defended him, sent him to the Tower. But Bacon was released after two days; and the heavy fine which had been laid upon him was remitted by the King. His pride was not quite broken. "I was the justest judge that was in England these fifty years," he said; "but it was the justest judgment that was in Parliament these two hundred years."

He spent the five years that remained to him in the obscurity and peace of his home, harassed by an unwonted poverty, but solaced by the active pursuit of philosophy. In these five years he wrote his greatest Latin work, *De Augmentis Scientiarum,* published an enlarged edition of the Essays, a fragment called *Sylva Sylvarum,* and a *History of Henry VII.* He mourned that he had not sooner abandoned politics and given all his time to literature and science. To the very last moment he was occupied with work, and died, so to speak, on the field of battle. In his essay "Of Death" he had voiced a wish to die "in an earnest pursuit, which is like one wounded in hot blood, who for the time scarce feels the hurt." Like Cæsar, he was granted his choice.

In March, 1626, while riding from London to Highgate, and turning over in his mind the question how far flesh might be preserved from putrefaction by being covered with snow, he resolved to put the matter to a test at once. Stopping off at a cottage, he bought a fowl, killed it, and stuffed it with snow. While he was doing this he was seized with chills and weakness; and finding himself too ill to ride back to town, he gave directions that he should be taken to the nearby home of Lord Arundel, where he took to bed. He did not yet resign life; he wrote cheerfully that "the experiment . . . succeeded excellently well." But it was his last. The fitful fever of his varied life had quite consumed him; he

[114]*Ibid.,* p. 13 note.

was all burnt out now, too weak to fight the disease that crept up slowly to his heart. He died on the ninth of April, 1626, at the age of sixty-five.

He had written in his will these proud and characteristic words: "I bequeath my soul to God. . . . My body to be buried obscurely. My name to the next ages and to foreign nations." The ages and the nations have accepted him.

CHAPTER IV

Spinoza

I. HISTORICAL AND BIOGRAPHICAL

I. THE ODYSSEY OF THE JEWS

THE story of the Jews since the Dispersion is one of the epics of European history. Driven from their natural home by the Roman capture of Jerusalem (70 A. D.), and scattered by flight and trade among all the nations and to all the continents; persecuted and decimated by the adherents of the great religions—Christianity and Mohammedanism—which had been born of their scriptures and their memories; barred by the feudal system from owning land, and by the guilds from taking part in industry; shut up within congested ghettoes and narrowing pursuits, mobbed by the people and robbed by the kings; building with their finance and trade the towns and cities indispensable to civilization; outcast and excommunicated, insulted and injured;—yet, without any political structure, without any legal compulsion to social unity, without even a common language, this wonderful people has maintained itself in body and soul, has preserved its racial and cultural integrity, has guarded with jealous love its oldest rituals and traditions, has patiently and resolutely awaited the day of its deliverance, and has emerged greater in number than ever before, renowned in every field for the contributions of its geniuses, and triumphantly restored, after two thousand years of wandering, to its ancient and unforgotten home. What drama could rival the grandeur of these sufferings, the variety of these scenes, and the glory and justice of this fulfillment? What fiction could match the romance of this reality?

The dispersion had begun many centuries before the fall of the Holy City; through Tyre and Sidon and other ports the Jews had spread abroad into every nook of the Mediterranean—to Athens and Antioch, to Alexandria and Carthage, to Rome and Marseilles, and even to distant Spain. After the destruction of the Temple the dispersion became almost a mass migration. Ultimately the movement followed two streams: one along the Danube and the Rhine, and thence later into Poland and Russia; the other into Spain and Portugal with the conquering Moors (711 A. D.). In Central Europe the Jews distinguished themselves as merchants and financiers; in the Peninsula they absorbed gladly the mathematical, medical and philosophical lore of the Arabs, and developed their own culture in the great schools of Cordova, Barcelona and Seville. Here in the twelfth and thirteenth centuries the Jews played a prominent part in transmitting ancient and Oriental culture to western Europe. It was at Cordova that Moses Maimonides (1135–1204), the greatest physician of his age, wrote his famous Biblical commentary, the *Guide to the Perplexed;* it was at Barcelona that Hasdai Crescas (1370–1430) propounded heresies that shook all Judaism.

The Jews of Spain prospered and flourished until the conquest of Granada by Ferdinand in 1492 and the final expulsion of the Moors. The Peninsular Jews now lost the liberty which they had enjoyed under the lenient ascendency of Islam; the Inquisition swept down upon them with the choice of baptism and the practice of Christianity, or exile and the confiscation of their goods. It was not that the Church was violently hostile to the Jews—the popes repeatedly protested against the barbarities of the Inquisition; but the King of Spain thought he might fatten his purse with the patiently-garnered wealth of this alien race. Almost in the year that Columbus discovered America, Ferdinand discovered the Jews.

The great majority of the Jews accepted the harder alternative, and looked about them for a place of refuge. Some took ship and sought entry into Genoa and other Italian ports; they were refused, and sailed on in growing misery and disease till they reached the coast of Africa, where many of them were murdered for the jewels they were believed to have swallowed. A few were received into Venice, which knew how much of its maritime ascendency it owed to its Jews. Others financed the voyage of Columbus, a man perhaps of their own race, hoping that the great navigator would find them a new home. A large number of them embarked in the frail vessels of that day and sailed up the Atlantic, between hostile England and hostile France, to find at last some measure of welcome in little big-souled Holland. Among these was a family of Portuguese Jews named Espinoza.

Thereafter Spain decayed, and Holland prospered. The Jews built their first synagogue in Amsterdam in 1598; and when, seventy-five years later, they built another, the most magnificent in Europe, their Christian neighbors helped them to finance the enterprise. The Jews were happy now, if we may judge from the stout content of the merchants and rabbis to whom Rembrandt has given immortality. But towards the middle of the seventeenth century the even tenor of events was interrupted by a bitter controversy within the synagogue. Uriel a Costa, a passionate youth who had left, like some other Jews, the sceptical influence of the Renaissance, wrote a treatise vigorously attacking the belief in another life. This negative attitude was not necessarily contrary to older Jewish doctrine; but the Synagogue compelled him to retract publicly, lest it should incur the disfavor of a community that had welcomed them generously, but would be unappeasably hostile to any heresy striking so sharply at what was considered the very essence of Christianity. The formula of retraction and penance required the proud author to lie down athwart the threshold of the synagogue while the members of the con, gregation walked over his body. Humiliated beyond sufferance, Uriel went home, wrote a fierce denunciation of his persecutors, and shot him, self.[1]

This was 1640. At that time Baruch Spinoza, "the greatest Jew of modern times,"[2] and the greatest of modern philosophers, was a child of eight, the favorite student of the synagogue.

2. THE EDUCATION OF SPINOZA

It was this Odyssey of the Jews that filled the background of Spinoza's mind, and made him irrevocably, however excommunicate, a Jew. Though his father was a successful merchant, the youth had no leaning to such a career, and preferred to spend his time in and around the synagogue, absorbing the religion and the history of his people. He was a brilliant scholar, and the elders looked upon him as a future light of their community and their faith. Very soon he passed from the Bible itself to the exactingly subtle commentaries of the Talmud; and from these to the writings of Maimonides, Levi ben Gerson, Ibn Ezra, and Hasdai Crescas; and his promiscuous voracity extended even to the mystical philosophy of Ibn Gebirol and the Cabbalistic intricacies of Moses of Cordova.

He was struck by the latter's identification of God and the universe; he followed up the idea in Ben Gerson, who taught the eternity of the world; and in Hasdai Crescas, who believed the universe of matter to be the body of God. He read in Maimonides a half-favorable discussion of the doctrine of Averroës, that immortality is impersonal; but he found in the *Guide to the Perplexed* more perplexities than guidance. For the great Rabbi propounded more questions than he answered; and Spinoza found the contradictions and improbabilities of the Old Testament linger-ing in his thought long after the solutions of Maimonides had dissolved into forgetfulness. The cleverest defenders of a faith are its greatest enemies; for their subtleties engender doubt and stimulate the mind. And if this was so with the writings of Maimonides, so much the more was it the case with the commentaries of Ibn Ezra, where the problems of the old faith were more directly expressed, and sometimes abandoned as un-answerable. The more Spinoza read and pondered, the more his simple certainties melted away into wondering and doubt.

His curiosity was aroused to inquire what the thinkers of the Christian

[1] Gutzkow has turned this story into a drama which still finds place in European repertoires.

[2] Renan, *Marc Aurèle;* Paris, Calmann-Levy: p. 65.

world had written on those great questions of God and human destiny. He took up the study of Latin with a Dutch scholar, Van den Ende, and moved into a wider sphere of experience and knowledge. His new teacher was something of a heretic himself, a critic of creeds and governments, an adventurous fellow who stepped out of his library to join a conspiracy against the king of France, and adorned a scaffold in 1674. He had a pretty daughter who became the successful rival of Latin for the affections of Spinoza; even a modern collegian might be persuaded to study Latin by such inducements. But the young lady was not so much of an intellectual as to be blind to the main chance; and when another suitor came, bearing costly presents, she lost interest in Spinoza. No doubt it was at that moment that our hero became a philosopher.

At any rate he had conquered Latin; and through Latin he entered into the heritage of ancient and medieval European thought. He seems to have studied Socrates and Plato and Aristotle; but he preferred to them the great atomists, Democritus, Epicurus and Lucretius; and the Stoics left their mark upon him ineffaceably. He read the Scholastic philosophers, and took from them not only their terminology, but their geometrical method of exposition by axiom, definition, proposition, proof, scholium and corollary. He studied Bruno (1548-1600), that magnificent rebel whose fires "not all the snows of the Caucasus could quench," who wandered from country to country and from creed to creed, and evermore "came out by the same door wherein he went,"—searching and wondering; and who at last was sentenced by the Inquisition to be killed "as mercifully as possible, and without the shedding of blood"—i. e., to be burned alive. What a wealth of ideas there was in this romantic Italian! First of all the master idea of unity: all reality is one in substance, one in cause, one in origin; and God and this reality are one. Again, to Bruno, mind and matter are one; every particle of reality is composed inseparably of the physical and the psychical. The object of philosophy, therefore, is to perceive unity in diversity, mind in matter, and matter in mind; to find the synthesis in which opposites and contradictions meet and merge; to rise to that highest knowledge of universal unity which is the intellectual equivalent of the love of God. Every one of these ideas became part of the intimate structure of Spinoza's thought.

Finally and above all, he was influenced by Descartes (1596-1650), father of the subjective and idealistic (as was Bacon of the objective and realistic) tradition in modern philosophy. To his French followers and English enemies the central notion in Descartes was the primacy of consciousness—his apparently obvious proposition that the mind knows itself more immediately and directly than it can ever know anything else; that it knows the "external world" only through that world's impress upon the mind in sensation and perception; that all philosophy must in consequence (though it should doubt everything else) begin with the individual mind and self, and make its first argument in three words: "I think, therefore I am" (*Cogito, ergo sum*). Perhaps there was something of Renaissance individualism in this starting-point; certainly there was in it a whole magician's-hatful of consequences for later speculation. Now began the great game of epistemology,[3] which in Leibniz, Locke, Berkeley, Hume and Kant waxed into a Three Hundred Years' War that at once stimulated and devastated modern philosophy.

But this side of Descartes' thought did not interest Spinoza; he would not lose himself in the labyrinths of epistemology. What a.tracted him was Descartes' conception of a homogeneous "substance" underlying all forms of matter, and another homogeneous substance underlying all forms of mind; this separation of reality into two ultimate substances was a challenge to the unifying passion of Spinoza, and acted like a fertilizing sperm upon the accumulations of his thought. What attracted him again was Descartes' desire to explain all of the world except God and the soul by mechanical and mathematical laws,—an idea going back to Leonardo and Galileo, and perhaps reflecting the development of machinery and industry in the cities of Italy. Given an initial push by God, said Descartes (very much as Anaxagoras had said two thousand years before), and the rest of astronomic, geologic and all non-mental processes and developments can be explained from a homogeneous substance existing at first in a disintegrated form (the "nebular hypothesis" of Laplace and Kant); and every movement of every animal, and even of the human body, is a mechanical movement,—the circulation of the blood, for example, and reflex action. All the world, and every body, is a machine; but outside the world is God, and within the body is the spiritual soul.

Here Descartes stopped; but Spinoza eagerly passed on.

3. Excommunication

These were the mental antecedents of the externally quiet but internally disturbed youth who in 1656 (he had been born in 1632) was summoned before the elders of the synagogue on the charge of heresy. Was it true, they asked him, that he had said to his friends that God might have a body—the world of matter; that angels might be hallucinations; that the soul might be merely life; and that the Old Testament said nothing of immortality?

We do not know what he answered. We only know that he was offered an annuity of $500 if he would consent to maintain at least an external loyalty to his synagogue and his faith;[4] that he refused the offer; and that on July 27, 1656, he was excommunicated with all the sombre

---

[3] Epistemology means, etymologically, the logic (*logos*) of understanding (*episteme*),—i. e., the origin, nature and validity of knowledge.

[4] Graetz, *History of the Jews;* New York, 1919; vol. v. p. 140.

formalities of Hebrew ritual. "During the reading of the curse, the wailing and protracted note of a great horn was heard to fall in from time to time; the lights, seen brightly burning at the beginning of the ceremony, were extinguished one by one as it proceeded, till at the end the last went out—typical of the extinction of the spiritual life of the excommunicated man—and the congregation was left in total darkness."[5]

Van Vloten has given us the formula used for excommunication:[6]

The heads of the Ecclesiastical Council hereby make known, that, already well assured of the evil opinions and doings of Baruch de Espinoza, they have endeavored in sundry ways and by various promises to turn him from his evil courses. But as they have been unable to bring him to any better way of thinking; on the contrary, as they are every day better certified of the horrible heresies entertained and avowed by him, and of the insolence with which these heresies are promulgated and spread abroad, and many persons worthy of credit having borne witness to these in the presence of the said Espinoza, he has been held fully convicted of the same. Review having therefore been made of the whole matter before the chiefs of the Ecclesiastical Council, it has been resolved, the Councillors assenting thereto, to anathematize the said Spinoza, and to cut him off from the people of Israel, and from the present hour to place him in Anathema with the following malediction:

With the judgment of the angels and the sentence of the saints, we anathematize, execrate, curse and cast out Baruch de Espinoza, the whole of the sacred community assenting, in presence of the sacred books with the six-hundred-and-thirteen precepts written therein, pronouncing against him the malediction wherewith Elisha cursed the children, and all the maledictions written in the Book of the Law. Let him be accursed by day, and accursed by night; let him be accursed in his lying down, and accursed in his rising up; accursed in going out and accursed in coming in. May the Lord never more pardon or acknowledge him; may the wrath and displeasure of the Lord burn henceforth against this man, load him with all the curses written in the Book of the Law, and blot out his name from under the sky; may the Lord sever him from evil from all the tribes of Israel, weight him with all the maledictions of the firmament contained in the Book of Law; and may all ye who are obedient to the Lord your God be saved this day.

Hereby then are all admonished that none hold converse with him by word of mouth, none hold communication with him by writing; that no one do him any service, no one abide under the same roof with him, no one approach within four cubits length of him, and no one read any document dictated by him, or written by his hand.

Let us not be too quick to judge the leaders of the synagogue; for they faced a delicate situation. No doubt they hesitated to subject themselves to the charge that they were as intolerant of heterodoxy as the Inquisition which had exiled them from Spain. But they felt that gratitude to

[5]Willis, Benedict de Spinoza; London, 1870; n. 35.
[6]Translation by Willis, p. 34.

their hosts in Holland demanded the excommunication of a man whose doubts struck at Christian doctrine quite as vitally as at Judaism. Protestantism was not then the liberal and fluent philosophy which it now becomes; the wars of religion had left each group entrenched immovably in its own creed, cherished now all the more because of the blood just shed in its defense. What would the Dutch authorities say to a Jewish community which repaid Christian toleration and protection by turning out in one generation an A Costa, and in the next a Spinoza? Furthermore, religious unanimity seemed to the elders their sole means of preserving the little Jewish group in Amsterdam from distegration, and almost the last means of preserving the unity, and so ensuring the survival, of the scattered Jews of the world. If they had had their own state, their own civil law, their own establishments of secular force and power, to compel internal cohesion and external respect, they might have been more tolerant; but their religion was to them their patriotism as well as their faith, the synagogue was their center of social and political life as well as of ritual and worship; and the Bible whose veracity Spinoza had impugned was the "portable Fatherland" of their people; under these circumstances, they thought, heresy was treason, and toleration suicide.

One feels that they should have bravely run these risks; but it is as hard to judge another justly as it is to get out of one's skin. Perhaps' Menasseh ben Israel, spiritual head of the whole Amsterdam community of Jews, could have found some conciliatory formula within which both the synagogue and the philosopher might have found room to live in mutual peace; but the great rabbi was then in London, persuading Cromwell to open England to the Jews. Fate had written that Spinoza should belong to the world.

4. RETIREMENT AND DEATH

He took the excommunication with quiet courage, saying: "It compels me to nothing which I should not have done in any case." But this was whistling in the dark; in truth the young student now found himself bitterly and pitilessly alone. Nothing is so terrible as solitude; and few forms of it so difficult as the isolation of a Jew from all his people. Spinoza had already suffered in the loss of his old faith; to so uproot the contents of one's mind is a major operation, and leaves many wounds. Had Spinoza entered another fold, embraced another of the orthodoxies in which men were grouped like kine huddling together for warmth, he might have found in the rôle of distinguished convert some of the life which he had lost by being utterly outcast from his family and his race. But he joined no other sect, and lived his life alone. His father, who had looked forward to his son's preeminence in Hebrew learning, sent him away; his sister

'As suggested by Israel Abrahams, art. *Jews,* Encyclopedia Britannica.

tried to cheat him of a small inheritance;[8] his former friends shunned him. No wonder there is little humor in Spinoza! And no wonder he breaks out with some bitterness occasionally when he thinks of the Keepers of the Law.

> Those who wish to seek out the causes of miracles, and to understand the things of nature as philosophers, and not to stare at them in astonishment like fools, are soon considered heretical and impious, and proclaimed as such by those whom the mob adore as the interpreters of nature and the gods. For these men know that once ignorance is put aside, that wonderment would be taken away which is the only means by which their authority is preserved.[9]

The culminating experience came shortly after the excommunication. One night as Spinoza was walking through the streets, a pious ruffian bent on demonstrating his theology by murder, attacked the young student with drawn dagger. Spinoza, turning quickly, escaped with a slight wound on the neck. Concluding that there are few places in this world where it is safe to be a philosopher, he went to live in a quiet attic room on the Outerdek road outside of Amsterdam. It was now, probably, that he changed his name from Baruch to Benedict. His host and hostess were Christians of the Mennonite sect, and could in some measure understand a heretic. They liked his sadly kind face (those who have suffered much become very bitter or very gentle), and were delighted when, occasionally, he would come down of an evening, smoke his pipe with them, and tune his talk to their simple strain. He made his living at first by teaching children in Van den Ende's school, and then by polishing lenses, as if he had an inclination for dealing with refractory material. He had learned the optical trade while living in the Jewish community; it was in accord with Hebrew canon that every student should acquire some manual art; not only because study and honest teaching can seldom make a livelihood, but, as Gamaliel had said, work keeps one virtuous, whereas "every learned man who fails to acquire a trade will at last turn out a rogue."

Five years later (1660) his host moved to Rhynsburg, near Leyden; and Spinoza moved with him. The house still stands, and the road bears the philosopher's name. These were years of plain living and high thinking. Many times he stayed in his room for two or three days together, seeing nobody, and having his modest meals brought up to him. The lenses were well done, but not so continuously as to earn for Spinoza more than merely enough; he loved wisdom too much to be a "successful" man. Colerus, who followed Spinoza in these lodgings, and wrote a short life of the philosopher from the reports of those who had known him,

---

[8] He contested the case in court; won it; and then turned over the bequest to the sister.

[9] *Ethics*, Part I, Appendix.

says, "He was very careful to cast up his accounts every quarter; which he did that he might spend neither more nor less than what he had to spend for each year. And he would say sometimes, to the people of the house, that he was like the serpent who forms a circle with his tail in his mouth; to denote that he had nothing left at the year's end."[10] But in his modest way he was happy. To one who advised him to trust in revelation rather than in reason, he answered: "Though I were at times to find the fruit unreal which I gather by my natural understanding, yet this would not make me otherwise than content; because in the gathering I am happy, and pass my days not in sighing and sorrow, but in peace, serenity and joy."[11] "If Napoleon had been as intelligent as Spinoza," says a great sage, "he would have lived in a garret and written four books."[12]

To the portraits of Spinoza which have come down to us we may add a word of description from Colerus. "He was of a middle size. He had good features in his face, the skin somewhat black, the hair dark and curly, the eyebrows long and black, so that one might easily know by his looks that he was descended from Portuguese Jews. As for his clothes, he was very careless of them, and they were not better than those of the meanest citizen. One of the most eminent councilors of state went to see him, and found him in a very untidy morning-gown; whereupon the councillor reproached him for it, and offered him another. Spinoza answered that a man was never the better for having a fine gown, and added, 'It is unreasonable to wrap up things of little or no value in a precious cover.' "[13] Spinoza's sartorial philosophy was not always so ascetic. "It is not a disorderly or slovenly carriage that makes us sages," he writes; "for affected indifference to personal appearance is rather evidence of a poor spirit in which true wisdom could find no worthy dwelling-place, and science could only meet with disorder and disarray."[14]

It was during this five years' stay at Rhynsburg that Spinoza wrote the little fragment "On the Improvement of the Intellect" (De Intellectus Emendatione), and the Ethics Geometrically Demonstrated (Ethica More Geometrico Demonstrata). The latter was finished in 1665; but for ten years Spinoza made no effort to publish it. In 1668 Adrian Koerbagh, for printing opinions similar to Spinoza's, was sent to jail for ten years; and died there after serving eighteen months of his sentence. When, in 1675, Spinoza went to Amsterdam trusting that he might now safely publish his chef-d'œuvre, "a rumor was spread about," as he writes to his friend Oldenburg, "that a book of mine was soon to appear, in which I endeavored to prove that there is no God. This report, I regret to add, was by many received as true. Certain theologians (who probably were them-

[10]In Pollock, Life and Philosophy of Spinoza; London, 1899; p. 393.
[11]Epistle 34, ed. Willis.
[12]Anatole France: M. Bergeret in Paris; New York, 1921; p. 180.
[13]In Pollock, p. 394.   [14]In Willis, p. 72.

selves the author of the rumor) took occasion upon this to lodge a complaint against me with the prince and the magistrates. . . . Having received a hint of this state of things from some trustworthy friends, who
assured me, further, that the theologians were everywhere lying in wait
for me, I determined to put off my attempted publication until such
time as I should see what turn affairs would take."[15]

Only after Spinoza's death did the *Ethics* appear (1677), along with an
unfinished treatise on politics (*Tractatus Politicus*) and a *Treatise on the
Rainbow*. All these works were in Latin, as the universal language of
European philosophy and science in the seventeenth century. *A Short
Treatise on God and Man,* written in Dutch, was discovered by Van
Vloten in 1852; it was apparently a preparatory sketch for the *Ethics.*
The only books published by Spinoza in his lifetime were *The Principles
of the Cartesian Philosophy* (1663), and *A Treatise on Religion and the
State* (*Tractatus Theologico-Politicus*), which appeared anonymously in
1670. It was at once honored with a place in the *Index Expurgatorius,*
and its sale was prohibited by the civil authorities; with this assistance it
attained to a considerable circulation under cover of title-pages which
disguised it as a medical treatise or an historical narrative. Countless
volumes were written to refute it; one called Spinoza "the most impious
atheist that ever lived upon the face of the earth"; Colerus speaks of
another refutation as "a treasure of infinite value, which shall never
perish";[16]—only this notice remains of it. In addition to such public
chastisement Spinoza received a number of letters intended to reform
him; that of a former pupil, Albert Burgh, who had been converted to
Catholicism, may be taken as a sample:

You assume that you have at last found the true philosophy. How do you
know that your philosophy is the best of all those which have ever been
taught in the world, are now taught, or shall be taught hereafter? To say
nothing of what may be devised in the future, have you examined all those
philosophies, both ancient and modern, which are taught here, in India,
and all the world over? And even supposing that you have duly examined
them, how do you know that you have chosen the best? . . . How dare you
set yourself up above all the patriarchs, prophets, apostles, martyrs, doctors,
and confessors of the Church? Miserable man and worm upon the earth
that you are, yea, ashes and food for worms, how can you confront the
eternal wisdom with your unspeakable blasphemy? What foundation have
you for this rash, insane, deplorable, accursed doctrine? What devilish pride
puffs you up to pass judgment on mysteries which Catholics themselves
declare to be incomprehensible? Etc., etc.[17]

To which Spinoza replied:

You who assume that you have at last found the best religion, or rather the
best teachers, and fixed your credulity upon them, how do you know that they

[15]Epistle 19.   [16]Pollock, 406.   [17]Epistle 73.

are the best among those who have taught religions, or now teach, or shall hereafter teach them? Have you examined all those religions, ancient and modern, which are taught here, and in India, and all the world over? And even supposing that you have duly examined them, how do you know that you have chosen the best?[18]

Apparently the gentle philosopher could be firm enough when occasion called for it.

Not all the letters were of this uncomfortable kind. Many of them were from men of mature culture and high position. Most prominent of these correspondents were Henry Oldenburg, secretary of the recently established Royal Society of England; Von Tschirnhaus, a young German inventor and nobleman; Huygens, the Dutch scientist; Leibnitz the philosopher, who visited Spinoza in 1676; Louis Meyer, a physician of the Hague; and Simon De Vries, a rich merchant of Amsterdam. The latter so admired Spinoza that he begged him to accept a gift of $1000. Spinoza refused; and later, when De Vries, making his will, proposed to leave his entire fortune to him, Spinoza persuaded De Vries instead to bequeath his wealth to his brother. When the merchant died it was found that his will required that an annuity of $250 should be paid to Spinoza out of the income of the property. Spinoza wished again to refuse saying, "Nature is satisfied with little; and if she is, I am also"; but he was at last prevailed upon to accept $150 a year. Another friend, Jan de Witt, chief magistrate of the Dutch republic, gave him a state annuity of $50. Finally, the Grand Monarch himself, Louis XIV, offered him a substantial pension, with the implied condition that Spinoza should dedicate his next book to the King. Spinoza courteously declined.

To please his friends and correspondents, Spinoza moved to Voorburg, a suburb of the Hague, in 1665; and in 1670 to the Hague itself. During these later years he developed an affectionate intimacy with Jan de Witt; and when De Witt and his brother were murdered in the streets by a mob which believed them responsible for the defeat of the Dutch troops by the French in 1672, Spinoza, on being apprised of the infamy, burst into tears, and but for the force which was used to restrain him, would have sallied forth, a second Anthony, to denounce the crime on the spot where it had been committed. Not long afterward, the Prince de Condé, head of the invading French army, invited Spinoza to his headquarters, to convey to him the offer of a royal pension from France and to introduce certain admirers of Spinoza who were with the Prince. Spinoza, who seems to have been rather a "good European" than a nationalist, thought it nothing strange for him to cross the lines and go to Condé's camp. When he returned to the Hague the news of his visit spread about, and there were angry murmurs among the people. Spinoza's host, Van den Spyck, was in fear of an attack upon his house; but Spinoza calmed him,

[18]Epistle 74.

saying: "I can easily clear myself of all suspicion of treason; . . . but should the people show the slightest disposition to molest you, should they even assemble and make a noise before your house, I will go down to them, though they should serve me as they did poor De Witt."[19] But when the crowd learned that Spinoza was merely a philosopher they concluded that he must be harmless; and the commotion quieted down.

Spinoza's life, as we see it in these little incidents, was not as impoverished and secluded as it has been traditionally pictured. He had some degree of economic security, he had influential and congenial friends, he took an interest in the political issues of his time, and he was not without adventures that came close to being matters of life and death. That he had made his way, despite excommunication and interdict, into the respect of his contemporaries, appears from the offer which came to him, in 1673, of the chair of philosophy at the University of Heidelberg; an offer couched in the most complimentary terms, and promising "the most perfect freedom in philosophizing, which His Highness feels assured you would not abuse by calling in question the established religion of the state." Spinoza replied characteristically:

> *Honored sir:* Had it ever been my wish to undertake the duties of a professor in any faculty, my desires would have been amply gratified in accepting the position which his Serene Highness the Prince Palatine does me the honor to offer me through you. The offer, too, is much enhanced in value in my eyes by the freedom of philosophizing attached to it. . . . But I do not know within what precise limits that the same liberty of philosophizing would have to be restrained, so that I would not seem to interfere with the established religion of the principality. . . . You see, therefore, honored sir, that I do not look for any higher worldly position than that which I now enjoy; and that for love of the quiet which I think I cannot otherwise secure, I must abstain from entering upon the career of a public teacher. . . .[20]

The closing chapter came in 1677. Spinoza was now only forty-four, but his friends knew that he had not many years left to him. He had come of consumptive parentage; and the comparative confinement in which he had lived, as well as the dust-laden atmosphere in which he had labored, were not calculated to correct this initial disadvantage. More and more he suffered from difficulty in breathing; year by year his sensitive lungs decayed. He reconciled himself to an early end, and feared only that the book which he had not dared to publish during his lifetime would be lost or destroyed after his death. He placed the MS. in a small writing desk, locked it, and gave the key to his host, asking him to transmit desk and key to Jan Rieuwertz, the Amsterdam publisher, when the inevitable should come.

On Sunday, February 20, the family with whom Spinoza lived went to church after receiving his assurance that he was not unusually ill. Dr.

[19]Willis, 67.   [20]Epistle 54.

Meyer alone remained with him. When they returned they found the philosopher lying dead in the arms of his friend. Many mourned him; for the simple folk had loved him as much for his gentleness as the learned had honored him for his wisdom. Philosophers and magistrates joined the people in following him to his final rest; and men of varied faiths met at his grave.

Nietzsche says somewhere that the last Christian died upon the cross. He had forgotten Spinoza.

II. THE TREATISE ON RELIGION AND THE STATE

Let us study his four books in the order in which he wrote them. The *Tractatus Theologico-Politicus* is perhaps the least interesting of them to us today, because the movement of higher criticism which Spinoza initiated has made into platitudes the propositions for which Spinoza risked his life. It is unwise of an author to prove his point too thoroughly; his conclusions pass into the currency of all educated minds, and his works no longer have that mystery about them which draws us ever on. So it has been with Voltaire; and so with Spinoza's treatise on religion and the state.

The essential principle of the book is that the language of the Bible is deliberately metaphorical or allegorical; not only because it partakes of the Oriental tendency to high literary color and ornament, and exaggerated descriptive expressions; but because, too, the prophets and the apostles, to convey their doctrine by arousing the imagination, were compelled to adapt themselves to the capacities and predispositions of the popular mind. "All Scripture was written primarily for an entire people, and secondarily for the whole human race; consequently its contents must necessarily be adapted, as far as possible, to the understanding of the masses."[21] "Scripture does not explain things by their secondary causes, but only narrates them in the order and style which has most power to move men, and especially uneducated men, to devotion. . . . Its object is not to convince the reason, but to attract and lay hold of the imagination."[22] Hence the abundant miracles and the repeated appearances of God. "The masses think that the power and providence of God are most clearly displayed by events that are extraordinary, and contrary to the conception which they have formed of nature. . . . They suppose, indeed, that God is inactive so long as nature works in her accustomed order; and *vice versa,* that the power of nature, and natural causes, are idle so long as God is acting; thus they imagine two powers distinct from one another, the power of God and the power of nature."[23] (Here enters the basic idea of Spinoza's philosophy—that God and the processes of nature are one.) Men love to believe that God breaks the natural order

[21]*Tractatus Theologico-Politicus,* ch. 5.   [22]*Ch. 6.*   [23]*Ibid.*

of events for them; so the Jews gave a miraculous interpretation of the lengthening of the day in order to impress others (and perhaps themselves) with the conviction that the Jews were the favorites of God: and similar incidents abound in the early history of every people.[24] Sober and literal statements do not move the soul; if Moses had said that it was merely the East wind (as we gather from a later passage) that cleared a path for them through the Red Sea, it would have made little impression on the minds of the masses he was leading. Again, the apostles resorted to miracle stories for the same reason that they resorted to parables; it was a necessary adaptation to the public mind. The greater influence of such men as compared with philosophers and scientists is largely attributable to the vivid and metaphorical forms of speech which the founders of religion, by the nature of their mission and their own emotional intensity, are driven to adopt.

Interpreted on this principle, the Bible, says Spinoza, contains nothing contrary to reason.[25] But interpreted literally, it is full of errors, contradictions, and obvious impossibilities—as that the Pentateuch was written by Moses. The more philosophical interpretation reveals, through the mist of allegory and poetry, the profound thought of great thinkers and leaders, and makes intelligible the persistence of the Bible and its immeasurable influence upon men. Both interpretations have a proper place and function: the people will always demand a religion phrased in imagery and haloed with the supernatural; if one such form of faith is destroyed they will create another. But the philosopher knows that God and nature are one being, acting by necessity and according to invariable law; it is this majestic Law which he will reverence and obey.[26] He knows that in the Scriptures "God is described as a law-giver or prince, and styled just, merciful, etc., merely in concession to the understanding of the people and their imperfect knowledge; that in reality God acts . . . by the necessity of his nature, and his decree . . . are eternal truths."[27]

Spinoza makes no separation between Old and New Testament, and looks upon the Jewish and the Christian religion as one, when popular hatred and misunderstandings are laid aside, and philosophical interpretation finds the hidden core and essence of the rival faiths. "I have often wondered that persons who make boast of professing the Christian religion—namely, love, joy, peace, temperance, and charity to all men—should quarrel with such rancorous animosity, and display daily toward one another such bitter hatred, that this, rather than the virtues which they profess, is the readiest criterion of their faith."[28] The Jews have survived chiefly because of Christian hatred of them; persecution gave them the unity and solidarity necessary for continued racial existence; without persecution they might have mingled and married with the peoples of Europe, and been engulfed in the majorities with which they

[24]*Ibid.*   [25]*Introd.*   [26]*Ch. 5.*   [27]*Ch. 4.*   [28]*Ch. 6.*

were everywhere surrounded. But there is no reason why the philosophic Jew and the philosophic Christian, when all nonsense is discarded, should not agree sufficiently in creed to live in peace and coöperation.

The first step toward this consummation, Spinoza thinks, would be a mutual understanding about Jesus. Let improbable dogmas be withdrawn, and the Jews would soon recognize in Jesus the greatest and noblest of the prophets. Spinoza does not accept the divinity of Christ, but he puts him first among men. "The eternal wisdom of God . . . has shown itself forth in all things, but chiefly in the mind of man, and most of all in Jesus Christ."[29] "Christ was sent to teach not only the Jews, but the whole human race"; hence "he accommodated himself to the comprehension of the people . . . and most often taught by parables."[30] He considers that the ethics of Jesus are almost synonymous with wisdom; in reverencing him one rises to "the intellectual love of God." So noble a figure, freed from the impediment of dogmas that lead only to divisions and disputes, would draw all men to him; and perhaps in his name a world torn with suicidal wars of tongue and sword might find a unity of faith and a possibility of brotherhood at last.

III. THE IMPROVEMENT OF THE INTELLECT

Opening Spinoza's next book, we come at the outset upon one of the gems of philosophic literature. Spinoza tells why he gave up everything for philosophy:

> After experience had taught me that all things which frequently take place in ordinary life are vain and futile, and when I saw that all the things I feared, and which feared me, had nothing good or bad in them save in so far as the mind was affected by them; I determined at last to inquire whether there was anything which might be truly good, and able to communicate its goodness, and by which the mind might be affected to the exclusion of all other things; I determined, I say, to inquire whether I might discover and attain the faculty of enjoying throughout eternity continual supreme happiness. . . . I could see the many advantages acquired from honor and riches, and that I should be debarred from acquiring these things if I wished seriously to investigate a new matter. . . . But the more one possesses of either of them, the more the pleasure is increased, and the more one is in consequence encouraged to increase them; whereas if at any time our hope is frustrated, there arises in us the deepest pain. Fame has also this great drawback, that if we pursue it we must direct our lives in such a way as to please the fancy of men, avoiding what they dislike and seeking what pleases them. . . . But the love towards a thing eternal and infinite alone feeds the mind with a pleasure secure from all pain. . . . The greatest good is the knowledge of the union which the mind has with the whole of nature. . . . The more the mind knows, the better it understands its forces and the

[29] Epistle 21.   [30] Ch. 4.

order of nature; the more it understands its forces or strength, the better it will be able to direct itself and lay down the rules for itself; and the more it understands the order of nature, the more easily it will be able to liberate itself from useless things; this is the whole method.

Only knowledge, then, is power and freedom; and the only permanent happiness is the pursuit of knowledge and the joy of understanding. Meanwhile, however, the philosopher must remain a man and a citizen; what shall be his mode of life during his pursuit of truth? Spinoza lays down a simple rule of conduct to which, so far as we know, his actual behavior thoroughly conformed:

> 1. To speak in a manner comprehensible to the people, and to do for them all things that do not prevent us from attaining our ends. . . . 2. To enjoy only such pleasures as are necessary for the preservation of health. 3. Finally, to seek only enough money . . . as is necessary for the maintenance of our life and health, and to comply with such customs as are not opposed to what we seek.[31]

But in setting out upon such a quest, the honest and clearheaded philosopher comes at once upon the problem: How do I know that my knowledge is knowledge, that my senses can be trusted in the material which they bring to my reason, and that my reason can be trusted with the conclusions which it derives from the material of sensation? Should we not examine the vehicle before abandoning ourselves to its directions? Should we not do all that we can to perfect it? "Before all things," says Spinoza, Baconianly, "a means must be devised for improving and clarifying the intellect."[32] We must distinguish carefully the various forms of knowledge, and trust only the best.

First, then, there is hearsay knowledge, by which, for example, I know the day of my birth. Second, vague experience, "empirical" knowledge in the derogatory sense, as when a physician knows a cure not by any scientific formulation of experimental tests, but by a "general impression" that it has "usually" worked. Third, immediate deduction, or knowledge reached by reasoning, as when I conclude to the immensity of the sun from seeing that in the case of other objects distance decreases the apparent size. This kind of knowledge is superior to the other two, but is yet precariously subject to sudden refutation by direct experience; so science for a hundred years reasoned its way to an "ether" which is now in high disfavor with the physicist élite. Hence the highest kind of knowledge is the fourth form, which comes by immediate deduction and direct perception, as when we see at once that 6 is the missing number in the proportion, 2:4::3:x; or as when we perceive that the whole is greater than the part. Spinoza believes that men versed in mathematics know most of Euclid in this intuitive way; but he admits ruefully that "the

[31] *De Emendatione,* Everyman edition. p. 231.   [32] *Ibid.*

things which I have been able to know by this knowledge so far have been very few."[33]

In the *Ethics* Spinoza reduces the first two forms of knowledge to one; and calls intuitive knowledge a perception of things *sub specie eternitatis* —in their eternal aspects and relations,—which gives in a phrase a definition of philosophy. *Scientia intuitiva,* therefore, tries to find behind things and events their laws and eternal relations. Hence Spinoza's very fundamental distinction (the basis of his entire system) between the "temporal order"—the "world" of things and incidents—and the "eternal order"— the world of laws and structure. Let us study this distinction carefully:

> It must be noted that I do not understand here by the series of causes and real entities a series of individual mutable things, but rather the series of fixed and eternal things. For it would be impossible for human weakness to follow up the series of individual mutable things, not only because their number surpasses all count, but because of the many circumstances, in one and the same thing, each of which may be the cause of the thing's existence. For indeed, the existence of particular things has no connection with their essence, and is not an eternal truth. However, there is no need that we should understand the series of individual mutable things, for their essence . . . is only to be found in fixed and eternal things, and from the laws inscribed in those things as their true codes, according to which all individual things are made and arranged; nay, these individual and mutable things depend so intimately and essentially on these fixed ones that without them they can neither exist nor be conceived.[34]

If we will keep this passage in mind as we study Spinoza's masterpiece, it will itself be clarified, and much in the *Ethics* that is discouragingly complex will unravel itself into simplicity and understanding.

IV. THE ETHICS

The most precious production in modern philosophy is cast into geometrical form, to make the thought Euclideanly clear; but the result is a laconic obscurity in which every line requires a Talmud of commentary. The Scholastics had formulated their thought so, but never so pithily; and they had been helped to clarity by their fore-ordained conclusions. Descartes had suggested that philosophy could not be exact until it expressed itself in the forms of mathematics; but he had never grappled with his own ideal. Spinoza came to the suggestion with a mind trained in mathematics as the very basis of all rigorous scientific pro-

[33]*Ibid.,* P. 233.

[34]P. 259. Cf. Bacon, *Novum Organum,* II, 2: "For although nothing exists in nature except individual bodies, exhibiting clear individual effects according to particular laws; yet, in each branch of learning, those very laws—their investigation, discovery and development—are the foundation both of theory and of practice." Fundamentally, all philosophers agree.

cedure, and impressed with the achievements of Copernicus, Kepler and Galileo. To our more loosely textured minds the result is an exhausting concentration of both matter and form; and we are tempted to console ourselves by denouncing this philosophic geometry as an artificial chess-game of thought in which axioms, definitions, theorems and proofs are manipulated like kings and bishops, knights and pawns; a logical solitaire invented to solace Spinoza's loneliness. Order is against the grain of our minds; we prefer to follow the straggling lines of fantasy, and to weave our philosophy precariously out of our dreams. But Spinoza had but one compelling desire—to reduce the intolerable chaos of the world to unity and order. He had the northern hunger for truth rather than the southern lust for beauty; the artist in him was purely an architect, building a system of thought to perfect symmetry and form.

Again, the modern student will stumble and grumble over the terminology of Spinoza. Writing in Latin, he was compelled to express his essentially modern thought in medieval and scholastic terms; there was no other language of philosophy which would then have been understood. So he uses the term *substance* where we should write *reality* or *essence; perfect* where we should write *complete; ideal* for our *object; objectively* for *subjectively,* and *formally* for *objectively.* These are hurdles in the race, which will deter the weakling but will stimulate the strong.

In short, Spinoza is not to be read, he is to be studied; you must approach him as you would approach Euclid, recognizing that in these brief two hundred pages a man has written down his lifetime's thought with stoic sculptury of everything superfluous. Do not think to find its core by running over it rapidly; never in a work of philosophy was there so little that could be skipped without loss. Every part depends upon preceding parts; some obvious and apparently needless proposition turns out to be the cornerstone of an imposing development of logic. You will not understand any important section thoroughly till you have read and pondered the whole; though one need not say, with Jacobi's enthusiastic exaggeration, that "no one has understood Spinoza to whom a single line of the Ethics remains obscure." "Here, doubtless," says Spinoza, in the second part of his book, "the reader will become confused, and will recollect many things which will bring him to a standstill; and therefore I pray him to proceed gently with me and form no judgment concerning these things until he shall have read all."[85] Read the book not all at once, but in small portions at many sittings. And having finished it, consider that you have but begun to understand it. Read then some commentary, like Pollock's *Spinoza,* or Martineau's *Study of Spinoza;* or, better, both. Finally, read the *Ethics* again; it will be a new book to you. When you have finished it a second time you will remain forever a lover of philosophy.

*Part II, proposition 11, note.

1. NATURE AND GOD

Page one plunges us at once into the maelstrom of metaphysics. Our modern hard-headed (or is it soft-headed?) abhorrence of metaphysics captures us, and for a moment we wish we were anywhere except in Spinoza. But then metaphysics, as William James said, is nothing but an attempt to think things out clearly to their ultimate significance, to find their substantial essence in the scheme of reality,—or, as Spinoza puts it, their essential substance; and thereby to unify all truth and reach that "highest of all generalizations" which, even to the practical Englishman,[36] constitutes philosophy. Science itself, which so superciliously scorns metaphysics, assumes a metaphysic in its every thought. It happens that the metaphysic which it assumes is the metaphysic of Spinoza.

There are three pivotal terms in Spinoza's system: *substance, attribute,* and *mode.* Attribute we put aside temporarily, for simplicity's sake. A mode is any individual thing or event, any particular form or shape, which reality transiently assumes; you, your body, your thoughts, your group, your species, your planet, are modes; all these are forms, modes, almost literally fashions, of some eternal and invariable reality lying behind and beneath them.

What is this underlying reality? Spinoza calls it *substance,* as literally that which stands beneath. Eight generations have fought voluminous battles over the meaning of this term; we must not be discouraged if we fail to resolve the matter in a paragraph. One error we should guard against: *substance* does not mean the constituent material of anything, as when we speak of wood as the substance of a chair. We approach Spinoza's use of the word when we speak of "the substance of his remarks." If we go back to the Scholastic philosophers from whom Spinoza took the term, we find that they used it as a translation of the Greek *ousia,* which is the present participle of *einai,* to be, and indicates the inner being or essence. Substance then is that which is (Spinoza had not forgotten the impressive "I am who am" of *Genesis*); that which eternally and unchangeably is, and of which everything else must be a transient form or mode. If now we compare this division of the world into substance and modes with its division, in *The Improvement of the Intellect,* into the eternal order of *laws* and invariable relations on the one hand, and the temporal order of time-begotten and death-destined *things* on the other, we are impelled to the conclusion that Spinoza means by substance here very nearly what he meant by the eternal order there. Let us provisionally take it as one element in the term substance, then, that it betokens the very structure of existence, underlying all events and things, and constituting the essence of the world.

[36]Spencer, *First Principles,* Part II, ch. 1.

But further Spinoza identifies substance with nature and God. After the manner of the Scholastics, he conceives nature under a double aspect: as active and vital process, which Spinoza calls *natura naturans*—nature begetting, the *élan vital* and creative evolution of Bergson; and as the passive product of this process, *natura naturata*—nature begotten, the material and contents of nature, its woods and winds and waters, its hills and fields and myriad external forms. It is in the latter sense that he denies, and in the former sense that he affirms, the identity of nature and substance and God. Substance and modes, the eternal order and the temporal order, active nature and passive nature, God and the world, —all these are for Spinoza coincident and synonymous dichotomies; each divides the universe into essence and incident. That substance is insubstantial, that it is form and not matter, that it has nothing to do with that mongrel and neuter composite of matter and thought which some interpreters have supposed it to be, stands out clearly enough from this identification of substance with creative but not with passive or material nature. A passage from Spinoza's correspondence may help us:

> I take a totally different view of God and Nature from that which the later Christians usually entertain, for I hold that God is the immanent, and not the extraneous, cause of all things. I say, All is in God; all lives and moves in God. And this I maintain with the Apostle Paul, and perhaps with every one of the philosophers of antiquity, although in a way other than theirs. I might even venture to say that my view is the same as that entertained by the Hebrews of old, if so much may be inferred from certain traditions, greatly altered or falsified though they be. It is however a complete mistake on the part of those who say that my purpose . . . is to show that God and Nature, under which last term they understand a certain mass of corporeal matter, are one and the same. I had no such intention.[37]

Again, in the *Treatise on Religion and the State,* he writes: "By the help of God I mean the fixed and unchangeable order of nature, or the *chain* of natural events";[38] the universal laws of nature and the eternal decrees of God are one and the same thing. "From the infinite nature of God all things . . . follow by the same necessity, and in the same way, as it follows from the nature of a triangle, from eternity to eternity, that its three angles are equal to two right angles."[39] What the laws of the circle are to all circles, God is to the world. Like substance, God is the causal chain or process,[40] the underlying condition of all things,[41] the law and structure of the world.[42] This concrete universe of modes and things is to God as a bridge is to its design, its structure, and the laws of mathematics and mechanics according to which it is built; these are the sustain-

[37]Epistle 21.   [38]Ch. 3.   [39]*Ethics,* I, 17, note.
[40]Höffding, *History of Modern Philosophy,* vol. i.
[41]Martineau, *Study of Spinoza;* London, 1822, p. 171.
[42]Prof. Woodbridge.

ing basis, the underlying condition, the substance, of the bridge; without them it would fall. And like the bridge, the world itself is sustained by its structure and its laws; it is upheld in the hand of God.

The will of God and the laws of nature being one and the same reality diversely phrased,[43] it follows that all events are the mechanical operation of invariable laws, and not the whim of an irresponsible autocrat seated in the stars. The mechanism which Descartes saw in matter and body alone, Spinoza sees in God and mind as well. It is a world of determinism, not of design. Because we act for conscious ends, we suppose that all processes have such ends in view; and because we are human we suppose that all events lead up to man and are designed to subserve his needs. But this is an anthropocentric delusion, like so much of our thinking.[44] The root of the greatest errors in philosophy lies in projecting our human purposes, criteria and preferences into the objective universe. Hence our "problem of evil": we strive to reconcile the ills of life with the goodness of God, forgetting the lesson taught to Job, that God is beyond our little good and evil. *Good* and *bad* are relative to human and often individual tastes and ends, and have no validity for a universe in which individuals are ephemera, and in which the Moving Finger writes even the history of the race in water.

> Whenever, then, anything in nature seems to us ridiculous, absurd or evil, it is because we have but a partial knowledge of things, and are in the main ignorant of the order and coherence of nature as a whole, and because we want everything to be arranged according to the dictates of our own reason; although in fact, what our reason pronounces bad is not bad as regards the order and laws of universal nature, but only as regards the laws of our own nature taken separately.[45] . . . As for the terms *good* and *bad,* they indicate nothing positive considered in themselves. . . . For one and the same thing can at the same time be good, bad, and indifferent. For example, music is good to the melancholy, bad to mourners, and indifferent to the dead.[46]

Bad and good are prejudices which the eternal reality cannot recognize; "it is right that the world should illustrate the full nature of the infinite, and not merely the particular ideals of man."[47] And as with good and bad, so with the ugly and the beautiful; these too are subjective and personal terms, which, flung at the universe, will be returned to the sender unhonored. "I would warn you that I do not attribute to nature either beauty or deformity, order or confusion. Only in relation to our imagination can things be called beautiful or ugly, well-ordered or confused."[48] "For example, if motion which the nerves receive by means of the eyes from objects before us is conducive of health, those objects are called

[43]*T. T-P.,* ch. 3.   [44]*Ethics,* Part I, Appendix.
[45]*Tractatus Politicus,* ch. 2.   [46]*Ethics,* IV. pref.
[47]Santayana, Introduction to the *Ethics,* Everyman ed., p. xx.
[48]Epistle 15, ed. Pollock.

beautiful; if it is not, those objects are called ugly."[49] In such passages Spinoza passes beyond Plato, who thought that his esthetic judgments must be the laws of creation and the eternal decrees of God.

Is God a person? Not in any human sense of this word. Spinoza notices "the popular belief which still pictures God as of the male, not of the female sex";[50] and he is gallant enough to reject a conception which mirrored the earthly subordination of woman to man. To a correspondent who objected to his impersonal conception of Deity, Spinoza writes in terms reminiscent of the old Greek sceptic Xenophanes:

> When you say that if I allow not in God the operations of seeing, hearing, observing, willing, and the like . . . you know not what sort of God mine is, I thence conjecture that you believe there is no greater perfection than such as can be explained by the attributes aforesaid. I do not wonder at it; for I believe that a triangle, if it could speak, would in like manner say that God is eminently triangular, and a circle that the divine nature is eminently circular; and thus would every one ascribe his own attributes to God.[51]

Finally, "neither intellect nor will pertains to the nature of God,"[52] in the usual sense in which these human qualities are attributed to the Deity; but rather the will of God is the sum of all causes and all laws, and the intellect of God is the sum of all mind. "The mind of God," as Spinoza conceives it, "is all the mentality that is scattered over space and time, the diffused consciousness that animates the world."[53] "All things, in however diverse degree, are animated."[54] Life or mind is one phase or aspect of everything that we know, as material extension or body is another; these are the two phases or attributes (as Spinoza calls them) through which we perceive the operation of substance or God; in this sense God—the universal process and eternal reality behind the flux of things—may be said to have both a mind and a body. Neither mind nor matter is God; but the mental processes and the molecular processes which constitute the double history of the world—these, and their causes and their laws, are God.

2. MATTER AND MIND

But what is mind, and what is matter? Is the mind material, as some unimaginative people suppose; or is the body merely an idea, as some imaginative people suppose? Is the mental process the cause, or the effect, of the cerebral process?—or are they, as Malebranche taught, unrelated and independent, and only providentially parallel?

Neither is mind material, answers Spinoza, nor is matter mental; neither is the brain-process the cause, nor is it the effect, of thought; nor

"Ethics, I, App. "Epistle 58, ed. Willis. "Epistle 60, ed. Willis.
"Ethics, I, 17, note. "Santayana, loc. cit., p. x. "Ethics, II, 13, note.

are the two processes independent and parallel. For there are not two processes, and there are not two entities; there is but one process, seen now inwardly as thought, and now outwardly as motion; there is but one entity, seen now inwardly as mind, now outwardly as matter, but in reality an inextricable mixture and unity of both. Mind and body do not act upon each other, because they are not other, they are one. "The body cannot determine the mind to think; nor the mind determine the body to remain in motion or at rest, or in any other state," for the simple reason that "the decision of the mind, and the desire and determination of the body . . . are one and the same thing."[55] And all the world is unifiedly double in this way; wherever there is an external "material" process, it is but one side or aspect of the real process, which to a fuller view would be seen to include as well an internal process correlative, in however differ- ent a degree, with the mental process which we see within ourselves. The inward and "mental" process corresponds at every stage with the external and "material" process; "the order and connection of ideas is the same as the order and connection of things."[56] "Thinking substance and extended substance are one and the same thing, comprehended now through this, now through that, attribute" or aspect. "Certain of the Jews seem to have perceived this, though confusedly, for they said that God and his intellect, and the things conceived by his intellect, were one and the same thing."[57]

If "mind" be taken in a large sense to correspond with the nervous system in all its ramifications, then every change in the "body" will be ac- companied by—or, better, form a whole with—a correlative change in the "mind." "Just as thoughts and mental processes are connected and ar- ranged in the mind, so in the body its modifications, and the modifications of things" affecting the body through sensations, "are arranged according to their order";[58] and "nothing can happen to the body which is not per- ceived by the mind," and consciously or unconsciously felt.[59] Just as the emotion as felt is part of a whole, of which changes in the circulatory and respiratory and digestive systems are the basis; so an idea is a part, along with "bodily" changes, of one complex organic process; even the infinitesimal subtleties of mathematical reflection have their correlate in the body. (Have not the "behaviorists" proposed to detect a man's thoughts by recording those involuntary vibrations of the vocal cords that seem to accompany all thinking?)

After so trying to melt away the distinction between body and mind, Spinoza goes on to reduce to a question of degree the difference between intellect and will. There are no "faculties" in the mind, no separate entities called intellect or will, much less imagination or memory; the mind is not an agency that deals with ideas, but it is the ideas themselves in their process and concatenation.[60] *Intellect* is merely an abstract and

[55]*Ethics*, III, 2.   [56]II, 17.   [57]*Ibid., note.*   [58]V, 1.   [59]II, 12, 13.
[60]For Spinoza's anticipation of the association theory cf. II, 18, note.

short-hand term for a series of ideas; and *will* an abstract term for a series of actions or volitions: "the intellect and the will are related to this or that idea or volition as rockiness to this or that rock."[61] Finally, "will and intellect are one and the same thing;[62] for a volition is merely an idea which, by richness of associations (or perhaps through the absence of competitive ideas), has remained long enough in consciousness to pass over into action. Every idea becomes an action unless stopped in the transition by a different idea; the idea is itself the first stage of a unified organic process of which external action is the completion.

What is often called will, as the impulsive force which determines the duration of an idea in consciousness, should be called desire,—which "is the very essence of man."[63] Desire is an appetite or instinct of which we are conscious; but instincts need not always operate through conscious desire.[64] Behind the instincts is the vague and varied effort for self-preservation (*conatus sese preservandi*); Spinoza sees this in all human and even infra-human activity, just as Schopenhauer and Nietzsche were to see the will to live or the will to power everywhere. Philosophers seldom disagree.

"Everything, in so far as it is in itself, endeavors to persist in its own being; and the endeavor wherewith a thing seeks to persist in its own being is nothing else than the actual essence of that thing";[65] the power whereby a thing persists is the core and essence of its being. Every instinct is a device developed by nature to preserve the individual (or, as our solitary bachelor fails to add, the species or the group.) Pleasure and pain are the satisfaction or the hindrance of an instinct; they are not the causes of our desires, but their results; we do not desire things because they give us pleasure; but they give us pleasure because we desire them;[66] and we desire them because we must.

There is, consequently, no free will; the necessities of survival determine instinct, instinct determines desire, and desire determines thought and action. "The decisions of the mind are nothing save desires, which vary according to various dispositions."[67] "There is in the mind no absolute or free will; but the mind is determined in willing this or that by a cause which is determined in its turn by another cause, and this by another, and so on to infinity."[68] "Men think themselves free because they are conscious of their volitions and desires, but are ignorant of the causes by which they are led to wish and desire."[69] Spinoza compares the feeling of free will to a stone's thinking, as it travels through space, that it determines its own trajectory and selects the place and time of its fall.[70]

---

[61]II, 48, note. [62]II, 49, corollary. [63]IV, 18.
[64]Spinoza is alive to the power of the "unconscious," as seen in somnambulism. (II, 2, note); and notes the phenomena of double personality (IV, 39, note).
[65]III, 6, 7. [66]III, 57. [67]III, 2, note.
[68]II, 48. [69]I, App. [70]Epistle 58, ed. Pollock.

Since human actions obey laws as fixed as those of geometry, psychology should be studied in geometrical form, and with mathematical objectivity. "I will write about human beings as though I were concerned with lines and planes and solids."[71] "I have labored carefully not to mock, lament, or execrate, but to understand, human actions; and to this end I have looked upon passions . . . not as vices of human nature, but as properties just as pertinent to it as are heat, cold, storm, thunder and the like to the nature of the atmosphere."[72] It is this impartiality of approach that gives to Spinoza's study of human nature such superiority that Froude called it "the most complete by far which has ever been made by any moral philosopher."[73] Taine knew no better way of praising Beyle's analysis than to compare it with Spinoza's; while Johannes Müller, coming to the subject of the instincts and emotions, wrote: "With regard to the relations of the passions to one another apart from their physiological conditions, it is impossible to give any better account than that which Spinoza has laid down with unsurpassed mastery,"—and the famous physiologist, with the modesty which usually accompanies real greatness, went on to quote *in extenso* the third book of the *Ethics*. It is through that analysis of human conduct that Spinoza approaches at last the problems which give the title to his masterpiece.

3. INTELLIGENCE AND MORALS

Ultimately there are but three systems of ethics, three conceptions of the ideal character and the moral life. One is that of Buddha and Jesus, which stresses the feminine virtues, considers all men to be equally precious, resists evil only by returning good, identifies virtue with love, and inclines in politics to unlimited democracy. Another is the ethic of Machiavelli and Nietzsche, which stresses the masculine virtues, accepts the inequality of men, relishes the risks of combat and conquest and rule, identifies virtue with power, and exalts an hereditary aristocracy. A third, the ethic of Socrates, Plato, and Aristotle, denies the universal applicability of either the feminine or the masculine virtues; considers that only the informed and mature mind can judge, according to diverse circumstance, when love should rule, and when power; identifies virtue, therefore, with intelligence; and advocates a varying mixture of aristocracy and democracy in government. It is the distinction of Spinoza that his ethic unconsciously reconciles these apparently hostile philosophies, weaves them into a harmonious unity, and gives us in consequence a system of morals which is the supreme achievement of modern thought.

He begins by making happiness the goal of conduct; and he defines happiness very simply as the presence of pleasure and the absence of pain. But pleasure and pain are relative, not absolute; and they are not states

[71] *T. T-P.,* Introd.   [72] *Ibid.,* ch. 1.   [73] *Short Studies.* I, 308.

but transitions. "Pleasure is man's transition from a lesser state of perfection" (i. e., completeness, or fulfillment) "to a greater." "Joy consists
in this, that one's power is increased."[74] "Pain is man's transition from a
greater state of perfection to a lesser. I say transition; for pleasure is
not perfection itself: if a man were born with the perfection to which he
passes he would be without . . . the emotion of pleasure. And the contrary of this makes it still more apparent."[75] All passions are passages, all
emotions are motions, towards or from completeness and power.

"By emotion (*affectus*) I understand the modifications of the body by
which the power of action in the body is increased or diminished, aided
or restrained, and at the same time the ideas of these modifications."[76]
(This theory of emotion is usually credited to James and Lange; it is here
formulated more precisely than by either of these psychologists, and accords remarkably with the findings of Professor Cannon.) A passion or
an emotion is bad or good not in itself, but only as it decreases or enhances our power. "By virtue and power I mean the same thing";[77] a
virtue is a power of acting, a form of ability;[78] "the more a man can preserve his being and seek what is useful to him, the greater is his virtue."[79]
Spinoza does not ask a man to sacrifice himself to another's good; he is
more lenient than nature. He thinks that egoism is a necessary corollary
of the supreme instinct of self-preservation; "no one ever neglects anything which he judges to be good, except with the hope of gaining a
greater good."[80] This seems to Spinoza perfectly reasonable. "Since
reason demands nothing against nature, it concedes that each man must
love himself, and seek what is useful to him, and desire whatever leads
him truly to a greater state of perfection; and that each man should
endeavor to preserve his being so far as in him lies."[81] So he builds his
ethic not on altruism and the natural goodness of man, like utopian re-
formers; nor on selfishness and the natural wickedness of man, like cynical
conservatives, but on what he considers to be an inevitable and justifiable
egoism. A system of morals that teaches a man to be weak is worthless;
"the foundation of virtue is no other than the effort to maintain one's
being; and man's happiness consists in the power of so doing."[82]

Like Nietzsche, Spinoza has not much use for humility;[83] it is either
the hypocrisy of a schemer or the timidity of a slave; it implies the absence of power—whereas to Spinoza all virtues are forms of ability and
power. So is remorse a defect rather than a virtue: "he who repents is
twice unhappy and doubly weak."[84] But he does not spend so much time
as Nietzsche in inveighing against humility; for "humility is very rare";[85]

---

[74]Cf. Nietzsche: "What is happiness? The feeling that power increases that
resistance is overcome."—*Antichrist*, sect. 2.
[75]III, App.   [77]III, def. 3.   [78]IV, def. 8.   [76]III, 55, cor. 2.
[79]IV, 20.   [80]*T. T.-P.*, ch. 16.   [81]IV, 18 note.   [82]*Ibid.*
[83]III, 55.   [84]IV, 54.   [85]III, App., def. 29.

and as Cicero said, even the philosophers who write books in its praise take care to put their names on the title-page. "One who despises himself is the nearest to a proud man," says Spinoza (putting in a sentence a pet theory of the psychoanalysts, that every conscious virtue is an effort to conceal or correct a secret vice). And whereas Spinoza dislikes humility he admires modesty, and objects to a pride that is not "tenoned and mortised" in deeds. Conceit makes men a nuisance to one another: "the conceited man relates only his own great deeds, and only the evil ones of others";[86] he delights in the presence of his inferiors, who will gape at his perfections and exploits; and becomes at last the victim of those who praise him most; for "none are more taken in by flattery than the proud."[87]

So far our gentle philosopher offers us a rather Spartan ethic; but he strikes in other passages a softer tone. He marvels at the amount of envy, recrimination, mutual belittlement, and even hatred, which agitates and separates men; and sees no remedy for our social ills except in the elimination of these and similar emotions. He believes it is a simple matter to show that hatred, perhaps because it trembles on the verge of love, can be more easily overcome by love than by reciprocated hate. For hatred is fed on the feeling that it is returned; whereas "he who believes himself to be loved by one whom he hates is a prey to the conflicting emotions of hatred and love, since (as Spinoza perhaps too optimistically believes) love tends to beget love; so that his hatred disintegrates and loses force. To hate is to acknowledge our inferiority and our fear; we do not hate a foe whom we are confident we can overcome. "He who wishes to revenge injuries by reciprocal hatred will live in misery. But he who endeavors to drive away hatred by means of love, fights with pleasure and confidence; he resists equally one or many men, and scarcely needs at all the help of fortune. Those whom he conquers yield joyfully."[88] "Minds are conquered not by arms but by greatness of soul."[89] In such passages Spinoza sees something of the light which shone on the hills of Galilee.

But the essence of his ethic is rather Greek than Christian. "The endeavor to understand is the first and only basis of virtue"[90]—nothing could be more simply and thoroughly Socratic. For "we are tossed about by external causes in many ways, and like waves driven by contrary winds, we waver and are unconscious of the issue and our fate."[91] We think we are most ourselves when we are most passionate, whereas it is then we are most passive, caught in some ancestral torrent of impulse or feeling, and swept on to a precipitate reaction which meets only part of the situation because without thought only part of a situation can be perceived. A passion is an "inadequate idea"; thought is response delayed till every vital angle of a problem has aroused a correlative reaction, inherited or

[86]*Ibid.;* and III, 55, note.   [87]IV, App., def. 21.   [88]IV, 45.
[90]IV, App. 11.   [91]IV, 26.   [89]III, 59, note.

acquired; only so is the idea adequate, the response all that it can be.[92] The instincts are magnificent as a driving force, but dangerous as guides; for by what we may call the individualism of the instincts, each of them seeks its own fulfilment, regardless of the good of the whole personality. What havoc has come to men, for example, from uncontrolled greed, pugnacity, or lust, till such men have become but the appendages of the instinct that has mastered them. "The emotions by which we are daily assailed have reference rather to some part of the body which is affected beyond the others, and so the emotions as a rule are in excess, and detain the mind in the contemplation of one object so that it cannot think of others."[93] But "desire that arises from pleasure or pain which has reference to one or certain parts of the body has no advantage to man as a whole."[94] To be ourselves we must complete ourselves.

All this is, of course, the old philosophic distinction between reason and passion; but Spinoza adds vitally to Socrates and the Stoics. He knows that as passion without reason is blind, reason without passion is dead. "An emotion can neither be hindered nor removed except by a contrary and stronger emotion."[95] Instead of uselessly opposing reason to passion—a contest in which the more deeply rooted and ancestral element usually wins—he opposes reasonless passions to passions coördinated by reason, put into place by the total perspective of the situation. Thought should not lack the heat of desire, nor desire the light of thought. "A passion ceases to be a passion as soon as we form a clear and distinct idea of it, and the mind is subject to passions in proportion to the number of adequate ideas which it has."[96] "All appetites are passions only so far as they arise from inadequate ideas; they are virtues . . . when generated by adequate ideas";[97] all intelligent behavior—i. e., all reaction which meets the total situation—is virtuous action; and in the end there is no virtue but intelligence.

Spinoza's ethics flows from his metaphysics: just as reason there lay in the perception of law in the chaotic flux of things, so here it lies in the establishment of law in the chaotic flux of desires; there it lay in seeing, here it lies in acting, sub specie eternitatis—under the form of eternity; in making perception and action fit the eternal perspective of the whole. Thought helps us to this larger view because it is aided by imagination, which presents to consciousness those distant effects of present actions

---

[92]To phrase it in later terms: reflex action is a local response to a local stimulus; instinctive action is a partial response to part of a situation; reason is total response to the whole situation.

[93]IV, 44, note.   [94]IV, 60.   [95]IV, 7, 14.   [96]V, 3.

[97]Notice the resemblance between the last two quotations and the psychoanalytic doctrine that desires are "complexes" only so long as we are not aware of the precise causes of these desires, and that the first element in treatment is therefore an attempt to bring the desire and its causes to consciousness—to form "adequate ideas" of it and them.

which could have no play upon reaction if reaction were thoughtlessly immediate. The great obstacle to intelligent behavior is the superior vividness of present sensations as compared with those projected memories which we call imagination. "In so far as the mind conceives a thing according to the dictates of reason, it will be equally affected whether the idea be of anything present, past, or future."[98] By imagination and reason we turn experience into foresight; we become the creators of our future, and cease to be the slaves of our past.

So we achieve the only freedom possible to man. The passivity of passion is "human bondage," the action of reason is human liberty. Freedom is not from causal law or process, but from partial passion or impulse; and freedom not from passion, but from uncoördinated and uncompleted passion. We are free only where we know.[99] To be a superman is to be free not from the restraints of social justice and amenity, but from the individualism of the instincts. With this completeness and integrity comes the equanimity of the wise man; not the aristocratic self-complaceny of Aristotle's hero, much less the supercilious superiority of Nietzsche's ideal, but a more comradely poise and peace of mind. "Men who are good by reason—i. e., men who, under the guidance of reason, seek what is useful to them—desire nothing for themselves which they do not also desire for the rest of mankind."[100] To be great is not to be placed above humanity, ruling others; but to stand above the partialities and futilities of uninformed desire, and to rule one's self.

This is a nobler freedom than that which men call free will; for the will is not free, and perhaps there is no "will." And let no one suppose that because he is no longer "free," he is no longer morally responsible for his behavior and the structure of his life. Precisely because men's actions are determined by their memories, society must for its protection form its citizens through their hopes and fears into some measure of social order and coöperation. All education presupposes determinism, and pours into the open mind of youth a store of prohibitions which are expected to participate in determining conduct. "The evil which ensues from evil deeds is not therefore less to be feared because it comes of necessity; whether our actions are free or not, our motives still are hope and fear. Therefore the assertion is false that I would leave no room for precepts and commands."[101] On the contrary, determinism makes for a better moral life: it teaches us not to despise or ridicule any one, or be angry with any one;[102] men are "not guilty"; and though we punish

---

[98]IV, 62.

[99]Cf. Professor Dewey: "A physician or engineer is free in his thought and his action in the degree in which he knows what he deals with. Possibly we find here the key to any freedom."—*Human Nature and Conduct;* New York, 1922; p. 303.

[100]IV, 18, note; cf. Whitman: "By God, I will not have anything that all cannot have their counterpart of on the same terms."

[101]Epistle 43. [102]II, end.

miscreants, it will be without hate; we forgive them because they know not what they do.

Above all, determinism fortifies us to expect and to bear both faces of fortune with an equal mind; we remember that all things follow by the eternal decrees of God. Perhaps even it will teach us the "intellectual love of God," whereby we shall accept the laws of nature gladly, and find our fulfillment within her limitations. He who sees all things as determined cannot complain, though he may resist; for he "perceives things under a certain species of eternity,"[103] and he understands that his mischances are not chances in the total scheme; that they find some justification in the eternal sequence and structure of the world. So minded, he rises from the fitful pleasures of passion to the high serenity of contemplation which sees all things as parts of an eternal order and development; he learns to smile in the face of the inevitable, and "whether he comes into his own now, or in a thousand years, he sits content."[104] He learns the old lesson that God is no capricious personality absorbed in the private affairs of his devotees, but the invariable sustaining order of the universe. Plato words the same conception beautifully in the *Republic*: "He whose mind is fixed upon true being has no time to look down upon the little affairs of men, or to be filled with jealousy and enmity in the struggle against them; his eye is ever directed towards fixed and immutable principles, which he sees neither injuring nor injured by one another, but all in order moving according to reason; these he imitates, and to these he would, as far as he can, conform himself."[105] "That which is necessary," says Nietzsche, "does not offend me. *Amor fati*"— love of late—"is the core of my nature."[106] Or Keats:

> *To bear all naked truths,*
> *And to envisage circumstance, all calm:*
> *That is the top of sovereignty.*[107]

Such a philosophy teaches us to say Yea to life, and even to death—"a free man thinks of nothing less than of death; and his wisdom is a meditation not on death but on life."[108] It calms our fretted egos with its large perspective; it reconciles us to the limitations within which our purposes must be circumscribed. It may lead to resignation and an Orientally supine passivity; but it is also the indispensable basis of all wisdom and all strength.

4. RELIGION AND IMMORTALITY

After all, as we perceive, Spinoza's philosophy was an attempt to love even a world in which he was outcast and alone; again like Job, he typified his people, and asked how it could be that even the just man, like the

---

[103]II, 44, cor. 2.   [104]Whitman.   [105]§500.
[106]*Ecce Homo*, p. 130. It was rather Nietzsche's hope than his attainment.
[107]*Hyperion*, II, 203.   [108]*Ethics*, IV, 67.

chosen people, should suffer persecution and exile and every desolation. For a time the conception of the world as a process of impersonal and invariable law soothed and sufficed him; but in the end his essentially religious spirit turned this mute process into something almost lovable. He tried to merge his own desires with the universal order of things, to become an almost indistinguishable part of nature. "The greatest good is the knowledge of the union which the mind has with the whole nature."[109] Indeed, our individual separateness is in a sense illusory; we are parts of the great stream of law and cause, parts of God; we are the flitting forms of a being greater than ourselves, and endless while we die. Our bodies are cells in the body of the race, our race is an incident in the drama of life; our minds are the fitful flashes of an eternal light. "Our mind, in so far as it understands, is an eternal mode of thinking, which is determined by another mode of thinking, and this one again by another, and so on to infinity; so that they all constitute at the same time the eternal and infinite intellect of God."[110] In this pantheistic merging of the individual with the All, the Orient speaks again: we hear the echo of Omar, who "never called the One two," and of the old Hindu poem: "Know in thyself and All one self-same soul; banish the dream that sunders part from whole."[111] "Sometimes," said Thoreau, "as I drift idly on Walden Pond, I cease to live and begin to be."

As such parts of such a whole we are immortal. "The human mind cannot be absolutely destroyed with the human body, but there is some part of it which remains eternal."[112] This is the part that conceives things *sub specie eternitatis;* the more we so conceive things, the more eternal our thought is. Spinoza is even more than usually obscure here; and after endless controversy among interpreters his language yet speaks differently to different minds. Sometimes one imagines him to mean George Eliot's immortality by repute, whereby that which is most rational and beautiful in our thought and our lives survives us to have an almost timeless efficacy down the years. Sometimes again Spinoza seems to have in mind a personal and individual immortality; and it may be that as death loomed up so prematurely in his path he yearned to console himself with this hope that springs eternally in the human breast. Yet he insistently differentiates eternity from everlastingness: "If we pay attention to the common opinion of men, we shall see that they are conscious of the eternity of their minds; but they confuse eternity with duration, and attribute it to imagination or memory, which they believe will remain after death."[113] But like Aristotle, Spinoza, though talking of immortality, denies the survival of personal memory. "The mind can neither imagine nor recollect anything save while in the body."[114] Nor does he believe

[109]*De Emendatione*, p. 230.   [110]*Ethics*, V, 40, note.
[111]In Pollock, 169, 145.   [112]*Ethics*, V, 23.
[113]V, 34, note.   [114]V, 21.

in heavenly rewards: "Those are far astray from a true estimate of virtue who expect for their virtue, as if it were the greatest slavery, that God will adorn them with the greatest rewards; as if virtue and the serving of God were not happiness itself and the greatest liberty."[115] "Blessedness," reads the last proposition of Spinoza's book, "is not the reward of virtue, but virtue itself." And perhaps in the like manner, immortality is not the reward of clear thinking, it is clear thought itself, as it carries up the past into the present and reaches out into the future, so overcoming the limits and narrowness of time, and catching the perspective that remains eternally behind the kaleidoscope of change; such thought is immortal because every truth is a permanent creation, part of the eternal acquisition of man, influencing him endlessly.

With this solemn and hopeful note the *Ethics* ends. Seldom has one book enclosed so much thought, and fathered so much commentary, while yet remaining so bloody a battleground for hostile interpretations. Its metaphysic may be faulty, its psychology imperfect, its theology unsatisfactory and obscure; but of the soul of the book, its spirit and essence, no man who has read it will speak otherwise than reverently. In the concluding paragraph that essential spirit shines forth in simple eloquence:

> Thus I have completed all I wished to show concerning the power of the mind over emotions, or the freedom of the mind. From which it is clear how much a wise man is in front of and how stronger he is than an ignorant one, who is guided by lust alone. For an ignorant man, besides being agitated in many ways by external causes, never enjoys one true satisfaction of the mind: he lives, moreover, almost unconscious of himself, God, and things, and as soon as he ceases to be passive, ceases to be. On the contrary the wise man, in so far as he is considered as such, is scarcely moved in spirit; he is conscious of himself, of God, and things by a certain eternal necessity; he never ceases to be, and always enjoys satisfaction of mind. If the road I have shown to lead to this is very difficult, it can yet be discovered. And clearly it must be very hard when it is so seldom found. For how could it be that it is neglected practically by all, if salvation were close at hand and could be found without difficulty? But all excellent things are as difficult as they are rare.

V. THE POLITICAL TREATISE

There remains for our analysis that tragic troso, the *Tractatus Politicus,* the work of Spinoza's maturest years, stopped suddenly short by his early death. It is a brief thing, and yet full of thought; so that one feels again how much was lost when this gentle life was closed at the very moment that it was ripening to its fullest powers. In the same generation which saw Hobbes exalting absolute monarchy and denouncing the uprising of the English people against their king almost as vigorously as Milton was defending it, Spinoza, friend of the republican De Witts, formulated

[115]II, 49, note.

a political philosophy which expressed the liberal and democratic hopes of his day in Holland, and became one of the main sources of that stream of thought which culminated in Rousseau and the Revolution.

All political philosophy, Spinoza thinks, must grow out of a distinction between the natural and the moral order—that is, between existence before, and existence after, the formation of organized societies. Spinoza supposes that men once lived in comparative isolation, without law or social organization; there were then, he says, no conceptions of right and wrong, justice or injustice; might and right were one.

> Nothing can exist in a natural state which can be called good or bad by common assent, since every man who is in a natural state consults only his own advantage, and determines what is good or bad according to his own fancy and in so far as he has regard for his own advantage alone, and holds himself responsible to no one save himself by any law; and therefore sin cannot be conceived in a natural state, but only in a civil state, where it is decreed by common consent what is good or bad, and each one holds himself responsible to the state.[116] . . . The law and ordinance of nature under which all men are born, and for the most part live, forbids nothing but what no one wishes or is able to do, and is not opposed to strife, hatred, anger, treachery, or, in general, anything that appetite suggests.[117]

We get an inkling of this law of nature, or this lawlessness of nature, by observing the behavior of states; "there is no altruism among nations,"[118] for there can be law and morality only where there is an accepted organization, a common and recognized authority. The "rights" of states are now what the "rights" of individuals used to be (and still often are), that is, they are *mights*, and the leading states, by some forgetful honesty of diplomats, are very properly called the "Great Powers." So it is too among species: there being no common organization, there is not among them any morality or law; each species does to the other what it wishes and can.[119]

But among men, as mutual need begets mutual aid, this natural order of powers passes into a moral order of rights. "Since fear of solitude exists in all men, because no one in solitude is strong enough to defend himself and procure the necessaries of life, it follows that men by nature tend towards social organization."[120] To guard against danger "the force or strength of one man would hardly suffice if men did not arrange mutual aid and exchange."[121] Men are not by nature, however, equipped for the mutual forbearance of social order; but danger begets association, which gradually nourishes and strengthens the social instincts: "men are not born for citizenship, but must be made fit for it."[122]

[116]*Ethics*, IV, 37, note 2.
[118]*Bismarck.*
[120]*T. T-P.*, ch. 6.
[122]*T. P.*, ch. 5.
[117]*Tractatus Politicus*, ch. 2.
[119]*Ethics*, IV, 37, note 1; and App., 27.
[121]*Ethics*, IV, App., 28.

Most men are at heart individualistic rebels against law or custom: the social instincts are later and weaker than the individualistic, and need reinforcement; man is not "good by nature," as Rousseau was so disastrously to suppose. But through association, if even merely in the family, sympathy comes, a feeling of kind, and at last of kindness. We like what is like us; "we pity not only a thing we have loved, but also one which we judge similar to ourselves";[123] out of this comes an "imitation of emotions,"[124] and finally some degree of conscience. Conscience, however, is not innate, but acquired; and varies with geography.[125] It is the deposit, in the mind of the growing individual, of the moral traditions of the group; through it society creates for itself an ally in the heart of its enemy —the naturally individualistic soul.

Gradually, in this development, it comes about that the law of individual power which obtains in a state of nature, yields in organized society to the legal and moral power of the whole. Might still remains right; but the might of the whole limits the might of the individual— limits it theoretically to his rights, to such exercise of his powers as agrees with the equal freedom of others. Part of the individual's natural might, or sovereignty, is handed over to the organized community, in return for the enlargement of the sphere of his remaining powers. We abandon, for example, the right to fly from anger to violence, and are freed from the danger of such violence from others. Law is necessary because men are subject to passions; if all men were reasonable, law would be superfluous. The perfect law would bear to individuals the same relation which perfect reason bears to passions: it would be the coördination of conflicting forces to avoid the ruin and increase the power of the whole. Just as, in metaphysics, reason is the perception of order in things, and in ethics the establishment of order among desires, so in politics it is the establishment of order among men. The perfect state would limit the powers of its citizens only as far as these powers were mutually destructive; it would withdraw no liberty except to add a greater one.

> The last end of the state is not to dominate men, nor to restrain them by fear; rather it is so to free each man from fear that he may live and act with full security and without injury to himself or his neighbor. The end of the state, I repeat, is not to make rational beings into brute beasts and machines. It is to enable their bodies and their minds to function safely. It is to lead men to live by, and to exercise, a free reason; that they may not waste their strength in hatred, anger and guile, nor act unfairly toward one another. Thus the end of the state is really liberty.[126]

Freedom is the goal of the state because the function of the state is to promote growth, and growth depends on capacity finding freedom. But

---

[123]*Ethics*, III, 22, note.   [124]*Ibid.*, 27, note 1.
[125]III, App. 27.   [126]*T. T-P.*, ch. 20.

what if laws stifle growth and freedom? What shall a man do if the state, seeking, like every organism or organization, to preserve its own existence (which ordinarily means that office-holders seek to keep themselves in office), becomes a mechanism of domineering and exploitation? Obey even the unjust law, answers Spinoza, if reasonable protest and discussion are allowed and speech is left free to secure a peaceful change. "I confess that from such freedom inconveniences may sometimes arise; but what question was ever settled so wisely that no abuses could spring therefrom?"[127] Laws against free speech are subversive of all law; for men will not long respect laws which they may not criticize.

> The more a government strives to curtail freedom of speech, the more obstinately is it resisted; not indeed by the avaricious, . . . but by those whom good education, sound morality, and virtue have rendered more free. Men in general are so constituted that there is nothing they will endure with so little patience as that views which they believe to be true should be counted crimes against the laws. . . . Under such circumstances they do not think it disgraceful, but most honorable, to hold the laws in abhorrence, and to refrain from no action against the government.[128] . . . Laws which can be broken without any wrong to one's neighbor are counted but a laughing-stock; and so far from such laws restraining the appetites and lusts of mankind, they rather heighten them. *Nitimur in vetitum semper, cupimusque negata.*[129]

And Spinoza concludes like a good American constitutionalist: "If actions only could be made the ground of criminal prosecutions, and words were always allowed to pass free, sedition would be divested of every semblance of justification."[130]

The less control the state has over the mind, the better for both the citizen and the state. Spinoza, while recognizing the necessity of the state, distrusts it, knowing that power corrupts even the incorruptible (was this not the name of Robespierre?); and he does not look with equanimity upon the extension of its authority from the bodies and actions to the souls and thoughts of men; that would be the end of growth and the death of the group. So he disapproves of state control of education, especially in the universities: "Academies that are founded at the public expense are instituted not so much to cultivate men's natural abilities as to restrain them. But in a free commonwealth arts and sciences will be better cultivated to the full if every one that asks leave is allowed to teach publicly, at his own cost and risk."[131] How to find a middle way between universities controlled by the state and universities controlled by private wealth, is a problem which Spinoza does not solve; private wealth had

[127] *Ibid.*   [128] *Ibid.*
[129] *T. P.,* ch. 10. ("We always resist prohibitions, and yearn for what is denied us.")
[130] *T. T-P.,* pref.   [131] *T. P.,* ch. 8.

not in his day grown to such proportions as to suggest the difficulty. His ideal, apparently, was higher education such as once flourished in Greece, coming not from institutions but from free individuals—"Sophists"—who traveled from city to city and taught independently of either public or private control.

These things premised, it makes no great difference what is the form of government; and Spinoza expresses only a mild preference for democracy. Any of the traditional political forms can be framed "so that every man . . . may prefer public right to private advantage; this is the task" of the law-giver.[182] Monarchy is efficient, but oppressive and militaristic.

> Experience is thought to teach that it makes for peace and concord to confer the whole authority on one man. For no dominion has stood so long without any notable change as that of the Turks; and on the other hand there were none so little lasting as those which were popular or democratic, nor any in which so many seditions arose. Yet if slavery, barbarism and desolation are to be called peace, men can have no worse misfortune. No doubt there are usually more and sharper quarrels between parents and children, than between masters and slaves; yet it advances not the art of household management to change a father's right into a right of property, and count children but as slaves. Slavery, then, and not peace, is furthered by handing over the whole authority to one man.[183]

To which he adds a word on secret diplomacy:

> It has been the one song of those who thirst after absolute power that the interest of the state requires that its affairs should be conducted in secret. . . . But the more such arguments disguise themselves under the mask of public welfare, the more oppressive is the slavery to which they will lead. . . . Better that right counsels be known to enemies than that the evil secrets of tyrants should be concealed from the citizens. They who can treat secretly of the affairs of a nation have it absolutely under their authority; and as they plot against the enemy in time of war, so do they against the citizens in time of peace.[184]

Democracy is the most reasonable form of government; for in it "every one submits to the control of authority over his actions, but not over his judgment and reason; i. e., seeing that all cannot think alike, the voice of the majority has the force of law."[185] The military basis of this democracy should be universal military service, the citizens retaining their arms during peace;[186] its fiscal basis should be the single tax.[187] The defect of democracy is its tendency to put mediocrity into power; and there is

---

[182] *T. T-P.*, ch. 17.   [183] *T. P.*, ch. 6.   [184] *T. P.*, ch. 7.
[185] *T. T-P.*, ch. 20.   [186] *T. P.*, ch. 7.

[187] "The fields and the whole soil, and (if it can be managed) the houses, should be public property, . . . let at a yearly rental to the citizen; . . . and with this exception let them all be free from every kind of taxation in time of peace."—*T. P.*, ch. 6.

no way of avoiding this except by limiting office to men of "trained skill."[138] Numbers by themselves cannot produce wisdom, and may give the best favors of office to the grossest flatterers. "The fickle disposition of the multitude almost reduces those who have experience of it to despair; for it is governed solely by emotions, and not by reason."[139] Thus democratic government becomes a procession of brief-lived demagogues, and men of worth are loath to enter lists where they must be judged and rated by their inferiors.[140] Sooner or later the more capable men rebel against such a system, though they be in a minority. "Hence I think it is that democracies change into aristocracies, and these at length into monarchies";[141] people at last prefer tyranny to chaos. Equality of power is an unstable condition; men are by nature unequal; and "he who seeks equality between unequals seeks an absurdity." Democracy has still to solve the problem of enlisting the best energies of men while giving to all alike the choice of those, *among the trained and fit,* by whom they wish to be ruled.

Who knows what light the genius of Spinoza might have cast upon this pivotal problem of modern politics had he been spared to complete his work? But even that which we have of this treatise was but the first and imperfect draft of his thought. While writing the chapter on democracy he died.

VI. THE INFLUENCE OF SPINOZA

"Spinoza did not seek to found a sect, and he founded none";[142] yet all philosophy after him is permeated with his thought. During the generation that followed his death, his name was held in abhorrence; even Hume spoke of his "hideous hypothesis"; "people talked of Spinoza," said Lessing, "as if he were a dead dog."

It was Lessing who restored him to repute. The great critic surprised Jacobi, in their famous conversation in 1780,[143] by saying that he had been a Spinozist throughout his mature life, and affirming that "there is no other philosophy than that of Spinoza." His love of Spinoza had strengthened his friendship with Moses Mendelssohn; and in his great play, *Nathan der Weise,* he poured into one mould that conception of the ideal Jew which had come to him from the living merchant and the dead philosopher. A few years later Herder's *Einige Gespräche über Spinoza's System* turned the attention of liberal theologians to the *Ethics;* Schleiermacher, leader of this school, wrote of "the holy and excommunicated Spinoza," while the Catholic poet, Novalis, called him "the god-intoxicated man."

Meanwhile Jacobi had brought Spinoza to the attention of Goethe; the

[138]*T. T-P.*, ch. 13. [139]*Ibid.*, ch. 17. [140]*Ethics*, IV, 58, note.
[141]*T. P.*, ch. 8. [142]Pollock, 78. [143]Printed in full in Willis.

great poet was converted, he tells us, at the first reading of the *Ethics;*[144] it was precisely the philosophy for which his deepening soul had yearned; henceforth it pervaded his poetry and his prose. It was here that he found the lesson *dass wir entsagen sollen*—that we must accept the limitations which nature puts upon us; and it was partly by breathing the calm air of Spinoza that he rose out of the wild romanticism of *Götz* and *Werther* to the classic poise of his later life.

It was by combining Spinoza with Kant's epistemology that Fichte, Schelling and Hegel reached their varied pantheisms; it was from *conatus sese preservandi,* the effort to preserve one's self, that Fichte's *Ich* was born, and Schopenhauer's "will to live," and Nietzsche's "will to power," and Bergson's *élan vital.* Hegel objected that Spinoza's system was too lifeless and rigid; he was forgetting this dynamic element of it and remembering only that majestic conception of God as law which he appropriated for his "Absolute Reason." But he was honest enough when he said, "To be a philosopher one must first be a Spinozist."

In England the influence of Spinoza rose on the tide of the Revolutionary movement; and young rebels like Coleridge and Wordsworth talked about "Spy-nosa" (which the spy set by the government to watch them took as a reference to his own nasal facilities) with the same ardor that animated the conversation of Russian intellectuals in the halcyon days of *Y Narod.* Coleridge filled his guests with Spinozist table-talk; and Wordsworth caught something of the philosopher's thought in his famous lines about

> *Something*
> *Whose dwelling is the light of setting suns,*
> *And the round ocean, and the living air,*
> *And the blue sky, and in the mind of man;—*
> *A motion and a spirit, which impels*
> *All thinking things, all objects of all thought,*
> *And rolls through all things.*

Shelley quoted the *Treatise on Religion and the State* in the original notes to *Queen Mab,* and began a translation of it for which Byron promised a preface. A fragment of this MS. came into the hands of C. S. Middleton, who took it for a work of Shelley's own, and called it "schoolboy speculation . . . too crude for publication entire." In a later and tamer age George Eliot translated the *Ethics,* though she never published the translation; and one may suspect that Spencer's conception of the Unknowable owes something to Spinoza through his intimacy with the novelist. "There are not wanting men of eminence of the present day," says Belfort Bax, "who declare that in Spinoza is contained the fulness of modern science."

[144]Brandes, *Main Currents in Nineteenth Century Literature;* New York, 1905; vol. vi, p. 10. Cf. Brandes, *Wolfgang Goethe;* New York, 1924; vol. I, pp. 432-7.

Perhaps so many were influenced by Spinoza because he lends himself to so many interpretations, and yields new riches at every reading. All profound utterances have varied facets for diverse minds. One may say of Spinoza what Ecclesiastes said of Wisdom: "The first man knew him not perfectly, no more shall the last find him out. For his thoughts are more than the sea, and his counsels profounder than the great deep."

On the second centenary of Spinoza's death subscriptions were collected for the erection of a statue to him at the Hague. Contributions came from every corner of the educated world; never did a monument rise upon so wide a pedestal of love. At the unveiling in 1882 Ernest Renan concluded his address with words which may fitly conclude also our chapter: "Woe to him who in passing should hurl an insult at this gentle and pensive head. He would be punished, as all vulgar souls are punished, by his very vulgarity, and by his incapacity to conceive what is divine. This man, from his granite pedestal, will point out to all men the way of blessedness which he found; and ages hence, the cultivated traveler, passing by this spot, will say in his heart, 'The truest vision ever had of God came, perhaps, here.' "[145]

[145] *Ethics*, Everyman ed., Introd., xxii, note.

CHAPTER V

Voltaire and the French Enlightenment

I. PARIS: *ŒDIPE*

At paris in 1742 Voltaire was coaching Mlle. Dumesnil to rise to tragic heights in a rehearsal of his play *Mérope*. She complained that she would have to have "the very devil" in her to simulate such passion as he required. "That is just it," answered Voltaire; "you must have the devil in you to succeed in any of the arts."[1] Even his critics and his enemies admitted that he himself met this requirement perfectly. "*Il avait le diable au corps*—he had the devil in his body," said Sainte-Beuve;[2] and De Maistre called him the man "into whose hands hell had given all its powers."[3]

Unprepossessing, ugly, vain, flippant, obscene, unscrupulous, even at times dishonest,—Voltaire was a man with the faults of his time and place, missing hardly one. And yet this same Voltaire turns out to have been tirelessly kind, considerate, lavish of his energy and his purse, as sedulous in helping friends as in crushing enemies, able to kill with a stroke of his pen and yet disarmed by the first advance of conciliation;—so contradictory is man.

But all these qualities, good and bad, were secondary, not of the essence of Voltaire; the astounding and basic thing in him was the inexhaustible fertility and brilliance of his mind. His works fill ninety-nine volumes, of which every page is sparkling and fruitful, though they range from subject to subject across the world as fitfully and bravely as in an encyclopedia. "My trade is to say what I think":[4] and what he thought was always worth saying, as what he said was always said incomparably well. If we do not read him now (though men like Anatole France have been formed to subtlety and wisdom by poring over his pages), it is because the theological battles which he fought for us no longer interest us intimately; we have passed on perhaps to other battle-fields, and are more absorbed with the economics of this life than with the geography of the next; the very thoroughness of Voltaire's victory over ecclesiasticism

[1]Tallentyre, *Life of Voltaire;* third edition; p. 145.
[2]*Portraits of the Eighteenth Century;* New York, 1905; vol. i, p. 196.
[3]Brandes, *Main Currents in Nineteenth Century Literature;* vol. iii, p. 107.
[4]Tallentyre, p. 32.

and superstition makes dead those issues which he found alive. Much of his fame, too, came of his inimitable conversation; but *scripta manent, verba volant*—written words remain, while spoken words fly away, the winged words of Voltaire with the rest. What is left to us is too much the flesh of Voltaire, too little the divine fire of his spirit. And yet, darkly as we see him through the glass of time, what a spirit!—"sheer intelligence transmuting anger into fun, fire into light";[5] "a creature of air and flame, the most excitable that ever lived, composed of more ethereal and more throbbing atoms than those of other men; there is none whose mental machinery is more delicate, nor whose equilibrium is at the same time more shifting and more exact."[6] Was he, perhaps, the greatest intellectual energy in all history?

Certainly he worked harder, and accomplished more, than any other man of his epoch. "Not to be occupied, and not to exist, amount to the same thing," he said. "All people are good except those who are idle." His secretary said that he was a miser only of his time.[7] "One must give one's self all the occupation one can to make life supportable in this world. . . . The further I advance in age, the more I find work necessary. It becomes in the long run the greatest of pleasures, and takes the place of the illusions of life."[8] "If you do not want to commit suicide always have something to do."[9]

Suicide must have been forever tempting him, for he was ever at work. "It was because he was so thoroughly alive that he filled the whole era with his life."[10] Contemporary with one of the greatest of centuries (1694–1778), he was the soul and essence of it. "To name Voltaire," said Victor Hugo, "is to characterize the entire eighteenth century."[11] Italy had a Renaissance, and Germany had a Reformation, but France had Voltaire; he was for his country both Renaissance and Reformation, and half the Revolution. He carried on the antiseptic scepticism of Montaigne, and the healthy earthy humor of Rabelais; he fought superstition and corruption more savagely and effectively than Luther or Erasmus, Calvin or Knox or Melanchthon; he helped to make the powder with which Mirabeau and Marat, Danton and Robespierre blew up the Old Régime. "If we judge of men by what they have done," said Lamartine, "then Voltaire is incontestably the greatest writer of modern Europe. . . . Destiny gave him eighty-three years of existence, that he might slowly decompose the decayed age; he had the time to combat time; and when he fell he was the conqueror."[12]

[5] J. M. Robertson, *Voltaire;* London, 1922; p. 67.
[6] Taine, *The Ancient Régime;* New York, 1876; p. 262.
[7] Voltaire, *Romances;* New York, 1889; p. 12.
[8] In Sainte-Beuve, i, 226.   [9] Tallentyre, 93.
[10] Morley, *Voltaire;* London, 1878; p. 14.   [11] Centenary address on Voltaire.
[12] *Romances,* pp. vi and ix.

No, never has a writer had in his lifetime such influence. Despite exile, imprisonment, and the suppression of almost every one of his books by the minons of church and state, he forged fiercely a path for his truth, until at last kings, popes and emperors catered to him, thrones trembled before him, and half the world listened to catch his every word. It was an age in which many things called for a destroyer. "Laughing lions must come," said Nietzsche; well, Voltaire came, and "annihilated with laughter."[18] He and Rousseau were the two voices of a vast process of economic and political transition from feudal aristocracy to the rule of the middle class. When a rising class is inconvenienced by existing law or custom it appeals from custom to reason and from law to nature—just as conflicting desires in the individual sparkle into thought. So the wealthy bourgeoisie supported the rationalism of Voltaire and the naturalism of Rousseau; it was necessary to loosen old habits and customs, to renovate and invigorate feeling and thought, to open the mind to experiment and change, before the great Revolution could come. Not that Voltaire and Rousseau were the causes of the Revolution; perhaps rather they were co-results with it of the forces that seethed and surged beneath the political and social surface of French life; they were the accompanying light and brilliance of the volcanic heat and conflagration. Philosophy is to history as reason is to desire: in either case an unconscious process determines from below the conscious thought above.

Yet we must not bend back too far in attempting to correct the philosopher's tendency to exaggerate the influence of philosophy. Louis XVI, seeing in his Temple prison the works of Voltaire and Rousseau, said, "Those two men have destroyed France,"[14]—meaning his dynasty. "The Bourbons might have preserved themselves," said Napoleon, "if they had controlled writing materials. The advent of cannon killed the feudal system; ink will kill the modern social organization."[15] "Books rule the world," said Voltaire, "or at least those nations in it which have a written language; the others do not count." "Nothing enfranchises like education";—and he proceeded to enfranchise France. "When once a nation begins to think, it is impossible to stop it."[16] But with Voltaire, France began to think.

"Voltaire," that is to say, François Marie Arouet, was born at Paris in 1694, the son of a comfortably successful notary and a somewhat aristocratic mother. He owed to his father, perhaps, his shrewdness and irascibility, and to his mother something of his levity and wit. He came into the world, so to speak, by a narrow margin: his mother did not survive his birth; and he was so puny and sickly an infant that the nurse did not give him more than a day to live. She was slightly in error, as he lived

[13]Brandes, 57.   [14]Tallentyre, 526.
[15]Bertaut, *Napoleon in His Own Words*; Chicago, 1916; p. 63.
[16]Tallentyre, 101.

almost to eighty-four; but throughout his life his frail body tormented with illness his unconquerable spirit.

He had for his edification a model elder brother, Armand, a pious lad who fell in love with the Jansenist heresy, and courted martyrdom for his faith. "Well," said Armand to a friend who advised the better part of valor, "if you do not want to be hanged, at least do not put off other people." The father said he had two fools for his sons—one in verse and the other in prose. The fact that François made verses almost as soon as he could write his name, convinced his very practical father that nothing good would come of him. But the famous hetaira, Ninon de l'Enclos, who lived in the provincial town to which the Arouets had returned after the birth of François, saw in the youth signs of greatness; and when she died she left him 2000 francs for the purchase of books. His early education came from these, and from a dissolute abbé (a Jérome Coignard in the flesh) who taught him scepticism along with his prayers. His later educators, the Jesuits, gave him the very instrument of scepticism by teaching him dialectic—the art of proving anything, and therefore at last the habit of believing nothing. François became an adept at argument: while the boys played games in the fields, he, aged twelve, stayed behind to discuss theology with the doctors. When the time came for him to earn his living, he scandalized his father by proposing to take up literature as profession. "Literature," said M. Arouet, "is the profession of the man who wishes to be useless to society and a burden to his relatives, and to die of hunger";—one can see the table trembling under his emphasis. So François went in for literature.

Not that he was a quiet and merely studious lad; he burnt the midnight oil—of others. He took to staying out late, frolicking with the wits and roisterers of the town, and experimenting with the commandments; until his exasperated father sent him off to a relative at Caen, with instructions to keep the youth practically in confinement. But his jailer fell in love with his wit, and soon gave him free rein. After imprisonment, now as later, came exile: his father sent him to the Hague with the French ambassador, requesting strict surveillance of the madcap boy; but François at once fell in love with a little lady, "Pimpette," held breathless clandestine interviews with her, and wrote to her passionate letters ending always with the refrain, "I shall certainly love you forever." The affair was discovered, and he was sent home. He remembered Pimpette for several weeks.

In 1715, proud of his twenty-one years, he went to Paris, just in time to be in at the death of Louis XIV. The succeeding Louis being too young to govern France, much less Paris, the power fell into the hands of a regent; and during this quasi-interregnum life ran riot in the capital of the world, and young Arouet ran with it. He soon achieved a reputation as a brilliant and reckless lad. When the Regent, for economy, sold half the horses that filled the royal stables, François remarked how much more sensible it would have been to dismiss half the asses that filled the royal court. At last all the bright and naughty things whispered about Paris were fathered upon him; and it was his ill luck that these included two poems accusing the Regent of desiring to usurp the throne. The Regent raged; and meeting the youth in the park one day, said to him: "M. Arouet, I will wager that I can show you something that you have never seen before." "What is that?" "The inside of the Bastille." Arouet saw it the next day, April 16, 1717.

While in the Bastille he adopted, for some unknown reason, the pen-name of Voltaire,[17] and became a poet in earnest and at length. Before he had served eleven months he had written a long and not unworthy epic, the *Henriade*, telling the story of Henry of Navarre. Then the Regent, having discovered, perhaps, that he had imprisoned an innocent man, released him and gave him a pension; whereupon Voltaire wrote thanking him for so taking care of his board, and begging permission hereafter to take care of his lodging himself.

He passed now almost with a bound from the prison to the stage. His tragedy, *Œdipe*, was produced in 1718, and broke all the records of Paris by running for forty-five consecutive nights. His old father, come to upbraid him, sat in a box, and covered his joy by grumbling, at every hit, "Oh, the rascal! the rascal!" When the poet Fontenelle met Voltaire after the play and damned it with high praise, saying it was "too brilliant for tragedy," Voltaire replied, smiling, "I must re-read your pastorals."[18] The youth was in no mood for caution or for courtesy; had he not put into the play itself these reckless lines?—

> Our priests are not what simple folk suppose;
> Their learning is but our credulity. (*Act iv, sc. 1*);

and into the mouth of Araspe this epoch-making challenge?—

> Let us trust to ourselves, see all with our own eyes;
> Let these be our oracles, our tripods and our gods. (*ii, 5*)

The play netted Voltaire 4000 francs, which he proceeded to invest with a wisdom unheard of in literary men; through all his tribulations he kept the art not merely of making a spacious income, but of putting it to work; he respected the classic adage that one must live before one can philosophize. In 1729 he bought up all the tickets in a poorly planned government lottery, and made a large sum, much to the anger of the Government. But as he became rich he became ever more generous; and a growing circle cf protégés gathered about him as he passed into the afternoon of life.

[17] Carlyle thought it an anagram for *A-r-o-u-e-t l. j.* (*le jeune*, the younger). But the name seems to have occurred among the family of Voltaire's mother.

[18] Robertson, 67.

It was well that he added an almost Hebraic subtlety of finance to his Gallic cleverness of pen; for his next play, *Artemire*, failed. Voltaire felt the failure keenly; every triumph sharpens the sting of later defeats. He was always painfully sensitive to public opinion, and envied the animals because they do not know what people say of them. Fate added to his dramatic failure a bad case of small-pox; he cured himself by drinking 120 pints of lemonade, and somewhat less of physic. When he came out of the shadow of death he found that his *Henriade* had made him famous; he boasted, with reason, that he had made poetry the fashion. He was received and feted everywhere; the aristocracy caught him up and turned him into a polished man of the world, an unequalled master of conversation, and the inheritor of the finest cultural tradition in Europe.

For eight years he basked in the sunshine of the salons; and then fortune turned away. Some of the aristocracy could not forget that this young man had no other title to place and honor than that of genius, and could not quite forgive him for the distinction. During a dinner at the Duc de Sully's chateau, after Voltaire had held forth for some minutes with unabashed eloquence and wit, the Chevalier de Rohan asked, not *sotto voce*, "Who is the young man who talks so loud?" "My Lord," answered Voltaire quickly, "he is one who does not carry a great name, but wins respect for the name he has." To answer the Chevalier at all was impertinence; to answer him unanswerably was treason. The honorable Lord engaged a band of ruffians to assault Voltaire by night, merely cautioning them, "Don't hit his head; something good may come out of that yet." The next day, at the theatre, Voltaire appeared, bandaged and limping, walked up to Rohan's box, and challenged him to a duel. Then he went home and spent all day practising with the foils. But the noble Chevalier had no mind to be precipitated into heaven, or elsewhere, by a mere genius; he appealed to his cousin, who was Minister of Police, to protect him. Voltaire was arrested, and found himself again in his old home, the Bastille, privileged once more to view the world from the inside. He was almost immediately released, on condition that he go into exile in England. He went; but after being escorted to Dover he recrossed the Channel in disguise, burning to avenge himself. Warned that he had been discovered, and was about to be arrested a third time, he took ship again, and reconciled himself to three years in England (1726–29).

II. LONDON: *LETTERS ON THE ENGLISH*

He set to work with courage to master the new language. He was displeased to find that *plague* had one syllable and *ague* two; he wished that plague would take one-half the language, and ague the other half. But soon he could read English well; and within a year he was master of the best English literature of the age. He was introduced to the literati by

Lord Bolingbroke, and dined with one after another of them, even with the elusive and corrosive Dean Swift. He pretended to no pedigree, and asked none of others: when Congreve spoke of his own plays as trifles, and desired to be considered rather a gentleman of leisure than an author, Voltaire said to him sharply, "If you had had the misfortune to be only a gentleman like any other, I should never have come to see you."

What surprised him was the freedom with which Bolingbroke, Pope, Addison, and Swift wrote whatever they pleased: here was a people that had opinions of its own; a people that had remade its religion, hanged its king, imported another, and built a parliament stronger than any ruler in Europe. There was no Bastille here, and no *lettres de cachet* by which titled pensioners or royal idlers could send their untitled foes to jail without cause and without trial. Here were thirty religions, and not one priest. Here was the boldest sect of all, the Quakers, who astonished all Christendom by behaving like Christians. Voltaire never to the end of his life ceased to wonder at them: in the *Dictionnaire Philosophique* he makes one of them say: "Our God, who has bidden us love our enemies and suffer evil without complaint, assuredly has no mind that we should cross the sea to go and cut the throats of our brothers because murderers in red clothes and hats two feet high enlist citizens by making a noise with two sticks on an ass's skin."

It was an England, too, that throbbed with a virile intellectual activity. Bacon's name was still in the air, and the inductive mode of approach was triumphing in every field. Hobbes (1588–1679) had carried out the sceptical spirit of the Renaissance, and the practical spirit of his master, into so complete and outspoken a materialism as would have won him in France the honor of martyrdom for a fallacy. Locke (1632–1704) had written a masterpiece of psychological analysis (the *Essay on the Human Understanding*, 1689), without any supernatural assumptions. Collins, Tyndal and other deists were re-affirming their faith in God while calling into question every other doctrine of the established church. Newton had just died: Voltaire attended the funeral, and often recalled the impression made upon him by the national honors awarded to this modest Englishman. "Not long ago," he writes, "a distinguished company were discussing the trite and frivolous question, who was the greatest man,— Cæsar, Alexander, Tamerlane, or Cromwell? Some one answered that without doubt it was Isaac Newton. And rightly: for it is to him who masters our minds by the force of truth, and not to those who enslave them by violence, that we owe our reverence."[19] Voltaire became a patient and thorough student of Newton's works, and was later the chief protagonist of Newton's views in France.

One must marvel at the quickness with which Voltaire absorbed almost all that England had to teach him—its literature, its science, and its

[19]*Letters on the English*, xiii; in Morley 52.

philosophy; he took all these varied elements, passed them through the fire of French culture and the French spirit, and transmuted them into the gold of Gallic wit and eloquence. He recorded his impressions in *Letters on the English,* which he circulated in manuscript among his friends; he did not dare to print them, for they praised "perfidious Albion" too highly to suit the taste of the royal censor. They contrasted English political liberty and intellectual independence with French tyranny and bondage;[20] they condemned the idle aristocracy and the tithe-absorbing clergy of France, with their perpetual recourse to the Bastille as the answer to every question and every doubt; they urged the middle classes to rise to their proper place in the state, as these classes had in England. Without quite knowing or intending it, these letters were the first cock's crow of the Revolution.

III. CIREY: *THE ROMANCES*

Nevertheless the Regent, not knowing of this chanticleer, sent Voltaire permission, in 1729, to return to France. For five years Voltaire enjoyed again that Parisian life whose wine flowed in his veins and whose spirit flowed from his pen. And then some miscreant of a publisher, getting hold of the *Letters on the English,* turned them without the author's permission into print, and sold them far and wide, to the horror of all good Frenchmen, including Voltaire. The Parliament of Paris at once ordered the book to be publicly burned as "scandalous, contrary to religion, to morals, and to respect for authority"; and Voltaire learned that he was again on the way to the Bastille. Like a good philosopher, he took to his heels—merely utilizing the occasion to elope with another man's wife.

The Marquise du Chatelet was twenty-eight; Voltaire, alas, was already forty. She was a remarkable woman: she had studied mathematics with the redoubtable Maupertuis, and then with Clairaut; she had written a learnedly annotated translation of Newton's *Principia;* she was soon to receive higher rating than Voltaire in a contest for a prize offered by the French Academy for an essay on the physics of fire; in short she was precisely the kind of woman who never elopes. But the Marquis was so dull, and Voltaire was so interesting—"a creature lovable in every way," she called him; "the finest ornament in France."[21] He returned her love

[20]Diderot was jailed six months for his *Letter on the Blind;* Buffon, in 1751, was made to retract publicly his teachings on the antiquity of the earth; Freret was sent to the Bastille for a critical inquiry into the origins of the royal power in France; books continued to be burned officially by the public hangman till 1788, as also after the Restoration in 1815; in 1757 an edict pronounced the death penalty for any author who should "attack religion,"—i. e., call in question any dogma of the traditional faith.—Robertson, 73, 84, 105, 107; Pellissier, *Voltaire Philosophe,* Paris, 1908, p. 92; Buckle, *History of Civilization,* New York, 1913; Vol. I, pp. 529 f.

[21]In Sainte-Beuve, i, 206.

with fervent admiration; called her "a great man whose only fault was being a woman"; formed from her, and from the large number of highly talented women then in France, his conviction of the native mental equality of the sexes;[22] and decided that her chateau at Cirey was an admirable refuge from the inclement political weather of Paris. The Marquis was away with his regiment, which had long been his avenue of escape from mathematics; and he made no objection to the new arrangements. Because of the *mariages de convenances* which forced rich old men on young women who had little taste for senility but much hunger for romance, the morals of the day permitted a lady to add a lover to her *ménage,* if it were done with a decent respect for the hypocrisies of mankind; and when she chose not merely a lover but a genius, all the world forgave her.

In the chateau at Cirey they did not spend their time billing and cooing. All the day was taken up with study and research; Voltaire had an expensive laboratory equipped for work in natural science; and for years the lovers rivaled each other in discovery and disquisition. They had many guests, but it was understood that these should entertain themselves all day long, till supper at nine. After supper, occasionally, there were private theatricals; or Voltaire would read to the guests one of his lively stories. Very soon Cirey became the Paris of the French mind; the aristocracy and the bourgeoisie joined in the pilgrimage to taste Voltaire's wine and wit, and see him act in his own plays. He was happy to be the centre of this corrupt and brilliant world; he took nothing too seriously, and for a while made *"Rire et faire rire"* his motto.[23] Catherine of Russia called him "the divinity of gayety." "If Nature had not made us a little frivolous," he said, "we should be most wretched. It is because one can be frivolous that the majority do not hang themselves." There was nothing of the dyspeptic Carlyle about him. *"Dulce est desipere in loco.*[24] Woe to philosophers who cannot laugh away their wrinkles. I look upon solemnity as a disease."[25]

It was now that he began to write those delightful romances—*Zadig, Candide, Micromégas, L'Ingenu, Le Monde comme il va,* etc.—which give the Voltairean spirit in purer form than anything else in his ninety-nine volumes. They are not novels, but humoresque-picaresque novelettes; the heroes are not persons but ideas, the villains are superstitions, and the events are thoughts. Some are mere fragments, like *L'Ingenu,* which is Rousseau before Jean Jacques. A Huron Indian comes to France with

[22]Tallentyre, 207. Contrast Voltaire's "God created woman only to tame mankind" (L'Ingenu, in *Romances,* 309), with Meredith's "Woman will be the last thing civilized by man" (*Ordeal of Richard Feverel,* p. 1). Sociologists would side with Voltaire. Man is woman's last domesticated animal.

[23]"To laugh and to make laugh."

[24]"It is sweet to be foolish on occasion."

[25]Letter to Frederick the Great, July, 1737.

some returning explorers; the first problem to which he gives rise is that of making him a Christian. An abbé gives him a copy of the New Testament, which the Huron likes so much that he soon offers himself not only for baptism but for circumcision as well. "For," he says, "I do not find in the book that was put into my hands a single person who was not circumcised. It is therefore evident that I must make a sacrifice to the Hebrew custom, and the sooner the better." Hardly has this difficulty been smoothed over when he has trouble over confession; he asks where in the Gospel this is commanded, and is directed to a passage in the Epistle of St. James: "Confess your sins to one another." He confesses; but when he had done he dragged the abbé from the confessional chair, placed himself in the seat, and bade the abbé confess in turn. "Come, my friend; it is said, 'We must confess our sins to one another'; I have related my sins to you, and you shall not stir till you recount yours." He falls in love with Miss St. Yves, but is told that he cannot marry her because she has acted as godmother at his baptism; he is very angry at this little trick of the fates, and threatens to get unbaptized. Having received permission to marry her, he is surprised to find that for marriage "notaries, priests, witnesses, contracts and dispensations are absolutely necessary. . . . 'You are then very great rogues, since so many precautions are required.'" And so, as the story passes on from incident to incident, the contradictions between primitive and ecclesiastical Christianity are forced upon the stage; one misses the impartiality of the scholar and the leniency of the philosopher; but Voltaire had begun his war against superstition, and in war we demand impartiality and leniency only of our foes.

Micromégas is an imitation of Swift, but perhaps richer than its model in cosmic imagination. The earth is visited by an inhabitant from Sirius; he is some 500,000 feet tall, as befits the citizen of so large a star. On his way through space he has picked up a gentleman from Saturn, who grieves because he is only a few thousand feet in height. As they walk through the Mediterranean the Sirian wets his heels. He asks his comrade how many senses the Saturnians have and is told: "We have seventy-two, but we are daily complaining of the smaller number." "To what age do you commonly live?" "Alas, a mere trifle; . . . very few on our globe survive 15,000 years. So you see that in a manner we begin to die the very moment we are born: our existence is no more than a point, our duration an instant, and our globe an atom. Scarce do we begin to learn a little when death intervenes before we can profit by experience."[26] As they stand in the sea they take up a ship as one might pick up some

[26]*Romances*, 339; cf. Shaw's *Back to Methuselah*. One of the most famous of Shaw's *bon mots* has its prototype in Voltaire's *Memnon the Philosopher*, who says, "I am afraid that our little terraqueous globe is the mad-house of those hundred thousand millions of worlds of which your lordship does me the honor to speak." —*Ibid.* 394.

animalcule, and the Sirian poises it on his thumb-nail, causing much commotion among the human passengers. "The chaplains of the ship repeated exorcisms, the sailors swore, and the philosophers formed a system" to explain this disturbance of the laws of gravity. The Sirian bends down like a darkening cloud and addresses them:

"O ye intelligent atoms, in whom the Supreme Being hath been pleased to manifest his omniscience and power, without doubt your joys on this earth must be pure and exquisite; for being unencumbered with matter, and—to all appearance—little else than soul, you must spend your lives in the delights of pleasure and reflection, which are the true enjoyments of a perfect spirit. True happiness I have nowhere found; but certainly here it dwells."

"We have matter enough," answered one of the philosophers, "to do abundance of mischief. . . . You must know, for example, that at this very moment, while I am speaking, there are 100,000 animals of our own species, covered with hats, slaying an equal number of their fellow-creatures, who wear turbans; at least they are either slaying or being slain; and this has usually been the case all over the earth from time immemorial."

"Miscreants!" cried the indignant Sirian; "I have a good mind to take two or three steps, and trample the whole nest of such ridiculous assassins under my feet."

"Don't give yourself the trouble," replied the philosopher; "they are industrious enough in securing their own destruction. At the end of ten years the hundredth part of these wretches will not survive. . . . Besides, the punishment should not be inflicted upon them, but upon those sedentary and slothful barbarians who, from their palaces, give orders for murdering a million of men, and then solemnly thank God for their success."[27]

Next to *Candide,* which belongs to a later period of Voltaire's life, the best of these tales is *Zadig*. Zadig was a Babylonian philosopher, "as wise as it is possible for men to be; . . . he knew as much of metaphysics as hath ever been known in any age,—that is, little or nothing at all." "Jealousy made him imagine that he was in love with Semira." In defending her against robbers he was wounded in the left eye.

A messenger was despatched to Memphis for the great Egyptian physician Hermes, who came with a numerous retinue. He visited Zadig, and declared that the patient would lose his eye. He even foretold the day and hour when this fatal event would happen. "Had it been the right eye," said he, "I could easily have cured it; but the wounds of the left eye are incurable." All Babylon lamented the fate of Zadig, and admired the profound knowledge of Hermes. In two days the abscess broke of its own accord, and Zadig was perfectly cured. Hermes wrote a book to prove that it ought not to have healed. Zadig did not read it.[28]

He hurried, instead, to Semira, only to find that upon hearing Hermes' first report she had betrothed herself to another man, having, she said, "an unconquerable aversion to one-eyed men." Zadig thereupon married a peasant woman, hoping to find in her the virtues which had been missing in the court lady Semira. To make sure of the fidelity of his wife, he arranged with a friend that he, Zadig, should pretend to die, and that the friend should make love to the wife an hour later. So Zadig had himself pronounced dead, and lay in the coffin while his friend first commiserated and then congratulated the widow, and at last proposed immediate marriage to her. She made a brief resistance; and then, "protesting she would ne'er consent, consented." Zadig rose from the dead and fled into the woods to console himself with the beauty of nature.

Having become a very wise man, he was made vizer to the king, to whose realm he brought prosperity, justice, and peace. But the queen fell in love with him; and the king, perceiving it, "began to be troubled. . . . He particularly remarked that the queen's shoes were blue, and that Zadig's shoes were blue; that his wife's ribbons were yellow, and that Zadig's bonnet was yellow." He resolved to poison them both; but the queen discovered the plot, and sent a note to Zadig: "Fly, I conjure thee, by our mutual love and our yellow ribbons!" Zadig again fled into the woods.

> He then represented to himself the human species, as it really is, as a parcel of insects devouring one another on a little atom of clay. This true image seemed to annihilate his misfortunes, by making him sensible of the nothingness of his own being and that of Babylon. His soul launched into infinity; and detached from the senses, contemplated the immutable order of the universe. But when, afterwards, returning to himself, . . . he considered that the Queen had perhaps died for him, the universe vanished from sight.

Passing out of Babylon he saw a man cruelly beating a woman; he responded to her cries for help, fought the man, and at last, to save himself, struck a blow which killed his enemy. Thereupon he turned to the lady and asked, "What further, madam, wouldst thou have me do for thee?" "Die, villain! for thou hast killed my lover. Oh, that I were able to tear out thy heart!"

Zadig was shortly afterward captured and enslaved; but he taught his master philosophy, and became his trusted counsellor. Through his advice the practice of suttee (by which a widow had herself buried with her husband) was abolished by a law which required that before such martyrdom the widow should spend an hour alone with a handsome man. Sent on a mission to the King of Serendib, Zadig taught him that an honest minister could best be found by choosing the lightest dancer among the applicants: he had the vestibule of the dance hall filled with loose valuables, easily stolen, and arranged that each candidate should pass through the vestibule alone and unwatched; when they had all entered, they were asked to dance. "Never had dancers performed more unwillingly or with less grace. Their heads were down, their backs bent, their hands pressed to their sides."—And so the story rushes on. We can imagine those evenings at Cirey!

IV. POTSDAM AND FREDERICK

Those who could not come to him wrote to him. In 1736 began his correspondence with Frederick, then Prince, and not yet Great. Frederick's first letter was like that of a boy to a king; its lavish flattery gives us an inkling of the reputation which Voltaire—though he had not yet written any of his masterpieces—had already won. It proclaims Voltaire as "the greatest man of France, and a mortal who does honor to language. . . . I count it one of the greatest honors of my life to be born the contemporary of a man of such distinguished attainments as yours . . . It is not given to every one to make the mind laugh"; and "what pleasures can surpass those of the mind?"[29] Frederick was a free-thinker, who looked upon dogmas as a king looks upon subjects; and Voltaire had great hopes that on the throne Frederick would make the Enlightenment fashionable, while he himself, perhaps, might play Plato to Frederick's Dionysius. When Frederick demurred to the flattery with which Voltaire answered his own, Voltaire replied: "A prince who writes against flattery is as singular as a pope who writes against infallibility." Frederick sent him a copy of the *Anti-Machiavel,* in which the prince spoke very beautifully of the iniquity of war, and of the duty of a king to preserve peace; Voltaire wept tears of joy over this royal pacifist. A few months later Frederick, made king, invaded Silesia and plunged Europe into a generation of bloodshed.

In 1745 the poet and his mathematician went to Paris, when Voltaire became a candidate for membership in the French Academy. To achieve this quite superfluous distinction he called himself a good Catholic, complimented some powerful Jesuits, lied inexhaustibly, and in general behaved as most of us do in such cases. He failed; but a year later he succeeded, and delivered a reception address which is one of the classics of the literature of France. For a while he lingered in Paris, flitting from salon to salon, and producing play after play. From *Œdipe* at eighteen to *Irène* at eighty-three he wrote a long series of dramas, some of them failures, most of them successes. In 1730 *Brutus* failed, and in 1732 *Eriphyle* failed; his friends urged him to abandon the drama; but in the same year he produced *Zaire,* which became his greatest success. *Mahomet* followed in 1741, *Mérope* in 1743, *Semiramis* in 1748, and *Tancrède* in 1760.

Meanwhile tragedy and comedy had entered his own life. After fifteen years, his love for Mme. du Chatelet had somewhat thinned; they had

[29] In Sainte-Beuve, i, 212–215.

even ceased to quarrel. In 1748 the Marquise fell in love with the handsome young Marquis de Saint-Lambert. When Voltaire discovered it he
raged; but when Saint-Lambert asked his forgiveness he melted into a
benediction. He had reached the crest of life now, and began to see death
in the distance: he could not take it ill that youth should be served. "Such
are women," he said philosophically (forgetting that there are such men
too): "I displaced Richelieu, Saint-Lambert turns me out! That is the
order of things; one nail drives out another; so goes the world."[80] He
wrote a pretty stanza to the third nail:

> Saint-Lambert, it is all for thee
> The flower grows;
> The rose's thorns are all for me;
> For thee the rose.

Then, in 1749, came the death of Mme. du Chatelet in childbirth. It
was characteristic of the age that her husband and Voltaire and Saint-
Lambert should meet at her death-bed with not one word of reproach,
and indeed made friends by their common loss.

Voltaire tried to forget his bereavement in work; for a time he busied
himself with his *Siècle de Louis XIV;* but what rescued him from despondency was the opportune renewal of Frederick's invitation to come to
his court at Potsdam. An invitation accompanied by 3000 francs for
traveling expenses was irresistible. Voltaire left for Berlin in 1750.

It soothed him to find himself assigned to a splendid suite in Frederick's palace, and accepted on equal terms by the most powerful monarch
of the age. At first his letters were full of satisfaction: writing on July 24
to d'Argental he describes Potsdam—"150,000 soldiers; . . . opera, comedy, philosophy, poetry, grandeur and graces, grenadiers and muses,
trumpets and violins, the suppers of Plato, society and liberty,—who
would believe it? Yet it is very true." Years before, he had written: *"Mon
Dieu!* . . . what a delightful life it would be to lodge with three or
four men of letters with talents and no jealousy" (what imagination!),
"to love one another, live quietly, cultivate one's art, talk of it, enlighten
ourselves mutually!—I picture to myself that I shall some day live in this
little Paradise."[81] And here it was!

Voltaire avoided the state dinners; he could not bear to be surrounded
with bristling generals; he reserved himself for the private suppers to
which Frederick, later in the evening, would invite a small inner circle
of literary friends; for this greatest prince of his age yearned to be a poet
and a philosopher. The conversation at these suppers was always in
French; Voltaire tried to learn German, but gave it up after nearly chok-
ing; and wished the Germans had more wit and fewer consonants.[82] One

[80]In Sainte-Beuve, i, 211.   [81]*Ibid.,* i, 193.
[82]Brandes, *Main Currents,* i, 3.

who heard the conversation said that it was better than the most interesting and best-written book in the world. They talked about everything,
and said what they thought. Frederick's wit was almost as sharp as Voltaire's; and only Voltaire dared to answer him, with that finesse which
could kill without giving offense. "One thinks boldly, one is free here,"
wrote Voltaire joyfully. Frederick "scratches with one hand, but caresses
with the other. . . . I am crossed in nothing . . . I find a port after
fifty years of storm. I find the protection of a king, the conversation of a
philosopher, the charms of an agreeable man, united in one who for sixteen years consoled me in misfortune and sheltered me from my enemies.
If one can be certain of anything it is of the character of the King of
Prussia."[33] However . . .

In November of this same year Voltaire thought he would improve
his finances by investing in Saxon bonds, despite Frederick's prohibition of
such investments. The bonds rose, and Voltaire profited; but his agent,
Hirsch, tried to blackmail him by threatening to publish the transaction.
Voltaire "sprang at his throat and sent him sprawling." Frederick learned
of the affair and fell into a royal rage. "I shall want him at the most
another year," he said to La Mettrie; "one squeezes the orange and throws
away the rind." La Mettrie, perhaps anxious to disperse his rivals, took
care to report this to Voltaire. The suppers were resumed, "but," wrote
Voltaire, "the orange rind haunts my dreams. . . . The man who fell
from the top of a steeple, and finding the falling through the air soft, said,
'Good, provided it lasts,' was not a little as I am."

He half desired a break; for he was as homesick as only a Frenchman
can be. The decisive trifle came in 1752. Maupertuis, the great mathematician whom Frederick had imported from France with so many others
in an attempt to arouse the German mind by direct contact with the "Enlightenment," quarreled with a subordinate mathematician, Koenig, over
an interpretation of Newton. Frederick entered into the dispute on the
side of Maupertuis; and Voltaire, who had more courage than caution,
entered it on the side of Koenig. "Unluckily for me," he wrote to Mme.
Denis, "I am also an author, and in the opposite camp to the King. I
have no sceptre, but I have a pen." About the same time Frederick was
writing to his sister: "The devil is incarnate in my men of letters; there
is no doing anything with them. These fellows have no intelligence except for society. . . . It must be a consolation to animals to see that
people with minds are often no better than they."[34] It was now that
Voltaire wrote against Maupertuis his famous "Diatribe of Dr. Akakia."
He read it to Frederick, who laughed all night over it, but begged Voltaire not to publish it. Voltaire seemed to acquiesce; but the truth was
that the thing was already sent to the printer, and the author could not
bring himself to practise infanticide on the progeny of his pen. When it

[33]Tallentyre, 226, 230.   [34]In Sainte-Beuve, i, 218.

appeared Frederick burst into flame, and Voltaire fled from the conflagration.

At Frankfort, though in territory quite outside Frederick's jurisdiction,
he was overtaken and arrested by the King's agents, and told that he could
not go on until he surrendered Frederick's poem, the *Palladium,* which
had not been adapted for polite society, and out-Pucelled Voltaire's
Pucelle itself. But the terrible manuscript was in a trunk which had been
lost on the way; and for weeks, till it came, Voltaire was kept almost in
prison. A book-seller to whom he owed something thought it an opportune
moment to come and press for the payment of his bill; Voltaire, furious,
gave him a blow on the ear; whereupon Voltaire's secretary, Collini, offered comfort to the man by pointing out, "Sir, you have received a box
on the ear from one of the greatest men in the world."[35]

Freed at last, he was about to cross the frontier into France, when word
came that he was exiled. The hunted old soul hardly knew where to turn;
for a time he thought of going to Pennsylvania—one may imagine his
desperation. He spent the March of 1754 seeking "an agreeable tomb" in
the neighborhood of Geneva, safe from the rival autocrats of Paris and
Berlin; at last he bought an old estate called *Les Délices;* settled down to
cultivate his garden and regain his health; and when his life seemed to be
ebbing away into senility, entered upon the period of his noblest and
greatest work.

V. LES DÉLICES: THE *ESSAY ON MORALS*

What was the cause of his new exile? That he had published in Berlin
"the most ambitious, the most voluminous, the most characteristic, and
the most daring of his works."[36] Its title was no small part of it: *Essai
sur les mœurs et l'esprit des Nations, et sur les principaux faits de l'histoire
depuis Charlemagne jusqu'à Louis XIII—an Essay on the Morals and
the Spirit of the Nations fom Charlemagne to Louis XIII.* He had begun
it at Cirey for Mme. du Chatelet, spurred on to the task by her denunciation of history as she is writ.

It is "an old almanac," she had said. "What does it matter to me, a
Frenchwoman living on my estate, to know that Egil succeeded Haquin
in Sweden, and that Ottoman was the son of Ortogrul? I have read with
pleasure the history of the Greeks and the Romans; they offered me
certain pictures which attracted me. But I have never yet been able
to finish any long history of our modern nations. I can see scarcely anything in them but confusion; a host of minute events without connection
or sequence, a thousand battles which settled nothing. I renounced a
study which overwhelms the mind without illuminating it."

Voltaire had agreed; he had made his *Ingenu* say, "History is nothing

[35]Morley, 146.   [36]Tallentyre, 291.

more than a picture of crimes and misfortunes"; and he was to write to Horace Walpole (July 15, 1768): "Truly the history of the Yorkists and Lancastrians, and many others, is much like reading the history of highway robbers." But he had expressed to Mme. du Chatelet the hope that a way out might lie in applying philosophy to history, and endeavoring to trace, beneath the flux of political events, the history of the human mind.[37] "Only philosophers should write history," he said.[38] "In all nations, history is disfigured by fable, till at last philosophy comes to enlighten man; and when it does finally arrive in the midst of this darkness, it finds the human mind so blinded by centuries of error, that it can hardly undeceive it; it finds ceremonies, facts and monuments, heaped up to prove lies."[39] "History," he concludes, "is after all nothing but a pack of tricks which we play upon the dead";[40] we transform the past to suit our wishes for the future, and in the upshot "history proves that anything can be proved by history."

He worked like a miner to find in this "Mississippi of falsehoods"[41] the grains of truth about the real history of mankind. Year after year he gave himself to preparatory studies: a *History of Russia,* a *History of Charles XII, The Age of Louis XIV,* and *The Age of Louis XIII;* and through these tasks he developed in himself that unflagging intellectual conscience which enslaves a man to make a genius. "The Jesuit Père Daniel, who produced a *History of France,* had placed before him in the Royal Library of Paris 1200 volumes of documents and manuscripts; spent an hour or so looking through them; and then, turning to Father Tournemine, the former teacher of Voltaire, dismissed the matter by declaring that all this material was 'useless old paper which he had no need of for the purpose of writing his history.' "[42] Not so Voltaire: he read everything on his subject that he could lay his hands on; he pored over hundreds of volumes of memoirs; he wrote hundreds of letters to survivors of famous events; and even after publishing his works he continued to study, and improved every edition.

But this gathering of material was only preparatory; what was needed was a new method of selection and arrangement. Mere facts would not do—even if, as so seldom happens, they were facts. "Details that lead to nothing are to history what baggage is to an army, *impedimenta;* we must look at things in the large, for the very reason that the human mind is so small, and sinks under the weight of minutiae."[43] "Facts" should be collected by annalists and arranged in some kind of historical dictionary where one might find them at need, as one finds words. What

[37]Robertson, 23; Morley, 215; Tallentyre, *Voltaire in His Letters,* New York, 1919, p. 222.
[38]Pellissier, 213.
[39]*Essai sur les Moeurs,* Introduction.
[40]In Morley, 220.
[41]Matthew Arnold's description of history.
[42]Brandes, *François de Voltaire.*
[43]In Morley, 275.

Voltaire sought was a unifying principle by which the whole history of civilization in Europe could be woven on one thread; and he was convinced that this thread was the history of culture. He was resolved that his history should deal not with kings but with movements, forces, and masses; not with nations but with the human race; not with wars but with the march of the human mind. "Battles and revolutions are the smallest part of the plan; squadrons and battalions conquering or being conquered, towns taken and retaken, are common to all history. . . . Take away the arts and the progress of the mind, and you will find nothing" in any age "rcmarkable enough to attract the attention of posterity."[44] "I wish to write a history not of wars, but of society; and to ascertain how men lived in the interior of their families, and what were the arts which they commonly cultivated. . . . My object is the history of the human mind, and not a mere detail of petty facts; nor am I concerned with the history of great lords . . . ; but I want to know what were the steps by which men passed from barbarism to civilization."[45] This rejection of Kings from history was part of that democratic uprising which at last rejected them from government; the *Essai sur les Mœurs* began the dethronement of the Bourbons.

And so he produced the first philosophy of history—the first systematic attempt to trace the streams of natural causation in the development of the European mind; it was to be expected that such an experiment should follow upon the abandonment of supernatural explanations: history could not come into its own until theology gave way. According to Buckle, Voltaire's book laid the basis of modern historical science; Gibbon, Niebuhr, Buckle and Grote were his grateful debtors and followers; he was the *caput Nili* of them all, and is still unsurpassed in the field which he first explored.

But why did his greatest book bring him exile? Because, by telling the truth, it offended everybody. It especially enraged the clergy by taking the view later developed by Gibbon, that the rapid conquest of paganism by Christianity had disintegrated Rome from within and prepared it to fall an easy victim to the invading and immigrating barbarians. It enraged them further by giving much less space than usual to Judea and Christendom, and by speaking of China, India and Persia, and of their faiths, with the impartiality of a Martian; in this new perspective a vast and novel world was revealed; every dogma faded into relativity; the endless East took on something of the proportions given it by geography; Europe suddenly became conscious of itself as the experimental peninsula of a continent and a culture greater than its own. How could it forgive a European for so unpatriotic a revelation? The King decreed that this Frenchman who dared to think of himself as a man first and a Frenchman afterward should never put foot upon the soil of France again.

[44]*Voltaire in His Letters*, 40–41.   [45]In Buckle, *History of Civilization*, I, 580.

VI. FERNEY: *CANDIDE*

Les Délices had been a temporary home, a centre from which Voltaire might prospect to find a shelter of more permanence. He found it in 1758 at Ferney, just inside the Swiss line near France; here he would be secure from the French power, and yet near to French refuge if the Swiss Government should trouble him. This last change ended his *Wanderjahre.* His fitful runnings to and fro had not been all the result of nervous restlessness; they had reflected, too, his ubiquitous insecurity from persecution; only at sixty-four did he find a house that could be also his home. There is a passage at the end of one of his tales, "The Travels of Scarmentado," which almost applies to its author: "As I had now seen all that was rare or beautiful on earth, I resolved for the future to see nothing but my own home; I took a wife, and soon suspected that she deceived me; but notwithstanding this doubt I still found that of all conditions of life this was much the happiest." He had no wife, but he had a niece—which is better for a man of genius. "We never hear of his wishing to be in Paris. . . . There can be no doubt that this wise exile prolonged his days."[46]

He was happy in his garden, planting fruit trees which he did not expect to see flourish in his lifetime. When an admirer praised the work he had done for posterity he answered, "Yes, I have planted 4000 trees." He had a kind word for everybody, but could be forced to sharper speech. One day he asked a visitor whence he came. "From Mr. Haller's." "He is a great man," said Voltaire; "a great poet, a great naturalist, a great philosopher, almost a universal genius." "What you say, sir, is the more admirable, as Mr. Haller does not do you the same justice." "Ah," said Voltaire, "perhaps we are both mistaken."[47]

Ferney now became the intellectual capital of the world; every learned man or enlightened ruler of the day paid his court either in person or by correspondence. Here came sceptical priests, liberal aristocrats, and learned ladies; here came Gibbon and Boswell from England; here came d'Alembert, Helvetius, and the other rebels of the Enlightenment; and countless others. At last the entertainment of this endless stream of visitors proved too expensive even for Voltaire; he complained that he was becoming the hotel-keeper for all Europe. To one acquaintance who announced that he had come to stay for six weeks, Voltaire said: "What is the difference between you and Don Quixote? He mistook inns for chateaux, and you mistake this chateau for an inn." "God preserve me from my friends," he concluded; "I will take care of my enemies myself."

Add to this perpetual hospitality, the largest correspondence the world has ever seen, and the most brilliant. Letters came from all sorts and

conditions of men: a burgomaster wrote from Germany asking "in confidence whether there is a God or not," and begging Voltaire to answer
by return post;[48] Gustavus III of Sweden was elated by the thought that
Voltaire sometimes glanced at the North, and told him that this was their
greatest encouragement to do their best up there; Christian VII of Den-
mark apologized for not establishing at once all reforms; Catherine II
of Russia sent him beautiful presents, wrote frequently, and hoped he
would not consider her importunate. Even Frederick, after a year of
doldrums, returned to the fold, and resumed his correspondence with
the King of Ferney.

> "You have done me great wrongs," he wrote. "I have forgiven them all,
> and I even wish to forget them. But if you had not had to do with a madman
> in love with your noble genius, you would not have gotten off so well. . . .
> Do you want sweet things? Very well; I will tell you some truths. I esteem
> in you the finest genius that the ages have borne; I admire your poetry, I love
> your prose. . . . Never has an author before you had a tact so keen, a taste
> so sure and delicate. You are charming in conversation; you know how to
> amuse and instruct at the same time. You are the most seductive being that
> I know, capable of making yourself loved by all the world when you choose.
> You have such graces of mind that you can offend and yet at the same time
> deserve the indulgence of those who know you. In short, you would be
> perfect if you were not a man."[49]

Who would have expected so gay a host to become the exponent of
pessimism? In youth, as a reveler in Paris's salons, he had seen the
sunnier side of life, despite the Bastille; and yet even in those careless days
he had rebelled against the unnatural optimism to which Leibnitz had
given currency. To an ardent young man who had attacked him in print,
and had contended with Leibnitz that this is "the best of all possible
worlds," Voltaire wrote, "I am pleased to hear, sir, that you have written
a little book against me. You do me too much honor. . . . When you
have shown, in verse or otherwise, why so many men cut their throats in
the best of all possible worlds, I shall be exceedingly obliged to you. I
await your arguments, your verses, and your abuse; and assure you from
the bottom of my heart that neither of us knows anything about the
matter. I have the honor to be," etc.

Persecution and disillusionment had worn down his faith in life; and
his experiences at Berlin and Frankfort had taken the edge from his hope.
But both faith and hope suffered most when, in November, 1755, came
the news of the awful earthquake at Lisbon, in which 30,000 people
had been killed. The quake had come on All Saints' Day; the churches
had been crowded with worshippers; and death, finding its enemies
in close formation, had reaped a rich harvest. Voltaire was shocked into
seriousness and raged when he heard that the French clergy were ex-

plaining the disaster as a punishment for the sins of the people of Lisbon. He broke forth in a passionate poem in which he gave vigorous expression to the old dilemma: Either God can prevent evil and he will not; or he wishes to prevent it and he cannot. He was not satisfied with Spinoza's answer that *good* and *evil* are human terms, inapplicable to the universe, and that our tragedies are trivial things in the perspective of eternity.

> *I am a puny part of the great whole.* 22
> *Yes; but all animals condemned to live,*
> *All sentient things, born by the same stern law,*
> *Suffer like me, and like me also die.*
> *The vulture fastens on his timid prey,*
> *And stabs with bloody beak the quivering limbs:*
> *All's well, it seems, for it. But in a while*
> *An eagle tears the vulture into shreds;*
> *The eagle is transfixed by shafts of man;*
> *The man, prone in the dust of battlefields,*
> *Mingling his blood with dying fellow men,*
> *Becomes in turn the food of ravenous birds.*
> *Thus the whole world in every member groans,*
> *All born for torment and for mutual death.*
> *And o'er this ghastly chaos you would say*
> *The ills of each make up the good of all!*
> *What blessedness! And as, with quaking voice,*
> *Mortal and pitiful ye cry, "All's well,"*
> *The universe belies you, and your heart*
> *Refutes a hundred times your mind's conceit. . . .*
> *What is the verdict of the vastest mind?*
> *Silence: the book of fate is closed to us.*
> *Man is a stranger to his own research;*
> *He knows not whence he comes, nor whither goes.*
> *Tormented atoms in a bed of mud,*
> *Devoured by death, a mockery of fate;*
> *But thinking atoms, whose far-seeing eyes,*
> *Guided by thoughts, have measured the faint stars.*
> *Our being mingles with the infinite;*
> *Ourselves we never see, or come to know.*
> *This world, this theatre of pride and wrong,*
> *Swarms with sick fools who talk of happiness. . . .*
>
> *Once did I sing, in less lugubrious tone,*
> *The sunny ways of pleasure's general rule;*
> *The times have changed, and, taught by growing age,*
> *And sharing of the frailty of mankind,*
> *Seeking a light amid the deepening gloom,*
> *I can but suffer, and will not repine.*[50]

Selected Works of Voltaire; London, 1911; pp. 3-5.

A few months later the Seven Years' War broke out; Voltaire looked upon it as madness and suicide, the devastation of Europe to settle whether England or France should win "a few acres of snow" in Canada. On the top of this came a public reply, by Jean Jacques Rousseau, to the poem on Lisbon. Man himself was to be blamed for the disaster, said Rousseau; if we lived out in the fields, and not in the towns, we should not be killed on so large a scale; if we lived under the sky, and not in houses, houses would not fall upon us. Voltaire was amazed at the popularity won by this profound theodicy; and angry that his name should be dragged into the dust by such a Quixote, he turned upon Rousseau "that most terrible of all the intellectual weapons ever wielded by man, the mockery of Voltaire."[51] In three days, in 1751, he wrote *Candide*.

Never was pessimism so gaily argued; never was man made to laugh so heartily while learning that this is a world of woe. And seldom has a story been told with such simple and hidden art; it is pure narrative and dialogue; no descriptions pad it out; and the action is riotously rapid. "In Voltaire's fingers," said Anatole France, "the pen runs and laughs."[52] It is perhaps the finest short story in all literature.

Candide, as his name indicates, is a simple and honest lad, son of the great Baron of Thunder-Ten-Trockh of Westphalia, and pupil of the learned Pangloss.

Pangloss was professor of metaphysicotheologicocosmonigology. . . . "It is demonstrable," said he, "that all is necessarily for the best end. Observe that the nose has been formed to bear spectacles . . . legs were visibly designed for stockings . . . stones were designed to construct castles . . . pigs were made so that we might have pork all the year round. Consequently, they who assert that all is well have said a foolish thing; they should have said all is for the best."

While Pangloss is discoursing, the castle is attacked by the Bulgarian army, and Candide is captured and turned into a soldier.

He was made to wheel about to the right and to the left, to draw his rammer, to return his rammer, to present, to fire, to march. . . . He resolved, one fine day in spring, to go for a walk, marching straight before him, believing that it was a privilege of the human as well as the animal species to make use of their legs as they pleased. He had advanced two leagues when he was overtaken by four heroes six feet tall, who bound him and carried him to a dungeon. He was asked which he would like the best, to be whipped six and thirty times through all the regiment, or to receive at once two balls of lead in his brain. He vainly said that human will is free, and that he chose neither the one nor the other. He was forced to make a choice; he determined, in virtue of that gift of God called liberty, to run the gauntlet six-and-thirty times. He bore this twice.[53]

[51]Tallentyre, 231.   [52]Introd. to *Candide*, Modern Library edition.
[53]*Candide*, p. 7.

Candide escapes, takes passage to Lisbon, and on board ship meets Professor Pangloss, who tells how the Baron and Baroness were murdered and the castle destroyed. "All this," he concludes, "was indispensable; for private misfortune makes the general good, so that the more private misfortunes there are, the greater is the general good." They arrive in Lisbon just in time to be caught in the earthquake. After it is over they tell each other their adventures and sufferings; whereupon an old servant assures them that their misfortunes are as nothing compared with her own. "A hundred times I was on the point of killing myself, but I loved life. This ridiculous foible is perhaps one of our most fatal characteristics; for is there anything more absurd than to wish to carry continually a burden which one can always throw down?" Or, as another character expresses it, "All things considered, the life of a gondolier is preferable to that of a doge; but I believe the difference is so trifling that it is not worth the trouble of examining."

Candide, fleeing from the Inquisition, goes to Paraguay; "there the Jesuit Fathers possess all, and the people nothing; it is a masterpiece of reason and justice." In a Dutch colony he comes upon a negro with one hand, one leg, and a rag for clothing. "When we work at the sugar canes," the slave explains, "and the mill snatches hold of a finger, they cut off a hand; and when we try to run away, they cut off a leg. . . . This is the price at which you eat sugar in Europe." Candide finds much loose gold in the unexplored interior; he returns to the coast and hires a vessel to take him to France; but the skipper sails off with the gold and leaves Candide philosophizing on the wharf. With what little remains to him, Candide purchases a passage on a ship bound for Bordeaux; and on board strikes up a conversation with an old sage, Martin.

"Do you believe," said Candide, "that men have always massacred one another as they do today, that they have always been liars, cheats, traitors, ingrates, brigands, idiots, thieves, scoundrels, gluttons, drunkards, misers, envious, ambitious, bloody-minded, calumniators, debauchees, fanatics, hypocrites and fools?"

"Do you believe," said Martin, "that hawks have always eaten pigeons when they have found them?"

"Without doubt," said Candide.

"Well, then," said Martin, "if hawks have always had the same character, why should you imagine that men have changed theirs?"

"Oh!" said Candide, "there is a vast deal of difference, for free will—" And reasoning thus they arrived at Bordeaux.[54]

We cannot follow Candide through the rest of his adventures, which form a rollicking commentary on the difficulties of medieval theology and Leibnitzian optimism. After suffering a variety of evils among a variety

[54] P. 104.

of men, Candide settles down as a farmer in Turkey; and the story ends
with a final dialogue between master and pupil:

> Pangloss sometimes said to Candide:
>
> "There is a concatenation of events in this best of all possible worlds: for
> if you had not been kicked out of a magnificent castle; . . . if you had not
> been put into the Inquisition; if you had not walked over America; . . . if
> you had not lost all your gold; . . . you would not be here eating preserved
> citrons and pistachio-nuts."
>
> "All that is very well," answered Candide; "but let us cultivate our
> garden."

VII. THE ENCYCLOPEDIA AND THE PHILOSOPHIC DICTIONARY

The popularity of so irreverent a book as *Candide* gives us some sense
of the spirit of the age. The lordly culture of Louis XIV's time, despite
the massive bishops who spoke so eloquent a part in it, had learned to
smile at dogma and tradition. The failure of the Reformation to capture
France had left for Frenchmen no half-way house between infallibility
and infidelity; and while the intellect of Germany and England moved
leisurely in the lines of religious evolution, the mind of France leaped
from the hot faith which had massacred the Huguenots to the cold hostility with which La Mettrie, Helvetius, Holbach and Diderot turned
upon the religion of their fathers. Let us look for a moment at the intellectual environment in which the later Voltaire moved and had his
being.

La Mettrie (1709–51) was an army physician who had lost his post
by writing a *Natural History of the Soul,* and had won exile by a work
called *Man a Machine.* He had taken refuge at the court of Frederick,
who was himself something of an advanced thinker and was resolved to
have the very latest culture from Paris. La Mettrie took up the idea of
mechanism where the frightened Descartes, like a boy who has burned his
fingers, had dropped it; and announced boldly that all the world, not
excepting man, was a machine. The soul is material, and matter is soul-
ful; but whatever they are they act upon each other, and grow and decay
with each other in a way that leaves no doubt of their essential similarity
and interdependence. If the soul is pure spirit, how can enthusiasm warm
the body, or fever in the body disturb the processes of the mind? All
organisms have evolved out of one original germ, through the reciprocal
action of organism and environment. The reason why animals have intelligence, and plants none, is that animals move about for their food,
while plants take what comes to them. Man has the highest intelligence
because he has the greatest wants and the widest mobility; "beings without wants are also without mind."

Though La Mettie was exiled for these opinions, Helvetius (1715-71), who took them as the basis of his book *On Man*, became one of the richest men in France, and rose to position and honor. Here we have the ethic, as in La Mettrie the metaphysic, of atheism. All action is dictated by egoism, self-love; "even the hero follows the feeling which for him is associated with the greatest pleasure"; and "virtue is egoism furnished with a spy-glass."[55] Conscience is not the voice of God, but the fear of the police; it is the deposit left in us from the stream of prohibitions poured over the growing soul by parents and teachers and press. Morality must be founded not on theology but on sociology; the changing needs of society, and not any unchanging revelation or dogma, must determine the good.

The greatest figure in this group was Denis Diderot (1713-84). His ideas were expressed in various fragments from his own pen, and in the *System of Nature* of Baron d'Holbach (1723-89), whose salon was the centre of Diderot's circle. "If we go back to the beginning," says Holbach, "we shall find that ignorance and fear created the gods; that fancy, enthusiasm or deceit adorned or disfigured them; that weakness worships them; that credulity preserves them; and that custom respects and tyranny supports them in order to make the blindness of men serve its own interests." Belief in God, said Diderot, is bound up with submission to autocracy; the two rise and fall together; and "men will never be free till the last king is strangled with the entrails of the last priest." The earth will come into its own only when heaven is destroyed. Materialism may be an over-simplification of the world—all matter is probably instinct with life, and it is impossible to reduce the unity of consciousness to matter and motion; but materialism is a good weapon against the Church, and must be used till a better one is found. Meanwhile one must spread knowledge and encourage industry; industry will make for peace, and knowledge will make a new and natural morality.

These are the ideas which Diderot and d'Alembert labored to disseminate through the great *Encyclopédie* which they issued, volume by volume, from 1752 to 1772. The Church had the first volumes suppressed; and, as the opposition increased, Diderot's comrades abandoned him; but he worked on angrily, invigorated by his rage. "I know nothing so indecent," he said, "as these vague declamations of the theologians against reason. To hear them one would suppose that men could not enter into the bosom of Christianity except as a herd of cattle enters a stable." It was, as Paine put it, the age of reason; these men never doubted that the intellect was the ultimate human test of all truth and all good. Let reason be freed, they said, and it would in a few generations build Utopia. Diderot did not suspect that the erotic and neurotic Jean Jacques Rousseau (1712-78), whom he had just introduced to Paris, was carrying in

*Taine. *The Ancient Régime*

his head, or in his heart, the seeds of a revolution against this enthronement of reason; a revolution which, armed with the impressive obscurities
of Immanuel Kant, would soon capture every citadel of philosophy.

Naturally enough, Voltaire, who was interested in everything, and had
a hand in every fight, was caught up for a time in the circle of the
Encyclopedists; they were glad to call him their leader; and he was not
averse to their incense, though some of their ideas needed a little pruning.
They asked him to write articles for their great undertaking, and he
responded with a facility and fertility which delighted them. When he
had finished this work he set about making an encyclopedia of his own,
which he called a *Philosophic Dictionary;* with unprecedented audacity
he took subject after subject as the alphabet suggested them, and poured
out under each heading part of his inexhaustible resources of knowledge
and wisdom. Imagine a man writing on everything, and producing a
classic none the less; the most readable and sparkling of Voltaire's works
aside from his romances; every article a model of brevity, clarity, and
wit. "Some men can be prolix in one small volume; Voltaire is terse
through a hundred."[56] Here at last Voltaire proves that he is a philosopher.

He begins, like Bacon, Descartes and Locke and all the moderns, with
doubt and a (supposedly) clean slate. "I have taken as my patron saint
St. Thomas of Didymus, who always insisted on an examination with his
own hands."[57] He thanks Bayle for having taught him the art of doubt. He
rejects all systems, and suspects that "every chief of a sect in philosophy
has been a little of a quack."[58] "The further I go, the more I am confirmed in the idea that systems of metaphysics are for philosophers what
novels are for women."[59] It is only charlatans who are certain. We know
nothing of first principles. It is truly extravagant to define God, angels,
and minds, and to know precisely why God formed the world, when we
do not know why we move our arms at will. Doubt is not a very agreeable
state, but certainty is a ridiculous one."[60] "I do not know how I was
made, and how I was born. I did not know at all, during a quarter of
my life, the causes of what I saw, or heard, or felt. . . . I have seen
that which is called matter, both as the star Sirius, and as the smallest
atom which can be perceived with the microscope; and I do not know
what this matter is."[61]

He tells a story of "The Good Brahmin," who says, "I wish I had never
been born!"

"Why so?" said I.

"Because," he replied, "I have been studying these forty years, and I find
that it has been so much time lost. . . . I believe that I am composed of

[56]Robertson, 87.   [57]*Philosophic Dictionary,* New York, 1901; vol. ix, p. 198.
[58]*Ibid.,* 42.   [59]In Pellissier, 11, note.
[60]Robertson. 122.   [61]*Dictionary,* article "Ignorance."

matter, but I have never been able to satisfy myself what it is that produces thought. I am even ignorant whether my understanding is a simple faculty like that of walking or digesting, or if I think with my head in the same manner as I take hold of a thing with my hands. . . . I talk a great deal, and when I have done speaking I remain confounded and ashamed of what I have said."

The same day I had a conversation with an old woman, his neighbor. I asked her if she had ever been unhappy for not understanding how her soul was made? She did not even comprehend my question. She had not, for the briefest moment in her life, had a thought about these subjects with which the good Brahmin had so tormented himself. She believed in the bottom of her heart in the metamorphoses of Vishnu, and provided she could get some of the sacred water of the Ganges in which to make her ablutions, she thought herself the happiest of women. Struck with the happiness of this poor creature, I returned to my philosopher, whom I thus addressed:

"Are you not ashamed to be thus miserable when, not fifty yards from you, there is an old automaton who thinks of nothing and lives contented?"

"You are right," he replied. "I have said to myself a thousand times that I should be happy if I were but as ignorant as my old neighbor; and yet it is a happiness which I do not desire."

This reply of the Brahmin made a greater impression on me than anything that had passed.[62]

Even if Philosophy should end in the total doubt of Montaigne's *"Que sais-je?"*[63] it is man's greatest adventure, and his noblest. Let us learn to be content with modest advances in knowledge, rather than be forever weaving new systems out of our mendacious imagination.

We must not say, Let us begin by inventing principles whereby we may be able to explain everything; rather we must say, Let us make an exact analysis of the matter, and then we shall try to see, with much diffidence, if it fits in with any principle.[64] . . . The Chancellor Bacon had shown the road which science might follow. . . . But then Descartes appeared and did just the contrary of what he should have done: instead of studying nature, he wished to divine her. . . . This best of mathematicians made only romances in philosophy.[65] . . . It is given us to calculate, to weigh, to measure, to observe; this is natural philosophy; almost all the rest is chimera.[66]

VIII. *ECRASEZ L'INFAME*

Under ordinary circumstances it is probable that Voltaire would never have passed out of the philosophic calm of this courteous scepticism to the arduous controversies of his later years. The aristocratic circles in which he moved agreed so readily with his point of view that there was no incentive to polemics; even the priests smiled with him over the dif-

[62]*Romances*, 450 f.   [63] "What do I know?"   [64]In Pellissier, 28, note.
[65]*Voltaire's Prose*, ed. Cohn and Woodward; Boston, 1918; p. 54.
[66]In Pellissier, 29-30.

ficulties of the faith, and cardinals considered whether, after all, they might not yet make him into a good Capuchin. What were the events that turned him from the polite persiflage of agnosticism to a bitter anti-clericalism which admitted no compromise, but waged relentless war to "crush the infamy" of ecclesiasticism?

Not far from Ferney lay Toulouse, the seventh city of France. In Voltaire's day the Catholic clergy enjoyed absolute sovereignty there; the city commemorated with frescoes the Revocation of the Edict of Nantes (an edict which had given freedom of worship to Protestants), and celebrated as a great feast the day of the Massacre of St. Bartholomew. No Protestant in Toulouse could be a lawyer, or a physician, or an apothecary, or a grocer, or a book-seller, or a printer; nor could a Catholic keep a Protestant servant or clerk—in 1748 a woman had been fined 3000 francs for using a Protestant midwife.

Now it happened that Jean Calas, a Protestant of Toulouse, had a daughter who became a Catholic, and a son who hanged himself, presumably because of disappointment in business. There was a law in Toulouse that every suicide should be placed naked on a hurdle, with face down, drawn thus through the streets, and then hanged on a gibbet. The father, to avert this, asked his relatives and his friends to testify to a natural death. In consequence, rumor began to talk of murder, and to hint that the father had killed the son to prevent his imminent conversion to Catholicism. Calas was arrested, put to the torture, and died soon after (1761). His family, ruined and hunted, fled to Ferney, and sought the aid of Voltaire. He took them into his home, comforted them, and marveled at the story of medieval persecution which they told.

About the same time (1762) came the death of Elizabeth Sirvens; again rumor charged that she had been pushed into a well just as she was about to announce her conversion to Catholicism. That a timid minority of Protestants would hardly dare to behave in this way was a rational consideration, and therefore out of the purview of rumor.—In 1765 a young man by the name of La Barre, aged sixteen, was arrested on the charge of having mutilated crucifixes. Subjected to torture, he confessed his guilt; his head was cut off, and his body was flung into the flames, while the crowd applauded. A copy of Voltaire's *Philosophic Dictionary*, which had been found on the lad, was burned with him.

For almost the first time in his life, Voltaire became a thoroughly serious man. When d'Alembert, disgusted equally with state, church and people, wrote that hereafter he would merely mock at everything, Voltaire answered, "This is not a time for jesting; wit does not harmonize with massacres. . . . Is this the country of philosophy and pleasure? It is rather the country of the Massacre of St. Bartholomew." It was with Voltaire now as with Zola and Anatole France in the case of Dreyfus; this tyrannous injustice lifted him up; he ceased to be merely a man of letters, and became a man of action too; he laid aside philosophy for war, or rather turned his philosophy into relentless dynamite. "During this time not a smile escaped me without my reproaching myself for it as for a crime." It was now that he adopted his famous motto, *Ecrasez l'infame,* and stirred the soul of France against the abuses of the church. He began to pour forth such intellectual fire and brimstone as melted mitres and sceptres, broke the power of the priesthood in France, and helped to overthrow a throne. He sent out a call to his friends and followers, summoning them to battle: "Come, brave Diderot, intrepid d'Alembert, ally yourselves; . . . overwhelm the fanatics and the knaves, destroy the insipid declamations, the miserable sophistries, the lying history, . . . the absurdities without number; do not let those who have sense be subjected to those who have none; and the generation which is being born will owe to us its reason and its liberty."[67]

Just at this crisis an effort was made to buy him off; through Mme. de Pompadour he received an offer of a cardinal's hat as the reward of reconciliation with the Church.[68] As if the rule of a few tongue-tied bishops could interest a man who was the undisputed sovereign of the world of intellect! Voltaire refused; and like another Cato, began to end all his letters with "Crush the infamy." He sent out his *Treatise on Toleration:* he said he would have borne with the absurdities of dogma had the clergy lived up to their sermons and had they tolerated differences; but "subtleties of which not a trace can be found in the Gospels are the source of the bloody quarrels of Christian history."[69] "The man who says to me, 'Believe as I do, or God will damn you,' will presently say, 'Believe as I do, or I shall assassinate you.' "[70] "By what right could a being created free force another to think like himself?"[71] "A fanaticism composed of superstition and ignorance has been the sickness of all the centuries."[72] No such perpetual peace as the Abbé de St.-Pierre had pleaded for could ever be realized unless men learned to tolerate one another's philosophic, political and religious differences. The very first step towards social health was the destruction of the ecclesiastical power in which intolerance had its root.

The *Treatise on Toleration* was followed up with a Niagara of pamphlets, histories, dialogues, letters, catechisms, diatribes, squibs, sermons, verses, tales, fables, commentaries and essays, under Voltaire's own name and under a hundred pseudonyms—"the most astonishing pell-mell of propaganda ever put out by one man."[73] Never was philosophy phrased so clearly, and with such life; Voltaire writes so well that one does not realize that he is writing philosophy. He said of himself, over-modestly, "I

[67]Correspondence, Nov. 11, 1765.   [68]Tallentyre, 319; questioned by some.
[69]Selected Works, p. 62.   [70]*Ibid.,* 65.
[71]*Essai sur les Moeurs;* Prose Works, p. 14.
[72]*Ibid.,* p. 26.   [73]Robertson, 112.

express myself clearly enough: I am like the little brooks, which are transparent because they are not deep."[74] And so he was read; soon everybody, even the clergy, had his pamphlets; of some of them 300,000 copies were sold, though readers were far fewer then than now; nothing like it had ever been seen in the history of literature. "Big books," he said, "are out of fashion." And so he sent forth his little soldiers, week after week, month after month, resolute and tireless, surprising the world with the fertility of his thought and the magnificent energy of his seventy years. As Helvetius put it, Voltaire had crossed the Rubicon, and stood before Rome.[75]

He began with a "higher criticism" of the authenticity and reliability of the Bible; he takes much of his material from Spinoza, more of it from the English Deists, most of it from the *Critical Dictionary* of Bayle (1647–1706); but how brilliant and fiery their material becomes in his hands! One pamphlet is called "The Questions of Zapata," a candidate for the priesthood; Zapata asks, innocently, "How shall we proceed to show that the Jews, whom we burn by the hundred, were for four thousand years the chosen people of God?"[76]—and he goes on with questions which lay bare the inconsistencies of narrative and chronology in the Old Testament. "When two Councils anathematize each other, as has often happened, which of them is infallible?" At last, "Zapata, receiving no answer, took to preaching God in all simplicity. He announced to men the common Father, the rewarder, punisher, and pardoner. He extricated the truth from the lies, and separated religion from fanaticism; he taught and practised virtue. He was gentle, kindly, and modest; and he was burned at Valladolid in the year of grace 1631."[77]

Under the article on "Prophecy" in the *Philosophic Dictionary,* he quotes Rabbin Isaac's *Bulwark of Faith* against the application of Hebrew prophecies to Jesus, and then goes on, ironically: "Thus these blind interpreters of their own religion and their own language, combated with the Church, and obstinately maintained that this prophecy cannot in any manner regard Jesus Christ."[78] Those were dangerous days, in which one was compelled to say what one meant without saying it, and the shortest line to one's purpose was anything but straight. Voltaire likes to trace Christian dogmas and rites to Greece, Egypt and India, and thinks that these adaptations were not the least cause of the success of Christianity in the ancient world. Under the article on "Religion" he asks, slyly, "After our own holy religion, which doubtless is the only good one, what religion would be the least objectionable?"—and he proceeds to describe a faith and worship directly opposed to the Catholicism of his

[74]In Sainte-Beuve, ii, 146.   [75]In Pellissier, 101.
[76]Selected Works, p. 26. Voltaire himself was something of an anti-Semite, chiefly because of his not quite admirable dealings with the financiers.
[77]*Ibid.,* 26-35.   [78]IX, 21.

day. "Christianity must be divine," he says, in one of his most unmeasured sallies, "since it has lasted 1,700 years despite the fact that it is so full of villainy and nonsense."[79] He shows how almost all ancient peoples had similar myths, and hastily concludes that the myths are thereby proved to have been the inventions of priests: "the first divine was the first rogue who met the first fool." However, it is not religion itself which he attributes to the priests, but theology. It is slight differences in theology that have caused so many bitter disputes and religious wars. "It is not the ordinary people . . . who have raised these ridiculous and fatal quarrels, the sources of so many horrors. . . . Men fed by your labors in a comfortable idleness, enriched by your sweat and your misery, struggled for partisans and slaves; they inspired you with a destructive fanaticism, that they might be your masters; they made you superstitious not that you might fear God but that you might fear them."[80]

Let it not be supposed from all this that Voltaire was quite without religion. He decisively rejects atheism;[81] so much so that some of the Encyclopedists turned against him, saying, "Voltaire is a bigot, he believes in God." In "The Ignorant Philosopher" he reasons towards Spinozist pantheism, but then recoils from it as almost atheism. He writes to Diderot:

I confess that I am not at all of the opinion of Saunderson, who denies a God because he was born sightless. I am, perhaps, mistaken; but in his place I should recognize a great Intelligence who had given me so many substitutes for sight; and perceiving, on reflection, the wonderful relations between all things, I should have suspected a Workman infinitely able. If it is very presumptuous to divine *what* He is, and *why* He has made everything that exists, so it seems to me very presumptuous to deny *that* He exists. I am exceedingly anxious to meet and talk with you, whether you think yourself one of His works, or a particle drawn, of necessity, from eternal and necessary matter. Whatever you are, you are a worthy part of that great whole which I do not understand.[82]

To Holbach he points out that the very title of his book, the *System of Nature,* indicates a divine organizing intelligence. On the other hand he stoutly denies miracles and the supernatural efficacy of prayer:

I was at the gate of the convent when Sister Fessue said to Sister Confite: "Providence takes a visible care of me; you know how I love my sparrow; he would have been dead if I had not said nine Ave-Marias to obtain his cure." . . . A metaphysician said to her: "Sister, there is nothing so good as Ave-Marias, especially when a girl pronounces them in Latin in the suburbs of Paris; but I cannot believe that God has occupied himself so

[79]*Essai sur les Moeurs,* part ii, ch. 9; in Morley 322.
[80]Selected Works, 63.
[81]Cf. *The Sage and the Atheist,* chs. 9 and 10.
[82]*Voltaire in His Letters.* p. 81.

much with your sparrow, pretty as it is; I pray you to believe that he has other things to attend to. . . ." Sister Fessue: "Sir, this discourse savors of heresy. My confessor . . . will infer that you do not believe in Providence." Metaphysician: "I believe in a general Providence, dear Sister, which has laid down from all eternity the law which governs all things, like light from the sun; but I believe not that a particular Providence changes the economy of the world for your sparrow."[83]

"His Sacred Majesty, Chance, decides everything."[84] True prayer lies not in asking for a violation of natural law but in the acceptance of natural law as the unchangeable will of God.[85]

Similarly, he denies free will.[86] As to the soul he is an agnostic: "Four thousand volumes of metaphysics will not teach us what the soul is."[87] Being an old man, he would like to believe in immortality, but he finds it difficult.

> Nobody thinks of giving an immortal soul to the flea; why then to an elephant, or a monkey, or my valet?[88] . . . A child dies in its mother's womb, just at the moment when it has received a soul. Will it rise again foetus, or boy, or man? To rise again—to be the same person that you were —you must have your memory perfectly fresh and present; for it is memory that makes your identity. If your memory be lost, how will you be the same man?[89] . . . Why do mankind flatter themselves that they alone are gifted with a spiritual and immortal principle? . . . Perhaps from their inordinate vanity. I am persuaded that if a peacock could speak he would boast of his soul, and would affirm that it inhabited his magnificent tail.[90]

And in this earlier mood he rejects also the view that belief in immortality is necessary for morality: the ancient Hebrews were without it, just when they were the "chosen people"; and Spinoza was a paragon of morality.

In later days he changed his mind. He came to feel that belief in God has little moral value unless accompanied by belief in an immortality of punishment and reward. Perhaps, "for the common people (*la canaille*) a rewarding and avenging God" is necessary. Bayle had asked, If a society of atheists could subsist?—Voltaire answers, "Yes, if they are also philosophers.[91] But men are seldom philosophers; "if there is a hamlet, to be good it must have a religion."[92] "I want my lawyer, my tailor, and my wife to believe in God," says "A" in "A, B, C"; "so, I imagine, I shall be less robbed and less deceived." "If God did not exist it would be necessary to invent him."[93] "I begin to put more store on happiness and life

[83]*Dictionary,* art. "Providence."
[85]*Romances,* p. 412.
[87]*Dictionary,* art. "Soul."
[89]*Dictionary,* art. "Resurrection."
[91]In Pellissier, 169.
[88]In Pellissier, 172.

[84]Correspondence, Feb. 26, 1767.
[86]*The Ignorant Philosopher.*
[88]In Morley, ed. 1886; p. 286.
[90]*Romances,* p. 411.
[93]*Dictionary,* art. "Religion."

than on truth";[94]—a remarkable anticipation, in the midst of the Enlightenment, of the very doctrine with which Immanuel Kant was later to combat the Enlightenment. He defends himself gently against his friends the atheists; he addresses Holbach in the article on "God" in the *Dictionary:*

> You yourself say that belief in God . . . has kept some men from crime; this alone suffices me. When this belief prevents even ten assassinations, ten calumnies, I hold that all the world should embrace it. Religion, you say, has produced countless misfortunes; say rather the superstition which reigns on our unhappy globe. This is the cruelest enemy of the pure worship due to the Supreme Being. Let us detest this monster which has always torn the bosom of its mother; those who combat it are the benefactors of the human race; it is a serpent which chokes religion in its embrace; we must crush its head without wounding the mother whom it devours."

This distinction between superstition and religion is fundamental with him. He accepts gladly the theology of the Sermon on the Mount, and acclaims Jesus in tributes which could hardly be matched even with the pages of saintly ecstasy. He pictures Christ among the sages, weeping over the crimes that have been committed in his name. At last he built his own church, with the dedication, "Deo erexit Voltaire"; the only church in Europe, he said, that was erected to God. He addresses to God a magnificent prayer; and in the article "Theist" he expounds his faith finally and clearly:

> The theist is a man firmly persuaded of the existence of a supreme being as good as he is powerful, who has formed all things . . . ; who punishes, without cruelty, all crimes, and recompenses with goodness all virtuous actions. . . . Reunited in this principle with the rest of the universe, he does not join any of the sects which all contradict one another. His religion is the most ancient and the most widespread; for the simple worship of a God preceded all the systems of the world. He speaks a language which all peoples understand, while they do not understand one another. He has brothers from Pekin to Cayenne, and he counts all the sages for his fellows. He believes that religion consists neither in the opinions of an unintelligible metaphysic, nor in vain shows, but in worship and in justice. To do good is his worship, to submit to God is his creed. The Mohammedan cries out to him, "Beware if you fail to make the pilgrimage to Mecca!"—the priest says to him, "Curses on you if you do not make the trip to Notre Dame de Lorette!" He laughs at Lorette and at Mecca: but he succors the indigent and defends the oppressed.

IX. VOLTAIRE AND ROUSSEAU

Voltaire was so engrossed in the struggle against ecclesiastical tyranny that during the later decades of his life he was compelled almost to with-

[94]Correspondence, Sept. 11, 1738.

draw from the war on political corruption and oppression. "Politics is not in my line: I have always confined myself to doing my little best to make men less foolish and more honorable." He knew how complex a matter political philosophy can become, and he shed his certainties as he grew. "I am tired of all these people who govern states from the recesses of their garrets";[95] "these legislators who rule the world at two cents a sheet; . . . unable to govern their wives or their households they take great pleasure in regulating the universe."[96] It is impossible to settle these matters with simple and general formulae, or by dividing all people into fools and knaves on the one hand, and on the other, ourselves. "Truth has not the name of a party"; and he writes to Vauvenargues: "It is the duty of a man like you to have preferences, but not exclusions."[97]

Being rich, he inclines towards conservatism, for no worse reason than that which impels the hungry man to call for a change. His panacea is the spread of property: ownership gives personality and an uplifting pride. "The spirit of property doubles a man's strength. It is certain that the possessor of an estate will cultivate his own inheritance better than that of another."[98]

He refuses to excite himself about forms of government. Theoretically he prefers a republic, but he knows its flaws: it permits factions which, if they do not bring on civil war, at least destroy national unity; it is suited only to small states protected by geographical situation, and as yet unspoiled and untorn with wealth; in general "men are rarely worthy to govern themselves." Republics are transient at best; they are the first form of society, arising from the union of families; the American Indians lived in tribal republics, and Africa is full of such democracies. But differentiation of economic status puts an end to these egalitarian governments; and differentiation is the inevitable accompaniment of development. "Which is better," he asks, "a monarchy or a republic?"—and he replies: "For four thousand years this question has been tossed about. Ask the rich for an answer—they all want aristocracy. Ask the people— they want democracy. Only the monarchs want monarchy. How then has it come about that almost the entire earth is governed by monarchs? Ask the rats who proposed to hang a bell about the neck of the cat."[99] But when a correspondent argues that monarchy is the best form of government he answers: "Provided Marcus Aurelius is monarch; for otherwise, what difference does it make to a poor man whether he is devoured by a lion or by a hundred rats?"[100]

Likewise, he is almost indifferent to nationalities, like a traveled man; he has hardly any patriotism in the usual sense of that word. Patriotism commonly means, he says, that one hates every country but one's own. If

[95]Correspondence, Sept. 18, 1763.   [96]In Pellissier, 237, note, and 236.
[97]Pellissier, 23; Morley, 86.   [98]*Dictionary*, art. "Property."
[99]*Dictionary*, art. "Fatherland."   [100]Correspondence. June 20, 1777.

a man wishes his country to prosper, but never at the expense of other countries, he is at the same time an intelligent patriot and a citizen of the universe.[101] Like a "good European" he praises England's literature and Prussia's king while France is at war with both England and Prussia. So long as nations make a practice of war, he says, there is not much to choose among them.

For he hates war above all else. "War is the greatest of all crimes; and yet there is no aggressor who does not color his crime with the pretext of justice."[102] "It is forbidden to kill; therefore all murderers are punished unless they kill in large numbers and to the sound of trumpets."[103] He has a terrible "General Reflection on Man," at the end of the article on "Man" in the *Dictionary:*

> Twenty years are required to bring man from the state of a plant, in which he exists in the womb of his mother, and from the state of an animal, which is his condition in infancy, to a state in which the maturity of reason begins to make itself felt. Thirty centuries are necessary in which to discover even a little of his structure. An eternity would be required to know anything of his soul. But one moment suffices in which to kill him.

Does he therefore think of revolution as a remedy? No. For first of all, he distrusts the people: "When the people undertake to reason, all is lost."[104] The great majority are always too busy to perceive the truth until change has made the truth an error; and their intellectual history is merely the replacement of one myth by another. "When an old error is established, politics uses it as a morsel which the people have put into their own mouths, until another superstition comes along to destroy this one, and politics profits from the second error as it did from the first."[105] And then again, inequality is written into the very structure of society, and can hardly be eradicated while men are men and life is a struggle. "Those who say that all men are equal speak the greatest truth if they mean that all men have an equal right to liberty, to the possession of their goods, and to the protection of the laws"; but "equality is at once the most natural and the most chimerical thing in the world: natural when it is limited to rights, unnatural when it attempts to level goods and powers."[106] "Not all citizens can be equally strong; but they can all be equally free; it is this which the English have won. . . . To be free is to be subject to nothing but the laws."[107] This was the note of the liberals, of Turgot and Condorcet and Mirabeau and the other followers of Voltaire who hoped to make a peaceful revolution; it could not quite satisfy the oppressed, who called not so much for liberty as for equality, equality even at the cost of liberty. Rousseau, voice of the common man,

[101]Pellissier, 222.
[103]*Dictionary*, art. "War."
[105]*Voltaire's Prose,* p. 15.
[107]Art. "Government."
[102]*The Ignorant Philosopher.*
[104]Correspondence, April 1, 1766.
[106]*Dictionary*, art. "Equality."

sensitive to the class distinctions which met him at every turn, demanded a leveling; and when the Revolution fell into the hands of his followers, Marat and Robespierre, equality had its turn, and liberty was guillotined.

Voltaire was sceptical of Utopias to be fashioned by human legislators who would create a brand new world out of their imaginations. Society is a growth in time, not a syllogism in logic; and when the past is put out through the door it comes in at the window. The problem is to show precisely by what changes we can diminish misery and injustice in the world in which we actually live.[108] In the "Historical Eulogy of Reason," Truth, the daughter of Reason, voices her joy at the accession of Louis XVI, and her expectation of great reforms; to which Reason replies: "My daughter, you know well that I too desire these things, and more. But all this requires time and thought. I am always happy when, amid many disappointments, I obtain some of the amelioration I longed for." Yet Voltaire too rejoiced when Turgot came to power, and wrote: "We are in the golden age up to our necks!"[109]—now would come the reforms he had advocated: juries, abolition of the tithe, an exemption of the poor from all taxes, etc. And had he not written that famous letter?—

Everything that I see appears to be throwing broadcast the seed of a revolution which must some day inevitably come, but which I shall not have the pleasure of witnessing. The French always come late to things, but they do come at last. Light extends so from neighbor to neighbor, that there will be a splendid outburst on the first occasion; and then there will be a rare commotion! The young are fortunate; they will see fine things.[110]

Yet he did not quite realize what was happening about him; and he never for a moment supposed that in this "splendid outburst" all France would accept enthusiastically the philosophy of this queer Jean Jacques Rousseau who, from Geneva and Paris, was thrilling the world with sentimental romances and revolutionary pamphlets. The complex soul of France seemed to have divided itself into these two men, so different and yet so French. Nietzsche speaks of "*la gaya scienza*, the light feet, wit, fire, grace, strong logic, arrogant intellectuality, the dance of the stars"—surely he was thinking of Voltaire. Now beside Voltaire put Rousseau: all heat and fantasy, a man with noble and jejune visions, the idol of *la bourgeoise gentile-femme*, announcing like Pascal that the heart has its reasons which the head can never understand.

In these two men we see again the old clash between intellect and instinct. Voltaire believed in reason always: "we can, by speech and pen, make men more enlightened and better."[111] Rousseau had little faith in reason; he desired action; the risks of revolution did not frighten him; he relied on the sentiment of brotherhood to re-unite the social elements

[108]Pellissier, 283.
[110]Correspondence, April 2, 1764.
[109]In Sainte-Beuve, i, 234.
[111]Selected Works, 62.

scattered by turmoil and the uprooting of ancient habits. Let laws be
removed, and men would pass into a reign of equality and justice. When
he sent to Voltaire his *Discourse on the Origin of Inequality*, with its
arguments against civilization, letters, and science, and for a return to
the natural condition as seen in savages and animals, Voltaire replied: "I
have received, sir, your new book against the human species, and I thank
you for it. . . . No one has ever been so witty as you are in trying to turn
us into brutes; to read your book makes one long to go on all fours. As,
however, it is now some sixty years since I gave up the practice, I feel
that it is unfortunately impossible for me to resume it."[112] He was
chagrined to see Rousseau's passion for savagery continue into the *Social
Contract*: "Ah, Monsieur," he writes to M. Bordes, "you see now that
Jean Jacques resembles a philosopher as a monkey resembles a man."[113]
He is the "dog of Diogenes gone mad."[114] Yet he attacked the Swiss
authorities for burning the book, holding to his famous principle: "I do
not agree with a word that you say, but I will defend to the death your
right to say it."[115] And when Rousseau was fleeing from a hundred
enemies Voltaire sent him a cordial invitation to come and stay with
him at Les Délices. What a spectacle that would have been!

Voltaire was convinced that all this denunciation of civilization was
boyish nonsense; that man was incomparably better off under civilization
than under savagery; he informs Rousseau that man is by nature a beast
of prey, and that civilized society means a chaining of this beast, a mitigation of his brutality, and the possibility of the development, through
social order, of the intellect and its joys. He agrees that things are bad:
"A government in which it is permitted a certain class of men to say,
'Let those pay taxes who work; we should not pay, because we do not
work,' is no better than a government of Hottentots." Paris has its re-
deeming features, even amidst its corruption. In "The World as It Goes,"
Voltaire tells how an angel sent Babouc to report on whether the city of
Persepolis should be destroyed; Babouc goes, and is horrified with the
vices he discovers; but after a time "he began to grow fond of a city the
inhabitants of which were polite, affable and beneficent, though they
were fickle, slanderous and vain. He was much afraid that Persepolis
would be condemned. He was even afraid to give in his account. This he
did, however, in the following manner. He caused a little statue, composed of different metals, of earth and of stones (the most precious and
the most vile) to be cast by one of the best founders of the city, and
carried it to the angel. 'Wilt thou break,' said he, 'this pretty statue because it is not wholly composed of gold and diamonds?' " The angel
resolved to think no more of destroying Persepolis, but to leave "the
world as it goes." After all, when one tries to change institutions without

---

[112]Correspondence, Aug. 30, 1755.   [113]*Ibid.*, Mar. 1765.
[114]In Sainte-Beuve, i, 230.   [115]*Voltaire in His Letters*, 65.

having changed the nature of men, that unchanged nature will soon resurrect those institutions.

Here was the old vicious circle; men form institutions, and institutions form men; where could change break into this ring? Voltaire and the liberals thought that intellect could break the ring by educating and changing men, slowly and peacefully; Rousseau and the radicals felt that the ring could be broken only by instinctive and passionate action that would break down the old institutions and build, at the dictates of the heart, new ones under which liberty, equality and fraternity would reign. Perhaps the truth lay above the divided camps: that instinct must destroy the old, but that only intellect can build the new. Certainly the seeds of reaction lay fertile in the radicalism of Rousseau: for instinct and sentiment are ultimately loyal to the ancient past which has begotten them, and to which they are stereotyped adaptations: after the catharsis of revolution the needs of the heart would recall supernatural religion and the "good old days" of routine and peace; after Rousseau would come Chateaubriand, and De Staël, and De Maistre, and Kant.

X. DÉNOUEMENT

Meanwhile the old "laughing philosopher" was cultivating his garden at Ferney; this "is the best thing we can do on earth." He had asked for a long life: "my fear is that I shall die before I have rendered service";[116] but surely now he had done his share. The records of his generosity are endless. "Everyone, far or near, claimed his good offices; people consulted him, related the wrongs of which they were the victims, and solicited the help of his pen and his credit."[117] Poor people guilty of some misdemeanor were his especial care; he would secure a pardon for them and then set them up in some honest occupation, meanwhile watching and counselling them. When a young couple who had robbed him went down on their knees to beg his forgiveness, he knelt to raise them, telling them that his pardon was freely theirs, and that they should kneel only for God's.[118] One of his characteristic undertakings was to bring up, educate, and provide a dowry for the destitute niece of Corneille. "The little good I have done," he said, "is my best work. . . . When I am attacked I fight like a devil; I yield to no one; but at bottom I am a good devil, and I end by laughing."[119]

In 1770 his friends arranged a subscription to have a bust made of him. The rich had to be forbidden to give more than a mite, for thousands asked the honor of contributing. Frederick inquired how much he should give; he was told, "A crown piece, sire, and your name." Voltaire congratulated him on adding to his cultivation of the other sciences this en-

[116]Correspondence, Aug. 25, 1766. [117]Sainte-Beuve, i, 235.
[118]Robertson, 71. [119]Ibid., 67.

couragement of anatomy by subscribing for the statue of a skeleton. He demurred to the whole undertaking on the ground that he had no face left to be modeled. "You would hardly guess where it ought to be. My eyes have sunk in three inches; my cheeks are like old parchment; . . . the few teeth I had are gone." To which d'Alembert replied: "Genius . . . has always a countenance which genius, its brother, will easily find."[120] When his pet, Bellet-Bonne, kissed him, he said it was "Life kissing Death."

He was now eighty-three; and a longing came over him to see Paris before he died. The doctors advised him not to undertake so arduous a trip; but "if I want to commit a folly," he answered, "nothing will prevent me"; he had lived so long, and worked so hard, that perhaps he felt he had a right to die in his own way, and in that electric Paris from which he had been so long exiled. And so he went, weary mile after weary mile, across France; and when his coach entered the capital his bones hardly held together. He went at once to the friend of his youth, d'Argental: "I have left off dying to come and see you," he said. The next day his room was stormed by three hundred visitors, who welcomed him as a king; Louis XVI fretted with jealousy. Benjamin Franklin was among the callers, and brought his grandson for Voltaire's blessing; the old man put his thin hands upon the youth's head and bade him dedicate himself to "God and Liberty."

He was so ill now that a priest came to shrive him. "From whom do you come, M. l'Abbé?" asked Voltaire. "From God Himself," was the answer. "Well, well, sir," said Voltaire; "your credentials?"[121] The priest went away without his prey. Later Voltaire sent for another abbé, Gautier, to come and hear his confession; Gautier came, but refused Voltaire absolution until he should sign a profession of full faith in Catholic doctrine. Voltaire rebelled; instead, he drew up a statement which he gave to his secretary, Wagner: "I die adoring God, loving my friends, not hating my enemies, and detesting superstition. (Signed) *Voltaire*. February 28, 1778."[122]

Though sick and tottering, he was driven to the Academy, through tumultuous crowds that clambered on his carriage and tore into souvenirs the precious pelisse which Catherine of Russia had given him. "It was one of the historic events of the century. No great captain returning from a prolonged campaign of difficulty and hazard crowned by the most glorious victory, ever received a more splendid and far-resounding greeting."[123] At the Academy he proposed a revision of the French dictionary; he spoke with youthful fire, and offered to undertake all such part of the work as would come under the letter A. At the close of the sitting he said, "Gentlemen, I thank you in the name of the alphabet." To which the chairman, Chastellux, replied: "And we thank you in the name of letters."

[120]Tallentyre, 497.   [121]Tallentyre, 535.
[122]*Ibid.*, 538.   [123]Morley, 262.

Meanwhile his play, *Irène,* was being performed at the theatre; against the advice of the physicians again, he insisted on attending. The play was poor; but people marveled not so much that a man of eighty-three should write a poor play, but that he should write any play at all;[124] and they drowned the speech of the players with repeated demonstrations in honor of the author. A stranger, entering, supposed himself to be in a madhouse, and rushed back frightened into the street.[125]

When the old patriarch of letters went home that evening he was almost reconciled to death. He knew that he was exhausted now; that he had used to the full that wild and marvelous energy which nature had given to him perhaps more than to any man before him. He struggled as he felt life being torn from him; but death could defeat even Voltaire. The end came on May 30, 1778.

He was refused Christian burial in Paris; but his friends set him up grimly in a carriage, and got him out of the city by pretending that he was alive. At Scellières they found a priest who understood that rules were not made for geniuses; and the body was buried in holy ground. In 1791 the National Assembly of the triumphant Revolution forced Louis XVI to recall Voltaire's remains to the Panthéon. The dead ashes of the great flame that had been were escorted through Paris by a procession of 100,000 men and women, while 600,000 flanked the streets. On the funeral car were the words: "He gave the human mind a great impetus; he prepared us for freedom." On his tombstone only three words were necessary:

HERE LIES VOLTAIRE

[124]Tallentyre, 525.   [125]*Ibid.,* 545.

CHAPTER VI

Immanuel Kant and German Idealism

I. ROADS TO KANT

NEVER has a system of thought so dominated an epoch as the philosophy of Immanuel Kant dominated the thought of the nineteenth century. After almost three-score years of quiet and secluded development, the uncanny Scot of Königsberg roused the world from its "dogmatic slumber," in 1781, with his famous *Critique of Pure Reason;* and from that year to our own the "critical philosophy" has ruled the speculative roost of Europe. The philosophy of Schopenhauer rose to brief power on the romantic wave that broke in 1848; the theory of evolution swept everything before it after 1859; and the exhilarating iconoclasm of Nietzsche won the center of the philosophic stage as the century came to a close. But these were secondary and surface developments; underneath them the strong and steady current of the Kantian movement flowed on, always wider and deeper; until today its essential theorems are the axioms of all mature philosophy. Nietzsche takes Kant for granted, and passes on;[1] Schopenhauer calls the *Critique* "the most important work in German literature," and considers any man a child until he has understood Kant;[2] Spencer could not understand Kant, and for precisely that reason, perhaps, fell a little short of the fullest philosophic stature. To adapt Hegel's phrase about Spinoza: to be a philosopher, one must first have been a Kantian.

Therefore let us become Kantians at once. But it cannot be done at once, apparently; for in philosophy, as in politics, the longest distance between two points is a straight line. Kant is the last person in the world whom we should read on Kant. Our philosopher is like and unlike Jehovah; he speaks through clouds, but without the illumination of the lightning-flash. He disdains examples and the concrete; they would have made his book too long, he argued.[3] (So abbreviated, it contains some 800 pages). Only professional philosophers were expected to read him; and these would not need illustrations. Yet when Kant gave the MS. of the *Critique* to his friend Herz, a man much versed in speculation, Herz

[1] *The Will to Power,* vol. ii, part I.
[2] *The World as Will and Idea,* London, 1883; vol. ii, p. 30.
[3] *The Critique of Pure Reason,* London, 1881; vol. ii, p. xxvii. All subsequent references are to volume two.

returned it half read, saying he feared insanity if he went on with it.
What shall we do with such a philosopher?

Let us approach him deviously and cautiously, beginning at a safe and
respectful distance from him; let us start at various points on the circum-
ference of the subject, and then grope our way towards that subtle centre
where the most difficult of all philosophies has its secret and its treasure.

1. FROM VOLTAIRE TO KANT

The road here is from theoretical reason without religious faith, to
religious faith without theoretical reason. Voltaire means the Enlightenment, the Encyclopedia, the Age of Reason. The warm enthusiasm of
Francis Bacon had inspired all Europe (except Rousseau) with unques-
tioning confidence in the power of science and logic to solve at last all
problems, and illustrate the "infinite perfectibility" of man. Condorcet,
in prison, wrote his *Historical Tableau of the Progress of the Human
Spirit* (1793), which spoke the sublime trust of the eighteenth century
in knowledge and reason, and asked no other key to Utopia than universal
education. Even the steady Germans had their *Aufklärung*, their rationalist, Christian Wolff, and their hopeful Lessing. And the excitable
Parisians of the Revolution dramatized this apotheosis of the intellect by
worshipping the "Goddess of Reason,"—impersonated by a charming
lady of the streets.

In Spinoza this faith in reason had begotten a magnificent structure
of geometry and logic: the universe was a mathematical system, and
could be described *à priori*, by pure deduction from accepted axioms.
In Hobbes the rationalism of Bacon had become an uncompromising
atheism and materialism; again nothing was to exist but "atoms and the
void." From Spinoza to Diderot the wrecks of faith lay in the wake of
advancing reason: one by one the old dogmas disappeared; the Gothic
cathedral of medieval belief, with its delightful details and grotesques,
collapsed; the ancient God fell from his throne along with the Bourbons,
heaven faded into mere sky, and hell became only an emotional expression. Helvetius and Holbach made atheism so fashionable in the salons
of France that even the clergy took it up; and La Mettrie went to peddle
it in Germany, under the auspices of Prussia's king. When, in 1784,
Lessing shocked Jacobi by announcing himself a follower of Spinoza, it
was a sign that faith had reached its nadir, and that Reason was triumphant.

David Hume, who played so vigorous a rôle in the Enlightenment
assault on supernatural belief, said that when reason is against a man,
he will soon turn against reason. Religious faith and hope, voiced in a
hundred thousand steeples rising out of the soil of Europe everywhere,
were too deeply rooted in the institutions of society and in the heart of

man, to permit their ready surrender to the hostile verdict of reason; it was inevitable that this faith and this hope, so condemned, would question the competence of the judge, and would call for an examination of reason as well as of religion. What was this intellect that proposed to destroy with a syllogism the beliefs of thousands of years and millions of men? Was it infallible? Or was it one human organ like any other, with strictest limits to its functions and its powers? The time had come to judge this judge, to examine this ruthless Revolutionary Tribunal that was dealing out death so lavishly to every ancient hope. The time had come for a critique of reason.

2. From Locke to Kant

The way had been prepared for such an examination by the work of Locke, Berkeley and Hume; and yet, apparently, their results too were hostile to religion.

John Locke (1632-1704) had proposed to apply to psychology the inductive tests and methods of Francis Bacon; in his great *Essay on Human Understanding* (1689) reason, for the first time in modern thought, had turned in upon itself, and philosophy had begun to scrutinize the instrument which it so long had trusted. This introspective movement in philosophy grew step by step with the introspective novel as developed by Richardson and Rousseau; just as the sentimental and emotional color of *Clarissa Harlowe* and *La Nouvelle Héloise* had its counterpart in the philosophic exaltation of instinct and feeling above intellect and reason.

How does knowledge arise? Have we, as some good people suppose, innate ideas, as, for example, of right and wrong, and God,—ideas inherent in the mind from birth, prior to all experience? Anxious theologians, worried lest belief in the Deity should disappear because God had not yet been seen in any telescope, had thought that faith and morals might be strengthened if their central and basic ideas were shown to be inborn in every normal soul. But Locke, good Christian though he was, ready to argue most eloquently for "The Reasonableness of Christianity," could not accept these suppositions; he announced, quietly, that all our knowledge comes from experience and through our senses—that "there is nothing in the mind except what was first in the senses." The mind is at birth a clean sheet, a *tabula rasa;* and sense-experience writes upon it in a thousand ways, until sensation begets memory and memory begets ideas. All of which seemed to lead to the startling conclusion that since only material things can effect our sense, we know nothing but matter, and must accept a materialistic philosophy. If sensations are the stuff of thought, the hasty argued, matter must be the material of mind.

Not at all, said Bishop George Berkeley (1684-1753); this Lockian analysis of knowledge proves rather that matter does not exist except as a form of mind. It was a brilliant idea—to refute materialism by the simple expedient of showing that we know of no such thing as matter; in all Europe only a Gaelic imagination could have conceived this metaphysical magic. But see how obvious it is, said the Bishop: has not Locke told us that all our knowledge is derived from sensation? Therefore all our knowledge of anything is merely our sensations of it, and the ideas derived from these sensations. A "thing" is merely a bundle of perceptions—i. e., classified and interpreted sensations. You protest that your breakfast is much more substantial than a bundle of perceptions; and that a hammer that teaches you carpentry through your thumb has a most magnificent materiality. But your breakfast is at first nothing but a congeries of sensations of sight and smell and touch; and then of taste; and then of internal comfort and warmth. Likewise, the hammer is a bundle of sensations of color, size, shape, weight, touch, etc.; its reality for you is not in its materiality, but in the sensations that come from your thumb. If you had no senses, the hammer would not exist for you at all; it might strike your dead thumb forever and yet win from you not the slightest attention. It is only a bundle of sensations, or a bundle of memories; it is a condition of the mind. All matter, so far as we know it, is a mental condition; and the only reality that we know directly is mind. So much for materialism.

But the Irish Bishop had reckoned without the Scotch sceptic. David Hume (1711–1776) at the age of twenty-six shocked all Christendom with his highly heretical *Treatise on Human Nature,*—one of the classics and marvels of modern philosophy. We know the mind, said Hume, only as we know matter: by perception, though it be in this case internal. Never do we perceive any such entity as the "mind"; we perceive merely separate ideas, memories, feelings, etc. The mind is not a substance, an organ that has ideas; it is only an abstract name for the series of ideas; the perceptions, memories and feelings *are* the mind; there is no observable "soul" behind the processes of thought. The result appeared to be that Hume had as effectually destroyed mind as Berkeley had destroyed matter. Nothing was left; and philosophy found itself in the midst of ruins of its own making. No wonder that a wit advised the abandonment of the controversy, saying: "No matter, never mind."

But Hume was not content to destroy orthodox religion by dissipating the concept of soul; he proposed also to destroy science by dissolving the concept of law. Science and philosophy alike, since Bruno and Galileo, had been making much of natural law, of "necessity" in the sequence of effect upon cause; Spinoza had reared his majestic metaphysics upon this proud conception. But observe, said Hume, that we never perceive causes, or laws; we perceive events and sequences, and *infer* causation and necessity; a law is not an eternal and necessary decree to which events are subjected, but merely a mental summary and shorthand of our kaleidoscopic experience; we have no guarantee that the sequences hitherto observed will re-appear unaltered in future experience. "Law" is an observed *custom* in the sequence of events; but there is no "necessity" in custom.

Only mathematical formulas have necessity—they alone are inherently and unchangeably true; and this merely because such formulae are tautological—the predicate is already contained in the subject; "$3 \times 3 = 9$" is an eternal and necessary truth only because "3×3" and "9" are one and the same thing differently expressed; the predicate adds nothing to the subject. Science, then, must limit itself strictly to mathematics and direct experiment; it cannot trust to unverified deduction from "laws." "When we run though libraries, persuaded of these principles," writes our uncanny sceptic, "what havoc must we make! If we take in our hands any volume of school metaphysics, for instance, let us ask, 'Does it contain any abstract reasoning concerning quantity or number?' No. 'Does it contain any experimental reasoning concerning matter of fact and existence?' No. Commit it then to the flames, for it can contain nothing but sophistry and illusion."[4]

Imagine how the ears of the orthodox tingled at these words. Here the epistemological tradition—the inquiry into the nature, sources, and validity of knowledge—had ceased to be a support to religion; the sword with which Bishop Berkeley had slain the dragon of materialism had turned against the immaterial mind and the immortal soul; and in the turmoil science itself had suffered severe injury. No wonder that when Immanuel Kant, in 1775, read a German translation of the works of David Hume, he was shocked by these results, and was roused, as he said, from the "dogmatic slumber" in which he had assumed without question the essentials of religion and the bases of science. Were both science and faith to be surrendered to the sceptic? What could be done to save them?

3. From Rousseau to Kant

To the argument of the Enlightenment, that reason makes for materialism, Berkeley had essayed the answer that matter does not exist. But this had led, in Hume, to the retort that by the same token mind does not exist either. Another answer was possible—that reason is no final test. There are some theoretical conclusions against which our whole being rebels; we have no right to presume that these demands of our nature must be stifled at the dictates of a logic which is after all but the recent construction of a frail and deceptive part of us. How often our instincts and feelings push aside the little syllogisms which would like us to behave like geometrical figures, and make love with mathematical precision! Sometimes, no doubt,—and particularly in the novel complexities and artificialities of urban life,—reason is the better guide; but in the great crises of life, and in the great problems of conduct and belief, we trust

[4]Quoted in Royce, *The Spirit of Modern Philosophy*, Boston, 1892; p. 98.

to our feelings rather than to our diagrams. If reason is against religion, so much the worse for reason!

Such, in effect, was the argument of Jean Jacques Rousseau (1712–1778), who almost alone, in France, fought the materialism and atheism of the Enlightenment. What a fate for a delicate and neurotic nature, to have been cast amidst the robust rationalism and the almost brutal hedonism[5] of the Encyclopedists! Rousseau had been a sickly youth, driven into brooding and introversion by his physical weakness and the unsympathetic attitude of his parents and teachers; he had escaped from the stings of reality into a hothouse world of dreams, where the victories denied him in life and love could be had for the imagining. His *Confessions* reveal an unreconciled complex of the most refined sentimentality with an obtuse sense of decency and honor; and through it all an unsullied conviction of his moral superiority.[6]

In 1749 the Academy of Dijon offered a prize for an essay on the question, "Has the Progress of the Sciences and the Arts Contributed to Corrupt, or to Purify, Morals?" Rousseau's essay won the prize. Culture is much more of an evil than a good, he argued—with all the intensity and sincerity of one who, finding culture out of his reach, proposed to prove it worthless. Consider the frightful disorders which printing has produced in Europe. Wherever philosophy arises, the moral health of the nation decays. "It was even a saying among the philosophers themselves that since learned men had appeared, honest men were nowhere to be found." "I venture to declare that a state of reflection is contrary to nature; and that a thinking man" (an "intellectual," as we would now say) "is a depraved animal." It would be better to abandon our over-rapid development of the intellect, and to aim rather at training the heart and the affections. Education does not make a man good, it only makes him clever—usually for mischief. Instinct and feeling are more trustworthy than reason.

In his famous novel, *La Nouvelle Héloïse* (1761), Rousseau illustrated at great length the superiority of feeling to intellect; sentimentality became the fashion among the ladies of the aristocracy, and among some of the men; France was for a century watered with literary, and then with actual, tears; and the great movement of the European intellect in the eighteenth century gave way to the romantic emotional literature of 1789–1848. The current carried with it a strong revival of religious feeling; the ecstasies of Chateaubriand's *Génie du Christianisme* (1802) were merely an echo of the "Confession of Faith of the Savoyard Vicar" which Rousseau included in his epochal essay on education—*Emile* (1762). The argument of the "Confession" was briefly this: that though reason might be against belief in God and immortality, feeling was over-

---

[5] The doctrine that all behavior is motived by the pursuit of pleasure.
[6] Cf. *Confessions*, bk. X; vol. ii, p. 184.

whelmingly in their favor; why should we not trust in instinct here, rather than yield to the despair of an arid scepticism?

When Kant read *Emile* he omitted his daily walk under the linden trees, in order to finish the book at once. It was an event in his life to find here another man who was groping his way out of the darkness of atheism, and who boldly affirmed the priority of feeling over theoretical reason in these supra-sensual concerns. Here at last was the second half of the answer to irreligion; now finally all the scoffers and doubters would be scattered. To put these threads of argument together, to unite the ideas of Berkeley and Hume with the feelings of Rousseau, to save religion from reason, and yet at the same time to save science from scepticism—this was the mission of Immanuel Kant.

But who was Immanuel Kant?

II. KANT HIMSELF

He was born at Königsberg, Prussia, in 1724. Except for a short period of tutoring in a nearby village, this quiet little professor, who loved so much to lecture on the geography and ethnology of distant lands, never left his native city. He came of a poor family, which had left Scotland some hundred years before Immanuel's birth. His mother was a Pietist,—i. e., a member of a religious sect which, like the Methodists of England, insisted on the full strictness and rigor of religious practice and belief. Our philosopher was so immersed in religion from morning to night that on the one hand he experienced a reaction which led him to stay away from church all through his adult life; and on the other hand he kept to the end the sombre stamp of the German Puritan, and felt, as he grew old, a great longing to preserve for himself and the world the essentials, at least, of the faith so deeply inculcated in him by his mother.

But a young man growing up in the age of Frederick and Voltaire could not insulate himself from the sceptical current of the time. Kant was profoundly influenced even by the men whom later he aimed to refute, and perhaps most of all by his favorite enemy, Hume; we shall see later the remarkable phenomenon of a philosopher transcending the conservatism of his maturity and returning in almost his last work, and at almost the age of seventy, to a virile liberalism that would have brought him martyrdom had not his age and his fame protected him. Even in the midst of his work of religious restoration we hear, with surprising frequency, the tones of another Kant whom we might almost mistake for a Voltaire. Schopenhauer thought it "not the least merit of Frederick the Great, that under his government Kant could develop himself, and dared to publish his *Critique of Pure Reason*. Hardly under any other government would a salaried professor" (therefore, in Germany, a government employee) "have ventured such a thing. Kant was obliged to promise the immediate successor of the great King that he would write no more."[7] It was in appreciation of this freedom that Kant dedicated the *Critique* to Zedlitz, Frederick's far-sighted and progressive Minister of Education.

In 1755 Kant began his work as private lecturer at the University of Königsberg. For fifteen years he was left in this lowly post; twice his applications for a professorship were refused. At last, in 1770, he was made professor of logic and metaphysics. After many years of experience as a teacher, he wrote a text-book of pedagogy, of which he used to say that it contained many excellent precepts, none of which he had ever applied. Yet he was perhaps a better teacher than writer; and two generations of students learned to love him. One of his practical principles was to attend most to those pupils who were of middle ability; the dunces, he said, were beyond all help, and the geniuses would help themselves.

Nobody expected him to startle the world with a new metaphysical system; to startle anybody seemed the very last crime that this timid and modest professor would commit. He himself had no expectations in that line; at the age of forty-two he wrote: "I have the fortune to be a lover of metaphysics; but my mistress has shown me few favors as yet." He spoke in those days of the "bottomless abyss of metaphysics," and of metaphysics as "a dark ocean without shores or lighthouse," strewn with many a philosophic wreck.[8] He could even attack the metaphysicians as those who dwelt on the high towers of speculation, "where there is usually a great deal of wind."[9] He did not foresee that the greatest of all metaphysical tempests was to be of his own blowing.

During these quiet years his interests were rather physical than metaphysical. He wrote on planets, earthquakes, fire, winds, ether, volcanoes, geography, ethnology, and a hundred other things of that sort, not usually confounded with metaphysics. His *Theory of the Heavens* (1755) proposed something very similar to the nebular hypothesis of Laplace, and attempted a mechanical explanation of all sidereal motion and development. All the planets, Kant thought, have been or will be inhabited; and those that are farthest from the sun, having had the longest period of growth, have probably a higher species of intelligent organisms than any yet produced on our planet. His *Anthropology* (put together in 1798 from the lectures of a life-time) suggested the possibility of the animal origin of man. Kant argued that if the human infant, in early ages when man was still largely at the mercy of wild animals, had cried as loudly upon entering the world as it does now, it would have been found out and devoured by beasts of prey; that in all probability, therefore, man was very different at first from what he had become under

[7] *The World as Will and Idea,* London, 1883; vol. ii, p. 133.
[8] In Paulsen, *Immanuel Kant;* New York, 1910; p. 82.
[9] *Ibid.,* p. 56.

civilization. And then Kant went on, subtly: "How nature brought about such a development, and by what causes it was aided, we know not. This remark carries us a long way. It suggests the thought whether the present period of history, on the occasion of some great physical revolution, may not be followed by a third, when an orang-outang or a chimpanzee would develop the organs which serve for walking, touching, speaking, into the articulated structure of a human being, with a central organ for the use of understanding, and gradually advance under the training of social institutions." Was this use of the future tense Kant's cautiously indirect way of putting forth his view of how man had really developed from the beast?[10]

So we see the slow growth of this simple little man, hardly five feet tall, modest, shrinking, and yet containing in his head, or generating there, the most far-reaching revolution in modern philosophy. Kant's life, says one biographer, passed like the most regular of regular verbs. "Rising, coffee-drinking, writing, lecturing, dining, walking," says Heine,—"each had its set time. And when Immanuel Kant, in his gray coat, cane in hand, appeared at the door of his house, and strolled towards the small avenue of linden trees which is still called 'The Philosopher's Walk,' the neighbors knew it was exactly half-past-three by the clock. So he promenaded up and down, during all seasons; and when the weather was gloomy, or the gray clouds threatened rain, his old servant Lampe was seen plodding anxiously after, with a large umbrella under his arm, like a symbol of Prudence."

He was so frail in physique that he had to take severe measures to regimen himself; he thought it safer to do this without a doctor; so he lived to the age of eighty. At seventy he wrote an essay "On the Power of the Mind to Master the Feeling of Illness by Force of Resolution." One of his favorite principles was to breathe only through the nose, especially when out-doors; hence, in autumn, winter and spring, he would permit no one to talk to him on his daily walks; better silence than a cold. He applied philosophy even to holding up his stockings—by bands passing up into his trousers' pockets, where they ended in springs contained in small boxes.[11] He thought everything out carefully before acting; and therefore remained a bachelor all his life long. Twice he thought of offering his hand to a lady; but he reflected so long that in one case the lady married a bolder man, and in the other the lady removed from Königsberg before the philosopher could make up his mind. Perhaps he felt, like Nietzsche, that marriage would hamper him in the honest pursuit of truth; "a married man," Talleyrand used to say, "will do anything for money." And Kant had written, at twenty-two, with all the fine enthusiasm of omnipotent youth: "I have already fixed upon the line which I am

[10] So Wallace suggests: Kant, Philadelphia, 1882: p. 115.
[11] Introd. to Kant's Critique of Practical Reason; London, 1909; p. xiii.

resolved to keep. I will enter on my course, and nothing shall prevent me from pursuing it."[12]

And so he persevered, through poverty and obscurity, sketching and writing and rewriting his *magnum opus* for almost fifteen years; finishing it only in 1781, when he was fifty-seven years old. Never did a man mature so slowly; and then again, never did a book so startle and upset the philosophic world.

III. THE CRITIQUE OF PURE REASON[13]

What is meant by this title? *Critique* is not precisely a criticism, but a critical analysis; Kant is not attacking "pure reason," except, at the end, to show its limitations; rather he hopes to show its possibility, and to exalt it above the impure knowledge which comes to us through the distorting channels of sense. For "pure" reason is to mean knowledge that does not come through our senses, but is independent of all sense experience; knowledge belonging to us by the inherent nature and structure of the mind.

At the very outset, then, Kant flings down a challenge to Locke and the English school: knowledge is not all derived from the senses. Hume thought he had shown that there is no soul, and no science; that our minds are but our ideas in procession and association; and our certainties but probabilities in perpetual danger of violation. These false conclusions, says Kant, are the result of false premises: you assume that all knowledge comes from "separate and distinct" sensations; naturally these cannot give you necessity, or invariable sequences of which you may be forever certain; and naturally you must not expect to "see" your soul, even with the eyes of the internal sense. Let us grant that absolute certainty of knowledge is impossible if all knowledge comes from sensation, from an independent external world which owes us no promise of regularity of behavior. But what if we have knowledge that is independent of sense-experience, knowledge whose truth is certain to us even before experience —*à priori?* Then absolute truth, and absolute science, would become possible, would it not? Is there such absolute knowledge? This is the problem of the first *Critique*. "My question is, what we can hope to achieve with reason, when all the material and assistance of experience are taken

[12]Wallace, p. 100.

[13]A word about what to read. Kant himself is hardly intelligible to the beginner, because his thought is insulated with a bizarre and intricate terminology (hence the paucity of direct quotation in this chapter). Perhaps the simplest introduction is Wallace's *Kant*, in the Blackwood Philosophical Classics. Heavier and more advanced is Paulsen's *Immanuel Kant*. Chamberlain's *Immanuel Kant* (2 vols.; New York, 1914) is interesting but erratic and digressive. A good criticism of Kant may be found in Schopenhauer's *World as Will and Idea;* vol. ii. pp. 1–159. But *caveat emptor*

away."[14] The *Critique* becomes a detailed biology of thought, an examina-tion of the origin and evolution of concepts, an analysis of the inherited structure of the mind. This, as Kant believes, is the entire problem of metaphysics. "In this book I have chiefly aimed at completeness; and I venture to maintain that there ought not to be one single metaphysical problem that has not been solved here, or to the solution of which the key at least has not here been supplied."[15] *Exegi monumentum aere perennius!* With such egotism nature spurs us on to creation.

The *Critique* comes to the point at once. "Experience is by no means the only field to which our understanding can be confined. Experience tells us what is, but not that it must be necessarily what it is and not otherwise. It therefore never gives us any really general truths; and our reason, which is particularly anxious for that class of knowledge, is roused by it rather than satisfied. General truths, which at the same time bear the character of an inward necessity, must be independent of ex-perience,—clear and certain in themselves."[16] That is to say, they must be true no matter what our later experience may be; true even *before* experience; true *à priori*. "How far we can advance independently of all experience, in *à priori* knowledge, is shown by the brilliant example of mathematics."[17] Mathematical knowledge is necessary and certain; we cannot conceive of future experience violating it. We may believe that the sun will "rise" in the west to-morrow, or that some day, in some con-ceivable asbestos world, fire will not burn stick; but we cannot for the life of us believe that two times two will ever make anything else than four. Such truths are true before experience; they do not depend on experience past, present, or to come. Therefore they are absolute and necessary truths; it is inconceivable that they should ever become untrue. But whence do we get this character of absoluteness and necessity? Not from experience; for experience gives us nothing but separate sensations and events, which may alter their sequence in the future.[18] These truths derive their necessary character from the inherent structure of our minds, from the natural and inevitable manner in which our minds must operate. For the mind of man (and here at last is the great thesis of Kant) is not passive wax upon which experience and sensation write their absolute and yet whimsical will; nor is it a mere abstract name for the series or group of mental states; it is an active organ which moulds and coördinates sensations into ideas, an organ which transforms the chaotic multiplicity of experience into the ordered unity of thought.

But how?

[14] *Critique of Pure Reason,* pref. p. xxiv.
[15] *Ibid.,* p. xxiii.   [16] *Ibid.,* p. i.   [17] P. 4.
[18] "Radical empiricism" (James, Dewey, etc.) enters the controversy at this point, and argues, against both Hume and Kant, that experience gives us relations and sequences as well as sensations and events.

1. TRANSCENDENTAL ESTHETIC

The effort to answer this question, to study the inherent structure of the mind, or the innate laws of thought, is what Kant calls "transcendental philosophy," because it is a problem transcending sense-experience. "I call knowledge transcendental which is occupied not so much with objects, as with our à priori concepts of objects."[19]—with our modes of correlating our experience into knowledge. There are two grades or stages in this process of working up the raw material of sensation into the finished product of thought. The first stage is the coördination of sensations by applying to them the forms of perception—space and time; the second stage is the coördination of the perceptions so developed, by applying to them the forms of conception—the "categories" of thought. Kant, using the word *esthetic* in its original and etymological sense, as connoting sensation or feeling, calls the study of the first of these stages "Transcendental Esthetic"; and using the word *logic* as meaning the science of the forms of thought, he calls the study of the second stage "Transcendental Logic." These are terrible words, which will take meaning as the argument proceeds; once over this hill, the road to Kant will be comparatively clear.

Now just what is meant by sensations and perceptions?—and how does the mind change the former into the latter? By itself a sensation is merely the awareness of a stimulus; we have a taste on the tongue, an odor in the nostrils, a sound in the ears, a temperature on the skin, a flash of light on the retina, a pressure on the fingers: it is the raw crude beginning of experience; it is what the infant has in the early days of its groping mental life; it is not yet knowledge. But let these various sensations group themselves about an object in space and time—say this apple; let the odor in the nostrils, and the taste on the tongue, the light on the retina, the shape-revealing pressure on the fingers and the hand, unite and group themselves about this "thing": and there is now an awareness not so much of a stimulus as of a specific object; there is a perception. Sensation has passed into knowledge.

But again, was this passage, this grouping, automatic? Did the sensations of themselves, spontaneously and naturally, fall into a cluster and an order, and so become perception? Yes, said Locke and Hume; not at all, says Kant.

For these varied sensations come to us through varied channels of sense, through a thousand "afferent nerves" that pass from skin and eye and ear and tongue into the brain; what a medley of messengers they must be as they crowd into the chambers of the mind, calling for attention! No wonder Plato spoke of "the rabble of the senses." And left to

[19]*Critique of Pure Reason.* p. 10.

themselves, they remain rabble, a chaotic "manifold," pitifully impotent, waiting to be ordered into meaning and purpose and power. As readily might the messages brought to a general from a thousand sectors of the battle-line weave themselves unaided into comprehension and command. No; there is a law-giver for this mob, a directing and coördinating power that does not merely receive, but takes these atoms of sensation and moulds them into sense.

Observe, first, that not all of the messages are accepted. Myriad forces play upon your body at this moment; a storm of stimuli beats down upon the nerve-endings which, amoebalike, you put forth to experience the external world: but not all that call are chosen; only those sensations are selected that can be moulded into perceptions suited to your present purpose, or that bring those imperious messages of danger which are always relevant. The clock is ticking, and you do not hear it; but that same ticking, not louder than before, will be heard at once if your purpose wills it so. The mother asleep at her infant's cradle is deaf to the turmoil of life about her; but let the little one move, and the mother gropes her way back to waking attention like a diver rising hurriedly to the surface of the sea. Let the purpose be addition, and the stimulus "two and three" brings the response, "five"; let the purpose be multiplication, and the same stimulus, the same auditory sensations, "two and three," bring the response, "six." Association of sensations or ideas is not merely by contiguity in space or time, nor by similarity, nor by recency, frequency or intensity of experience; it is above all determined by the purpose of the mind. Sensations and thoughts are servants, they await our call, they do not come unless we need them. There is an agent of selection and direction that uses them and is their master. In addition to the sensations and the ideas there is the *mind*.

This agent of selection and coördination, Kant thinks, uses first of all two simple methods for the classification of the material presented to it: the sense of space, and the sense of time. As the general arranges the messages brought him according to the place for which they come, and the time at which they were written, and so finds an order and a system for them all; so the mind allocates its sensations in space and time, attributes them to this object here or that object there, to this present time or to that past. Space and time are not things perceived, but modes of perception, ways of putting sense into sensation; space and time are organs of perception.

They are *à priori*, because all ordered experience involves and presupposes them. Without them, sensations could never grow into perceptions. They are *à priori* because it is inconceivable that we should ever have any future experience that will not also involve them. And because they are *à priori*, their laws, which are the laws of mathematics, are *à priori*, absolute and necessary, world without end. It is not merely probable, it is certain that we shall never find a straight line that is not the shortest distance between two points. Mathematics, at least, is saved from the dissolvent scepticism of David Hume.

Can all the sciences be similarly saved? Yes, if their basic principle, the law of causality—that a given cause must *always* be followed by a given effect—can be shown, like space and time, to be so inherent in all the processes of understanding that no future experience can be conceived that would violate or escape it. Is causality, too, à *priori*, an indispensable prerequisite and condition of all thought?

2. TRANSCENDENTAL ANALYTIC

So we pass from the wide field of sensation and perception to the dark and narrow chamber of thought; from "transcendental esthetic" to "transcendental logic." And first to the naming and analysis of those elements in our thought which are not so much given to the mind by perception as given to perception by the mind; those levers which raise the "perceptual" knowledge of objects into the "conceptual" knowledge of relationships, sequences, and laws; those tools of the mind which refine experience into science. Just as perceptions arranged sensations around objects in space and time, so conception arranges perceptions (objects and events) about the ideas of cause, unity, reciprocal relation, necessity, contingency, etc.; these and other "categories" are the structure into which perceptions are received, and by which they are classified and moulded into the ordered concepts of thought. These are the very essence and character of the mind; mind *is* the coördination of experience.

And here again observe the activity of this mind that was, to Locke and Hume, mere "passive wax" under the blows of sense-experience. Consider a system of thought like Aristotle's; is it conceivable that this almost cosmic ordering of data should have come by the automatic, anarchistic spontaneity of the data themselves? See this magnificent card-catalogue in the library, intelligently ordered into sequence by human purpose. Then picture all these card-cases thrown upon the floor, all these cards scattered pell-mell into riotous disorder. Can you now conceive these scattered cards pulling themselves up, Münchausen-like, from their disarray, passing quietly into their alphabetical and topical places in their proper boxes, and each box into its fit place in the rack,—until all should be order and sense and purpose again? What a miracle-story these sceptics have given us after all!

Sensation is unorganized stimulus, perception is organized sensation, conception is organized perception, science is organized knowledge, wisdom is organized life: each is a greater degree of order, and sequence, and unity. Whence this order, this sequence, this unity? Not from the things themselves; for they are known to us only by sensations that come through a thousand channels at once in disorderly multitude; it is our purpose that put order and sequence and unity upon this importunate lawlessness; it is ourselves, our personalities, our minds, that bring light upon these seas. Locke was wrong when he said, "There is nothing in the intellect except what was first in the senses"; Leibnitz was right when he added,—"nothing, except the intellect itself." "Perceptions without conceptions," says Kant, "are blind." If perceptions wove themselves automatically into ordered thought, if mind were not an active effort hammering out order from chaos, how could the same experience leave one man mediocre, and in a more active and tireless soul be raised to the light of wisdom and the beautiful logic of truth?

The world, then, has order, not of itself, but because the thought that knows the world is itself an ordering, the first stage in that classification of experience which at last is science and philosophy. The laws of thought are also the laws of things, for things are known to us only through this thought that must obey these laws, since it and they are one; in effect, as Hegel was to say, the laws of logic and the laws of nature are one, and logic and metaphysics merge. The generalized principles of science are necessary because they are ultimately laws of thought that are involved and presupposed in every experience, past, present, and to come. Science is absolute, and truth is everlasting.

3. TRANSCENDENTAL DIALECTIC

Nevertheless, this certainty, this absoluteness, of the highest generalizations of logic and science, is, paradoxically, limited and relative: limited strictly to the field of actual experience, and relative strictly to our human mode of experience. For if our analysis has been correct, the world as we know it is a construction, a finished product, almost—one might say—a manufactured article, to which the mind contributes as much by its moulding forms as the thing contributes by its stimuli. (So we perceive the top of the table as round, whereas our sensation is of an ellipse.) The object as it appears to us is a phenomenon, an appearance, perhaps very different from the external object before it came within the ken of our senses; what that original object was we can never know; the "thing-in-itself" may be an object of thought or inference (a "noumenon"), but it cannot be experienced,—for in being experienced it would be changed by its passage through sense and thought. "It remains completely unknown to us what objects may be by themselves and apart from the receptivity of our senses. We know nothing but our manner of perceiving them; that manner being peculiar to us, and not necessarily shared by every being, though, no doubt, by every human being."[20] The moon as

---

[20] *Critique*, p. 37. If Kant had not added the last clause, his argument for the necessity of knowledge would have fallen.

known to us is merely a bundle of sensations (as Hume saw), unified (as Hume did not see) by our native mental structure through the elaboration of sensations into perceptions, and of these into conceptions or ideas; in result, the moon is *for us* merely our ideas.[21]

Not that Kant ever doubts the existence of "matter" and the external world; but he adds that we know nothing certain about them except that they exist. Our detailed knowledge is about their appearance, their phenomena, about the sensations which we have of them. Idealism does not mean, as the man in the street thinks, that nothing exists outside the perceiving subject; but that a goodly part of every object is created by the forms of perception and understanding: we know the object as transformed into idea; what it is before being so transformed we cannot know. Science, after all, is naïve; it supposes that it is dealing with things in themselves, in their full-blooded external and uncorrupted reality; philosophy is a little more sophisticated, and realizes that the whole material of science consists of sensations, perceptions and conceptions, rather than of things. "Kant's greatest merit," says Schopenhauer, "is the distinction of the phenomenon from the thing-in-itself."[22]

It follows that any attempt, by either science or religion, to say just what the ultimate reality is, must fall back into mere hypothesis; "the understanding can never go beyond the limits of sensibility."[23] Such transcendental science loses itself in "antinomies," and such transcendental theology loses itself in "paralogisms." It is the cruel function of "transcendental dialectic" to examine the validity of these attempts of reason to escape from the enclosing circle of sensation and appearance into the unknowable world of things "in themselves."

Antinomies are the insoluble dilemmas born of a science that tries to overleap experience. So, for example, when knowledge attempts to decide whether the world is finite or infinite in space, thought rebels against either supposition: beyond any limit, we are driven to conceive something further, endlessly; and yet infinity is itself inconceivable. Again: did the world have a beginning in time? We cannot conceive eternity; but then, too, we cannot conceive any point in the past without feeling at once that before that, something was. Or has that chain of causes which science studies, a beginning, a First Cause? Yes, for an endless chain is inconceivable; no, for a first cause uncaused is inconceivable as well. Is there any exit from these blind alleys of thought? There is, says Kant, if we remember that space, time and cause are modes of perception and conception, which must enter into all our experience, since they are the web and structure of experience; these dilemmas arise from supposing that space, time and cause are external things independent of perception.

[21] So John Stuart Mill, with all his English tendency to realism, was driven at last to define matter as merely "a permanent possibility of sensations."

[22] *The World as Will and Idea;* vol. ii, p. 7.   [23] *Critique,* p. 215.

We shall never have any experience which we shall not interpret in terms of space and time and cause; but we shall never have any philosophy if we forget that these are not things, but modes of interpretation and understanding.

So with the paralogisms of "rational" theology—which attempts to prove by theoretical reason that the soul is an incorruptible substance, that the will is free and above the law of cause and effect, and that there exists a "necessary being," God, as the presupposition of all reality. Transcendental dialectic must remind theology that substance and cause and necessity are finite categories, modes of arrangement and classification which the mind applies to sense-experience, and reliably valid only for the phenomena that appear to such experience; we cannot apply these conceptions to the noumenal (or merely inferred and conjectural) world. Religion cannot be proved by theoretical reason.

So the first *Critique* ends. One could well imagine David Hume, un-cannier Scot than Kant himself, viewing the results with a sardonic smile. Here was a tremendous book, eight hundred pages long; weighted beyond bearing, almost, with ponderous terminology; proposing to solve all the problems of metaphysics, and incidentally to save the absoluteness of science and the essential truth of religion. What had the book really done? It had destroyed the naïve world of science, and limited it, if not in degree, certainly in scope,—and to a world confessedly of mere surface and appearance, beyond which it could issue only in farcical "antin-omies"; so science was "saved"! The most eloquent and incisive portions of the book had argued that the objects of faith—a free and immortal soul, a benevolent creator—could never be proved by reason; so religion was "saved"! No wonder the priests of Germany protested madly against this salvation, and revenged themselves by calling their dogs Immanuel Kant.[24]

And no wonder that Heine compared the little professor of Königsberg with the terrible Robespierre; the latter had merely killed a king, and a few thousand Frenchmen—which a German might forgive; but Kant, said Heine, had killed God, had undermined the most precious argu-ments of theology. "What a sharp contrast between the outer life of this man, and his destructive, world-convulsing thoughts! Had the citizens of Königsberg surmised the whole significance of those thoughts, they would have felt a more profound awe in the presence of this man than in that of an executioner, who merely slays human beings. But the good people saw in him nothing but a professor of philosophy; and when at the fixed hour he sauntered by, they nodded a friendly greeting, and set their watches."[25]

Was this caricature, or revelation?

[24]Wallace, p. 82.   [25]Heine. *Prose Miscellanies,* Philadelphia, 1876; p. 146.

IV. THE CRITIQUE OF PRACTICAL REASON

If religion cannot be based on science and theology, on what then? On morals. The basis in theology is too insecure; better that it should be abandoned, even destroyed; faith must be put beyond the reach or realm of reason. But therefore the moral basis of religion must be absolute, not derived from questionable sense-experience or precarious inference; not corrupted by the admixture of fallible reason; it must be derived from the inner self by direct perception and intuition. We must find a universal and necessary ethic; à priori principles of morals as absolute and certain as mathematics. We must show that "pure reason can be practical; i. e., can of itself determine the will independently of anything empirical,"[26] that the moral sense is innate, and not derived from experience. The moral imperative which we need as the basis of religion must be an absolute, a categorical, imperative.

Now the most astounding reality in all our experience is precisely our moral sense, our inescapable feeling, in the face of temptation, that this or that is wrong. We may yield; but the feeling is there nevertheless. *Le matin je fais des projets, et le soir je fais des sottises;*[27] but we know that they are *sottises,* and we resolve again. What is it that brings the bite of remorse, and the new resolution? It is the categorical imperative in us, the unconditional command of our conscience, to "act as if the maxim of our action were to become by our will a universal law of nature."[28] We know, not by reasoning, but by vivid and immediate feelings, that we must avoid behavior which, if adopted by all men, would render social life impossible. Do I wish to escape from a predicament by a lie? But "while I can will the lie, I can by no means will that lying should be a universal law. For with such a law there would be no promises at all."[29] Hence the sense in me, that I must not lie, even if it be to my advantage. Prudence is hypothetical; its motto is, Honesty when it is the best policy; but the moral law in our hearts is unconditional and absolute.

And an action is good not because it has good results, or because it is wise, but because it is done in obedience to this inner sense of duty, this moral law that does not come from our personal experience, but legislates imperiously and à priori for all our behavior, past, present, and future. The only thing unqualifiedly good in this world is a good will—the will to follow the moral law, regardless of profit or loss for ourselves. Never mind your happiness; do your duty. "Morality is not properly the doctrine how we may make ourselves happy, but how we may make ourselves worthy of happiness."[30] Let us seek the happiness in others; but for our-

[26]*Critique of Practical Reason,* p. 31.
[27]"In the morning I make good resolutions; in the evening I commit follies."
[28]*Practical Reason,* p. 139.   [29]*Ibid.,* p. 19.   [30]*Ibid.,* p. 227.

selves, perfection—whether it bring us happiness or pain.[31] To achieve perfection in yourself and happiness in others, "so act as to treat humanity, whether in thine own person or in that of another, in every case as an end, never only as a means":[32]—this too, as we directly feel, is part of the categorical imperative. Let us live up to such a principle, and we shall soon create an ideal community of rational beings; to create it we need only act as if we already belonged to it; we must apply the perfect law in the imperfect state. It is a hard ethic, you say,—this placing of duty above beauty, of morality above happiness; but only so can we cease to be beasts, and begin to be gods.

Notice, meanwhile, that this absolute command to duty proves at last the freedom of our wills; how could we ever have conceived such a notion as duty if we had not felt ourselves free? We cannot prove this freedom by theoretical reason; we prove it by feeling it directly in the crisis of moral choice. We feel this freedom as the very essence of our inner selves, of the "pure Ego"; we feel within ourselves the spontaneous activity of a mind moulding experience and choosing goals. Our actions, once we initiate them, seem to follow fixed and invariable laws, but only because we perceive their results through sense, which clothes all that it transmits in the dress of that causal law which our minds themselves have made. Nevertheless, we are beyond and above the laws we make in order to understand the world of our experience; each of us is a center of initiative force and creative power. In a way which we feel but cannot prove, each of us is free.

And again, though we cannot prove, we feel, that we are deathless. We perceive that life is not like those dramas so beloved by the people—in which every villain is punished, and every act of virtue meets with its reward; we learn anew every day that the wisdom of the serpent fares better here than the gentleness of the dove, and that any thief can triumph if he steals enough. If mere worldly utility and expediency were the justification of virtue, it would not be wise to be too good. And yet, knowing all this, having it flung into our faces with brutal repetition, we still feel the command to righteousness, *we know that we ought* to do the inexpedient good. How could this sense of right survive if it were not that in our hearts we feel this life to be only a part of life, this earthly dream only an embryonic prelude to a new birth, a new awakening; if we did not vaguely know that in that later and longer life the balance will be redressed, and not one cup of water given generously but shall be returned a hundred-fold?

Finally, and by the same token, there is a God. If the sense of duty involves and justifies belief in rewards to come, "the postulate of immortality . . . must lead to the supposition of the existence of a cause

[31]Preface to The Metaphysical Elements of Ethics.
[32]Metaphysics of Morals, London, 1909; p. 47.

adequate to this effect; in other words, it must postulate the existence of God."[33] This again is no proof by "reason"; the moral sense, which has to do with the world of our actions, must have priority over that theoretical logic which was developed only to deal with sense-phenomena. Our reason leaves us free to believe that behind the thing-in-itself there is a just God; our moral sense commands us to believe it. Rousseau was right: above the logic of the head is the feeling in the heart. Pascal was right: the heart has reasons of its own, which the head can never understand.

V. ON RELIGION AND REASON

Does this appear trite, and timid, and conservative? But it was not so; on the contrary, this bold denial of "rational" theology, this frank reduction of religion to moral faith and hope, aroused all the orthodox of Germany to protests. To face this "forty-parson-power" (as Byron would have called it) required more courage than one usually associates with the name of Kant.

That he was brave enough appeared in all clarity when he published, at sixty-six, his *Critique of Judgment,* and, at sixty-nine, his *Religion within the Limits of Pure Reason.* In the earlier of these books Kant returns to the discussion of that argument from design which, in the first *Critique,* he had rejected as an insufficient proof of the existence of God. He begins by correlating design and beauty; the beautiful he thinks, is anything which reveals symmetry and unity of structure, as if it had been designed by intelligence. He observes in passing (and Schopenhauer here helped himself to a good deal of his theory of art) that the contemplation of symmetrical design always gives us a disinterested pleasure; and that "an interest in the beauty of nature for its own sake is always a sign of goodness."[34] Many objects in nature show such beauty, such symmetry and unity, as almost to drive us to the notion of supernatural design. But on the other hand, says Kant, there are also in nature many instances of waste and chaos, of useless repetition and multiplication; nature preserves life, but at the cost of how much suffering and death! The appearance of external design, then, is not a conclusive proof of Providence. The theologians who use the idea so much should abandon it, and the scientists who have abandoned it should use it; it is a magnificent clue, and leads to hundreds of revelations. For there is design, undoubtedly; but it is internal design, the design of the parts by the whole; and if science will interpret the parts of an organism in terms of their meaning for the whole, it will have an admirable balance for that other heuristic principle—the mechanical conception of life—which also is fruitful for discovery, but which, alone, can never explain the growth of even a blade of grass.

[33]*Practical Reason,* p. 220.   [34]*Critique of Judgment,* sect. 29.

The essay on religion is a remarkable production for a man of sixty-nine; it is perhaps the boldest of all the books of Kant. Since religion must be based not on the logic of theoretical reason but on the practical reason of the moral sense, it follows that any Bible or revelation must be judged by its value for morality, and cannot itself be the judge of a moral code. Churches and dogmas have value only in so far as they assist the moral development of the race. When mere creeds or ceremonies usurp priority over moral excellence as a test of religion, religion has disappeared. The real church is a community of people, however scattered and divided, who are united by devotion to the common moral law. It was to establish such a community that Christ lived and died; it was this real church which he held up in contrast to the ecclesiasticism of the Pharisees. But another ecclesiasticism has almost overwhelmed this noble conception. "Christ has brought the kingdom of God nearer to earth; but he has been misunderstood; and in place of God's kingdom the kingdom of the priest has been established among us."[35] Creed and ritual have again replaced the good life; and instead of men being bound together by religion, they are divided into a thousand sects; and all manner of "pious nonsense" is inculcated as "a sort of heavenly court service by means of which one may win through flattery the favor of the ruler of heaven."[36]—Again, miracles cannot prove a religion, for we can never quite rely on the testimony which supports them; and prayer is useless if it aims at a suspension of the natural laws that hold for all experience. Finally, the nadir of perversion is reached when the church becomes an instrument in the hands of a reactionary government; when the clergy, whose function it is to console and guide a harassed humanity with religious faith and hope and charity, are made the tools of theological obscurantism and political oppression.

The audacity of these conclusions lay in the fact that precisely this had happened in Prussia. Frederick the Great had died in 1786, and had been succeeded by Frederick William II, to whom the liberal policies of his predecessor seemed to smack unpatriotically of the French Enlightenment. Zedlitz, who had been Minister of Education under Frederick, was dismissed; and his place was given to a Pietist, Wöllner. Wöllner had been described by Frederick as "a treacherous and intriguing priest," who divided his time between alchemy and Rosicrucian mysteries, and climbed to power by offering himself as "an unworthy instrument" to the new monarch's policy of restoring the orthodox faith by compulsion.[37] In 1788 Wöllner issued a decree which forbade any teaching, in school or university, that deviated from the orthodox form of Lutheran Protestantism; he established a strict censorship over all forms of publication, and ordered the discharge of every teacher suspected of any heresy. Kant was

[35]Quoted in Chamberlain, *Immanuel Kant;* vol. i, p. 510.
[36]In Paulsen, 366.
[37]*Encyclopedia Britannica,* article "Frederick William II."

at first left unmolested, because he was an old man, and—as one royal adviser said—only a few people read him, and these did not understand him. But the essay on religion was intelligible; and though it rang true with religious fervor, it revealed too strong a strain of Voltaire to pass the new censorship. The *Berliner Monatsschrift*, which had planned to publish the essay, was ordered to suppress it.

Kant acted now with a vigor and courage hardly credible in a man who had almost completed three score years and ten. He sent the essay to some friends at Jena, and through them had it published by the press of the university there. Jena was outside of Prussia, under the jurisdiction of that same liberal Duke of Weimar who was then caring for Goethe. The result was that in 1794 Kant received an eloquent cabinet order from the Prussian King, which read as follows: "Our highest person has been greatly displeased to observe how you misuse your philosophy to undermine and destroy many of the most important and fundamental doctrines of the Holy Scriptures and of Christianity. We demand of you immediately an exact account, and expect that in future you will give no such cause of offense, but rather that, in accordance with your duty, you will employ your talents and authority so that our paternal purpose may be more and more attained. If you continue to oppose this order you may expect unpleasant consequences."[38] Kant replied that every scholar should have the right to form independent judgments on religious matters, and to make his opinions known; but that during the reign of the present king he would preserve silence. Some biographers who can be very brave by proxy, have condemned him for this concession; but let us remember that Kant was seventy, that he was frail in health, and not fit for a fight; and that he had already spoken his message to the world.

VI. ON POLITICS AND ETERNAL PEACE

The Prussian government might have pardoned Kant's theology, had he not been guilty of political heresies as well. Three years after the accession of Frederick William II, the French Revolution had set all the thrones of Europe trembling. At a time when most of the teachers in the Prussian universities had rushed to the support of legitimate monarchy, Kant, sixty-five years young, hailed the Revolution with joy; and with tears in his eyes said to his friends: "Now I can say like Simeon, 'Lord, let now Thy servant depart in peace; for mine eyes have seen Thy salvation.' "[39]

He had published, in 1784, a brief exposition of his political theory under the title of "The Natural Principle of the Political Order considered in connection with the Idea of a Universal Cosmopolitical History." Kant begins by recognizing, in that strife of each against all which

<hr />

[38] In Paulsen, p. 49.   [39] Wallace, p. 40.

had so shocked Hobbes, nature's method of developing the hidden
capacities of life; struggle is the indispensable accompaniment of
progress. If men were entirely social, man would stagnate; a certain alloy
of individualism and competition is required to make the human species
survive and grow. "Without qualities of an unsocial kind . . . men might
have led an Arcadian shepherd life in complete harmony, contentment,
and mutual love; but in that case all their talents would have forever
remained hidden in their germ." (Kant, therefore, was no slavish follower
of Rousseau.) "Thanks be then to nature for this unsociableness, for this
envious jealousy and vanity, for this insatiable desire for possession and
for power. . . . Man wishes concord; but nature knows better what is
good for his species; and she wills discord, in order that man may be
impelled to a new exertion of his powers, and to the further development
of his natural capacities."

The struggle for existence, then, is not altogether an evil. Nevertheless,
men soon perceive that it must be restricted within certain limits, and
regulated by rules, customs, and laws; hence the origin and development
of civil society. But now "the same unsociableness which forced men into
society becomes again the cause of each commonwealth's assuming the
attitude of uncontrolled freedom in its external relations,—i. e., as one
state in relation to other states; and consequently, any one state must
expect from any other the same sort of evils as formerly oppressed
individuals and compelled them to enter into a civil union regulated by
law."[40] It is time that nations, like men, should emerge from the wild
state of nature, and contract to keep the peace. The whole meaning and
movement of history is the ever greater restriction of pugnacity and
violence, the continuous enlargement of the area of peace. "The history
of the human race, viewed as a whole, may be regarded as the realization
of a hidden plan of nature to bring about a political constitution, internally and externally perfect, as the only state in which all the capacities
implanted by her in mankind can be fully developed."[41] If there is no
such progress, the labors of successive civilizations are like those of
Sisyphus, who again and again "up the high hill heaved a huge round
stone," only to have it roll back as it was almost at the top. History would
be then nothing more than an endless and circuitous folly; "and we
might suppose, like the Hindu, that the earth is a place for the expiation
of old and forgotten sins."[42]

The essay on "Eternal Peace" (published in 1795, when Kant was
seventy-one) is a noble development of this theme. Kant knows how easy
it is to laugh at the phrase; and under his title he writes: "These words
were once put by a Dutch inn-keeper on his sign-board as a satirical
inscription, over the representation of a church-yard" cemetery.[43] Kant

[40] *Eternal Peace and Other Essays;* Boston, 1914; p. 14.
[41] *Ibid.*, p. 19.   [42] P. 58.   [43] P. 68.

had before complained, as apparently every generation must, that "our rulers have no money to spend on public education . . . because all their resources are already placed to the account of the next war."[44] The nations will not really be civilized until all standing armies are abolished. (The audacity of this proposal stands out when we remember that it was Prussia itself which, under the father of Frederick the Great, had been the first to establish conscription.) "Standing armies excite states to out-rival one another in the number of their armed men, which has no limit. Through the expense occasioned thereby, peace becomes in the long run more oppressive than a short war; and standing armies are thus the cause of aggressive wars undertaken in order to get rid of this burden."[45] For in time of war the army would support itself on the country, by requisitioning, quartering, and pillaging; preferably in the enemy's territory, but if necessary, in one's own land; even this would be better than supporting it out of government funds.

Much of this militarism, in Kant's judgment, was due to the expansion of Europe into America and Africa and Asia; with the resultant quarrels of the thieves over their new booty. "If we compare the barbarian in-stances of inhospitality . . . with the inhuman behavior of the civilized, and especially the commercial, states of our continent, the injustice practiced by them even in their first contact with foreign lands and peoples fills us with horror; the mere visiting of such peoples being regarded by them as equivalent to a conquest. America, the negro lands, the Spice Islands, the Cape of Good Hope, etc., on being discovered, were treated as countries that belonged to nobody; for the aboriginal inhabitants were reckoned as nothing. . . . And all this has been done by nations who make a great ado about their piety, and who, while drinking up iniquity like water, would have themselves regarded as the very elect of the orthodox faith."[46]—The old fox of Königsberg was not silenced yet!

Kant attributed this imperialistic greed to the oligarchical constitution of European states; the spoils went to a select few, and remained sub-stantial even after division. If democracy were established, and all shared in political power, the spoils of international robbery would have to be so subdivided as to constitute a resistible temptation. Hence the "first definitive article in the conditions of Eternal Peace" is this: "The civil constitution of every state shall be republican, and war shall not be declared except by a plebiscite of all the citizens."[47] When those who must do the fighting have the right to decide between war and peace, history will no longer be written in blood. "On the other hand, in a constitution where the subject is not a voting member of the state, and which is there-fore not republican, the resolution to go to war is a matter of the smallest concern in the world. For in this case the ruler, who, as such, is not a mere citizen, but the owner of the state, need not in the least suffer per-

[44] P. 21.   [45] P. 71.   [46] P. 68.   [47] Pp. 76-77.

sonally by war, nor has he to sacrifice his pleasures of the table or the chase, or his pleasant palaces, court festivals, or the like. He can, therefore, resolve for war from insignificant reasons, as if it were but a hunting expedition; and as regards its propriety, he may leave the justification of it without concern to the diplomatic corps, who are always too ready to give their services for that purpose."[48] How contemporary truth is!

The apparent victory of the Revolution over the armies of reaction in 1795 led Kant to hope that republics would now spring up throughout Europe, and that an international order would arise based upon a democracy without slavery and without exploitation, and pledged to peace. After all, the function of government is to help and develop the individual, not to use and abuse him. "Every man is to be respected as an absolute end in himself; and it is a crime against the dignity that belongs to him as a human being, to use him as a mere means for some external purpose."[49] This too is part and parcel of that categorical imperative without which religion is a hypocritical farce. Kant therefore calls for equality: not of ability, but of opportunity for the development and application of ability; he rejects all prerogatives of birth and class, and traces all hereditary privilege to some violent conquest in the past. In the midst of obscurantism and reaction and the union of all monarchical Europe to crush the Revolution, he takes his stand, despite his seventy years, for the new order, for the establishment of democracy and liberty everywhere. Never had old age so bravely spoken with the voice of youth.

But he was exhausted now; he had run his race and fought his fight. He withered slowly into a childlike senility that came at last to be a harmless insanity: one by one his sensibilities and his powers left him; and in 1804, aged seventy-nine, he died, quietly and naturally, like a leaf falling from a tree.

VII. CRITICISM AND ESTIMATE

And now how does this complex structure of logic, metaphysics, psychology, ethics, and politics stand today, after the philosophic storms of a century have beaten down upon it? It is pleasant to answer that much of the great edifice remains; and that the "critical philosophy" represents an event of permanent importance in the history of thought. But many details and outworks of the structure have been shaken.

First, then, is space a mere "form of sensibility," having no objective reality independent of the perceiving mind? Yes and no. Yes: for space is an empty concept when not filled with perceived objects; "space" merely means that certain objects are, for the perceiving mind, at such and such a position, or distance, with reference to other perceived objects; and no external perception is possible except of objects in space;

[48]*Ibid.*   [49]In Paulsen, p. 340.

space then is assuredly a "necessary form of the external sense." And no: for without doubt, such spatial facts as the annual elliptical circuit of sun by earth, though statable only by a mind, are independent of any perception whatever; the deep and dark blue ocean rolled on before Byron told it to, and after he had ceased to be. Nor is space a "construct" of the mind through the coördination of spaceless sensations; we perceive space directly through our simultaneous perception of different objects and various points—as when we see an insect moving across a still background. Likewise: time as a sense of before and after, or a measurement of motion, is of course subjective, and highly relative; but a tree will age, wither and decay whether or not the lapse of time is measured or perceived. The truth is that Kant was too anxious to prove the subjectivity of space, as a refuge from materialism; he feared the argument that if space is objective and universal, God must exist in space, and be therefore spatial and material. He might have been content with the critical idealism which shows that all reality is known to us primarily as our sensations and ideas. The old fox bit off more than he could chew.[50]

He might well have contented himself, too, with the relativity of scientific truth, without straining towards that mirage, the absolute. Recent studies like those of Pearson in England, Mach in Germany, and Henri Poincaré in France, agree rather with Hume than with Kant: all science, even the most rigorous mathematics, is relative in its truth. Science itself is not worried about the matter; a high degree of probability contents it. Perhaps, after all, "necessary" knowledge is not necessary?

The great achievement of Kant is to have shown, once for all, that the external world is known to us only as sensation; and that the mind is no mere helpless *tabula rasa,* the inactive victim of sensation, but a positive agent, selecting and reconstructing experience as experience arrives. We can make subtractions from this accomplishment without injuring its essential greatness. We may smile, with Schopenhauer, at the exact baker's dozen of categories, so prettily boxed into triplets, and then stretched and contracted and interpreted deviously and ruthlessly to fit and surround all things.[51] And we may even question whether these categories, or interpretive forms of thought, are innate, existing before sensation and experience; perhaps so in the individual, as Spencer con-

[50]The persistent vitality of Kant's theory of knowledge appears in its complete acceptance by so matter-of-fact a scientist as the late Charles P. Steinmetz: "All our sense-perceptions are limited by, and attached to, the conceptions of time and space. Kant, the greatest and most critical of all philosophers, denies that time and space are the product of experience, but shows them to be categories—conceptions in which our minds clothe the sense perceptions. Modern physics has come to the same conclusion in the relativity theory, that absolute space and absolute time have no existence, but time and space exist only as far as things or events fill them; that is, they are forms of perception."—Address at the Unitarian Church, Schenectady, 1923.

[51]*Op. cit.,* vol. ii, p. 23.

ceded, though acquired by the race; and then, again, probably acquired even by the individual: the categories may be grooves of thought, habits of perception and conception, gradually produced by sensations and perceptions automatically arranging themselves,—first in disorderly ways, then, by a kind of natural selection of forms of arrangement, in orderly and adaptive and illuminating ways. It is memory that classifies and interprets sensations into perceptions, and perceptions into ideas; but memory is an accretion. That unity of the mind which Kant thinks native (the "transcendental unity of apperception") is acquired—and not by all; and can be lost as well as won—in amnesia, or alternating personality, or insanity. Concepts are an achievement, not a gift.

The nineteenth century dealt rather hardly with Kant's ethics, his theory of an innate, à priori, absolute moral sense. The philosophy of evolution suggested irresistibly that the sense of duty is a social deposit in the individual, the content of conscience is acquired, though the vague disposition to social behavior is innate. The moral self, the social man, is no "special creation" coming mysteriously from the hand of God, but the late product of a leisurely evolution. Morals are not absolute; they are a code of conduct more or less haphazardly developed for group survival, and varying with the nature and circumstances of the group: a people hemmed in by enemies, for example, will consider as immoral that zestful and restless individualism which a nation youthful and secure in its wealth and isolation will condone as a necessary ingredient in the exploitation of natural resources and the formation of national character. No action is good in itself, as Kant supposes.[52]

His pietistic youth, and his hard life of endless duty and infrequent pleasure, gave him a moralistic bent; he came at last to advocate duty for duty's sake, and so fell unwittingly into the arms of Prussian absolutism.[53] There is something of a severe Scotch Calvinism in this opposition of duty to happiness; Kant continues Luther and the Stoic Reformation, as Voltaire continues Montaigne and the Epicurean Renaissance. He represented a stern reaction against the egoism and hedonism in which Helvetius and Holbach had formulated the life of their reckless era, very much as Luther had reacted against the luxury and laxity of Mediterranean Italy. But after a century of reaction against the absolutism of Kant's ethics, we find ourselves again in a welter of urban sensualism and immorality, of ruthless individualism untempered with democratic conscience or aristocratic honor; and perhaps the day will soon come when a disintegrating civilization will welcome again the Kantian call to duty.

The marvel in Kant's philosophy is his vigorous revival, in the second *Critique,* of those religious ideas of God, freedom, and immortality, which the first *Critique* had apparently destroyed. "In Kant's works," says

[52]*Practical Reason,* p. 31.
[53]Cf. Prof. Dewey: *German Philosophy and Politics.*

Nietzsche's critical friend, Paul Ree, "you feel as though you were at a country fair. You can buy from him anything you want—freedom of the will and captivity of the will, idealism and a refutation of idealism, atheism and the good Lord. Like a juggler out of an empty hat, Kant draws out of the concept of duty a God, immortality, and freedom,—to the great surprise of his readers."[54] Schopenhauer too takes a fling at the derivation of immortality from the need of reward: "Kant's virtue, which at first bore itself so bravely towards happiness, loses its independence later, and holds out its hand for a tip."[55] The great pessimist believes that Kant was really a sceptic who, having abandoned belief himself, hesitated to destroy the faith of the people, for fear of the consequences to public morals. "Kant discloses the groundlessness of speculative theology, and leaves popular theology untouched, nay even establishes it in a nobler form as a faith based upon moral feeling." This was afterwards distorted by the philosophasters into rational apprehension and consciousness of God, etc. . . . ; while Kant, as he demolished old and revered errors, and knew the danger of doing so, rather wished through the moral theology merely to substitute a few weak temporary supports, so that the ruin might not fall upon him, but that he might have time to escape."[56] So too Heine, in what is no doubt an intentional caricature, represents Kant, after having destroyed religion, going out for a walk with his servant Lampe, and suddenly perceiving that the old man's eyes are filled with tears. "Then Immanuel Kant has compassion, and shows that he is not only a great philosopher, but also a good man; and half kindly, half ironically, he speaks: 'Old Lampe must have a God or else he cannot be happy, says the practical reason; for my part, the practical reason may, then, guarantee the existence of God.' "[57] If these interpretations were true we should have to call the second *Critique* a Transcendental Anesthetic.

But these adventurous reconstructions of the inner Kant need not be taken too seriously. The fervor of the essay on "Religion within the Limits of Pure Reason" indicates a sincerity too intense to be questioned, and the attempt to change the base of religion from theology to morals, from creeds to conduct, could have come only from a profoundly religious mind. "It is indeed true," he wrote to Moses Mendelssohn in 1766, "that I think many things with the clearest conviction, . . . which I never have the courage to say; but I will never say anything which I do not think."[58] Naturally, a long and obscure treatise like the great *Critique* lends itself to rival interpretations; one of the first reviews of the book, written by Reinhold a few years after it appeared, said as much as we can say today:

[54]In Untermann, *Science and Revolution,* Chicago, 1905; p. 81.
[55]In Paulsen, p. 317.
[56]*The World as Will and Idea,* vol. ii, p. 129.
[57]Quoted by Paulsen, p. 8.   [58]In Paulsen, p. 53.

"The *Critique of Pure Reason* has been proclaimed by the dogmatists as
the attempt of a sceptic who undermines the certainty of all knowledge;—
by the sceptics as a piece of arrogant presumption that undertakes to erect
a new form of dogmatism upon the ruins of previous systems;—by the
supernaturalists as a subtly plotted artifice to displace the historical
foundations of religion, and to establish naturalism without polemic;—
by the naturalists as a new prop for the dying philosophy of faith;—by
the materialists as an idealistic contradiction of the reality of matter;—
by the spiritualists as an unjustifiable limitation of all reality to the
corporeal world, concealed under the name of the domain of experience."[59] In truth the glory of the book lay in its appreciation of all these
points of view; and to an intelligence as keen as Kant's own, it might well
appear that he had really reconciled them all, and fused them into such
a unity of complex truth as philosophy had not seen in all its history
before.

As to his influence, the entire philosophic thought of the nineteenth
century revolved about his speculations. After Kant, all Germany began to
talk metaphysics: Schiller and Goethe studied him; Beethoven quoted
with admiration his famous words about the two wonders of life—"the
starry heavens above, the moral law within"; and Fichte, Schelling,
Hegel and Schopenhauer produced in rapid succession great systems of
thought reared upon the idealism of the old Königsberg sage. It was in
these balmy days of German metaphysics that Jean Paul Richter wrote:
"God has given to the French the land, to the English the sea, to the
Germans the empire of the air." Kant's criticism of reason, and his exaltation of feeling, prepared for the voluntarism of Schopenhauer and
Nietzsche, the intuitionism of Bergson, and the pragmatism of William
James; his identification of the laws of thought with the laws of reality
gave to Hegel a whole system of philosophy; and his unknowable "thing-
in-itself" influenced Spencer more than Spencer knew. Much of the
obscurity of Carlyle is traceable to his attempt to allegorize the already
obscure thought of Goethe and Kant—that diverse religions and philosophies are but the changing garments of one eternal truth. Caird and
Green and Wallace and Watson and Bradley and many others in England
owe their inspiration to the first *Critique;* and even the wildly innovating
Nietzsche takes his epistemology from the "great Chinaman of Königsberg" whose static ethics he so excitedly condemns. After a century of
struggle between the idealism of Kant, variously reformed, and the
materialism of the Enlightenment, variously redressed, the victory seems
to lie with Kant. Even the great materialist Helvetius wrote, paradoxically: "Men, if I may dare say it, are the creators of matter."[60] Philosophy
will never again be so naïve as in her earlier and simpler days; she must
always be different hereafter, and profounder, because Kant lived.

Ibid., p. 114.   [60] In Chamberlain. vol. i, p. 86.

VIII. A NOTE ON HEGEL

Not very long ago it was the custom for historians of philosophy to give to the immediate successors of Kant—to Fichte, Schelling, and Hegel—as much honor and space as to all his predecessors in modern thought from Bacon and Descartes to Voltaire and Hume. Our perspective today is a little different, and we enjoy perhaps too keenly the invective leveled by Schopenhauer at his successful rivals in the competition for profes-sional posts. By reading Kant, said Schopenhauer, "the public was com-pelled to see that what is obscure is not always without significance." Fichte and Schelling took advantage of this, and excogitated magnificent spider-webs of metaphysics. "But the height of audacity in serving up pure nonsense, in stringing together senseless and extravagant mazes of words, such as had previously been known only in madhouses, was finally reached in Hegel, and became the instrument of the most bare-faced general mystification that has ever taken place, with a result which will appear fabulous to posterity, and will remain as a monument to German stupidity."[61] Is this fair?

Georg Wilhelm Friedrich Hegel was born at Stuttgart in 1770. His father was a subordinate official in the department of finances of the state of Würtemberg; and Hegel himself grew up with the patient and me-thodical habits of those civil servants whose modest efficiency has given Germany the best-governed cities in the world. The youth was a tireless student: he made full analyses of all the important books he read, and copied out long passages. True culture, he said, must begin with resolute self-effacement; as in the Pythagorean system of education, where the pupil, for the first five years, was required to keep his peace.

His studies of Greek literature gave him an enthusiasm for Attic culture which remained with him when almost all other enthusiasms had died away. "At the name of Greece," he wrote, "the cultivated German finds himself at home. Europeans have their religion from a further source, from the East; . . . but what is here, what is present,—science and art, all that makes life satisfying, and elevates and adorns it—we derive, directly or indirectly, from Greece." For a time he preferred the religion of the Greeks to Christianity; and he anticipated Strauss and Renan by writing a *Life of Jesus* in which Jesus was taken as the son of Mary and Joseph, and the miraculous element was ignored. Later he destroyed the book.

In politics too he showed a spirit of rebellion hardly to be suspected from his later sanctification of the *status quo*. While studying for the ministry at Tübingen, he and Schelling hotly defended the French Revo-

[61]Caird, *Hegel*, in the Blackwood Philosophical Classics; pp. 5-8. The biographi-cal account follows Caird throughout.

lution, and went out early one morning to plant a Liberty Tree in the market-place. "The French nation, by the bath of its revolution," he wrote, "has been freed from many institutions which the spirit of man has left behind like its baby shoes, and which therefore weighed upon it, as they still weigh upon others, like lifeless feathers." It was in those hopeful days, "when to be young was very heaven," that he flirted, like Fichte, with a kind of aristocratic socialism, and gave himself, with characteristic vigor, to the Romantic current in which all Europe was engulfed.

He was graduated from Tübingen in 1793 with a certificate stating that he was a man of good parts and character, well up in theology and philology, but with no ability in philosophy. He was poor now, and had to earn his bread by tutoring in Berne and Frankfort. These were his chrysalis years: while Europe tore itself into nationalist pieces, Hegel gathered himself together and grew. Then (1799) his father died, and Hegel, falling heir to some $1500, considered himself a rich man, and gave up tutoring. He wrote to his friend Schelling for advice as to where to settle, and asked for a place where there would be simple food, abundant books, and "ein gutes Bier." Schelling recommended Jena, which was a university town under the jurisdiction of the Duke of Weimar. At Jena Schiller was teaching history; Tieck, Novalis and the Schlegels were preaching romanticism; and Fichte and Schelling were propounding their philosophies. There Hegel arrived in 1801, and in 1803 became a teacher at the University.

He was still there in 1806 when Napoleon's victory over the Prussians threw the scholarly little city into confusion and terror. French soldiers invaded Hegel's home, and he took to his heels like a philosopher, carrying with him the manuscript of his first important book, *The Phenomenology of Spirit*. For a while he was so destitute that Goethe told Knebel to lend him a few dollars to tide him over. Hegel wrote almost bitterly to Knebel: "I have made my guiding-star the Biblical saying, the truth of which I have learned by experience, Seek ye first food and clothing, and the kingdom of heaven shall be added unto you." For a while he edited a paper at Bamberg; then, in 1812, he became head of the gymnasium at Nürnburg. It was there, perhaps, that the stoic necessities of administrative work cooled the fires of romanticism in him, and made him, like Napoleon and Goethe, a classic vestige in a romantic age. And it was there that he wrote his *Logic* (1812–16), which captivated Germany by its unintelligibility, and won him the chair of philosophy at Heidelberg. At Heidelberg he wrote his immense *Encyclopedia of the Philosophical Sciences* (1817), on the strength of which he was promoted, in 1818, to the University of Berlin. From that time to the end of his life he ruled the philosophic world as indisputably as Goethe the world of literature, and Beethoven the realm of music. His birthday came on the day after Goethe's; and proud Germany made a double holiday for them every year.

A Frenchman once asked Hegel to put his philosophy into one sentence; and he did not succeed so well as the monk who, asked to define Christianity while standing on one foot, said, simply, "Thou shalt love thy neighbor as thyself." Hegel preferred to answer in ten volumes; and when they were written and published, and all the world was talking about them, he complained that "only one man understands me, and even he does not."[62] Most of his writings, like Aristotle's, consist of his lecture-notes; or, worse, of the notes taken by students who heard his lectures. Only the *Logic* and the *Phenomenology* are from his hand, and these are masterpieces of obscurity, darkened by abstractness and condensation of style, by a weirdly original terminology, and by an overcareful modification of every statement with a Gothic wealth of limiting clauses. Hegel described his work as "an attempt to teach philosophy to speak in German."[63] He succeeded.

The *Logic* is an analysis not of methods of reasoning, but of the concepts used in reasoning. These Hegel takes to be the categories named by Kant—Being, Quality, Quantity, Relation, etc. It is the first business of philosophy to dissect these basic notions that are so bandied about in all our thinking. The most pervasive of them all is Relation; every idea is a group of relations; we can think of something only by relating it to something else, and perceiving its similarities and its differences. An idea without relations of any kind is empty; this is all that is meant by saying that "Pure Being and Nothing are the same": Being absolutely devoid of relations or qualities does not exist, and has no meaning whatever. This proposition led to an endless progeny of witticisms which still breed; and it proved to be at once an obstacle and a lure to the study of Hegel's thought.

Of all relations, the most universal is that of contrast or opposition. Every condition of thought or of things—every idea and every situation in the world—leads irresistibly to its opposite, and then unites with it to form a higher or more complex whole. This "dialectical movement" runs through everything that Hegel wrote. It is an old thought, of course, foreshadowed by Empedocles, and embodied in the "golden mean" of Aristotle, who wrote that "the knowledge of opposites is one." The truth (like an electron) is an organic unity of opposed parts. The truth of conservatism and radicalism is liberalism—an open mind and a cautious hand, an open hand and a cautious mind; the formation of our opinions on large issues is a decreasing oscillation between extremes; and in all debatable questions *veritas in medio stat*. The movement of evolution is

---

[62] Ruthless critics, as we might have expected, challenge the authenticity of this story.

[63] Wallace: *Prolegomena to the Logic of Hegel*, p. 16.

a continuous development of oppositions, and their merging and reconciliation. Schelling was right—there is an underlying "identity of opposites"; and Fichte was right—thesis, antithesis and synthesis constitute
the formula and secret of all development and all reality.

For not only do thoughts develop and evolve according to this "dialectical movement," but things do equally; every condition of affairs contains
a contradiction which evolution must resolve by a reconciling unity. So,
no doubt, our present social system secretes a self-corroding contradiction:
the stimulating individualism required in a period of economic adolescence and unexploited resources, arouses, in a later age, the aspiration
for a coöperative commonwealth; and the future will see neither the
present reality nor the visioned ideal, but a synthesis in which something
of both will come together to beget a higher life. And that higher stage too
will divide into a productive contradiction, and rise to still loftier levels
of organization, complexity, and unity. The movement of thought, then,
is the same as the movement of things; in each there is a dialectical progression from unity through diversity to diversity-in-unity. Thought and
being follow the same law; and logic and metaphysics are one.

Mind is the indispensable organ for the perception of this dialectical
process, and this unity in difference. The function of the mind, and the
task of philosophy, is to discover the unity that lies potential in diversity;
the task of ethics is to unify character and conduct; and the task of politics
is to unify individuals into a state. The task of religion is to reach and feel
that Absolute in which all opposites are resolved into unity, that great
sum of being in which matter and mind, subject and object, good and
evil, are one. God is the system of relationships in which all things move
and have their being and their significance. In man the Absolute rises to
self-consciousness, and becomes the Absolute Idea—that is, thought
realizing itself as part of the Absolute, transcending individual limitations
and purposes, and catching, underneath the universal strife, the hidden
harmony of all things. "Reason is the substance of the universe; . . . the
design of the world is absolutely rational."[64]

Not that strife and evil are mere negative imaginings; they are real
enough; but they are, in wisdom's perspective, stages to fulfilment and
the good. Struggle is the law of growth; character is built in the storm
and stress of the world; and a man reaches his full height only through
compulsions, responsibilities, and suffering. Even pain has its rationale;
it is a sign of life and a stimulus to reconstruction. Passion also has a place
in the reason of things: "nothing great in the world has been accomplished without passion";[65] and even the egoistic ambitions of a Napoleon
contribute unwittingly to the development of nations. Life is not made
for happiness, but for achievement. "The history of the world is not the
theatre of happiness; periods of happiness are blank pages in it, for they

[64] Hegel: *Philosophy of History.* Bohn ed., pp. 9, 13.　　　[65] *Ibid.*. p. 26.

are periods of harmony";[66] and this dull content is unworthy of a man. History is made only in those periods in which the contradictions of reality are being resolved by growth, as the hesitations and awkwardness of youth pass into the ease and order of maturity. History is a dialectical movement, almost a series of revolutions, in which people after people, and genius after genius, become the instrument of the Absolute. Great men are not so much begetters, as midwives, of the future; what they bring forth is mothered by the *Zeitgeist,* the Spirit of the Age. The genius merely places another stone on the pile, as others have done; "somehow his has the good fortune to come last, and when he places his stone the arch stands self-supported." "Such individuals had no consciousness of the general Idea they were unfolding; . . . but they had an insight into the requirements of the time—what was ripe for development. This was the very Truth for their age, for their world; the species next in order, so to speak, and which was already formed in the womb of time."[67]

Such a philosophy of history seems to lead to revolutionary conclusions. The dialectical process makes change the cardinal principle of life; no condition is permanent; in every stage of things there is a contradiction which only the "strife of opposites" can resolve. The deepest law of politics, therefore, is freedom—an open avenue to change; history is the growth of freedom, and the state is, or should be, freedom organized. On the other hand, the doctrine that "the real is rational" has a conservative color: every condition, though destined to disappear, has the divine right that belongs to it as a necessary stage in evolution; in a sense it is brutally true that "whatever is, is right." And as unity is the goal of development, order is the first requisite of liberty.

If Hegel inclined, in his later years, to the conservative rather than to the radical implications of his philosophy, it was partly because the Spirit of the Age (to use his own historic phrase) was weary of too much change. After the Revolution of 1830 he wrote: "Finally, after forty years of war and immeasurable confusion, an old heart might rejoice to see an end of it all, and the beginning of a period of peaceful satisfaction."[68] It was not quite in order that the philosopher of strife as the dialectic of growth should become the advocate of content; but at sixty a man has a right to ask for peace. Nevertheless, the contradictions in Hegel's thought were too deep for peace; and in the next generation his followers split with dialectical fatality into the "Hegelian Right" and the "Hegelian Left." Weisse and the younger Fichte found, in the theory of the real as rational, a philosophical expression of the doctrine of Providence, and justification for a politics of absolute obedience. Feuerbach, Moleschott, Bauer and Marx returned to the scepticism and "higher criticism" of Hegel's youth, and developed the philosophy of history into a theory of class struggles leading by Hegelian necessity to "socialism inevitable." In

[66]*Ibid.,* p. 28.   [67]*Ibid.,* p. 31.   [68]In Caird, p. 93.

place of the Absolute as determining history through the *Zeitgeist*, Marx offered mass movements and economic forces as the basic causes of every fundamental change, whether in the world of things or in the life of thought. Hegel, the imperial professor, had hatched the socialistic eggs.

The old philosopher denounced the radicals as dreamers, and carefully hid away his early essays. He allied himself with the Prussian Government, blessed it as the latest expression of the Absolute, and basked in the sun of its academic favors. His enemies called him "the official philosopher." He began to think of the Hegelian system as part of the natural laws of the world; he forgot that his own dialectic condemned his thought to impermanence and decay. "Never did philosophy assume such a lofty tone, and never were its royal honors so fully recognized and secured, as in 1830" in Berlin.[69]

But Hegel aged rapidly in those happy years. He became as absent-minded as a story-book genius; once he entered the lecture-room with only one shoe, having left the other, unnoticed, in the mud. When the cholera epidemic came to Berlin in 1831, his weakened body was one of the first to succumb to the contagion. After only a day's illness he passed away suddenly and quietly in his sleep. Just as the space of a year had seen the birth of Napoleon, Beethoven and Hegel, so in the years from 1827 to 1832 Germany lost Goethe, Hegel, and Beethoven. It was the end of an epoch, the last fine effort of Germany's greatest age.

[69]Paulsen, *Immanuel Kant*, p. 385.

CHAPTER VII

Schopenhauer

I. THE AGE

WHY did the first half of the nineteenth century lift up, as voices of the age, a group of pessimistic poets—Byron in England, De Musset in France, Heine in Germany, Leopardi in Italy, Pushkin and Lermontof in Russia; a group of pessimistic composers—Schubert, Schumann, Chopin, and even the later Beethoven (a pessimist trying to convince himself that he is an optimist); and above all, a profoundly pessimistic philosopher—Arthur Schopenhauer?

That great anthology of woe, *The World as Will and Idea,* appeared in 1818. It was the age of the "Holy" Alliance. Waterloo had been fought, the Revolution was dead, and the "Son of the Revolution" was rotting on a rock in a distant sea. Something of Schopenhauer's apotheosis of Will was due to that magnificent and bloody apparition of the Will made flesh in the little Corsican; and something of his despair of life came from the pathetic distance of St. Helena—Will defeated at last, and dark Death the only victor of all the wars. The Bourbons were restored, the feudal barons were returning to claim their lands, and the pacific idealism of Alexander had unwittingly mothered a league for the suppression of progress everywhere. The great age was over. "I thank God," said Goethe, "that I am not young in so thoroughly finished a world."

All Europe lay prostrate. Millions of strong men had perished; millions of acres of land had been neglected or laid waste; everywhere on the Continent life had to begin again at the bottom, to recover painfully and slowly the civilizing economic surplus that had been swallowed up in war. Schopenhauer, traveling through France and Austria in 1804, was struck by the chaos and uncleanliness of the villages, the wretched poverty of the farmers, the unrest and misery of the towns. The passage of the Napoleonic and counter-Napoleonic armies had left scars of ravage on the face of every country. Moscow was in ashes. In England, proud victor in the strife, the farmers were ruined by the fall in the price of wheat; and the industrial workers were tasting all the horrors of the nascent and uncontrolled factory-system. Demobilization added to unemployment. "I have heard my father say," wrote Carlyle, "that in the years when oatmeal was as high as ten shillings a stone, he had noticed the laborers retire

227

each separately to a brook, and there drink instead of dining, anxious only to hide their misery from one another."[1] Never had life seemed so meaningless, or so mean.

Yes, the Revolution was dead; and with it the life seemed to have gone out of the soul of Europe. That new heaven, called Utopia, whose glamour had relieved the twilight of the gods, had receded into a dim future where only young eyes could see it; the older ones had followed that lure long enough, and turned away from it now as a mockery of men's hopes. Only the young can live in the future, and only the old can live in the past; men were most of them forced to live in the present, and the present was a ruin. How many thousands of heroes and believers had fought for the Revolution! How the hearts of youth everywhere in Europe had turned towards the young republic, and had lived on the light and hope of it,— until Beethoven tore into shreds the dedication of his Heroic Symphony to the man who had ceased to be the Son of the Revolution and had become the son-in-law of reaction. How many had fought even then for the great hope, and had believed, with passionate uncertainty, to the very end? And now here was the very end: Waterloo, and St. Helena, and Vienna; and on the throne of prostrate France a Bourbon who had learned nothing and forgotten nothing. This was the glorious denouement of a generation of such hope and effort as human history had never known before. What a comedy this tragedy was—for those whose laughter was yet bitter with tears!

Many of the poor had, in these days of disillusionment and suffering, the consolation of religious hope; but a large proportion of the upper classes had lost their faith, and looked out upon a ruined world with no alleviating vision of a vaster life in whose final justice and beauty these ugly ills would be dissolved. And in truth it was hard enough to believe that such a sorry planet as men saw in 1818 was held up in the hand of an intelligent and benevolent God. Mephistopheles had triumphed, and every Faust was in despair. Voltaire had sown the whirlwind, and Schopenhauer was to reap the harvest.

Seldom had the problem of evil been flung so vividly and insistently into the face of philosophy and religion. Every martial grave from Boulogne to Moscow and the Pyramids lifted a mute interrogation to the indifferent stars. How long, O Lord, and Why? Was this almost universal calamity the vengeance of a just God on the Age of Reason and unbelief? Was it a call to the penitent intellect to bend before the ancient virtues of faith, hope and charity? So Schlegel thought, and Novalis, and Chateaubriand, and De Musset, and Southey, and Wordsworth, and Gogol; and they turned back to the old faith like wasted prodigals happy to be home again. But some others made harsher answer: that the chaos of Europe but reflected the chaos of the universe; that there was no divine

[1]Froude: *Life and Letters of Thomas Carlyle,* I, p. 52.

order after all, nor any heavenly hope; that God, if God there was, was blind, and Evil brooded over the face of the earth. So Byron, and Heine, and Lermontof, and Leopardi, and our philosopher.

II. THE MAN

Schopenhauer was born at Dantzig on February 22, 1788. His father was a merchant noted for ability, hot temper, independence of character, and love of liberty. He moved from Dantzig to Hamburg when Arthur was five years old, because Dantzig lost its freedom in the annexation of Poland in 1793. Young Schopenhauer, therefore, grew up in the midst of business and finance; and though he soon abandoned the mercantile career into which his father had pushed him, it left its mark upon him in a certain bluntness of manner, a realistic turn of mind, a knowledge of the world and of men; it made him the antipodes of that closet or academic type of philosopher whom he so despised. The father died, apparently by his own hand, in 1805. The paternal grandmother had died insane.

"The character or will," says Schopenhauer, "is inherited from the father; the intellect from the mother."[2] The mother had intellect—she became one of the most popular novelists of her day—but she had temperament and temper too. She had been unhappy with her prosaic husband; and when he died she took to free love, and moved to Weimar as the fittest climate for that sort of life. Arthur Schopenhauer reacted to this as Hamlet to his mother's re-marriage; and his quarrels with his mother taught him a large part of those half-truths about women with which he was to season his philosophy. One of her letters to him reveals the state of their affairs: "You are unbearable and burdensome, and very hard to live with; all your good qualities are overshadowed by your conceit, and made useless to the world simply because you cannot restrain your propensity to pick holes in other people."[3] So they arranged to live apart; he was to come only to her "at homes," and be one guest among others; they could then be as polite to each other as strangers, instead of hating each other like relatives. Goethe, who liked Mme. Schopenhauer because she let him bring his Christiane with him, made matters worse by telling the mother that her son would become a very famous man; the mother had never heard of two geniuses in the same family. Finally, in some culminating quarrel, the mother pushed her son and rival down the stairs; whereupon our philosopher bitterly informed her that she would be known to posterity only through him. Schopenhauer quitted Weimar soon afterward; and though the mother lived twenty-four years more, he never saw her again. Byron, also a child of 1788, seems to have

[2] *The World as Will and Idea;* London, 1883; iii, 300.
[3] In Wallace: *Life of Schopenhauer;* London, no date; p. 59.

had similar luck with his mother. These men were almost by this circumstance doomed to pessimism; a man who has not known a mother's love—
and worse, has known a mother's hatred—has no cause to be infatuated
with the world.

Meanwhile Schopenhauer had gone through "gymnasium" and university, and had learned more than was on their schedules. He had his
fling at love and the world, with results that affected his character and
his philosophy.[4] He became gloomy, cynical, and suspicious; he was obsessed with fears and evil fancies; he kept his pipes under lock and key,
and never trusted his neck to a barber's razor; and he slept with loaded
pistols at his bedside—presumably for the convenience of the burglar. He
could not bear noise: "I have long held the opinion," he writes, "that the
amount of noise which anyone can bear undisturbed stands in inverse
proportion to his mental capacity, and may therefore be regarded as a
pretty fair measure of it. . . . Noise is a torture to all intellectual people.
. . . The superabundant display of vitality which takes the form of
knocking, hammering, and tumbling things about, has proved a daily
torment to me all my life long."[5] He had an almost paranoiac sense of
unrecognized greatness; missing success and fame, he turned within and
gnawed at his own soul.

He had no mother, no wife, no child, no family, no country. "He was
absolutely alone, with not a single friend; and between one and none there
lies an infinity."[6] Even more than Goethe he was immune to the nationalistic fevers of his age. In 1813 he so far fell under the sway of Fichte's
enthusiasm for a war of liberation against Napoleon, that he thought of
volunteering, and actually bought a set of arms. But prudence seized him
in time; he argued that "Napoleon gave after all only concentrated and
untrammeled utterance to that self-assertion and lust for more life which
weaker mortals feel but must perforce disguise."[7] Instead of going to
war he went to the country and wrote a doctor's thesis in philosophy.

After this dissertation *On the Fourfold Root of Sufficient Reason*
(1813),[8] Schopenhauer gave all his time, and devoted all his power, to
the work which was to be his masterpiece—*The World as Will and Idea*.

---

[4]Cf. Wallace, 92.
[5]*The World as Will and Idea*, ii, 199; *Essays*, "On Noise."
[6]Nietzsche: *Schopenhauer as Educator;* London, 1910; p. 122.
[7]Wallace: Article "Schopenhauer" in the *Encyclopedia Brittanica*.
[8]Schopenhauer insists, hardly with sufficient reason, and almost to the point of
salesmanship, that this book must be read before the *World as Will and Idea* can
be understood. The reader may nevertheless rest content with knowing that the
"principle of sufficient reason" is the "law of cause and effect," in four forms:
1—Logical, as the determination of conclusion by premises; 2—Physical, as the
determination of effect by cause; 3—Mathematical, as the determination of structure by the laws of mathematics and mechanics; and 4—Moral, as the determination of conduct by character.

He sent the MS. to the publisher *magna cum laude;* here, he said, was no mere rehash of old ideas, but a highly coherent structure of original thought, "clearly intelligible, vigorous, and not without beauty"; a book "which would hereafter be the source and occasion of a hundred other books."[9] All of which was outrageously egotistic, and absolutely true. Many years later Schopenhauer was so sure of having solved the chief problems of philosophy that he thought of having his signet ring carved with an image of the Sphinx throwing herself down the abyss, as she had promised to do on having her riddles answered.

Nevertheless, the book attracted hardly any attention; the world was too poor and exhausted to read about its poverty and exhaustion. Sixteen years after publication Schopenhauer was informed that the greater part of the edition had been sold as waste paper. In his essay on Fame, in "The Wisdom of Life," he quotes, with evident allusion to his masterpiece, two remarks of Lichtenberger's: "Works like this are as a mirror: if an ass looks in you cannot expect an angel to look out"; and "when a head and a book come into collision, and one sounds hollow, is it always the book?" Schopenhauer goes on, with the voice of wounded vanity: "The more a man belongs to posterity—in other words, to humanity in general—so much the more is he an alien to his contemporaries; for since his work is not meant for them as such, but only in so far as they form part of mankind at large, there is none of that familiar local color about his productions which would appeal to them." And then he becomes as eloquent as the fox in the fable: "Would a musician feel flattered by the loud applause of an audience if he knew that they were nearly all deaf, and that to conceal their infirmity he saw one or two persons applauding? And what would he say if he discovered that those one or two persons had often taken bribes to secure the loudest applause for the poorest player?" —In some men egotism is a compensation for the absence of fame; in others, egotism lends a generous coöperation to its presence.

So completely did Schopenhauer put himself into this book that his later works are but commentaries on it; he became Talmudist to his own Torah, exegete to his own Jeremiads. In 1836 he published an essay *On the Will in Nature,* which was to some degree incorporated into the enlarged edition of *The World as Will and Idea* which appeared in 1844. In 1841 came *The Two Ground-Problems of Ethics,* and in 1851 two substantial volumes of *Parerga et Parliapomena*—literally, "By-products and Leavings"—which have been translated into English as the *Essays.* For this, the most readable of his works, and replete with wisdom and wit, Schopenhauer received, as his total remuneration, ten free copies. Optimisim is difficult under such circumstances.

Only one adventure disturbed the monotony of his studious seclusion

[9] In Wallace, *Life,* p. 107.

after leaving Weimar. He had hoped for a chance to present his philosophy at one of the great universities of Germany; the chance came in 1822, when he was invited to Berlin as *privat-docent*. He deliberately chose for his lectures the very hours at which the then mighty Hegel was scheduled to teach; Schopenhauer trusted that the students would view him and Hegel with the eyes of posterity. But the students could not so far anticipate, and Schopenhauer found himself talking to empty seats. He resigned, and revenged himself by those bitter diatribes against Hegel which mar the later editions of his *chef-d'œuvre*. In 1831 a cholera epidemic broke out in Berlin; both Hegel and Schopenhauer fled; but Hegel returned prematurely, caught the infection, and died in a few days. Schopenhauer never stopped until he reached Frankfort, where he spent the remainder of his seventy-two years.

Like a sensible pessimist, he had avoided that pitfall of optimists— the attempt to make a living with the pen. He had inherited an interest in his father's firm, and lived in modest comfort on the revenue which this brought him. He invested his money with a wisdom unbecoming a philosopher. When a company in which he had taken shares failed, and the other creditors agreed to a 70% settlement, Schopenhauer fought for full payment, and won. He had enough to engage two rooms in a boarding-house; there he lived the last thirty years of his life, with no comrade but a dog. He called the little poodle Atma (the Brahmins' term for the World-Soul), but the wags of the town called it "Young Schopenhauer." He ate his dinners, usually, at the Englischer Hof. At the beginning of each meal he would put a gold coin upon the table before him; and at the end of each meal he would put the coin back into his pocket. It was, no doubt, an indignant waiter who at last asked him the meaning of this invariable ceremony. Schopenhauer answered that it was his silent wager to drop the coin into the poor-box on the first day that the English officers dining there should talk of anything else than horses, women, or dogs.[19]

The universities ignored him and his books, as if to substantiate his claim that all advances in philosophy are made outside of academic walls. "Nothing," says Nietzsche, "so offended the German savants as Schopenhauer's unlikeness to them." But he had learned some patience; he was confident that, however belated, recognition would come. And at last, slowly, it came. Men of the middle classes—lawyers, physicians, merchants—found in him a philosopher who offered them no mere pretentious jargon of metaphysical unrealities, but an intelligible survey of the phenomena of actual life. A Europe disillusioned with the ideals and efforts of 1848 turned almost with acclamation to this philosophy that had voiced the despair of 1815. The attack of science upon theology, the socialist indictment of poverty and war, the biological stress on the

[19]Wallace, 171.

struggle for existence,—all these factors helped to lift Schopenhauer finally to fame.

He was not too old to enjoy his popularity: he read with avidity all the articles that appeared about him; he asked his friends to send him every bit of printed comment they could find—he would pay the postage. In 1854 Wagner sent him a copy of *Der Ring der Nibelugen,* with a word in appreciation of Schopenhauer's philosophy of music. So the great pessimist became almost an optimist in his old age; he played the flute assiduously after dinner, and thanked Time for ridding him of the fires of youth. People came from all over the world to see him; and on his seventieth birthday, in 1858, congratulations poured in upon him from all quarters and every continent.

It was not too soon; he had but two more years to live. On September 21, 1860, he sat down alone to breakfast, apparently well. An hour later his landlady found him still seated at the table, dead.

III. THE WORLD AS IDEA

What strikes the reader at once upon opening *The World as Will and Idea* is its style. Here is no Chinese puzzle of Kantian terminology, no Hegelian obfuscation, no Spinozist geometry; everything is clarity and order; and all is admirably centered about the leading conception of the world as will, and therefore strife, and therefore misery. What blunt honesty, what refreshing vigor, what uncompromising directness! Where his predecessors are abstract to the point of invisibility, with theories that give out few windows of illustration upon the actual world, Schopenhauer, like the son of a business man, is rich in the concrete, in examples, in applications, even in humor.[11] After Kant, humor in philosophy was a startling innovation.

But why was the book rejected? Partly because it attacked just those who could have given it publicity—the university teachers. Hegel was philosophic dictator of Germany in 1818; yet Schopenhauer loses no time in assailing him. In the preface to the second edition he writes:

> No time can be more unfavorable to philosophy than that in which it is shamefully misused on the one hand to further political objects, on the other as a means of livelihood. . . . Is there then nothing to oppose to the maxim, *Primum vivere, deinde philosophari?*[12] These gentlemen desire to live, and

[11]One instance of his humor had better be buried in the obscurity of a foot-note. "The actor Unzelmann," notorious for adding remarks of his own to the lines of the playwright, "was forbidden, at the Berlin theatre, to improvise. Soon afterwards he had to appear upon the stage on horseback." Just as they entered, the horse was guilty of conduct seriously unbecoming a public stage. "The audience began to laugh; whereupon Unzelmann severely reproached the horse:—'Do you not know that we are forbidden to improvise?' "—Vol. ii, p. 273.

[12]First one must live, then one may philosophize.

indeed to live by philosophy. To philosophy they are assigned, with their wives and children. . . . The rule, "I sing the song of him whose bread I eat," has always held good; the making of money by philosophy was regarded by the ancients as the characteristic of the sophists. . . . Nothing is to be had for gold but mediocrity. . . . It is impossible that an age which for twenty years has applauded a Hegel—that intellectual Caliban—as the greatest of the philosophers, . . . could make him who has looked on at that desirous of its approbation. . . . But rather, truth will always be *paucorum hominum*,[13] and must therefore quietly and modestly wait for the few whose unusual mode of thought may find it enjoyable. . . . Life is short, but truth works far and lives long; let us speak the truth.

These last words are nobly spoken; but there is something of sour grapes in it all; no man was ever more anxious for approbation than Schopenhauer. It would have been nobler still to say nothing ill of Hegel; *de vivis nil nisi bonum*—of the living let us say nothing but good. And as for modestly awaiting recognition,—"I cannot see," says Schopenhauer, "that between Kant and myself anything has been done in philosophy."[14] "I hold this thought—that the world is will—to be that which has long been sought for under the name of philosophy, and the discovery of which is therefore regarded, by those who are familiar with history, as quite as impossible as the discovery of the philosopher's stone."[15] "I only intend to impart a single thought. Yet, notwithstanding all my endeavors, I could find no shorter way of imparting it than this whole book. . . . Read the book twice, and the first time with great patience."[16] So much for modesty! "What is modesty but hypocritical humility, by means of which, in a world swelling with envy, a man seeks to obtain pardon for excellences and merits from those who have none?"[17] "No doubt, when modesty was made a virtue, it was a very advantageous thing for the fools; for everybody is expected to speak of himself as if he were one."[18]

There was no humility about the first sentence of Schopenhauer's book. "The world," it begins, "is my idea." When Fichte had uttered a similar proposition even the metaphysically sophisticated Germans had asked,—"What does his wife say about this?" But Schopenhauer had no wife. His meaning, of course, was simple enough: he wished to accept at the outset the Kantian position that the external world is known to us only through our sensations and ideas. There follows an exposition of idealism which is clear and forceful enough, but which constitutes the least original part of the book, and might better have come last than

[13]Of few men.   [14]Vol. ii, p. 5.   [15]Vol. i, p. vii.
[16]*Ibid.*, viii. In fact, this is just what one must do; many have found even a third reading fruitful. A great book is like a great symphony, which must be heard many times before it can be really understood.
[17]I, 303.   [18]*Essays*, "On Pride."

first. The world took a generation to discover Schopenhauer because he put his worst foot forward, and hid his own thought behind a two-hundred-page barrier of second-hand idealism.[19]

The most vital part of the first section is an attack on materialism. How can we explain mind as matter, when we know matter only through mind?

If we had followed materialism thus far with clear ideas, when we reached its highest point we would suddenly be seized with a fit of the inextinguishable laughter of the Olympians. As if waking from a dream, we would all at once become aware that its fatal result—knowledge—which it had reached so laboriously, was presupposed as the indispensable condition of its very starting-point. Mere matter; and when we imagined that we thought matter, we really thought only the subject that perceives matter: the eye that sees it, the hand that feels it, the understanding that knows it. Thus the tremendous *petitio principii* reveals itself unexpectedly; for suddenly the last link is seen to be the starting-point, the chain of a circle; and the materialist is like Baron Münchausen, who, when swimming on horseback, drew the horse into the air with his legs, and himself by his queue.[20] . . . The crude materialism which even now, in the middle of the nineteenth century,[21] has been served up again under the ignorant delusion that it is original, . . . stupidity denies vital force, and first of all tries to explain the phenomena of life from physical and chemical forces, and those again from the mechanical effects of matter.[22] . . . But I will never believe that even the simplest chemical combination will ever admit of mechanical explanation; much less the properties of light, heat, and electricity. These will always require a dynamical explanation.[23]

No: it is impossible to solve the metaphysical puzzle, to discover the secret essence of reality, by examining matter first, and then proceeding to examine thought: we must begin with that which we know directly and intimately—ourselves. "We can never arrive at the real nature of things from without. However much we may investigate, we can never reach anything but images and names. We are like a man who goes round a castle seeking in vain for an entrance, and sometimes sketching the façades."[24] Let us enter within. If we can ferret out the ultimate nature of our own minds we shall perhaps have the key to the external world.

---

[19]Instead of recommending books about Schopenhauer it would be better to send the reader to Schopenhauer himself: all three volumes of his main work (with the exception of Part I in each volume) are easy reading, and full of matter; and all the Essays are valuable and delightful. By way of biography Wallace's *Life* should suffice. In this essay it has been thought desirable to condense Schopenhauer's immense volumes not by rephrasing their ideas, but by selecting and coördinating the salient passages, and leaving the thought in the philosopher's own clear and brilliant language. The reader will have the benefit of getting Schopenhauer at first hand, however briefly.

[20]I, 34.   [21]Vogt, Büchner, Moleschott, Feuerbach, etc.
[22]I, 159.   [23]III, 43.   [24]I, 128.

IV. THE WORLD AS WILL

1. THE WILL TO LIVE

Almost without exception, philosophers have placed the essence of mind in thought and consciousness; man was the knowing animal, the *animal rationale.* "This ancient and universal radical error, this enormous *proton pseudos,*[25] . . . must before everything be set aside."[26] "Consciousness is the mere surface of our minds, of which, as of the earth, we do not know the inside but only the crust."[27] Under the conscious intellect is the conscious or unconscious *will,* a striving, persistent vital force, a spontaneous activity, a will of imperious desire. The intellect may seem at times to lead the will, but only as a guide leads his master; the will "is the strong blind man who carries on his shoulders the lame man who can see."[28] We do not want a thing because we have found reasons for it, we find reasons for it because we want it; we even elaborate philosophies and theologies to cloak our desires.[29] Hence Schopenhauer calls man the "metaphysical animal": other animals desire without metaphysics. "Nothing is more provoking, when we are arguing against a man with reasons and explanations, and taking all pains to convince him, than to discover at last that he *will* not understand, that we have to do with his *will.*"[30] Hence the uselessness of logic: no one ever convinced anybody by logic; and even logicians use logic only as a source of income. To convince a man, you must appeal to his self-interest, his desires, his will. Observe how long we remember our victories, and how soon we forget our defeats; memory is the menial of *will.*[31] "In doing accounts we make mistakes much oftener in our own favor than to our disadvantage; and this without the slightest dishonest intention."[32] "On the other hand, the understanding of the stupidest man becomes keen when objects are in question that closely concern his wishes";[33] in general, the intellect is developed by danger, as in the fox, or by want, as in the criminal. But always it seems subordinate and instrumental to desire; when it attempts to displace the will, confusion follows. No one is more liable to mistakes than he who acts only on reflection.[34]

Consider the agitated strife of men for food, mates, or children; can this be the work of reflection? Certainly not; the cause is the half con-

---

[25]First lie, initial mistake.

[26]II, 409. Schopenhauer forgets (or does he take his lead from?) Spinoza's emphatic statement: "Desire is the very essence of man."—*Ethics,* part iv, prop. 18. Fichte had also emphasized the will.

[27]II, 328.   [28]II, 421.

[29]A source of Freud.   [30]III, 443.

[31]*Essays,* "Counsels and Maxims," p. 126.   [32]II, 433.

[33]II, 437.   [34]II, 251.

scious will to live, and to live fully. "Men are only apparently drawn
from in front; in reality they are pushed from behind";[85] they think they
are led on by what they see, when in truth they are driven on by what
they feel,—by instincts of whose operation they are half the time unconscious. Intellect is merely the minister of foreign affairs; "nature has
produced it for the service of the individual will. Therefore it is only
designed to know things so far as they afford motives for the will, but not
to fathom them or to comprehend their true being."[86] "The will is the
only permanent and unchangeable element in the mind; . . . it is the
will which," through continuity of purpose, "gives unity to consciousness
and holds together all its ideas and thoughts, accompanying them like a
continuous harmony."[87] It is the organ-point of thought.

Character lies in the will, and not in the intellect; character too is
continuity of purpose and attitude: and these are will. Popular language
is correct when it prefers the "heart" to the "head"; it knows (because it
has not reasoned about it) that a "good will" is profounder and more
reliable than a clear mind; and when it calls a man "shrewd," "knowing,"
or "cunning" it implies its suspicion and dislike. "Brilliant qualities of
mind win admiration, but never affection"; and "all religions promise a
reward . . . for excellences of the *will* or heart, but none for excellences
of the head or understanding."[88]

Even the body is the product of the will. The blood, pushed on by that
will which we vaguely call life, builds its own vessels by wearing grooves
in the body of the embryo; the grooves deepen and close up, and become
arteries and veins.[89] The will to know builds the brain just as the will to
grasp forms the hand, or as the will to eat develops the digestive tract.[40]
Indeed, these pairs—these forms of will and these forms of flesh—are but
two sides of one process and reality. The relation is best seen in emotion,
where the feeling and the internal bodily changes form one complex unit.[41]

The act of will and the movement of the body are not two different things
objectively known, which the bond of causality unites; they do not stand
in the relation of cause and effect; they are one and the same, but they are
given in entirely different ways,—immediately, and again in perception.
. . . The action of the body is nothing but the act of the will objectified.
This is true of every movement of the body; . . . the whole body is nothing
but objectified will. . . . The parts of the body must therefore completely
correspond to the principal desires through which the will manifests itself;
they must be the visible expression of these desires. Teeth, throat and bowels
are objectified hunger; the organs of generation are objectified sexual desire.
. . . The whole nervous system constitutes the antennae of the will, which is

[85]III, 118.   [86]II, 463, 326; a source of Bergson.
[87]II, 333.   [88]II, 450, 449.   [89]II, 479.
[40]II, 486. This is the Lamarckian view of growth and evolution as due to desires
and functions compelling structures and begetting organs.
[41]I, 132. A source for the James-Lange theory of emotion?

stretches within and without. . . . As the human body generally corresponds
to the human will generally, so the individual bodily structure corresponds to
the individually modified will, the character of the individual.[42]

The intellect tires, the will never; the intellect needs sleep, but the
will works even in sleep. Fatigue, like pain, has its seat in the brain;
muscles not connected with the cerebrum (like the heart) never tire.[48]
In sleep the brain feeds; but the will requires no food. Hence the need
for sleep is greatest in brain-workers. (This fact, however, "must not mis-
lead us into extending sleep unduly; for then it loses in intensity . . . and
becomes mere loss of time.") [44] In sleep the life of man sinks to the vege-
tative level, and then "the will works according to its original and essential
nature, undisturbed from without, with no diminution of its power
through the activity of the brain and the exertion of knowing, which is
the heaviest organic function; . . . therefore in sleep the whole power
of the will is directed to the maintenance and improvement of the organism. Hence all healing, all favorable crises, take place in sleep."[45] Burdach
was right when he declared sleep to be the original state. The embryo
sleeps almost continuously, and the infant most of the time. Life is "a
struggle against sleep: at first we win ground from it, which in the end
it recovers. Sleep is a morsel of death borrowed to keep up and renew
that part of life which has been exhausted by the day."[46] It is our eternal
foe; even when we are awake it possesses us partly. After all, what is to
be expected of heads even the wisest of which is every night the scene
of the strangest and the most senseless dreams, and which has to take up
its meditations again on awakening from them?"[47]

Will, then, is the essence of man. Now what if it is also the essence of
life in all its forms, and even of "inanimate" matter? What if will is the
long-sought-for, the long-despaired-of, "thing-in-itself,"—the ultimate
inner reality and secret essence of all things?

Let us try, then, to interpret the external world in terms of will. And
let us go at once to the bottom; where others have said that will is a form
of force let us say that force is a form of will.[48] To Hume's question—
What is causality?—we shall answer, Will. As will is the universal cause
in ourselves, so is it in things; and unless we so understand cause as will,
causality will remain only a magic and mystic formula, really meaningless. Without this secret we are driven to mere occult qualities like "force,"
or "gravity," or "affinity"; we do not know what these forces are, but we
know—at least a little more clearly—what will is; let us say, then, that

<hr/>

[42]I, 130–141; II, 482. Cf. Spinoza, *Ethics,* III, 2.
[43]II, 424. But is there no such thing as the satiation or exhaustion of desire? In
profound fatigue or sickness even the will to live fades.
[44]II, 468.   [45]II, 463.
[46]"Counsels and Maxims," essay "On Our Relations to Ourselves."
[47]II, 333.   [48]I, 144.

repulsion and attraction, combination and decomposition, magnetism and electricity, gravity and crystallization, are Will.[49] Goethe expressed this idea in the title of one of his novels, when he called the irresistible attraction of lovers *die Wahlverwandschaften*—"elective affinities." The force which draws the lover, and the force which draws the planet, are one.

So in plant life. The lower we go among the forms of life the smaller we find the rôle of intellect; but not so with will.

> That which in us pursues its ends by the light of knowledge, but here . . . only strives blindly and dumbly in a one-sided and unchangeable manner, must yet in both cases come under the name of Will. . . . Unconsciousness is the original and natural condition of all things, and therefore also the basis from which, in particular species of beings, consciousness results as their highest efflorescence; wherefore even then unconsciousness always continue: to predominate. Accordingly, most existences are without consciousness; but yet they act according to the laws of their nature,—i. e., of their will. Plants have at most a very weak analogue of consciousness; the lowest species of animals only the dawn of it. But even after it has ascended through the whole series of animals to man and his reason, the unconsciousness of plants, from which it started, still remains the foundation, and may be traced in the necessity for sleep.[50]

Aristotle was right: there is a power within that moulds every form, in plants and planets, in animals and men. "The instinct of animals in general gives us the best illustration of what remains of teleology in nature. For as instinct is an action similar to that which is guided by the conception of an end, and yet is entirely without this; so all construction in nature resembles that which is guided by the conception of an end, and yet is entirely without it."[51] The marvelous mechanical skill of animals shows how prior the will is to the intellect. An elephant which had been led through Europe, and had crossed hundreds of bridges, refused to advance upon a weak bridge, though it had seen many horses and men crossing it. A young dog fears to jump down from the table; it foresees the effect of the fall not by reasoning (for it has no experience of such a fall) but by instinct. Orang-outangs warm themselves by a fire which they find, but they do not feed the fire; obviously, then, such actions are instinctive, and not the result of reasoning; they are the expression not of intellect but of will.[52]

The will, of course, is a will to live, and a will to maximum life. How dear life is to all living things!—and with what silent patience it will bide its time! "For thousands of years galvanism slumbered in copper and zinc, and they lay quietly beside silver, which must be consumed in flame as soon as all three are brought together under the required conditions. Even in the organic kingdom we see a dry seed preserve the slumbering force of life through three thousand years, and, when at last the favorable circumstances occur, grow up as a plant." Living toads found in limestone lead to the conclusion that even animal life is capable of suspension for thousands of years.[53] The will is a will to live; and its eternal enemy is death.

But perhaps it can defeat even death?

2. The Will to Reproduce

It can, by the strategy and martyrdom of reproduction.

Every normal organism hastens, at maturity, to sacrifice itself to the task of reproduction: from the spider who is eaten up by the female he has just fertilized, or the wasp that devotes itself to gathering food for offspring it will never see, to the man who wears himself to ruin in the effort to feed and clothe and educate his children. Reproduction is the ultimate purpose of every organism, and its strongest instinct; for only so can the will conquer death. And to ensure this conquest of death, the will to reproduce is placed almost entirely beyond control of knowledge or reflection: even a philosopher, occasionally, has children.

The will shows itself here as independent of knowledge, and works blindly, as in unconscious nature. . . . Accordingly, the reproductive organs are properly the focus of will, and form the opposite pole to the brain, which is the representative of knowledge. . . . The former are the life-sustaining principle,—they ensure endless life; "for this reason they were worshipped by the Greeks in the *phallus* and by the Hindus in the *lingam*. . . . Hesiod and Parmenides said very significantly that Eros is the first, the creator, the principle from which all things proceed. The relation of the sexes . . . is really the invisible central point of all action and conduct, and peeps out everywhere in spite of all veils thrown over it. It is the cause of war and the end of peace; the basis of what is serious, and the aim of the jest; the inexhaustible source of wit, the key of all illusions, and the meaning of all mysterious hints.[54] . . . We see it at every moment seat itself, as the true and hereditary lord of the world, out of the fullness of its own strength, upon the ancestral throne; and looking down thence with scornful glance, laugh at the preparations made to bind it, or imprison it, or at least limit it and, wherever possible, keep it concealed, and even so to master it that it shall only appear as a subordinate, secondary concern of life.[55]

The "metaphysics of love" revolves about this subordination of the father to the mother, of the parent to the child, of the individual to the species. And first, the law of sexual attraction is that the choice of mate

---

[53] I, 178.

[54] "A source of Freud's theory of "wit and the unconscious."

[55] I, 426, 525; III, 314. Schopenhauer, like all who have suffered from sex, exaggerates its rôle; the parental relation probably outweighs the sexual in the minds of normal adults.

is to a large extent determined, however unconsciously, by mutual fitness to procreate.

> Each seeks a mate that will neutralize his defects, lest they be inherited; . . . a physically weak man will seek a strong woman. . . . Each one will especially regard as beautiful in another individual those perfections which he himself lacks, nay, even those imperfections which are the opposite of his own.[56] . . . The physical qualities of two individuals can be such that for the purpose of restoring as far as possible the type of the species, the one is quite specially and perfectly the completion and supplement of the other, which therefore desires it exclusively. . . . The profound consciousness with which we consider and ponder every part of the body, . . . the critical scrupulosity with which we look at a woman who begins to please us . . . the individual here acts, without knowing it, by order of something higher than himself. . . . Every individual loses attraction for the opposite sex in proportion as he or she is removed from the fittest period for begetting or conceiving: . . . youth without beauty has still always attraction; beauty without youth has none. . . . That in every case of falling in love, . . . what alone is looked to is the production of an individual of a definite nature, is primarily confirmed by the fact that the essential matter is not the reciprocation of love, but possession.[57]

Nevertheless, no unions are so unhappy as these love marriages—and precisely for the reason that their aim is the perpetuation of the species, and not the pleasure of the individual.[58] "He who marries from love must live in sorrow," runs a Spanish proverb. Half the literature of the marriage problem is stultified because it thinks of marriage as mating, instead of thinking of it as an arrangement for the preservation of the race. Nature does not seem to care whether the parents are "happy forever afterwards," or only for a day, so long as reproduction is achieved. Marriages of convenience, arranged by the parents of the mates, are often happier than marriages of love. Yet the woman who marries for love, against the advice of her parents, is in a sense to be admired; for "she has preferred what is of most importance, and has acted in the spirit of nature (more exactly, of the species), while the parents advised in the spirit of individual egoism."[59] Love is the best eugenics.

Since love is a deception practiced by nature, marriage is the attrition of love, and must be disillusioning. Only a philosopher can be happy in marriage, and philosophers do not marry.

> Because the passion depended upon an illusion which represented that which has value only for the species as valuable for the individual, the deception must vanish after the attainment of the end of the species. The individual discovers that he has been the dupe of the species. If Petrarch's passion had been gratified, his song would have been silenced.[60]

[56] A source of Weininger.   [57] III, 342, 357, 347, 360, 359, 352, 341.
[58] III, 372.   [59] III, 371.   [60] III, 370.

The subordination of the individual to the species as instrument of its continuance, appears again in the apparent dependence of individual vitality on the condition of the reproductive cells.

The sexual impulse is to be regarded as the inner life of the tree (the species) upon which the life of the individual grows, like a leaf that is nourished by the tree and assists in nourishing the tree; this is why that impulse is so strong, and springs from the depths of our nature. To castrate an individual means to cut him off from the tree of the species upon which he grows, and thus severed, leaves him to wither; hence the degradation of his mental and physical powers. That the service of the species, i. e., fecundation, is followed in the case of every animal individual by momentary exhaustion and debility of all the powers, and in the case of most insects, indeed, by speedy death,—on account of which Celsus said, *Seminis emissio est partis animae jactura;* that in the case of man the extinction of the generative power shows that the individual approaches death; that excessive use of this power at every age shortens life, while on the other hand, temperance in this respect increases all the powers, and especially the muscular powers, on which account it was part of the training of the Greek athletes; that the same restraint lengthens the life of the insect even to the following spring; all this points to the fact that the life of the individual is at bottom only borrowed from that of the species. . . . Procreation is the highest point; and after attaining to it, the life of the first individual quickly or slowly sinks, while a new life ensures to nature the endurance of the species, and repeats the same phenomena. . . . Thus the alternation of death and reproduction is as the pulsebeat of the species. . . . Death is for the species what sleep is for the individual; . . . this is nature's great doctrine of immortality. . . . For the whole world, with all its phenomena, is the objectivity of the one indivisible will, the Idea, which is related to all other Ideas as harmony is related to the single voice. . . . In Eckermann's *Conversations with Goethe* (vol. i, p. 161), Goethe says: "Our spirit is a being of a nature quite indestructible, and its activity continues from eternity to eternity. It is like the sun, which seems to set only to our earthly eyes, but which, in reality, never sets, but shines on unceasingly." Goethe has taken the simile from me, not I from him.[61]

Only in space and time do we seem to be separate beings; they constitute the "principle of individuation" which divides life into distinct organisms as appearing in different places or periods; space and time are the Veil of Maya,—Illusion hiding the unity of things. In reality there is only the species, only life, only will. "To understand clearly that the individual is only the phenomenon, not the thing-in-itself," to see in "the constant change of matter the fixed permanence of form,"—this is the essence of philosophy.[62] "The motto of history should run: *Eadem, sed aliter.*"[63] The more things change, the more they remain the same.

[61]III, 310; I, 214; III, 312, 270, 267; I, 206, 362.
[62]I, 357-8.
[63]III, 227. "The same things, but in different ways."

He to whom men and all things have not at all times appeared as mere phantoms or illusions, has no capacity for philosophy. . . . The true philosophy of history lies in perceiving that, in all the endless changes and motley complexity of events, it is only the self-same unchangeable being that is before us, which today pursues the same ends as it did yesterday and ever will. The historical philosopher has accordingly to recognize the identical character in all events, . . . and in spite of all the variety of special circumstances, of costumes and manners and customs, has to see everywhere the same humanity. . . . To have read Herodotus is, from a philosophical point of view, to have studied enough history. . . . Throughout and everywhere the true symbol of nature is the circle, because it is the schema or type of recurrence.[64]

We like to believe that all history is a halting and imperfect preparation for the magnificent era of which we are the salt and summit; but this notion of progress is mere conceit and folly. "In general, the wise in all ages have always said the same things, and the fools, who at all times form the immense majority, have in their way too acted alike, and done the opposite; and so it will continue. For, as Voltaire says, we shall leave the world as foolish and wicked as we found it."[65]

In the light of all this we get a new and grimmer sense of the inescapable reality of determinism. "Spinoza says (Epistle 62) that if a stone which has been projected through the air had consciousness, it would believe that it was moving of its own free will. I add to this only that the stone would be right. The impulse given it is for the stone what the motive is for me; and what in the stone appears as cohesion, gravitation, rigidity, is in its inner nature the same as that which I recognize in myself as well, and what the stone also, if knowledge were given to it, would recognize as will."[66] But in neither the stone nor the philosopher is the will "free." Will as a whole is free, for there is no other will beside it that could limit it; but each part of the universal Will—each species, each organism, each organ—is irrevocably determined by the whole.

Everyone believes himself à *priori* to be perfectly free, even in his individual actions, and thinks that at every moment he can commence another manner of life, which just means that he can become another person. But à *posteriori*, through experience, he finds to his astonishment that he is not free, but subjected to necessity; that in spite of all his resolutions and reflections he does not change his conduct, and that from the beginning of his life to the end of it, he must carry out the very character which he himself condemns, and as it were, play the part which he has undertaken, to the very end.[67]

[64] III, 227, 267; Wallace, 97. Cf. Nietzsche's "eternal recurrence."
[65] Introduction to "The Wisdom of Life."
[66] II, 164.　　[67] I, 147.

V. THE WORLD AS EVIL

But if the world is will, it must be a world of suffering.

And first, because will itself indicates want, and its grasp is always greater than its reach. For every wish that is satisfied there remain ten that are denied. Desire is infinite, fulfilment is limited—"it is like the alms thrown to a beggar, that keeps him alive today in order that his misery may be prolonged tomorrow. . . . As long as our consciousness is filled by our will, so long as we are given up to the throng of desires with their constant hopes and fears, so long as we are subject to willing, we can never have lasting happiness or peace."[68] And fulfilment never satisfies; nothing is so fatal to an ideal as its realization. "The satisfied passion oftener leads to unhappiness than to happiness. For its demands often conflict so much with the personal welfare of him who is concerned that they undermine it."[69] Each individual bears within himself a disruptive contradiction; the realized desire develops a new desire, and so on endlessly. "At bottom this results from the fact that the will must live on itself, for there exists nothing besides it, and it is a hungry will."[70]

In every individual the measure of the pain essential to him was determined once for all by his nature; a measure which could neither remain empty, nor be more than filled . . . If a great and pressing care is lifted from our breast, . . . another immediately replaces it, the whole material of which was already there before, but could not come into consciousness as care because there was no capacity left for it. . . . But now that there is room for this it comes forward and occupies the throne.[71]

Again, life is evil because pain is its basic stimulus and reality, and pleasure is merely a negative cessation of pain. Aristotle was right: the wise man seeks not pleasure, but freedom from care and pain.

All satisfaction, or what is commonly called happiness, is, in reality and essence, negative only. . . . We are not properly conscious of the blessings and advantages we actually possess, nor do we prize them, but think of them merely as a matter of course, for they gratify us only negatively, by restraining suffering. Only when we have lost them do we become sensible of their value; for the want, the privation, the sorrow, is the positive thing, communicating itself directly to us. . . . What was it that led the Cynics to repudiate pleasure in any form, if it was not the fact that pain is, in a greater or less degree, always bound up with pleasure? . . . The same truth is contained in that fine French proverb: *le mieux est l'ennemi du bien* —leave well enough alone.[72]

Life is evil because "as soon as want and suffering permit rest to a man, *ennui* is at once so near that he necessarily requires diversion,"[73]—

---

[68] I, 253.   [69] III, 368.   [70] I, 201.   [71] I, 409.
[71] I, 411; "Counsels and Maxims," p. 5. "The better is enemy of the good."
[72] I, 404.

i. e., more suffering. Even if the socialist Utopia were attained, innumerable evils would be left, because some of them—like strife—are essential to life; and if every evil were removed, and strife were altogether ended, boredom would become as intolerable as pain. So "life swings like a pendulum backward and forward between pain and *ennui*. . . . After man had transformed all pains and torments into the conception of hell, there remained nothing for heaven except *ennui*."[74] The more successful we become, the more we are bored. "As want is the constant scourge of the people, so *ennui* is the scourge of the fashionable world. In middle-class the *ennui* is represented by the Sundays and want by the week-days."[75]

Life is evil because the higher the organism the greater the suffering. The growth of knowledge is no solution.

> For as the phenomenon of will becomes more complete, the suffering becomes more and more apparent. In the plant there is as yet no sensibility, and therefore no pain. A certain very small degree of suffering is experienced by the lowest species of animal life—Infusoria and Radiata; even in insects the capacity to feel and suffer is still limited. It first appears in a high degree with the complete nervous system of vertebrate animals, and always in a higher degree the more intelligence develops. Thus, in proportion as knowledge attains to distinctness, as consciousness ascends, pain also increases, and reaches its highest degree in man. And then, again, the more distinctly a man knows—the more intelligent he is—the more pain he has; the man who is gifted with genius suffers most of all.[76]

He that increaseth knowledge, therefore, increaseth sorrow. Even memory and foresight add to human misery; for most of our suffering lies in retrospect or anticipation; pain itself is brief. How much more suffering is caused by the thought of death than by death itself!

Finally, and above all, life is evil because life is war. Everywhere in nature we see strife, competition, conflict, and a suicidal alternation of victory and defeat. Every species "fights for the matter, space, and time of the others."

> The young hydra, which grows like a bud out of the old one, and afterwards separates itself from it, fights, while it is still joined to the old one, for the prey that offers itself, so that the one snatches it out of the mouth of the other. But the bull-dog ant of Australia affords us the most extraordinary example of this kind; for if it is cut in two, a battle begins between the head and the tail. The head seizes the tail with its teeth, and the tail defends itself bravely by stinging the head; the battle may last for half an hour, until they die or are dragged away by other ants. This contest takes place every time the experiment is tried. . . . Yunghahn relates that he saw in Java a plain, as far as the eye could reach, entirely covered with skeletons, and took it for a battle-field; they were, however, merely the

[74] I, 402.   [75] I, 404.   [76] I, 400.

skeletons of large turtles, . . . which come this way out of the sea to lay their eggs, and are then attacked by wild dogs who with their united strength lay them on their backs, strip off the small shell from the stomach, and devour them alive. But often then a tiger pounces upon the dogs. . . . For this these turtles are born. . . . Thus the will to live everywhere preys upon itself, and in different forms is its own nourishment, till finally the human race, because it subdues all the others, regards nature as a manufactory for its own use. Yet even the human race . . . reveals in itself with most terrible distinctness this conflict, this variance of the will with itself; and we find *homo homini lupus.*[77]

The total picture of life is almost too painful for contemplation; life depends on our not knowing it too well.

If we should bring clearly to a man's sight the terrible sufferings and miseries to which his life is constantly exposed, he would be seized with horror; and if we were to conduct the confirmed optimist through the hospitals, infirmaries, and surgical operating-rooms, through the prisons, torture-chambers, and slave kennels, over battle-fields and places of execution; if we were to open to him all the dark abodes of misery, where it hides itself from the glance of cold curiosity, and, finally, allow him to look into the starving dungeons of Ugolino, he too would understand at last the nature of this "best of all possible worlds." For whence did Dante take the materials of his hell but from our actual world? And yet he made a very proper hell out of it. But when, on the other hand, he came to describe heaven and its delights, he had an insurmountable difficulty before him, for our world affords no materials at all for this. . . . Every epic and dramatic poem can only represent a struggle, an effort, a fight for happiness; never enduring and complete happiness itself. It conducts its heroes through a thousand dangers and difficulties to the goal; as soon as this is reached it hastens to let the curtain fall; for now there would remain nothing for it to do but to show that the glittering goal in which the hero expected to find happiness had only disappointed him, and that after its attainment he was no better off than before.[78]

We are unhappy married, and unmarried we are unhappy. We are unhappy when alone, and unhappy in society: we are like hedge-hogs clustering together for warmth, uncomfortable when too closely packed, and yet miserable when kept apart. It is all very funny; and "the life of every individual, if we survey it as a whole, . . . and only lay stress on its most significant features, is really always a tragedy; but gone through in detail it has the character of a comedy."[79] Think of it:

At the age of five years to enter a spinning-cotton or other factory, and from that time forth to sit there daily, first ten, then twelve, and ultimately fourteen hours, performing the same mechanical labor, is to purchase dearly the satisfaction of drawing breath. But this is the fate of millions, and that

[77] I, 192; III, 112; I, 191. "Man is a wolf to man."
[78] I, 419, 413.   [79] I, 415.

of millions more is analogous to it. . . . Again, under the firm crust of the planet dwell powerful forces of nature, which, as soon as some accident affords them free play, must necessarily destroy the crust, with everything living upon it, as has already taken place at least three times upon our planet, and will probably take place oftener still. The earthquake of Lisbon, the earthquake of Haiti, the destruction of Pompeii, are only small playful hints of what is possible.[80]

In the face of all this, "optimism is a bitter mockery of men's woes";[81] and "we cannot ascribe to the *Theodicy* of Leibnitz, "as a methodical and broad unfolding of optimism, any other merit than this, that it gave occasion later for the immortal *Candide* of the great Voltaire; whereby Leibnitz' oft-repeated and lame excuse for the evil of the world—that the bad sometimes brings about the good—received a confirmation which was unexpected by him."[82] In brief, "the nature of life throughout presents itself to us as intended and calculated to awaken the conviction that nothing at all is worth our striving, our efforts and struggles; that all good things are vanity, the world in all its ends bankrupt, and life a business which does not cover expenses."[83]

To be happy, one must be as ignorant as youth. Youth thinks that willing and striving are joys; it has not yet discovered the weary insatiableness of desire, and the fruitlessness of fulfilment; it does not yet see the inevitableness of defeat.

> The cheerfulness and vivacity of youth are partly due to the fact that when we are ascending the hill of life, death is not visible; it lies down at the bottom of the other side. . . . Towards the close of life, every day we live gives us the same kind of sensation as the criminal experiences at every step on his way to the gallows. . . . To see how short life is, one must have lived long. . . . Up to our thirty-sixth year we may be compared, in respect to the way in which we use our vital energy, to people who live on the interest of their money; what they spend today they have again tomorrow. But from the age of thirty-six onward, our position is like that of the investor who begins to entrench on his capital. . . . It is the dread of this calamity that makes love of possession increase with age. . . . So far from youth being the happiest period of life, there is much more truth in the remark made by Plato, at the beginning of the *Republic,* that the prize should rather be given to old age, because then at last a man is freed from the animal passion which has hitherto never ceased to disquiet him. . . . Yet it should not be forgotten that, when this passion is extinguished, the true kernel of life is gone, and nothing remains but the hollow shell; or, from another point of view, life then becomes like a comedy which, begun by real actors, is continued and brought to an end by automata dressed in their clothes.[84]

At the end, we meet death. Just as experience begins to coördinate itself into wisdom, brain and body begin to decay. "Everything lingers

[80]III, 389, 395.   [81]I, 420.   [82]III, 394.   [83]III, 383.
[84]"Counsels and Maxims," 124–138.

for but a moment, and hastens on to death."[85] And if death bides its time, it is but playing with us as a cat with a helpless mouse. "It is clear that as our walking is admittedly nothing but a constantly-prevented falling, so the life of our bodies is nothing but a constantly-prevented dying, an ever-postponed death."[86] "Among the magnificent ornaments and apparel of Eastern despots there is always a costly vial of poison."[87] The philosophy of the East understands the omnipresence of death, and gives to its students that calm aspect and dignified slowness of carriage, which comes of a consciousness of the brevity of personal existence. The fear of death is the beginning of philosophy, and the final cause of religion. The average man cannot reconcile himself to death; therefore he makes innumerable philosophies and theologies; the prevalence of a belief in immortality is a token of the awful fear of death.

Just as theology is a refuge from death, so insanity is a refuge from pain. "Madness comes as a way to avoid the memory of suffering";[88] it is a saving break in the thread of consciousness; we can survive certain experiences or fears only by forgetting them.

> How unwillingly we think of things which powerfully injure our interests, wound our pride, or interfere with our wishes; with what difficulty do we determine to lay such things before our intellects for careful and serious investigation. . . . In that resistance of the will to allowing what is contrary to it to come under the examination of the intellect lies the place at which madness can break in upon the mind. . . . If the resistance of the will against the apprehension of some knowledge reaches such a degree that that operation is not performed in its entirety, then certain elements or circumstances become for the intellect completely suppressed, because the will cannot endure the sight of them; and then, for the sake of the necessary connections, the gaps that thus arise are filled up at pleasure; thus madness appears. For the intellect has given up its nature to please the will; the man now imagines what does not exist. Yet the madness which has thus arisen is the lethe of unendurable suffering; it was the last remedy of harassed nature, i. e., of the will.[89]

The final refuge is suicide. Here at last, strange to say, thought and imagination conquer instinct. Diogenes is said to have put an end to himself by refusing to breathe;—what a victory over the will to live! But this triumph is merely individual; the will continues in the species. Life laughs at suicide, and smiles at death; for every deliberate death there are thousands of indeliberate births. "Suicide, the wilful destruction of the single phenomenal existence, is a vain and foolish act, for the thing-in-itself—the species, and life, and will in general—remains unaffected by it, even as the rainbow endures however fast the drops which support

---

[85] II, 454; III, 269. [86] "Counsels and Maxims," 28, note.
[87] I, 119. [88] I, 250.
[89] III, 167-9. A source of Freud.

it for the moment may chance to fall."[90] Misery and strife continue after the death of the individual, and must continue, so long as will is dominant in man. There can be no victory over the ills of life until the will has been utterly subordinated to knowledge and intelligence.

VI. THE WISDOM OF LIFE

1. PHILOSOPHY

Consider, first, the absurdity of the desire for material goods. Fools believe that if they can only achieve wealth, their wills can be completely gratified; a man of means is supposed to be a man with means for the fulfilment of every desire. "People are often reproached for wishing for money above all things, and for loving it more than anything else; but it is natural and even inevitable for people to love that which, like an unwearied Proteus, is always ready to turn itself into whatever object their wandering wishes or their manifold desires may fix upon. Everything else can satisfy only *one* wish; money alone is absolutely good, . . . because it is the abstract satisfaction of every wish."[91] Nevertheless, a life devoted to the acquisition of wealth is useless unless we know how to turn it into joy; and this is an art that requires culture and wisdom. A succession of sensual pursuits never satisfies for long; one must understand the ends of life as well as the art of acquiring means. "Men are a thousand times more intent on becoming rich than on acquiring culture, though it is quite certain that what a man *is* contributes more to his happiness than what he *has*."[92] "A man who has no mental needs is called a Philistine";[93] he does not know what to do with his leisure— *difficilis in otio quies;*[94] he searches greedily from place to place for new sensations; and at last he is conquered by that nemesis of the idle rich or the reckless voluptuary—*ennui.*[95]

Not wealth but wisdom is the Way. "Man is at once impetuous striving of will (whose focus lies in the reproductive system), and eternal, free, serene subject of pure knowledge (of which the focus is the brain)."[96] Marvelous to say, knowledge, though born of the will, may yet master the will. The possibility of the independence of knowledge first appears in the indifferent way in which the intellect occasionally responds to the dictates of desire. "Sometimes the intellect refuses to obey the will: e. g., when we try in vain to fix our minds upon something, or when we call in vain upon the memory for something that was entrusted to it. The anger of the will against the intellect on such occasions makes its relation to it,

---

[90] I, 515.
[92] *Ibid.,* p. 11.
[94] P. 39. "Quiet in leisure is difficult."
[95] I, 262.

[91] *Essays,* "Wisdom of Life," p. 47.
[93] P. 41.
[96] P. 22.

and the difference of the two. very plain. Indeed, vexed by this anger, the intellect sometimes officiously brings what was asked of it hours afterward, or even the following morning, quite unexpectedly and unseasonably."[97] From this imperfect subservience the intellect may pass to domination. "In accordance with previous reflection, or a recognized necessity, a man suffers, or accomplishes in cold blood, what is of the utmost, and often terrible, importance to him: suicide, execution, the duel, enterprises of every kind fraught with danger to life; and in general, things against which his whole animal nature rebels. Under such circumstances we see to what an extent reason has mastered the animal nature."[98]

This power of the intellect over the will permits of deliberate development; desire can be moderated or quieted by knowledge; and above all by a determinist philosophy which recognizes everything as the inevitable result of its antecedents. "Of ten things that annoy us, nine would not be able to do so if we understood them thoroughly in their causes, and therefore knew their necessity and true nature. . . . For what bridle and bit are to an unmanageable horse, the intellect is for the will in man."[99] "It is with inward as with outward necessity: nothing reconciles us so thoroughly as distinct knowledge."[100] The more we know of our passions, the less they control us; and "nothing will protect us from external compulsion so much as the control of ourselves."[101] *Si vis tibi omnia subjicere, subjice te rationi.*[102] The greatest of all wonders is not the conqueror of the world, but the subduer of himself.

So philosophy purifies the will. But philosophy is to be understood as experience and thought, not as mere reading or passive study.

The constant streaming in of the thoughts of others must confine and suppress our own; and indeed in the long run paralyze the power of thought. . . . The inclination of most scholars is a kind of *fuga vacui*[103] from the poverty of their own minds, which forcibly draws in the thoughts of others. . . . It is dangerous to read about a subject before we have thought about it ourselves. . . . When we read, another person thinks for us; we merely repeat his mental process. . . . So it comes about that if anyone spends almost the whole day in reading, . . . he gradually loses the capacity for thinking. . . . Experience of the world may be looked upon as a kind of text, to which reflection and knowledge form the commentary. Where there is a great deal of reflection and intellectual knowledge, and very little experience, the result is like those books which have on each page two lines of text to forty lines of commentary.[104]

[97] II, 439.   [98] I, 112.
[99] II, 426.   [100] I, 396.
[101] "Counsels and Maxims," p. 51.
[102] "If you would subject all things to yourself, subject yourself to reason."—Henaca.
[103] Vacuum suction.
[104] II, 254: *Essays*, "Books and Reading"; "Counsels and Maxims," p. 21.

The first counsel, then, is Life before books; and the second is, Text before commentary. Read the creators rather than the expositors and the critics. "Only from the authors themselves can we receive philosophic thoughts: therefore whoever feels himself drawn to philosophy must seek out its immortal teachers in the still sanctuary of their own works."[105] One work of genius is worth a thousand commentaries.

Within these limitations, the pursuit of culture, even through books, is valuable, because our happiness depends on what we have in our heads rather than on what we have in our pockets. Even fame is folly; "other people's heads are a wretched place to be the home of a man's true happiness."[106]

> What one human being can be to another is not a very great deal; in the end everyone stands alone; and the important thing is, who it is that stands alone. . . . The happiness which we receive from ourselves is greater than that which we obtain from our surroundings. . . . The world in which a man lives shapes itself chiefly by the way in which he looks at it. . . . Since everything which exists or happens for a man exists only in his consciousness, and happens for him alone, the most essential thing for a man is the constitution of his consciousness. . . . Therefore it is with great truth that Aristotle says, "To be happy means to be self-sufficient."[107]

The way out of the evil of endless willing is the intelligent contemplation of life, and converse with the achievements of the great of all times and countries; it is only for such loving minds that these great ones have lived. "Unselfish intellect rises like a perfume above the faults and follies of the world of Will."[108] Most men never rise above viewing things as objects of desire—hence their misery; but to see things purely as objects of understanding is to rise to freedom.

> When some external cause or inward disposition lifts us suddenly out of the endless stream of willing, and delivers knowledge out of the slavery of the will, the attention is no longer directed to the motives of willing, but comprehends things free from their relation to the will, and thus observes them without personal interest, without subjectivity, purely objectively, —gives itself entirely up to them so far as they are ideas, but not in so far as they are motives. Then all at once the peace which we were always seeking, but which always fled from us on the former path of the desires, comes to us of its own accord, and it is well with us. It is the painless state which Epicurus prized as the highest good and as the state of the gods; for we are for the moment set free from the miserable striving of the will; we keep the Sabbath of the penal servitude of willing; the wheel of Ixion stands still.[109]

[105] I, xxvii.   [106] "Wisdom of Life," p. 117.
[107] Ibid., pp. 27, 4-9.   [108] "Wisdom of Life," 34, 108.
[109] I, 254. Ixion, according to classical mythology, tried to win Juno from Jupiter, nd was punished by being bound to a forever-revolving wheel.

2. GENIUS

Genius is the highest form of this will-less knowledge. The lowest forms of life are entirely made up of will, without knowledge; man in general is mostly will and little knowledge; genius is mostly knowledge and little will. "Genius consists in this, that the knowing faculty has received a considerably greater development than the service of the will demands."[110] This involves some passage of force out of reproductive into intellectual activity. "The fundamental condition of genius is an abnormal predominance of sensibility and irritability over reproductive power."[111] Hence the enmity between genius and woman, who represents reproduction and the subjugation of the intellect to the will to live and make live. "Women may have great talent, but no genius, for they always remain subjective";[112] with them everything is personal, and is viewed as a means to personal ends. On the other hand,

> genius is simply the completest objectivity,—i. e., the objective tendency of the mind. . . . Genius is the power of leaving one's own interests, wishes and aims entirely out of sight, of entirely renouncing one's own personality for a time, so as to remain pure knowing subject, clear vision of the world. . . . Therefore the expression of genius in a face consists in this, that in it a decided predominance of knowledge over will is visible. In ordinary countenances there is a predominant expression of will, and we see that knowledge only comes into activity under the impulse of the will, and is directed merely by motives of personal interest and advantage.[113]

Freed from will, the intellect can see the object as it is; "genius holds up to us the magic glass in which all that is essential and significant appears to us collected and placed in the clearest light, and what is accidental and foreign is left out."[114] Thought pierces through passion as sunlight pours through a cloud, and reveals the heart of things; it goes behind the individual and particular to the "Platonic Idea" or universal essence of which it is a form—just as the painter sees, in the person whom he paints, not merely the individual character and feature, but some universal quality and permanent reality for whose unveiling the individual is only a symbol and a means. The secret of genius, then, lies in the clear and impartial perception of the objective, the essential, and the universal.

It is this removal of the personal equation which leaves the genius so maladapted in the world of will-ful, practical, personal activity. By seeing so far he does not see what is near; he is imprudent and "queer"; and while his vision is hitched to a star he falls into a well. Hence, partly, the

[110]III, 139.   [111]III, 159.   [113]*Ibid.*
[112]I, 240, 243.   [114]I, 321.

unsociability of the genius; he is thinking of the fundamental, the universal, the eternal; others are thinking of the temporary, the specific, the immediate; his mind and theirs have no common ground, and never meet. "As a rule, a man is sociable just in the degree in which he is intellectually poor and generally vulgar."[115] The man of genius has his compensations, and does not need company so much as people who live in perpetual dependence on what is outside them. "The pleasure which he receives from all beauty, the consolation which art affords, the enthusiasm of the artist, . . . enable him to forget the cares of life," and "repay him for the suffering that increases in proportion to the clearness of consciousness, and for his desert loneliness among a different race of men."[116]

The result, however, is that the genius is forced into isolation, and sometimes into madness; the extreme sensitiveness which brings him pain along with imagination and intuition, combines with solitude and maladaptation to break the bonds that hold the mind to reality. Aristotle was right again: "Men distinguished in philosophy, politics, poetry or art appear to be all of a melancholy temperament."[117] The direct connection of madness and genius "is established by the biographies of great men, such as Rousseau, Byron, Alfieri, etc."[118] "By a diligent search in lunatic asylums, I have found individual cases of patients who were unquestionably endowed with great talents, and whose genius distinctly appeared through their madness."[119]

Yet in these semi-madmen, these geniuses, lies the true aristocracy of mankind. "With regard to the intellect, nature is highly aristocratic. The distinctions which it has established are greater than those which are made in any country by birth, rank, wealth, or caste."[120] Nature gives genius only to a few because such a temperament would be a hindrance in the normal pursuits of life, which require concentration on the specific and immediate. "Nature really intended even learned men to be tillers of the soil; indeed, professors of philosophy should be estimated according to this standard; and then their achievements will be found to come up to all fair expectations."[121]

3. ART

This deliverance of knowledge from servitude to the will, this forgetting of the individual self and its material interest, this elevation of the mind

[115]"Wisdom of Life," p. 24. *An apologia pro vita sua.*
[116]I, 345. [117]In "Wisdom of Life," p. 19.
[118]The source of Lombroso—who adds Schopenhauer to the list.
[119]I, 247. [120]II, 342.
[121]III, 20. The professor of philosophy might avenge himself by pointing out that by nature we seem to be hunters rather than tillers; that agriculture is a human invention, not a natural instinct.

to the will-less contemplation of truth, is the function of art. The object of science is the universal that contains many particulars; the object of art is the particular that contains a universal. "Even the portrait ought to be, as Winckelmann says, the ideal of the individual."[122] In painting animals the most characteristic is accounted the most beautiful, because it best reveals the species. A work of art is successful, then, in proportion as it suggests the Platonic Idea, or universal, of the group to which the represented object belongs. The portrait of a man must aim, therefore, not at photographic fidelity, but at exposing, as far as possible, through one figure, some essential or universal quality of man."[123] Art is greater than science because the latter proceeds by laborious accumulation and cautious reasoning, while the former reaches its goal at once by intuition and presentation; science can get along with talent, but art requires genius.

Our pleasure in nature, as in poetry or painting, is derived from con-templation of the object without admixture of personal will. To the artist the Rhine is a varied series of bewitching views, stirring the senses and the imagination with suggestions of beauty; but the traveler who is bent on his personal affairs "will see the Rhine and its banks only as a line, and the bridges only as lines cutting the first line."[124] The artist so frees himself from personal concerns that "to artistic perception it is all one whether we see the sunset from a prison or from a palace."[125] "It is this blessedness of will-less perception which casts an enchanting glamour over the past and the distant, and presents them to us in so fair a light."[126] Even hostile objects, when we contemplate them without excitation of the will, and without immediate danger, become sublime. Similarly, tragedy may take an esthetic value, by delivering us from the strife of the in-dividual will, and enabling us to see our suffering in a larger view. Art alleviates the ills of life by showing us the eternal and universal behind the transitory and the individual. Spinoza was right: "in so far as the mind sees things in their eternal aspect it participates in eternity."[127]

This power of the arts to elevate us above the strife of wills is possessed above all by music.[128] "Music is by no means like the other arts, the copy of the Ideas" or essences of things, but it is "the copy of the will itself"; it shows us the eternally moving, striving, wandering will, always at last

[122]I, 290.

[123]So in literature, character-portrayal rises to greatness—other things equal—in proportion as the clearly-delineated individual represents also a universal type, like Faust and Marguerite or Quixote and Sancho Panza.

[124]III, 145.   [125]I, 265.   [126]I, 256.

[127]I, 230. Cf. Goethe: "There is no better deliverance from the world" of strife "than through art."—Elective Affinities, New York, 1902, p. 336.

[128]"Schopenhauer was the first to recognize and designate with philosophic clear-ness the position of music with reference to the other fine arts."—Wagner, Beethoven, Boston, 1872, p. 23.

returning to itself to begin its striving anew. "This is why the effect of music is more powerful and penetrating than the other arts, for they speak only of shadows, while it speaks of the things itself."[129] It differs too from the other arts because it affects our feelings directly,[130] and not through the medium of ideas; it speaks to something subtler than the intellect. What symmetry is to the plastic arts, rhythm is to music; hence music and architecture are antipodal; architecture, as Goethe said, is frozen music; and symmetry is rhythm standing still.

4. RELIGION

It dawned upon Schopenhauer's maturity that his theory of art—as the withdrawal of the will, and the contemplation of the eternal and universal —was also a theory of religion. In youth he had received very little religious training; and his temper did not incline him to respect the ecclesiastical organizations of his time. He despised theologians: "As *ultima ratio*," or the final argument, "of theologians we find among many nations the stake";[181] and he described religion as "the metaphysics of the masses."[182] But in later years he began to see a profound significance in certain religious practices and dogmas. "The controversy which is so perseveringly carried on in our own day between supernaturalists and rationalists rests on the failure to recognize the allegorical nature of all religion."[183] Christianity, for example, is a profound philosophy of pessimism; "the doctrine of original sin (assertion of the will) and of salvation (denial of the will) is the great truth which constitutes the essence of Christianity."[184] Fasting is a remarkable expedient for weakening those desires that lead never to happiness but either to disillusionment or to further desire. "The power by virtue of which Christianity was able to overcome first Judaism, and then the heathenism of Greece and Rome, lies solely in its pessimism, in the confession that our state is both exceedingly wretched and sinful, while Judaism and heathenism were both optimistic":[185] they thought of religion as a bribe to the heavenly powers for aid towards earthly success; Christianity thought of religion as a deterrent from the useless quest of earthly happiness. In the midst of worldly luxury and power it has held up the ideal of the saint, the Fool in Christ, who refuses to fight, and absolutely overcomes the individual will.[186]

Buddhism is profounder than Christianity, because it makes the destruc-

---

[129]I, 333.
[130]Hanslick (*The Beautiful in Music*, London, 1891, p. 23) objects to this, and argues that music affects only the imagination directly. Strictly, of course, it affects only the senses directly.
[181]II, 365.   [182]*Essays*, "Religion," p. 2.   [183]II, 369.
[184]I, 524.   [185]II, 372.   [186]I, 493.

tion of the will the entirety of religion, and preaches Nirvana as the goal of all personal development. The Hindus were deeper than the thinkers of Europe, because their interpretation of the world was internal and intuitive, not external and intellectual; the intellect divides everything, intuition unites everything; the Hindus saw that the "I" is a delusion; that the individual is merely phenomenal, and that the only reality is the Infinite One—"That art thou." "Whoever is able to say this to himself, with regard to every being with whom he comes in contact,"—whoever is clear-eyed and clear-souled enough to see that we are all members of one organism, all of us little currents in an ocean of will,—he "is certain of all virtue and blessedness, and is on the direct road to salvation."[137] Schopenhauer does not think that Christianity will ever displace Buddhism in the East: "it is just the same as if we fired a bullet against a cliff."[138] Rather, Indian philosophy streams into Europe, and will profoundly alter our knowledge and our thought. "The influence of the Sanskrit literature will penetrate not less deeply than did the revival of Greek letters in the fifteenth century."[139]

The ultimate wisdom, then, is Nirvana: to reduce one's self to a minimum of desire and will. The world-will is stronger than ours; let us yield at once. "The less the will is excited, the less we suffer."[140] The great masterpieces of painting have always represented countenances in which "we see the expression of the completest knowledge, which is not directed to particular things, but has . . . become the quieter of all will."[141] "That peace which is above all reason, that perfect calm of the spirit, that deep rest, that inviolable confidence and serenity, . . . as Raphael and Correggio have represented it, is an entire and certain gospel; only knowledge remains, the will has vanished."[142]

VII. THE WISDOM OF DEATH

And yet, something more is needed. By Nirvana the individual achieves the peace of will-lessness, and finds salvation; but after the individual? Life laughs at the death of the individual; it will survive him in his offspring, or in the offspring of others; even if his little stream of life runs dry there are a thousand other streams that grow broader and deeper with every generation. How can *Man* be saved? Is there a Nirvana for the race as well as for the individual?

Obviously, the only final and radical conquest of the will must lie in stopping up the source of life—the will to reproduce. "The satisfaction of the reproductive impulse is utterly and intrinsically reprehensible be-

[137] I, 483.   [138] I, 460.
[139] I, xiii. Perhaps we are witnessing a fulfillment of this prophecy in the growth of theosophy and similar faiths.
[140] "Counsels and Maxims," p. 19.   [141] I. 200.   [142] 521.

cause it is the strongest affirmation of the lust for life."[143] What crime have these children committed that they should be born?

If, now, we contemplate the turmoil of life, we behold all occupied with its want and misery, straining all their powers to satisfy its infinite needs and to ward off its multifarious sorrows, yet without daring to hope for anything else than simply the preservation of this tormented existence for a short span of time. In between, however, and in the midst of this tumult, we see the glance of two lovers meet longingly; yet why so secretly, fearfully, and stealthily? Because these lovers are the traitors who seek to perpetuate the whole want and drudgery which would otherwise speedily reach an end; . . . here lies the profound reason for the shame connected with the process of generation.[144]

It is woman that is the culprit here; for when knowledge has reached to will-lessness, her thoughtless charms allure man again into reproduction. Youth has not intelligence enough to see how brief these charms must be; and when the intelligence comes, it is too late.

With young girls Nature seems to have had in view what, in the language of the drama, is called a *striking effect;* as for a few years she dowers them with a wealth of beauty and is lavish in her gift of charm, at the expense of all the rest of their lives; so that during those years they may capture the fancy of some man to such a degree that he is hurried away into undertaking the honorable care of them . . . as long as they live—a step for which there would not seem to be any sufficient warrant if only reason directed man's thoughts. . . . Here, as elsewhere, Nature proceeds with her usual economy; for just as the female ant, after fecundation, loses her wings, which are then superfluous, nay, actually a danger to the business of breeding; so, after giving birth to one or two children, a woman generally loses her beauty; probably, indeed, for similar reasons.[145]

Young men ought to reflect that "if the object which inspires them today to write madrigals and sonnets had been born eighteen years earlier, it would scarcely have won a glance from them."[146] After all, men are much more beautiful in body than women.

It is only a man whose intellect is clouded by his sexual impulse that could give the name of the *fair sex* to that under-sized, narrow-shouldered, broad-hipped, and short-legged race; for the whole beauty of the sex is bound up with this impulse. Instead of calling them beautiful there would be more warrant for describing women as the unesthetic sex. Neither for music, nor for poetry, nor for the fine arts, have they really and truly any sense of susceptibility; it is a mere mockery if they make a pretense of it in order to assist their endeavor to please. . . . They are incapable of taking a purely objective interest in anything. . . . The most distinguished intellects among the whole sex have never managed to produce a single achieve-

[143] In Wallace, p. 29.   [144] III, 374; I, 423.
[145] Essay on Women, p. 73.   [146] III, 339.

ment in the fine arts that is really genuine and original; or given to the world any work of permanent value in any sphere.[147]

This veneration of women is a product of Christianity and of German sentimentality; and it is in turn a cause of that Romantic movement which exalts feeling, instinct and will above the intellect.[148] The Asiatics know better, and frankly recognize the inferiority of woman. "When the laws gave women equal rights with men, they ought also to have endowed them with masculine intellects."[149] Asia again shows a finer honesty than ours in its marriage institutions; it accepts as normal and legal the custom of polygamy, which, though so widely practiced among us, is covered with the fig-leaf of a phrase. "Where are there any real monogamists?"[150]—And how absurd it is to give property-rights to women! "All women are, with rare exceptions, inclined to extravagance," because they live only in the present, and their chief out-door sport is shopping. "Women think that it is men's business to earn money, and theirs to spend it";[151] this is their conception of the division of labor. "I am therefore of opinion that women should never be allowed altogether to manage their own concerns, but should always stand under actual male supervision, be it of father, of husband, of son, or of the state—as is the case in Hindostan; and that consequently they should never be given full power to dispose of any property they have not themselves acquired."[152] It was probably the luxury and extravagance of the women of Louis XIII's court that brought on the general corruption of government which culminated in the French Revolution.[153]

The less we have to do with women, then, the better. They are not even a "necessary evil";[154] life is safer and smoother without them. Let men recognize the snare that lies in women's beauty, and the absurd comedy of reproduction will end. The development of intelligence will weaken or frustrate the will to reproduce, and will thereby at last achieve the extinction of the race. Nothing could form a finer denouement to the insane tragedy of the restless will;—why should the curtain that has just fallen upon defeat and death always rise again upon a new life, a new struggle, and a new defeat? How long shall we be lured into this much-ado-about-nothing, this endless pain that leads only to a painful end? When shall we have the courage to fling defiance into the face of the Will,—to tell it that the loveliness of life is a lie, and that the greatest boon of all is death?

[147]Essay on Women, p. 79.   [148]III, 209–14.
[149]Essay on Women, p. 84.   [150]Ibid., p. 86.
[151]Ibid., p. 75.
[152]In Wallace, p. 80. An echo of Schopenhauer's dissatisfaction with his mother's extravagance.
[153]Essay on Women, p. 89.
[154]Carlyle's phrase.

VIII. CRITICISM

The natural response to such a philosophy is a medical diagnosis, of the age and of the man.

Let us realize again that we have here a phenomenon akin to that which, in the days after Alexander and after Caesar, brought first to Greece and then to Rome a flood of Oriental faiths and attitudes. It is characteristic of the East to see the external Will in nature as so much more powerful than the will in man, and to come readily to a doctrine of resignation and despair. As the decay of Greece brought the pallor of Stoicism and the hectic flush of Epicureanism upon the cheeks of Hellas, so the chaos of the Napoleonic wars brought into the soul of Europe that plaintive weariness which made Schopenhauer its philosophic voice. Europe had a terrible headache in 1815.[155]

The personal diagnosis can take its lead from Schopenhauer's admission that a man's happiness depends on what he is, rather than on external circumstance. Pessimism is an indictment of the pessimist. Given a diseased constitution and a neurotic mind, a life of empty leisure and gloomy *ennui*, and there emerges the proper physiology for Schopenhauer's philosophy. One must have leisure to be a pessimist; an active life almost always brings good spirits in body and in mind. Schopenhauer admires the serenity that comes of modest aims and a steady life,[156] but he could hardly speak of these from personal experience. *Difficilis in otio quies,* truly; he had money enough for continuous leisure, and he found continuous leisure to be more intolerable than continuous work. Perhaps the tendency of philosophers toward melancholy is due to the unnaturalness of sedentary occupations; too often an attack upon life is merely a symptom of the lost art of excretion.

Nirvana is the ideal of a listless man, a Childe Harold or a Réné, who has begun by desiring too much, by staking all on one passion, and then, having lost, spends the remainder of his life in a passionless and petulant boredom. If intellect arises as the servant of will, it is quite likely that the particular product of the intellect which we know as the philosophy of Schopenhauer was the cover and apology of a diseased and indolent will. And no doubt his early experiences with women and with men developed an abnormal suspiciousness and sensitivity, as it did in Stendhal and Flaubert and Nietzsche. He became cynical and solitary. He writes: "A friend in need is not a friend indeed; he is merely a borrower";[157] and, "Do not tell a friend anything that you would conceal from an enemy."[158]

---

[155]Compare the apathy and despondency of Europe today (1924), and the popularity of such books as Spengler's *Downfall of the Western World.*

[156]I, 422.

[157]"Counsels and Maxims," p. 86.   [158]*Ibid.,* p. 96.

He advises a quiet, monotonous, hermit life; he fears society, and has no sense of the values or joys of human association.[159] But happiness dies when it is not shared.

There is, of course, a large element of egotism in pessimism: the world is not good enough for us, and we turn up our philosophic noses to it. But this is to forget Spinoza's lesson, that our terms of moral censure and approbation are merely human judgments, mostly irrelevant when applied to the cosmos as a whole. Perhaps our supercilious disgust with existence is a cover for a secret disgust with ourselves: we have botched and bungled our lives, and we cast the blame upon the "environment," or the "world," which have no tongues to utter a defense. The mature man accepts the natural limitations of life; he does not expect Providence to be prejudiced in his favor; he does not ask for loaded dice with which to play the game of life. He knows, with Carlyle, that there is no sense in vilifying the sun because it will not light our cigars. And perhaps, if we are clever enough to help it, the sun will do even that; and this vast neutral cosmos may turn out to be a pleasant place enough if we bring a little sunshine of our own to help it out. In truth the world is neither with us nor against us; it is but raw material in our hands, and can be heaven or hell according to what we are.

Part of the cause of pessimism, in Schopenhauer and his contemporaries, lay in their romantic attitudes and expectations. Youth expects too much of the world; pessimism is the morning after optimism, just as 1815 had to pay for 1789. The romantic exaltation and liberation of feeling, instinct and will, and the romantic contempt for intellect, restraint, and order, brought their natural penalties; for "the world," as Horace Walpole said, "is a comedy for those who think, but a tragedy for those who feel." "Perhaps no movement has been so prolific of melancholy as emotional romanticism. . . . When the romanticist discovers that his ideal of happiness works out into actual unhappiness, he does not blame his ideal. He simply assumes that the world is unworthy of a being so exquisitely organized as himself."[160] How could a capricious universe ever satisfy a capricious soul?

The spectacle of Napoleon's rise to empire, Rousseau's denunciation—and Kant's critique—of the intellect, and his own passionate temperament and experiences, conspired to suggest to Schopenhauer the primacy and ultimacy of the will. Perhaps, too, Waterloo and St. Helena helped to develop a pessimism born, no doubt, of bitter personal contact with the stings and penalties of life. Here was the most dynamic individual will in all history, imperiously commanding continents; and yet its doom was as certain and ignominious as that of the insect to which the day of its birth brings ineviable death. It never occurred to Schopenhauer that it was better to have fought and lost than never to have fought at

---

[159]*Ibid.,* pp. 24, 37.   [160]Babbitt, *Rousseau and Romanticism,* p. 208.

all; he did not feel, like the more masculine and vigorous Hegel, the glory and desirability of strife; he longed for peace, and lived in the midst of war. Everywhere he saw strife; he could not see, behind the strife, the friendly aid of neighbors, the rollicking joy of children and young men, the dances of vivacious girls, the willing sacrifices of parents and lovers, the patient bounty of the soil, and the renaissance of spring.

And what if desire, fulfilled, leads only to another desire? Perhaps it is better that we should never be content. Happiness, says an old lesson, lies rather in achievement than in possession or satiation. The healthy man asks not so much for happiness as for an opportunity to exercise his capacities; and if he must pay the penalty of pain for this freedom and this power he makes the forfeit cheerfully; it is not too great a price. We need resistance to raise us, as it raises the airplane or the bird; we need obstacles against which to sharpen our strength and stimulate our growth. Life without tragedy would be unworthy of a man.[161]

Is it true that "he that increaseth knowledge increaseth sorrow," and that it is the most highly organized beings that suffer most? Yes; but it is also true that the growth of knowledge increases joy as well as sorrow, and that the subtlest delights, as well as the keenest pains, are reserved for the developed soul. Voltaire rightly preferred the Brahmin's "unhappy" wisdom to the blissful ignorance of the peasant woman; we wish to experience life keenly and deeply, even at the cost of pain; we wish to venture into its innermost secrets, even at the cost of disillusionment.[162] Virgil, who had tasted every pleasure, and knew the luxuries of imperial favor, at last "tired of everything except the joys of understanding." When the senses cease to satisfy, it is something to have won access, however arduously, to comradeship with those artists, poets and philosophers whom only the mature mind can comprehend. Wisdom is a bitter-sweet delight, deepened by the very discords that enter into its harmony.

Is pleasure negative? Only a sorely wounded soul, drawing itself in from contact with the world, could have uttered so fundamental a blasphemy against life. What is pleasure but the harmonious operation of our instincts?—and how can pleasure be negative except where the instinct at work makes for retreat rather than for approach? The pleasures

[161]Cf. Schopenhauer himself: "To have no regular work, no set sphere of activity, —what a miserable thing it is! . . . Effort, struggles with difficulties! that is as natural to a man as grubbing in the ground is to a mole. To have all his wants satisfied is something intolerable—the feeling of stagnation which comes from pleasures that last too long. To overcome difficulties is to experience the full delight of existence."—"Counsels and Maxims," p. 53. One would like to know more of what the maturer Schopenhauer thought of the brilliant philosophy of his youth.

[162]Anatole France (Voltaire's last avatar) has dedicated one of his masterpieces —The Human Tragedy—to the task of showing that though "the joy of understanding is a sad joy," yet "those who have once tasted it would not exchange it for all the frivolous gaieties and empty hopes of the vulgar herd." Cf. The Garden of Epicurus, New York, 1908, p. 120.

of escape and rest, of submission and security, of solitude and quiet are no
doubt negative, because the instincts that impel us to them are essentially
negative—forms of flight and fear; but shall we say the same of the
pleasures that come when positive instincts are in command—instincts of
acquisition and possession, of pugnacity and mastery, of action and play,
of association and love? Is the joy of laughter negative, or the romping of
the child, or the song of the mating bird, or the crow of Chanticleer, or
the creative ecstasy of art? Life itself is a positive force, and every normal
function of it holds some delight.

It remains true, no doubt, that death is terrible. Much of its terror dis-
appears if one has lived a normal life; one must have lived well in order
to die well. And would deathlessness delight us? Who envies the fate of
Ahasuerus, to whom immortal life was sent as the heaviest punishment
that could be inflicted upon man? And why is death terrible if not because
life is sweet? We need not say with Napoleon that all who fear death are
atheists at heart; but we may surely say that a man who lives to three-
score years and ten has survived his pessimism. No man, said Goethe, is a
pessimist after thirty. And hardly before twenty; pessimism is a luxury of
self-conscious and self-important youth; youth that comes out of the
warm bosom of the communistic family into the cold atmosphere of
individualistic competition and greed, and then yearns back to its
mother's breast; youth that hurls itself madly against the windmills and
evils of the world, and sadly sheds utopias and ideals with every year. But
before twenty is the joy of the body, and after thirty is the joy of the
mind; before twenty is the pleasure of protection and security; and after
thirty, the joy of parentage and home.

How should a man avoid pessimism who has lived almost all his life
in a boarding-house? And who abandoned his only child to illegitimate
anonymity?[163] At the bottom of Schopenhauer's unhappiness was his rejection of the normal life,—his rejection of women and marriage and
children. He finds in parentage the greatest of evils, where a healthy man
finds in it the greatest of life's satisfactions. He thinks that the stealthiness
of love is due to shame in continuing the race—could anything be more
pedantically absurd? He sees in love only the sacrifice of the individual to
the race, and ignores the delights with which the instinct repays the
sacrifice,—delights so great that they have inspired most of the poetry of
the world.[164] He knows woman only as shrew and as sinner, and he
imagines that there are no other types. He thinks that the man who undertakes to support a wife is a fool;[165] but apparently such men are not much

---

[163]Finot, *The Science of Happiness*, New York, 1914, p. 70.

[164]Cf., again, Schopenhauer himself: "It is just this not seeking of one's own
things (which is everywhere the stamp of greatness) that gives to passionate love
the touch of sublimity."—III, 368.

[165]Essay on Women. p. 75.

more unhappy than our passionate apostle of single infelicity; and (as Balzac said) it costs as much to support a vice as it does to support a family. He scorns the beauty of woman,—as if there were any forms of beauty that we could spare, and that we should not cherish as the color and fragrance of life. What hatred of women one mishap had generated in this unfortunate soul!

There are other difficulties, more technical and less vital, in this remarkable and stimulating philosophy. How can suicide ever occur in a world where the only real force is the will to live? How can the intellect, begotten and brought up as servant of the will, ever achieve independence and objectivity? Does genius lie in knowledge divorced from will, or does it contain, as its driving force, an immense power of will, even a large alloy of personal ambition and conceit?[166] Is madness connected with genius in general, or rather with only the "romantic" type of genius (Byron, Shelley, Poe, Heine, Swinburne, Strindberg, Dostoievski, etc.); and is not the "classic" and profounder type of genius exceptionally sound (Socrates, Plato, Spinoza, Bacon, Newton, Voltaire, Goethe, Darwin, Whitman, etc.)? What if the proper function of intellect and philosophy is not the denial of the will but the coördination of desires into a united and harmonious will? What if "will" itself, except as the unified product of such coördination, is a mythical abstraction, as shadowy as "force"?

Nevertheless there is about this philosophy a blunt honesty by the side of which most optimistic creeds appear as soporific hypocrisies. It is all very well to say, with Spinoza, that good and bad are subjective terms, human prejudices; and yet we are compelled to judge this world not from any "impartial" view, but from the standpoint of actual human sufferings and needs. It was well that Schopenhauer should force philosophy to face the raw reality of evil, and should point the nose of thought to the human tasks of alleviation. It has been harder, since his day, for philosophy to live in the unreal atmosphere of a logic-chopping metaphysics; thinkers begin to realize that thought without action is a disease.

After all, Schopenhauer opened the eyes of psychologists to the subtle depth and omnipresent force of instinct. Intellectualism—the conception of man as above all a thinking animal, consciously adapting means to rationally chosen ends—fell sick with Rousseau, took to its bed with Kant, and died with Schopenhauer. After two centuries of introspective analysis philosophy found, behind thought, desire; and behind the intellect, instinct;—just as, after a century of materialism, physics finds, behind matter, energy. We owe it to Schopenhauer that he revealed our secret hearts to us, showed us that our desires are the axioms of our philosophies, and cleared the way to an understanding of thought as no mere abstract cal-

[166]Cf. Schopenhauer: "The greatest intellectual capacities are only found in connection with a vehement and passionate will."—II, 413.

culation of impersonal events, but as a flexible instrument of action and desire.

Finally, and despite exaggerations, Schopenhauer taught us again the necessity of genius, and the value of art. He saw that the ultimate good is beauty, and that the ultimate joy lies in the creation or cherishing of the beautiful. He joined with Goethe and Carlyle in protest against the attempt of Hegel and Marx and Buckle to eliminate genius as a fundamental factor in human history; in an age when all the great seemed dead he preached once more the ennobling worship of heroes. And with all his faults he succeeded in adding another name to theirs.

CHAPTER VIII

Herbert Spencer

I. COMTE AND DARWIN

THE KANTIAN PHILOSOPHY which announced itself as "prolegomena to all future metaphysics," was, by malicious intent, a murderous thrust at traditional modes of speculation; and, contrary to intent, a damaging blow to all metaphysics whatsoever. For metaphysics had meant, throughout the history of thought, an attempt to discover the ultimate nature of reality; now men learned, on the most respectable authority, that reality could never be experienced; that it was a "noumenon," conceivable but not knowable; and that even the subtlest human intelligence could never pass beyond phenomena, could never pierce the veil of Maya. The metaphysical extravagances of Fichte, Hegel and Schelling, with their various readings of the ancient riddle, their Ego and Idea and Will, had canceled one another into zero; and by the eighteen-thirties the universe was generally conceded to have guarded its secret well. After a generation of Absolute intoxication, the mind of Europe reacted by taking a pledge against metaphysics of any kind.

Since the French had made a specialty of scepticism, it was natural that they should produce the founder (if there are such persons in philosophy, where every idea is hallowed with years) of the "positivist" movement. Auguste Comte—or, as his parents called him, Isidore Auguste Marie François Xavier Comte—was born at Montpellier in 1798. The idol of his youth was Benjamin Frankin, whom he called the modern Socrates. "You know that at five-and-twenty he formed the design of becoming perfectly wise, and that he fulfilled his design. I have dared to undertake the same thing, though I am not yet twenty." He made a fair start by becoming secretary to the great Utopian, Saint-Simon, who passed on to him the reforming enthusiasm of Turgot and Condorcet, and the idea that social, like physical phenomena, might be reduced to laws and science, and that all philosophy should be focused upon the moral and political improvement of mankind. But, like most of us who set out to reform the world, Comte found it difficult enough to manage his own home; in 1827, after two years of marital infelicity, he suffered a mental break-down, and attempted suicide in the Seine. To his rescuer, therefore, we owe something of the five volumes of *Positive Philosophy* which appeared between 1830 and 1842, and the four volumes of *Positive Polity* which appeared between 1851 and 1854.

This was an undertaking which, in scope and patience, was second in modern times only to Spencer's "Synthetic Philosophy." Here the sciences were classified according to the decreasing simplicity and generality of their subject-matter: mathematics, astronomy, physics, chemistry, biology, and sociology; each rested on the results of all the sciences before it; therefore sociology was the apex of the sciences, and the others had their reason for existence only in so far as they could provide illumination for the science of society. Science, in the sense of exact knowledge, had spread from one subject-matter to another in the order given; and it was natural that the complex phenomena of social life should be the last to yield to scientific method. In each field of thought the historian of ideas could observe a Law of Three Stages: at first the subject was conceived in the *theological* fashion, and all problems were explained by the will of some deity—as when the stars were gods, or the chariots of gods; later, the same subject reached the *metaphysical* stage, and was explained by metaphysical abstractions—as when the stars moved in circles because circles were the most perfect figure; finally the subject was reduced to *positive* science by precise observation, hypothesis, and experiment, and its phenomena were explained through the regularities of natural cause and effect. The "Will of God" yields to such airy entities as Plato's "Ideas" or Hegel's "Absolute Idea," and these in turn yield to the laws of science. Metaphysics is a stage of arrested development: the time had come, said Comte, to abandon these puerilities. Philosophy was not something different from science; it was the coördination of all the sciences with a view to the improvement of human life.

There was a certain dogmatic intellectualism about this positivism which perhaps reflected the disillusioned and isolated philosopher. When, in 1845, Mme. Clotilde de Vaux (whose husband was spending his life in jail) took charge of Comte's heart, his affection for her warmed and colored his thought, and led to a reaction in which he placed feeling above intelligence as a reforming force, and concluded that the world could be redeemed only by a new religion, whose function it should be to nourish and strengthen the feeble altruism of human nature by exalting Humanity as the object of a ceremonial worship. Comte spent his old age devising for this Religion of Humanity an intricate system of priesthood, sacraments, prayers, and discipline; and proposed a new calendar in which the names of pagan deities and medieval saints should be replaced by the heroes of human progress. As a wit put it, Comte offered the world all of Catholicism except Christianity.

The positivist movement fell in with the flow of English thought, which took its spirit from a life of industry and trade, and looked up to matters of fact with a certain reverence. The Baconian tradition had turned thought in the direction of things, mind in the direction of matter; the materialism of Hobbes, the sensationalism of Locke, the scepticism of Hume, the ultilitarianism of Bentham, were so many variations on the theme of a practical and busy life. Berkeley was an Irish discord in this domestic symphony. Hegel laughed at the English habit of honoring physical and chemical equipment with the name of "philosophical instruments"; but such a term came naturally to men who agreed with Comte and Spencer in defining philosophy as a generalization of the results of all the sciences. So it was that the positivist movement found more adherents in England than in the land of its birth; adherents perhaps not so fervent as the generous Littré, but endowed with that English tenacity which kept John Stuart Mill (1806–73) and Frederick Harrison (1831–1923) faithful all their lives to Comte's philosophy, while their English caution kept them aloof from his ceremonious religion.

Meanwhile the Industrial Revolution, born of a little science, was stimulating science in return. Newton and Herschel had brought the stars to England, Boyle and Davy had opened the treasures of chemistry, Faraday was making the discoveries that would electrify the world, Rumford and Joule were demonstrating the transformability and equivalence of force and the conservation of energy. The sciences were reaching a stage of complexity which would make a bewildered world welcome a synthesis. But above all these intellectual influences that stirred England in the youth of Herbert Spencer was the growth of biology, and the doctrine of evolution. Science had been exemplarily international in the development of this doctrine: Kant had spoken of the possibility of apes becoming men; Goethe had written of "the metamorphosis of plants; Erasmus Darwin and Lamarck had propounded the theory that species had evolved from simpler forms by the inheritance of the effects of use and disuse; and in 1830 St. Hilaire shocked Europe, and gladdened old Goethe, by almost triumphing against Cuvier in that famous debate on evolution which seemed like another *Ernani*, another revolt against classic ideas of changeless rules and orders in a changeless world.

In the eighteen-fifties evolution was in the air. Spencer expressed the idea, long before Darwin, in an essay on "The Development Hypothesis" (1852), and in his *Principles of Psychology* (1855). In 1858 Darwin and Wallace read their famous papers before the Linnaean Society; and in 1859 the old world, as the good bishops thought, crashed to pieces with the publication of the *Origin of Species*. Here was no mere vague notion of evolution, of higher species evolving somehow from lower ones; but a detailed and richly documented theory of the actual mode and process of evolution "by means of natural selection, or the preservation of favored races in the struggle for life." In one decade all the world was talking about evolution. What lifted Spencer to the crest of this wave of thought was the clarity of mind which suggested the application of the evolution idea to every field of study, and the range of mind which brought almost all knowledge to pay tribute to his theory. As mathematics had dominated philosophy in the seventeenth century, giving to the world Descartes, Hobbes, Spinoza, Leibnitz and Pascal; and as psychology had written philosophy in Berkeley and Hume and Condillac and Kant; so in the nineteenth century, in Schelling and Schopenhauer, in Spencer and Nietzsche and Bergson, biology was the background of philosophic thought. In each case the epochal ideas were the piece-meal production of separate men, more or less obscure; but the ideas are attached to the men who coördinated and clarified them, as the New World took the name of Amerigo Vespucci because he drew a map. Herbert Spencer was the Vespucci of the age of Darwin, and something of its Columbus too.

II. THE DEVELOPMENT OF SPENCER

He was born at Derby in 1820. In both lines his ancestors were Non-conformists or Dissenters. His father's mother had been a devoted follower of John Wesley; his father's brother, Thomas, though an Anglican clergyman, led a Wesleyan movement within the Church, never attended a concert or a play, and took an active part in movements for political reform. This drive to heresy became stronger in the father, and culminated in the almost obstinate individualism of Herbert Spencer himself. The father never used the supernatural to explain anything; he was described by one acquaintance (though Herbert considered this an exaggeration) as "without faith or religion whatever, so far as one could see."[1] He was inclined to science, and wrote an *Inventional Geometry*. In politics he was an individualist like his son and "would never take off his hat to anyone, no matter of what rank."[2] "If he did not understand some question my mother put, he would remain silent; not asking what the question was, and letting it go unanswered. He continued this course all through his life, notwithstanding its futility; there resulted no improvement."[3] One is reminded (except for the silence) of Herbert Spencer's resistance, in his later years, to the extension of State functions.

The father, as well as an uncle and the paternal grandfather, were teachers of private schools; and yet the son, who was to be the most famous English philosopher of his century, remained till forty an uneducated man. Herbert was lazy, and the father was indulgent. At last, when he was thirteen, Herbert was sent to Hinton to study under his uncle, who had a reputation for severity. But Herbert promptly ran away from the uncle, and trudged all the way back to the paternal home at Derby—48 miles the first day, 47 the next, and 20 the third, all on a little bread and beer. Nevertheless he returned to Hinton after a few weeks,

[1] Spencer, *Autobiography*, New York, 1904; vol. 1, p. 51.
[2] P. 53.   [3] P. 61.

and stayed for three years. It was the only systematic schooling that he ever received. He could not say, later, just what it was he learned there; no history, no natural science, no general literature. He says, with characteristic pride: "That neither in boyhood nor youth did I receive a single lesson in English, and that I have remained entirely without formal knowledge of syntax down to the present hour, are facts which should be known; since their implications are at variance with assumptions universally accepted."[4] At the age of forty he tried to read the *Iliad,* but "after reading some six books I felt what a task it would be to go on—felt that I would rather give a large sum than read to the end."[5] Collier, one of his secretaries, tells us that Spencer never finished any book of science.[6] Even in his favorite fields he received no systematic instruction. He burnt his fingers and achieved a few explosions in chemistry; he browsed entomologically among the bugs about school and home; and he learned something about strata and fossils in his later work as a civil engineer; for the rest he picked his science casually as he went along. Until he was thirty he had no thought at all of philosophy.[7] Then he read Lewes, and tried to pass on to Kant; but finding, at the outset, that Kant considered space and time to be forms of sense-perception rather than objective things, he decided that Kant was a dunce, and threw the book away.[8] His secretary tells us that Spencer composed his first book, *Social Statics,* "having read no other ethical treatise than an old and now forgotten book by Jonathan Dymond." He wrote his *Psychology* after reading only Hume, Mansel and Reid; his *Biology* after reading only Carpenter's *Comparative Physiology* (and not the *Origin of Species*); his *Sociology* without reading Comte or Tylor, his *Ethics* without reading Kant or Mill or any other moralist than Sedgwick.[9] What a contrast to the intensive and relentless education of John Stuart Mill!

Where, then, did he find those myriad facts with which he propped up his thousand arguments? He "picked them up," for the most part, by direct observation rather than by reading. "His curiosity was ever awake, and he was continually directing the attention of his companion to some notable phenomenon . . . until then seen by his eyes alone." At the Athenaeum Club he pumped Huxley and his other friends almost dry of their expert knowledge; and he ran through the periodicals at the Club as he had run through those that passed through his father's hands for the Philosophical Society at Derby, "lynx-eyed for every fact that was grist to his mill."[10] Having determined what he wanted to do, and having found the central idea, evolution, about which all his work would turn, his brain became a magnet for relevant material, and the unprecedented

[4]P. vii.
[6]Appendix to Royce's *Herbert Spencer.*
[8]Pp. 289, 291.
[10]*Ibid.*

[5]P. 300.
[7]*Autob.,* i, 438.
[9]Collier, in Royce, 210 f.

orderliness of his thought classified the material almost automatically as it came. No wonder the proletaire and the business man heard him gladly; here was just such a mind as their own—a stranger to book-learning, innocent of "culture" and yet endowed with the natural, matter-of-fact knowledge of the man who learns as he works and lives.

For he was working for his living: and his profession intensified the practical tendency of his thought. He was surveyor, supervisor and designer of railway lines and bridges, and in general an engineer. He dripped inventions at every turn; they all failed, but he looked back upon them, in his *Autobiography,* with the fondness of a father for a wayward son; he sprinkled his reminiscent pages with patent salt-cellars, jugs, candle-extinguishers, invalid-chairs, and the like. As most of us do in youth, he invented new diets too; for a time he was vegetarian; but he abandoned it when he saw a fellow-vegetarian develop anemia, and him-self losing strength; "I found that I had to rewrite what I had written during the time I was a vegetarian, because it was so wanting in vigor."[11] He was ready in those days to give everything a trial; he even thought of migrating to New Zealand, forgetting that a young country has no use for philosophers. It was characteristic of him that he made parallel lists of reasons for and against the move, giving each reason a numerical value. The sums being 110 points for remaining in England and 301 for going, he remained.

His character had the defects of its virtues. He paid for his resolute realism and practical sense by missing the spirit and zest of poetry and art. The only poetical touch in his twenty volumes was due to a printer who made Spencer speak of "the daily versification of scientific predic-tions." He had a fine persistence whose other side was an opinionated obstinacy; he could sweep the entire universe for proofs of his hypotheses, but he could not see with any insight another's point of view; he had the egotism that bears up the nonconformer, and he could not carry his great-ness without some conceit. He had the limitations of the pioneer: a dog-matic narrowness accompanying a courageous candor and an intense originality; sternly resisting all flattery, rejecting proffered governmental honors, and pursuing his painful work for forty years in chronic ill-health and modest seclusion; and yet marked, by some phrenologist who gained access to him—"Self-esteem very large."[12] The son and grandson of teachers, he wielded the ferule in his books, and struck a high didactic tone. "I am never puzzled," he tells us.[13] His solitary bachelor life left him lacking in the warmly human qualities, though he could be in-dignantly humane. He had an affair with that great Englishwoman, George Eliot, but she had too much intellect to please him.[14] He lacked humor, and had no subtlety or nuances in his style. When he lost at his favorite

[11]*Autob.,* i, 401.   [12]P. 228.
[13]P. 464.   [14]I, 457–62; II, 44.

game of billiards, he denounced his opponent for devoting so much time to such a game as to have become an expert in it. In his *Autobiography* he writes reviews of his own early books, to show how it should have been done.[15]

Apparently the magnitude of his task compelled him to look upon life with more seriousness than it deserves. "I was at the *Fête* of St. Cloud on Sunday," he writes from Paris; "and was much amused by the juvenility of the adults. The French never entirely cease to be boys; I saw gray-haired people riding on whirligigs such as we have at our own fairs."[16] He was so busy analyzing and describing life that he had no time to live it. After seeing Niagara Falls he jotted down in his diary: "Much what I had expected."[17] He describes the most ordinary incidents with the most magnificent pedantry—as when he tells us of the only time he ever swore.[18] He suffered no crises, felt no romance (if his memoirs record him well); he had some intimacies, but he writes of them almost mathematically; he plots the curves of his tepid friendships without any uplifting touch of passion. A friend said of himself that he could not write well when dictating to a young woman stenographer; Spencer said that it did not bother him at all. His secretary says, "The passionless thin lips told of a total lack of sensuality, and the light eyes betrayed a lack of emotional depth."[19] Hence the monotonous levelness of his style: he never soars, and needs no exclamation-points; in a romantic century he stands like a sculptured lesson in dignity and reserve.

He had an exceptionally logical mind; he marshalled his *à prioris* and his *à posterioris* with the precision of a chess player. He is the clearest expositor of complex subjects that modern history can show; he wrote of difficult problems in terms so lucid that for a generation all the world was interested in philosophy. "It has been remarked," he says, "that I have an unusual faculty of exposition—set forth my data and reasonings and conclusions with a clearness and coherence not common."[20] He loved spacious generalizations, and made his works interesting rather with his hypotheses than with his proofs. Huxley said that Spencer's idea of a tragedy was a theory killed by a fact;[21] and there were so many theories in Spencer's mind that he was bound to have a tragedy every day or two. Huxley, struck by the feeble and undecided gait of Buckle, said of him to Spencer: "Ah, I see the kind of man; he is top-heavy." "Buckle," Spencer adds, "had taken in a much larger quantity of matter than he could organize."[22] With Spencer it was the other way: he organized much more than he had taken in. He was all for coördination and synthesis; he depreciated Carlyle for lacking a similar turn. The fondness for order be-

---

[15]I, 415, 546.   [16]I, 533.   [17]II, 465.
[18]Tyndall once said of him what a much better fellow he would be if he had a good swear now and again.—Elliott, *Herbert Spencer*, p. 61.
[19]Royce, 188.   [20]*Autob.*, ii, 511.   [21]I, 467.   [22]II, 4.

came in him an enslaving passion; a brilliant generalization over-mastered him. But the world was calling for a mind like his; one who could transform the wilderness of facts with sunlit clarity into civilized meaning; and the service which Spencer performed for his generation entitled him to the failings that made him human. If he has been pictured here rather frankly, it is because we love a great man better when we know his faults, and suspiciously dislike him when he shines in unmitigated perfection.

"Up to this date," wrote Spencer at forty, "my life might fitly have been characterized as miscellaneous."[23] Seldom has a philosopher's career shown such desultory vacillation. "About this time" (age twenty-three) "my attention turned to the construction of watches."[24] But gradually he found his field, and tilled it with honest husbandry. As early as 1842 he wrote, for the *Non-conformist* (note the medium he chose), some letters on "The Proper Sphere of Government," which contained his later *laissez-faire* philosophy *in ovo*. Six years later he dropped engineering to edit *The Economist*. At the age of thirty, when he spoke disparagingly of Jonathan Dymond's *Essays on the Principles of Morality*, and his father challenged him to do as well with such a subject, he took the dare, and wrote his *Social Statics*. It had only a small sale, but it won him access to the magazines. In 1852 his essay on "The Theory of Population" (one of the many instances of Malthus' influence on the thought of the nineteenth century) suggested that the struggle for existence leads to a survival of the fittest, and coined those historic phrases. In the same year his essay on "The Development Hypothesis" met the trite objection —that the origin of new species by progressive modification of older ones had never been seen—by pointing out that the same argument told much more strongly against the theory of the "special creation" of new species by God; and it went on to show that the development of new species was no more marvelous or incredible than the development of a man from ovum and sperm, or of a plant from a seed. In 1855 his second book, *The Principles of Psychology*, undertook to trace the evolution of mind. Then, in 1857, came an essay on "Progress, Its Law and Cause," which took up Von Baer's idea of the growth of all living forms from homogeneous beginnings to heterogeneous developments, and lifted it into a general principle of history and progress. In short Spencer had grown with the spirit of his age, and was ready now to become the philosopher of universal evolution.

When, in 1858, he was revising his essays for collective publication, he was struck by the unity and sequence of the ideas he had expressed; and the notion came to him, like a burst of sunlight through opened doors, that the theory of evolution might be applied in every science as well as in biology; that it could explain not only species and genera but planets and strata, social and political history, moral and esthetic conceptions. He was fired with the thought of a series of works in which he would show the evolution of matter and mind from nebula to man, and from savage to Shakespeare. But he almost despaired when he thought of his nearly forty years. How could one man, so old, and an invalid, traverse all the sphere of human knowledge before his death? Only three years back he had had a complete break-down; for eighteen months he had been incapacitated, broken in mind and courage, wandering aimlessly and hopelessly from place to place. The consciousness of his latent powers made his weakness a bitter thing to him. He knew that he would never be quite healthy again, and that he could not bear mental work for more than an hour at a time. Never was a man so handicapped for the work he chose, and never did a man choose, so late in life, so great a work.

He was poor. He had not given much thought to getting a living. "I don't mean to get on," he said; "I don't think getting on is worth the bother."[25] He had resigned the editorship of *The Economist* on receiving $2,500 as bequest from an uncle; but his idleness had consumed this gift. It occurred to him now that he might seek advance subscriptions for his intended volumes, and so live from hand to mouth, and pay his way as he went. He prepared an outline, and submitted it to Huxley, Lewes, and other friends; they secured him an imposing list of initial subscribers whose names might adorn his prospectus: Kingsley, Lyell, Hooker, Tyndall, Buckle, Froude, Bain, Herschel and others. Published in 1860, this prospectus brought 440 subscriptions from Europe, and 200 from America; the total promising a modest $1,500 a year. Spencer was satisfied, and set to work with a will.

But after the publication of *First Principles*, in 1862, many subscribers withdrew their names because of the famous "Part One," which, attempting to reconcile science and religion, offended bishops and pundits alike. The way of the peacemaker is hard. *First Principles* and *The Origin of Species* became the center of a great Battle of the Books, in which Huxley served as generalissimo for the forces of Darwinism and agnosticism. For a time the evolutionists were severely ostracised by respectable people; they were denounced as immoral monsters, and it was thought good form to insult them publicly. Spencer's subscribers fell away with every instalment, and many defaulted on payments due for instalments received. Spencer went on as long as he could, paying out of his pocket the deficit which every issue involved. At last his funds and his courage were exhausted, and he issued to the remaining subscribers an announcement that he could no longer continue his work.

Then came one of the encouraging incidents of history. Spencer's greatest rival, who had held the field of English philosophy before the

[25] J. A. Thomson, *Herbert Spencer*, p. 71.

publication of *First Principles,* and now saw himself superseded by the philosopher of evolution, wrote to him as follows, on February 4, 1866:

> Dear Sir:
>
> On arriving here last week, I found the December *livraison* of your *Biology,* and I need hardly say how much I regretted the announcement in the paper annexed to it. . . . I propose that you should write the next of your treatises, and that I should guarantee the publisher against loss. . . . I beg that you will not consider this proposal in the light of a personal favor, though even if it were I should still hope to be permitted to offer it. But it is nothing of the kind—it is a simple proposal of coöperation for an important public purpose, for which you give your labor and have given your health. I am, Dear Sir,
>
> Very truly yours,
J. S. Mill.[26]

Spencer courteously refused; but Mill went out among his friends and persuaded several of them to subscribe for 250 copies each. Spencer again objected, and could not be moved. Then suddenly came a letter from Prof. Youmans, saying that Spencer's American admirers had bought, in his name, $7000 of public securities, of which the interest or dividends were to go to him. This time he yielded. The spirit of the gift renewed his inspiration; he resumed his task; and for forty years he kept his shoulder to the wheel, until all the Synthetic Philosophy had arrived safely into print. This triumph of mind and will over illness and a thousand obstacles is one of the sunny spots in the book of man.

III. FIRST PRINCIPLES

1. THE UNKNOWABLE

"We too often forget," says Spencer at the outset, "that not only is there 'a soul of goodness in things evil,' but generally also a soul of truth in things erroneous." He proposes, therefore, to examine religious ideas, with a view to finding that core of truth which under the changing form of many faiths, has given to religion its persistent power over the human soul.

What he finds at once is that every theory of the origin of the universe drives us into inconceivabilities. The atheist tries to think of a self-existent world, uncaused and without beginning; but we cannot conceive of anything beginningless or uncaused. The theist merely puts back the difficulty by a step; and to the theologian who says, "God made the world," the child's unanswerable query comes, "Who made God?" All ultimate religious ideas are logically inconceivable.

---

[26] *Autob.,* ii, 156.

All ultimate scientific ideas are equally beyond rational conception. What is matter? We reduce it to atoms, and then find ourselves forced to divide the atom as we had divided the molecule; we are driven into the dilemma that matter is infinitely divisible,—which is inconceivable; or that there is a limit to its divisibility,—which also is inconceivable. So with the divisibility of space and time; both of these are ultimately irrational ideas. Motion is wrapped in a triple obscurity, since it involves matter changing, in time, its position in space. When we analyze matter resolutely we find nothing at last but force—a force impressed upon our organs of sense, or a force resisting our organs of action; and who shall tell us what force is? Turn from physics to psychology, and we come upon mind and consciousness: and here are greater puzzles than before. "Ultimate scientific ideas," then, "are all representations of realities that cannot be comprehended. . . . In all directions the scientist's investigations bring him face to face with an insoluble enigma; and he ever more clearly perceives it to be an insoluble enigma. He learns at once the greatness and the littleness of the human intellect—its power in dealing with all that comes within the range of experience, its impotence in dealing with all that transcends experience. He, more than any other, truly *knows* that in its ultimate nature nothing can be known."[27] The only honest philosophy, to use Huxley's word, is agnosticism.

The common cause of these obscurities is the relativity of all knowledge. "Thinking being relating, no thought can express more than relatons. . . . Intellect being framed simply by and for converse with phenomena, involves us in nonsense when we try to use it for anything beyond phenomena."[28] And yet the relative and phenomenal imply by their names and natures something beyond them, something ultimate and absolute. "On watching our thoughts we see how impossible it is to get rid of the consciousness of an Actuality lying behind Appearances, and how from this impossibility results our indestructible belief in that Actuality."[29] But what that Actuality is we cannot know.

From this point of view the reconciliation of science and religions is no longer very difficult. "Truth generally lies in the coördination of antagonistic opinions."[30] Let science admit that its "laws" apply only to phenomena and the relative; let religion admit that its theology is a rationalizing myth for a belief that defies conception. Let religion cease to picture the Absolute as a magnified man; much worse, as a cruel and blood-thirsty and treacherous monster, afflicted with "a love of adulation such as would be despised in a human being."[31] Let science cease to deny deity, or to take materialism for granted. Mind and matter are, equally,

[27]*First Principles,* New York, 1910; p. 56.
[28]Pp. 107–108. This unconsciously follows Kant, and succinctly anticipates Bergson.
[29]P. 83.   [30]*Autob.,* ii. 16.   [31]*F. P.,* 103.

relative phenomena, the double effect of an ultimate cause whose nature must remain unknown. The recognition of this Inscrutable Power is the core of truth in every religion, and the beginning of all philosophy.

2. EVOLUTION

Having indicated the unknowable, philosophy surrenders it, and turns its face to what can be known. Metaphysics is a mirage: as Michelet put it, it is "the art of befuddling one's self methodically." The proper field and function of philosophy lies in the summation and unification of the results of science. "Knowledge of the lowest kind is un-unified knowledge; science is partially-unified knowledge; philosophy is completely-unified knowledge."[32] Such complete unification requires a broad and universal principle that will include all experience, and will describe the essential features of all knowledge. Is there a principle of this kind?

We may perhaps approach such a principle by trying to unify the highest generalizations of physics. These are the indestructibility of matter, the conservation of energy, the continuity of motion, the persistence of relations among forces (i. e., the inviolability of natural law), the transformability and equivalence of forces (even of mental and physical forces), and the rhythm of motion. This last generalization, not usually recognized, needs only to be pointed out. All nature is rhythmical, from the pulsations of heat to the vibrations of violin strings; from the undulations of light, heat and sound to the tides of the sea; from the periodicities of sex to the periodicities of planets and comets and stars; from the alternation of night and day to the succession of the seasons, and perhaps to the rhythms of climatic change; from the oscillations of molecules to the rise and fall of nations and the birth and death of stars.

All these "laws of the knowable" are reducible (by an analysis which must not here be followed in detail) to the final law of the persistence of force. But there is something static and inert about this principle; it does not so much as hint at the secret of life. What is the dynamic principle of reality? What is the formula of the growth and decay of all things? It must be a formula of evolution and dissolution, for "an entire history of anything must include its appearance out of the imperceptible and its disappearance into the imperceptible."[33]

So Spencer offers us his famous formula of evolution, which made the intellect of Europe gasp for breath, and required ten volumes and forty years for its explanation. "Evolution is an integration of matter and a concomitant dissipation of motion; during which the matter passes from an indefinite, incoherent homogeneity to a definite, coherent heterogeneity; and during which the retained motion undergoes a parallel transformation."[34] What does this mean?

[32] P. 119.   [33] P. 253.   [34] P. 367.

The growth of planets out of nebulae; the formation of oceans and mountains on the earth; the metabolism of elements by plants, and of animal tissues by men; the development of the heart in the embryo, and the fusion of bones after birth; the unification of sensations and memories into knowledge and thought, and of knowledge into science and philosophy; the development of families into clans and gentes and cities and states and alliances and the "federation of the world": here is the integration of matter,—the aggregation of separate items into masses and groups and wholes. Such integration of course involves a lessening of motion in the parts, as the growing power of the state lessens the freedom of the individual; but at the same time it gives to the parts an interdependence, a protective tissue of relationships, which constitute "coherence" and promote corporate survival. The process brings, too, a greater definiteness of forms and functions: the nebula is shapeless, nebulous; and yet out of it come the elliptical regularity of the planets, the sharp lines of mountain-chains, the specific form and character of organisms and organs, the division of labor and specialization of function in physiological and political structures, etc. And the parts of this integrating whole become not merely definite but diverse, heterogeneous in nature and operation. The primeval nebula is homogeneous—i. e., it consists of parts that are alike; but soon it is differentiated into gases and liquids and solids; the earth becomes here green with grass, there white with mountain-tops, or blue with the multitudinous sea; evolving life begets, out of a relatively homogeneous protoplasm, the varied organs of nutrition, reproduction, locomotion, and perception; a simple language fills whole continents with its multiplying dialects; a single science breeds a hundred, and the folk-lore of a nation flowers into a thousand forms of literary art; individuality grows, character stands out uniquely, and every race and people develops its peculiar genius. Integration and heterogeneity, aggregation of parts into ever larger wholes and differentiation of parts into ever more varied forms: these are the foci of the orbit of evolution. Whatever passes from diffusion to integration and unity, and from a homogeneous simplicity to a differentiated complexity (cf. America, 1600–1900), is in the flow of evolution; whatever is returning from integration to diffusion, and from complexity to simplicity (cf. Europe 200–600 A. D.), is caught in the ebb of dissolution.

Not content with this synthetic formula, Spencer endeavors to show how it follows by inevitable necessity from the natural operation of mechanical forces. There is, first, a certain "Instability of the Homogeneous": i. e., similar parts cannot long remain similar because they are unevenly subjected to external forces; outer parts, e. g., are sooner attacked, like coast-line towns in war; and the variety of occupations moulds similar men into the varied embodiments of a hundred professions and trades. There is, again, a "Multiplication of Effects": one cause may produce a vast variety of results, and help to differentiate the world; a word amiss, like Marie Antoinette's, or an altered telegram at Ems, or a wind at Salamis, may play an endless rôle in history. And there is the law of "Segregation": the parts of a relatively homogeneous whole, being driven separate into different areas, are shaped by diverse environments into dissimilar products,—as the English become Americans, or Canadians, or Australians, according to the genius of the place. In these many ways the forces of nature build the variety of this evolving world.

But finally, and inescapably, comes "Equilibration." Every motion, being motion under resistance, must sooner or later come to an end; every rhythmic oscillation (unless externally reinforced) suffers some loss of rate and amplitude. The planets ride through a lesser orbit, or will ride, than once they rode; the sun will shine less warmly and brightly as the centuries pass away; the friction of the tides will retard the rotation of the earth. This globe, that throbs and murmurs with a million motions, and luxuriates into a million forms of riotously breeding life, will some day move more leisurely in its orbit and its parts; the blood will run cooler and more slowly in our desiccated veins; we shall not hurry any more; like dying races, we shall think of heaven in terms of rest and not of life; we shall dream of Nirvana. Gradually, and then rapidly, equilibration will become dissolution, the unhappy epilogue of evolution. Societies will disintegrate, masses will migrate, cities will fade into the dark hinterland of peasant life; no government will be strong enough to hold the loosened parts together; social order will cease to be even remembered. And in the individual too, integration will give way to disruption; and that coördination which is life will pass into that diffuse disorder which is death. The earth will be a chaotic theatre of decay, a gloomy drama of energy in irreversible degradation; and it will itself be resolved into the dust and nebula from which it came. The cycle of evolution and dissolution will be complete. The cycle will begin again, and endless times again; but always this will be the denouement. *Memento mori* is written upon the face of life; and every birth is a prelude to decay and death.

First Principles is a magnificent drama, telling with almost classic calm the story of the rise and fall, the evolution and dissolution, of planets and life and man; but it is a tragic drama, for which the fittest epilogue is Hamlet's word—"The rest is silence." Is there any wonder that men and women nurtured on faith and hope rebelled against this summary of existence? We know that we must die; but as it is a matter that will take care of itself, we prefer to think of life. There was in Spencer an almost Schopenhauerian sense of the futility of human effort. At the end of his triumphant career he expressed his feeling that life was not worth living.

He had the philosopher's disease of seeing so far ahead that all the little pleasant shapes and colors of existence passed under his nose unseen.

He knew that people would not relish a philosophy whose last word was not God and heaven, but equilibration and dissolution; and in concluding this First Part he defended with unusual eloquence and fervor his right to speak the dark truths that he saw.

Whoever hesitates to utter that which he thinks the highest truth, lest it should be too much in advance of the time, may reassure himself by looking at his acts from an impersonal point of view. Let him remember that opinion is the agency through which character adapts external arrangements to itself, and that his opinion rightly forms part of this agency—is a unit of force constituting, with other such units, the general power which works out social changes; and he will perceive that he may properly give utterance to his innermost conviction; leaving it to produce what effect it may. It is not for nothing that he has in him these sympathies with some principles and repugnance to others. He, with all his capacities, and aspirations, and beliefs, is not an accident but a product of the time. While he is a descendant of the past he is a parent of the future; and his thoughts are as children born to him, which he may not carelessly let die. Like every other man he may properly consider himself as one of the myriad agencies through whom works the Unknown Cause; and when the Unknown Cause produces in him a certain belief, he is thereby authorized to profess and act out that belief. . . . Not as adventitious therefore will the wise man regard the faith that is in him. The highest truth he sees he will fearlessly utter; knowing that, let what may come of it, he is thus playing his right part in the world—knowing that if he can effect the change he aims at—well; if not —well also; though not so well.

IV. BIOLOGY: THE EVOLUTION OF LIFE

The second and third volumes of the Synthetic Philosophy appeared in 1872 under the title of *Principles of Biology.* They revealed the natural limitations of a philosopher invading a specialist's field; but they atoned for errors or detail by illuminating generalizations that gave a new unity and intelligibility to vast areas of biological fact.

Spencer begins with a famous definition: "Life is the continuous adjustment of internal relations to external relations."[85] The completeness of life depends on the completeness of this correspondence; and life is perfect when the correspondence is perfect. The correspondence is not a merely passive adaptation; what distinguishes life is the adjustment of internal relations in anticipation of a change in external relations, as when an animal crouches to avoid a blow, or a man makes a fire to warm his food. The defect of the definition lies not merely in its tendency to neglect the remoulding activity of the organism upon the environment,

Principles of Biology; New York. 1910; i, 99.

but in its failure to explain what is that subtle power whereby an organism is enabled to make these prophetic adjustments that characterize
vitality. In a chapter added to later editions, Spencer was forced to discuss "The Dynamic Element in Life," and to admit that his definition
had not really revealed the nature of life. "We are obliged to confess that
Life in its essence cannot be conceived in physico-chemical terms."[36] He
did not realize how damaging such an admission was to the unity and
completeness of his system.

As Spencer sees in the life of the individual an adjustment of internal
to external relations, so he sees in the life of the species a remarkable
adjustment of reproductive fertility to the conditions of its habitat. Reproduction arises originally as a readaptation of the nutritive surface to
the nourished mass; the growth of an amoeba, for example, involves an
increase of mass much more rapid than the increase in the surface through
which the mass must get its nourishment. Division, budding, spore-forma-
tion, and sexual reproduction have this in common, that the ratio of mass
to surface is reduced, and the nutritive balance is restored. Hence the
growth of the individual organism beyond a certain point is dangerous;
and normally growth gives way, after a time, to reproduction.

On the average, growth varies inversely with the rate of energy-ex-
penditure; and the rate of reproduction varies inversely with the degree
of growth. "It is well known to breeders that if a filly is allowed to bear a
foal, she is thereby prevented from reaching her proper size. . . . As a
converse fact, castrated animals, as capons and notably cats, often become larger than their unmutilated associates."[37] The rate of reproduction tends to fall as the development and capability of the individual
progress. "When, from lowness of organization, the ability to contend
with external dangers is small, there must be great fertility to compensate
for the consequent mortality; otherwise the race must die out. When,
on the contrary, high endowments give much capacity for self-preservation, a correspondingly low degree of fertility is requisite," lest the rate
of multiplication should outrun the supply of food.[38] In general, then,
there is an opposition of individuation and genesis, or individual development and fertility. The rule holds for groups and species more regularly
than for individuals: the more highly developed the species or the group,
the lower will its birth-rate be. But it holds for individuals too, on the
average. For example, intellectual development seems hostile to fertility.
"Where exceptional fertility exists, there is sluggishness of mind, and
where there has been, during education, excessive expenditure in mental
action, there frequently follows a complete or partial infertility. Hence
the particular kind of further evolution which Man is hereafter to undergo is one which, more than any other, may be expected to cause a
decline in his power of reproduction."[39] Philosophers are notorious for

[36] I, 120.   [37] II, 459.   [38] II, 421.   [39] II, 530.

shirking parentage. In woman, on the other hand, the arrival of motherhood normally brings a diminution of intellectual activity;[40] and perhaps her shorter adolescence is due to her earlier sacrifice to reproduction.

Despite this approximate adaptation of birth-rate to the needs of group survival, the adaptation is never complete, and Malthus was right in his general principle that population tends to outrun the means of subsistence. "From the beginning this pressure of population has been the proximate cause of progress. It produced the original diffusion of the race. It compelled men to abandon predatory habits and take to agriculture. It led to the clearing of the earth's surface. It forced men into the social state, . . . and developed the social sentiments. It has stimulated to progressive improvements in production, and to increased skill and intelligence."[41] It is the chief cause of that struggle for existence through which the fittest are enabled to survive, and through which the level of the race is raised.

Whether the survival of the fittest is due chiefly to spontaneous favorable variations, or to the partial inheritance of characters or capacities repeatedly acquired by successive generations, is a question on which Spencer took no dogmatic stand; he accepted Darwin's theory gladly, but felt that there were facts which it could not explain, and which compelled a modified acceptance of Lamarckian views. He defended Lamarck with fine vigor in his controversy with Weismann, and pointed out certain defects in the Darwinian theory. In those days Spencer stood almost alone on the side of Lamarck; it is of some interest to note that today the neo-Lamarckians include descendants of Darwin, while the greatest contemporary English biologist gives it as the view of present-day students of genetics that Darwin's *particular* theory (not, of course the general theory) of evolution must be abandoned.[42]

V. PSYCHOLOGY: THE EVOLUTION OF MIND

The two volumes on *The Principles of Psychology* (1873) are the weakest links in Spencer's chain. There had been an earlier volume on the subject (1855), a youthfully vigorous defense of materialism and determinism; but age and thought revised this into a milder form, and padded it out with hundreds of pages of painstaking but unilluminating analysis. Here, even more than elsewhere, Spencer is rich in theories and poor in proofs. He has a theory of the origin of nerves out of intercellular connective tissue; and a theory of the genesis of instinct by the compounding of reflexes and the transmission of acquired character; and a theory of the origin of mental categories out of the experience of the race; and

[40] *Autob.,* i, 62.   [41] *Biology,* ii, 536.
[42] Cf., address of Sir Wm. Bateson before the American Association for the Advancement of Science (Toronto, Dec. 28, 1921), in *Science,* Jan. 20, 1922.

a theory of "transfigured realism";[43] and a hundred other theories that have all the obfuscating power of metaphysics rather than the clarifying virtue of a matter-of-fact psychology. In these volumes we leave realistic England and go "back to Kant."

What strikes us at once is that for the first time in the history of psychology, we get here a resolutely evolutionist point of view, an attempt at genetic explanations, an effort to trace the bewildering complexities of thought down to the simplest of nervous operations, and finally to the motions of matter. It is true that this effort fails; but who has ever succeeded in such an attempt? Spencer sets out with a magnificent program for the unveiling of the processes whereby consciousness has been evolved; in the end he is compelled to posit consciousness everywhere,[44] in order to evolve it. He insists that there has been one continuous evolution from nebula to mind, and at last confesses that matter is known only through mind. Perhaps the most significant paragraphs in these volumes are those in which the materialist philosophy is abandoned:

> Can the oscillation of a molecule be represented in consciousness side by side with a nervous shock, and the two be recognized as one? No effort enables us to assimilate them. That a unit of feeling has nothing in common with a unit of motion, becomes more than ever manifest when we bring the two into juxtaposition. And the immediate verdict of consciousness thus given, might be analytically justified; . . . for it might be shown that the conception of an oscillating molecule is built out of many units of feeling." (I. e., our knowledge of matter is built up out of units of mind—sensations and memories and ideas). ". . . Were we compelled to choose between the alternatives of translating mental phenomena into physical phenomena, or of translating physical phenomena into mental phenomena, the latter alternative would seem the more acceptable of the two.[45]

Nevertheless there is of course an evolution of mind; a development of modes of response from simple to compound to complex, from reflex to tropism to instinct, through memory and imagination to intellect and reason. To the reader who can pass alive through these 1400 pages of physiological and psychological analysis there will come an overwhelming sense of the continuity of life and the continuity of mind; he will see, as on a retarded cinematograph, the formation of nerves, the development of adaptive reflexes and instincts, and the production of consciousness and thought through the clash of conflicting impulses. "Intelligence has neither distinct grades nor is it constituted by faculties that are truly independent, but its highest manifestations are the effects of a complica-

---

[43] Spencer means by this that although the objects of experience may very well be transfigured by perception, and be quite other than they seem, they have an existence which does not all depend upon perceiving them.—II, 494.
[44] *Autob.*, ii, 549.
[45] *Principles of Psychology*, New York, 1910; i, 158-9.

tion that has arisen by insensible steps out of the simplest elements."[46] There is no hiatus between instinct and reason; each is an adjustment of inner relations to outer relations, and the only difference is one of degree, in so far as the relations responded to by instinct are comparatively stereotyped and simple, while those met by reason are comparatively novel and complex. A rational action is simply an instinctive response which has survived in a struggle with other instinctive responses aroused by a situation; "deliberation" is merely the internecine strife of rival impulses.[47] At bottom, reason and instinct, mind and life, are one.

Will is an abstract term which we give to the sum of our active impulses, and a volition is the natural flow of an unimpeded idea into action.[48] An idea is the first stage of an action, an action is the last stage of an idea. Similarly, an emotion is the first stage of an instinctive action, and the expression of the emotion is a useful prelude to the completed response; the baring of the teeth in anger gives a substantial hint of that tearing of the enemy to pieces which used to be the natural termination of such a beginning.[49] "Forms of thought" like the perception of space and time, or the notions of quantity and cause, which Kant supposed innate, are merely instinctive ways of thinking; and as instincts are habits acquired by the race but native to the individual, so these categories are mental habits slowly acquired in the course of evolution, and now part of our intellectual heritage.[50] All these age-long puzzles of psychology can be explained by "the inheritance of continually-accumulating modifications."[51]—It is of course just this all-pervading assumption that makes so much of these laborious volumes questionable, and perhaps vain.

VI. SOCIOLOGY: THE EVOLUTION OF SOCIETY

With sociology the verdict is quite different. These stout volumes, whose publication ranged over twenty years, are Spencer's masterpiece: they cover his favorite field, and show him at his best in suggestive generalization and political philosophy. From his first book, *Social Statics,* to the last fascicle of *The Principles of Sociology,* over a stretch of almost half a century, his interest is predominantly in the problems of economics and government; he begins and ends, like Plato, with discourses on moral and political justice. No man, not even Comte (founder of the science and maker of the word), has done so much for sociology.

In a popular introductory volume, *The Study of Sociology* (1873), Spencer argues eloquently for the recognition and development of the new science. If determinism is correct in psychology, there must be regularities of cause and effect in social phenomena; and a thorough student of man and society will not be content with a merely chronological his-

[46]I, 388.   [47]I, 453–5.   [48]I, 496–7.
[49]I, 482 f; ii, 540 f.   [50]I, 466.   [51]I, 491.

tory, like Livy's, nor with a biographical history like Carlyle's; he will look in human history for those general lines of development, those causal sequences, those illuminating correlations, which transform the wilderness of facts into the chart of science. What biography is to anthropology, history is to sociology.[52] Of course there are a thousand obstacles that the study of society must yet overcome before it can deserve the name of science.[53] The young study is harassed by a multitude of prejudices— personal, educational, theological, economic, political, national, religious; and by the ready omniscience of the uninformed. "There is a story of a Frenchman who, having been three weeks here, proposed to write a book on England; who, after three months, found that he was not quite ready; and who, after three years, concluded that he knew nothing about it."[54] Such a man was ripe to *begin* the study of sociology. Men prepare themselves with life-long study before becoming authorities in physics or chemistry or biology; but in the field of social and political affairs every grocer's boy is an expert, knows the solution, and demands to be heard.

Spencer's own preparation, in this case, was a model of intellectual conscience. He employed three secretaries to gather data for him, and to classify the data in parallel columns giving the domestic, ecclesiastical, professional, political, and industrial institutions of every significant people. At his own expense he published these collections in eight large volumes, so that other students might verify or modify his conclusions; and the publication being unfinished at his death, he left part of his little savings to complete the undertaking. After seven years of such preparation, the first volume of the *Sociology* appeared in 1876; not until 1896 was the last one ready. When everything else of Spencer's has become a task for the antiquarian, these three volumes will still be rich in reward for every student of society.

Nevertheless, the initial conception of the work is typical of Spencer's habit of rushing into generalizations. Society, he believes, is an organism, having organs of nutrition, circulation, coördination and reproduction,[55] very much as in the case of individuals. It is true that in the individual, consciousness is localized, while in society each of the parts retains its own consciousness and its own will; but the centralization of government and authority tends to reduce the scope of this distinction. "A social organism is like an individual organism in these essential traits: that it grows; that while growing it becomes more complex; that while becoming more complex, its parts acquire increasing mutual dependence; that

---

[52] *The Study of Sociology*, New York, 1910; p. 52.

[53] *The Principles of Ethics*, New York, 1910; i, 464. If Spencer's critics had read this passage they would not have accused him of over-rating sociology.

[54] *Study*, 9.

[55] Cf. budding with colonization, and sexual reproduction with the inter-marriage of races.

its life is immense in length compared with the lives of its component units; . . . that in both cases there is increasing integration accompanied by increasing heterogeneity.[56] Thus the development of society liberally carries out the formula of evolution: the growing size of the political unit, from family to state and league, the growing size of the economic unit, from petty domestic industry to monopolies and cartels, the growing size of the population unit, from villages to towns and cities—surely these show a process of integration; while the division of labor, the multiplication of professions and trades, and the growing economic interdependence of city with country, and of nation with nation, amply illustrate the development of coherence and differentiation.

The same principle of the integration of the heterogeneous applies to every field of social phenomena, from religion and government to science and art. Religion is at first the worship of a multitude of gods and spirits, more or less alike in every nation; and the development of religion comes through the notion of a central and omnipotent deity subordinating the others, and coördinating them into their hierarchy of special rôles. The first gods were probably suggested by dreams and ghosts.[57] The word *spirit* was, and is, applied equally to ghosts and gods. The primitive mind believed that in death, or sleep, or trance, the ghost or spirit left the body; even in a sneeze the forces of expiration might expel the spirit, so that a protective "God bless you!"—or its equivalent—became attached to this dangerous adventure. Echoes and reflections were sounds and sights of one's ghost or double; the Basuto refuses to walk by a stream, lest a crocodile should seize his shadow and consume it. God was, at first, only "a permanently existing ghost."[58] Persons who had been powerful during their earthly lives were believed to keep their power in their ghostly appearance. Among the Tannese the word for god means, literally, a dead man.[59] "Jehovah" meant "the strong one," "the warrior": he had been a local potentate, perhaps, who was worshiped after his death as the "god of hosts." Such dangerous ghosts had to be propitiated: funeral rites grew into worship, and all the modes of currying favor with the earthly chief were applied to the ceremonial of prayer and the appeasement of the gods. Ecclesiastical revenues originated in gifts to the gods, just as state revenues began as presents to the chief. Obeisances to kings became prostration and prayer at the altar of the god. The derivation of the god from the dead king shows clearly in the case of the Romans, who deified rulers before their death. In such ancestor-worship all religion seems to have its origin. The power of this custom may be illustrated by the story of the chief who refused baptism because he was not satisfied with the answer to his query as to whether he would meet his

[56] *Autob.,* ii, 56.
[57] *Principles of Sociology,* New York, 1910; i, 286.
[58] I, 296. [59] I, 303.

unbaptized ancestors in heaven.[60] (Something of this belief entered into the bravery of the Japanese in the war of 1905; death was made easier for them by the thought that their ancestors were looking down upon them from the skies.)

Religion is probably the central feature in the life of primitive men; existence is so precarious and humble among them that the soul lives rather in the hope of things to come than in the reality of things seen. In some measure, supernatural religion is a concomitant of militarist societies; as war gives way to industry, thought turns from death to life, and life runs out of the grooves of reverent authority into the open road of initiative and freedom. Indeed, the most far-reaching change that has taken place in all the history of western society is the gradual replacement of a military by an industrial régime. Students of the state habitually classify societies according as their governments are monarchical, aristocratic, or democratic; but these are superficial distinctions; the great dividing line is that which separates militant from industrial societies, nations that live by war from those that live by work.

The military state is always centralized in government, and almost always monarchical; the coöperation it inculcates is regimental and compulsory; it encourages authoritarian religion, worshiping a warrior god; it develops rigid class distinctions and class codes; it props up the natural domestic absolutism of the male. Because the death rate in warlike societies is high, they tend to polygamy and a low status of women. Most states have been militant because war strengthens the central power and makes for the subordination of all interests to those of the state. Hence "history is little more than the Newgate calendar of nations," a record of robbery, treachery, murder and national suicide. Cannibalism is the shame of primitive societies; but some modern societies are sociophagous, and enslave and consume whole peoples. Until war is outlawed and overcome, civilization is a precarious interlude between catastrophes; "the possibility of a high social . . . state fundamentally depends on the cessation of war."[61]

The hope of such a consummation lies not so much in the spiritual conversion of the hearts of men (for men are what the environment makes them), as in the development of industrial societies. Industry makes for democracy and peace: as life ceases to be dominated by war, a thousand centers of economic development arise, and power is beneficently spread over a large portion of the members of the group. Since production can prosper only where initiative is free, an industrial society breaks down those traditions of authority, hierarchy, and caste, which flourish in military states, and under which military states flourish. The occupation of the soldier ceases to be held in high repute; and patriotism becomes a

<hr/>

[60] I, 284, 422; *Encycl. Brit.*, "Ancestor-worship."
[61] II, 663.

love of one's country rather than a hatred of every other.[62] Peace at home becomes the first need of prosperity, and as capital becomes international, and a thousand investments cross every frontier, international peace becomes a necessity as well. As foreign war diminishes, domestic brutality decreases; monogamy replaces polygamy because the life-tenure of men becomes almost equal to that of women; the status of women rises, and the "emancipation of women" becomes a matter of course.[63] Superstitious religions give way to liberal creeds whose focus of effort is the amelioration and ennoblement of human life and character on this earth. The mechanisms of industry teach men the mechanisms of the universe, and the notion of invariable sequences in cause and effect; exact investigation of natural causes replaces the easy resort to supernatural explanation.[64] History begins to study the people at work rather than the kings at war; it ceases to be a record of personalities and becomes the history of great inventions and new ideas. The power of government is lessened, and the power of productive groups within the state increases; there is a passage "from status to contract," from equality in subordination to freedom in initiative, from compulsory coöperation to coöperation in liberty. The contrast between the militant and the industrial types of society is indicated by "inversion of the belief that individuals exist for the benefit of the State into the belief that the State exists for the benefit of the individuals."[65]

While protesting vigorously against the growth of an imperialistic militarism in England, Spencer chose his country as a type of approach to the industrial society, and pointed to France and Germany as instances of the militant state.

From time to time newspapers remind us of the competition between Germany and France in their military developments. The body politic, in either case, expends most of its energies in growths of teeth and claws—every increase on the one side prompting an increase on the other. . . . Recently the French Minister for Foreign Affairs, referring to Tunis, Tongking, the Congo, and Madagascar, enlarged on the need there had been for competing in political burglaries with other nations; and held that, by taking forcible possession of territories owned by inferior peoples, 'France has regained a certain portion of the glory which so many noble enterprises during previous centuries has insured her.' . . . Hence we see why, in France, as in Germany, a scheme of social re-organization under which each citizen, while maintained by the community, is to labor for the community, has obtained so wide an adhesion as to create a formidable political body—why among the French, St. Simon, Fourier, Proudhon, Cabet, Louis Blanc, Pierre Leroux, now by word and now by deed, have sought to bring about some form of communistic working and living. . . . Verification by contrast meets us on observing that in England, where the extent of ownership by others has been less than in France and Germany, alike under its military

[62]II, 634-5.   [63]I, 681.   [64]II, 599.   [65]I, 575.

form and under its civil form, there has been less progress in sentiment and idea towards that form of ownership by others which socialism implies.[66]

As this passage indicates, Spencer believes that socialism is a derivative of the militant and feudal type of state, and has no natural affiliation with industry. Like militarism, socialism involves the development of centralization, the extension of governmental power, the decay of initiative, and the subordination of the individual. "Well may Prince Bismarck display leanings towards State Socialism."[67] "It is the law of all organization that as it becomes complete it becomes rigid."[68] Socialism would be in industry what a rigid instinctive equipment is in animals; it would produce a community of human ants and bees, and would issue in a slavery far more monotonous and hopeless than the present condition of affairs.

> Under the compulsory arbitration which socialism would necessitate, . . . the regulators, pursuing their personal interests, . . . would not be met by the combined resistance of all workers; and their power, unchecked as now by refusals to work save on prescribed terms, would grow and ramify and consolidate until it became irresistible. . . . When from regulation of the workers by the bureaucracy we turn to the bureaucracy itself, and ask how it is to be regulated, there is no satisfactory answer. . . . Under such conditions there must arise a new aristocracy, for the support of which the masses would toil; and which, being consolidated, would wield a power far beyond that of any past aristocracy.[69]

Economic relationships are so different from political relationships, and so much more complex, that no government could regulate them all without such an enslaving bureaucracy. State interference always neglects some factor of the intricate industrial situation, and has failed whenever tried; note the wage-fixing laws of medieval England, and the price-fixing laws of Revolutionary France. Economic relations must be left to the automatic self-adjustment (imperfect though it may be) of supply and demand. What society most wants it will pay for most heavily; and if certain men, or certain functions, receive great rewards it is because they have taken, or have involved, exceptional risks or pains. Men as now constituted will not tolerate a compulsory equality. Until an automatically-changed environment automatically changes human character, legislation enacting artificial changes will be as futile as astrology.[70]

Spencer was almost made sick by the thought of a world ruled by the wage-earning class. He was not enamored of trade-union leaders so far as he could know them through the refractory medium of the London Times.[71] He pointed out that strikes are useless unless most strikes fail; for if all workers should, at various times, strike and win, prices would

[66]III, 596–9.   [67]Social Statics, p. 329.   [68]Sociology, i, 571.
[69]III, 588. There is danger of this in Russia to-day.
[70]Cf. The Man vs. the State.   [71]III. 589.

presumably rise in accord with the raised wages, and the situation would be as before.[72] "We shall presently see the injustices once inflicted by the employing classes paralleled by the injustices inflicted by the employed classes."[73]

Nevertheless his conclusions were not blindly conservative. He realized the chaos and brutality of the social system that surrounded him, and he looked about with evident eagerness to find a substitute. In the end he gave his sympathies to the coöperative movement; he saw in this the culmination of that passage from status to contract in which Sir Henry Maine had found the essence of economic history. "The regulation of labor becomes less coercive as society assumes a higher type. Here we reach a form in which the coerciveness has diminished to the smallest degree consistent with combined action. Each member is his own master in respect of the work he does; and is subject only to such rules, established by majority of the members, as are needful for maintaining order. The transition from the compulsory coöperation of militancy to the voluntary coöperation of industrialism is completed."[74] He doubts if human beings are yet honest and competent enough to make so democratic a system of industry efficient; but he is all for trying. He foresees a time when industry will no longer be directed by absolute masters, and men will no longer sacrifice their lives in the production of rubbish. "As the contrast between the militant and the industrial types is indicated by inversion of the belief that individuals exist for the benefit of the state into the belief that the state exists for the benefit of individuals; so the contrast between the industrial type and the type likely to be evolved from it is indicated by inversion of the belief that life is for work into the belief that work is for life."[75]

VII. ETHICS: THE EVOLUTION OF MORALS

So important does this problem of industrial reconstruction seem to Spencer that he devotes to it again the largest section of *The Principles of Ethics* (1893)—"this last part of my task . . . , to which I regard all the preceding parts as subsidiary."[76] As a man with all the moral severity of the mid-Victorian, Spencer was especially sensitive to the problem of finding a new and natural ethic to replace the moral code which had been associated with the traditional faith. "The supposed supernatural sanctions of right conduct do not, if rejected, leave a blank. There exist natural sanctions no less pre-emptory, and covering a much wider field."[77]

The new morality must be built upon biology. "Acceptance of the doctrine of organic evolution determines certain ethical conceptions."[78]

[72]III, 545.   [73]*Autob.*, ii, 433.   [74]III, 572.
[75]I, 575.   [76]*Ethics*, vol. i, p. xiii.   [77]I, 7.
[78]I, 25.

Huxley, in his Romanes lectures at Oxford in 1893, argued that biology could not be taken as an ethical guide; that "nature red in tooth and claw" (as Tennyson was phrasing it) exalted brutality and cunning rather than justice and love; but Spencer felt that a moral code which could not meet the tests of natural selection and the struggle for existence, was from the beginning doomed to lipservice and futility. Conduct, like anything else, should be called good or bad as it is well adapted, or maladapted, to the ends of life; "the highest conduct is that which conduces to the greatest length, breadth, and completeness of life."[79] Or, in terms of the evolution formula, conduct is moral according as it makes the individual or the group more integrated and coherent in the midst of a heterogeneity of ends. Morality, like art, is the achievement of unity in diversity; the highest type of man is he who effectively unites in himself the widest variety, complexity, and completeness of life.

This is a rather vague definition, as it must be; for nothing varies so much, from place to place and from time to time, as the specific necessities of adaptation, and therefore the specific content of the idea of good. It is true that certain forms of behavior have been stamped as good—as adapted, in the large, to the fullest life—by the sense of pleasure which natural selection has attached to these preservative and expansive actions. The complexity of modern life has multiplied exceptions, but normally, pleasure indicates biologically useful, and pain indicates biologically dangerous, activities.[80] Nevertheless, within the broad bounds of this principle, we find the most diverse, and apparently the most hostile, conceptions of the good. There is hardly any item of our Western moral code which is not somewhere held to be immoral; not only polygamy, but suicide, murder of one's own countrymen, even of one's parents, finds in one people or another a lofty moral approbation.

The wives of the Fijian chiefs consider it a sacred duty to suffer strangulation on the death of their husbands. A woman who had been rescued by Williams 'escaped during the night, and, swimming across the river, and presenting herself to her own people, insisted on the completion of the sacrifice which she had in a moment of weakness reluctantly consented to forego'; and Wilkes tells of another who loaded her rescuer 'with abuse,' and ever afterwards manifested the most deadly hatred towards him."[81] "Livingstone says of the Makololo women, on the shores of the Zambesi, that they were quite shocked to hear that in England a man had only one wife: to have only one was not 'respectable.' So, too, in Equatorial Africa, according to Reade, 'If a man marries, and his wife thinks that he can afford another spouse, she pesters him to marry again; and calls him a "stingy fellow" if he declines to do so.'[82]

Such facts, of course, conflict with the belief that there is an inborn moral sense which tells each man what is right and what is wrong. But

[79]I, 22, 26; ii, 3.   [80]I, 98.   [81]I, 469.   [82]I, 327.

the association of pleasure and pain, on the average, with good or evil conduct, indicates a measure of truth in the idea; and it may very well be that certain moral conceptions, acquired by the race, become hereditary with the individual.[83] Here Spencer uses his favorite formula to reconcile the intuitionist and the utilitarian, and falls back once more upon the inheritance of acquired characters.

Surely, however, the innate moral sense, if it exists, is in difficulties today; for never were ethical notions more confused. It is notorious that the principles which we apply in our actual living are largely opposite to those which we preach in our churches and our books. The professed ethic of Europe and America is a pacifistic Christianity; the actual ethic is the militaristic code of the marauding Teutons from whom the ruling strata, almost everywhere in Europe, are derived. The practice of duelling, in Catholic France and Protestant Germany, is a tenacious relic of the original Teutonic code.[84] Our moralists are kept busy apologizing for these contradictions, just as the moralists of a later monogamic Greece and India were hard put to it to explain the conduct of gods who had been fashioned in a semi-promiscuous age.[85]

Whether a nation develops its citizens on the lines of Christian morality or the Teutonic code depends on whether industry or war is its dominant concern. A militant society exalts certain virtues and condones what other peoples might call crimes; aggression and robbery and treachery are not so unequivocally denounced among peoples accustomed to them by war, as among peoples who have learned the value of honesty and non-aggression through industry and peace. Generosity and humanity flourish better where war is infrequent and long periods of productive tranquillity inculcate the advantages of mutual aid.[86] The patriotic member of a militant society will look upon bravery and strength as the highest virtues of a man; upon obedience as the highest virtue of the citizen; and upon silent submission to multiple motherhood as the highest virtue of a woman.[87] The Kaiser thought of God as the leader of the German army, and followed up his approbation of duelling by attending divine service.[88] The North American Indians "regarded the use of the bow and arrow, the war-club and spear, as the noblest employments of man. . . . They looked upon agricultural and mechanical labor as degrading. . . . Only during recent times—only now that national welfare is becoming more and more dependent on superior powers of production," and these "on the higher mental faculties, are other occupations than militant ones rising into respectability."[89]

Now war is merely wholesale cannibalism; and there is no reason why it should not be classed with cannibalism and unequivocally denounced. "The sentiment and the idea of justice can grow only as fast as the

[83]I, 471.   [84]I, 323.   [85]I, 458.   [86]I, 391 f.
[87]Cf. the philosophy of Nietzsche.   [88]I, 318.   [89]I, 423-4.

external antagonisms of societies decrease, and the internal harmonious coöperations of their members increase."[90] How can this harmony be promoted? As we have seen, it comes more readily through freedom than through regulation. The formula of justice should be: "Every man is free to do that which he wills, provided he infringes not the equal freedom of any other man."[91] This is a formula hostile to war, which exalts authority, regimentation and obedience; it is a formula favorable to peaceful industry, for it provides a maximum of stimulus with an absolute equality of opportunity; it is conformable to Christian morals, for it holds every person sacred, and frees him from aggression;[92] and it has the sanction of that ultimate judge—natural selection—because it opens up the resources of the earth on equal terms to all, and permits each individual to prosper according to his ability and his work.

This may seem, at first, to be a ruthless principle; and many will oppose to it, as capable of national extension, the family principle of giving to each not according to his ability and product, but according to his need. But a society governed on such principles would soon be eliminated.

During immaturity benefits received must be inversely proportionate to capacities possessed. Within the family-group most must be given where least is deserved, if desert is measured by worth. Contrariwise, after maturity is reached benefit must vary directly as worth: worth being measured by fitness to the conditions of existence. The ill-fitted must suffer the evils of unfitness, and the well-fitted profit by their fitness. These are the two laws which a species must conform to if it is to be preserved. . . . If, among the young, benefit were proportioned to efficiency, the species would disappear forthwith; and if, among adults, benefit were proportioned to inefficiency, the species would disappear by decay in a few generations. . . . The only justification for the analogy between parent and child, and government and people, is the childishness of the people who entertain the analogy.[93]

Liberty contends with Evolution for priority in Spencer's affections;[94] and Liberty wins. He thinks that as war decreases, the control of the individual by the state loses most of its excuse;[95] and in a condition of permanent peace the state would be reduced within Jeffersonian bounds, acting only to prevent breaches of equal freedom. Such justice should be administered without cost, so that wrong-doers might know that the poverty of their victims would not shield them from punishment; and all the expenses of the state should be met by direct taxation, lest the invisibility of taxation should divert public attention from governmental extravagance.[96] But "beyond maintaining justice, the state cannot do any-

---

[90]I, 377.
[92]I, 257.
[94]Elliott, *Herbert Spencer*, p. 81.
[96]II, 200.

[91]II, 46.
[93]II, 4, 217.
[95]I, 148, 420.

thing else without transgressing justice";[97] for it would then be protecting inferior individuals from that natural apportionment of reward and capacity, penalty and incapacity, on which the survival and improvement of the group depend.

The principle of justice would require common ownership of land, if we could separate the land from its improvements.[98] In his first book, Spencer had advocated nationalization of the soil, to equalize economic opportunity; but he withdrew his contention later (much to the disgust of Henry George, who called him "the perplexed philosopher"), on the ground that land is carefully husbanded only by the family that owns it, and that can rely on transmitting to its own descendants the effects of the labor put into it. As for private property, it derives immediately from the law of justice, for each man should be equally free to retain the products of his thrift. The justice of bequests is not so obvious; but the "right to bequeath is included in the right of ownership, since otherwise the ownership is not complete."[99] Trade should be as free among nations as among individuals; the law of justice should be no merely tribal code, but an inviolable maxim of international relations.

These are, in outline, the real "rights of man"—the right to life, liberty, and the pursuit of happiness on equal terms with all. Besides these economic rights, political rights are unimportant unrealities. Changes in the form of government amount to nothing where economic life is not free; and a *laissez-faire* monarchy is much better than a socialistic democracy.

> Voting being simply a method of creating an appliance for the preservation of rights, the question is whether universality of votes conduces to creation of the best appliance for the preservation of rights. We have seen that it does not effectually secure this end. . . . Experience makes obvious that which should have been obvious without experience, that with a universal distribution of votes the larger class will inevitably profit at the expense of the smaller class. . . . Evidently the constitution of the state appropriate to that industrial type of society in which equity is fully realized, must be one in which there is not a representation of individuals but a representation of interests. . . . It may be that the industrial type, perhaps by the development of coöperative organizations, which theoretically, though not at present practically, obliterate the distinction between employer and employed, may produce social arrangements under which antagonistic class-interests will either not exist, or will be so far mitigated as not seriously to complicate matters. . . . But with such humanity as now exists, and must for a long time exist, the possession of what are called equal rights will not insure the maintenance of equal rights properly so-called.[100]

Since political rights are a delusion, and only economic rights avail, women are misled when they spend so much time seeking the franchise. Spencer fears that the maternal instinct for helping the helpless may lead

[97]II, 222.   [98]II, 81.   [99]II, 120.   [100]II, 192–3.

women to favor a paternalistic state.[101] There is some confusion in his mind on this point; he argues that political rights are of no importance, and then that it is very important that women should not have them; he denounces war, and then contends that women should not vote because they do not risk their lives in battle[102]—a shameful argument for any man to use who has been born of a woman's suffering. He is afraid of women because they may be too altruistic; and yet the culminating conception of his book is that industry and peace will develop altruism to the point where it will balance egoism and so evolve the spontaneous order of a philosophic anarchism.

The conflict of egoism and altruism (this word, and something of this line of thought, Spencer takes, more or less unconsciously, from Comte) results from the conflict of the individual with his family, his group, and his race. Presumably egoism will remain dominant; but perhaps that is desirable. If everybody thought more of the interests of others than of his own we should have a chaos of curtsies and retreats; and probably "the pursuit of individual happiness within the limits prescribed by social conditions is the first requisite to the attainment of the greatest general happiness."[103] What we may expect, however, is a great enlargement of the sphere of sympathy, a great development of the impulses to altruism. Even now the sacrifices entailed by parentage are gladly made; "the wish for children among the childless, and the occasional adoption of children, show how needful for the attainment of certain egoistic satisfactions are these altruistic activities."[104] The intensity of patriotism is another instance of the passionate preference of larger interests to one's immediate concerns. Every generation of social living deepens the impulses to mutual aid.[105] "Unceasing social discipline will so mould human nature that eventually, sympathetic pleasures will be spontaneously pursued to the fullest extent advantageous to all."[106] The sense of duty which is the echo of generations of compulsion to social behavior, will then disappear; altruistic actions, having become instinctive through their natural selection for social utility, will, like every instinctive operation, be performed without compulsion, and with joy. The natural evolution of human society brings us ever nearer to the perfect state.

VIII. CRITICISM

The intelligent reader, in the course of this brief analysis,[107] will have perceived certain difficulties in the argument, and will need no more

[101]II, 196–7. [102]II, 166. [103]I, 196, 190.
[104]I, 242–3. [105]I, 466. [106]I, 250.

[107]The analysis, of course, is incomplete. "Space forbids" (the author has often smiled at this cloak for laziness, but must offer it here), a discussion of the *Education*, the *Essays*, and large sections of the *Sociology*. The lesson of the *Education* has been too well learned; and we require today some corrective of Spencer's

than some scattered reminders as to where the imperfections lie. Negative criticism is always unpleasant, and most so in the face of a great achievement; but it is part of our task to see what time has done to Spencer's synthesis.

1. First Principles

The first obstacle, of course, is the Unknowable. We may cordially recognize the probable limitations of human knowledge; we cannot quite fathom that great sea of existence of which we are merely a transient wave. But we must not dogmatize on the subject, since in strict logic the assertion that anything is unknowable already implies some knowledge of the thing. Indeed, as Spencer proceeds through his ten volumes, he shows "a prodigious knowledge of the unknowable."[108] As Hegel put it: to limit reason by reasoning is like trying to swim without entering the water. And all this logic-chopping about "inconceivability"—how far away that seems to us now, how like those sophomoric days when to be alive was to debate! And for that matter, an unguided machine is not much more conceivable than a First Cause, particularly if, by this latter phrase, we mean the sum total of all causes and forces in the world. Spencer, living in a world of machines, took mechanism for granted; just as Darwin, living in an age of ruthless individual competition, saw only the struggle for existence.

What shall we say of that tremendous definition of evolution? Does it explain anything? "To say, 'first there was the simple, and then the complex was evolved out of it,' and so on, is not to explain nature."[109] Spencer, says Bergson, repieces, he does not explain;[110] he misses, as he at last perceives, the vital element in the world. The critics, evidently, have been irritated by the definition: its Latinized English is especially arresting in a man who denounced the study of Latin, and defined a good style as that which requires the least effort of understanding. Something must be conceded to Spencer, however; no doubt he chose to sacrifice immediate clarity to the need of concentrating in a brief statement the flow of all existence. But in truth he is a little too fond of his definition; he rolls it over his tongue like a choice morsel, and takes it apart and puts it together again interminably. The weak point of the definition lies in the supposed "instability of the homogeneous." Is a whole composed of like parts more unstable, more subject to change, than a whole composed of unlike parts? The heterogeneous, as more complex, would presumably be more unstable than the homogeneously simple. In ethnology and politics it is

victorious assertion of the claims of science as against letters and the arts. Of the essays, the best are those on style, laughter, and music. Hugh Elliott's *Herbert Spencer* is an admirable exposition.

[108]Browne: *Kant and Spencer*, p. 253.
[109]Ritchie: *Darwin and Hegel*, p. 60.
[110]*Creative Evolution*, p. 64.

taken for granted that heterogeneity makes for instability, and that the fusion of immigrant stocks into one national type would strengthen a society. Tarde thinks that civilization results from an increase of similarity among the members of a group through generations of mutual imitation; here the movement of evolution is conceived as a progress towards homogeneity. Gothic architecture is surely more complex than that of the Greeks; but not necessarily a higher stage of artistic evolution. Spencer was too quick to assume that what was earlier in time was simpler in structure; he underrated the complexity of protoplasm, and the intelligence of primitive man.[111] Finally, the definition fails to mention the very item which in most minds today is inalienably associated with the idea of evolution—namely, natural selection. Perhaps (imperfect though this too would be) a description of history as a struggle for existence and a survival of the fittest—of the fittest organisms, the fittest societies, the fittest moralities, the fittest languages, ideas, philosophies—would be more illuminating than the formula of incoherence and coherence, of homo- and heterogeneity, of dissipation and integration?

"I am a bad observer of humanity in the concrete," says Spencer, "being too much given to wandering into the abstract."[112] This is dangerous honesty. Spencer's method, of course, was too deductive and à priori, very different from Bacon's ideal or the actual procedure of scientific thought. He had, says his secretary, "an inexhaustible faculty of developing à priori and à posteriori, inductive and deductive, arguments in support of any imaginable proposition"; [113] and the à priori arguments were probably prior to the others. Spencer began, like a scientist, with observation; he proceeded, like a scientist, to make hypotheses; but then, unlike a scientist, he resorted not to experiment, nor to impartial observation, but to the selective accumulation of favorable data. He had no nose at all for "negative instances." Contrast the procedure of Darwin, who, when he came upon data unfavorable to his theory, hastily made note of them, knowing that they had a way of slipping out of the memory a little more readily than the welcome facts!

2. BIOLOGY AND PSYCHOLOGY

In a foot-note to his essay on "Progress," Spencer candidly confesses that his ideas of evolution were based on Lamarck's theory of the transmissibility of acquired characters, and were not really an anticipation of Darwin, whose essential idea was the theory of natural selection. He is rather the philosopher of Lamarckianism, then, than the philosopher of Darwinism. He was almost forty when the *Origin of Species* appeared; and at forty, one's categories are hardened into immutability.

[111]Cf. Boas: *The Mind of Primitive Man.*
[112]*Autob.*, ii, 461.   [113]Royce, 194.

Aside from lesser difficulties, like the failure to reconcile his illuminating principle—that reproduction decreases as development advances—with such facts as the higher rate of reproduction in civilized Europe as compared with savage peoples, the major defects of his biological theory are his reliance on Lamarck and his failure to find a dynamic conception of life. When he confesses that life "cannot be conceived in physicochemical terms,"[114] the "admission is fatal to his formula of evolution, to his definition of life, and to the coherence of the Synthetic Philosophy."[115] The secret of life might better have been sought in the power of mind to adjust external to internal relations than in the almost passive adjustment of the organism to the environment. On Spencer's premises, complete adaptation would be death.

The volumes on psychology formulate rather than inform. What we knew is reshaped into an almost barbarously complex terminology, which obscures where it should clarify. The reader is so fatigued with formulas and definitions and questionable reductions of psychological facts to neural structures that he may fail to observe that the origin of mind and consciousness is left quite unexplained. It is true that Spencer tries to cover up this gaping chasm in his system of thought by arguing that mind is the subjective accompaniment of nerve processes evolved mechanically, somehow, out of the primeval nebula; but why there should be this subjective accompaniment in addition to the neural mechanism, he does not say. And that, of course, is just the point of all psychology.

3. SOCIOLOGY AND ETHICS

Magnificent as the Sociology is, its 2000 pages give many an opening for attack. Running through it is Spencer's usual assumption that evolution and progress are synonymous, whereas it may well be that evolution will give to insects and bacteria the final victory in their relentless war with man. It is not quite evident that the industrial state is either more pacific or more moral than the "militant" feudalism that preceded it. Athens' most destructive wars came long after her feudal lords had yielded power to a commercial bourgeoisie; and the countries of modern Europe seem to make war with blithe indifference as to whether they are industrial or not; industrial imperialism may be as militaristic as land-hungry dynasties. The most militaristic of modern states was one of the two leading industrial nations of the world. Further, the rapid industrial development of Germany seems to have been aided, rather than impeded, by state control of certain phases of transport and trade. Socialism is obviously a development not of militarism but of industrialism. Spencer wrote at a time when the comparative isolation of England made her pacifist (in Europe), and when her supremacy in commerce

[114]*Biology*, i, 120.   [115]J. A. Thomson, *Herbert Spencer*, p. 109.

and industry made her a firm believer in free trade; he would have been shocked had he lived to see how readily the free trade theory would disappear along with commercial and industrial supremacy, and how the pacifism would disappear as soon as Germany's assault on Belgium threatened English isolation. And of course Spencer exaggerated the virtues of the industrial régime; he was almost blind to the brutal exploitation that flourished in England before the state interfered to mitigate it; all that he could see "in the middle of our century, especially in England," was "a degree of individual freedom greater than ever before existed."[116] No wonder that Nietzsche reacted in disgust from industrialism, and exaggerated, in his turn, the virtues of the military life.[117]

The analogy of the social organism would have driven Spencer into state socialism had his logic been more powerful than his feelings; for state socialism represents, in a far higher degree than a *laissez-faire* society, the integration of the heterogeneous. By the yard-stick of his own formula Spencer would have been compelled to acclaim Germany as the most highly evolved of modern states. He tried to meet this point by arguing that heterogeneity involves the freedom of the parts, and that such freedom implies a minimum of government; but this is quite a different note than that which we heard in "*coherent* heterogeneity." In the human body integration and evolution leave rather little freedom to the parts. Spencer replies that in a society consciousness exists only in the parts, while in the body consciousness exists only in the whole. But social consciousness—consciousness of the interests and processes of the group— is as centralized in society as personal consciousness is in the individual; very few of us have any "sense of the state." Spencer helped to save us from a regimental state socialism, but only by the sacrifice of his consistency and his logic.

And only by individualistic exaggerations. We must remember that Spencer was caught between two eras; that his political thinking had been formed in the days of *laissez-faire,* and under the influence of Adam Smith; while his later years were lived in a period when England was struggling to correct, by social control, the abuses of her industrial régime. He never tired of reiterating his arguments against state-interference; he objected to state-financed education, or to governmental protection of citizens against fraudulent finance;[118] at one time he argued that even the management of war should be a private, and not a state, concern;[119] he wished, as Wells put it, "to raise public shiftlessness to the dignity of a national policy." He carried his MSS. to the printer himself, having too little confidence in a government institution to entrust them

---

[116]*Sociology*, iii, 607. Cf. *The Study of Sociology*, p. 335: "The testimony is that higher wages commonly result only in more extravagant living or in drinking to greater excess."

[117]Cf. *The Joyful Wisdom*, sect. 40.   [118]*Autob.*, ii, 5.   [119]I, 239.

to the Post Office.[120] He was a man of intense individuality, irritably in-sistent on being let alone; and every new act of legislation seemed to him an invasion of his personal liberty. He could not understand Benjamin Kidd's argument, that since natural selection operates more and more upon groups, in class and international competition, and less and less upon individuals, a widening application of the family-principle (whereby the weak are aided by the strong) is indispensable for the maintenance of group unity and power. Why a state should protect its citizens from unsocial physical strength and refuse protection against unsocial economic strength is a point which Spencer ignores. He scorned as childish the analogy of government and citizen with parent and child; but the real analogy is with brother helping brother. His politics were more Darwinian than his biology.

But enough of these criticisms. Let us turn back to the man again, and see in fairer perspective the greatness of his work.

IX. CONCLUSION

First Principles made Spencer almost at once the most famous philoso-pher of his time. It was soon translated into most of the languages of Europe; even in Russia, where it had to face and defeat a government prosecution. He was accepted as the philosophic exponent of the spirit of the age; and not only did his influence pass everywhere into the thought of Europe, but it strongly affected the realistic movement in literature and art. In 1869 he was astounded to find that *First Principles* had been adopted as a text-book at Oxford.[121] More marvelous still, his books began, after 1870, to bring him returns that made him financially secure. In some cases admirers sent him substantial gifts, which he always re-turned. When Czar Alexander II visited London, and expressed to Lord Derby a desire to meet the distinguished savants of England, Derby in-vited Spencer, Huxley, Tyndall, etc. The others attended, but Spencer declined. He associated with only a few intimates. "No man is equal to his book," he wrote. "All the best products of his mental activity go into his book, where they come separated from the mass of inferior products with which they are mingled in his daily talk."[122] When people insisted on coming to see him he inserted stopping into his ears, and listened placidly to their conversation.

Strange to say, his fame vanished almost as suddenly as it had come. He outlived the height of his own repute, and was saddened, in his last years, by seeing what little power his tirades had had to stop the tide of "paternalistic" legislation. He had become unpopular with almost every class. Scientific specialists whose privileged fields he had invaded damned him with faint praise, ignoring his contributions and emphasizing his

[120]Collier. in Royce, 221.   [121]*Autob.*, ii, 242.   [122]*Autob.*, i, 423.

errors; and bishops of all creeds united in consigning him to an eternity of punishment. Laborites who liked his denunciations of war turned from him in anger when he spoke his mind on socialism and on trade-union politics; while conservatives who liked his views on socialism shunned him because of his agnosticism. "I am more Tory than any Tory and more radical than any Radical," he said, wistfully.[123] He was incorrigibly sincere, and offended every group by speaking candidly on every subject: after sympathizing with the workers as victims of their employers, he added that the workers would be as domineering if positions were reversed; and after sympathizing with women as victims of men, he did not fail to add that men were the victims of women so far as the women could manage it. He grew old alone.

As he aged he became more gentle in opposition, and more moderate in opinion. He had always laughed at England's ornamental king, but now he expressed the view that it was no more right to deprive the people of their king than it was to deprive a child of its doll.[124] So in religion he felt it absurd and unkind to disturb the traditional faith where it seemed a beneficent and cheering influence.[125] He began to realize that religious beliefs and political movements are built upon needs and impulses beyond the reach of intellectual attack; and he reconciled himself to seeing the world roll on without much heeding the heavy books he hurled in its direction. Looking back over his arduous career, he thought himself foolish for having sought literary fame instead of the simpler pleasures of life.[126] When he died, in 1903, he had come to think that his work had been done in vain.[127]

We know now, of course, that it was not so. The decay of his repute was part of the English-Hegelian reaction against positivism; the revival of liberalism will raise him again to his place as the greatest English philosopher of his century. He gave to philosophy a new contact with things, and brought to it a realism which made German philosophy seem, beside it, weakly pale and timidly abstract. He summed up his age as no man had ever summed up any age since Dante; and he accomplished so masterly a coördination of so vast an area of knowledge that criticism is almost shamed into silence by his achievement. We are standing now on heights which his struggles and his labors won for us; we seem to be above him because he has raised us on his shoulders. Some day, when the sting of his opposition is forgotten, we shall do him better justice.

[123]II, 431. [124]Elliott, p. 66. [126]*Autob.*, ii, 547.
[126]II, 534. [127]Thomson, p. 51.

CHAPTER IX

Friedrich Nietzsche

I. THE LINEAGE OF NIETZSCHE

NIETZSCHE was the child of Darwin and the brother of Bismarck.

It does not matter that he ridiculed the English evolutionists and the German nationalists: he was accustomed to denounce those who had most influenced him; it was his unconscious way of covering up his debts.

The ethical philosophy of Spencer was not the most natural corollary of the theory of evolution. If life is a struggle for existence in which the fittest survive, then strength is the ultimate virtue, and weakness the only fault. *Good* is that which survives, which wins; *bad* is that which gives way and fails. Only the mid-Victorian cowardice of the English Darwinians, and the bourgeois respectability of French positivists and German socialists, could conceal the inevitableness of this conclusion. These men were brave enough to reject Christian theology, but they did not dare to be logical, to reject the moral ideas, the worship of meekness and gentleness and altruism, which had grown out of that theology. They ceased to be Anglicans, or Catholics, or Lutherans; but they did not dare cease to be Christians.—So argued Friedrich Nietzsche.

"The secret stimulus of the French free-thinkers from Voltaire to August Comte was not to remain behind the Christian ideal, . . . but to outbid it if possible. Comte, with his 'Live for others,' out-Christianizes Christianity. In Germany it was Schopenhauer, and in England John Stuart Mill, who gave the greatest fame to the theory of sympathetic affections, of pity, and of usefulness to others as the principle of action. . . . All the systems of socialism placed themselves unwittingly . . . upon the common ground of these doctrines."[1]

Darwin unconsciously completed the work of the Encyclopedists: they had removed the theological basis of modern morals, but they had left that morality itself untouched and inviolate, hanging miraculously in the air; a little breath of biology was all that was needed to clear away this remnant of imposture. Men who could think clearly soon perceived what the profoundest minds of every age had known: that in this battle

[1] Quoted in Faguet, *On Reading Nietzsche*, New York, 1918; p. 71.

we call life, what we need is not goodness but strength, not humility but pride, not altruism but resolute intelligence; that equality and democracy are against the grain of selection and survival; that not masses but geniuses are the goal of evolution; that not "justice" but power is the arbiter of all differences and all destinies.—So it seemed to Friedrich Nietzsche.

Now if all this were true, nothing could be more magnificent or significant than Bismarck. Here was a man who knew the realities of life, who said bluntly that "there is no altruism among nations," and that modern issues are to be decided not by votes and rhetoric, but by blood and iron. What a cleansing whirlwind he was for a Europe rotten with delusions and democracy and "ideals"! In a few brief months he had brought decadent Austria to accept his leadership; in a few brief months he had humbled a France drunk with the legend of Napoleon; and in those brief months had he not also forced all those little German "states," all those petty potentates, principalities and powers to fuse themselves into a mighty empire, the very symbol of the new morality of strength? The growing military and industrial vigor of this new Germany needed a voice; the arbitrament of war needed a philosophy to justify it. Christianity would not justify it, but Darwinism could. Given a little audacity, and the thing could be done.

Nietzsche had the audacity, and became the voice.

II. YOUTH

Nevertheless, his father was a minister; a long line of clergymen lay behind each of his parents; and he himself remained a preacher to the end. He attacked Christianity because there was so much of its moral spirit in him; his philosophy was an attempt to balance and correct, by violent contradiction, an irresistible tendency to gentleness and kindness and peace; was it not the final insult that the good people of Genoa should call him *Il Santo*—"the Saint"? His mother was a pious and Puritan lady, of the same sort that had fostered Immanuel Kant; and, with perhaps one disastrous exception, Nietzsche remained pious and Puritan, chaste as a statue, to the last: therefore his assault on Puritanism and piety. How he longed to be a sinner, this incorrigible saint!

He was born at Röcken, Prussia, on October 15, 1844,—which happened to be the birthday of the reigning Prussian king, Frederick William IV. His father, who had tutored several members of the royal family, rejoiced at this patriotic coincidence, and named the boy after the King. "There was at all events one advantage in the choice of this day for my birth; my birthday throughout the whole of my childhood was a day of public rejoicing."[2]

The early death of his father left him a victim to the holy women of

[2]*Ecce Homo*, English translation, ed. Levy, p. 15.

the household, who petted him into an almost feminine delicacy and sensibility. He disliked the bad boys of the neighborhood, who robbed birds' nests, raided orchards, played soldier, and told lies. His schoolmates called him "the little minister," and one of them described him as "a Jesus in the Temple." It was his delight to seclude himself and read the Bible, or to read it to others so feelingly as to bring tears to their eyes. But there was a hidden nervous stoicism and pride in him: when his school-fellows doubted the story of Mutius Scaevola he ignited a batch of matches in the palm of his hand and let them lie there till they were burnt out.[3] It was a typical incident: all his life long he was to seek physical and intellectua. means of hardening himself into an idealized masculinity. "What I am not, that for me is God and virtue."[4]

At eighteen he lost his faith in the God of his fathers, and spent the remainder of his life looking for a new deity; he thought he found one in the Superman. He said later that he had taken the change easily; but he had a habit of easily deceiving himself, and is an unreliable autobiographer. He became cynical, like one who had staked all on a single throw of the dice, and had lost; religion had been the very marrow of his life, and now life seemed empty and meaningless. He passed suddenly into a period of sensual riot with his college mates at Bonn and Leipzig, and even overcame the fastidiousness that had made so difficult for him the male arts of smoking and drinking. But soon wine, woman and tobacco disgusted him; he reacted into a great scorn of the whole *biergemütlichkeit* of his country and his time; people who drank beer and smoked pipes were incapable of clear perception or subtle thought.

It was about this time, in 1865, that he discovered Schopenhauer's *World as Will and Idea,* and found in it "a mirror in which I espied the world, life, and my own nature depicted with frightful grandeur."[5] He took the book to his lodgings, and read every word of it hungrily. "It seemed as if Schopenhauer were addressing me personally. I felt his enthusiasm, and seemed to see him before me. Every line cried aloud for renunciation, denial, resignation."[6] The dark color of Schopenhauer's

[3]Mencken, *The Philosophy of Friedrich Nietzsche,* Boston, 1913; p. 10.

[4]*Thus Spake Zarathustra,* p. 129. This work will be referred to hereafter as "Z"; and the following (in the English translation) will be referred to by their initials: *The Birth of Tragedy* (1872), *Thoughts Out of Season* (1873-76), *Human All Too Human* (1876-80), *The Dawn of Day* (1881), *The Joyful Wisdom* (1882), *Beyond Good and Evil* (1886), *The Genealogy of Morals* (1887), *The Case of Wagner* (1888), *The Twilight of the Idols* (1888), *Antichrist* (1889), *Ecce Homo* (1889), *The Will to Power* (1889). Perhaps the best of these as an introduction to Nietzsche himself is *Beyond Good and Evil. Zarathustra* is obscure, and its latter half tends towards elaboration. *The Will to Power* contains more meat than any of the other books. The most complete biography is by Frau Förster-Nietzsche; Halévy's, much shorter, is also good. Salter's *Nietzsche the Thinker* (New York, 1917) is a scholarly exposition.

[5]B. T., introd., p. xvii.

[6]Quoted by Mencken, p. 18.

philosophy impressed itself permanently upon his thought: and not only when he was a devoted follower of "Schopenhauer as Educator" (the title of one of his essays), but even when he came to denounce pessimism as a form of decadence, he remained at bottom an unhappy man, whose nervous system seemed to have been carefully designed for suffering, and whose exaltation of tragedy as the joy of life was but another self-deception. Only Spinoza or Goethe could have saved him from Schopenhauer; but though he preached *æquanimitas* and *amor fati,* he never practised them; the serenity of the sage and the calm of the balanced mind were never his.

At the age of twenty-three he was conscripted into military service. He would have been glad to get exemption as near-sighted and the only son of a widow, but the army claimed him nevertheless; even philosophers were welcomed as cannon-fodder in the great days of Sadowa and Sedan. However, a fall from a horse so wrenched his breast-muscles that the recruiting-sergeant was forced to yield up his prey. Nietzsche never quite recovered from that hurt. His military experience was so brief that he left the army with almost as many delusions about soldiers as he had had on entering it; the hard Spartan life of commanding and obeying, of endurance and discipline, appealed to his imagination, now that he was free from the necessity of realizing this ideal himself; he came to worship the soldier because his health would not permit him to become one.

From military life he passed to its antipodes—the academic life of a philologist; instead of becoming a warrior he became a Ph.D. At twenty-five he was appointed to the chair of classical philology at the University of Basle, from whose safe distance he could admire the bloody ironies of Bismarck. He had queer regrets on taking up this unheroically sedentary work: on the one hand he wished he had gone into a practical and active profession, such as medicine; and at the same time he found himself drawn towards music. He had become something of a pianist, and had written sonatas; "without music," he said, "life would be a mistake."[7]

Not far from Basle was Tribschen, where that giant of music, Richard Wagner, was living with another man's wife. Nietzsche was invited to come and spend his Christmas there, in 1869. He was a warm enthusiast for the music of the future, and Wagner did not despise recruits who could lend to his cause something of the prestige that goes with scholarship and universities. Under the spell of the great composer, Nietzsche began to write his first book, which was to begin with the Greek drama and end with *The Ring of the Nibelungs,* preaching Wagner to the world as the modern Æschylus. He went up into the Alps to write in peace, far from the madding crowd; and there, in 1870, came to him the news that Germany and France had gone to war.

He hesitated; the spirit of Greece, and all the muses of poetry and

[7]Letter to Brandes, in Huneker, *Egoists,* New York, 1910; p. 251.

drama and philosophy and music had laid their consecrating hands upon him. But he could not resist the call of his country; here was poetry too. "Here," he wrote, "you have the state, of shameful origin; for the greater part of men a well of suffering that is never dried, a flame that consumes them in its frequent crises. And yet when it calls, our souls become forgetful of themselves; at its bloody appeal the multitude is urged to courage and uplifted to heroism."[8] At Frankfort, on his way to the front, he saw a troop of cavalry passing with magnificent clatter and display through the town; there and then, he says, came the perception, the vision, out of which was to grow his entire philosophy. "I felt for the first time that the strongest and highest Will to Life does not find expression in a miserable struggle for existence, but in a Will to War, a Will to Power, a Will to Overpower!"[9] Bad eyesight disqualified him from active soldiering, and he had to be content with nursing; and though he saw horrors enough, he never knew the actual brutality of those battle-fields which his timid soul was later to idealize with all the imaginative intensity of inexperience. Even for nursing he was too sensitively delicate; the sight of blood made him ill; he fell sick, and was sent home in ruins. Ever afterward he had the nerves of a Shelley and the stomach of a Carlyle; the soul of a girl under the armor of a warrior.

III. NIETZSCHE AND WAGNER

Early in 1872 he published his first, and his only complete, book—*The Birth of Tragedy out of the Spirit of Music*.[10]

Never had a philologist spoken so lyrically. He told of the two gods whom Greek art had worshipped: at first Dionysus (or Bacchus), the god of wine and revelry, of ascending life, of joy in action, of ecstatic emotion and inspiration, of instinct and adventure and dauntless suffering, the god of song and music and dance and drama;—and then, later, Apollo, the god of peace and leisure and repose, of esthetic emotion and intellectual contemplation, of logical order and philosophic calm, the god of painting and sculpture and epic poetry. The noblest Greek art was a union of the two ideals,—the restless masculine power of Dionysus and the quiet feminine beauty of Apollo. In drama Dionysus inspired the chorus, and Apollo the dialogue; the chorus grew directly out of the procession of the satyr-dressed devotees of Dionysus; the dialogue was an after-thought, a reflective appendage to an emotional experience.

The profoundest feature of Greek drama was the Dionysian conquest of pessimism through art. The Greeks were not the cheerful and optimis-

---

[8] In Halévy, *Life of Friedrich Nietzsche*, London, 1911; p. 106.

[9] In Förster-Nietzsche, *The Young Nietzsche*, London, 1912; p. 235.

[10] It falls in with their later break that Wagner wrote about the same time an essay "On the Evolution of Music Out of the Drama" (*Prose Works*, vol. x).

tic people whom we meet with in modern rhapsodies about them; they knew the stings of life intimately, and its tragic brevity. When Midas asked Silenus what fate is best for a man, Silenus answered: "Pitiful race of a day, children of accidents and sorrow, why do you force me to say what were better left unheard? The best of all is unobtainable—not to be born, to be nothing. The second best is to die early." Evidently these men had little to learn from Schopenhauer, or from the Hindus. But the Greeks overcame the gloom of their disillusionment with the brilliance of their art: out of their own suffering they made the spectacle of the drama, and found that "it is only as an esthetic phenomenon," as an object of artistic contemplation or reconstruction, "that existence and the world appear justified."[11] "The sublime is the artistic subjugation of the awful."[12] Pessimism is a sign of decay, optimism is a sign of superficiality; "tragic optimism" is the mood of the strong man who seeks intensity and extent of experience, even at the cost of woe, and is delighted to find that strife is the law of life. "Tragedy itself is the proof of the fact that the Greeks were not pessimists." The days when this mood begot the Æschylean drama and the pre-Socratic philosophy were the "tremendous days of Greece."[13]

Socrates—"the type of the theoretical man"[14]—was a sign of the loosened fibre of the Greek character; "the old Marathonian stalwart capacity of body and soul was more and more sacrificed to a dubious enlightenment, involving progressive degeneration of the physical and mental powers."[15] Critical philosophy replaced the philosophical poetry of the pre-Socratics; science replaced art; intellect replaced instinct; dialectic replaced the games. Under the influence of Socrates, Plato the athlete became an esthete, Plato the dramatist became a logician, an enemy of passion, a deporter of poets, a "pre-Christian Christian," an epistemologist. On the temple of Apollo at Delphi those words of passionless wisdom were inscribed—*gnothe seauton* and *meden agan*[16]—which became, in Socrates and Plato, the delusion that intelligence is the only virtue, and in Aristotle the enervating doctrine of the golden mean. In its youth a people produce mythology and poetry; in its decadence, philosophy and logic. In its youth Greece produced Homer and Æschylus; in its decay it gave us Euripides—the logician turned dramatist, the rationalist destroying myth and symbol, the sentimentalist destroying the tragic optimism of the masculine age, the friend of Socrates who replaces the Dionysian chorus with an Apollonian galaxy of dialecticians and orators.

No wonder the Delphic oracle of Apollo had named Socrates the wisest of the Greeks, and Euripides the wisest after him; and no wonder that

[11]B. T., 50, 183.   [12]P. 62.

[13]*The Wagner-Nietzsche Correspondence*, New York, 1921; p. 167.

[14]B. T., 114.   [15]P. 102.   [16]"Know thyself" and "nothing in excess."

"the unerring instinct of Aristophanes . . . comprised Socrates and Euripides . . . in the same feeling of hatred, and saw in them the symptoms of a degenerate culture."[17] It is true that they recanted; that Euripides' last play—*The Bacchœ*—is his surrender to Dionysus, and the prelude to his suicide; and that Socrates in prison took to practicing the music of Dionysus to ease his conscience. " 'Perhaps'—thus he had to ask himself—'what is not intelligible to me is not therefore unreasonable? Perhaps there is a realm of wisdom from which the logician is banished? Perhaps art is even a necessary correlative of and supplement to science?' "[18] But it was too late; the work of the logician and the rationalist could not be undone; Greek drama and Greek character decayed. "The surprising thing had happened: when the poet" and the philosopher "recanted, their tendency had already conquered."[19] With them ended the age of heroes, and the art of Dionysus.

But perhaps the age of Dionysus may return? Did not Kant destroy once and for all the theoretical reason and the theoretical man?—and did not Schopenhauer teach us again the profundity of instinct and the tragedy of thought?—and is not Richard Wagner another Æschylus, restoring myths and symbols, and uniting music and drama again in Dionysian ecstasy? "Out of the Dionysian root of the German spirit a power has arisen which has nothing in common with the primitive conditions of Socratic culture, . . . —namely, German music, . . . in its vast solar orbit from Bach to Beethoven, from Beethoven to Wagner."[20] The German spirit has too long reflected passively the Apollonian art of Italy and France; let the German people realize that their own instincts are sounder than these decadent cultures; let them make a Reformation in music as in religion, pouring the wild vigor of Luther again into art and life. Who knows but that out of the war-throes of the German nation another age of heroes dawns, and that out of the spirit of music tragedy may be reborn?

In 1872 Nietzsche returned to Basle, still weak in body, but with a spirit burning with ambition, and loath to consume itself in the drudgery of lecturing. "I have before me work enough for fifty years, and I must mark time under the yoke."[21] Already he was a little disillusioned with the war: "the German Empire is extirpating the German spirit," he wrote.[22] The victory of 1871 had brought a certain coarse conceit into the soul of Germany; and nothing could be more hostile to spiritual growth. An impish quality in Nietzsche made him restless before every idol; and he determined to assail this dulling complacency by attacking its most respected exponent—David Strauss. "I enter society with a duel: Stendhal gave that advice."[23]

[17]B. T., 182 [18]P. 113. [19]P. 95. [20]B. T., 150.
[21]In Halévy, 169. [22]Ibid., 151. [23]Ibid.

In the second of his well-named *Thoughts out of Season*—"Schopen-hauer as Educator"—he turned his fire upon the chauvinistic universities. "Experience teaches us that nothing stands so much in the way of developing great philosophers as the custom of supporting bad ones in state universities. . . . No state would ever dare to patronize such men as Plato and Schopenhauer. . . . The state is always afraid of them."[24] He renewed the attack in "The Future of Our Educational Institutions"; and in "The Use and Abuse of History" he ridiculed the submergence of the German intellect in the minutiæ of antiquarian scholarship. Already in these essays two of his distinctive ideas found expression: that morality, as well as theology, must be reconstructed in terms of the evolution theory; and that the function of life is to bring about "not the betterment of the majority, who, taken as individuals, are the most worthless types," but "the creation of genius," the development and elevation of superior personalities.[25]

The most enthusiastic of these essays was called "Richard Wagner in Bayreuth." It hailed Wagner as a Siegfried "who has never learned the meaning of fear,"[26] and as founder of the only real art, because the first to fuse all the arts into a great esthetic synthesis; and it called upon Germany to realize the majestic significance of the coming Wagner festival —"Bayreuth signifies for us the morning sacrament on the day of battle."[27] This was the voice of youthful worship, the voice of an almost femininely refined spirit who saw in Wagner something of that masculine decisiveness and courage which went later into the conception of the Superman. But the worshipper was a philosopher too, and recognized in Wagner a certain dictatorial egotism offensive to an aristocratic soul. He could not bear Wagner's attack upon the French in 1871 (Paris had not been kind to *Tannhäuser!*); and he was astounded at Wagner's jealousy of Brahms.[28] The central theme even of this laudatory essay boded no good for Wagner: "The world has been Orientalized long enough; and men now yearn to be Hellenized."[29] But Nietzsche already knew that Wagner was half Semitic.

And then, in 1876, came Bayreuth itself, and Wagnerian opera night after night,—without cuts,—and *Wagnériennes*, and emperors and princes and princelets, and the idle rich crowding out the impecunious devotees. Suddenly it dawned upon Nietzsche how much of Geyer there was in Wagner,[30] how much *The Ring of the Nibelungs* owed to the theatrical effects which abounded in it, and how far the *melos* that some missed in the music had passed into the drama. "I had had visions of a drama

[24]"Schopenhauer as Educator," sect. 8.
[26]*Ibid.*, sect. 6.
[27]*T. O. S.*, i, 117.
[27]*Ibid.*, 104.
[28]*The Wagner-Nietzsche Correspondence*, p. 223.
[29]*T. O. S.*, i, 122.
[30]Nietzsche considered Wagner's father to be Ludwig Geyer, a Jewish actor.

overspread with a symphony, a form growing out of the *Lied*. But the alien appeal of the opera drew Wagner irresistibly in the other direction."[31] Nietzsche could not go in that direction; he detested the dramatic and the operatic. "I should be insane to stay here," he wrote. "I await with terror each of these long musical evenings . . . I can bear no more."[32]

And so he fled, without a word to Wagner and in the midst of Wagner's supreme triumph, while all the world worshipped; fled, "tired with disgust of all that is feminism and undisciplined rhapsody in that romanticism, that idealistic lying, that softening of the human conscience, which had conquered here one of the bravest souls."[33] And then, in faraway Sorrento, whom should he encounter but Wagner himself, resting from his victory, and full of a new opera he was writing—*Parsifal*. It was to be an exaltation of Christianity, pity, and fleshless love, and a world redeemed by a "pure fool," "the fool in Christ." Nietzsche turned away without a word, and never spoke to Wagner thereafter. "It is impossible for me to recognize *greatness* which is not united with candor and sincerity towards one's self. The moment I make a discovery of this sort, a man's achievements count for absolutely nothing with me."[34] He preferred Siegfried the rebel to Parsifal the saint, and could not forgive Wagner for coming to see in Christianity a moral value and beauty far outweighing its theological defects. In *The Case of Wagner* he lays about him with neurotic fury:

> Wagner flatters every nihilistic Buddhistic instinct, and disguises it in music; he flatters every kind of Christianity and every religious form and expression of decadence. . . . Richard Wagner, . . . a decrepit and desperate romantic, collapsed suddenly before the Holy Cross. Was there no German then with eyes to see, with pity in his conscience to bewail, this horrible spectacle? Am I then the only one he caused to suffer? . . . And yet I was one of the most corrupt Wagnerians. . . . Well, I am the child of this age, just like Wagner,—i. e., a decadent; but I am conscious of it; I defended myself against it.[35]

Nietzsche was more "Apollonian" than he supposed: a lover of the subtle and delicate and refined, not of wild Dionysian vigor, nor of the tenderness of wine and song and love. "Your brother, with his air of delicate distinction, is a most uncomfortable fellow," said Wagner to Frau Förster-Nietzsche; ". . . sometimes he is quite embarrassed at my jokes—and then I crack them more madly than ever."[36] There was so

[31] *The Wagner-Nietzsche Correspondence,* p. 279.
[32] In Halévy, p. 191.
[33] *Correspondence,* p. 310.
[34] *Ibid.,* p. 295.
[35] C. W., pp. 46, 27, 9, 2; cf. Faguet, p. 21.
[36] Quoted in Ellis, *Affirmations,* London, 1898; p. 27.

much of Plato in Nietzsche; he feared that art would unteach men to be hard;[37] being tender-minded, he supposed that all the world was like himself,—dangerously near to practising Christianity. There had not been wars enough to suit this gentle professor. And yet, in his quiet hours, he knew that Wagner was as right as Nietzsche, that Parsifal's gentleness was as necessary as Siegfried's strength, and that in some cosmic way these cruel oppositions merged into wholesome creative unities. He liked to think of this "stellar friendship"[38] that still bound him, silently, to the man who had been the most valuable and fruitful experience of his life. And when, in a lucid moment of his final insanity, he saw a picture of the long-dead Wagner, he said softly, "Him I loved much."

IV. THE SONG OF ZARATHUSTRA

And now from art, which seemed to have failed him, he took refuge in science—whose cold Apollonian air cleansed his soul after the Dionysian heat and riot of Tribschen and Bayreuth—and in philosophy, which "offers an asylum where no tyranny can penetrate."[39] Like Spinoza, he tried to calm his passions by examining them; we need, he said, "a chemistry of the emotions." And so, in his next book, *Human All Too Human* (1878-80), he became psychologist, and analyzed with a surgeon's ruthlessness the tenderest feelings and the most cherished beliefs,—dedicating it all bravely, in the midst of reaction, to the scandalous Voltaire. He sent the volumes to Wagner, and received in return the book of *Parsifal*. They never communicated again.

And then, at the very prime of life, in 1879, he broke down, physically and mentally, and sank into the vicinity of death. He prepared for the end defiantly: "Promise me," he said to his sister, "that when I die only my friends shall stand about my coffin, and no inquisitive crowd. See that no priest or anyone else utter falsehoods at my graveside, when I can no longer protect myself; and let me descend into my tomb as an honest pagan."[40] But he recovered, and this heroic funeral had to be postponed. Out of such illness came his love of health and the sun, of life and laughter and dance, and *Carmen's* "music of the south"; out of it too came a stronger will, born of fighting death, a "Yea-saying" that felt life's sweetness even in its bitterness and pain; and out of it perhaps a pitiful effort to rise to Spinoza's cheerful acceptance of natural limitations and human destiny. "My formula for greatness is *Amor fati:* . . . not only to bear up under every necessity, but to love it." Alas, it is more easily said than done.

[37]Cf. Z., pp. 258–264, and 364–374, which refer to Wagner.
[38]Cf. *Correspondence*, p. 311.
[39]T. O. S., ii, 122.
[40]*The Lonely Nietzsche*, p. 65.

The titles of his next books—*The Dawn of Day* (1881) and *The Joyful Wisdom* (1882)—reflect a grateful convalescence; here is a kindlier tone and a gentler tongue than in the later books. Now he had a year of quiet days, living modestly on the pension his university had given him. The proud philosopher could even thaw into a pretty frailty, and find himself suddenly in love. But Lou Salomé did not return his love; his eyes were too sharp and deep for comfort. Paul Rée was less dangerous, and played Dr. Pagello to Nietzsche's de Musset. Nietzsche fled in despair, composing aphorisms against women as he went. In truth he was naïve, enthusiastic, romantic, tender to simplicity; his war against tenderness was an attempt to exorcise a virtue which had led to a bitter deception and to a wound that never healed.

He could not find solitude enough now: "it is difficult to live with men, because silence is difficult."[41] He passed from Italy to the heights of the Alps at Sils-Maria in the Upper Engadine,—loving not man nor woman neither, and praying that Man might be surpassed. And there on the lonely heights came the inspiration of his greatest book.

> *I sat there waiting—waiting for nothing,*
> *Enjoying, beyond good and evil, now*
> *The light, now the shade; there was only*
> *The day, the lake, the noon, time without end.*
> *Then, my friend, suddenly one became two,*
> *And Zarathustra passed by me.*[42]

Now his "soul rose and overflowed all its margins."[43] He had found a new teacher—Zoroaster; a new god—the Superman; and a new religion —eternal recurrence: he must sing now—philosophy mounted into poetry under the ardor of his inspiration. "I could sing a song, and *will* sing it, although I am alone in an empty house and must sing it into mine own ears."[44] (What loneliness is in that phrase!) "Thou great star!—what would be thy happiness, were it not for those for whom thou shinest? . . . Lo! I am weary of my wisdom, like the bee that hath collected too much honey; I need hands reaching out for it."[45] So he wrote *Thus Spake Zarathustra* (1883) and finished it in that "hallowed hour when Richard Wagner gave up the ghost in Venice."[46] It was his magnificent answer to *Parsifal;* but the maker of *Parsifal* was dead.

It was his masterpiece, and he knew it. "This work stands alone," he wrote of it later. "Do not let us mention the poets in the same breath; nothing perhaps had ever been produced out of such a superabundance of strength. . . . If all the spirit and goodness of every great soul were collected together, the whole could not create a single one of Zarathustra's discourses."[47] A slight exaggeration!—but assuredly it is one of the great

41 Z., 212.   43 In Halévy, 234.   43 Z., 315.   44 Z., 279.
45 Z., 1.   46 E. H., 97.   47 E. H., 106.

books of the nineteenth century. Yet Nietzsche had a bitter time getting
it into print; the first part was delayed because the publisher's presses
were busy with an order for 500,000 *hymn-books,* and then by a stream of
anti-Semitic pamphlets;[48] and the publisher refused to print the last part
at all, as quite worthless from the point of view of shekels; so that the
author had to pay for its publication himself. Forty copies of the book
were sold; seven were given away; one acknowledged it; no one praised
it. Never was a man so much alone.

Zarathustra, aged thirty, comes down from his meditative mountain to
preach to the crowd, like his Persian prototype Zoroaster; but the crowd
turns from him to see a rope-walker perform. The rope-walker falls, and
dies. Zarathustra takes him upon his shoulders and carries him away;
"because thou hast made danger thy calling, therefore shall I bury thee
with my own hands." "Live dangerously," he preaches. "Erect your cities
beside Vesuvius. Send out your ships to unexplored seas. Live in a state
of war."

And remember to disbelieve. Zarathustra, coming down from the
mountain, meets an old hermit who talks to him about God. But when
Zarathustra was alone, he spake thus with his heart: "Can it actually be
possible? This old saint in his forest hath not yet heard aught of God
being dead!"[49] But of course God was dead, all the Gods were dead.

> For the old Gods came to an end long ago. And verily it was a good and
> joyful end of Gods!
> They did not die lingering in the twilight,—although that lie is told![50]
> On the contrary, they once upon a time—laughed themselves unto death!
> That came to pass when, by a God himself, the most ungodly word was
> uttered, the word: "there is but one God! Thou shalt have no other gods
> before me."
> An old grim beard of a God, a jealous one, forgot himself thus.
> And then all Gods laughed and shook on their chairs and cried: "Is god-
> liness not just that there are Gods, but no God?"
> Whoever hath ears let him hear.
> Thus spake Zarathustra.[51]

What hilarious atheism! "Is not just this godliness, that there are *no*
gods?" "What could be created if there were Gods? . . . If there were
Gods, how could I bear to be no God? *Consequently* there are no Gods."[52]
"Who is more ungodly than I, that I may enjoy his teachings?"[53] "I conjure you, my brethren, remain faithful to earth, and do not believe those
who speak unto you of superterrestrial hopes! Poisoners they are, whether
they know it or not."[54] Many an erstwhile rebel returns to this sweet
poison at last, as a necessary anesthesia for life. The "higher men" gather

[48]Halévy, 261. [49]Z., 4. [50]A hit at Wagner's *Götterdämmerung.*
[51]Z., 263. [52]Z., 116-8. [53]Z., 245. [54]Z., 5.

in Zarathustra's cave to prepare themselves to preach his doctrine; he leaves them for a while, and returns to find them offering incense to a donkey who has "created the world in his own image—i. e., as stupid as possible."[55] This is not edifying; but then, says our text:

> He who must be a creator in good and evil—verily, he must first be a destroyer, and break values into pieces.
>
> Thus the highest evil is part of the highest goodness. But that is creative goodness.
>
> Let us speak thereon, ye wisest men, however bad it be. To be silent is worse; all unuttered truths become poisonous.
>
> And whatever will break on our truths, let it break! Many a house hath yet to be built.
>
> Thus spake Zarathustra.[56]

Is this irreverent? But Zarathustra complains that "nobody knoweth any longer how to revere,"[57] and he calls himself "the most pious of all those who believe not in God."[58] He longs for belief, and pities "all who, like myself, suffer from the great loathing, for whom the old God died and no new God yet lieth in cradles and napkins."[59] And then he pronounces the name of the new God:

> Dead are all Gods; now we will that superman live. . . .
>
> I teach you superman. Man is a something that shall be surpassed. What have ye done to surpass him? . . .
>
> What is great in man is that he is a bridge and not a goal: what can be loved in man is that he is a *transition* and a *destruction*.
>
> I love those who do not know how to live except in perishing, for they are those going beyond.
>
> I love the great despisers because they are the great adorers, they are arrows of longing for the other shore.
>
> I love those who do not seek beyond the stars for a reason to perish and be sacrificed, but who sacrifice themselves to earth in order that earth may some day become superman's. . . .
>
> It is time for man to mark his goal. It is time for man to plant the germ of his highest hope. . . .
>
> Tell me, my brethren, if the goal be lacking to humanity, is not humanity itself lacking? . . .
>
> Love unto the most remote man is higher than love unto your neighbor.[60]

Nietzsche appears to foresee that every reader will think himself the superman; and tries to guard against this by confessing that the superman is not yet born; we can only be his fore-runners and his soil. "Will nothing beyond your capacity. . . . Be not virtuous beyond your ability; and demand nothing of yourselves contrary to probability."[61] Not for us is the happiness which only the superman will know; our best goal is work.

[55]Z., 457.   [56]Z., 162.   [57]Z., 354.   [58]Z., 376.
[59]Z., 434.   [60]Z., 108 (and 419), 5, 8, 11. 79, 80.   [61]Z., 423-6.

"For a long time I ceased not to strive for my happiness; now I strive for my work."[62]

Nietzsche is not content with having created God in his own image; he must make himself immortal. After the superman comes Eternal Recurrence. All things will return, in precise detail, and an infinite number of times; even Nietzsche will return, and this Germany of blood and iron and sack-cloth and ashes, and all the travail of the human mind from ignorance to Zarathustra. It is a terrible doctrine, the last and most courageous form of Yea-saying and the acceptance of life; and yet how could it not be? The possible combinations of reality are limited, and time is endless; some day, inevitably, life and matter will fall into just such a form as they once had, and out of that fatal repetition all history must unwind its devious course again. To such a pass determinism brings us. No wonder Zarathustra feared to speak this his last lesson; feared and trembled and held back, until a voice spoke to him: "What matter about thyself, Zarathustra? Say thy word and break in pieces!"[63]

V. HERO–MORALITY

Zarathustra became for Nietzsche a Gospel whereon his later books were merely commentaries. If Europe would not appreciate his poetry perhaps it would understand his prose. After the song of the prophet, the logic of the philosopher; what though the philosopher himself should disbelieve in logic?—it is a tool of clarity, if not the seal of proof.

He was more than ever alone now, for Zarathustra had seemed a little queer even to Nietzsche's friends. Scholars like Overbeck and Burckhardt, who had been his colleagues at Basle, and had admired The Birth of Tragedy, mourned the loss of a brilliant philologist, and could not celebrate the birth of a poet. His sister (who had almost justified his view that for a philosopher a sister is an admirable substitute for a wife) left him suddenly, to marry one of those anti-Semites whom Nietzsche despised, and went off to Paraguay to found a communistic colony. She asked her pale, frail brother to come along, for the sake of his health; but Nietzsche valued the life of the mind more than the health of the body; he wished to stay where the battle was; Europe was necessary to him "as a culture museum."[64] He lived irregularly in place and time; he tried Switzerland and Venice and Genoa and Nice and Turin. He liked to write amid the doves that flock about the lions of St. Mark—"this Piazza San Marco is my finest work-room." But he had to follow Hamlet's advice about staying out of the sun, which hurt his ailing eyes; he shut himself up in dingy, heatless attics, and worked behind closed blinds. Because of his failing eyes he wrote henceforth no books, but only aphorisms.

[62]Z., 341.   [63]Z., 210.
[64]In Figgis, The Will to Freedom, New York, 1917; p. 249.

He gathered some of these fragments together under the titles *Beyond Good and Evil* (1886) and *The Genealogy of Morals* (1887); he hoped, in these volumes, to destroy the old morality, and prepare the way for the morality of the superman. For a moment he became the philologist again, and sought to enforce his new ethic with etymologies that are not quite beyond reproach. He observes that the German language contains two words for *bad: schlecht* and *böse. Schlecht* was applied by the upper to the lower classes, and meant ordinary, common; later it came to mean vulgar, worthless, bad. *Böse* was applied by the lower to the upper classes, and meant unfamiliar, irregular, incalculable, dangerous, harmful, cruel; Napoleon was *böse.* Many simple peoples feared the exceptional individual as a disintegrating force; there is a Chinese proverb that "the great man is a public misfortune. Likewise, *gut* had two meanings, as opposite to *schlecht* and *böse:* as used by the aristocracy it meant strong, brave, powerful, warlike, godlike (*gut* from *Gott*); as used by the people it meant familiar, peaceful, harmless, kind.

Here then were two contradictory valuations of human behavior, two ethical standpoints and criteria: a *Herren-moral* and a *Heerden-moral*— a morality of masters and a morality of the herd. The former was the accepted standard in classical antiquity, especially among the Romans; even for the ordinary Roman, virtue was *virtus*—manhood, courage, enterprise, bravery. But from Asia, and especially from the Jews in the days of their political subjection, came the other standard; subjection breeds humility, helplessness breeds altruism—which is an appeal for help. Under this herd-morality love of danger and power gave way to love of security and peace; strength was replaced by cunning, open by secret revenge, sternness by pity, initiative by imitation, the pride of honor by the whip of conscience. Honor is pagan, Roman, feudal, aristocratic; conscience is Jewish, Christian, bourgeois, democratic.[65] It was the eloquence of the prophets, from Amos to Jesus, that made the view of a subject class an almost universal ethic; the "world" and the "flesh" became synonyms of evil, and poverty a proof of virtue.[66]

This valuation was brought to a peak by Jesus: with him every man was of equal worth, and had equal rights; out of his doctrine came democracy, utilitarianism, socialism; progress was now defined in terms of these plebeian philosophies, in terms of progressive equalization and vulgarization, in terms of decadence and descending life.[67] The final stage in this decay is the exaltation of pity and self-sacrifice, the sentimental comforting of criminals, "the inability of a society to excrete." Sympathy is legitimate if it is active; but pity is a paralyzing mental luxury, a waste of feeling for the irremediably botched, the incompetent, the defective, the vicious, the culpably diseased and the irrevocably criminal. There is

[65]Cf. Taine, *The French Revolution,* New York, 1885; vol. iii, p. 94.
[66]B. G. E., 117. [67]*Ibid.,* 121-3.

a certain indelicacy and intrusiveness in pity; "visiting the sick" is an orgasm of superiority in the contemplation of our neighbor's helplessness."[68]

Behind all this "morality" is a secret will to power. Love itself is only a desire for possession; courtship is combat and mating is mastery: Don José kills Carmen to prevent her from becoming the *property* of another. "People imagine that they are unselfish in love because they seek the advantage of another being, often in opposition to their own. But for so doing they want to *possess* the other being. . . . *L'amour est de tous les sentiments le plus égoiste, et, par conséquent, lorsqu'il est blessé, le moins généreux.*"[69] Even in the love of truth is the desire to possess it, perhaps to be its first possessor, to find it virginal. Humility is the protective coloration of the will to power.

Against this passion for power, reason and morality are helpless; they are but weapons in its hands, dupes of its game. "Philosophical systems are shining mirages"; what we see is not the long-sought truth, but the reflection of our own desires. "The philosophers all pose as though their real opinions had been discovered through the self-evolving of a cold, pure, divinely indifferent dialectic; . . . whereas in fact a prejudicial proposition, idea or 'suggestion,' which is generally their heart's desire abstracted and refined, is defended by them with arguments sought out after the event."

It is these underground desires, these pulsations of the will to power, that determine our thoughts. "The greater part of our intellectual activity goes on unconsciously, and unfelt by us; . . . conscious thinking . . . is the weakest." Because instinct is the direct operation of the will to power, undisturbed by consciousness, "instinct is the most intelligent of all kinds of intelligence which have hitherto been discovered." Indeed, the rôle of consciousness has been senselessly over-estimated; "consciousness may be regarded as secondary, almost as indifferent and superfluous, probably destined to disappear and to be superseded by perfect automatism."[70]

In strong men there is very little attempt to conceal desire under the cover of reason; their simple argument is, "I will." In the uncorrupted vigor of the master soul, desire is its own justification; and conscience,

---

[68]D. D., 232.

[69]C. W., 9, quoting Benjamin Constant: "Love is of all feelings the most egoistic; and in consequence it is, when crossed, the least generous." But Nietzsche can speak more gently of love. "Whence arises the sudden passion of a man for a woman? . . . Least of all from sensuality only: but when a man finds weakness, need of help, and high spirits, all united in the same creature, he suffers a sort of over-flowing of soul, and is touched and offended at the same moment. At this point arises the source of great love" (H. A. H., ii, 287). And he quotes from the French "the chastest utterance I ever heard: *Dans le veritable amour c'est l'âme qui enveloppe le corps*"—"in true love it is the soul that embraces the body."

[70]H. A. H., ii, 26; B. G. E., 9; J. W., 258; B. G. E., 162; W. P., ii, 38.

pity or remorse can find no entrance. But so far has the Judaeo-Christian-democratic point-of-view prevailed in modern times, that even the strong are now ashamed of their strength and their health, and begin to seek "reasons." The aristocratic virtues and valuations are dying out. "Europe is threatened with a new Buddhism"; even Schopenhauer and Wagner become pity-ful Buddhists. "The whole of the morality of Europe is based upon the values which are useful to the herd." The strong are no longer permitted to exercise their strength; they must become as far as possible like the weak; "goodness is to do nothing for which we are not strong enough." Has not Kant, that "great Chinaman of Königsberg," proved that men must never be used as means? Consequently the instincts of the strong—to hunt, to fight, to conquer and to rule—are introverted into self-laceration for lack of outlet; they beget asceticism and the "bad conscience"; "all instincts which do not find a vent turn inward—this is what I mean by the growing 'internalization' of man: here we have the first form of what came to be called the *soul*."[71]

The formula for decay is that the virtues proper to the herd infect the leaders, and break them into common clay. "Moral systems must be compelled first of all to bow before the *gradations of rank;* their presumption must be driven home to their conscience—until they thoroughly understand at last that it is *immoral* to say that 'what is right for one is proper for another.'" Different functions require different qualities; and the "evil" virtues of the strong are as necessary in a society as the "good" virtues of the weak. Severity, violence, danger, war, are as valuable as kindliness and peace; great individuals appear only in times of danger and violence and merciless necessity. The best thing in man is strength of will, power and permanence of passion; without passion one is mere milk, incapable of deeds. Greed, envy, even hatred, are indispensable items in the process of struggle, selection and survival. Evil is to good as variation to heredity, as innovation and experiment to custom; there is no development without an almost-criminal violation of precedents and "order." If evil were not good it would have disappeared. We must beware of being too good; "man must become better and more evil."[72]

Nietzsche is consoled to find so much evil and cruelty in the world; he takes a sadistic pleasure in reflecting on the extent to which, he thinks, "cruelty constituted the great joy and delight of ancient man"; and he believes that our pleasure in the tragic drama, or in anything sublime, is a refined and vicarious cruelty. "Man is the cruelest animal," says Zara-

[71] B. G. E., 128, 14, 177; W. P., i, 228; G. M., 46, 100. The student of psychology may be interested to follow up psychoanalytic sources in H. A. H., i, 23–27 and D. D., 125–131 (theory of dreams); H. A. H., i, 215 (Adler's theory of the neurotic constitution); and D. D., 293 ("overcorrection"). Those who are interested in pragmatism will find a fairly complete anticipation of it in B. G. E., 9, 50, 53; and W. P., ii, 20, 24, 26, 50.

[72] B. G. E., 165 (quoting John Stuart Mill), 59; W. P., i, 308; Z., 421.

thustra. "When gazing at tragedies, bull-fights and crucifixions he hath
hitherto felt happier than at any other time on earth. And when he invented hell . . . lo, hell was his heaven on earth"; he could put up with
suffering now, by contemplating the eternal punishment of his oppressors
in the other world.[73]

The ultimate ethic is biological; we must judge things according to
their value for life; we need a physiological "transvaluation of all values."
The real test of a man, or a group, or a species, is energy, capacity, power.
We may be partly reconciled to the nineteenth century—otherwise so
destructive of all the higher virtues—by its emphasis on the physical. The
soul is a function of an organism. One drop of blood too much or too
little in the brain may make a man suffer more than Prometheus suffered
from the vulture. Varying foods have varying mental effects: rice makes
for Buddhism, and German metaphysics is the result of beer. A philosophy therefore is true or false according as it is the expression and exaltation of ascending or of descending life. The decadent says, "Life is worth
nothing"; let him rather say, "*I* am worth nothing." Why should life be
worth living when all the heroic values in it have been permitted to decay,
and democracy—that is, disbelief in all great men—ruins, with every
decade, another people?

> The gregarious European man nowadays assumes an air as if he were the
> only kind of man that is allowable; he glorifies his qualities, such as public
> spirit, kindness, deference, industry, temperance, modesty, indulgence, sym-
> pathy,—by virtue of which he is gentle, endurable, and useful to the herd,—
> as the peculiarly human virtues. In cases, however, where it is believed that
> the leader and bell-wether cannot be dispensed with, attempt after attempt is
> made nowadays to replace commanders by the summoning together of clever
> gregarious men; all representative constitutions, for example, are of this
> origin. In spite of all, what a blessing, what a deliverance from a weight be-
> coming unendurable, is the appearance of an absolute ruler for these gregari-
> ous Europeans—of this fact the effect of the appearance of Napoleon was
> the last great proof; the history of the influence of Napoleon is almost the
> history of the higher happiness to which the entire century has attained in its
> worthiest individuals and periods.[74]

VI. THE SUPERMAN

Just as morality lies not in kindness but in strength, so the goal of
human effort should be not the elevation of all but the development of
finer and stronger individuals. "Not mankind, but superman is the goal."
The very last thing a sensible man would undertake would be to improve
mankind: mankind does not improve, it does not even exist—it is an
abstraction; all that exists is a vast ant-hill of individuals. The aspect of

[73]G. M., 73; B. G. E., 177; Z., 317.   [74]D. D., 84; Ellis, 50; B. G. E., 121.

the whole is much more like that of a huge experimental work-shop where some things in every age succeed, while most things fail; and the aim of all the experiments is not the happiness of the mass but the improvement of the type. Better that societies should come to an end than that no higher type should appear. Society is an instrument for the enhancement of the power and personality of the individual; the group is not an end in itself. "To what purpose then are the machines, if all individuals are only of use in maintaining them? Machines"—or social organizations—"that are ends in themselves—is that the *umana commedia?*"[75]

At first Nietzsche spoke as if his hope were for the production of a new species;[76] later he came to think of his superman as the superior individual rising precariously out of the mire of mass mediocrity, and owing his existence more to deliberate breeding and careful nurture than to the hazards of natural selection. For the biological process is biased against the exceptional individual; nature is most cruel to her finest products; she loves rather, and protects, the average and the mediocre; there is in nature a perpetual reversion to type, to the level of the mass,—a recurrent mastery of the best by the most.[77] The superman can survive only by human selection, by eugenic foresight and an ennobling education.

How absurd it is, after all, to let higher individuals marry for love— heroes with servant girls, and geniuses with seamstresses! Schopenhauer was wrong; love is not eugenic; when a man is in love he should not be permitted to make decisions affecting his entire life; it is not given to man to love and be wise. We should declare invalid the vows of lovers, and should make love a legal impediment to marriage. The best should marry only the best; love should be left to the rabble. The purpose of marriage is not merely reproduction, it should also be development.

> Thou art young, and wishest for child and marriage. But I ask thee, art thou a man who dareth to wish for a child? Art thou the victorious one, the self-subduer, the commander of thy senses, the master of thy virtues?—or in thy wish doth there speak the animal, or necessity? Or solitude? Or discord with thyself? I would that thy victory and freedom were longing for a child. Thou shalt build living monuments unto thy victory and thy liberation. Thou shalt build beyond thyself. But first thou must build thyself square in body and soul. Thou shalt not only propagate thyself, but propagate thyself upward! Marriage: thus I call the will of two to create that one which is more than they who created it. I call marriage reverence unto each other as unto those who will such a will.[78]

Without good birth, nobility is impossible. "Intellect alone does not ennoble; on the contrary, something is always needed to ennoble intellect. What then is needed? Blood . . . (I do not refer here to the prefix

---

[75] W. P., ii, 387, 135; H. A. H., i, 375.
[76] Cf. Z., 104. [77] W. P., ii, 158. [78] Z., 94.

'Lords,' or the 'Almanac de Gotha': this is a parenthesis for donkeys)."
But given good birth and eugenic breeding, the next factor in the formula
of the superman is a severe school; where perfection will be exacted as a
matter of course, not even meriting praise; where there will be few
comforts and many responsibilities; where the body will be taught to
suffer in silence, and the will may learn to obey and to command. No
libertarian nonsense!—no weakening of the physical and moral spine by
indulgence and "freedom"! And yet a school where one will learn to
laugh heartily; philosophers should be graded according to their capacity
for laughter; "he who strideth across the highest mountains laugheth at
all tragedies." And there will be no moralic acid in this education of the
superman; an asceticism of the will, but no condemnation of the flesh.
"Cease not to dance, ye sweet girls! No spoil-sport hath come unto you
with an evil eye, . . . no enemy of girls with beautiful ankles."⁷⁹ Even
a superman may have a taste for beautiful ankles.

A man so born and bred would be beyond good and evil; he would not
hesitate to be *böse* if his purpose should require it; he would be fearless
rather than good. "What is good? . . . To be brave is good." "What is
good? All that increases the feeling of power, the will to power, power
itself, in man. What is bad (*schlecht*)? All that comes from weakness."
Perhaps the dominant mark of the superman will be love of danger and
strife, provided they have a purpose; he will not seek safety first; he will
leave happiness to the greatest number. "Zarathustra was fond of all such
as makes distant voyages, and like not to live without danger."⁸⁰ Hence
all war is good, despite the vulgar pettiness of its causes in modern times;
"a good war halloweth any cause." Even revolution is good: not in itself,
for nothing could be more unfortunate than the supremacy of the masses;
but because times of strife bring out the latent greatness of individuals
who before had insufficient stimulus or opportunity; out of such chaos
comes the dancing star; out of the turmoil and nonsense of the French
Revolution, Napoleon; out of the violence and disorder of the Renaissance such powerful individualities, and in such abundance, as Europe
has hardly known since, and could no longer bear.

Energy, intellect, and pride,—these make the superman. But they
must be harmonized: the passions will become powers only when they
are selected and unified by some great purpose which moulds a chaos
of desires into the power of a personality. "Woe to the thinker who is
not the gardener but the soil of his plants!" Who is it that follows his
impulses? The weakling: he lacks the power to inhibit; he is not strong
enough to say No; he is a discord, a decadent. To discipline one's self—
that is the highest thing. "The man who does not wish to be merely one
of the mass only needs to cease to be easy on himself." To have a purpose

⁷⁹W. P., ii, 353; B. G. E., 260; Z., 49, 149.
⁸⁰Z., 60, 222; *Antichrist*, 128; W. P., ii, 257.

for which one can be hard upon others, but above all upon one's self; to have a purpose for which one will do almost anything *except betray a friend,*—that is the final patent of nobility, the last formula of the super-man.[81]

Only by seeing such a man as the goal and reward of our labors can we love life and live upward. "We must have an aim for whose sake we are all dear to one another."[82] Let us be great, or servants and instruments to the great; what a fine sight it was when millions of Europeans offered themselves as means to the ends of Bonaparte, and died for him gladly, singing his name as they fell! Perhaps those of us who understand can become the prophets of him whom we cannot be, and can straighten the way for his coming; we, indifferent of lands, indifferent of times, can work together, however separated, for this end. Zarathustra will sing, even in his suffering, if he can but hear the voices of these hidden helpers, these lovers of the higher man. "Ye lonely ones of to-day, ye who stand apart, ye shall one day be a people; from you who have chosen yourselves, a chosen people shall arise; and from it the superman."[83]

VII. DECADENCE

Consequently, the road to the superman must lie through aristocracy. Democracy—"this mania for counting noses"—must be eradicated before it is too late. The first step here is the destruction of Christianity so far as all higher men are concerned. The triumph of Christ was the beginning of democracy; "the first Christian was in his deepest instincts a rebel against everything privileged; he lived and struggled unremittingly for 'equal rights' "; in modern times he would have been sent to Siberia. "He that is greatest among you, let him be your servant"—this is the inversion of all political wisdom, of all sanity; indeed, as one reads the Gospel one feels the atmosphere of a Russian novel; they are a sort of plagiarism from Dostoievski. Only among the lowly could such notions take root; and only in an age whose rulers had degenerated and ceased to rule. "When Nero and Caracalla sat on the throne, the paradox arose that the lowest man was worth more than the man on top."[84]

As the conquest of Europe by Christianity was the end of ancient aristocracy, so the overrunning of Europe by Teutonic warrior barons brought a renewal of the old masculine virtues, and planted the roots of the modern aristocracies. These men were not burdened with "morals": they "were free from every social restraint; in the innocence of their wild-beast conscience they returned as exultant monsters from a horrible train

---

[81]D. D., 295, 194-7; T. I., 57; W. P., ii, 221-2, 369, 400; "Schopenhauer as Educator," sect. 1.

[82]Quoted in Salter, 446.   [83]Z., 107.

[84]*Antichrist*, 195; Ellis, 49-50; W. P., ii, 313.

of murder, incendiarism, rapine, torture, with an arrogance and compromise as if nothing but a student's freak had been perpetrated." It was
such men who supplied the ruling classes for Germany, Scandinavia,
France, England, Italy, and Russia.

A herd of blond beasts of prey, a race of conquerors and masters, with
military organization, with the power to organize, unscrupulously placing
their fearful paws upon a population perhaps vastly superior in numbers,
. . . this herd founded the State. The dream is dispelled which made
the State begin with a contract. What has he to do with contracts who can
command, who is master by nature, who comes on the scene with violence in
deed and demeanour?[85]

This splendid ruling stock was corrupted, first by the Catholic lauda-
tion of feminine virtues, secondly by the Puritan and plebeian ideals of
the Reformation, and thirdly by inter-marriage with inferior stock. Just
as Catholicism was mellowing into the aristocratic and unmoral culture
of the Renaissance, the Reformation crushed it with a revival of Judaic
rigor and solemnity. "Does anybody at last understand, *will* anybody
understand what the Renaissance was? *The transvaluation of Christian
values,* the attempt undertaken with all means, all instincts and all genius
to make the *opposite* values, the *noble* values triumph . . . I see before
me a possibility perfectly magical in its charm and glorious coloring. . . .
Cæsar Borgia as Pope. . . . Do you understand me?"[86]

Protestantism and beer have dulled German wit; add, now, Wagnerian
opera. As a result, "the present-day Prussian is one of the most dangerous
enemies of culture." "The presence of a German retards my digestion."
"If, as Gibbon says, nothing but time—though a long time—is required
for a world to perish; so nothing but time—though still more time—is
required for a false idea to be destroyed in Germany." When Germany
defeated Napoleon it was as disastrous to culture as when Luther defeated
the Church; thenceforward Germany put away her Goethes, her Schopen-
hauers and her Beethovens, and began to worship "patriots"; *"Deutsch-
land über Alles*—I fear that was the end of German philosophy."[87] Yet
there is a natural seriousness and depth in the Germans that gives ground
for the hope that they may yet redeem Europe; they have more of the
masculine virtues than the French or the English; they have perseverance,
patience, industry—hence their scholarship, their science, and their military discipline; it is delightful to see how all Europe is worried about the
German army. If the German power of organization could coöperate with
the potential resources of Russia, in materials and in men, then would
come the age of great politics. "We require an intergrowth of the German
and Slav races; and we require, too, the cleverest financiers, the Jews,
that we may become the masters of the world. . . . We require an un-

conditional union with Russia." The alternative was encirclement and strangulation.

The trouble with Germany is a certain stolidity of mind which pays for this solidity of character; Germany misses the long traditions of culture which have made the French the most refined and subtle of all the peoples of Europe. "I believe only in French culture, and I regard everything else in Europe which calls itself culture as a misunderstanding." "When one reads Montaigne, La Rochefoucauld, . . . Vauvenargues, and Chamfort, one is nearer to antiquity than with any group of authors in any other nation." Voltaire is "a grand seigneur of the mind"; and Taine is "the first of living historians." Even the later French writers Flaubert, Bourget, Anatole France, etc.—are infinitely beyond other Europeans in clarity of thought and language—"what clearness and delicate precision in these Frenchmen!" European nobility of taste, feeling and manners is the work of France. But of the old France, of the sixteenth and seventeenth centuries; the Revolution, by destroying the aristocracy, destroyed the vehicle and nursery of culture, and now the French soul is thin and pale in comparison with what it used to be. Nevertheless it has still some fine qualities; "in France almost all psychological and artistic questions are considered with incomparably more subtlety and thoroughness than they are in Germany. . . . At the very moment when Germany arose as a great power in the world of politics, France won new importance in the world of culture."[88]

Russia is the blond beast of Europe. Its people have a "stubborn and resigned fatalism which gives them even nowadays the advantage over us Westerners." Russia has a strong government, without "parliamentary imbecility." Force of will has long been accumulating there, and now threatens to find release; it would not be surprising to find Russia becoming master of Europe. "A thinker who has at heart the future of Europe will in all his perspectives concerning the future calculate upon the Jews and the Russians as above all the surest and the likeliest factors in the great play and battle of forces." But all in all it is the Italians who are the finest and most vigorous of existing peoples; the man-plant grows strongest in Italy, as Alfieri boasted. There is a manly bearing, an aristocratic pride in even the lowliest Italian; "a poor Venetian gondolier is always a better figure than a Berlin Geheimrath, and in the end, indeed, a better man."[89]

Worst of all are the English; it is they who corrupted the French mind with the democratic delusion; "shop-keepers, Christians, cows, women, Englishmen, and other democrats belong together." English utilitarianism and philistinism are the nadir of European culture. Only in a land of cut-throat competition could anyone conceive of life as a struggle for mere

[88]Salter, 464-7; E. H., 37, 83; B. G. E., 213-6; T. I., 54; Faguet, 10-11.
[89]G. M., 98; B. G. E., 146, 208; Salter, 469.

existence. Only in a land where shop-keepers and ship-keepers had multiplied to such a number as to overcome the aristocracy could democracy be fabricated; this is the gift, the Greek gift, which England has given the modern world. Who will rescue Europe from England, and England from democracy?

VIII. ARISTOCRACY

Democracy means drift; it means permission given to each part of an organism to do just what it pleases; it means the lapse of coherence and interdependence, the enthronement of liberty and chaos. It means the worship of mediocrity, and the hatred of excellence. It means the impossibility of great men—how could great men submit to the indignities and indecencies of an election? What chance would they have? "What is hated by the people, as a wolf by the dogs, is the free spirit, the enemy of all fetters, the not-adorer," the man who is not a "regular party-member." How can the superman arise in such a soil? And how can a nation become great when its greatest men lie unused, discouraged, perhaps unknown? Such a society loses character; imitation is horizontal instead of vertical—not the superior man but the majority man becomes the ideal and the model; everybody comes to resemble everybody else; even the sexes approximate—the men become women and the women become men.[90]

Feminism, then, is the natural corollary of democracy and Christianity. "Here is little of man; therefore women try to make themselves manly. For only he who is enough of a man will save the woman in woman." Ibsen, "that typical old maid," created the "emancipated woman." "Woman was created out of man's rib?—'wonderful is the poverty of my ribs!' says man." Woman has lost power and prestige by her "emancipation"; where have women now the position they enjoyed under the Bourbons? Equality between man and woman is impossible, because war between them is eternal; there is here no peace without victory—peace comes only when one or the other is acknowledged master. It is dangerous to try equality with a woman; she will not be content with that; she will be rather content with subordination if the man is a man. Above all, her perfection and happiness lie in motherhood. "Everything in woman is a riddle, and everything in woman hath one answer: its name is child-bearing." "Man is for woman a means; the end is always the child. But what is woman for man? . . . A dangerous toy." "Man shall be educated for war, and woman for the recreation of the warrior; everything else is folly." Yet "the perfect woman is a higher type of humanity than the perfect man, and also something much rarer. . . . One cannot be gentle enough towards women."[91]

[90] W. P., i, 382-4; ii, 206; Z., 141.   [91] Z., 248, 169; Huneker, *Egoists*, 266.

Part of the tension of marriage lies in its fulfilment of the woman and its narrowing and emptying of the man. When a man woos a woman he offers to give all the world for her; and when she marries him he does; he must forget the world as soon as the child comes; the altruism of love becomes the egoism of the family. Honesty and innovation are luxuries of celibacy. "Where the highest philosophical thinking is concerned, all married men are suspect. . . . It seems to me absurd that one who has chosen for his sphere the assessment of existence as a whole should burden himself with the cares of a family, with winning bread, security, and social position for wife and children." Many a philosopher has died when his child was born. "The wind blew through my key hole, saying, 'Come!' My door cunningly opened of itself, saying, 'Go!' But I lay fettered by my love unto my children."[92]

With feminism come socialism and anarchism; all of them are of the litter of democracy; if equal political power is just, why not equal economic power? Why should there be leaders anywhere? There are socialists who will admire the book of Zarathustra; but their admiration is not wanted. "There are some that preach my doctrine of life but at the same time are preachers of equality. . . . I do not wish to be confounded with these preachers of equality. For within me justice saith, 'Men are not equal.' " "We wish to possess nothing in common." "Ye preachers of equality, the tyrant-insanity of impotence thus crieth out of yourselves for equality." Nature abhors equality, it loves differentiation of individuals and classes and species. Socialism is anti-biological: the process of evolution involves the utilization of the inferior species, race, class, or individual by the superior; all life is exploitation, and subsists ultimately on other life; big fishes catch little fishes and eat them, and that is the whole story. Socialism is envy: "they want something which we have."[93] It is however, an easily managed movement; all that is necessary to control it is to open occasionally the trap-door between masters and slaves and let the readers of discontent come up into paradise. It is not the leaders that must be feared, but those lower down, who think that by a revolution they can escape the subordination which is the natural result of their incompetence and sloth. Yet the slave is noble only when he revolts.

In any case the slave is nobler than his modern masters—the bourgeoisie. It is a sign of the inferiority of nineteenth century culture that the man of money should be the object of so much worship and envy. But these business men too are slaves, puppets of routine, victims of busy-ness; they have no time for new ideas; thinking is taboo among them, and the

[92]*Lonely Nietzsche*, 77, 313; Z., 232.

[93]Z., 137-8; B. G. E., 226; W. P., i, 102 (which predicts a revolution "compared with which the Paris Commune . . . will seem to have been but a slight indigestion"); ii, 208; D. D., 362. Nietzsche, when he wrote these aristocratic passages, was living in a dingy attic on $1000 a year, most of which went into the publication of his books.

joys of the intellect are beyond their reach. Hence their restless and perpetual search for "happiness," their great houses which are never homes,
their vulgar luxury without taste, their picture-galleries of "originals,"
with cost attached, their sensual amusements that dull rather than refresh
or stimulate the mind. "Look at these superfluous! They acquire riches
and become poorer thereby"; they accept all the restraints of aristocracy
without its compensating access to the kingdom of the mind. "See how
they climb, these swift apes! They climb over one another, and thus drag
themselves into the mud and depths. . . . The stench of shop-keepers,
the wriggling of ambition, the evil breath." There is no use in such men
having wealth, for they cannot give it dignity by noble use, by the discriminating patronage of letters or the arts. "Only a man of intellect
should hold property"; others think of property as an end in itself, and
pursue it more and more recklessly,—look at "the present madness of
nations, which desire above all to produce as much as possible, and to be
as rich as possible." At last man becomes a bird of prey: "they live in
ambush for one another; they obtain things from each other by lying in
wait. That is called by them good neighborliness. . . . They seek the
smallest profits out of every sort of rubbish." "To-day, mercantile morality
is really nothing but a refinement on piratical morality—buying in the
cheapest market and selling in the dearest." And these men cry out for
laissez-faire, to be let alone,—these very men who most need supervision
and control. Perhaps even some degree of socialism, dangerous as that is,
would be justified here: "We should take all the branches of transport
and trade which favor the accumulation of large fortunes—especially
therefore the money market—out of the hands of private persons or
private companies, and look upon those who own too much, just as upon
those who own nothing, as types fraught with danger to the community."[94]

Higher than the bourgeois, and lower than the aristocrat, is the soldier.
A general who uses up soldiers on the battlefield, where they have the
pleasure of dying under the anesthesia of glory, is far nobler than the
employer who uses up men in his profit-machine; observe with what
relief men leave their factories for the field of slaughter. Napoleon was
not a butcher but a benefactor; he gave men death with military honors
instead of death by economic attrition; people flocked to his lethal
standard because they preferred the risks of battle to the unbearable
monotony of making another million collar-buttons. "It is to Napoleon
that the honor shall one day be given of having made for a time a world
in which the man, the warrior, outweighed the tradesman and the
Philistine." War is an admirable remedy for peoples that are growing
weak and comfortable and contemptible; it excites instincts that rot away

---

[94] T. O. S., i, 142; H. A. H., i, 360; ii, 147, 340; T. I., 100; Z., 64, 305, 355.

in peace. War and universal military service are the necessary antidotes to democratic effeminacy. "When the instincts of a society ultimately make it give up war and conquest, it is decadent; it is ripe for democracy and the rule of shop-keepers." Yet the causes of modern war are anything but noble; dynastic and religious wars were a little finer than settling trade disputes with guns.[95] "Within fifty years these Babel governments" (the democracies of Europe) "will clash in a gigantic war for the markets of the world."[96] But perhaps out of that madness will come the unification of Europe;—an end for which even a trade-war would not be too great a price to pay. For only out of a unified Europe can come that higher aristocracy by which Europe may be redeemed.

The problem of politics is to prevent the business man from ruling. For such a man has the short sight and narrow grasp of a politician, not the long view and wide range of the born aristocrat trained to statesmanship. The finer man has a divine right to rule—i. e., the right of superior ability. The simple man has his place, but it is not on the throne. In his place the simple man is happy, and his virtues are as necessary to society as those of the leader; "it would be absolutely unworthy a deeper mind to consider mediocrity in itself as an objection." Industriousness, thrift, regularity, moderation, strong conviction,—with such virtues the mediocre man becomes perfect, but perfect only as an instrument. "A high civilization is a pyramid; it can stand only upon a broad base; its prerequisite is a strongly and soundly consolidated mediocrity." Always and everywhere, some will be leaders and some followers; the majority will be compelled, and will be happy, to work under the intellectual direction of higher men.[97]

> Wherever I found living things, there also I heard the speech of obedience. All living things are things that obey. And this is the second: he is commanded who cannot obey his own self. This is the way of living things. But this is the third I heard: to command is more difficult than to obey. And not only that the commander beareth the burden of all who obey, and that this burden easily crusheth him:—an effort and a jeopardy appeared unto me to be contained in all commanding; and whenever living things command they risk themselves.[98]

The ideal society, then, would be divided into three classes: producers (farmers, prolétaires and business men), officials (soldiers and functionaries), and rulers. The latter would rule, but they would not officiate in government; the actual work of government is a menial task. The rulers will be philosopher-statesmen rather than office-holders. Their power

[95] J. W., 77–8; B. G. E., 121; Faguet, 22; H. A. H., ii, 288.
[96] G. M., 255 (this prediction was written in 1887).
[97] *Antichrist*, 219–220.   [98] Z., 159.

will rest on the control of credit and the army; but they themselves will
live more like soldiers than like financiers. They will be Plato's guardians
again; Plato was right—philosophers are the highest men. They will be
men of refinement as well as of courage and strength; scholars and generals in one. They will be united by courtesy and *corps d'esprit:* "These
men are kept rigorously within bounds by morality,[99] veneration, custom,
gratitude, still more by reciprocal surveillance, by jealousy *inter pares;*
and on the other hand, in their attitude towards one another they will be
inventive in consideration, self-command, delicacy, pride, and friendship."[100]

Will this aristocracy be a caste, and their power hereditary? For the
most part yes, with occasional openings to let in new blood. But nothing
can so contaminate and weaken an aristocracy as marrying rich vulgar-
ians, after the habit of the English aristocracy; it was such intermarriage
that ruined the greatest governing body the world has ever seen—the
aristocratic Roman senate. There is no "accident of birth"; every birth
is the verdict of nature upon a marriage; and the perfect man comes
only after generations of selection and preparation; "a man's ancestors
have paid the price of what he is."

Does this offend too much our long democratic ears? But "those races
that cannot bear this philosophy are doomed; and those that regard it as
the greatest blessing are destined to be the masters of the world." Only
such an aristocracy can have the vision and the courage to make Europe
a nation, to end this bovine nationalism, this petty *Vaterlanderei.* Let us
be "good Europeans," as Napoleon was, and Goethe, and Beethoven, and
Schopenhauer, and Stendhal, and Heine. Too long we have been fragments, shattered pieces of what might be a whole. How can a great culture grow in this air of patriotic prejudice and narrowing provincialism?
The time for petty politics is past; the compulsion to great politics has
come. When will the new race appear, and the new leaders? When will
Europe be born?

> Have ye not heard anything of my children? Speak to me of my garden,
> my Happy Isles, my new beautiful race. For their sake I am rich, for their
> sake I became poor. . . . What have I not surrendered? What would I not
> surrender that I might have one thing: those children, that living plantation,
> those life-trees of my highest will and my highest hope?[101]

IX. CRITICISM

It is a beautiful poem; and perhaps it is a poem rather than a philosophy. We know that there are absurdities here, and that the man went

[99]When did this poor exile re-enter?
[100]Quoted by Nordau, *Degeneration*, New York, 1895; p. 439.
[101]W. P., ii, 353, 362-4, 371, 422; B. G. E., 239; T. O. S., ii, 39; Z., 413.

too far in an attempt to convince and correct himself; but we can see him suffering at every line, and we must love him even where we question him. There is a time when we tire of sentimentality and delusion, and relish the sting of doubt and denial; and then Nietzsche comes to us as a tonic, like open spaces and fresh winds after a long ceremony in a crowded church. "He who knows how to breathe in the air of my writings is conscious that it is the air of the heights, that it is bracing. A man must be built for it; otherwise the chances are that it will kill him."[102] Let none mistake this acid for infant's milk.

And then what style! "People will say, some day, that Heine and I were the greatest artists, by far, that ever wrote in German, and that we left the best any mere German could do an incalculable distance behind us." And it is almost so.[103] "My style dances," he says; every sentence is a lance; the language is supple, vigorous, nervous,—the style of a fencer, too quick and brilliant for the normal eye. But on rereading him we perceive that something of this brilliance is due to exaggeration, to an interesting but at last neurotic egotism, to an over-facile inversion of every accepted notion, the ridicule of every virtue, the praise of every vice; he takes, we discover, a sophomore's delight in shocking; we conclude that it is easy to be interesting when one has no prejudices in favor of morality. These dogmatic assertions, these unmodified generalizations, these prophetic repetitions, these contradictions—of others not more than of himself— reveal a mind that has lost its balance, and hovers on the edge of madness. At last this brilliance tires us out and exhausts our nerves, like whips upon the flesh, or loud emphasis in conversation. There is a sort of Teutonic bluster in this violence of speech;[104] none of that restraint which is the first principle of art; none of that balance, harmony, and controversial urbanity, which Nietzsche so admired in the French. Nevertheless is it a powerful style; we are overwhelmed with the passion and iteration of it; Nietzsche does not prove, he announces and reveals; he wins us with his imagination rather than with his logic; he offers us not a philosophy merely, nor yet only a poem, but a new faith, a new hope, a new religion.

His thought, as much as his style, reveals him as a son of the Romantic movement. "What," he asks, "does a philosopher firstly and lastly require of himself? To overcome his age in himself, to become 'timeless.'" But this was a counsel of perfection which he more honored in the breach than in the observance; he was baptized with the spirit of his age, and by total immersion. He did not realize how Kant's subjectivism—"the world is my idea," as Schopenhauer honestly put it—had led to Fichte's "absolute ego," and this to Stirner's unbalanced individualism, and this to the unmoralism of the superman.[105] The superman is not merely Schopenhauer's "genius," and Carlyle's "hero," and Wagner's Siegfried; he looks

---

[102]E. H., 2.
[104]Figgis, 230, 56.
[103]E. H., 39. Nietzsche thought himself a Pole.
[105]Cf. Santayana, *Egotism in German Philosophy.*

suspiciously like Schiller's Karl Moor and Goethe's Götz; Nietzsche took more than the word *Uebermensch* from the young Goethe whose later Olympian calm he scorned so enviously. His letters are full of romantic sentiment and tenderness; "I suffer" recurs in them almost as frequently as "I die" in Heine.[106] He calls himself "a mystic and almost mænadic soul," and speaks of *The Birth of Tragedy* as "the confession of a romanticist."[107] "I am afraid," he writes to Brandes, "that I am too much of a musician not to be a romanticist."[108] "An author must become silent when his work begins to speak";[109] but Nietzsche never conceals himself, and rushes into the first person on every page. His exaltation of instinct against thought, of the individual against society, of the "Dionysian" against the "Apollonian" (i. e., the romantic against the classic type), betrays his time as definitely as the dates of his birth and his death. He was, for the philosophy of his age, what Wagner was for its music,—the culmination of the Romantic movement, the high tide of the Romantic stream; he liberated and exalted the "will" and the "genius" of Schopenhauer from all social restraint, as Wagner liberated and exalted the passion that had torn at its classic bonds in the Sonata Pathétique and the Fifth and Ninth Symphonies. He was the last great scion of the lineage of Rousseau.

Let us go back now on the road we have traveled with Nietzsche, and tell him, however ineffectually, some of the objections with which we were so often tempted to interrupt him. He was wise enough to see for himself, in his later years, how much absurdity had contributed to the originality of *The Birth of Tragedy*.[110] Scholars like Wilamowitz-Moellendorff laughed the book out of the philologic court. The attempt to deduce Wagner from Æschylus was the self-immolation of a young devotee before a despotic god. Who would have thought that the Reformation was "Dionysian"—i. e., wild, unmoral, vinous, Bacchanalian; and that the Renaissance was quite the opposite of these, quiet, restrained, moderate, "Apollonian"? Who would have suspected that "Socratism was the culture of the opera"?[111] The attack on Socrates was the disdain of a Wagnerian for logical thought; the admiration for Dionysus was a sedentary man's idolatry of action (hence also the apotheosis of Napoleon), and a bashful bachelor's secret envy of masculine bibulousness and sexuality.

Perhaps Nietzsche was right in considering the pre-Socratic age as the halcyon days of Greece; no doubt the Peloponnesian War undermined the economic and political basis of Periclean culture. But it was a little absurd to see in Socrates only a disintegrating criticism (as if Nietzsche's own function was not chiefly this) and not also a work of salvage for a society

[106]E. g., cf. Halévy, 231.
[108]Quoted by Huneker, *Egoists*, 251.
[110]Cf. B. T., pp. 1 and 4 of the Introduction.
[107]B. T., 6, xxv.
[109]Quoted by Faguet, 9.
[111]B. T., 142.

ruined less by philosophy than by war and corruption and immorality. Only a professor of paradox could rank the obscure and dogmatic fragments of Heraclitus above the mellowed wisdom and the developed art of Plato. Nietzsche denounces Plato, as he denounces all his creditors—no man is a hero to his debtor; but what is Nietzsche's philosophy but the ethics of Thrasymachus and Callicles, and the politics of Plato's Socrates? —With all his philology, Nietzsche never quite penetrated to the spirit of the Greeks; never learned the lesson that moderation and self-knowledge (as taught by the Delphic inscriptions and the greater philosophers) must bank, without extinguishing, the fires of passion and desire;[112] that Apollo must limit Dionysus. Some have described Nietzsche as a pagan; but he was not that: neither Greek pagan like Pericles nor German pagan like Goethe; he lacked the balance and restraint that made these men strong. "I shall give back to men the serenity which is the condition of all culture," he writes,[113] but alas, how can one give what one has not?

Of all Nietzsche's books, *Zarathustra* is safest from criticism, partly because it is obscure, and partly because its inexpugnable merits dwarf all fault-finding. The idea of eternal recurrence, though common to the "Apollonian" Spencer as well as to the "Dionysian" Nietzsche, strikes one as unhealthy fancy, a weird last-minute effort to recover the belief in immortality. Every critic has seen the contradiction between the bold preachment of egoism (Zarathustra "proclaims the Ego whole and holy, and selfishness blessed"—an unmistakable echo of Stirner) and the appeal to altruism and self-sacrifice in the preparation and service of the super man. But who, reading this philosophy, will classify himself as servant, and not as superman?

As for the ethical system of *Beyond Good and Evil* and *The Genealogy of Morals*, it is stimulating exaggeration. We acknowledge the need of asking men to be braver, and harder on themselves,—almost all ethical philosophies have asked that; but there is no urgent necessity for asking people to be crueler and "more evil"[114]—surely this is a work of supererogation? And there is no great call to complain that morality is a weapon used by the weak to limit the strong; the strong are not too deeply impressed by it, and make rather clever use of it in turn: most moral codes are imposed from above rather than from below; and the crowd praises and blames by prestige imitation. It is well, too, that humility should be occasionally maltreated; "we have had deprecation and ducking long enough," as the good gray poet said; but one does not observe any superabundance of this quality in modern character. Nietzsche here fell short of that historical sense which he lauded as so necessary to philosophy; or he would have seen the doctrine of meekness and humble-

[112]Cf. Santayana, 141.   [113]In Halévy, 192.
[114]Cf. Nordau, *Degeneration*, 451, for a rather hectic attack on Nietzsche as an imaginative sadist.

ness of heart as a necessary antidote to the violent and warlike virtues of the barbarians who nearly destroyed, in the first millennium of the Christian era, that very culture to which Nietzsche always returns for nourishment and refuge. Surely this wild emphasis on power and movement is the echo of a feverish and chaotic age? This supposedly universal "will to power" hardly expresses the quiescence of the Hindu, the calm of the Chinese, or the satisfied routine of the medieval peasant. Power is the idol of some of us; but most of us long rather for security and peace.

In general, as every reader will have perceived, Nietzsche fails to recognize the place and value of the social instincts; he thinks the egoistic and individualistic impulses need reinforcement by philosophy! One must wonder where were Nietzsche's eyes when all Europe was forgetting, in a slough of selfish wars, those cultural habits and acquisitions which he admired so much, and which depend so precariously on coöperation and social amenity and self-restraint. The essential function of Christianity has been to moderate, by the inculcation of an extreme ideal of gentleness, the natural barbarity of men; and any thinker who fears that men have been corrupted out of egoism into an excess of Christian virtue needs only to look about him to be comforted and reassured.

Made solitary by illness and nervousness, and forced into war against the sluggishness and mediocrity of men, Nietzsche was led to suppose that all the great virtues are the virtues of men who stand alone. He reacted from Schopenhauer's submergence of the individual in the species to an unbalanced liberation of the individual from social control. Foiled in his search for love, he turned upon woman with a bitterness unworthy of a philosopher, and unnatural in a man; missing parentage and losing friendship, he never knew that the finest moments of life come through mutuality and comradeship, rather than from domination and war. He did not live long enough, or widely enough, to mature his half-truths into wisdom. Perhaps if he had lived longer he would have turned his strident chaos into a harmonious philosophy. Truer of him than of the Jesus to whom he applied them, were his own words: "He died too early; he himself would have revoked his doctrine had he reached" a riper age; "noble enough to revoke he was!"[115] But death had other plans.

Perhaps in politics his vision is sounder than in morals. Aristocracy is the ideal government; who shall deny it? "O ye kind heavens! there is in every nation . . . a fittest, a wisest, bravest, best; whom could we find and make king over us, all were in truth well. . . . By what art discover him? Will the heavens in their pity teach us no art? For our need of him is great!"[116] But who are the best? Do the best appear only in certain families, and must we therefore have hereditary aristocracy? But we had it; and it led to clique-pursuits, class-irresponsibility, and stagnation. Perhaps aristocracies have been saved, as often as destroyed, by

[115]Z., 99–100.   [116]Carlyle, Past and Present, New York, 1901.

intermarriage with the middle classes; how else has the English aristocracy maintained itself? And perhaps inbreeding degenerates? Obviously
there are many sides to these complex problems, at which Nietzsche has
flung so lustily his Yeas and Nays.[117] Hereditary aristocracies do not like
world-unification; they tend to a narrowly nationalistic policy, however
cosmopolitan they may be in conduct; if they abandoned nationalism
they would lose a main source of their power—the manipulation of foreign
relations. And perhaps a world-state would not be so beneficial to culture
as Nietzsche thinks; large masses move slowly; and Germany probably did
more for culture when she was merely "a geographical expression," with
independent courts rivalling one another in the patronage of art, than
in her days of unity and empire and expansion; it was not an emperor
who cherished Goethe and rescued Wagner.

It is a common delusion that the great periods of culture have been
ages of hereditary aristocracy: on the contrary, the efflorescent periods of
Pericles and the Medici and Elizabeth and the Romantic age were
nourished with the wealth of a rising bourgeoisie; and the creative work
in literature and art was done not by aristocratic families but by the offspring of the middle class;—by such men as Socrates, who was the son of
a midwife, and Voltaire, who was the son of an attorney, and Shakespeare,
who was the son of a butcher. It is ages of movement and change that
stimulate cultural creation; ages in which a new and vigorous class is rising
to power and pride. And so in politics: it would be suicidal to exclude
from statesmanship such genius as lacked aristocratic pedigree; the better
formula, surely, is a "career open to talent" wherever born; and genius
has a way of getting born in the most outlandish places. Let us be ruled
by *all* the best. An aristocracy is good only if it is a fluent body of men
whose patent to power lies not in birth but in ability,—an aristocracy continually selected and nourished out of a democracy of open and equal
opportunity to all.

After these deductions (if they must be made), what remains? Enough
to make the critic uncomfortable. Nietzsche has been refuted by every
aspirant to respectability; and yet he stands as a milestone in modern
thought, and a mountain-peak in German prose. No doubt he was guilty
of a little exaggeration when he predicted that the future would divide
the past into "Before Nietzsche" and "After Nietzsche"; but he did succeed in effecting a wholesome critical review of institutions and opinions
that for centuries had been taken for granted. It remains that he opened
a new vista into Greek drama and philosophy; that he showed at the
outset the seeds of romantic decadence in the music of Wagner; that he
analyzed our human nature with a subtlety as sharp as a surgeon's knife,
and perhaps as salutary; that he laid bare some hidden roots of morality

---

[117]"In my youth," says Nietzsche somewhere, "I flung at the world with Yea and
Nay; now in my old age I do penance for it."

as no other modern thinker had done;[118] that "he introduced a value
hitherto practically unknown in the realms of ethics—namely, aristocracy";[119] that he compelled an honest taking of thought about the ethical
implications of Darwinism; that he wrote the greatest prose poem in the
literature of his century; and (this above all) that he conceived of man
as something that man must surpass. He spoke with bitterness, but with
invaluable sincerity; and his thought went through the clouds and cobwebs of the modern mind like cleansing lightning and a rushing wind.
The air of European philosophy is clearer and fresher now because
Nietzsche wrote.[120]

X. FINALE

"I love him who willeth the creation of something beyond himself,
and then perisheth," said Zarathustra.[121]

Undoubtedly Nietzsche's intensity of thought consumed him prematurely. His battle against his time unbalanced his mind; "it has always
been found a terrible thing to war with the moral system of one's age;
it will have its revenge . . . from within and from without."[122] Towards
the end Nietzsche's work grew in bitterness; he attacked persons as well
as ideas,—Wagner, Christ, etc. "Growth in wisdom," he wrote, "may be
exactly measured by decrease in bitterness":[123] but he could not convince
his pen. Even his laughter became neurotic as his mind broke down;
nothing could better reveal the poison that was corroding him than the
reflection: "Perhaps I know best why man is the only animal that laughs:
he alone suffers so excruciatingly that he was compelled to invent laughter."[124] Disease and increasing blindness were the physiological side ot
his breakdown.[125] He began to give way to paranoiac delusions of grandeur
and persecution; he sent one of his books to Taine with a note assuring
the great critic that it was the most marvelous book ever written;[126] and
he filled his last book, *Ecce Homo*, with such mad self-praise as we have
seen.[127] *Ecce homo!*—alas, we behold the man here only too well!

Perhaps a little more appreciation by others would have forestalled
this compensatory egotism, and given Nietzsche a better hold upon
perspective and sanity. But appreciation came too late. Taine sent him a

---

[118]Though of course the essentials of Nietzsche's ethic are to be found in Plato,
Machiavelli, Hobbes, La Rochefoucauld, and even in the Vautrin of Balzac's *Père
Goriot.*

[119]Simmel.

[120]The extensive influence of Nietzsche on contemporary literature will need no
pointing out to those who are familiar with the writings of Artzibashef, Strindberg,
Przybyszewski, Hauptmann, Dehmel, Hamsun, and d'Annunzio.

[121]Z., 86.   [122]Ellis, 39.

[123]Quoted by Ellis, 80.   [124]W. P., i, 24.

[125]Cf. the essay on Nietzsche in Gould's *Biographical Clinic.*

[126]Figgis, 43.   [127]E. H., 20; cf. Nordau, 465.

generous word of praise when almost all others ignored or reviled him;
Brandes wrote to tell him that he was giving a course of lectures on the
"aristocratic radicalism" of Nietzsche at the University of Copenhagen;
Strindberg wrote to say that he was turning Nietzsche's ideas to dramatic
use; perhaps best of all, an anonymous admirer sent a check for $400.
But when these bits of light came, Nietzsche was almost blind in sight
and soul; and he had abandoned hope. "My time is not yet," he wrote;
"only the day after tomorrow belongs to me."[128]

The last blow came at Turin in January, 1889, in the form of a stroke
of apoplexy. He stumbled blindly back to his attic room, and dashed off
mad letters: to Cosima Wagner four words—"Ariadne, I love you"; to
Brandes a longer message, signed "The Crucified"; and to Burckhardt
and Overbeck such fantastic missives that the latter hurried to his aid.
He found Nietzsche ploughing the piano with his elbows, singing and
crying his Dionysian ecstasy.

They took him at first to an asylum,[129] but soon his old mother came
to claim him and take him under her own forgiving care. What a picture!
—the pious woman who had borne sensitively but patiently the shock of
her son's apostasy from all that she held dear, and who, loving him none
the less, received him now into her arms, like another *Pietà*. She died in
1897, and Nietzsche was taken by his sister to live in Weimar. There a
statue of him was made by Kramer—a pitiful thing, showing the once
powerful mind broken, helpless, and resigned. Yet he was not all unhappy; the peace and quiet which he had never had when sane were his
now; Nature had had mercy on him when she made him mad. He
caught his sister once weeping as she looked at him, and he could not
understand her tears: "Lisbeth," he asked, "why do you cry? Are we
not happy?" On one occasion he heard talk of books; his pale face lit up:
"Ah!" he said, brightening, "I too have written some good books"—and
the lucid moment passed.

He died in 1900. Seldom has a man paid so great a price for genius.

[128] E. H., 55.
[129] "The right man in the right place," says the brutal Nordau.

CHAPTER X

Contemporary European Philosophers:
Bergson, Croce and Bertrand Russell

I. HENRI BERGSON

1. THE REVOLT AGAINST MATERIALISM

THE history of modern philosophy might be written in terms of the warfare of physics and psychology. Thought may begin with its object, and at last, in consistency, try to bring its own mystic reality within the circle of material phenomena and mechanical law; or it may begin with itself, and be driven, by the apparent necessities of logic, to conceive all things as forms and creatures of mind. The priority of mathematics and mechanics in the development of modern science, and the reciprocal stimulation of industry and physics under the common pressure of expanding needs, gave to speculation a materialistic impulsion; and the most successful of the sciences became the models of philosophy. Despite Descartes' insistence that philosophy should begin with the self and travel outward, the industrialization of Western Europe drove thought away from thought and in the direction of material things.

Spencer's system was the culminating expression of this mechanical point of view. Hailed though he was as "the philosopher of Darwinism," he was more truly the reflex and exponent of industrialism; he endowed industry with glories and virtues which to our hind-sight seem ridiculous; and his outlook was rather that of a mechanician and an engineer absorbed in the motions of matter, than that of a biologist feeling the *élan* of life. The rapid obsolescence of his philosophy is due largely to the replacement of the physical by the biological stand-point in recent thought; by the growing disposition to see the essence and secret of the world in the movement of life rather than in the inertia of things. And indeed, matter itself has in our days almost taken on life: the study of electricity, magnetism, and the electron has given a vitalistic tinge to physics; so that instead of a reduction of psychology to physics—which was the more or less conscious ambition of English thought—we approach a vitalized physics and an almost spiritualized matter. It was Schopenhauer who first, in modern thought, emphasized the possibility of making the concept of life more fundamental and inclusive than that of force; it is Bergson who in our own generation has taken up this idea, and has almost converted a sceptical world to it by the force of his sincerity and his eloquence.

Bergson was born in Paris, in 1859, of French and Jewish parentage. He was an eager student, and seems to have taken every prize that turned up. He did homage to the traditions of modern science by specializing at first in mathematics and physics, but his faculty for analysis soon brought him face to face with the metaphysical problems that lurk behind every science; and he turned spontaneously to philosophy. In 1878 he entered the École Normale Supèrieure, and on graduating, was appointed to teach philosophy at the Lycée of Clermont-Ferrand. There, in 1888, he wrote his first major work—the *Essai sur les données immèdiates de la conscience,* translated as *Time and Free-will.* Eight quiet years intervened before the appearance of his next (and his most difficult) book —*Matière et mémoire.* In 1898 he became professor at the École Normale, and in 1900 at the Collège de France, where he has been ever since. In 1907 he won international fame with his masterpiece—*L'Évolution créatrice (Creative Evolution)*; he became almost overnight the most popular figure in the philosophic world; and all that was needed for his success was the placing of his books upon the Index Expurgatorius in 1914. In that same year he was elected to the French Academy.

It is a remarkable thing that Bergson, the David destined to slay the Goliath of materialism, was in youth a devotee of Spencer. But too much knowledge leads to scepticism; early devotees are the likeliest apostates, as early sinners are senile saints. The more he studied Spencer, the more keenly conscious Bergson became of the three rheumatic joints of the materialist mechanism: between matter and life, between body and mind, and between determinism and choice. The patience of Pasteur had discredited the belief in abiogenesis (the generation of life by non-living matter); and after a hundred years of theory, and a thousand vain experiments, the materialists were no nearer than before to solving the problem of the origin of life Again, though thought and brain were obviously connected, the mode of connection was as far from obvious as it had ever been. If mind was matter, and every mental act a mechanical resultant of neural states, of what use was consciousness? Why could not the material mechanism of the brain dispense with this "epiphenomenon," as the honest and logical Huxley called it, this apparently useless flame thrown up by the heat of cerebral commotion? Finally, was determinism any more intelligible than free will? If the present moment contains no living and creative choice, and is totally and mechanically the product of the matter and motion of the moment before, then so was that moment the mechanical effect of the moment that preceded it, and that again of the one before . . . and so on, until we arrive at the primeval nebula as the total cause of every later event, of every line of Shakespeare's plays, and every suffering of his soul; so that the sombre rhetoric of Hamlet and Othello, of Macbeth and Lear, in every clause and every phrase, was written far off there in the distant skies and the distant æons, by the structure and content of that legendary cloud. What a draft upon credulity! What an exercise of faith such a theory must demand in this unbelieving generation! What mystery or miracle, of Old Testament or New, could be half so incredible as this monstrous fatalistic myth, this nebula composing tragedies? There was matter enough for rebellion here; and if Bergson rose so rapidly to fame it was because he had the courage to doubt where all the doubters piously believed.

2. MIND AND BRAIN

We naturally incline to materialism, Bergson argues, because we tend to think in terms of space; we are geometricians all. But time is as fundamental as space; and it is time, no doubt, that holds the essence of life, and perhaps of all reality. What we have to understand is that time is an accumulation, a growth, a *duration*. "Duration is the continuous progress of the past which gnaws into the future and which swells as it advances"; it means that "the past in its entirety is prolonged into the present and abides there actual and acting." Duration means that the past endures, that nothing of it is quite lost. "Doubtless we think with only a small part of our past; but it is with our entire past . . . that we desire, will, and act." And since time is an accumulation, the future can never be the same as the past, for a new accumulation arises at every step. "Each moment is not only something new, but something unforeseeable; . . . change is far more radical than we suppose"; and that geometrical predictability of all things which is the goal of a mechanist science is only an intellectualist delusion. At least "for a conscious being, to exist is to change, to change is to mature, to mature is to go on creating one's self endlessly." What if this is true of all things? Perhaps all reality is time and duration, becoming and change?[1]

In ourselves, memory is the vehicle of duration, the handmaiden of time; and through it so much of our past is actively retained that rich alternatives present themselves for every situation. As life grows richer in its scope, its heritage and its memories, the field of choice widens, and at last the variety of possible responses generates consciousness, which is the rehearsal of response. "Consciousness seems proportionate to the living being's power of choice. It lights up the zone of potentialities that surrounds the act. It fills the interval between what is done and what might be done." It is no useless appendage; it is a vivid theatre of imagination, where alternative responses are pictured and tested before the irrevocable

[1] *Creative Evolution*, New York, 1911; pp. 7, 15, 5, 6, 1.

choice. "In reality," then, "a living being is a center of action; it represents a sum of contingency entering into the world; that is to say, a certain quantity of possible action." Man is no passively adaptive machine; he is a focus of redirected force, a center of creative evolution.[2]

Free will is a corollary of consciousness; to say that we are free is merely to mean that we know what we are doing.

> The primary function of memory is to evoke all those past perceptions which are analogous to the present perception, to recall to us what preceded and what followed them, and so to suggest to us that decision which is the most useful. But this is not all. By allowing us to grasp in a single intuition multiple moments of duration, it frees us from the movement of the flow of things, that is to say, from the rhythm of necessity. The more of these moments memory can contract into one, the firmer is the hold which it gives to us on matter; so that the memory of a living being appears indeed to measure, above all, its powers of action upon things.[3]

If determinists were right, and every act were the automatic and mechanical resultant of pre-existent forces, motive would flow into action with lubricated ease. But on the contrary, choice is burdensome and effortful, it requires resolution, a lifting up of the power of personality against the spiritual gravitation of impulse or habit or sloth. Choice is creation, and creation is labor. Hence the worried features of men; and their weary envy of the choiceless routine of animals, who "are so placid and self-contained." But the Confucian peacefulness of your dog is no philosophic calm, no quiet surface of unfathomed depth; it is the certainty of instinct, the orderliness of an animal that need not, and cannot, choose. "In the animal, invention is never anything but a variation on the theme of routine. Shut up in the habits of the species, it succeeds, no doubt, in enlarging them by its individual initiative; but it escapes automatism only for an instant, for just the time to create a new automatism. The gates of its prison close as soon as they are opened; by pulling at its chain it succeeds only in stretching it. With man, consciousness breaks the chain. In man, and man alone, it sets itself free."[4]

Mind, then, is not identical with brain. Consciousness depends upon the brain, and falls with it; but so does a coat fall with the nail on which it hangs,—which does not prove that the coat is an "epiphenomenon," an ornamental ectoplasm of the nail. The brain is the system of images and reaction-patterns; consciousness is the recall of images and the choice of reactions. "The direction of the stream is distinct from the river bed,

---

[2]*Ibid.,* 179, 262.   [3]*Matter and Memory,* London, 1919; p. 303.
[4]*Creative Evolution,* p. 264. This is an example of Bergson's facility in replacing argument with analogy, and of his tendency to exaggerate the gap between animals and men. Philosophy should not flatter. Jérome Coignard was wiser, and "would have refused to sign the Declaration of the Rights of Man, because of the sharp and unwarranted distinction it drew between man and the gorilla."

although it must adopt its winding course. Consciousness is distinct from the organism which it animates, although it must undergo its vicissitudes."[5]

It is sometimes said that in ourselves, consciousness is directly connected with a brain, and that we must therefore attribute consciousness to living beings which have a brain, and deny it to those which have none. But it is easy to see the fallacy of such an argument. It would be just as though we should say that because in ourselves digestion is directly connected with a stomach, therefore only living beings with a stomach can digest. We should be entirely wrong, for it is not necessary to have a stomach, nor even to have special organs, in order to digest. An amoeba digests, although it is an almost undifferentiated protoplasmic mass. What is true is that in proportion to the complexity and perfection of an organism, there is a division of labor; special organs are assigned special functions, and the faculty of digesting is localized in the stomach, or rather is a general digestive apparatus, which works better because confined to that one function alone. In like manner, consciousness in man is unquestionably connected with the brain; but it by no means follows that a brain is indispensable to consciousness. The lower we go in the animal series, the more nervous centers are simplified and separate from one another, and at last they disappear altogether, merged in the general mass of an organism with hardly any differentiation. If, then, at the top of the scale of living beings, consciousness is attached to very complicated nervous centers, must we not suppose that it accompanies the nervous system down its whole descent, and that when at last the nerve stuff is merged in the yet undifferentiated living matter, consciousness is still there, diffused, confused, but not reduced to nothing? Theoretically, then, everything living might be conscious. *In principle,* consciousness is coextensive with life.[6]

Why is it, nevertheless, that we seem to think of mind and thought in terms of matter and the brain? It is because that part of our minds which we call the "intellect" is a constitutional materialist; it was developed, in the process of evolution, to understand and deal with material, spatial objects; from this field it derives all its concepts and its "laws," and its notion of a fatalistic and predictable regularity everywhere. "Our intellect, in the narrow sense of the word, is intended to secure the perfect fitting of our body to its environment, to represent the relations of external things among themselves,—in short, to think matter."[7] It is at home with solids, inert things; it sees all becoming as being,[8] as a series of states; it misses the connective tissue of things, the flow of duration that constitutes their very life.

Look at the moving-picture; it seems to our tired eyes to be alive with

[5] *Ibid.,* p. 270.
[6] *Mind-Energy,* New York, 1920; p. 11.
[7] *Creative Evolution,* p. ix.
[8] Cf. Nietzsche: "Being is a fiction invented by those who suffer from becoming."—*Birth of Tragedy,* p. xxvii.

motion and action; here, surely, science and mechanism have caught the continuity of life. On the contrary, it is just here that science and the intellect reveal their limitations. The moving picture does not move, is not a picture of motion; it is only a series of instantaneous photographs, "snap-shots," taken in such rapid succession that when they are thrown in rapid succession upon the screen, the willing spectator enjoys the illusion of continuity, as he did in his boyhood with thumb-nail movies of his pugilistic heroes. But it is an illusion none the less; and the cinema film is obviously a series of pictures in which everything is as still as if eternally congealed.

And as the "motion"-picture camera divides into static poses the vivid current of reality, so the human intellect catches a series of states, but loses the continuity that weaves them into life. We see matter and we miss energy; we think that we know what matter is; but when at the heart of the atom we find energy, we are bewildered, and our categories melt away. "No doubt, for greater strictness, all considerations of motion may be eliminated from mathematical processes; but the introduction of motion into the genesis of figures is nevertheless the origin of modern mathematics";[9]—nearly all the progress of mathematics in the nineteenth century was due to the use of the concepts of time and motion in addition to the traditional geometry of space. All through contemporary science, as one sees in Mach and Pearson and Henri Poincaré, there runs the uncomfortable suspicion that "exact" science is merely an approximation, which catches the inertia of reality better than its life.

But it is our own fault if, by insisting on the application of physical concepts in the field of thought, we end in the *impasse* of determinism, mechanism, and materialism. The merest moment of reflection might have shown how inappropriate the concepts of physics are in the world of mind: we think as readily of a mile as of half a mile, and one flash of thought can circumnavigate the globe; our ideas elude every effort to picture them as material particles moving in space, or as limited by space in their flight and operation. Life escapes these *solid* concepts; for life is a matter of time rather than of space; it is not position, it is change; it is not quantity so much as quality; it is not a mere redistribution of matter and motion, it is fluid and persistent creation.

A very small element of a curve is very near to being a straight line. And the smaller it is, the nearer. In the limit it may be termed a part of the straight line, as you please, for in each of its points a curve coincides with its tangent. So, likewise, 'vitality' is tangent, at any and every point, to physical and chemical forces; but such points are, in fact, only views taken by a mind which imagines stops at various moments of the movement that generates the curve. In reality, life is no more made-up of physico-chemical elements than a curve is composed of straight lines.[10]

[9]*Creative Evolution*, p. 32.   [10]*Ibid.*, p. 31.

How then shall we catch the flow and essence of life if not by thinking and the intellect? But is the intellect all? Let us for a while stop
thinking, and just gaze upon that inner reality—our selves—which is
better known to us than all things else: what do we see? Mind, not
matter; time, not space; action, not passivity; choice, not mechanism.
We see life in its subtle and penetrating flow, not in its "states of mind,"
not in its devitalized and separated parts, as when the zoologist examines
a dead frog's legs, or studies preparations under a microscope, and thinks
that he is a *biologist* studying *life!* This direct perception, this simple and
steady looking-upon (*intueor*) a thing, is intuition; not any mystic process, but the most direct examination possible to the human mind. Spinoza
was right: reflective thought is not by any means the highest form of
knowledge; it is better, no doubt, than hearsay; but how weak it is beside
the direct perception of the thing itself! "A true empiricism is one that
sets itself the task of getting as close as possible to the original, of sound-
ing the depths of life, of feeling the pulse of its spirit by a sort of intellectual auscultation";[11] we "listen in" on the current of life. By direct
perception we feel the presence of *mind;* by intellectual circumlocution
we arrive at the notion that thought is a dance of molecules in the brain.
Is there any doubt that intuition here beholds more truly the heart of life?

This does not mean that thinking is a disease, as Rousseau held, or that
the intellect is a treacherous thing which every decent citizen should for-
swear. The intellect retains its normal function of dealing with the
material and spatial world, and with the material aspects or spatial expressions of life and mind; intuition is limited to the direct feeling of life
and mind, not in their external embodiments but in their inner being. "I
have never maintained that it was necessary 'to put something different
in the place of intellect,' or to set instinct above it. I have simply tried
to show that when we leave the domain of mathematics and physics to
enter that of life and consciousness, we must make our appeal to a certain
sense of life which cuts across pure understanding and has its origin in
the same vital impulse as instinct—although instinct, properly so-called,
is quite a different thing." Nor do we try "to refute intellect by intellect";
we merely "adopt the language of the understanding, since only the
understanding has a language"; we cannot help it if the very words that
we use are psychological only by symbolism, and still reek with the
material connotations forced upon them by their origin. *Spirit* means
breath, and *mind* means a *measure,* and *thinking* points to a *thing;* nevertheless these are the crass media through which the soul must express
itself. "It will be said that we do not transcend our intellect, for it is still
with our intellect, and through our intellect, that we see the other forms
of consciousness"; even introspection and intuition are materialist metaphors. And this would be a legitimate objection, "if there did not remain,

<hr />

[11] *Introduction to Metaphysics,* p. 14.

around our conceptual and logical thought, a vague nebulosity, made of the very substance out of which has been formed the luminous nucleus that we call the intellect." The new psychology is revealing in us a mental region incomparably wider than the intellect. "To explore the most sacred depths of the unconscious, to labor in the sub-soil of consciousness: that will be the principal task of psychology in the century which is opening. I do not doubt that wonderful discoveries await it there."[12]

3. CREATIVE EVOLUTION

With this new orientation, evolution appears to us as something quite different from the blind and dreary mechanism of struggle and destruction which Darwin and Spencer described. We sense duration in evolution, the accumulation of vital powers, the inventiveness of life and mind, "the continual elaboration of the absolutely new." We are prepared to understand why the most recent and expert investigators, like Jennings and Maupas, reject the mechanical theory of protozoan behavior, and why Professor E. B. Wilson, dean of contemporary cytologists, concludes his book on the cell with the statement that "the study of the cell has, on the whole, seemed to widen rather than to narrow the enormous gap that separates even the lowest forms of life from the inorganic world." And everywhere, in the world of biology, one hears of the rebellion against Darwin.[13]

Darwinism means, presumably, the origin of new organs and functions, new organisms and species, by the natural selection of favorable variations. But this conception, hardly half a century old, is already worm-eaten with difficulties. How, on this theory, did the instincts originate? It would be convenient to conceive them as the inherited accumulation of acquired habits; but expert opinion closes that door in our faces,—though some day that door may be opened. If only congenital powers and qualities are transmissible, every instinct must have been, on its first appearance, as strong as it natively is now; it must have been born, so to speak, adult, in full panoply for action; else it could not have favored its possessor in the struggle for existence. If, on its first appearance, it was weak, it could have achieved survival value only through that acquired strength which (by current hypothesis) is not inherited. Every origin is here a miracle.

And, as with the first instincts, so with every variation: one wonders how the change could have offered, in its first form, a handle to selection. In the case of such complex organs as the eye, the difficulty is discouraging: either the eye appeared at once, full-formed and competent (which is as credible as Jonah's introspection of the whale); or it began with a series of "fortuitous" variations which, by a still more fortuitous survival,

---

[12]In Ruhe, *The Philosophy of Bergson*, p. 37; *Creative Evolution*, pp. 258 and xii.
[13]*Ibid.*, pp. 11 and 25.

produced the eye. At every step the theory of a mechanical production of complicated structures by a blind process of variation and selection presents us with fairy-tales that have all the incredibility of childhood's lore, and little of its beauty.

The most decisive difficulty, however, is the appearance of similar effects, brought about by different means, in widely divergent lines of evolution. Take as example the invention of sex as a mode of reproduction, both in plants and in animals; here are lines of evolution as divergent as could be, and yet the same complex "accident" occurs in both. Or take the organs of sight in two very distinct phyla—the molluscs and the vertebrates; "how could the same small variations, incalculable in number, have ever occurred in the same order on two independent lines of evolution, if they were purely accidental?" More remarkable still,

> nature arrives at identical results, in sometimes neighboring species, by entirely different embryogenic processes. . . . The retina of the vertebrate is produced by an expansion of the rudimentary brain of the embryo. . . . In the mollusc, on the contrary, the retina is derived from the ectoderm[14] directly. . . . If the crystalline lens of a Triton be removed, it is regenerated by the iris. Now the original lens was built out of the ectoderm, while the iris is of mesodermal origin. What is more, in the Salamandra maculata, if the lens be removed and the iris left, the regeneration of the lens takes place at the upper part of the iris; but if this upper part of the iris itself be taken away, the regeneration takes place in the inner or retinal layer of the remaining region. Thus parts differently situated, differently constituted, meant normally for different functions, are capable of performing the same duties and even of manufacturing, when necessary, the same pieces of the machine.[15]

So, in amnesia and aphasia, "lost" memories and functions reappear in regenerated or substituted tissues.[16] Surely we have here overwhelming evidence that there is something more in evolution than a helpless mechanism of material parts. Life is more than its machinery; it is a power that can grow, that can restore itself, that can mould to its own will some measure of environing circumstance. Not that there is any external design determining these marvels; that would be merely an inverted mechanism, a fatalism as destructive of human initiative and of creative evolution as the sombre surrender of Hindu thought to India's heat. "We must get beyond both points of view—mechanism and finalism—as being, at bottom, only standpoints to which the human mind has been led by considering the work of men": we thought at first that all things moved because of some quasi-human will using them as instruments in a cosmic

---

[14]The organs of the growing embryo are built up out of one or another of three layers of tissues; the external layer, or ectoderm; the intermediate layer, or mesoderm; and the internal layer, or endoderm.

[15]*Creative Evolution*, pp. 64 and 75.   [16]*Matter and Memory*, ch. ii.

game; and then we thought that the cosmos itself was a machine because we had been dominated, in character and philosophy, by our mechanical age. There is a design in things; but in them, not outside; an *entelechy,* an inward determination of all the parts by the function and purpose of the whole.[17]

Life is that which makes efforts, which pushes upwards and outwards and on; "always and always the procreant urge of the world." It is the opposite of inertia, and the opposite of accident; there is a direction in the growth to which it is self-impelled. Against it is the undertow of matter, the lag and slack of things towards relaxation and rest and death; at every stage life has had to fight with the inertia of its vehicle; and if it conquers death through reproduction, it does so only by yielding every citadel in turn, and abandoning every individual body at last to inertia and decay. Even to stand is to defy matter and its "laws": while to move about, to go forth and seek, and not, plant-like, to wait, is a victory purchased at every moment by effort and fatigue. And consciousness slips, as soon as it is permitted, into the restful automatism of instinct, habit, and sleep.

At the outset life is almost as inert as matter; it takes a stationary form, as if the vital impulse were too weak to risk the adventure of motion. And in one great avenue of development this motionless stability has been the goal of life: the bending lily and the majestic oak are altars to the god Security. But life was not content with this stay-at-home existence of the plant; always its advances have been away from security towards freedom; away from carapaces, scales and hides, and other burdensome protections, to the ease and perilous liberty of the bird. "So the heavy hoplite was supplanted by the legionary; the knight, clad in armor, had to give place to the light free-moving infantryman; and in a general way, in the evolution of life, just as in the evolution of human societies and of individual destinies, the greatest successes have been for those who accepted the heaviest risks."[18] So, too, man has ceased to evolve new organs on his body; he makes tools and weapons instead, and lays them aside when they are not needed, rather than carry all his armament at every step, like those gigantic fortresses, the mastodon and the megatherium, whose heavy security lost them the mastery of the globe. Life may be impeded, as well as aided, by its instruments.

It is with instincts as with organs; they are the tools of the mind; and like all organs that are attached and permanent, they become burdens when the environment that needed them has disappeared. Instinct comes ready-made, and gives decisive—and usually successful—responses to stereotyped and ancestral situations; but it does not adapt the organism to change, it does not enable man to meet flexibly the fluid complexities of modern life. It is the vehicle of security, while intellect is the organ of an

[17]*Creative Evolution,* p. 89.   [18]*Ibid.,* p. 132.

adventurous liberty. It is life taking on the blind obedience of the machine.

How significant it is that we laugh, usually, when a living thing behaves like matter, like a mechanism; when the clown tumbles about aimlessly, and leans against pillars that are not there; or when our best beloved falls on an icy path, and we are tempted to laugh first and ask questions afterward. That geometrical life which Spinoza almost confused with deity is really a reason for humor and tears; it is ridiculous and shameful that men should be machines; and ridiculous and shameful that their philosophy should describe them so.

Life has taken three lines in its evolution: in one it relapsed into the almost material torpor of plants, and found there, occasionally, a supine security, and the cowardly tenure of a thousand years; in another avenue its spirit and effort congealed into instinct as in the ants and bees; but in the vertebrates it took the dare of freedom, cast off its ready-made instincts and marched bravely into the endless risks of thought. Instinct still remains the profounder mode of visioning reality and catching the essence of the world; but intelligence grows ever stronger and bolder, and wider in its scope; it is at last in intelligence that life has placed its interests and its hopes.

This persistently creative life, of which every individual and every species is an experiment, is what we mean by God; God and Life are one. But this God is finite, not omnipotent,—limited by matter, and overcoming its inertia painfully, step by step; and not omniscient, but groping gradually towards knowledge and consciousness and "more light." "God, thus defined, has nothing of the ready-made; He is unceasing life, action, freedom. Creation, so conceived, is not a mystery; we experience it in ourselves when we act freely," when we consciously choose our actions and plot our lives.[19] Our struggles and our sufferings, our ambitions and our defeats, our yearnings to be better and stronger than we are, are the voice and current of the *Élan Vital* in us, that vital urge which makes us grow, and transforms this wandering planet into a theatre of unending creation.

And who knows but that at last life may win the greatest victory of all over its ancient enemy, matter, and learn even to elude mortality? Let us have an open mind, even to our hopes.[20] All things are possible to life if time is generous. Consider what life and mind have done in the mere moment of a millennium, with the forests of Europe and America; and then see how foolish it is to put up barriers to life's achievements. "The animal takes its stand on the plant, man bestrides animality, and the

[19]*Ibid.*, p. 248.
[20]Bergson thinks the evidence for telepathy is overwhelming. He was one of those who examined Eusapia Palladino and reported in favor of her sincerity. In 1913 he accepted the presidency of the Society for Physical Research. Cf. *Mind-Energy*, p. 81.

whole of humanity, in space and time, is one immense army galloping beside and before and behind each of us in an overwhelming charge able to beat down every resistance and clear the most formidable obstacles, perhaps even death."[21]

4. CRITICISM

"I believe," says Bergson, "that the time given to refutation in philosophy is usually time lost. Of the many attacks directed by the many thinkers against each other, what now remains? Nothing, or assuredly very little. That which counts and endures is the modicum of positive truth which each contributes. The true statement is of itself able to displace the erroneous idea, and becomes, without our having taken the trouble of refuting anyone, the best of refutations."[22] This is the voice of Wisdom herself. When we "prove" or "disprove" a philosophy we are merely offering another one, which, like the first, is a fallible compound of experience and hope. As experience widens and hope changes, we find more "truth" in the "falsehoods" we denounced, and perhaps more falsehood in our youth's eternal truths. When we are lifted upon the wings of rebellion we like determinism and mechanism, they are so cynical and devilish; but when death looms up suddenly at the foot of the hill we try to see beyond it into another hope. Philosophy is a function of age. Nevertheless . . .

What strikes one first in reading Bergson is the style: brilliant not with the paradox-fireworks of Nietzsche, but with a steady brightness, as of a man who is resolved to live up to the fine traditions of luminous French prose. It is harder to be wrong in French than in some other languages; for the French will not tolerate obscurity, and truth is clearer than fiction. If Bergson is occasionally obscure it is by the squandered wealth of his imagery, his analogies, and his illustrations; he has an almost Semitic passion for metaphor, and is apt at times to substitute ingenious simile for patient proof. We have to be on our guard against this image-maker, as one bewares of a jeweler, or a real-estate poet—while recognizing gratefully, in *Creative Evolution,* our century's first philosophic masterpiece.[28]

Perhaps Bergson would have been wiser to base his criticism of the intellect on the grounds of a broader intelligence, rather than on the ukases of intuition. Introspective intuition is as fallible as external sense; each must be tested and corrected by matter-of-fact experience; and each can be trusted only so far as its findings illumine and advance our action. Bergson presumes too much in supposing that the intellect catches only

[21]*Creative Evolution,* p. 271.   [22]In Ruhe, p. 47.

[28]As with Schopenhauer, so with Bergson, the reader will do well to pass by all summaries and march resolutely through the philosopher's chef-d'œuvre itself. Wildon Carr's exposition is unduly worshipful, Hugh Elliott's unduly disparaging; they cancel each other into confusion. The *Introduction to Metaphysics* is as simple as one may expect of metaphysics; and the essay on *Laughter,* though one-sided, is enjoyable and fruitful.

the states, and not the flux, of reality and life; thought is a *stream* of *transitive* ideas, as James had shown before Bergson wrote;[24] "ideas" are merely points that memory selects in the flow of thought; and the mental current adequately reflects the continuity of perception and the movement of life.

It was a wholesome thing that this eloquent challenge should check the excesses of intellectualism; but it was as unwise to offer intuition in the place of thought as it would be to correct the fancies of youth with the fairy-tales of childhood. Let us correct our errors forward, not backward. To say that the world suffers from too much intellect would require the courage of a madman. The romantic protest against thinking, from Rousseau and Chateaubriand to Bergson and Nietzsche and James, has done its work; we will agree to dethrone the Goddess of Reason if we are not asked to re-light the candles before the ikon of Intuition. Man exists by instinct, but he progresses by intelligence.

That which is best in Bergson is his attack upon materialist mechanism. Our pundits of the laboratory had become a little too confident of their categories, and thought to squeeze all the cosmos into a test-tube. Materialism is like a grammar that recognizes only nouns; but reality, like language, contains action as well as objects, verbs as well as substantives, life and motion as well as matter. One could understand, perhaps, a merely molecular memory, like the "fatigue" of overburdened steel; but molecular foresight, molecular planning, molecular idealism?—Had Bergson met these new dogmas with a cleansing scepticism he might have been a little less constructive, but he would have left himself less open to reply. His doubts melt away when his system begins to form; he never stops to ask what "matter" is; whether it may not be somewhat less inert than we have thought; whether it may be, not life's enemy, but life's willing menial if life but knew its mind. He thinks of the world and the spirit, of body and soul, of matter and life, as hostile to each other; but matter and body and the "world" are merely the materials that wait to be formed by intelligence and will. And who knows that these things too are not forms of life, and auguries of mind? Perhaps here too, as Heraclitus would say, there are gods.

Bergson's critique of Darwinism issues naturally from his vitalism. He carries on the French tradition established by Lamarck, and sees impulse and desire as active forces in evolution; his spirited temper rejects the Spencerian conception of an evolution engineered entirely by the mechanical integration of matter and dissipation of motion; life is a positive power, an effort that builds its organs through the very persistence of its desires. We must admire the thoroughness of Bergson's biological preparation, his familiarity with the literature, even with the periodicals

---

[24] Cf. the famous pages on "The Stream of Thought" in James's *Principles of Psychology*, New York, 1890; vol. i. ch. 9.

in which current science hides itself for a decade of probation. He offers his erudition modestly, never with the elephantine dignity that weighs down the pages of Spencer. All in all, his criticism of Darwin has proved effective; the specifically Darwinian features of the evolution theory are now generally abandoned.[25]

In many ways the relation of Bergson to the age of Darwin is a replica of Kant's relation to Voltaire. Kant strove to repulse that great wave of secular, and partly atheistic, intellectualism which had begun with Bacon and Descartes, and had ended in the scepticism of Diderot and Hume; and his effort took the line of denying the finality of intellect in the field of transcendental problems. But Darwin unconsciously, and Spencer consciously, renewed the assaults which Voltaire, and his more-than-Voltairean followers, had leveled at the ancient faith; and mechanist materialism, which had given ground before Kant and Schopenhauer, had won all of its old power at the beginning of our century. Bergson attacked it, not with a Kantian critique of knowledge, nor with the idealist contention that matter is known only through mind; but by following the lead of Schopenhauer, and seeking, in the objective as well as in the subjective world, an energizing principle, an active *entelechy*, which might make more intelligible the miracles and subtleties of life. Never was vitalism so forcefully argued, or so attractively dressed.

Bergson soared to an early popularity because he had come to the defense of hopes which spring eternally in the human breast. When people found that they could believe in immortality and deity without losing the respect of philosophy, they were pleased and grateful; and Bergson's lecture-room became the salon of splendid ladies happy to have their heart's desires upheld with such learned eloquence. Strangely mingled with them were the ardent syndicalists who found in Bergson's critique of intellectualism a justification of their gospel of "less thought and more action." But this sudden popularity exacted its price; the contradictory nature of Bergson's support disintegrated his following; and Bergson may share the fate of Spencer, who lived to be present at the burial of his own reputation.

Yet, of all contemporary contributions to philosophy, Bergson's is the most precious. We needed his emphasis on the elusive contingency of things, and the remoulding activity of mind. We were near to thinking of the world as a finished and pre-determined show, in which our initiative was a self-delusion, and our efforts a devilish humor of the gods; after Bergson we come to see the world as the stage and the material of our

[25]Bergson's arguments, however, are not all impregnable: the appearance of similar effects (like sex or sight) in different lines might be the mechanical resultant of similar environmental exigencies; and many of the difficulties of Darwinism would find a solution if later research should justify Darwin's belief in the partial transmission of characters repeatedly acquired by successive generations.

own originative powers. Before him we were cogs and wheels in a vast and dead machine; now, if we wish it, we can help to write our own parts in the drama of creation.

II. BENEDETTO CROCE

1. The Man

From Bergson to Croce is an impossible transition: there is hardly a parallel in all their lines. Bergson is a mystic who translates his visions into deceptive clarity; Croce is a sceptic with an almost German gift for obscurity. Bergson is religiously-minded, and yet talks like a thorough-going evolutionist; Croce is an anti-clerical who writes like an American Hegelian. Bergson is a French Jew who inherits the traditions of Spinoza and Lamarck; Croce is an Italian Catholic who has kept nothing of his religion except its scholasticism and its devotion to beauty.

Perhaps the comparative infertility of Italy in the philosophy of the last hundred years is due in some part to the retention of scholastic attitudes and methods even by thinkers who have abandoned the old theology. (More of it, doubtless, is due to the northward movement of industry and wealth.) Italy might be described as the land that had a Renaissance, but never a Reformation; it will destroy itself for beauty's sake, but it is as sceptical as Pilate when it thinks of truth. Perhaps the Italians are wiser than the rest of us, and have found that truth is a mirage, while beauty—however subjective—is a possession and a reality. The artists of the Renaissance (excepting the sombre and almost Protestant Michelangelo, whose brush was the echo of Savonarola's voice) never worried their heads about morals or theology; it was enough for them that the Church recognized their genius, and paid their bills. It became an unwritten law in Italy that men of culture would make no trouble for the Church. How could an Italian be unkind to a Church that had brought all the world to Canossa, and had levied imperial tribute on every land to make Italy the art-gallery of the world?

So Italy remained loyal to the old faith, and contented itself with the *Summa* of Aquinas for philosophy. Giambattista Vico came, and stirred the Italian mind again; but Vico went, and philosophy seemed to die with him. Rosmini thought for a time that he would rebel; but he yielded. Throughout Italy men became more and more irreligious, and more and more loyal to the Church.

Benedetto Croce is an exception. Born in 1866 in a small town in the province of Aquila, and the only son of a well-to-do Catholic and conservative family, he was given so thorough a training in Catholic theology that at last, to restore the balance, he became an atheist. In countries that have had no Reformation there is no half-way house between orthodoxy and absolute unbelief. Benedetto was at first so pious that he insisted on studying every phase of religion, until at last he reached its philosophy and its anthropology; and insensibly his studies were substituted for his faith.

In 1883 life dealt him one of those ruthless blows which usually turn men's minds back to belief. An earthquake overwhelmed the little town of Casamicciola where the Croces were staying; Benedetto lost both his parents, and his only sister; he himself remained buried for hours under the ruins, with many broken bones. It took him several years to recover his health; but his later life and work showed no breaking of his spirit. The quiet routine of convalescence gave him, or strengthened in him, the taste for scholarship; he used the modest fortune which the catastrophe left him to collect one of the finest libraries in Italy; he became a philosopher without paying the usual penalty of poverty or a professorship; he realized Ecclesiastes' cautious counsel, that "wisdom is good with an inheritance."

He has remained throughout his life a student, a lover of letters and of leisure. It was against his protests that he was drawn into politics and made minister of Public Education, perhaps to lend an air of philosophic dignity to a cabinet of politicians. He was chosen to the Italian senate; and as the rule in Italy is, once a senator always a senator (the office being for life), Croce provides the spectacle, not unusual in ancient Rome, but rather unique in our day, of a man who can be a senator and a philosopher at the same time. He would have interested Iago. But he does not take his politics too seriously; his time goes chiefly to the editing of his internationally famous periodical, *La Critica,* in which he and Giovanni Gentile dissect the world of thought and *belles lettres.*

When the war of 1914 came, Croce, angered at the thought that a mere matter of economic conflict should be permitted to interrupt the growth of the European mind, denounced the outbreak as suicidal mania; and even when Italy had, of necessity, thrown in her lot with the Allies, he remained aloof, and became as unpopular in Italy as Bertrand Russell in England or Romain Rolland in France. But Italy has forgiven him now; and all the youth of the land look up to him as their unbiased guide, philosopher, and friend; he has become for them an institution as important as the universities. It is nothing unusual now to hear judgments of him like Giuseppe Natoli's: "The system of Benedetto Croce remains the highest conquest in contemporary thought." Let us inquire into the secret of this influence.

2. The Philosophy of the Spirit

His first book, in its original form, was a leisurely series of articles (1895–1900) on *Historical Materialism and the Economics of Karl Marx.*

He had been immensely stimulated by Antonio Labriola, his professor at the University of Rome; under his guidance Croce had plunged into the labyrinths of Marx's *Kapital.* "This intercourse with the literature of Marxism, and the eagerness with which for some time I followed the socialistic press of Germany and Italy, stirred my whole being, and for the first time awakened in me a feeling of political enthusiasm, yielding a strange taste of newness to me; I was like a man who, having fallen in love for the first time when no longer young, should observe in himself the mysterious process of the new passion."[26] But the wine of social reform did not quite go to his head; he soon reconciled himself to the political absurdities of mankind, and worshipped again at the altar of philosophy.

One result of this adventure was his elevation of the concept Utility to a parity with Goodness, Beauty and Truth. Not that he conceded to economic affairs the supreme importance given to them in the system of Marx and Engels. He praised these men for a theory which, however incomplete, had drawn attention to a world of data before underrated and almost ignored; but he rejected the absolutism of the economic interpretation of history, as an unbalanced surrender to the suggestions of an industrial environment. He refused to admit materialism as a philosophy for adults or even as a method for science; mind was to him the primary and ultimate reality. And when he came to write his system of thought he called it, almost pugnaciously, "The Philosophy of the Spirit."

For Croce is an idealist, and recognizes no philosophy since Hegel's. All reality is idea; we know nothing except in the form it takes in our sensations and our thoughts. Hence all philosophy is reducible to logic; and truth is a perfect relationship in our ideas. Perhaps Croce likes this conclusion a bit too well; he is nothing if not logical; even in his book on *Esthetics* he cannot resist the temptation to intrude a chapter on logic. It is true that he calls philosophy the study of the concrete universal, and science the study of the abstract universal; but it is the reader's misfortune that Croce's concrete universal is universally abstract. He is, after all, a product of the scholastic tradition; he delights in abstruse distinctions and classifications that exhaust both the subject and the reader; he slides easily into logical casuistry, and refutes more readily than he can conclude. He is a Germanized Italian, as Nietzsche is an Italianized German.

Nothing could be more German, or more Hegelian, than the title of the first of the trilogy that makes up the *Filosofia dello Spirito*—the *Logic as the Science of the Pure Concept* (1905). Croce wants every idea to be as pure as possible—which seems to mean as ideological as possible, as abstract and unpragmatic as possible; there is nothing here of that passion for clarity and practical content which made William James

[26] In Piccoli: *Benedetto Croce.* New York, 1922: p. 72.

ⅎ beacon-light amid the mists of philosophy. Croce does not care to define an idea by reducing it to its practical consequences; he prefers to reduce practical affairs to ideas, relations, and categories. If all abstract or technical words were removed from his books they would not so suffer from obesity.

By a "pure concept" Croce means a universal concept, like quantity, quality, evolution, or any thought which may conceivably be applied to all reality. He proceeds to juggle these concepts as if the spirit of Hegel had found in him another avatar, and as if he were resolved to rival the reputation of the master for obscurity. By calling all this "logic," Croce convinces himself that he scorns metaphysics, and that he has kept himself immaculate from it; metaphysics, he thinks, is an echo of theology, and the modern university professor of philosophy is just the latest form of the medieval theologian. He mixes his idealism with a certain hardness of attitude towards tender beliefs: he rejects religion; he believes in the freedom of the will, but not in the immortality of the soul; the worship of beauty and the life of culture are to him a substitute for religion. "Their religion was the whole intellectual patrimony of primitive peoples; our intellectual patrimony is our religion. . . . We do not know what use could be made of religion by those who wish to preserve it side by side with the theoretic activity of man, with his art, his criticism, and his philosophy. . . . Philosophy removes from religion all reason for existing. . . . As the science of the spirit, it looks upon religion as a phenomenon, a transitory historical fact, a psychic condition that can be surpassed."[27] One wonders if La Gioconda's smile did not hover over the face of Rome when it read these words.

We have here the unusual occurrence of a philosophy that is at once naturalistic and spiritualistic, agnostic and indeterministic, practical and idealistic, economic and esthetic. It is true that Croce's interest is caught more surely by the theoretical than by the pragmatic aspects of life; but the very subjects he has essayed bear witness to an honorable effort to overcome his scholastic inclinations. He has written an immense volume on *The Philosophy of the Practical*, which turns out to be in part another logic under another name, and in part a metaphysical discussion of the old problem of free will. And in a more modest tome *On History* he has achieved the fruitful conception of history as philosophy in motion, and of the historian as one who shows nature and man not in theory and abstraction but in the actual flow and operation of causes and events. Croce loves his Vico, and warmly seconds the earlier Italian's plea that history should be written by philosophers. He believes that the fetish of a perfectly scientific history has led to a microscopic erudition in which the historian loses the truth because he knows too much. Just as Schliemann exhumed not only one Troy but seven after scientific historians

Esthetic. Engl. tr., p. 63.

had shown that there had been no Troy at all, so Croce thinks the hyper-critical historian exaggerates our ignorance of the past.

I recollect the remark made to me when I was occupied with research work in my young days, by a friend of but slight literary knowledge, to whom I had lent a very critical, indeed hypercritical, history of ancient Rome. When he had finished reading it he returned the book to me, remarking that he had acquired the proud conviction of being 'the most learned of philologists': for the latter arrive at the conclusion that they know nothing, as the result of exhausting toil; while he knew nothing without any effort at all, simply as a generous gift of nature.[28]

Croce recognizes the difficulty of finding out the actual past, and quotes Rousseau's definition of history as "the art of choosing, from among many lies, that one which most resembles the truth."[29] He has no sympathy with the theorist who, like Hegel, or Marx, or Buckle, distorts the past into a syllogism that will conclude with his prejudice. There is no foreordained plan in history; and the philosopher who writes history must devote himself not to the tracing of cosmic designs, but to the revelation of causes and consequences and correlations. And he will also remember that only that part of the past is of value which is contemporary in its significance and its illumination. History might at last be what Napoleon called it,—"the only true philosophy and the only true psychology"—if historians would write it as the apocalypse of nature and the mirror of man.

3. WHAT IS BEAUTY?

Croce came to philosophy from historical and literary studies; and it was natural that his philosophic interest should be deeply colored by the problems of criticism and esthetics. His greatest book is his *Esthetic* (1902). He prefers art to metaphysics and to science: the sciences give us utility but the arts give us beauty; the sciences take us away from the individual and the actual, into a world of increasingly mathematical abstractions, until (as in Einstein) they issue in momentous conclusions of no practical importance; but art takes us directly to the particular person and the unique fact, to the philosophical universal intuited in the form of the concrete individual. "Knowledge has two forms: it is either *intuitive* knowledge or *logical* knowledge; knowledge obtained through the imagination or knowledge obtained through the intellect; knowledge of the individual or knowledge of the universal; of individual things or of the relations between them; it is the production either of images or of concepts."[30] The origin of art, therefore, lies in the power of forming images. "Art is ruled uniquely by the imagination. Images are its only wealth. It does not classify objects, it does not pronounce them real or imaginary, does not qualify them, does not define them; it feels and presents them—nothing more."[31] Because imagination precedes thought, and is necessary to it, the artistic, or image-forming, activity of the mind is prior to the logical, concept-forming, activity. Man is an artist as soon as he imagines, and long before he reasons.

The great artists understood the matter so. "One paints not with the hands but with the brain," said Michelangelo; and Leonardo wrote: "The minds of men of lofty genius are most active in invention when they are doing the least external work." Everybody knows the story told of da Vinci, that when he was painting the "Last Supper," he sorely displeased the Abbot who had ordered the work, by sitting motionless for days before an untouched canvas; and revenged himself for the importunate Abbot's persistent query—When would he begin to work?—by using the gentleman as an unconscious model for the figure of Judas.

The essence of the esthetic activity lies in this motionless effort of the artist to conceive the perfect image that shall express the subject he has in mind; it lies in a form of intuition that involves no mystic insight, but perfect sight, complete perception, and adequate imagination. The miracle of art lies not in the externalization but in the conception of the idea; externalization is a matter of mechanical technique and manual skill.

"When we have mastered the internal word, when we have vividly and clearly conceived a figure or a statue, when we have found a musical theme, expression is born and is complete, nothing more is needed. If, then, we open our mouth, and speak or sing, . . . what we do is to say aloud what we have already said within, to sing aloud what we have already sung within. If our hands strike the keyboard of the pianoforte, if we take up pencil or chisel, such actions are willed" (they belong to the practical, not to the esthetic, activity), "and what we are then doing is executing in great movements what we have already executed briefly and rapidly within."[32]

Does this help us to answer that baffling question, What is beauty? Here certainly there are as many opinions as there are heads; and every lover, in this matter, thinks himself an authority not to be gainsaid. Croce answers that beauty is the mental formation of an image (or a series of images) that catches the essence of the thing perceived. The beauty belongs, again, rather to the inward image than to the outward form in which it is embodied. We like to think that the difference between ourselves and Shakespeare is largely a difference in technique of external expression; that we have thoughts that lie too deep for words. But this is a fond illusion: the difference lies not in the power of externalizing the image but in the power of inwardly forming an image that expresses the object.

Even that esthetic sense which is contemplation rather than creation

[31] In Carr; *The Philosophy of Benedetto Croce*, London, 1917; p. 35.
[32] *Esthetic*, p. 50.

is also inward expression; the degree in which we understand or appreciate a work of art depends upon our ability to see by direct intuition the reality portrayed,—our power to form for ourselves an expressive image. "It is always our own intuition we express when we are enjoying a beautiful work of art. . . . It can only be my own intuition when, reading Shakespeare, I form the image of Hamlet or Othello."[33] Both in the artist creating and in the spectator contemplating beauty, the esthetic secret is the expressive image. Beauty is adequate expression: and since there is no real expression if it be not adequate, we may answer very imply the ancient question, and say, Beauty is expression.[34]

4. CRITICISM

All this is as clear as a starless night; and not wiser than it should be. The *Philosophy of the Spirit* lacks spirit, and discourages a sympathetic exposition. The *Philosophy of the Practical* is unpractical, and lacks the breath of living reference. The essay *On History* catches one leg of the truth, by proposing a union of history and philosophy; but it misses the other by failing to see that history can become philosophy only by being not analytic but synthetic; not shredded history (giving in separate books the separate story of the supposedly insulated activities of men—economic, political, scientific, philosophical, religious, literary, and artistic) but what one might call, not too seriously, wedded history,—history in which all the phases of human life in a given period—made as brief as individual frailty may require—shall be studied in their correlation, in their common response to similar conditions, and in their varied mutual influence. That would be the picture of an age, the image of the complexity of man; it would be such history as a philosopher would consent to write.

As to the *Esthetic*, let others judge. At least one student cannot understand it. Is man an artist as soon as he forms images? Does the essence of art lie only in the conception, and not in the externalization? Have we never had thoughts and feelings more beautiful than our speech? How do we know what the inward image was, in the artist's mind, or whether the work that we admire realizes or misses his idea? How shall we call Rodin's "Harlot" beautiful, except because it is the *expressive embodiment* of an adequate conception?—conception though it be of an ugly and distressing subject? Aristotle notes that it pleases us to see the faithful images of things that are repugnant to us in reality; why, except that we reverence the art that has so well embodied the idea?

It would be interesting, and no doubt disconcerting, to know what artists think of these philosophers who tell them what beauty is. The greatest living artist has abandoned the hope of answering the question. "I believe," he writes, "that we shall never know exactly why a thing is

[33] In Carr, p. 79.   [34] *Esthetic,* p. 79.

beautiful." But the same mellow wisdom offers us a lesson which we learn, usually, too late. "No one has ever been able to show me precisely the right way. . . . As for me, I follow my feeling for the beautiful. What man is certain of having found a better guide? . . . If I had to choose between beauty and truth, I should not hesitate; it is beauty I should keep. . . . There is nothing true in the world except beauty."[35] Let us hope that we need not choose. Perhaps we shall some day be strong enough and clear enough in soul to see the shining beauty of even the darkest truth.

III. BERTRAND RUSSELL

1. THE LOGICIAN

We have kept for the last the youngest and the most virile of the European thinkers of our generation.

When Bertrand Russell spoke at Columbia University in 1914, he looked like his subject, which was epistemology—thin, pale, and moribund; one expected to see him die at every period. The Great War had just broken out, and this tender-minded, peace-loving philosopher had suffered from the shock of seeing the most civilized of continents disintegrate into barbarism. One imagined that he spoke of so remote a subject as "Our Knowledge of the External World" because he knew it was remote, and wished to be as far as possible from actualities that had become so grim. And then, seeing him again, ten years later, one was happy to find him, though fifty-two, hale and jolly, and buoyant with a still rebellious energy. This despite an intervening decade that had destroyed almost all his hopes, loosened all his friendships, and broken almost all the threads of his once sheltered and aristocratic life.

For he belongs to the Russells, one of the oldest and most famous families in England or the world, a family that has given statesmen to Britain for many generations. His grandfather, Lord John Russell, was a great Liberal Prime Minister who fought an unyielding battle for free-trade, for universal free education, for the emancipation of the Jews, for liberty in every field. His father, Viscount Amberley, was a free-thinker, who did not over-burden his son with the hereditary theology of the West. He is now heir presumptive to the second Earl Russell but he rejects the institution of inheritance, and proudly earns his own living. When Cambridge dismissed him for his pacifism he made the world his university, and became a traveling Sophist (in the original sense of that once noble word), whom the world supported gladly.

There have been two Bertrand Russells: one who died during the war; and another who rose out of that one's shroud, an almost mystic com-

[35]Anatole France, *On Life and Letters*, Engl. tr., vol. ii, pp. 113 and 176.

munist born out of the ashes of a mathematical logician. Perhaps there was a tender mystic strain in him always; represented at first by a mountain of algebraic formulae; and then finding a distorted expression in a socialism that has the ear-marks rather of a religion than of a philosophy. The most characteristic title among his books is *Mysticism and Logic:* a merciless attack on the illogicality of mysticism, followed by such a glorification of scientific method as makes one think of the mysticism of logic. Russell inherits the English positivist tradition, and is resolved to be tough-minded, because he knows that he cannot.

Perhaps it was by an over-correction that he emphasized the virtues of logic, and made a divinity of mathematics. He impressed one, in 1914, as cold-blooded, as a temporarily animated abstraction, a formula with legs. He tells us that he never saw a motion-picture till he read Bergson's cinematographic analogy for the intellect; then he reconciled himself to one performance, merely as a task in philosophy. Bergson's vivid sense of time and motion, his feeling that all things were alive with a vital impetus, made no impression on Russell; it seemed to him a pretty poem and nothing more; for his part he would have no other god than mathematics. He had no liking for the classics; he argued vigorously, like another Spencer, for more science in education. The world's woes, he felt, were largely due to mysticism, to culpable obscurity of thought; and the first law of morality should be, to think straight. "Better the world should perish than that I, or any other human being, should believe a lie; . . . that is the religion of thought, in whose scorching flames the dross of the world is being burnt away."[86]

His passion for clarity drove him inevitably to mathematics; he was almost thrilled at the calm precision of this aristocratic science. "Mathematics, rightly viewed, possesses not only truth but supreme beauty—a beauty cold and austere, like that of sculpture, without appeal to any part of our weaker nature, without the gorgeous trappings of painting or music, yet sublimely pure, and capable of a stern perfection such as only the greatest art can show."[87] He believes that the progress of mathematics was the finest feature of the nineteenth century; specifically, "the solution of the difficulties which formerly surrounded the mathematical infinite is probably the greatest achievement of which our age can boast."[88] In one century the old geometry which had held the fortress of mathematics for two thousand years was almost entirely destroyed; and Euclid's text, the oldest school-book in the world, was at last superseded. "It is nothing less than a scandal that he should still be taught to boys in England."[89]

Perhaps the source of most of the innovations in modern mathematics is the rejection of axioms; and Russell delights in men who challenge "self-evident truths" and insist upon the demonstration of the obvious.

[86]*Mysticism and Logic,* London, 1919; p. 241.
[87]*Ibid.,* p. 60.   [88]P. 64.   [89]P. 95.

He was rejoiced to hear that parallel lines may somewhere meet, and that the whole may be no greater than one of its parts. He likes to startle the innocent reader with such puzzles as this: the even numbers are but half of all numbers, and yet there are just as many of them as there are numbers altogether,—since for every number there is its even double. Indeed, this is the whole point about that hitherto indefinable thing, the mathematical infinite: it is a whole containing parts that have as many terms or items as the whole.—The reader may follow this tangent if the spirit moves him.[40]

What draws Russell to mathematics is, again, its rigid impersonality and objectivity; here, and here alone, is eternal truth, and absolute knowledge; these *à priori theorems* are the "Ideas" of Plato, the "eternal order" of Spinoza, the substance of the world. The aim of philosophy should be to equal the perfection of mathematics by confining itself to statements similarly exact, and similarly true before all experience. "Philosophical propositions . . . must be *à priori*," says this strange positivist. Such propositions will refer not to things but to relations, and to universal relations. They will be independent of specific "facts" and events; if every particular in the world were changed, these proportions would still be true. E. g., "if all A's are B's, and X is A, then X is a B": this is true whatever A may be; it reduces to a universal and *à priori* form the old syllogism about the mortality of Socrates; and it would be true if no Socrates, even if nobody at all, had ever existed. Plato and Spinoza were right: "the world of universals may also be described as the world of being. The world of being is unchangeable, rigid, exact, delightful to the mathematician, the logician, the builder of metaphysical systems, and all who love perfection more than life."[41] To reduce all philosophy to such mathematical form, to take all specific content out of it, to compress it (voluminously) into mathematics—this was the ambition of this new Pythagoras.

"People have discovered how to make reasoning symbolic, as it is in algebra, so that deductions can be effected by mathematical rules. . . .

[40] Not that one would recommend Russell's mathematical volumes to the lay reader. The *Introduction to Mathematical Philosophy* sets out with a specious intelligibility, but soon makes demands which only a specialist in mathematics can meet. Even the little book on *The Problems of Philosophy,* though intended to be popular, is difficult, and unnecessarily epistemological; the larger volume, *Mysticism and Logic,* is much clearer and closer to the earth. The *Philosophy of Leibnitz* is a fine exposition of a great thinker, ignored in these limited pages. The twin volumes on *The Analysis of Mind* and *The Analysis of Matter* will serve to bring the reader up to date with certain aspects of psychology and physics. The post-war books are easy reading; and though they suffer from the confusion natural to a man whose idealism is slipping into disillusionment, they are interesting and worth while. *Why Men Fight* is still the best of these tracts for the times. *Roads to Freedom* is a genial survey of social philosophies as old as Diogenes, which Russell rediscovers with all the enthusiasm of a Columbus.

[41] *Mysticism and Logic,* p. 111; *The Problems of Philosophy,* p. 156.

Pure mathematics consists entirely of assertions to the effect that if such and such a proposition is true of anything, then such and such another proposition is true of that thing. It is essential not to discuss whether the first proposition is really true, and not to mention what the anything is of which it is supposed to be true. . . . Thus mathematics may be defined as the subject in which we never know what we are talking about, nor whether what we are saying is true."[42]

And perhaps (if one may rudely interrupt exposition with opinion) this description does no great injustice to mathematical philosophy. It is a splendid game for those who like it; guaranteed to "kill time" as rapidly as chess; it is a new form of solitaire, and should be played as far as possible from the contaminating touch of things. It is remarkable that after writing several volumes of this learned moonshine, Bertrand Russell should suddenly come down upon the surface of this planet, and begin to reason very passionately about war, and government, and socialism, and revolution,—and never once make use of the impeccable formulae piled like Pelion upon Ossa in his *Principia Mathematica*. Nor has anyone else, observably, made use of them. To be useful, reasoning must be about things, and must keep in touch with them at every step. Abstractions have their use as summaries; but as implements of argument they require the running test and commentary of experience. We are in danger here of a scholasticism beside which the giant *Summa's* of medieval philosophy would be models of pragmatic thought.

From such a starting point, Bertrand Russell was almost fated to pass into agnosticism. He found so much in Christianity that could not be phrased in mathematics, that he abandoned it all except its moral code. He speaks scornfully of a civilization that persecutes men who deny Christianity, and imprisons those who take it seriously.[43] He can find no God in such a contradictory world; rather, only a humorus Mephistopheles could have produced it, and in a mood of exceptional deviltry.[44] He follows Spencer in his vision of the end of the world, and rises to eloquence in describing the Stoic's resignation to the ultimate defeat of every individual and every species. We talk of evolution and progress; but progress is an egotistical phrase and evolution is but one half of an unmoral cycle of events terminating in dissolution and death. "Organic life, we are told, has developed gradually from the protozoon to the philosopher; and this development, we are assured, is indubitably an advance. Unfortunately, it is the philosopher, not the protozoon, who gives us this assurance."[45] The "free man" cannot comfort himself with childish hopes and anthropomorphic gods; he has to keep his courage up even

[42]*Mysticism and Logic*, pp. 76 and 75.
[43]*Why Men Fight*, New York, 1917; p. 45.
[44]*Mysticism and Logic*, pp. 76 and 75.
[45]*Ibid.*, p. 106.

though he knows that in the end he too must die, that all things must die. Nevertheless, he will not surrender; if he cannot win, he can at least enjoy the fight; and by the knowledge that foresees his own defeat he stands superior to the blind forces that will destroy him. His worship will go not to these brute powers without, that by their aimless persistence conquer him, and tear down every home and every civilization that he builds; but to those creative powers within him that struggle on in the face of failure, and raise for at least some centuries the frail beauty of carved and pictured things, and the majestic ruins of the Parthenon.

Such was the philosophy of Bertrand Russell—before the war.

2. THE REFORMER

And then the Great Madness came; and the Bertrand Russell who had lain so long buried and mute under the weight of logic and mathematics and epistemology, suddenly burst forth, like a liberated flame, and the world was shocked to find that this slim and anemic-looking professor was a man of infinite courage, and a passionate lover of humanity. Out of the recesses of his formulae the scholar stepped forth, and poured out upon the most exalted statesmen of his country a flood of polemic that did not stop even when they ousted him from his chair at the University, and isolated him, like another Galileo, in a narrow quarter of London. Men who doubted his wisdom admitted his sincerity; but they were so disconcerted by this amazing transformation that they slipped for a moment into a very un-British intolerance. Our embattled pacifist, despite his most respectable origins, was outlawed from society, and denounced as a traitor to the country which had nourished him, and whose very existence seemed to be threatened by the maelstrom of the war.

Back of this rebellion lay a simple horror of all bloody conflict. Bertrand Russell, who had tried to be a disembodied intellect, was really a system of feelings; and the interests of an empire seemed to him not worth the lives of the young men whom he saw so proudly marching forth to kill and die. He set to work to ferret out the causes of such a holocaust; and thought he found in socialism an economic and political analysis that at once revealed the sources of the disease and indicated its only cure. The cause was private property, and the cure was communism.

All property, he pointed out, in his genial way, had had its origin in violence and theft; in the Kimberley diamond mines and the Rand gold mines the transition of robbery into property was going on under the nose of the world. "No good to the community, of any sort or kind, results from the private ownership of land. If men were reasonable they would decree that it should cease tomorrow, with no compensation beyond a moderate life-income to the present holders."[46]

Why Men Fight, p. 134.

Since private property is protected by the state, and the robberies that make property are sanctioned by legislation and enforced by arms and war, the state is a great evil; and it would be well if most of its functions were taken over by cooperatives and producers' syndicates. Personality and individuality are crushed into a rote conformity by our societies; only the greater safety and orderliness of modern life can reconcile us to the state.

Freedom is the supreme good; for without it personality is impossible. Life and knowledge are today so complex, that only by free discussion can we pick our way through errors and prejudices to that total perspective which is truth. Let men, let even teachers, differ and debate; out of such diverse opinions will come an intelligent relativity of belief which will not readily fly to arms; hatred and war come largely of fixed ideas or dogmatic faith. Freedom of thought and speech would go like a cleansing draught through the neuroses and superstitions of the "modern" mind.

For we are not so educated as we think; we are but beginning the great experiment of universal schooling; and it has not had time to affect profoundly our ways of thinking and our public life. We are building the equipment, but we are still primitive in methods and technique; we think of education as the transmission of a certain body of settled knowledge, when it should be rather the development of a scientific habit of mind. The distinctive feature of the unintelligent man is the hastiness and absoluteness of his opinions; the scientist is slow to believe, and never speaks without modification. The larger use of science, and of scientific method, in education would give to us a measure of that intellectual conscience which believes only up to the evidence in hand, and is always ready to concede that it may be wrong. With such methods, education may prove the great solvent of our ills; it may even make of our children's children the new men and women who must come before the new society can appear. "The instinctive part of our character is very malleable. It may be changed by beliefs, by material circumstances, by social circumstances, and by institutions." It is quite conceivable, for example, that education could mould opinion to admire art more than wealth, as in the days of the Renaissance, and could guide itself by the resolution "to promote all that is creative, and so to diminish the impulses and desires that center round possession." This is the Principle of Growth, whose corollaries would be the two great commandments of a new and natural morality: first, the Principle of Reverence, that "the vitality of individuals and communities is to be promoted as far as possible"; and second, the Principle of Tolerance, that "the growth of one individual or one community is to be as little as possible at the expense of another."[47]

There is nothing that man might not do if our splendid organization

[47] *Ibid.*, pp. 101, 248, 256; *Mysticism and Logic*, p. 108.

of schools and universities were properly developed and properly manned, and directed intelligently to the reconstruction of human character. This, and not violent revolution, or paper legislation, is the way out of economic greed and international brutality. Man has come to control all other forms of life because he has taken more time in which to grow up; when he takes still more time, and spends that time more wisely, he may learn even to control and remake himself. Our schools are the open sesame to Utopia.

3. Epilogue

All this, of course, is rather optimistic,—though it is better to err on the side of hope than in favor of despair. Russell has poured into his social philosophy the mysticism and the sentiment which he had so resolutely repressed in his attitude towards metaphysics and religion. He has not applied to his economic and political theories the same rigid scrutiny of assumptions, the same scepticism of axioms, which gave him such satisfaction in mathematics and logic. His passion for the *à priori*, his love of "perfection more than life," leads him here to splendid pictures that serve rather as poetic relief to the prose of the world than as practicable approaches to the problems of life. It is delightful, for example, to contemplate a society in which art shall be better respected than wealth; but so long as nations rise and fall, in the flux of natural group-selection, according to their economic rather than their artistic power, it is economic and not artistic power which, having the greater survival value, will win the greater plaudits and the large rewards. Art can only be the flower that grows out of wealth; it cannot be wealth's substitute. The Medici came before Michelangelo.

But it is not necessary to pick more flaws in Russell's brilliant vision; his own experience has been his severest critic. In Russia he found himself face to face with an effort to create a socialist society; and the difficulties encountered by the experiment almost destroyed Russell's faith in his own gospel. He was disappointed to find that the Russian Government could not risk such a measure of democracy as had seemed to him the axiom of a liberal philosophy; and he was so angered by the suppression of free speech and free press, and by the resolute monopoly and systematic use of every avenue of propaganda, that he rejoiced in the illiteracy of the Russian people;—the ability to read being, in this age of subsidized newspapers, an impediment to the acquisition of truth. He was shocked to find that nationalization of the land had been forced (except on paper) to yield to private ownership; and it dawned upon him that men, as made today, will not properly till and husband their holdings unless they can rely on transmitting them, and the improvements which they put into them, to their children. "Russia seems on the way to becoming a greater France, a great nation of peasant proprietors. The old feudalism has disappeared." He began to understand that this dramatic overturn, with all its sacrifices and all its heroism, was only Russia's 1789.

Perhaps he was more at home when he went for a year to teach in China; there was less mechanism there, and a slower pace; one could sit down and reason, and life would stand still while one dissected it. In that vast sea of humanity new perspectives came to our philosopher; he realized that Europe is but the tentative pseudopodium of a greater continent and an older—and perhaps profounder—culture; all his theories and syllogisms melted into a modest relativity before this mastodon of the nations. One sees his system loosening as he writes:

> I have come to realize that the white race isn't as important as I used to think it was. If Europe and America kill themselves off in war it will not necessarily mean the destruction of the human species, nor even an end to civilization. There will still be a considerable number of Chinese left; and in many ways China is the greatest country I have ever seen. It is not only the greatest numerically and the greatest culturally, but it seems to me the greatest intellectually. I know of no other civilization where there is such open-mindedness, such realism, such a willingness to face the facts as they are, instead of trying to distort them into a particular pattern.[48]

It is a little difficult to pass from England to America, and then to Russia, and then to India and China, and yet keep one's social philosophy unchanged. The world has convinced Bertrand Russell that it is too big for his formulae, and perhaps too large and heavy to move very rapidly towards his heart's desire. And there are so many hearts, and so many different desires! One finds him now "an older and a wiser man," mellowed by time and a varied life; as wide awake as ever to all the ills that flesh is heir to and yet matured into the moderation that knows the difficulties of social change. All in all, a very lovable man: capable of the profoundest metaphysics and the subtlest mathematics, and yet speaking always simply, with the clarity which comes only to those who are sincere; a man addicted to fields of thought that usually dry up the springs of feeling, and yet warmed and illumined with pity, full of an almost mystic tenderness for mankind. Not a courtier, but surely a scholar and a gentleman, and a better Christian than some who mouth the word. Happily, he is still young and vigorous, the flame of life burns brightly in him yet; who knows but this next decade will see him grow out of disillusionment into wisdom, and write his name among the highest in "the serene brotherhood of philosophs"?

[48]Interview in *New York World*, May 4, 1924.

CHAPTER XI

Contemporary American Philosophers:
Santayana, James and Dewey

INTRODUCTION

THERE ARE, as everybody knows, two Americas, of which one is European. European America is chiefly the eastern states, where the older stocks look up respectfully to foreign aristocracies, and more recent immigrants look back with a certain nostalgia to the culture and traditions of their native lands. In this European America there is an active conflict between the Anglo-Saxon soul, sober and genteel, and the restless and innovating spirit of the newer peoples. The English code of thought and manners must eventually succumb to the continental cultures that encompass and inundate it here; but for the present that British mood dominates the literature, though no longer the morals, of the American East. Our standard of art and taste in the Atlantic states is English; our literary heritage is English; and our philosophy, when we have time for any, is in the line of British thought. It is this new England that produced Washington and Irving and Emerson and even Poe; it is this new England that wrote the books of the first American philosopher, Jonathan Edwards; and it is this new England that captured and remade that strange, exotic figure, America's latest thinker, George Santayana. For Santayana, of course, is an American philosopher only by grace of geography; he is a European who, having been born in Spain, was transported to America in his unknowing childhood, and who now, in his ripe age, returns to Europe as to a paradise for which his years with us were a probation. Santayana is steeped in the "genteel tradition" of the old America.[1]

[1]Cf. his own analysis of the two Americas: "America is not simply a young country with an old mentality; it is a country with two mentalities, one a survival of the beliefs and standards of the fathers, the other an expression of the instincts, practices and discoveries of the younger generations. In all the higher things of the mind—in religion, in literature, in the moral emotions—it is the hereditary spirit that prevails, so much so that Mr. Bernard Shaw finds that America is a hundred years behind the times. The truth is that one-half of the American mind has remained, I will not say high and dry, but slightly becalmed; it has floated gently in the back-water, while alongside, in invention and industry and social organization, the other half of the mind was leaping down a sort of Niagara Rapids. This may be found symbolized in American architecture. . . . The American Will inhabits the

The other America is American. It consists of those people, whether Yankees or Hoosiers or cowboys, whose roots are in this soil, and not in Europe; whose manners, ideas and ideals are a native formation; whose souls are touched neither with the gentility of the families that adorn Boston, or New York, or Philadelphia, or Richmond, nor with the volatile passions of the southern or eastern European; men and women moulded into physical ruggedness and mental directness and simplicity by their primitive environment and tasks. This is the America that produced Lincoln and Thoreau and Whitman and Mark Twain; it is the America of "horse sense," of "practical men," of "hard-headed business men"; it is the America which so impressed itself upon William James that he became its exponent in philosophy while his brother became more British than an Englishman; and it is the America that made John Dewey.

We shall study Santayana first, despite chronology; because, though he is the youngest of our greater philosophers, he represents an older and a foreign school; and the subtlety of his thought, and the fragrance of his style, are like the perfume that lingers in a room from which the flowers have been taken away. We shall have, very probably, no more Santayanas; for hereafter it is America, and not Europe, that will write America's philosophies.

I. GEORGE SANTAYANA

1. BIOGRAPHICAL

Santayana was born at Madrid in 1863. He was brought to America in 1872, and remained here till 1912. He took his degrees at Harvard, and taught there from his twenty-seventh to his fiftieth year. One of his students describes him vividly:

> Those who remember him in the class room will remember him as a spirit solemn, sweet, and withdrawn, whose Johannine face by a Renaissance painter held an abstract eye and a hieratic smile, half mischief, half content; whose rich voice flowed evenly, in cadences smooth and balanced as a liturgy; whose periods had the intricate perfection of a poem and the import of a prophecy; who spoke somehow for his hearers and not to them, stirring the depths in their natures and troubling their minds, as an oracle might, to whom pertained mystery and reverence, so compact of remoteness and fascination was he, so moving and so unmoved.[2]

He was not quite content with the country of his choice; his soul, softened with much learning, and sensitive as a poet's soul must be (for he was poet first, and philosopher afterward), suffered from the noisy skyscraper; the American Intellect inhabits the colonial mansion."—*Winds of Doctrine*, New York, 1913; p. 188.

[2]Horace Kallen in *The Journal of Philosophy*, Sept. 29, 1921; vol. 18, p. 534.

haste of American city-life; instinctively he shrank back to Boston, as if to be as near to Europe as he could; and from Boston to Cambridge and Harvard, and a privacy that preferred Plato and Aristotle to James and Royce. He smiled with a little bitterness at the popularity of his colleagues, and remained aloof from the crowd and the press; but he knew that he was fortunate to have found a home in the finest School of Philosophy that any American university had ever known. "It was a fresh morning in the life of reason, cloudy but brightening."[3]

His first essay in philosophy was *The Sense of Beauty* (1896), which even the matter-of-fact Münsterberg rated as the best American contribution to esthetics. Five years later came a more fragmentary, and more readable, volume, *Interpretations of Poetry and Religion*. Then, for seven years, like Jacob serving for his love, he worked silently, publishing only occasional verse; he was preparing his *magnum opus, The Life of Reason*. These five volumes (*Reason in Common Sense, Reason in Society, Reason in Religion, Reason in Art*, and *Reason in Science*) at once lifted Santayana to a fame whose quality fully atoned for what it lacked in spread. Here was the soul of a Spanish grandee grafted upon the stock of the gentle Emerson; a refined mixture of Mediterranean aristocracy with New England individualism; and, above all, a thoroughly emancipated soul, almost immune to the spirit of his age, speaking as if with the accent of some pagan scholar come from ancient Alexandria to view our little systems with unwondering and superior eye, and to dash our new-old dreams with the calmest reasoning and the most perfect prose. Hardly since Plato had philosophy phrased itself so beautifully; here were words full of a novel tang, phrases of delicate texture, perfumed with subtlety and barbed with satiric wit; the poet spoke in these luxuriant metaphors, the artist in these chiseled paragraphs. It was good to find a man who could feel at once the lure of beauty and the call of truth.

After this effort Santayana rested on his fame, contenting himself with poems and minor volumes.[4] Then, strange to say, after he had left Harvard and gone to live in England, and the world presumed that he looked upon his work as finished, he published, in 1923, a substantial volume on *Scepticism and Animal Faith*, with the blithe announcement that this was merely the introduction to a new system of philosophy, to be called "Realms of Being." It was exhilarating to see a man of sixty sailing forth on distant voyages anew, and producing a book as vigorous

[3]*Character and Opinion in the United States*, New York, 1921; end of chapter first.

[4]These are, chiefly: *Three Philosophical Poets* (1910)—classic lectures on Lucretius, Dante and Goethe: *Winds of Doctrine* (1913); *Egotism in German Philosophy* (1916); *Character and Opinion in the United States* (1921); and *Soliloquies in England* (1922). All of these are worth reading, and rather easier than the *Life of Reason*. Of this the finest volume is *Reason in Religion*. *Little Essays from the Writings of George Santayana*, edited by L. P. Smith, and arranged by Santayana himself, is an admirable selection.

in thought, and as polished in style, as any that he had written. We must begin with this latest product, because it is in truth the open door to all of Santayana's thinking.

2. SCEPTICISM AND ANIMAL FAITH

"Here," says the preface, "is one more system of philosophy. If the reader is tempted to smile, I can assure him that I smile with him. . . . I am merely attempting to express for the reader the principles to which he appeals when he smiles." Santayana is modest enough (and this is strange in a philosopher) to believe that other systems than his own are possible. "I do not ask anyone to think in my terms if he prefers others. Let him clean better, if he can, the windows of his soul, that the variety and beauty of the prospect may spread more brightly before him."[5]

In this last and introductory volume he proposes to clear away, first of all, the epistemological cobwebs that have enmeshed and arrested the growth of modern philosophy. Before he delineates the Life of Reason he is willing to discuss, with all the technical paraphernalia dear to the professional epistemologist, the origin, validity and limits of human reason. He knows that the great snare of thought is the uncritical acceptance of traditional assumptions: "criticism surprises the soul in the arms of convention," he says, unconventionally. He is willing to doubt almost everything: the world comes to us dripping with the qualities of the senses through which it has flowed, and the past comes down to us through a memory treacherously colored with desire. Only one thing seems certain to him, and that is the experience of the moment—this color, this form, this taste, this odor, this quality; these are the "real" world, and their perception constitutes "the discovery of essence."[6]

Idealism is correct, but of no great consequence: it is true that we know the world only through our ideas; but since the world has behaved, for some thousands of years, substantially as if our combined sensations were true, we may accept this pragmatic sanction without worry for the future. "Animal faith" may be faith in a myth, but the myth is a good myth, since life is better than any syllogism. The fallacy of Hume lay in supposing that by discovering the origin of ideas he had destroyed their validity: "A natural child meant for him an illegitimate one; his philosophy had not yet reached the wisdom of the French lady who asked if all children were not natural."[7] This effort to be sceptically strict in doubting the veracity of experience has been carried by the Germans to the point of a disease, like a madman forever washing his hands to clean away dirt that is not there. But even these philosophers "who look for the

[5]*Scepticism and Animal Faith,* pp. v and vi.
[6]*Ibid.,* pp. 11f.
[7]*Reason in Common Sense,* New York, 1911; p. 93.

foundations of the universe in their own minds" do not live as if they really believed that things cease to exist when not perceived.

> We are not asked to abolish our conception of the natural world, nor even, in our daily life, to cease to believe in it; we are to be idealists only north-northwest, or transcendentally; when the wind is southerly we are to remain realists. . . . I should be ashamed to countenance opinions which, when not arguing, I did not believe. It would seem to me dishonest and cowardly to militate under other colors than those under which I live. . . . Therefore no modern writer is altogether a philosopher in my eyes, except Spinoza. . . . I have frankly taken nature by the hand, accepting as a rule, in my farthest speculation, the animal faith I live by from day to day.[8]

And so Santayana is through with epistemology; and we breathe more easily as we pass on with him to that magnificent reconstruction of Plato and Aristotle which he calls "The Life of Reason." This epistemological introduction was apparently a necessary baptism for the new philosophy. It is a transitional concession; philosophy still makes its bow in epistemological dress, like the labor leaders who for a time wear silk breeches at the king's court. Some day, when the middle ages are really over, philosophy will come down from these clouds, and deal with the affairs of men.

3. REASON IN SCIENCE

The Life of Reason is "a name for all practical thought and action justified by its fruits in consciousness." Reason is no foe of the instincts, it is their successful unison; it is nature become conscious in us, illuminating its own path and goal. It "is the happy marriage of two elements—impulse and ideation—which, if wholly divorced, would reduce man to a brute or a maniac. The rational animal is generated by the union of these two monsters. He is constituted by ideas which have ceased to be visionary and actions which have ceased to be vain." Reason is "man's imitation of divinity."[9]

The Life of Reason bases itself frankly on science, because "science contains all trustworthy knowledge." Santayana knows the precariousness of reason, and the fallibility of science; he accepts the modern analysis of scientific method as merely a shorthand description of regularities observed in our experience, rather than "laws" governing the world and guaranteed unchangeable. But even so modified, science must be our only reliance; "faith in the intellect . . . is the only faith yet sanctioned by its fruits."[10] So Santayana is resolved to understand life, feeling like Socrates that life without discourse is unworthy of a man; he will subject all "the

---

[8]*Scepticism and Animal Faith*, pp. 192, 298, 305, 308.
[9]*R. in C. S.*, pp. 3, 6 and 17.
[10]*R. in Science*, New York, 1906, p. 318; *R. in C. S.*, p. 96.

phases of human progress," all the pageant of man's interests and history, to the scrutiny of reason.

He is modest enough nevertheless; he proposes no new philosophy, but only an application of old philosophies to our present life; he thinks the first philosophers were the best; and of them all he ranks highest Democritus[11] and Aristotle; he likes the plain blunt materialism of the first, and the unruffled sanity of the second. "In Aristotle the conception of human nature is perfectly sound: everything ideal has a natural basis, and everything natural an ideal development. His ethics, when thoroughly digested and weighed, will seem perfectly final. The Life of Reason finds there its classic explication." And so, armed with the atoms of Democritus and the golden mean of Aristotle, Santayana faces the problems of contemporary life.

> In natural philosophy I am a decided materialist—apparently the only one living. . . . But I do not profess to know what matter is in itself. . . . I wait for the men of science to tell me. . . . But whatever matter may be, I call it matter boldly, as I call my acquaintances Smith and Jones without knowing their secrets.[12]

He will not permit himself the luxury of pantheism, which is merely a subterfuge for atheism; we add nothing to nature by calling it God; "the word *nature* is poetical enough; it suggests sufficiently the generative and controlling function, the endless vitality and changeful order of the world in which I live." To be forever clinging to the old beliefs in these refined and denatured forms is to be like Don Quixote, tinkering with obsolete armor. Yet Santayana is poet enough to know that a world quite divested of deity is a cold and uncomfortable home. "Why has man's conscience in the end invariably rebelled against naturalism and reverted in some form or other to a cultus of the unseen?" Perhaps "because the soul is akin to the eternal and ideal"; it is not content with that which is, and yearns for a better life; it is saddened by the thought of death, and clings to the hope of some power that may make it permanent amid the surrounding flux. But Santayana concludes, bluntly: "I believe there is nothing immortal. . . . No doubt the spirit and energy of the world is what is acting in us, as the sea is what rises in every little wave; but it passes through us; and, cry out as we may, it will move on. Our privilege is to have perceived it as it moved."[13]

Mechanism is probably universal; and though "physics cannot account for that minute motion and pullulation in the earth's crust of which human affairs are a portion," the best method in psychology is to suppose that mechanism prevails even in the inmost recesses of the soul. Psychol-

[11] He makes Democritus the hero of his latest volume, *Dialogues in Limbo.*
[12] *S. and A. F.,* pp. viii and vii.
[13] *Ibid.,* pp. 237 and 271; *R. in C. S.,* p. 189; *Winds of Doctrine,* p. 199.

ogy graduates from literature into science only when it seeks the mechanical and material basis of every mental event. Even the splendid work of Spinoza on the passions is merely "literary psychology," a dialectic of deduction, since it does not seek for each impulse and emotion its physiological and mechanical ground. The "behaviorists" of today have found the right road, and should follow it unfrightened.[14]

So thoroughly mechanical and material is life that consciousness, which is not a thing but a condition and a process, has no causal efficacy; the efficacy lies in the heat with which impulse and desire move brain and body, not in the light which flashes up as thought. "The value of thought is ideal, not causal"; that is, it is not the instrument of action but the theatre of pictured experience and the recipient of moral and esthetic delights.

Is it the mind that controls the bewildered body and points out the way to physical habits uncertain of their affinities? Or is it not much rather an automatic inward machinery that executes the marvelous work, while the mind catches here and there some glimpse of the operation, now with delight and adhesion, now with impotent rebellion? . . . Lalande, or whoever it was, who searched the heavens with his telescope and could find no God, would not have found the human mind if he had searched the brain with a microscope. . . . Belief in such a spirit is simply belief in magic. . . . The only facts observed by the psychologist are physical facts. . . . The soul is only a fine quick organization within the material animal; . . . a prodigious network of nerves and tissues, growing in each generation out of a seed.[15]

Must we accept this buoyant materialism? It is astounding that so subtle a thinker and so ethereal a poet as Santayana should tie to his neck the millstone of a philosophy which after centuries of effort is as helpless as ever to explain the growth of a flower or the laughter of a child. It may be true that the conception of the world as "a bisectible hybrid," half material and half mental, is "the clumsy conjunction of an automaton with a ghost";[16] but it is logic and lucidity personified alongside of Santayana's conception of himself as an automaton automatically reflecting on its own automatism. And if consciousness has no efficacy, why was it evolved, so slowly and so painfully, and why does it survive in a world in which useless things so soon succumb? Consciousness is an organ of judgment as well as a vehicle of delight; its vital function is the rehearsal of response and the coördination of reaction. It is because of it that we are men. Perhaps the flower and its seed, and the child and its laughter, contain more of the mystery of the universe than any machine

[14]R. in S., pp. 75, 131, 136.
[15]R. in C. S., pp. 219, 214, 212; Winds, p. 150; S. and A. F., pp. 287, 257, 218–9.
[16]R. in C. S., p. 211.

that ever was on land or sea; and perhaps it is wiser to interpret nature in terms of life rather than try to understand her in terms of death.

But Santayana has read Bergson too, and turns away from him in scorn.

> Bergson talks a great deal about life, he feels that he has penetrated deeply into its nature; and yet death, together with birth, is the natural analysis of what life is. What is this creative purpose that must wait for sun and rain to set in motion? What is this life that in any individual can be suddenly extinguished by a bullet? What is this *élan vital* that a little fall in temperature would banish altogether from the universe?[17]

4. Reason in Religion

Sainte-Beuve remarked of his countrymen that they would continue to be Catholics long after they had ceased to be Christians. This is the analysis of Renan and Anatole France, and of Santayana too. He loves Catholicism as one may still long for the woman who has deceived him—"I do believe her though I know she lies." He mourns for his lost faith, that "splendid error, which conforms better to the impulses of the soul" than life itself. He describes himself at Oxford, in the midst of some ancient ritual:

> *Exile that I am,*
> *Exile not only from the wind-swept moor,*
> *Where Guadaranna lifts his purple crest,*
> *But from the spirit's realm, celestial, sure,*
> *Goal of all hope, and vision of the best.*

It is because of this secret love, this believing unbelief, that Santayana achieves his masterpiece in *Reason in Religion*, filling his sceptical pages with a tender sadness, and finding in the beauty of Catholicism plentiful cause for loving it still. He smiles, it is true, at "the traditional orthodoxy, the belief, namely, that the universe exists and is good for the sake of man or of the human spirit"; but he scorns "the enlightenment common to young wits and worm-eaten old satirists, who plume themselves on detecting the scientific ineptitude of religion—something which the blindest half see—but leave unexplored the habits of thought from which those tenets sprang, their original meaning and their true function." Here, after all, is a remarkable phenomenon—that men everywhere have had religions; how can we understand man if we do not understand religion? "Such studies would bring the sceptic face to face with the mystery and pathos of mortal existence. They would make him understand why religion is so profoundly moving and in a sense so profoundly just."[18]

[17] *Winds*, p. 107.
[18] *R. in Religion*, New York, 1913; p. 4.

Santayana thinks, with Lucretius, that it was fear which first made the gods.

> Faith in the supernatural is a desperate wager made by man at the lowest ebb of his fortunes; it is as far as possible from being the source of that normal vitality which subsequently, if his fortunes mend, he may gradually recover. . . . If all went well, we should attribute it only to ourselves. . . . The first things which a man learns to distinguish and repeat are things with a will of their own, things which resist his casual demands; and so the first sentiment with which he confronts reality is a certain animosity, which becomes cruelty toward the weak, and fear and fawning before the powerful. . . . It is pathetic to observe how lowly are the motives that religion, even the highest, attributes to the deity, and from what a hardpressed and bitter existence they have been drawn. To be given the best morsel, to be remembered, to be praised, to be obeyed blindly and punctiliously—these have been thought points of honor with the gods, for which they would dispense favors and punishments on the most exorbitant scale.[19]

Add to fear, imagination: man is an incorrigible animist, and interprets all things anthropomorphically; he personifies and dramatises nature, and fills it with a cloud of deities; "the rainbow is taken . . . for a trace left in the sky by the passage of some beautiful and elusive goddess." Not that people quite literally believe these splendid myths; but the poetry of them helps men to bear the prose of life. This mythopoetic tendency is weak today, and science has led to a violent and suspicious reaction against imagination; but in primitive peoples, and particularly in the near East, it was unchecked. The Old Testament abounds in poetry and metaphor; the Jews who composed it did not take their own figures literally; but when European peoples, more literal and less imaginative, mistook these poems for science, our Occidental theology was born. Christianity was at first a combination of Greek theology with Jewish morality; it was an unstable combination, in which one or the other element would eventually yield; in Catholicism the Greek and pagan element triumphed, in Protestantism, the stern Hebraic moral code. The one had a Renaissance, the other a Reformation.[20]

The Germans—the "northern barbarians," Santayana calls them—had never really accepted Roman Christianity. "A non-Christian ethics of valor and honor, a non-Christian fund of superstition, legend and sentiment, subsisted always among medieval peoples." The Gothic cathedrals were barbaric, not Roman. The warlike temper of the Teutons raised its head above the peacefulness of the Oriental, and changed Christianity from a religion of brotherly love to a stern inculcation of business virtues, from a religion of poverty to a religion of prosperity and power. "It was this youthful religion—profound, barbaric, poetical—that the Teutonic

---

[19] *R. in S.,* p. 297; *R. in R.,* pp. 28, 34.
[20] *S. and A. F.,* p. 6; *R. in C. S.,* p. 128; *R. in R.,* pp. 27f.

races insinuated into Christianity, and substituted for that last sigh of two expiring worlds."[21]

Nothing would be so beautiful as Christianity, Santayana thinks, if it were not taken literally; but the Germans insisted on taking it literally. The dissolution of Christian orthodoxy in Germany was thereafter inevitable. For taken literally, nothing could be so absurd as some of the ancient dogmas, like the damnation of innocents, or the existence of evil in a world created by omnipotent benevolence. The principle of individual interpretation led naturally to a wild growth of sects among the people, and to a mild pantheism among the élite—pantheism being nothing more than "naturalism poetically expressed." Lessing and Goethe, Carlyle and Emerson, were the landmarks of this change. In brief, the moral system of Jesus had destroyed that militaristic Yahveh who by an impish accident of history had been transmitted to Christianity along with the pacifism of the prophets and of Christ.[22]

Santayana is by constitution and heredity incapable of sympathy with Protestantism; he prefers the color and incense of his youthful faith. He scolds the Protestants for abandoning the pretty legends of medievaldom, and above all for neglecting the Virgin Mary, whom he considers, as Heine did, the "fairest flower of poesy." As a wit has put it, Santayana believes that there is no God, and that Mary is His mother. He adorns his room with pictures of the Virgin and the saints.[23] He likes the beauty of Catholicism more than the truth of any other faith, for the same reason that he prefers art to industry.

> There are two stages in the criticism of myths. . . . The first treats them angrily as superstitions; the second treats them smilingly as poetry. . . . Religion is human experience interpreted by human imagination. . . . The idea that religion contains a literal, not a symbolic, representation of truth and life is simply an impossible idea. Whoever entertains it has not come within the region of profitable philosophizing on that subject. . . . Matters of religion should never be matters of controversy. . . . We seek rather to honor the piety and understand the poetry embodied in these fables.[24]

The man of culture, then, will leave undisturbed the myths that so comfort and inspire the life of the people; and perhaps he will a little envy them their hope. But he will have no faith in another life. "The fact of having been born is a bad augury for immortality."[25] The only immortality that will interest him is that which Spinoza describes.

"He who lives in the ideal," says Santayana, "and leaves it expressed in society or in art enjoys a double immortality. The eternal has absorbed

[21]*R. in R.*, pp. 103, 125.   [22]*R. in R.*, pp. 137, 130, 172.
[23]Margaret Münsterberg in *The American Mercury*, Jan., 1924, p. 74.
[24]*The Sense of Beauty*, New York, 1896, p. 189; *R. and A. F.*, p. 247; *Winds*, p. 46; *R. in R.*, pp. 98, 97.
[25]*R. in R.*, p. 240.

him while he lived, and when he is dead his influence brings others to the same absorption, making them, through that ideal identity with the best in him, reincarnations and perennial seats of all in him which he could rationally hope to rescue from destruction. He can say, without any subterfuge or desire to delude himself, that he shall not wholly die; for he will have a better notion than the vulgar of what constitutes his being. By becoming the spectator and confessor of his own death and of universal mutation, he will have identified himself with what is spiritual in all spirits and masterful in all apprehension; and so conceiving himself, he may truly feel and know that he is eternal."[26]

5. Reason in Society

The great problem of philosophy is to devise a means whereby men may be persuaded to virtue without the stimulus of supernatural hopes and fears. Theoretically it solved this problem twice; both in Socrates and in Spinoza it gave the world a sufficiently perfect system of natural or rational ethics. If men could be moulded to either philosophy, all would be well. But "a truly rational morality or social regimen has never existed in the world, and is hardly to be looked for"; it remains the luxury of philosophers. "A philosopher has a haven in himself, of which I suspect the fabled bliss to follow in other lives . . . is only a poetic symbol; he has pleasure in truth, and an equal readiness to enjoy the scene or quit it" (though one may observe a certain obstinate longevity in him). For the rest of us the avenue of moral development must lie, in the future as in the past, in the growth of those social emotions which bloom in the generous atmosphere of love and the home."[27]

It is true, as Schopenhauer argued, that love is a deception practised upon the individual by the race; that "nine-tenths of the cause of love are in the lover, for one-tenth that may be in the object"; and that love "fuses the soul again into the impersonal blind flux." Nevertheless, love has its recompenses; and in his greatest sacrifice man finds his happiest fulfilment. "Laplace is reported to have said on his deathbed that science was mere trifling, and that nothing was real but love." After all, romantic love, despite its poetical delusions, ends normally in a relationship—of parent and child—far more satisfying to the instincts than any celibate security. Children are our immortality; and "we commit the blotted manuscript of our lives more willingly to the flames, when we find the immortal text half engrossed in a fairer copy."[28]

The family is the avenue of human perpetuity, and therefore still the basic institution among men; it could carry on the race even if all other

---

[26]*Ibid.*, p. 273.   [27]*R. in S.*, p. 239; *S. and A. F.*, p. 54.
[28]*R. in Society*, New York, 1915, pp. 22, 6, 195, 41; *R. in C. S.*, p. 57; *R. in S.,* p. 258

institutions failed. But it can conduct civilization only to a certain simple pitch; further development demands a larger and more complex system in which the family ceases to be the productive unit, loses its control over the economic relations of its members, and finds its authority and its powers more and more appropriated by the state. The state may be a monster, as Nietzsche called it; a monster of unnecessary size; but its centralized tyranny has the virtue of abolishing the miscellaneous and innumerable petty tyrannies by which life was of old pestered and confined. One master pirate, accepting tribute quietly, is better than a hundred pirates, taking toll without warning and without stint.[29]

Hence, in part, the patriotism of the people; they know that the price they pay for government is cheaper than the cost of chaos. Santayana wonders whether such patriotism does more harm than good; for it tends to attach the stigma of disloyalty to advocates of change. "To love one's country, unless that love is quite blind and lazy, must involve a distinction between the country's actual condition and its inherent ideal; and this distinction in turn involves a demand for changes and for effort." On the other hand, race patriotism is indispensable. "Some races are obviously superior to others. A more thorough adjustment to the conditions of existence has given their spirit victory, scope, and a relative stability." Hence intermarriage is perilous, except between races of acknowledged equality and stability. "The Jews, the Greeks, the Romans, the English, were never so great as when they confronted other nations, reacting against them and at the same time, perhaps, adopting their culture; but this greatness fails inwardly whenever contact leads to amalgamation."[30]

The great evil of the state is its tendency to become an engine of war, a hostile fist shaken in the face of a supposedly inferior world. Santayana thinks that no people has ever won a war.

> Where parties and governments are bad, as they are in most ages and countries, it makes practically no difference to a community, apart from local ravages, whether its own army or the enemy's is victorious in war. . . . The private citizen in any event continues in such countries to pay a maximum of taxes and to suffer, in all his private interests, a maximum of vexation and neglect. Nevertheless . . . the oppressed subject will glow like the rest with patriotic ardor, and will decry as dead to duty and honor anyone who points out how perverse is this helpless allegiance to a government representing no public interest.[31]

This is strong language for a philosopher; but let us have our Santayana unexpurgated. Often enough, he thinks, conquest and absorption by a larger state is a step forward toward the organization and pacification of mankind; it would be a boon to all the world if all the world were

[29]*R. in Society*, pp. 45, 77, 79.
[30]*Ibid.*, pp. 164–167.   [31]*Ibid.*, p. 171.

ruled by some great power or group of powers, as all the world was once ruled by Rome, first with the sword and then with the word.

> The universal order once dreamt of and nominally almost established, the empire of universal peace, all-permeating rational art, and philosophical worship, is mentioned no more. . . . Those dark ages, from which our political practice is derived, had a political theory we should do well to study; for their theory about a universal empire and a catholic church was in turn the echo of a former age of reason when a few men conscious of ruling the world had for a moment sought to survey it as a whole and to rule it justly.[32]

Perhaps the development of international sports may give some outlet to the spirit of group rivalry, and serve in some measure as "a moral equivalent for war"; and perhaps the cross-investments of finance may overcome the tendency of trade to come to blows for the markets of the world. Santayana is not so enamored of industry as Spencer was; he knows its militant as well as its pacific side: and all in all, he feels more at ease in the atmosphere of an ancient aristocracy than in the hum of a modern metropolis. We produce too much, and are swamped with the things we make; "things are in the saddle and ride mankind," as Emerson put it. "In a world composed entirely of philosophers an hour or two a day of manual labor—a very welcome quality—would provide for material wants." England is wiser than the United States; for though she too is obsessed with the mania for production, she has in at least a portion of her people realized the value and the arts of leisure.[33]

He thinks that such culture as the world has known has always been the fruit of aristocracies.

> Civilization has hitherto consisted in the diffusion and dilution of habits arising in privileged centres. It has not sprung from the people; it has arisen in their midst by a variation from them, and it has afterward imposed itself on them from above. . . . A state composed exclusively of such workers and peasants as make up the bulk of modern nations would be an utterly barbarous state. Every liberal tradition would perish in it; and the rational and historic essence of patriotism itself would be lost. The emotion of it, no doubt, would endure, for it is not generosity that the people lack. They possess every impulse; it is experience that they cannot gather, for in gathering it they would be constituting those higher organs that make up an aristocratic society.[34]

He dislikes the ideal of equality, and argues with Plato that the equality of unequals is inequality. Nevertheless he does not quite sell himself to aristocracy; he knows that history has tried it and found its virtues very

[32] *Ibid.*, p. 81; *R. in S.*, p. 255, referring, no doubt, to the age of the Antonines, and implicitly accepting the judgment of Gibbon and Renan that this was the finest period in the history of government.

[33] *R. in Society*. pp. 87, 66, 69.   [34] *Ibid.*, pp. 125, 124; *R. in Science*, p. 255

well balanced by its defects; that it closes career to unpedigreed talent, that it chokes the growth, in all but a narrow line, of just those superiorities and values that aristocracy would, in theory, develop and use. It makes for culture, but also it makes for tyranny; the slavery of millions pays for the liberty of a few. The first principle of politics should be that a society is to be judged by the measure in which it enhances the life and capacities of its constituent individuals;—"but for the excellence of the typical single life no nation deserves to be remembered more than the sands of the sea."[35] From this point of view, democracy is a great improvement on aristocracy. But it too has its evils; not merely its corruption and its incompetence, but worse, its own peculiar tyranny, the fetich of uniformity. "There is no tyranny so hateful as a vulgar, anonymous tyranny. It is all-permeating, all-thwarting; it blasts every budding novelty and sprig of genius with its omnipresent and fierce stupidity."[36]

What Santayana despises above all is the chaos and indecent haste of modern life. He wonders was there not more happiness for men in the old aristocratic doctrine that the good is not liberty, but wisdom, and contentment with one's natural restrictions; the classical tradition knew that only a few can win. But now that democracy has opened the great free-for-all, catch-as-catch-can wrestling match of *laissez-faire* industrialism, every soul is torn with climbing, and no one knows content. Classes war against one another without restraint; and "whoever is victorious in this struggle (for which liberalism cleared the field) will make an end of liberalism."[37] This is the nemesis of revolutions, too: that in order to survive they must restore the tyranny which they destroyed.

> Revolutions are ambiguous things. Their success is generally proportionate to their power of adaptation and to the reabsorption within them of what they rebelled against. A thousand reforms have left the world as corrupt as ever, for each successful reform has founded a new institution, and this institution has bred its new and congenial abuses.[38]

What form of society, then, shall we strive for? Perhaps for none; there is not much difference among them. But if for any one in particular, for "timocracy." This would be government by men of merit and honor; it would be an aristocracy, but not hereditary; every man and woman would have an open road according to ability, to the highest offices in the state; but the road would be closed to incompetence, no matter how richly furnished it might be with plebiscites. "The only equality subsisting would be equality of opportunity."[39] Under such a government corruption would be at a minimum, and science and the arts would flourish through discriminating encouragement. It would be just that synthesis of democ-

---

[35] *R. in Society*, p. 52.   [36] *Ibid.*, p. 217; *Sense of Beauty*, p. 110.
[37] Herbert W. Smith in *American Review*, March, 1923; p. 195.
[38] *R. in R.*, p. 83; but cf. *R. in Science*, p. 233.   [39] *R. in Society*, p. 123f.

racy and aristocracy which the world pines for in the midst of its political chaos today: only the best would rule; but every man would have an equal chance to make himself worthy to be numbered among the best — It is, of course, Plato over again, the philosopher-kings of the *Republic* appearing inevitably on the horizon of every far-seeing political philosophy. The longer we think about these matters the more surely we return to Plato. We need no new philosophy; we need only the courage to live up to the oldest and the best.

6. COMMENT

There is in all these pages something of the melancholy of a man separated from all that he loves and was accustomed to, a man *déraciné*, a Spanish aristocrat exiled to middle-class America. A secret sadness sometimes breaks forth: "That life is worth living," he says, "is the most necessary of assumptions, and, were it not assumed, the most impossible of conclusions."[40] In the first volume of "The Life of Reason" he talks of the plot and meaning of human life and history as the subject of philosophy; in the last volume he wonders is there a meaning, or a plot?[41] He has unconsciously described his own tragedy: "There is tragedy in perfection, because the universe in which perfection arises is itself imperfect."[42] Like Shelley, Santayana has never felt at home on this middling planet; his keen esthetic sense seems to have brought to him more suffering from the ugliness of things than delight in the scattered loveliness of the world. He becomes at times bitter and sarcastic; he has never caught the hearty cleansing laughter of paganism, nor the genial and forgiving humanity of Renan or Anatole France. He stands aloof and superior, and therefore alone. "What is the part of wisdom?" he asks; and answers —"To dream with one eye open; to be detached from the world without being hostile to it; to welcome fugitive beauties and pity fugitive sufferings, without forgetting for a moment how fugitive they are."[43]

But perhaps this constant *memento mori* is a knell to joy; to live, one must remember life more than death; one must embrace the immediate and actual thing as well as the distant and perfect hope. "The goal of speculative thinking is none other than to live as much as may be in the eternal, and to absorb and be absorbed in the truth."[44] But this is to take philosophy more seriously than even philosophy deserves to be taken; and a philosophy which withdraws one from life is as much awry as any celestial superstition in which the eye, rapt in some vision of another world, loses the meat and wine of this one. "Wisdom comes by disillusionment," says Santayana;[45] but again that is only the beginning of wisdom,

[40]*R. in C. S.,* p. 252.   [41]*Ibid.,* p. 9.   [42]*R. in Science,* p. 237.
[43]Herbert W. Smith in *American Review,* March, 1923; p. 191.
[44]*R. in C. S.,* p. 28.   [45]*Ibid.,* p. 202.

as doubt is the beginning of philosophy; it is not also the end and fulfilment. The end is happiness, and philosophy is only a means; if we take it
as an end we become like the Hindu mystic whose life-purpose is to concentrate upon his navel.

Perhaps Santayana's conception of the universe as merely a material
mechanism has something to do with this sombre withdrawal into himself; having taken life out of the world, he seeks for it in his own bosom.
He protests that it is not so; and though we may not believe him, his
too-much-protesting disarms us with its beauty:

> A theory is not an unemotional thing. If music can be full of passion,
> merely by giving form to a single sense, how much more beauty or terror
> may not a vision be pregnant with which brings order and method into
> everything that we know. . . . If you are in the habit of believing in special
> providences, or of expecting to continue your romantic adventures in a second
> life, materialism will dash your hopes most unpleasantly, and you may think
> for a year or two that you have nothing left to live for. But a thorough
> materialist, one born to the faith and not half plunged into it by an un-
> expected christening in cold water, will be like the superb Democritus, a
> laughing philosopher. His delight in a mechanism that can fall into so many
> marvellous and beautiful shapes, and can generate so many exciting passions,
> should be of the same intellectual quality as that which the visitor feels in a
> museum of natural history, where he views the myriad butterflies in their
> cases, the flamingoes and shell-fish, the mammoths and gorillas. Doubtless
> there were pangs in that incalculable life; but they were soon over; and how
> splendid meantime was the pageant, how infinitely interesting the universal
> interplay, and how foolish and inevitable those absolute little passions.[46]

But perhaps the butterflies, if they could speak, would remind us that
a museum (like a materialist philosophy) is only a show-case of lifeless
things; that the reality of the world eludes these tragic preservations, and
resides again in the pangs of passion, in the ever-changing and never-
ending flow of life.

"Santayana," says an observant friend,

> had a natural preference for solitude. . . . I remember leaning over the
> railing of an ocean liner anchored at Southampton and watching passengers
> from the English tender crowd up the gang-plank to the steamer; one only
> stood apart at the edge of the tender, with calm and amused detachment
> observed the haste and struggle of his fellow-passengers, and not till the deck
> had been cleared, followed himself. 'Who could it be but Santayana?' a
> voice said beside me; and we all felt the satisfaction of finding a character
> true to himself.[47]

After all, we must say just that, too, of his philosophy: it is a veracious
and fearless self-expression; here a mature and subtle, though too sombre,

[46]R. in Science, pp. 89–90.
[47]Margaret Münsterberg in The American Mercury, Jan., 1924, p. 69.

soul has written itself down quietly, in statuesque and classic prose. And though we may not like its minor key, its undertone of sweet regret for a vanished world, we see in it the finished expression of this dying and nascent age, in which men cannot be altogether wise and free, because they have abandoned their old ideas and have not yet found the new ones that shall lure them nearer to perfection.

II. WILLIAM JAMES

1. Personal

The reader will not need to be reminded that the philosophy which we have just summarized is a European philosophy in everything but the place of its composition. It has the nuances and polish and mellow resignation characteristic of an old culture; one could tell from any paragraph in the *Life of Reason* that this is no native American voice.

In William James the voice and the speech and the very turn of phrase are American. He pounced eagerly upon such characteristic expressions as "cash-value," and "results," and "profits," in order to bring his thought within the ken of the "man in the street"; he spoke not with the aristocratic reserve of a Santayana or a Henry James, but in a racy vernacular and with a force and directness, which made his philosophy of "pragmatism" and "reserve energy" the mental correlate of the "practical" and "strenuous" Roosevelt. And at the same time he phrased for the common man that "tender-minded" trust in the essentials of the old theology which lives side by side, in the American soul, with the realistic spirit of commerce and finance, and with the tough persistent courage that turned a wilderness into the promised land.

William James was born in New York City in 1842. His father was a Swedenborgian mystic, whose mysticism did no damage to his wit and humor; and the son was not lacking in any of the three. After some seasons in American private schools, William was sent with his brother Henry (one year his junior) to private schools in France. There they fell in with the work of Charcot and other psychopathologists, and took, both of them, a turn to psychology; one of them, to repeat an old phrase, proceeded to write fiction like psychology, while the other wrote psychology like fiction. Henry spent most of his life abroad, and finally became a British citizen. Through his more continuous contact with European culture he acquired a maturity of thought which his brother missed; but William, returning to live in America, felt the stimulation of a nation young in heart and rich in opportunity and hope, and caught so well the spirit of his age and place that he was lifted on the wings of the *Zeitgeist* to a lonely pinnacle of popularity such as no other American philosopher had ever known.

He took his M.D. at Harvard in 1870, and taught there from 1872 to his death in 1910, at first anatomy and physiology, and then psychology, and at last philosophy. His greatest achievement was almost his first —*The Principles of Psychology* (1890); a fascinating mixture of anatomy, philosophy and analysis; for in James psychology still drips from the foetal membranes of its mother, metaphysics. Yet the book remains the most instructive, and easily the most absorbing, summary of its subject; something of the subtlety which Henry put into his clauses helped William James to the keenest introspection which psychology had witnessed since the uncanny clarity of David Hume.

This passion for illuminating analysis was bound to lead James from psychology to philosophy, and at last back to metaphysics itself; he argued (against his own positivist inclinations) that metaphysics is merely an effort to think things out clearly; and he defined philosophy, in his simple and pellucid manner, as "only thinking about things in the most comprehensive possible way."[48] So, after 1900, his publications were almost all in the field of philosophy. He began with *The Will to Believe* (1897); then, after a masterpiece of psychological interpretation—*Varieties of Religious Experience* (1902)—he passed on to his famous books on *Pragmatism* (1907), *A Pluralistic Universe* (1909), and *The Meaning of Truth* (1909). A year after his death came *Some Problems of Philosophy* (1911); and later, an important volume of *Essays in Radical Empiricism* (1912). We must begin our study with this last book, because it was in these essays that James formulated most clearly the bases of his philosophy.[49]

2. PRAGMATISM

The direction of his thought is always to things; and if he begins with psychology it is not as a metaphysician who loves to lose himself in ethereal obscurities, but as a realist to whom thought, however distinct it may be from matter, is essentially a mirror of external and physical reality. And it is a better mirror than some have believed; it perceives and reflects not merely separate things, as Hume supposed, but their relations too; it sees everything in a context; and the context is as immediately given in perception as the shape and touch and odor of the thing. Hence the meaninglessness of Kant's "problem of knowledge" (how do we put sense and order into our sensations?)—the sense and the order, in outline at least, are already there. The old atomistic psychology

---

[48] *Some Problems of Philosophy,* p. 25.

[49] The reader who has leisure for but one book of James's should go directly to *Pragmatism,* which he will find a fountain of clarity as compared with most philosophy. If he has more time, he will derive abundant profit from the brilliant pages of the (unabbreviated) *Psychology.* Henry James has written two volumes of autobiography, in which there is much delightful gossip about William. Flournoy has a good volume of exposition, and Schinz's *Anti-Pragmatism* is a vigorous criticism.

of the English school, which conceived thought as a series of separate ideas mechanically associated, is a misleading copy of physics and chemistry; thought is not a series, it is a stream, a continuity of perception and feeling, in which ideas are passing nodules like corpuscles in the blood We have mental "states" (though this is again a misleadingly static term) that correspond to prepositions, verbs, adverbs and conjunctions, as well as "states" that reflect the nouns and pronouns of our speech; we have feelings of *for* and *to* and *against* and *because* and *behind* and *after* as well as of matter and men. It is these "transitive" elements in the *flow* of thought that constitute the thread of our mental life, and give us some measure of the continuity of things.

Consciousness is not an entity, not a thing, but a flux and system of relations; it is a point at which the sequence and relationship of thoughts coincide illuminatingly with the sequence of events and the relationship of things. In such moments it is reality itself, and no mere "phenomenon," that flashes into thought; for beyond phenomena and "appearances" there is nothing. Nor is there any need of going beyond the experience-process to a soul; the soul is merely the sum of our mental life, as the "Noumenon" is simply the total of all phenomena, and the "Absolute" the web of the relationships of the world.

It is this same passion for the immediate and actual and real that led James to pragmatism. Brought up in the school of French clarity, he abominated the obscurities and pedantic terminology of German metaphysics; and when Harris and others began to import a moribund Hegelianism into America, James reacted like a quarantine officer who has detected an immigrant infection. He was convinced that both the terms and the problems of German metaphysics were unreal; and he cast about him for some test of meaning which would show, to every candid mind, the emptiness of these abstractions.

He found the weapon which he sought when, in 1878, he came upon an essay by Charles Peirce, in the *Popular Science Monthly*, on "How to Make Our Ideas Clear." To find the meaning of an idea, said Peirce, we must examine the consequences to which it leads in action; otherwise dispute about it may be without end, and will surely be without fruit. This was a lead which James was glad to follow; he tried the problems and ideas of the old metaphysics by this test, and they fell to pieces at its touch like chemical compounds suddenly shot through with a current of electricity. And such problems as had meaning took on a clearness and a reality as if, in Plato's famous figure, they had passed out of the shadows of a cave into the brilliance of a sun-lit noon.

This simple and old-fashioned test led James on to a new definition of truth. Truth had been conceived as an objective relation, as once good and beauty had been; now what if truth, like these, were also relative to human judgment and human needs? "Natural laws" had been taken as "objective" truths, eternal and unchangeable; Spinoza had made them the very substance of his philosophy; and yet what were these truths but formulations of experience, convenient and successful in practice; not copies of an object, but correct calculations of specific consequences? Truth is the "cash-value" of an idea.

> The true . . . is only the expedient in the way of our thinking, just as "the right" is only the expedient in the way of our behaving. Expedient is almost any fashion; and expedient in the long run and on the whole, of course; for what meets expediently all the experiences in sight won't necessarily meet all further experiences equally satisfactorily. . . . Truth is *one species* of good, and not, as is usually supposed, a category distinct from good, and coördinate with it. The true is the name of whatever proves itself to be good in the way of belief.[50]

Truth is a process, and "happens to an idea"; verity is verification. Instead of asking whence an idea is derived, or what are its premises, pragmatism examines its results; it "shifts the emphasis and looks forward"; it is "the attitude of looking away from first things, principles, 'categories,' supposed necessities, and of looking towards last things, fruits, consequences, facts."[51] Scholasticism asked, What *is* the thing,—and lost itself in "quiddities"; Darwinism asked, What is its origin?—and lost itself in nebulas; pragmatism asks, What are its consequences?—and turns the face of thought to action and the future.

3. Pluralism

Let us apply this method to the oldest problem in philosophy—the existence and nature of God. The Scholastic philosophers described the deity as "*Ens a se extra et supra omne genus, necessarium, unum, infinite, perfectum, simplex, immutabile, immensum, eternum, intelligens.*"[52] This is magnificent; what deity would not be proud of such a definition? But what does it mean?—what are its consequences for mankind? If God is omniscient and omnipotent, we are puppets; there is nothing that we can do to change the course of destiny which His will has from the beginning delineated and decreed; Calvinism and fatalism are the logical corollaries of such a definition. The same test applied to mechanistic determinism issues in the same results: if we really believed in determinism we would become Hindu mystics and abandon ourselves at once to the immense fatality which uses us as marionettes. Of course we do not accept these sombre philosophies; the human intellect repeatedly proposes them because of their logical simplicity and symmetry, but life ignores and overflows them, and passes on.

A philosophy may be unimpeachable in other respects, but either of two defects will be fatal to its universal adoption. First, its ultimate principle

[50]*Pragmatism*, pp. 222, 75, 53. 45.   [51]*Ibid.*, p. 54.   [52]P. 121.

must not be one that essentially baffles and disappoints our dearest desires and most cherished hopes. . . . But a second and worse defect in a philosophy than contradicting our active propensities is to give them no object whatever to press against. A philosophy whose principle is so incommensurate with our most intimate powers as to deny them all relevancy in universal affairs, as to annihilate their motives at one blow, will be even more unpopular than pessimism. . . . That is why materialism will always fail of universal adoption.[53]

Men accept or reject philosophies, then, according to their needs and their temperaments, not according to "objective truth"; they do not ask, Is this logical?—they ask, What will the actual practice of this philosophy mean for our lives and our interests? Arguments for and against may serve to illuminate, but they never prove.

> Logic and sermons never convince;
> The damp of the night drives deeper into my soul. . . .
> Now I re-examine philosophies and religions.
> They may prove well in lecture rooms, yet not prove at all under the spacious clouds, and along the landscape and flowing currents.[54]

We know that arguments are dictated by our needs, and that our needs cannot be dictated to by arguments.

The history of philosophy is to a great extent that of a certain clash of human temperaments. . . . Of whatever temperament a professional philosopher is, he tries, when philosophizing, to sink the fact of his temperament. Temperament is no conventionally recognized reason, so he urges impersonal reasons only for his conclusions. Yet his temperament really gives him a stronger bias than any of his more strictly objective premises.[55]

These temperaments which select and dictate philosophies may be divided into the tender-minded and the tough-minded. The tender-minded temperament is religious, it likes to have definite and unchanging dogmas and à priori truths; it takes naturally to free will, idealism, monism, and optimism. The tough-minded temperament is materialistic, irreligious, empiricist (going only on "facts"), sensationalistic (tracing all knowledge to sensation), fatalistic, pluralistic, pessimistic, sceptical. In each group there are gaping contradictions; and no doubt there are temperaments that select their theories partly from one group and partly from the other. There are people (William James, for example) who are "tough-minded" in their addiction to facts and in their reliance on the senses, and yet "tender-minded" in their horror of determinism and their need for religious belief. Can a philosophy be found that will harmonize these apparently contradictory demands?

[53]*Principles of Psychology*, New York, 1890, vol. ii, p. 312.
[54]Whitman, *Leaves of Grass* Philadelphia. 1900, pp. 61, 172.
[55]*Pragmatism*, p. 6.

James believes that pluralistic theism affords us such a synthesis. He offers a finite God, not an Olympian thunderer sitting aloof on a cloud, "but one helper, *primus inter pares,* in the midst of all the shapers of the great world's fate."[56] The cosmos is not a closed and harmonious system; it is a battle-ground of cross-currents and conflicting purposes; it shows itself, with pathetic obviousness, as not a uni- but a multi-verse. It is useless to say that this chaos in which we live and move is the result of one consistent will; it gives every sign of contradiction and division within itself. Perhaps the ancients were wiser than we, and polytheism may be truer than monotheism to the astonishing diversity of the world. Such polytheism "has always been the real religion of common people, and is so still today."[57] The people are right, and the philosophers are wrong. Monism is the natural disease of philosophers, who hunger and thirst not (as they think) for truth, but for unity. " 'The world is One!'—the formula may become a sort of number-worship. 'Three' and 'seven' have, it is true, been reckoned as sacred numbers; but abstractly taken, why is 'one' more excellent than 'forty-three,' or than 'two million and ten'?"[58]

The value of a multiverse, as compared with a universe, lies in this, that where there are cross-currents and warring forces our own strength and will may count and help decide the issue; it is a world where nothing is irrevocably settled, and all action matters. A monistic world is for us a dead world; in such a universe we carry out, willy-nilly, the parts assigned to us by an omnipotent deity or a primeval nebula; and not all our tears can wipe out one word of the eternal script. In a finished universe individuality is a delusion; "in reality," the monist assures us, we are all bits of one mosaic substance. But in an unfinished world we can write some lines of the parts we play, and our choices mould in some measure the future in which we have to live. In such a world we can be free; it is a world of chance, and not of fate; everything is "not quite"; and what we are or do may alter everything. If Cleopatra's nose, said Pascal, had been an inch longer or shorter, all history would have been changed.

The theoretical evidence for such free will, or such a multiverse, or such a finite God, is as lacking as for the opposite philosophies. Even the practical evidence may vary from person to person; it is conceivable that some may find better results, for their lives, from a deterministic than from a libertarian philosophy. But where the evidence is indecisive, our vital and moral interests should make the choice.

If there be any life that it is really better that we should lead, and if there be any idea which, if believed in, would help us to lead that life, then

---

[56] *Ibid.,* p. 298.
[57] *Varieties of Religious Experience,* New York, 1902, p. 526.
[58] *Pragmatism,* p. 312. The answer, of course, is that unity, or one system of laws holding throughout the universe, facilitates explanation, prediction, and control.

it would be really *better for us* to believe in that idea, *unless, indeed, belief in it incidentally clashed with other greater vital benefits.*[59]

Now the persistence of the belief in God is the best proof of its almost universal vital and moral value. James was amazed and attracted by the endless varieties of religious experience and belief; he described them with an artist's sympathy, even where he most disagreed with them. He saw some truth in every one of them, and demanded an open mind toward every new hope. He did not hesitate to affiliate himself with the Society for Psychical Research; why should not such phenomena, as well as others, be the object of patient examination? In the end, James was convinced of the reality of another—a spiritual—world.

I firmly disbelieve, myself, that our human experience is the highest form of experience extant in the universe. I believe rather that we stand in much the same relation to the whole of the universe as our canine and feline pets do to the whole of human life. They inhabit our drawing rooms and libraries. They take part in scenes of whose significance they have no inkling. They are merely tangent to curves of history, the beginnings and ends and forms of which pass wholly beyond their ken. So we are tangent to the wider life of things.[60]

Nevertheless he did not think of philosophy as a meditation on death; no problems had value for him unless they could guide and stimulate our terrestrial career. "It was with the excellencies, not the duration, of our natures, that he occupied himself."[61] He did not live in his study so much as in the current of life; he was an active worker in a hundred efforts for human betterment; he was always helping somebody, lifting men up with the contagion of his courage. He believed that in every individual there were "reserve energies" which the occasional midwifery of circumstance would bring forth; and his constant sermon, to the individual and to society, was a plea that these resources should be entirely used. He was horrified at the waste of human energy in war; and he suggested that these mighty impulses of combat and mastery could find a better outlet in a "war against nature." Why should not every man, rich or poor, give two years of his life to the state, not for the purpose of killing other people, but to conquer the plagues, and drain the marshes, and irrigate the deserts, and dig the canals, and democratically do the physical and social engineering which builds up so slowly and painfully what war so quickly destroys?

He sympathized with socialism, but he disliked its deprecation of the individual and the genius. Taine's formula, which reduced all cultural manifestations to "race, environment, and time," was inadequate precisely because it left out the individual. But only the individual has value;

---

[59] *Ibid.,* p. 78.   [60] *Ibid.,* p. 299.
[61] Kallen, *William James and Henri Bergson,* p. 240.

everything else is a means—even philosophy. And so we need on the one
hand a state which shall understand that it is the trustee and servant of
the interests of individual men and women; and on the other a philosophy
and a faith which shall "offer the universe as an adventure rather than a
scheme,"[62] and shall stimulate every energy by holding up the world as a
place where, though there are many defeats, there are also victories waiting to be won.

> *A shipwrecked sailor, buried on this coast,*
> *Bids you set sail.*
> *Full many a gallant bark, when we were lost,*
> *Weathered the gale.*[63]

4. COMMENT

The reader needs no guide to the new and the old elements in this
philosophy. It is part of the modern war between science and religion;
another effort, like Kant's and Bergson's, to rescue faith from the uni-
versalized mechanics of materialism. Pragmatism has its roots in Kant's
"practical reason"; in Schopenhauer's exaltation of the will; in Darwin's
notion that the fittest (and therefore also the fittest and truest idea) is
that which survives; in utilitarianism, which measured all goods in terms
of use; in the empirical and inductive traditions of English philosophy;
and finally in the suggestions of the American scene.

Certainly, as everyone has pointed out, the manner, if not the substance, of James's thinking was specifically and uniquely American. The
American lust for movement and acquisition fills the sails of his style and
thought, and gives them a buoyant and almost aerial motility. Huneker
calls it "a philosophy for philistines," and indeed there is something that
smacks of salesmanship in it: James talks of God as of an article to be
sold to a materialistically-minded consumer by every device of optimistic
advertising; and he counsels us to believe as if he were recommending
long-term investments, with high dividends, in which there was nothing
to lose, and all the (other) world to win. It was young America's defense-
reaction against European metaphysics and European science.

The new test of truth was of course an ancient one; and the honest
philosopher described pragmatism modestly as "a new name for old ways
of thinking." If the new test means that truth is that which has been
tried, by experience and experiment, the answer is, Of course. If it means
that personal utility is a test of truth, the answer is, Of course not; personal utility is merely personal utility; only universal permanent utility
would constitute truth. When some pragmatists speak of a belief having
been true once because then useful (though now disproved), they utter

[62]Chesterton.
[63]Quoted by James (*Pragmatism*, p. 297) from the Greek Anthology.

nonsense learnedly; it was a useful error, not a truth. Pragmatism is cor-. rect only if it is a platitude.

What James meant to do, however, was to dispel the cobwebs that had entangled philosophy; he wished to reiterate in a new and startling way the old English attitude towards theory and ideology. He was but carrying on the work of Bacon in turning the face of philosophy once more towards the inescapable world of things. He will be remembered for this empirical emphasis, this new realism, rather than for his theory of truth; and he will be honored perhaps more as a psychologist than as a philosopher. He knew that he had found no solution for the old questions; he frankly admitted that he had expressed only another guess, another faith. On his desk, when he died, there lay a paper on which he had written his last, and perhaps his most characteristic, sentences: "There is no conclusion. What has concluded that we might conclude in regard to it? There are no fortunes to be told and there is no advice to be given. Farewell."

III. JOHN DEWEY

1. EDUCATION

After all, pragmatism was "not quite" an American philosophy; it did not catch the spirit of the greater America that lay south and west of the New England states. It was a highly moralistic philosophy, and betrayed the Puritanic origins of its author. It talked in one breath of practical results and matters of fact, and in the next it leaped, with the speed of hope, from earth to heaven. It began with a healthy reaction against metaphysics and epistemology, and one expected from it a philosophy of nature and of society; but it ended as an almost apologetic plea for the intellectual respectability of every dear belief. When would philosophy learn to leave to religion these perplexing problems of another life, and to psychology these subtle difficulties of the knowledge-process, and give itself with all its strength to the illumination of human purposes and the coördination and elevation of human life?

Circumstances left nothing undone to prepare John Dewey to satisfy this need, and to outline a philosophy that should express the spirit of an informed and conscious America. He was born in the "effete East" (in Burlington, Vermont, 1859), and had his schooling there, as if to absorb the old culture before adventuring into the new. But soon he took Greeley's counsel and went West teaching philosophy at the universities of Minnesota (1888-9), Michigan (1889-94), and Chicago (1894-1904). Only then did he return East, to join—and later to head—the department of philosophy at Columbia University. In his first twenty years the Vermont environment gave him that almost rustic simplicity which characterizes him even now that all the world acclaims him. And then, in his twenty years in the Middle West, he saw that vast America of which the Eastern mind is so proudly ignorant; he learned its limitations and its powers; and when he came to write his own philosophy he gave to his students and his readers an interpretation of the sound and simple naturalism which underlies the superficial superstitions of the "provinces" of America. He wrote the philosophy, as Whitman wrote the poetry, not of one New-English state, but of the continent.[64]

Dewey first caught the eyes of the world by his work in the School of Education at Chicago. It was in those years that he revealed the resolute experimental bent of his thought; and now, thirty years later, his mind is still open to every new move in education, and his interest in the "schools of tomorrow" never flags. Perhaps his greatest book is *Democracy and Education;* here he draws the varied lines of his philosophy to a point, and centres them all on the task of developing a better generation. All progressive teachers acknowledge his leadership; and there is hardly a school in America that has not felt his influence. We find him active everywhere in the task of remaking the schools of the world; he spent two years in China lecturing to teachers on the reform of education, and made a report to the Turkish Government on the reorganization of their national schools.

Following up Spencer's demand for more science, and less literature. in education, Dewey adds that even the science should not be book, learning, but should come to the pupil from the actual practice of useful occupations. He has no great regard for a "liberal" education; the term was used, originally, to denote the culture of a "free man,"—i. e., a man who never worked; and it was natural that such an education should be fitted rather to a leisure class in an aristocracy than to an industrial and democratic life. Now that we are nearly all of us caught up in the industrialization of Europe and America, the lessons we must learn are those that come through occupation rather than through books. Scholastic culture makes for snobbishness, but fellowship in occupations makes for democracy. In an industrial society the school should be a miniature workshop and a miniature community; it should teach through practice, and through trial and error, the arts and discipline necessary for economic and social order. And finally, education must be re-conceived, not as merely a preparation for maturity (whence our absurd idea that it should stop after adolescence), but as a continuous growth of the mind and a continuous illumination of life. In a sense, the schools can give us only

---

[64]The most important of Dewey's books are: *The School and Society* (1900); *Studies in Logical Theory* (1903); *Ethics* (with Tufts, 1908); *How We Think* (1909); *The Influence of Darwin on Philosophy* (1910); *Democracy and Education* (1913); *Schools of Tomorrow* (with his daughter Evelyn, 1915); *Essays in Experimental Logic* (1916); *Creative Intelligence* (1917); *Reconstruction in Philosophy* (1920); *Human Nature and Conduct* (1922). The last two are the easiest approaches to his thought.

the instrumentalities of mental growth; the rest depends upon our absorp‹ tion and interpretation of experience. Real education comes after we leave school; and there is no reason why it should stop before our death.

2. INSTRUMENTALISM

What distinguishes Dewey is the undisguised completeness with which he accepts the evolution theory. Mind as well as body is to him an organ evolved, in the struggle for existence, from lower forms. His starting-point in every field is Darwinian.

When Descartes said, "The nature of physical things is much more easily conceived when they are beheld coming gradually into existence, than when they are only considered as produced at once in a finished and perfect state," the modern world became self-conscious of the logic that was hence-forth to control it, the logic of which Darwin's *Origin of Species* is the latest scientific achievement. . . . When Darwin said of species what Galileo had said of the earth, *e pur si muove*, he emancipated, once for all, genetic and experimental ideas as an organon of asking questions and look-ing for explanations.[65]

Things are to be explained, then, not by supernatural causation, but by their place and function in the environment. Dewey is frankly naturalis-tic; he protests that "to idealize and rationalize the universe at large is a confession of inability to master the courses of things that specifically concern us."[66] He distrusts, too, the Schopenhauerian Will and the Bergso-nian *élan;* these may exist, but there is no need to worship them; for these world-forces are as often as not destructive of everything that man creates and reverences.[67] Divinity is within us, not in these neutral cosmic powers. "Intelligence has descended from its lonely isolation at the remote edge of things, whence it operated as unmoved mover and ultimate good, to take its seat in the moving affairs of men."[68] We must be faithful to the earth.

Like a good positivist, scion of the stock of Bacon and Hobbes and Spencer and Mill, Dewey rejects metaphysics as the echo and disguise of theology. The trouble with philosophy has always been that its problems were confused with those of religion. "As I read Plato, philosophy began with some sense of its essentially political basis and mission—a recognition that its problems were those of the organization of a just social order. But it soon got lost in dreams of another world."[69] In German philosophy the interest in religious problems deflected the course of philosophic develop-ment; in English philosophy the social interest outweighed the super-

---

[65] *The Influence of Darwin on Philosophy,* New York, 1910, p. 8.
[66] *Ibid.,* p. 17.
[67] *Human Nature and Conduct,* New York, 1922, p. 74.
[68] *I. of D. on P.,* p. 55. [69] *Ibid.,* p. 21.

natural. For two centuries the war raged between an idealism that reflected authoritarian religion and feudal aristocracy, and a sensationalism
that reflected the liberal faith of a progressive democracy.

This war is not yet ended; and therefore we have not quite emerged
from the Middle Ages. The modern era will begin only when the naturalist
point of view shall be adopted in every field. This does not mean that
mind is reduced to matter, but only that mind and life are to be understood not in theological but in biological terms, as an organ or an organism in an environment, acted upon and reacting, moulded and moulding.
We must study not "states of consciousness" but modes of response. "The
brain is primarily an organ of a certain kind of behavior, not of knowing
the world."[70] Thought is an instrument of re-adaptation; it is an organ
as much as limbs and teeth. Ideas are imagined contacts, experiments in
adjustment. But this is no passive adjustment, no merely Spencerian
adaptation. "Complete adaptation to environment means death. The
essential point in all response is the desire to control the environment."[71]
The problem of philosophy is not how we can come to know an external
world, but how we can learn to control it and remake it, and for what
goals. Philosophy is not the analysis of sensation and knowledge (for that
is psychology), but the synthesis and coordination of knowledge and
desire.

To understand thought we must watch it arise in specific situations.
Reasoning, we perceive, begins not with premises, but with difficulties;
then it conceives an hypothesis which becomes the conclusion for which
it seeks the premises; finally it puts the hypothesis to the test of observation or experiment. "The first distinguishing characteristic of thinking is
facing the facts—inquiry, minute and extensive scrutinizing, observation."[72] There is small comfort for mysticism here.

And then again, thinking is social; it occurs not only in specific situations, but in a given cultural *milieu*. The individual is as much a product
of society as society is a product of the individual; a vast network of
customs, manners, conventions, language, and traditional ideas lies ready
to pounce upon every new-born child, to mould it into the image of the
people among whom it has appeared. So rapid and thorough is the
operation of this social heredity that it is often mistaken for physical or
biological heredity. Even Spencer believed that the Kantian categories,
or habits and forms of thought, were native to the individual, whereas in
all probability they are merely the product of the social transmission of
mental habits from adults to children.[73] In general the rôle of instinct
has been exaggerated, and that of early training under-rated; the most

[70]*Creative Intelligence*, New York, 1917, p. 36.
[71]Class lectures on "Psychological Ethics," Sept. 29, 1924.
[72]*Reconstruction in Philosophy*, New York, 1920, p. 140.
[73]*Ibid.* p. 92.

powerful instincts, such as sex and pugnacity, have been considerably modified and controlled by social training; and there is no reason why other instincts, like those of acquisition and mastery, should not be similarly modified by social influence and education. We must unlearn our ideas about an unchangeable human nature and an omnipotent environment. There is no knowable limit to change or growth; and perhaps there is nothing impossible but thinking makes it so.

3. Science and Politics

What Dewey sees and reverences as the finest of all things, is growth; so much so, that he makes this relative but specific notion, and no absolute "good," his ethical criterion.

Not perfection as a final goal, but the ever-enduring process of perfecting, maturing, refining, is the aim in living . . . The bad man is the man who, no matter how good he has been, is beginning to deteriorate, to grow less good. The good man is the man who, no matter how morally unworthy he *has* been, is moving to become better. Such a conception makes one severe in judging himself and humane in judging others.[74]

And to be good does not merely mean to be obedient and harmless; goodness without ability is lame; and all the virtue in the world will not save us if we lack intelligence. Ignorance is not bliss, it is unconsciousness and slavery; only intelligence can make us sharers in the shaping of our fates. Freedom of the will is no violation of causal sequences, it is the illumination of conduct by knowledge. "A physician or engineer is free in his thoughts or his actions in the degree in which he knows what he deals with. Perhaps we find here the key to any freedom."[75] Our trust must after all be in thought, and not in instinct;—how could instinct adjust us to the increasingly artificial environment which industry has built around us, and the maze of intricate problems in which we are enmeshed?

Physical science has for the time being far outrun psychical. We have mastered the physical mechanism sufficiently to turn out possible goods; we have not gained a knowledge of the conditions through which possible values become actual in life, and so are still at the mercy of habit, of haphazard, and hence of force. . . . With tremendous increase in our control of nature, in our ability to utilize nature for human use and satisfaction, we find the actual realization of ends, the enjoyment of values, growing unassured and precarious. At times it seems as though we were caught in a contradiction; the more we multiply means the less certain and general is the use we are able to make of them. No wonder a Carlyle or a Ruskin puts our whole industrial civilization under a ban, while a Tolstoi proclaims a return to the

[74] *Reconstruction in Philosophy*, pp. 177, 176.
[75] *Human Nature and Conduct*, p. 303.

desert. But the only way to see the situation steadily and see it whole is to keep in mind that the entire problem is one of the development of science and its application to life. . . . Morals, philosophy, returns to its first love; love of the wisdom that is nurse of good. But it returns to the Socratic principle equipped with a multitude of special methods of inquiry and tests; with an organized mass of knowledge, and with control of the arrangements by which industry, law and education may concentrate upon the problem of the participation by all men and women, up to the capacity of absorption, in all attained values.[76]

Unlike most philosophers, Dewey accepts democracy, though he knows its faults. The aim of political order is to help the individual to develop himself completely; and this can come only when each shares, up to his capacity, in determining the policy and destiny of his group. Fixed classes belong with fixed species; the fluidity of classes came at the same time as the theory of the transformation of species.[77] Aristocracy and monarchy are more efficient than democracy, but they are also more dangerous. Dewey distrusts the state, and wishes a pluralistic order, in which as much as possible of the work of society would be done by voluntary associations. He sees in the multiplicity of organizations, parties, corporations, trade unions, etc., a reconciliation of individualism with common action. As these

develop in importance, the state tends to become more and more a regulator and adjustor among them; defining the limits of their actions, preventing and settling conflicts. . . . Moreover, the voluntary associations . . . do not coincide with political boundaries. Associations of mathematicians, chemists, astronomers, business corporations, labor organizations, churches, are trans-national because the interests they represent are world-wide. In such ways as these, internationalism is not an aspiration but a fact, not a sentimental ideal but a force. Yet these interests are cut across and thrown out of gear by the traditional doctrine of exclusive national sovereignty. It is the vogue of this doctrine or dogma that presents the strongest barrier to the effective formation of an international mind which alone agrees with the moving forces of present-day labor, commerce, science, art, and religion.[78]

But political reconstruction will come only when we apply to our social problems the experimental methods and attitudes which have succeeded so well in the natural sciences. We are still in the metaphysical stage of political philosophy; we fling abstractions at one another's heads, and when the battle is over nothing is won. We cannot cure our social ills with wholesale ideas, magnificent generalizations like individualism or order, democracy or monarchy or aristocracy, or what not. We must meet each problem with a specific hypothesis, and no universal theory; theories are tentacles, and fruitful progressive living must rely on trial and error.

[76] "Psychology and Social Science"; *I. of D. on P.*, p. 71.
[77] *Reconstruction*, p. 75.   [78] *Ibid.*, pp. 203, 205.

The experimental attitude . . . substitutes detailed analysis for whole-sale assertions, specific inquiries for temperamental convictions, small facts for opinions whose size is in precise ratio to their vagueness. It is within the social sciences, in morals, politics and education, that thinking still goes on by large antitheses, by theoretical oppositions of order and freedom, in-dividualism and socialism, culture and utility, spontaneity and discipline, actuality and tradition. The field of the physical sciences was once occu-pied by similar "total" views, whose emotional appeal was inversely as thei: intellectual clarity. But with the advance of the experimental method, the question has ceased to be which one of two rival claimants has a right to the field. It has become a question of clearing up a confused subject-matter by attacking it bit by bit. I do not know a case where the final result was anything like victory for one or another among the pre-experimental notions. All of them disappeared because they became increasingly irrelevant to the situation discovered, and with their detected irrelevance they became un-meaning and uninteresting.[79]

It is in this field, in this application of human knowledge to our social antagonisms, that the work of philosophy should lie. Philosophy clings like a timid spinster to the old-fashioned problems and ideas; "direct pre-occupation with contemporary difficulties is left to literature and politics."[80] Philosophy is in flight today before the sciences, one after another of which have run away from her into the productive world, until she is left chill and alone, like a forsaken mother with the vitals gone from her and almost all her cupboards empty. Philosophy has withdrawn herself timidly from her real concerns—men and their life in the world—into a crum-bling corner called epistemology, and is in danger every moment of being ousted by the laws that prohibit habitation in flimsy and rickety struc-tures. But these old problems have lost their meaning for us: "we do not solve them, we get over them";[81] they evaporate in the heat of social friction and living change. Philosophy, like everything else, must secularize itself; it must stay on the earth and earn its keep by illuminating life.

What serious-minded men not engaged in the professional business of philosophy most want to know is what modifications and abandonments of intellectual inheritance are required by the newer industrial, political, and scientific movements. . . . The task of future philosophy is to clarify men's ideas as to the social and moral strifes of their own day. Its aim is to be-come, so far as is humanly possible, an organ for dealing with these con-flicts. . . . A catholic and far-sighted theory of the adjustment of the con-flicting factors of life is philosophy.[82]

A philosophy so understood might at last produce philosophers worthy to be kings.

[79] *New Republic*, Feb. 3, 1917.
[80] *Creative Intelligence*, p. 4.
[81] *I. of D. on P.*, p. 19.
[82] *Creative Intelligence*, p. 5: *Reconstruction*, p. 26; *I. of D. on P.*, p. 45.

Conclusion

If THE READER will now summarize for himself these three philosophies, he will perhaps see more justice than at first in that disregard of chronology which placed Santayana before James and Dewey. It is clearer, in retrospect, that the most eloquent and subtle of our living thinkers belongs almost wholly to the cultural traditions of Europe; that William James, though attached in many ways to that tradition, caught the spirit of at least the Eastern America in his thinking, and the spirit of all America in his style; and that John Dewey, product of East and West alike, has given philosophic form to the realistic and democratic temper of his people. It becomes evident that our ancient dependence on European thought is lessening, that we are beginning to do our own work in philosophy, literature and science, and in our own way. Merely beginning, of course: for we are still young, and we have not yet learned to walk entirely without the assistance of our European ancestry. But if we find it hard to surpass ourselves, and are sometimes discouraged with our own superficiality, our provincialism, our narrowness and our bigotry, our immature intolerance and our timid violence against innovation and .periment—let us remember that England needed eight hundred years between her foundation and her Shakespeare; and that France needed eight hundred years between her foundation and her Montaigne. We have drawn to us from Europe, and selected for survival and imitation among ourselves, rather the initiative individualist and the acquisitive pioneer than the meditative and artistic souls; we have had to spend our energies in clearing our great forests and tapping the wealth of our soil; we have had no time yet to bring forth a native literature and a mature philosophy.

But we have become wealthy, and wealth is the prelude to art. In every country where centuries of physical effort have accumulated the means for luxury and leisure, culture has followed as naturally as vegetation grows in a rich and watered soil. To have become wealthy was the first necessity; a people too must live before it can philosophize. No doubt we have grown faster than nations usually have grown; and the disorder of our souls is due to the rapidity of our development. We are like youths disturbed and unbalanced, for a time, by the sudden growth and experiences of puberty. But soon our maturity will come; our minds will catch up with our bodies, our culture with our possessions. Perhaps there are greater souls than Shakespeare's, and greater minds than Plato's, waiting to be born. When we have learned to reverence liberty as well as wealth, we too shall have our Renaissance.

Glossary

Note: This glossary comprises chiefly the more important
and more difficult words which recur rather frequently.

Anthropomorphism: the interpretation of God in the likeness of man.
Apollonian: having the calm, "classic" beauty of Apollo, as against the emotional
and "romantic" qualities associated with Dionysus.
A posteriori: reasoning from observed facts to general conclusions.
A priori: reasoning from general propositions to particular conclusions.
Attribute: in Spinoza, one of the infinite aspects of Substance or reality, like ex-
tension (matter) or thought.

Behaviorist: one who restricts psychology to objective observation, ignoring introspection and consciousness.

Calvinism: a form of Protestantism emphasizing the eternal predestination of every
individual to damnation or to salvation.
Causality: the operation of cause and effect.
Concept: an idea; often used specifically of philosophical ideas.
Consciousness: awareness.
Cosmology: a study of the origin and nature of the world.

Determinism: the doctrine that all events are the inevitable result of antecedent
conditions, and that the human being, in acts of apparent choice, is the
mechanical expression of his heredity and his past environment.
Dialectic: any logical process; in Hegel, the development of one idea or condition
into another by the process of thesis, antithesis and synthesis.

Entelechy: the inner nature of anything, which determines its development
Epicurean: one who believes that pleasure is the highest good.
Epistemology: the study of the origin, processes, and validity of knowledge.
Essence: the most important and significant aspect.
Esthetics: the study of the nature of beauty; in Kant, the study of sensation.
Ethics: the study of right and wrong in conduct.

Fatalism: the doctrine that nothing which the individual can do can in any way
affect the fate to which he is destined.
Finalism: the doctrine that events are caused by the purposes they serve.
First Cause: the beginning of the entire series of causes; usually identified with God,
Formally: in a technical way; according to the form or structure.
Free will: the partial freedom of the agent, in acts of conscious choice, from the de-
termining compulsion of heredity, environment, and circumstance.

Hedonism: the doctrine that pleasure is the actual, and also the proper, motive of every choice.
Heuristic: a method of research.

Idealism: in metaphysics, the doctrine that ideas, or thought, are the fundamental reality; in ethics, the devotion to moral ideals.
Ideation: the process of thought.
Instrumentalism: the doctrine that ideas are instruments of response and adaptation, and that their truth is to be judged in terms of their effectiveness.
Intuitionism: in metaphysics, the doctrine that intuition, rather than reason, reveals the reality of things; in ethics, the doctrine that man has an innate sense of right and wrong.

Lamarckianism: the belief in the transmissibility of acquired characters.
Logic: the study of reasoning; in Hegel, the study of the origin and natural sequence of fundamental ideas.

Materialism: the doctrine that matter is the only reality.
Mechanism: the doctrine that all events and all thoughts occur according to the laws of mechanics.
Metaphysics: the inquiry into the ultimate and fundamental reality.
Mode: in Spinoza, a particular thing, form, event, or idea.

Naturalism: the doctrine that all reality comes under the "laws of Nature."
Neurosis: a mental disturbance or disease.
Nirvana: in Hindu theory, a condition of happiness arising out of the absolute cessation of desire.
Noumenon: in Kant, the ultimate reality, or Thing-in-Itself, which can be conceived by thought, but cannot be perceived in experience.

Objective: independent of the perceiving individual; in Spinoza, as existing in thought.
Ontology: a study of the ultimate nature of things.

Pantheism: the doctrine that God is immanent in all things.
Pluralism: the doctrine that the world is not a unit in law and structure, but the scene of contrary forces and processes.
Polytheism: the worship of many gods.
Positivism: the restriction of philosophical inquiry to problems open to scientific methods.
Pragmatism: the doctrine that truth is the practical efficacy of an idea.
Prolegomena: introductory studies.

Realism: in epistemology, the doctrine that the external world exists independently of perception, and substantially as perceived by us; in logic, the doctrine that universal ideas have objective realities corresponding to them.

Scholasticism: the philosophy of the medieval theologians; in general, the divorce of speculation from observation and practice.
Sociology: the study of social institutions and processes.
Subjective: as existing in thought; in Spinoza, as the object of thought.
Substance: in Spinoza, the basic and eternal reality, the structure and law of the world.

Transcendental: beyond the realm and reach of the senses.

Theist: a believer in a personal God.

Teleology: the theory or study of development as caused by the purposes which things serve.

Tropism: an invariable response.

Utilitarianism: the doctrine that all actions are to be judged in terms of their utility in promoting the greatest happiness of the greatest number.

Vitalism: the doctrine that life is the basic reality, of which everything else is a form or manifestation.

Voluntarism: the doctrine that will is the basic factor, both in the universe and in human conduct.

Bibliography

Diogenes Laertius: Lives of the Philosophers. Loeb Classical Library. (Putnam.) 2 volumes. $2.50 each.

Xenophon: Memorabilia. Loeb Classical Library. (Putnam.) $2.50.

Plato: Works of, edited by Prof. Irwin Edman. (Simon & Schuster.) $2.50.

Plato: Republic. Translated by Jowett. (Oxford.) 2 volumes. $2.85.

Plato: Republic. Translated by H. Spens. Everyman's Library. (Dutton.) $.80.

Plato: Dialogues. Everyman's Library. (Dutton.) $.80.

Plato: Four Socratic Dialogues. Translated by Jowett. (Oxford.) $1.70.

Aristotle: Ethics. Translated by D. P. Chase. Everyman's Library. (Dutton.) $.80.

Aristotle: Ethics. Translated by Bishop Welldon. (Macmillan.) $2.75.

Aristotle: Politics. Translated by Jowett. (Oxford.) $1.70.

Aristotle: Politics. Translated by William Ellis. Everyman's Library. (Dutton.) $.80.

Lucretius: On the Nature of Things. Translated by W. E. Leonard. Everyman's Library. (Dutton.) $.80.

Lucretius: On the Nature of Things. Translated by C. Bailey. (Oxford.) $1.70.

Epictetus: Book of Epictetus containing Enchiridion. (Dodge.) $1.50.

Marcus Aurelius: Meditations. Translated by Casaubon. Everyman's Library. (Dutton.) $.80.

Marcus Aurelius: Meditations. Translated by John Jackson. (Oxford.) $1.70.

Bacon, Francis: Novum Organum. (Oxford.) $5.00.

Bacon, Francis: Advancement of Learning. Everyman's Library. (Dutton.) $.80.

Descartes, René: Discourse on Method. (Open Court.) $1.00.

Hobbes, Thomas: Leviathan. Everyman's Library. (Dutton.) $.80.

Locke, John: Essay on the Human Understanding. (Dutton.) $2.50.

Spinoza, Benedictus: Ethics. Everyman's Library. (Dutton.) $.80.

Leibnitz, G. W.: Essays Concerning Human Understanding. (Open Court.) $3.00.

Voltaire, François M.: Prose Works. (Black.) $3.00.

Holbach, Paul H.: System of Nature. No edition now in print.

Hume, David: Enquiry Concerning the Principles of Human Morals. (Open Court.) $1.00.

Hume, David: Enquiry Concerning Human Understanding. (Open Court.) $1.00.

Hume, David: Treatise of Human Nature. Everyman's Library. 2 volumes. (Dutton.) $.80 each.

Kant, Immanuel: Critique of Pure Reason. (Macmillan.) $5.00.

Kant, Immanuel: Critique of Aesthetic Judgment. (Oxford.) $4.20.

Kant, Immanuel: Selections from Kant's Philosophy by John Watson. (Macmillan.) $2.50.

Hegel, G. M. F.: Philosophy of History. No edition now in print.

Schopenhauer, Arthur: The World as Will and Idea. (Scribner's.) 3 volumes. $19.50.

Schopenhauer, Arthur: Works of, edited by Will Durant. (Simon & Schuster.) $2.50.

Schopenhauer, Arthur: Essays. (Willy Book.) $3.00.

Comte, Auguste: Positive Philosophy. (George Bell.) 3 volumes. Volume 1 is now out of print. $2.40 each.

Mill, J. S.: System of Logic. (Longmans, Green.) $2.50.

Spencer, Herbert: First Principles. (Appleton.) $3.00.

Nietzsche, Friedrich: The Will to Power. (Macmillan.) 2 volumes. $3.50 each.

Nietzsche, Friedrich: Thus Spake Zarathustra. (Macmillan.) $4.00 (Modern Library.) $.95.

Bradley, F. H.: Appearance and Reality. (Macmillan.) $6.50.

Bergson, Henri: Creative Evolution. (Holt.) $3.50.

Croce, Benedetto: History. (Harcourt, Brace.) $4.50.

Russell, B. A.: Mysticism and Logic. (Longmans, Green.) $3.00.

Russell, B. A.: Selected Papers. (Modern Library.) $.95.

James, William: Pragmatism. (Longmans, Green.) $2.00.

Dewey, John: Human Nature and Conduct. (Holt.) $2.25.

Dewey, John: Reconstruction in Philosophy. (Holt.) $2.00.

Santayana, George: Life of Reason. (Scribner's.) 5 volumes. $2.00 each.

INDEX

405